GREENBERG'S®

GUIDE TO

GILBERT ERECTOR SETS

Volume Two • 1933—1962

William M. Bean

KALMBACH BOOKS

 Published by Kalmbach Publishing Co., 21027 Crossroads Circle, Waukesha, WI 53187.

Printed in Hong Kong

97 98 99 00 01 02 03 04 05 06   10 9 8 7 6 5 4 3 2 1

For more information, visit our website at
http://www.kalmbach.com

Publisher's Cataloging-in-Publication
(Provided by Quality Books, Inc.)

Bean, William M. (William Montague), 1947–
Greenberg's guide to Gilbert Erector sets. Volume Two, 1933–1962 / William M. Bean. — 1st ed.
p. cm
ISBN: 0-89778-418-9

1. A.C. Gilbert Company—Catalogs. 2. Toys—United States—Collectors and collecting—Catalogs. I. Title. II. Title: Guide to Gilbert erector sets III. Title: Gilbert erector sets

TS2301.T7B43 1997   688.7'25
QBI97-40703

Book design: Sabine Beaupré
Cover design: Kristi Ludwig

CONTENTS

Dedication 4

Introduction: How to Use Volume Two 5

1 Early Transition Period: 1933–37 9

2 Late Transition Period and World War II: 1938–45 53

3 The Erector Renaissance: 1946–56 80

4 The Post-Renaissance Decline of Erector: 1957–62 138

5 Special Erector Sets for American Wholesalers 182

This book is dedicated
To my daughters, Becky and Mandy,
for all the time I missed with them
while I was concentrating
on this madness I call a hobby;
and
To Alfred Carlton Gilbert, who, in his wildest dreams,
could never have imagined the contribution
he would make to the world.

William M. Bean

INTRODUCTION: HOW TO USE VOLUME TWO

The second volume of *Greenberg's Guide to Gilbert Erector Sets* has been designed to help you learn about the Erector Sets produced by The A. C. Gilbert Company between 1933 and 1962. In addition, I have included specific technical information to help you in five areas:

To establish when a set was manufactured
To specify which parts belong in a set
To identify the correct "period" parts that belong in a set
To know how a set was organized
To establish a realistic value for a set.

Techniques for Dating Erector Sets

One of the most interesting facets of collecting Erector Sets is tracking the changes that occurred in the sets over the years. Sets were added to and later deleted from the lineup. New component parts of the Erector System were invented, modified, and sometimes dropped. Experiments were made with color schemes and packaging techniques. Finally, different materials were used to manufacture Erector parts at different times. One of the most challenging aspects of Erector collecting is being able to assign specific dates to these changes.

The ability to assign the correct production year to a given set is also critical when selecting the contents list to use for the set inventory. Subtle changes that occurred from year to year affected the set contents, and unless the date of production can be established, there is no way to be sure which list to use.

Fortunately, Gilbert left us some clues. The company added copyright dates to the instruction manuals as well as to the inner lid labels on sets made after 1935. However, the help these dates give is limited because in most cases a copyrighted piece was used for many years. What we can learn from the copyright date is the earliest date of manufacture, but not necessarily the actual date of manufacture.

This table of instruction manual copyright dates shows the years specific dates were used:

Copyright Date	**Years of Use**
1929	1929–33*
1933	1933–34*
1934	1934–35*
1935	1935
1936	1936–37
1938	1938–48*
1948	1948–50
1951	1951–53
1954	1954–60*
1959	1959–62

* More than one copyrighted manual used. For example, sets from 1933 may have the 1929 manual or the 1933 manual.

The best clue we have for dating Erector Sets is a section usually found at the end of each instruction manual entitled "Erector Separate Parts Prices." This section was regularly updated, usually once each year and sometimes more often. These sections are so important that you'll find them reproduced in this reference guide. Assuming an Erector Set still contains the instruction manual, the list of separate parts is the best way to establish the year that set was produced.

A third clue to establishing a manufacture date for a set comes from an examination of the component parts, for over the years the parts were modified in many ways. In certain years, paint color varied or different materials were used to manufacture a specific part. From time to time, a part was modified, with an improved shape or hole pattern. I have noted these changed in detail.

Before concluding this section on dating techniques, please understand that dating sets is not an exact science. Changes occurred throughout a given year and not on January 1. We can be sure that when a change was made, old inventory was exhausted before modified parts were used. To clarify, when I write, "the color of part (X) was changed from red to blue in 1944," I do not mean that *all* 1944 sets came with blue part (X). Instead, I mean that the earliest sets observed with blue part (X) are from 1944. There may be earlier 1944 sets with red part (X).

Techniques for Completing Erector Sets

One objective shared by most Erector collectors when adding a set to their collection is the desire to replenish any missing parts. At the end of each section of this book, you will find a detailed contents list that provides a complete inventory for each set.

Contents lists are hard to come by. Those printed here have been developed by studying mint sets and painstakingly examining instruction manuals to calculate the maximum number of parts required to build each model. Also, in some cases, factory-produced inventory lists have survived. When adding parts, take care that you use the correct variation of a specific part (see below).

Techniques for Identifying Correct "Period" Parts

The component parts in the Erector system were repeatedly modified over the years. Detailed information is given at the end of each section of this book relating to such changes. Studying these changes will help you learn which variation of a part was used in a particular year.

Techniques for Organizing Erector Sets

A second objective shared by most Erector enthusiasts when adding a set to their collection is the desire to organize it and repack it in the same way as when it was new. This is no surprise, as Gilbert was a true showman and recognized the market value of displaying the sets in the most spectacular fashion. The duplication of original packaging makes for a superb display in any Erector collection.

When an Erector set was new and first shipped from the Gilbert factory, its parts were highly organized. Most of them were clipped in place to a cardboard parts display or to a tray constructed from the large base plates. The challenge for Erector collectors is to know how a set was organized and where its parts were located. This challenge is compounded because Erector catalogs, the primary source for such information, were not regularly updated with new set pictures, even when major changes were made in the sets and their appearance.

Very few sets survive with the original cardboard packing inserts. Many of these inserts were destroyed on Christmas or whenever the set was first used. Others were discarded over the years when the owner had difficulty fitting all the parts back in the box and shutting the lid. Nevertheless, these inserts are essential to reorganizing a set into "show" condition. Many collectors reproduce inserts using materials from art supply stores or other sources.

While it is beyond the scope of this reference guide to picture each set correctly for each year, I have tried to illustrate a representative cross section. In addition, clubs of enthusiasts, notably the A. C. Gilbert Heritage Society, seek to publish organizational diagrams in their newsletters. (For more information about this organization, contact the author in care of the publisher.)

Techniques for Appraising Erector Sets

Perhaps nothing could be more discouraging to a fledgling Erector collector than to pay twice the going price for a set, unless it would be selling a set for half its current value. To prevent newcomers from making errors of this magnitude, I have included information on set values. The pricing of Erector Sets is more complicated than that for other collectible toys, primarily because of the factors of completeness and organization. Therefore, I urge readers to become very familiar with this section before using the set values in the chapters that follow.

A key point to recall about the values listed in this guide is that they are top prices. That is, they represent the price knowledgeable collectors would pay for a set they intended to keep. If you purchase an incomplete set at a flea market and expect to quickly find a buyer willing to pay the prices listed here, you may be disappointed, especially when dealing in the low or mid-range sets.

The four main factors to consider when placing a value on an Erector Set are desirability, condition, completeness, and organization.

Desirability: A combination of factors contributes to the desirability of a set, including rarity, uniqueness, and size. By itself, the factor of rarity contributes little to set value. A No. 1½ from 1935 may be rare, but few if any collectors are actively searching for one. However, when rarity is combined with uniqueness, desirability and value increase substantially. A Skyscraper Set from 1935 may be as rare as a No. 1½ from that year, but it is far more valuable because of the uniqueness of that set and its contents.

Size also influences desirability. Throughout the fifty-four years of traditional Erector production, sets were offered in a wide range of sizes: small sets with low numbers and large sets with high numbers. There is true value to be found in the smaller sets; they generate the same feelings of nostalgia as the large ones do and offer an opportunity for those with limited resources to take part in this wonderful hobby. But large sets have more parts, which means they make more impressive displays. Even more significant, large sets generally have a greater variety of parts. Most collectors place the highest premium on the largest set offered in a given year, since it will contain the full range of the parts available at that point in Erector history.

Condition: As with all collectibles, condition is a major factor in determining the value of an item. For the low and mid-range Erector Sets, condition tends to be *the* key factor. However, the most significant point to remember, which is perhaps unique to Erector collecting, is that the condition of the set box is usually more important than the condition of the parts it contains. Missing or damaged parts, especially those common to the small and mid-range sets, are easy to replace, but be sure to use those from the correct period.

In describing an Erector Set, the condition of the parts should be mentioned as well as that of the box. I use three different grades of condition in this book—Good (Gd), Very Good (VG), and Excellent (Exc)—and define them as follows:

Good (Gd)

Cardboard Box Sets: The box is complete, although the aprons (sides of the box) may be missing or the corners may be loose. Box lids may be worn, dirty, or stained, but are legible.

Metal Box Sets: The box is sound, but paint may be worn or scratched. Light corrosion may be present, but not heavy rust. Labels or lithography may be worn, dirty, stained, or less than complete, but should be clearly legible.

Wood Box Sets: The box is complete, although there may be cracks. Labels may be worn, dirty, or stained, but should be clearly legible. All hardware and trays are present and may have light corrosion, but not heavy rust.

Parts: The parts show signs of usage and wear. Painted

parts may be scratched or worn or have screw marks. Plated parts may have light surface corrosion, but not heavy rust. Girders may have modest bends that can be straightened, but not twists.

Very Good (VG)

Cardboard Box Sets: The box is complete and sound with all aprons present. Box lids may have light wear, stains, or scratches.

Metal Box Sets: The box has no significant damage or rust. Labels or lithography may have light wear or scratches, or labels may be less than complete.

Wood Box Sets: The box is sound with no cracks or damage; it may show slight signs of wear or scratches, but no major defects in the finish. Labels may have slight wear or scratches.

Parts: The parts are clean with no bends or rust. Painted parts may show light rubbing and screw marks. Plated parts have no corrosion, but are not necessarily shiny.

Excellent (Exc)

Cardboard Box Sets: The box may show light rubbing on the edges and corners, but otherwise should be clean and bright.

Metal Box Sets: The box may show light rubbing and wear, but its overall finish is clean, bright, and shiny. All labels and lithography are clean and complete.

Wood Box Sets: The box may show light rubbing and wear, but its overall finish is clean and bright. All labels are clean and complete.

Parts: The parts are bright, shiny, and clean and appear nearly new. They have no scratches or screw marks.

The values given for these three gradings are based on the assumption that all the major components (instruction manual, motor, and all rare or special parts) are present, and the set appears to be fairly complete.

Gradings lower than Good (such as Fair or Poor) are not given because, except for any highly desirable parts, a set in such condition is worth only the value of any salvageable parts.

Gradings higher than Excellent (such as Like New or Mint) are not given because, unless a set was never used or was saved in its original factory shipping carton, such a rating probably would not apply. On rare occasions, such a set does surface, and its value increases accordingly.

Completeness: A significant element of value will be added to a set if the seller can assure the buyer that the set is complete; that is, the set contains every part, down to the last nut and bolt, that it had when it was new. Such an assurance implies, first, that the seller has knowledge of the contents of the set (an inventory list) and, second, that the seller has done the inventory, filling in any missing parts with correct period replacements.

I have included a complete series of contents lists, but should point out that doing an inventory for a large Erector Set is no small task. It involves many, many hours of concentrated effort. So, if you are buying a set, you should be skeptical when a dealer at a flea market says, "It's all there!" They always do, and it never is! But add value and appreciate the knowledgeable collector who has taken the time to study the contents list, count all the parts, and make the correct replacements in order to sell a set with the same assurance.

Organization: Some people still buy Erector Sets to build with; the vast majority of collectors do not. They want to pack the parts back in the box, use cardboard inserts, and make the set look as it did when it left the Gilbert factory. The ability to reorganize a set in this fashion implies, first, that the original cardboard parts display inserts are present (or that suitable reproductions have been obtained) and, second, that the parts are correctly organized and clipped in the proper places.

Knowing how to reassemble a set can best be determined by examining an original set in mint condition, but since such sets are few and far between, collectors usually have to rely on Erector catalogs and advertisements showing the sets. These pictures lack detail, however, and often areas are hidden by instruction manuals or parts trays. They can cause frustration because Gilbert tended to use the same photograph year after year, even after he made changes in the set.

With completeness and organization in mind, I have added two more values for each set. Inventoried (Inv) means that a set has been inventoried and is complete. Organized (Org) means that it has the cardboard parts display inserts and is correctly reassembled and organized.

It will become clear as you read on that despite all the obstacles collectors face, they have developed the knowledge to correctly repack most Erector Sets. Those pictured in this book are correctly displayed and may offer some assistance to you. As with completeness, organization is a time-consuming activity, yet one that adds significantly to the value of a set.

Listings of Erector Sets

It would be difficult and cumbersome to give a value for every possible combination of factors, but using the values given herein and a little common sense, you should be able to determine a reasonable price for any set.

For example, a typical listing might read as follows:

	Gd	Vg	Exc	Inv	Org

No. 4½ **Famous No. 4½**

Featured battery-operated (P58) Motor and (MN) Base Plates. Came in a cardboard box 18¼" x 10¼" x 1¼"; two-layer set with removable cardboard parts display tray; sold for $3.00 in 1936.

60	**90**	**150**	**+30**	**+40**

The approximate value of No. 4½, if it is in Good condition and inventoried and made complete, would be $90 ($60 + $30). In Excellent condition, if the set has been inventoried, made complete, and reassembled with the original cardboard insert, the approximate value would be $240 ($150 + $30 + $40).

Most of all, remember that the pricing guide is just that—a guide. The value of a collectible is always a subjective figure, one that represents a compromise between the person who would rather have the set than the money and the person who would rather have the money than the set. I hope this volume, like its companion, adds to the enjoyment of buyers and sellers of Erector Sets.

Author Bill Bean amid his collection of Erector Sets. Good hunting to all of you!

1

EARLY TRANSITION PERIOD: 1933–37

Most Erector historians agree that there were two major periods in the evolution of Erector when all the correct elements came together and the sets that Gilbert produced were nearly perfect. These were the Classic Period (1924–32) and what I refer to as the Renaissance Period (1946–56).

What occurred between the Classic Period and the Renaissance Period is the Transition Period, and it is also a wonderful part of Erector history to explore. This era is full of new ideas and techniques, some quickly discarded but others becoming a permanent part of Erector development. The Transition Period was a time of experimentation and renewal, as Erector survived the Great Depression and blossomed into the age of the Baby Boomer.

There is little similarity between sets from the Classic Period and those from the Renaissance Period, but the refinement and the success of each is unquestionable. The Transition Period takes us from one to the other.

Set No. 4 from 1933. Note the unusual method of securing the disc wheels to the cardboard insert with flaps. These flaps fit inside the back rim of the wheel.

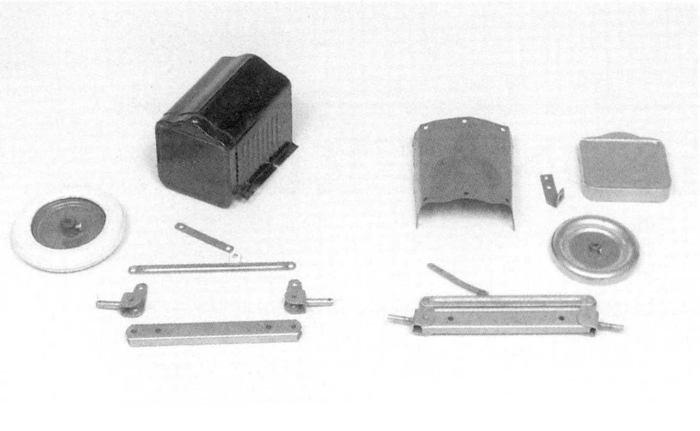

Even with the downsizing that occurred in 1933, Gilbert still included parts to build truck models in the larger sets. The old radiator hood was split into three separate components, which fit into the new metal boxes. Just the opposite occurred with the new front axle unit, however. It came assembled and was composed of five pre-1933 truck parts. In 1933, the smaller (MH) Disc Wheel replaced the old (DM) Disc Wheel and (OR) Rubber Tire.

THE 1933 ERECTOR LINE

In the history of Erector Sets, 1933 stood out as a significant year. With the American economy deep in the grips of the Great Depression, the market for toys had dramatically changed. Many business enterprises were failing, and the A. C. Gilbert Company was operating in the red. If the firm was going to survive, A. C. Gilbert, the inventor of Erector and the driving force in the business, knew that Erector, his primary product, would have to change. So change it he did.

- Metal box sets were introduced, and the appearance of the cardboard box sets was changed.
- The components of the Erector system were modified with the addition of some new parts but the deletion of nearly half of the old ones.
- Many of the large sets were eliminated, as well as the specialized parts created for them.

A detailed examination of these changes is in order, and the changes will become apparent as I review the 1933 line.

First of all, there is some question as to the number of different sets Gilbert offered in that line. *The Erector Look-em-over Book* (the Erector catalog for the year, item no. D1008) identifies three sets offered in cardboard boxes (Nos. 1, 3, and 4), two offered in metal boxes (Nos. 6 and 7), and three offered in wood boxes (Nos. A, 8, and 8½). Each of these eight sets was pictured, described, and promoted. But the 1933 price list (item no. D1010) gives prices for these eight and two additional sets: Nos. 9 and 10. While those two sets probably represented leftover, unsold inventories from the previous year, it would appear that Gilbert was reluctant to see an end to the colossal sets and models that had evolved during the late 1920s and early '30s. At the time, he could not have known that the Classic Era was finished.

While 1933 will always be remembered as the year with the greatest number of deletions from the Erector System (more than 100 parts were eliminated), there were significant additions as well. Many of the new parts come from modification of Classic Period parts, and this practice was unique to 1933.

Six new "truck parts" were added to the Erector System this year. The (LX) Steering Column Bracket, (MA) New Radiator, and (MG) Radiator Hood were all descended from the old (DD) Hood and Radiator. What had been one part was now divided into three. The (MG) Radiator Hood was not as well proportioned as it had been when it was part of the old (DD); now it was painted red instead of black. There were actually two versions of the (MA) New Radiator in 1933. The earlier one was still embossed "White" just as (DD) had been, but this variation is rare. The embossing was dropped early in 1933, and most (MA)s have no lettering. Both versions of the (MA) were nickel-plated, as was the (LX) Steering Column Bracket.

While these three new truck parts were created by disassembling a Classic Period part, the (MI) Front Axle Unit did just the opposite. It was formed by combining five Classic Period truck parts into a single unit. That is, it was composed of an old (DF) Tie Rod, a (DG) Drag Link, two (DH) Steering Knuckles, and a (DI) Front Axle.

The remaining two 1933 truck parts were the (MH) 3" Disc Wheel, Nickel Rim, which replaced last year's (DM) Disc Wheel and (DR) Rubber Tire, and the (MB) 18½" Angle Girder. This angle girder was adopted directly from the Meccano line. Although it had numerous other applications, the (MB) was added this year specifically for building the truck chassis.

Other interesting parts joined the Erector ranks in 1933. A new series of base plates was developed: (MC) Base Plate, 1" x 2½", (MD) Base Plate, 2½" x 5", (MD) Flat Plate 1" x 4", and (MF) Flat Plate 1" x 5". The 1933 versions of the (MC) and (MD) Base Plates are noteworthy, for they were made from heavy-gauge steel in this and the next year only.

Also new in 1933 was the (LV) 3" Disc Wheel, Red. It was identical to the (MH) Disc Wheel, except it was painted solid red. The (MH) was nickel-plated, with the hubcap painted red. The (MH), which was designed to look like a truck tire, came only with sets having the truck parts. The (LV) was less expensive to produce and was packed in all but the smallest of the other sets.

A wonderful addition to the 1933 line was the (MJ) Electro Magnet With Cord. Used mainly on crane models, it required a 6-volt battery (not included in the set) to operate. A (BY) 11 Hole Fiber Strip was also included with the electro magnet, and boys used it to construct an "on-off" switch. The 1933 and 1934 version of the (MJ), which came in a housing painted red, gave a new element of action to Erector.

Another noteworthy change occurred with the sections of display track that came with the Hudson Locomotive sets. In the past, this display track was part (LO) Track Section, and it was composed of ties and rails, welded together. Now, however, these components had to be separated to fit them in the set boxes. So two new parts, the (LP) Railroad Tie and (ML) Railroad Rail, replaced the old (LO). When assembled, the (ML) and (LP) were identical to the (LO).

One final new addition to Erector in 1933 was the introduction of "parts cans." In the past, nuts, bolts, and other small parts had been packed in small cardboard boxes that had lids. Beginning now, parts cans were substituted for the boxes in all but the smallest sets. Gilbert apparently was in the mood to make things out of steel this year.

Cardboard Box Sets

It is rather surprising that the picture on the lids of the cardboard box sets was changed in 1933, for Gilbert had never been a stickler for accuracy with these smaller sets in the past. Through half of the Classic Period (1924–32), the picture on the lids of the cardboard box sets had shown a bridge built of "Style 1" girders, which had been dropped in 1924. In 1928, this out-of-date label was replaced with a more colorful one picturing the White Truck and a coal loader model. It was a beautiful piece of artwork, but the problem with using this picture in 1933 was that Gilbert had eliminated the White truck and many of the elaborate parts used in the coal loader. So, in spite of the cost (hardly a small point in 1933), Gilbert created a new lid label for the cardboard box sets.

This new label was somewhat disappointing, as it was not nearly as colorful or striking as its predecessor. Pictured on this label was a man pointing to a partially completed model of a suspension bridge that a boy was assembling. An actual suspension bridge furnished the background for the scene. The most colorful part of the label was the name "Erector" in red lettering, followed by the caption "100 Toys in One." Gilbert still got it wrong, however, because this label shows the bridge being built with (Q) Base Plates, which were deleted in 1933! Good or bad, Gilbert must have liked this picture, because it would be used on the cardboard box sets for twenty-five straight years.

Gilbert offered three cardboard box sets in its 1933 lineup. Because of the revisions in the 1933 parts, these sets were completely redesigned this year. Although similar in size and price to their 1932 precursors, the set contents and the models illustrated in the instruction manuals were drastically changed. All of these sets were upgraded with at least some of the new base plates.

Set No. 1 was called "The Dandy Beginner's Set." It was a one-layer set with a mustard yellow cardboard insert and featured the (FP) Small Disc Wheels.

Next in the 1933 lineup was No. 3, which featured the new (LV) 3" Red Disc Wheels. Incidentally, Gilbert began to use a clever technique for packing the small parts with this set. A small, shallow cardboard box was created, just the right size to fit into the new (MD) Base Plate. This box had a small hole in the bottom. The nuts, bolts, and other small parts were packed in this box, and, using a paper fastener, it was clipped to the inside of the (MD), which acted as a lid. Gilbert continued to use this packing technique with cardboard sets into the 1950s.

Gilbert called No. 4 "The Famous 4"; it was a two-layer set with a removable cardboard parts display. It was the smallest set in the lineup to contain a battery-operated electric motor, a tradition for this set that began in 1913. The apron on the lid extended to the bottom of the box, a feature unique to No. 4 sets from 1933 as well as the sets made for Sears, Roebuck & Co. (see Chapter Five).

Designers used an interesting packaging technique to secure the red (LW) 3" Disc Wheels in No. 4. Instead of using the traditional paper fasteners to hold them in place, they relied on "flaps" added to the lower-level inserts. There were two flaps per wheel, and they were cut into the insert and folded up at a shallow angle. (Someone described them as "elephant ears.") The flaps then fit into the backs of the wheels to hold them in place. As far as I know, this was the only set to use this unusual packaging technique.

Metal Box Sets

Undoubtedly, the most important development that occurred in 1933 for Erector collectors was the introduction of metal boxes to house the sets. Toy collecting is driven by nostalgia, and most of us under the age of seventy probably remember our childhood set coming in a metal box.

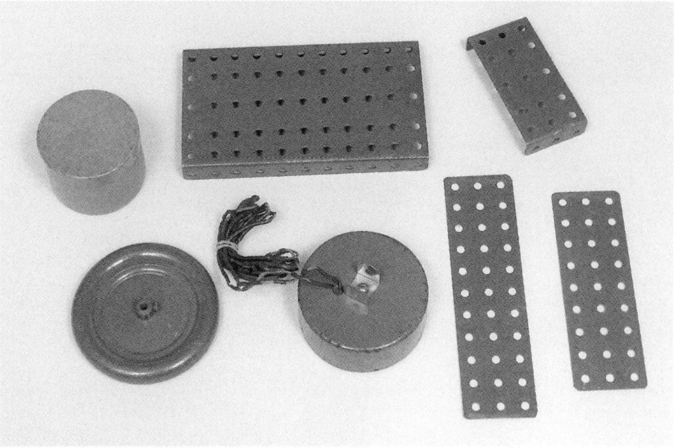

New components for 1933 included a new series of base plates, the electro magnet, the (LV) Disc Wheel, and metal cans for storing small parts.

No one knows when Gilbert began to consider making the containers for the larger sets out of metal instead of wood. Perhaps the idea formed almost a decade before the first true metal box appeared, when the company packaged No. 7 from 1924 in a container having a wood body and a steel lid. What is clear is that the evolution of the metal box Erector Set, which began in 1933, would progress until the demise of traditional Erector in 1962.

Actually, the transition to metal box sets began quite modestly this year. Of the eight sets identified in the Erector catalog, only two came in metal boxes. They were middle-of-the-line sets designated as Nos. 6 and 7. But these two sets are fascinating, not just because they represent a dramatic transition in the packaging and appearance of Erector, but also because they were modified several times during this year and the modifications are interesting in their own right.

The smaller of the two metal box sets was No. 6, which Gilbert named "The Super 6." The box measured 18" x 10" x 3". Painted green, it came with a brass handle and latches. There were no dividers in the body of the box, but the large green cardboard insert filling the center left space along

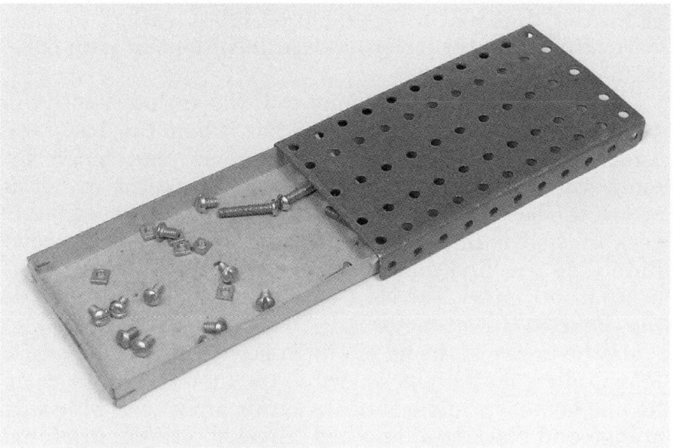

In 1933, Gilbert developed a clever method for housing nuts, bolts, and other small parts in the small sets. The (MD) Base Plate formed a lid for this shallow cardboard box. A paper fastener held the boxes in place on the cardboard insert.

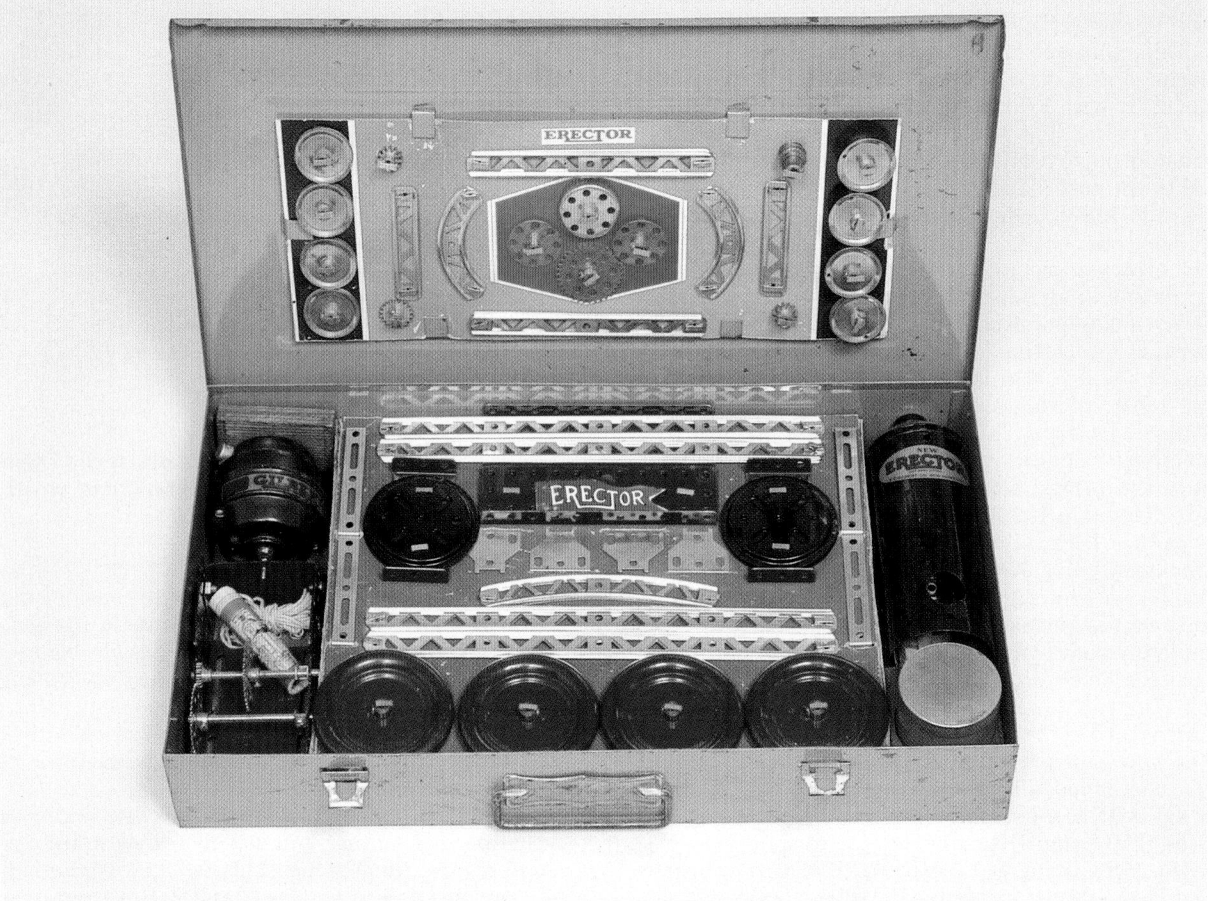

Here is No. 6, one of the metal box sets introduced in 1933. Only two sizes were offered, with No. 6 being smaller. Gilbert painted the boxes green, and because he abandoned this color after a few years, collectors prize the green box sets.

both sides for the larger parts, including the motor, boiler, assembled gearbox, and parts can. The can was mounted in a wood block that held it snug against the lid when the box was closed. The parts can and its lid were usually painted light blue, but some of the earliest sets came with a scarce green can that had a nickel-plated lid. A variety of parts were attached to the lower-level cardboard insert with paper fasteners.

Incidentally, the (P56G) Motor that was included with this set was too large to fit in the box when the base was attached to the motor, so the base came unattached and hung from the electrical cord. It was up to the owner to attach the base to the motor, though the motor would not fit back in the box unless the cardboard insert was discarded. Rarely do you find one of these sets with the lower cardboard insert intact. The No. 6 was the smallest set to contain the (P56G) 110-volt motor.

On the inside of the lid of The Super 6 was an innovation. Mounted via metal tabs welded to the lid was a large, colorful display insert made of heavy cardboard. It was blue with orange and black trim and had "Erector" printed in orange letters. Paper fasteners held pulleys, gears and additional parts to this insert. (While mounting parts on the inside of the lid was new to Erector, the idea was not new. Meccano, an English construction set manufacturer and Erector's chief rival in the 1910s and '20s, had been using this technique for years. Gilbert was free to capitalize on this idea for Erector because he had purchased the American Meccano Co. in 1929.) The metal tabs fit around the border of the display insert and had to be bent each time someone removed or reinstalled the insert. Many of these sets are found with the tabs missing, as the metal would break from repeated bending. The cardboard parts display usually was discarded as well.

A most interesting variation occurred in the way this display insert was mounted to the inside of the lid. The earliest of the No. 6 sets from 1933 were manufactured with long steel strips welded near the top and bottom of the inside of the lid. These strips were flanged to provide slots into which the display insert slid. Two metal tabs, one on either side, held the insert in place. These long metal strips were not used for long, and this method for mounting the parts display insert quickly gave way to an "all tabs" system, which was easier and less expensive to produce. The 1933 version of No. 7 underwent the same modification.

On the outside of the lid was a label, and two distinctive versions of it were used on the No. 6 from 1933. The first was not really a label, but a decal left over from the wood box sets of 1932. It measured 7½" x 2½" and had a red background. "The New Erector" was printed in black lettering with gold trim. This version of No. 6 is rare, because these decals were quickly replaced with a new label that was

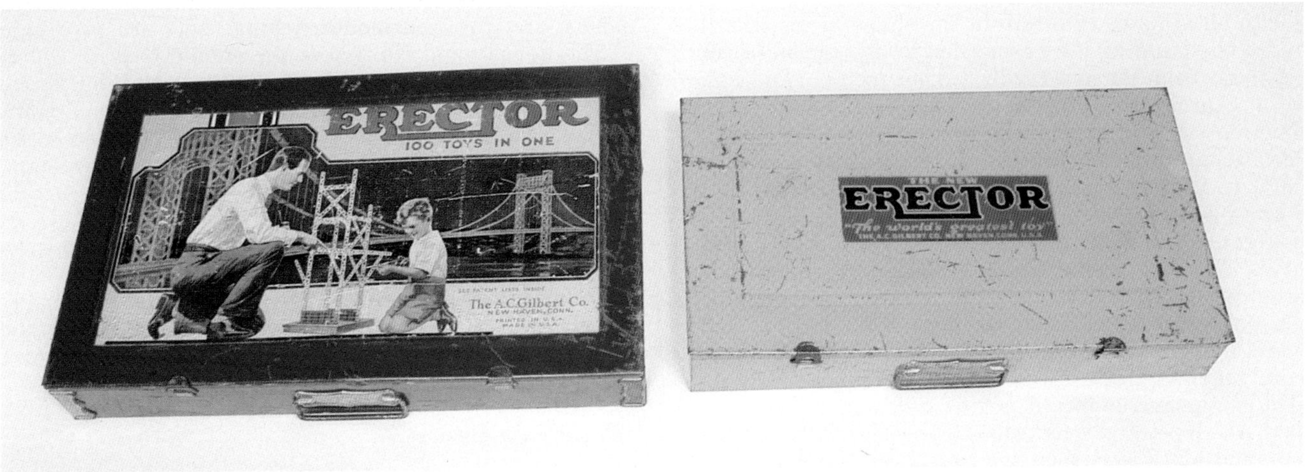

The very early versions of the Nos. 6 and 7 from 1933 had most unusual labels on the outside of the lids. Metal boxes were new this year, and obviously Gilbert was experimenting with different methods of adorning them. By midyear, oval labels were used.

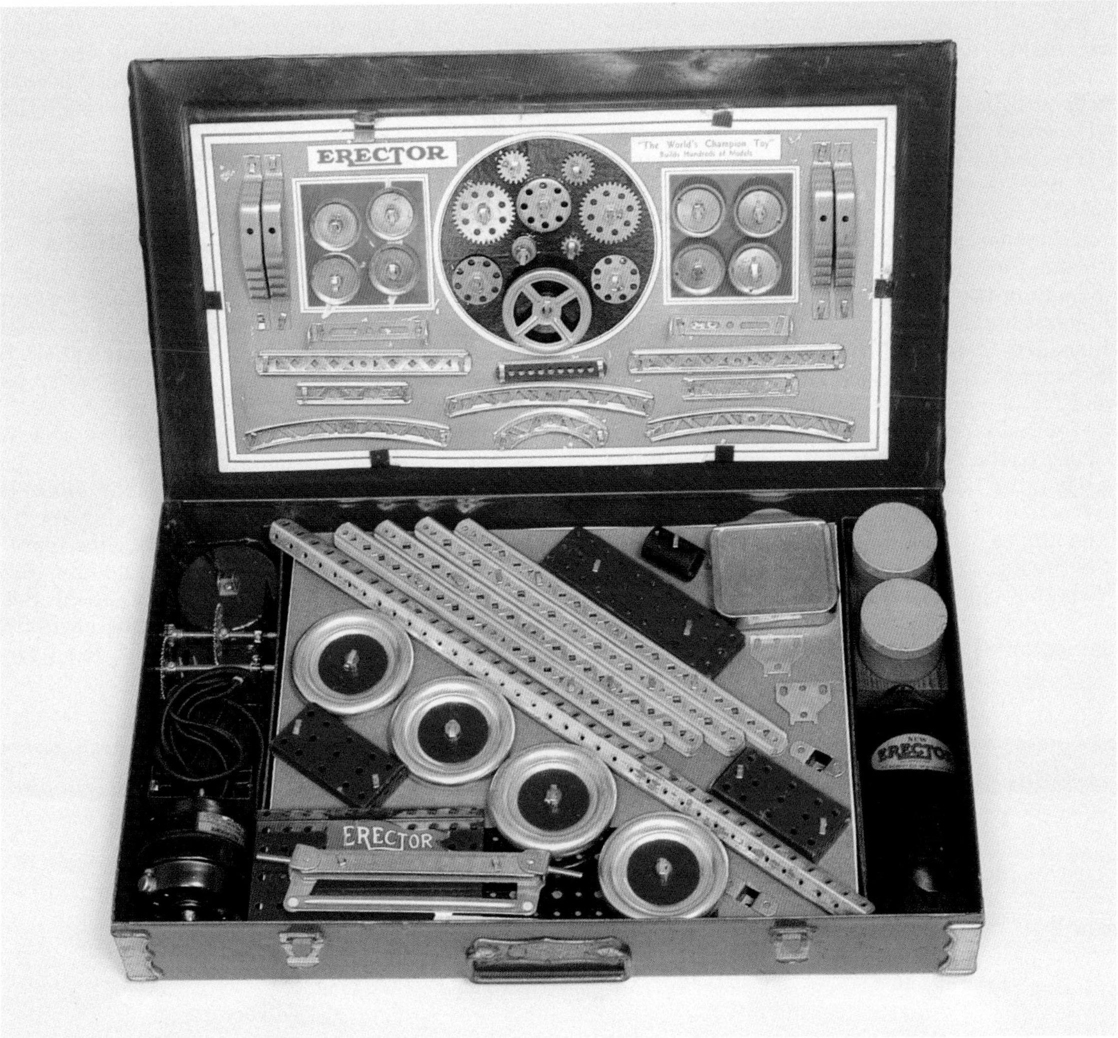

The Sensational No. 7 was the larger of the two metal box sets introduced in 1933. It featured the newly created truck parts and the electro-magnet.

familiar to all of us as children. In the shape of a circle, it pictured a boy building the suspension bridge model (a cut taken directly from the new cardboard box picture) and contained a caption that modestly stated, "Erector—The World's Greatest Toy." This label was printed in color, and in 1933 its background color was black (which may not be so familiar!). In 1934 that color was changed to the yellow that we all know so well.

The larger of the two metal box sets was No. 7, and Gilbert named it "The Sensational No. 7 Set." Its red-painted box measured 20" x 12" x 3" and came with a brass handle, latches, and corner trim. Inside the body of the box on each side were dividers that formed compartments for the large parts and motor. A green wood block held two parts cans. As with No. 6, the motor would not fit unless the base was removed. An elevated green cardboard insert fit between the dividers, and parts were fastened to it. Like No. 6, this set had a large cardboard parts display insert clipped to the inside of the lid. The insert was blue with orange and black trim and was lettered in orange "Erector—The World's Champion Toy."

As with The Super 6, Sensational No. 7 had some interesting and distinctive changes in the label used on the outside of the lid. The earliest version of this set came with a label whose size makes it unique in the development of Erector's metal boxes. It was the same label picture that was used on the cardboard box sets; it measured 17" x 9" and covered almost the entire lid. This was the only time a metal box set was adorned in this way. These sets are rare because the transition to oval labels with black background happened very quickly.

One final modification of the 1933 metal box sets is notable. It involves the manner in which the lids were attached to the body of the box. The very earliest of these sets came with small hinges identical to those used on the midsized wood box sets from 1932. These hinges connected the lid to the body across the back of the box. Set No. 7 had three hinges, and No. 6 had two. In conjunction with these hinges were two jointed strips, one on each side, which connected the box body to the lid. These jointed strips held the box lid upright when the lid was open.

But the construction of these earliest sets was quickly changed, with the hinges being moved to the sides of the box and made part of the lid. A loose-fitting rivet secured the lid to the body. With this change, the jointed strips were no longer required, so they were eliminated. This modification in hinge design occurred even before the change in lid labels, and the rear-mounted hinge sets are rare indeed.

The Sensational No. 7 was the smallest set in the 1933 line to contain the new, scaled down truck and chassis parts. As such, it is the direct descendent of the No. 7½ White Truck Set from the Classic Period. Also included in No. 7 was the (MJ) Electro Magnet, for use on crane models.

One other interesting item was included in the metal box sets: a small, corked glass vial of 3-in-One oil. It came wrapped in a small instruction sheet that indicated it was a free sample and gave directions for oiling the motor. Actually, all the sets (both metal box and wood) that contained the (P56G) 110-volt motor came with a vial of oil. This practice was continued in all the sets with electric motors through 1938 and in the Electric Train Set through 1942.

Wood Box Sets

This was the last year that Gilbert's Erector Sets came packed in wood boxes. These sets represented a last-ditch effort to retain the extravagance of the decade gone by. Only three of the five wood box sets were cataloged, all being Hudson sets: Nos. A, 8, and 8½. They are found in limited quantities today, undoubtedly owing to the low demand for such a high-priced toy during the poor economic climate of 1933. Set Nos. 9 and 10 (covered in the first volume of *Greenberg's Guide to Gilbert Erector Sets*) probably were not produced, but were listed in the price list to liquidate leftovers from the previous year.

Several distinctive features enable collectors to distinguish the 1933 wood box sets from their 1931–32 precursors. First, except for No. A, all included the new 1933 parts. That set, named "The Mile a Minute No. A Erector," was an accessory set that contained only the parts to build the Hudson locomotive. But "The 20th Century No. 8 Erector" contained all the parts from The Sensational No. 7 as well as those for the locomotive. "The World's Champion No. 8½ Erector" contained everything from No. 8, along with parts for the Hudson tender.

Incidentally, with the elimination of the White Truck model and the downsizing of the 1933 truck parts, Gilbert could again follow his old "Erector Rule." Since the inception of Erector in 1913, each set in the regular line had contained all the parts of the next smaller set, plus more. During the expansion of the Erector System in the late 1920s and early '30s, however, this had become impractical. Set Nos. 8 and 8½ from 1932 could not include all the parts from the (next smallest) No. 7½, "The White Truck Set." There was not

1933 METAL BOX VARIATIONS

	I	II	III	IV
Inner lid parts display mounting system	Slotted strips and tabs	Tabs only		
Hinge system	Rear-mounted hinges and jointed strips		Side-mounted hinges	
Lid Label	Large (17" x 9")			Oval with black background
	early 1933 ——————→			mid-1933 ——→

enough room in the box to hold the truck parts. So Gilbert fudged and included only the parts from No. 7, "The Steam Shovel Set." But in 1933, with the new, smaller truck parts, it was again feasible to follow this long-standing practice. So Nos. 8 and 8½ contained an instruction manual and all the parts from The Sensational No. 7 (now the truck set) as well as the Hudson parts.

The wood box sets had lid label modifications similar to the metal box sets. The earliest sets came with a 7½" x 2½" decal, identical to the one used on No. 6 and the 1932 wood box sets. But the wood box sets also got the black background circle labels when they first became available early in the year. Collectors prefer the circle label to the rectangular decal, because it is so unusual to see this label on a wood box. While all the 1933 sets are scarce, (this was the worst year for Erector sales during the Transition Period), the wood box sets are especially difficult to find because of their high initial prices.

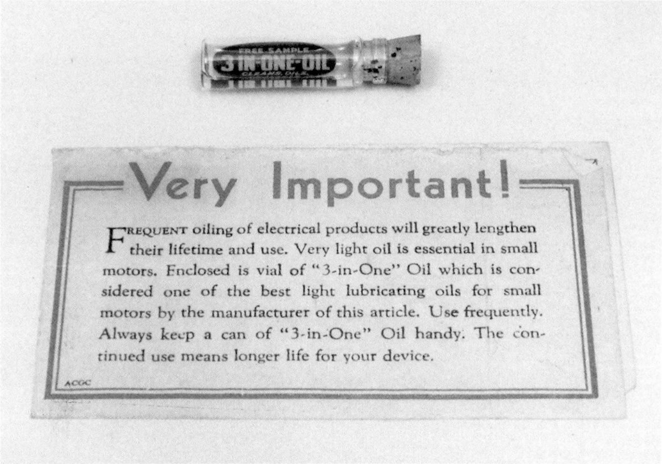

Gilbert included a vial of 3-in-One oil in the large sets that came with a 110-volt motor. If you are fortunate enough to see such a vial, don't discard it!

Erector System Modifications For 1933

I. New Parts

(LP) Railroad Tie
(LV) 3" Disc Wheel, Red
(LX) Steering Column Bracket, painted red
(MA) New Radiator, nickel-plated. Earliest version embossed "White" (rare); later one not embossed
(MB) 18½" Angle Girder, nickel-plated
(MC) Base Plate 1" x 2½", heavy-gauge steel painted red
(MD) Base Plate 2½" x 5", heavy-gauge steel painted red
(ME) Flat Plate 1" x 4", painted red
(MF) Flat Plate 1" x 5", painted red
(MG) Radiator Hood, painted red
(MH) 3" Disc Wheel, nickel rim and red hubcap
(MI) Front Axle Unit, nickel-plated
(MJ) Electro Magnet With Cord, housing painted red
(ML) Railroad Rail
( ) Parts Cans. The cylindrical parts can was new. It was made of steel, and both the can body and lid were painted blue. Some examples of green parts cans with nickel lids exist in No. 6 sets. These parts cans were used in the metal and wood box sets

II. Eliminated Parts

The real magnitude of the 1933 downsizing can best be seen by examining the parts dropped from the Erector System. In the previous year, 255 different parts were used in the lineup of sets (181 if those specific to the Hudson locomotive and tender are omitted). Of those 181 parts, 104 were dropped in 1933.

(P17) Red Wheel, large
(P50) 72 Tooth Gear
(P57E) 8" Axle Rod
(P57F) 12" Axle Rod
(K) 11 Hole Strip Bracket
(L) 21 Hole Strip Bracket
(P) Small Base Plate—5 Hole
(Q) Regular Base Plate—11 Hole
(R) Dash Plate
(V) Short Boiler
(X) Digger Scoop
(AB) One Hole Coupling
(AG) Large Hook
(AH) Small Triangle
(AI) Large Triangle
(AK) Pile Driver Weight
(AL) Collar Formed One Side
(AQ) Sheave Pulley
(AR) 8 Hole Strip
(AU) Mast Step
(AV) 7 Hole Strip Bracket
(AW) Foot Block
(AY) Bull Ring
(AZ) Bull Ring Plate
(BA) Bull Ring Center
(BAX) Bull Ring Center, ¼" Hub
(BB) Segment Plate
(BC) Left Fender
(BD) Right Fender
(BE) 6" Slotted Angle Strip
(BF) Ratchet
(BG) Truck Body
(BK) Wing Nut
(BM) Clam Shell Scoop
(BP) Tip Bucket
(BV) Chain Bucket, Large
(BX) Reflector
(BZ) Boiler Plate
(CA) Signal Arm
(CB) Wrench
(CC) Cab Top A
(CD) Cab Top B
(CF) Brass Brush
(CG) Miniature Light Bulb
(CK) Coil Magnet Wire
(CO) Miniature Socket
(CR) Special Turret Plate
(CS) Wheel Segment
(CU) Bell
(DA) 10" Axle Rod
(DD) Hood and Radiator
(DF) Tie Rod
(DG) Drag Link
(DH) Steering Knuckle
(DI) Front Axle
(DJ) Rear Axle
(DK) Flat Spring
(DL) Bumper

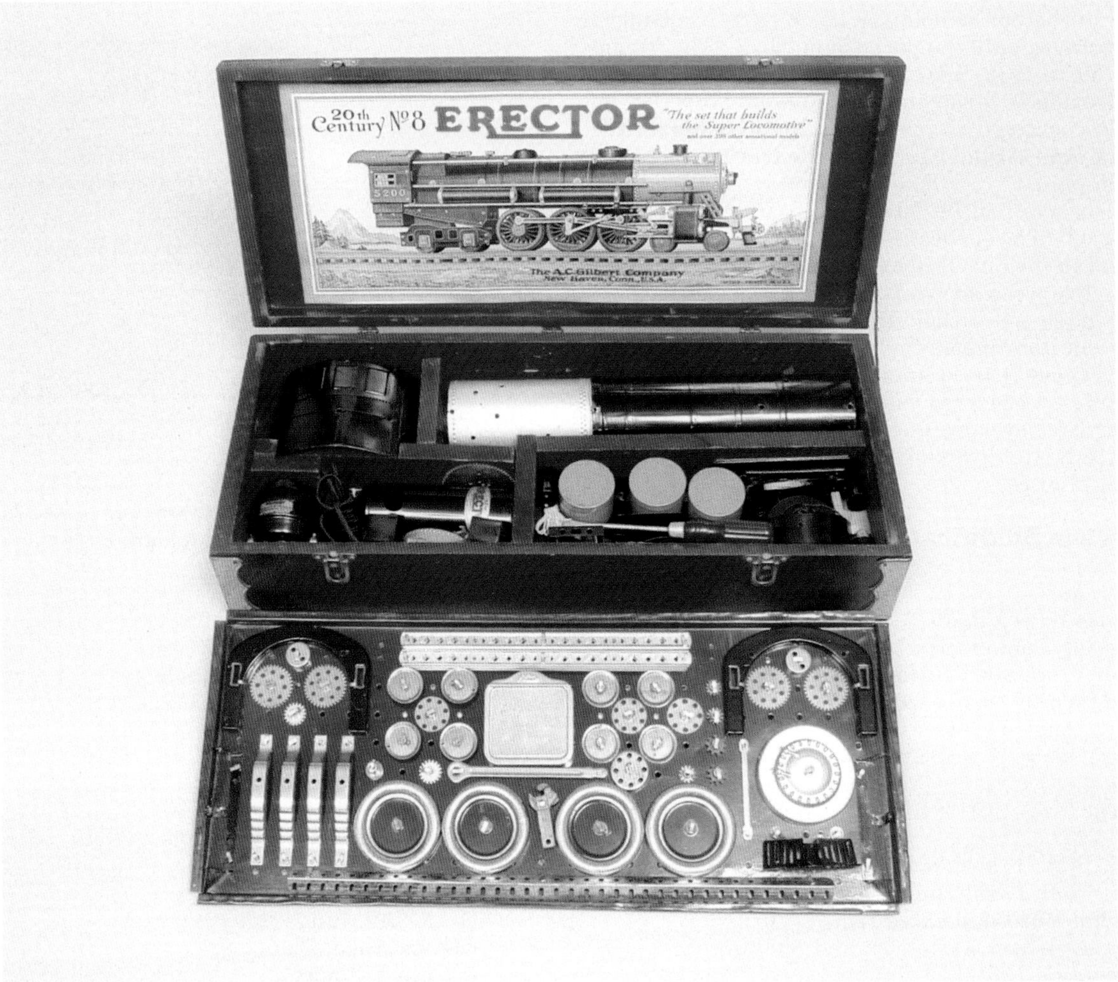

Set No. 8 from 1933, which was the last year Gilbert produced sets in wood boxes. The wood box offering was confined only to the Hudson locomotive sets, which were quite different from their predecessors from 1932. The new sets contained parts and parts cans from 1933 and often the black background oval label on the outside of the lid.

(DM) Disc Wheel
(DP) 12" Slotted Angle Strip
(DQ) Special Large Base Plate
(DR) Large Rubber Tire
(DY) Bushing
(DZ) Tackle Block
(EB) ¼" Collar
(EE) Double Angle Bracket
(EL) Brake Drum
(EM) Universal Car Truck
(EO) 6" Duplex Flat Base Plate
(EU) 3" Duplex Flat Base Plate
(EW) 12" Duplex Flat Base Plate
(EX) Big Channel Girder 12"
(EY) Big Channel Girder 6"
(EX) 6" Curved BC Girder
(FB) Cam
(FC) Machine Frame Right
(FH) 2" Slotted Angle Girder
(FJ) Rack
(FK) Machine Frame Left
(FL) Helical Gear
(FM) Cone Pulley
(FT) Ferris Wheel Support
(FU) Ferris Wheel Cab Roof
(FV) 13" Axle Rod, 5⁄16" Diameter
(FW) Slotted Crank
(FX) Quarter Gear
(FY) Universal Ball
(FZ) Internal Gear
(GA) 6" x 8" Duplex Flat Base Plate
(GS) Eccentric
(GU) Eccentric Loop
(HD) Gondola
(HE) Tail
(HG) Nose Cap
(HI) Gondola Strut
(HJ) Propeller
(HK) 5" Girder, Formed
(HL) Rudder—Left
(HM) Rudder—Right
(HN) Stabilizer
(HO) Cover For Zeppelin
(HP) 6" Ring
(HQ) Zeppelin Support Rod
(HS) Propeller Rod, 3"

Listings of 1933 Erector Sets

	Gd	VG	Exc	Inv	Org

NO. 1 The Dandy Beginner's Set

Built 50 different models and featured (FP) Small Disc Wheels. Came in a cardboard box 13½" x 9½" x 1"; sold for $1.00. **30 50 80 +15 +20**

NO. 3 The Set With The Long Girders

Built 75 different models and featured (LV) 3" Disc Wheels. Came in a cardboard box 18¼" x 10¼" x 1"; sold for $2.00. **40 60 100 +20 +25**

NO. 4 The Famous No. 4

Built more than 100 models and featured battery-operated (P58) Motor. Came in a cardboard box 18¼" x 10¼" x 2½". Two-layer set with removable parts tray; sold for $3.95.
80 120 200 +40 +50

NO. 6 The Super 6

Built more than 125 models and featured 110-volt (P56G) Motor and Boiler. Came in a green metal box 18" x 10" x 3" with parts display on inside of lid; sold for $5.95.

Early version (with rectangular decal)
160 240 400 +80 +100

Late version (with circle label)
120 180 300 +60 +75

NO. 7 The Sensational No. 7

Built more than 160 models and featured truck parts and (MJ) Electro Magnet. Came in a red metal box 20" x 12" x 3" with brass corner trim and parts display on inside of lid; sold for $10.00.

Early version (with large label)
320 480 800 +160 +200

Late version (with circle label)
240 360 600 +120 +150

NO. 8 The 20th Century No. 8 Erector

Built 199 models, including all models from No. 7, and contained 840 parts. Came in a wood box 25½" x 10¾" x 5½", finished in red with black corners, brass side grips and corner trim, suitcase catches, and recessed lid with a large, full-color inside lid label that pictured the Erector Hudson locomotive, the featured model. Two-layer set with removable metal parts tray; sold for $15.95.

Early version (with rectangular decal)
880 1320 2200 +440 +660

Late version (with circle label)
1000 1500 2500 +500 +750

NO. 8½ The World's Champion No. 8½ Erector

Built 207 models, including all models from No. 8, and contained 1180 parts. Came in a wood box 29¼" x 10¾" x 5½", finished in red with black corners, brass side grips and corner trim, suitcase catches, and recessed lid with a large, full-color inside lid label that pictured the Erector Hudson locomotive and tender, the featured model. Two-layer set with removable metal parts tray; sold for $25.00.

Early version (with rectangular decal)
1280 1920 3200 +640 +960

Late version (with circle label)
1400 2100 3500 +700 +1050

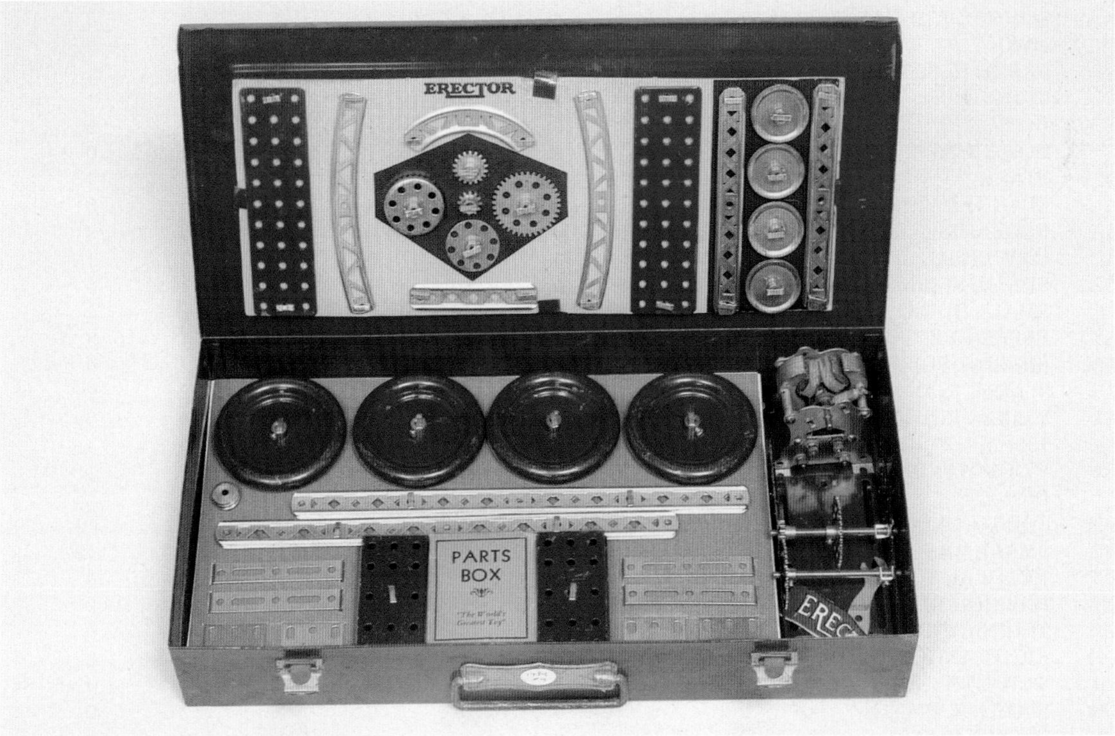

The charming little No. 4 from 1934 in a newly created metal box. The previous year's No. 4 (identical in contents) was packed in cardboard.

1933 CONTENTS LIST

Set No.		1	3	4	6	7	8	8½	A
P 7	SMALL WHEEL	4	4	4	4	4	4	4	0
P12	CROWN GEAR	0	0	1	1	1	1	1	0
P13	12 TOOTH PINION GEAR	0	0	2	2	2	2	2	1
P13A	12 TOOTH PINION (SPECIAL)	0	0	0	0	0	1	1	1
P14	WORM GEAR	0	0	1	1	1	1	1	0
P15	COUPLING	0	0	1	1	1	4	4	4
P20	5 HOLE STRIP—FORMED	0	0	0	2	4	4	4	0
P24	CRANK	1	1	1	2	2	2	2	0
P33	SMALL SCREW DRIVER	1	1	1	1	1	0	0	0
P34	HANK OF STRING	0	1	1	1	1	1	1	0
P37	COLLAR	1	4	6	8	10	10	10	8
P48	MITRE GEAR	0	0	0	0	0	2	2	2
P49	18 TOOTH GEAR	0	0	1	1	2	2	2	0
P50A	72 TOOTH GEAR (HUDSON)	0	0	0	0	0	1	1	1
P52	LADDER CHAIN	0	0	0	0	1	1	1	1
P56G	MOTOR	0	0	0	1	1	1	1	0
P57A	2⅛" AXLE ROD	1	1	1	1	1	3	3	3
P57D	6" AXLE ROD	0	1	1	1	2	2	2	1
P58	MOTOR	0	0	1	0	0	0	0	0
P79	CAR TRUCK	4	4	4	4	4	4	4	0
A	2½" GIRDER	4	4	4	4	4	4	4	0
B	5" GIRDER	4	4	8	8	12	12	12	0
C	10" GIRDER	4	8	12	16	48	48	48	0
D	2½" CURVED GIRDER	4	4	4	4	4	4	4	0
E	5" CURVED GIRDER	0	2	4	4	13	13	13	0
F	5 HOLE STRIP	0	0	2	2	3	6	6	0
G	7 HOLE STRIP	0	0	2	2	4	4	4	1
H	11 HOLE STRIP	0	0	4	4	4	4	4	1
I	21 HOLE STRIP	0	0	2	2	6	6	6	0
J	41 HOLE STRIP	0	0	0	0	2	2	6	0
M	SMALL DOUBLE ANGLE	0	0	2	2	6	6	10	0
N	LONG DOUBLE ANGLE	2	4	4	4	4	4	4	0
O	PAWL	0	0	1	1	4	4	4	0
S	LARGE BASE PLATE—21 HOLE	0	0	0	0	2	2	2	2
T	BOILER	0	0	0	1	1	1	1	0
U	BOILER TOP	0	0	0	1	1	1	1	0
W	STACK	0	0	0	3	3	3	3	1
Z	FLANGED WHEEL	0	0	0	4	4	4	4	0
AA	ECCENTRIC CRANK	0	0	0	0	0	3	3	3
AC	UNIVERSAL BRACKET	0	0	0	0	0	1	1	1
AE	SPIRAL SPRING	0	0	0	0	1	1	1	0
AF	SMALL HOOK	1	1	1	1	1	3	3	1
AJ	PAPER ERECTOR FLAG	0	0	1	1	1	1	1	0
AM	SPECIAL PULLEY—METAL	0	0	0	1	2	2	2	0
AS	3" AXLE ROD	0	0	2	3	3	3	3	0
AT	4" AXLE ROD	2	2	2	4	4	4	4	0
AX	19¾" AXLE ROD	0	0	0	0	0	4	4	4
B2	WOOD HANDLE SCREW DRIVER	0	0	0	0	0	1	1	1
BH	SOLID COLLAR	0	0	0	0	2	12	12	12
BL	SMALL WASHER	6	12	12	12	12	20	20	12
BN	REGULAR TURRET PLATE	0	0	2	4	4	4	4	0
BT	PIERCED DISC	1	1	1	2	2	2	2	2
BY	11 HOLE FIBRE STRIP	0	0	0	0	1	1	1	0
CH	RIGHT ANGLE	8	12	12	14	36	36	36	8
CJ	36 TOOTH GEAR	0	0	3	3	4	4	4	0
CQ	SLOT COUPLING	0	0	0	0	0	2	2	2
CY	5" AXLE ROD	0	2	2	2	2	2	2	0
CZ	7" AXLE ROD	0	0	0	0	2	2	2	0
DB	MOTOR PULLEY	0	0	1	1	1	1	1	0

1933 CONTENTS LIST

Set No.		1	3	4	6	7	8	8½	A
DE	STEERING COLUMN	0	0	0	0	1	1	1	0
DK	FLAT SPRING	0	0	0	0	4	4	4	0
DO	STEERING WHEEL WITH HUB	0	0	0	0	1	1	1	0
DS	COTTER PIN	0	0	0	0	1	1	1	0
DT	1-HOLE SET SCREW COUPLING	0	0	0	0	0	6	6	6
EH	GEAR BOX BRACKET	0	0	2	2	2	2	2	0
EI	STANDARD GEAR BOX SIDE PLATE	0	0	2	2	2	2	2	0
EJ	GEAR BOX BASE	0	0	1	1	1	1	1	0
EK	PLAIN DRUM	0	0	0	0	1	1	1	0
FA	1¾" x 8-32 SCREW	0	0	0	0	0	3	8	3
FD	HINGED LOOP	0	0	0	0	6	6	6	6
FP	SMALL DISC WHEEL	4	0	0	0	0	0	0	0
HF	BUTT ENDPLATE	0	0	0	0	0	1	1	1
IR	ENGINE FRAME	0	0	0	0	0	1	1	1
IS	DRIVER WHEEL	0	0	0	0	0	6	6	6
IT	COACH WHEEL	0	0	0	0	0	8	20	8
IU	SAND BOX	0	0	0	0	0	1	1	1
IV	STEAM DOME	0	0	0	0	0	1	1	1
IW	FEED WATER HEATER	0	0	0	0	0	1	1	1
IX	BELL	0	0	0	0	0	1	1	1
IY	BELL HANGER	0	0	0	0	0	1	1	1
IZ	SMOKE STACK	0	0	0	0	0	1	1	1
JA	COW CATCHER	0	0	0	0	0	1	1	1
JC	SMOKE BOX FRONT	0	0	0	0	0	1	1	1
JD	AXLE BOX	0	0	0	0	0	4	16	4
JE	PARALLEL ROD	0	0	0	0	0	2	2	2
JF	MAIN CONNECTING ROD	0	0	0	0	0	2	2	2
JG	REAR TRUCK FRAME, RIGHT	0	0	0	0	0	1	1	1
JH	REAR TRUCK FRAME, LEFT	0	0	0	0	0	1	1	1
JI	FRONT TRUCK FRAME	0	0	0	0	0	2	2	2
JJ	SMOKE BOX SHELL	0	0	0	0	0	1	1	1
JK	STEAM CHEST & CYLINDER PLATE	0	0	0	0	0	2	2	2
JL	STEAM CHEST & CYLINDER BAND	0	0	0	0	0	1	1	1
JM	STEAM CHEST END	0	0	0	0	0	13	13	13
JN	CYLINDER END	0	0	0	0	0	4	5	4
JO	CROSSHEAD GUIDE BAR	0	0	0	0	0	2	2	2
JP	CROSSHEAD	0	0	0	0	0	4	4	4
JQ	CROSSHEAD BEARER, RIGHT	0	0	0	0	0	1	1	1
JR	CROSSHEAD BEARER, LEFT	0	0	0	0	0	1	1	1
JS	LINK FRAME	0	0	0	0	0	2	2	2
JT	LINK ROD	0	0	0	0	0	2	2	2
JU	ROD CLAMP	0	0	0	0	0	2	2	2
JV	CROSSHEAD LINK	0	0	0	0	0	2	2	2
JW	COMBINING LEVER	0	0	0	0	0	2	2	2
JX	VALVE LEVER	0	0	0	0	0	4	4	4
JY	AIR DRUM SHELL	0	0	0	0	0	4	4	4
JZ	JACKET	0	0	0	0	0	1	1	1
KA	STEAM PIPE CASING	0	0	0	0	0	2	2	2
KB	MAIN BOILER	0	0	0	0	0	1	1	1
KC	BOILER FIRE BOX	0	0	0	0	0	1	1	1
KD	FIRE BOX FRONT	0	0	0	0	0	1	1	1
KE	BOILER BACKHEAD	0	0	0	0	0	1	1	1

1933 CONTENTS LIST

Set No.		1	3	4	6	7	8	8½	A
KF	FIRING DECK	0	0	0	0	0	1	1	1
KG	ASH PAN	0	0	0	0	0	1	1	1
KH	CAB	0	0	0	0	0	1	1	1
KI	CAB END	0	0	0	0	0	2	2	2
KJ	DRAW CASING	0	0	0	0	0	1	1	1
KK	FIRING DECK PLATE	0	0	0	0	0	1	1	1
KL	FRONT RUNNING BOARD, RIGHT	0	0	0	0	0	1	1	1
KM	FRONT RUNNING BOARD, LEFT	0	0	0	0	0	1	1	1
KN	REAR RUNNING BOARD	0	0	0	0	0	2	2	2
KO	RUNNING BOARD STEP	0	0	0	0	0	2	2	2
KP	FRONT BUMPER PLATE STEP	0	0	0	0	0	1	1	1
KQ	APRON	0	0	0	0	0	1	1	1
KR	M.C.B. COUPLING	0	0	0	0	0	1	3	1
KS	COUPLING PIN LIFTER	0	0	0	0	0	1	3	1
KT	¼" AXLE 3⁵⁄₃₂" LONG	0	0	0	0	0	5	5	5
KU	¼" AXLE 3⅝" LONG	0	0	0	0	0	2	8	2
KV	HEADLIGHT	0	0	0	0	0	1	1	1
KW	TRUCK FRAME	0	0	0	0	0	0	4	0
KX	TRUCK BOLSTER	0	0	0	0	0	0	2	0
KZ	TENDER BASE STEP	0	0	0	0	0	0	1	0
LA	TENDER SIDE PLATE	0	0	0	0	0	0	2	0
LB	TENDER BACK PLATE	0	0	0	0	0	0	2	0
LC	CORNER PLATE	0	0	0	0	0	0	4	0
LD	FRONT FUEL BOARD	0	0	0	0	0	0	1	0
LE	SIDE FUEL BOARD	0	0	0	0	0	0	2	0
LF	BACK FUEL BOARD WITH DECK	0	0	0	0	0	0	1	0
LG	FUEL SLIDE	0	0	0	0	0	0	1	0
LH	TENDER STEP	0	0	0	0	0	0	4	0
LI	COUPLING YOKE	0	0	0	0	0	0	2	0
LJ	TANK HANDLE	0	0	0	0	0	0	4	0
LK	TENDER STEP ANGLE	0	0	0	0	0	0	4	0
LL	REAR TIE FRAME	0	0	0	0	0	2	2	2
LP	RAILROAD TIE	0	0	0	0	0	6	12	6
LS	JACK	0	0	0	0	0	2	2	2
LT	MOTOR SUPPORT BRACKET	0	0	0	0	0	2	2	2
LV	3" DISC WHEEL, RED	0	4	4	4	0	0	0	0
LU	OFFSET WRENCH	0	0	0	0	0	2	2	2
LX	STEERING COLUMN BRACKET	0	0	0	0	1	1	1	0
MA	NEW RADIATOR	0	0	0	0	1	1	1	0
MB	18½" ANGLE GIRDER	0	0	0	0	4	4	4	0
MC	BASE PLATE (1" x 2½")	2	2	2	2	4	4	4	0
MD	BASE PLATE (2½" x 5")	1	1	1	1	1	1	1	0
ME	FLAT PLATE (1" x 4")	0	0	0	0	4	4	4	0
MF	FLAT PLATE (1" x 5")	0	2	4	4	11	11	11	0
MG	RADIATOR HOOD	0	0	0	0	1	1	1	0
MH	3" DISC WHEEL, NICKEL RIM	0	0	0	0	4	4	4	0
MI	FRONT AXLE UNIT	0	0	0	0	1	1	1	0
MJ	ELECTRO MAGNET WITH CORD	0	0	0	0	1	1	1	0
ML	RAILROAD RAIL	0	0	0	0	0	4	8	4
S51	¼" x 8-32 SCREW	20	35	48	88	125	125	250	114
S52	½" x 8-32 SCREW	0	0	0	0	0	18	28	18
S57	1⅜" x 8-32 SCREW	0	0	0	4	4	9	12	9
S62	⅞" x 8-32 SCREW	3	6	6	6	24	24	56	20
N21	8-32 SQUARE NUT	23	45	54	100	175	175	354	175

Form M 1503

ERECTOR SEPARATE PARTS PRICES

Most all dealers carry Separate Erector Parts. If unable to obtain in your city send us your check, Money Order or stamps for the parts you want and we will be glad to send your order direct.

A. C. GILBERT CO., NEW HAVEN, CONN., U. S. A.

Trade No.	Name of Part	Page	Price
*N1	4-40 Hex. Nut	2	$ .10 doz.
*N11	6-32 Hex. Nut	2	.10 doz.
*N21	8-32 Square Nut	2	.05 doz.
P7	Small Wheel	3	.10 ea.
P12	Crown Gear	3	.10 ea.
P13	12-Tooth Pinion Gear	3	.10 ea.
P14	Worm Gear	3	.20 ea.
P15	Coupling	2	.10 ea.
P17	Red Wheel—large	3	.10 ea.
P20	Five Hole Strip—formed	2	.05 ea.
P22	Slotted Strip	2	.01 ea.
P24	Crank	2	.10 ea.
P33	Small Screw Driver	4	.05 ea.
P34	Hank of String	1	.05 ea.
P37	Collar	2	.25 doz.
P38	3-hole Strip	2	.05 doz.
P39	Wood Screw	2	.15 doz.
P40	Screw Eye	2	.20 doz.
P48	Mitre Gear	3	.20 ea.
P49	18 Tooth Gear	3	.15 ea.
P50	72-Tooth Gear	3	.30 ea.
P52	Ladder Chain (22 in. lgt)	1	.15 ft.
P52A	Ladder Chain (10 ft. lgt)	1	.15 ft.
P54	Motor	6	1.75 ea.
P56G	Motor	6	3.95 ea.
P57	Motor	6	5.00 ea.
P50	110 v. Induction Motor listed only		1.25 ea.
P57A	2⅞ in. Axle	2	.02 ea.
P58	Motor	6	1.00 ea.
P59	Reverse Base	6	.75 ea.
P60C	Transformers	6	3.50 ea.
P57D	6 in. Axle	2	.06 ea.
P57E	8 in. Axle	2	.08 ea.
P57F	12 in. Axle	2	.12 ea.
P65	Disc Clutch Pow. Hoist	6	15.00 ea.
P79	Car Truck	2	.05 ea.
*P1133	Terminal Nut 4-40	2	.10 doz.
*S-3	⅛ in. x 4-40 Terminal Screw	2	.12 doz.
*S-11	Set Screw	2	.05 doz.
*S-14	¼ in. x 6-32 Screw	2	.05 doz.
*S-51	¼ in. x 8-32 Screw	2	.05 doz.
*S-57	1⅜ in. x 8-32 Screw	2	.15 doz.
*S-62	⅞ in. x 8-32 Screw	2	.10 doz.
A	2½ in. Girder	1	.20 doz.
B	5 in. Girder	1	.35 doz.
C	10 in. Girder	1	.50 doz.
D	2½ in. Curved Girder	1	.25 doz.
E	5 in. Curved Girder	1	.40 doz.
F	5 Hole Strip	2	.10 doz.
G	7 Hole Strip	2	.10 doz.
H	11 Hole Strip	2	.15 doz.
I	21 Hole Strip	2	.20 doz.
J	41 Hole Strip	2	.30 doz.
K	11 Hole Strip Bracket	2	.35 doz.
L	21 Hole Strip Bracket	2	.05 ea.
M	Small Double Angle	2	.25 doz.
N	Long Double Angle	2	.05 ea.

Trade No.	Name of Part	Page	Price
O	Pawl	2	.05 ea.
P	Small Base Plate—5 hole	6	.10 ea.
Q	Regular Base Plate—11 hole	6	.15 ea.
R	Dash Plate	4	.20 ea.
S	Large Base Plate—21 holes	6	.40 ea.
T	Boiler	4	.25 ea.
U	Boiler Top	4	.20 ea.
V	Short Boiler	4	.15 ea.
W	Stack	4	.05 ea.
X	Digger Scoop	4	.75 ea.
Y	(Discontinued—See B. M.)		
Z	Flanged Wheel	3	.15 ea.
AA	Eccentric Crank	2	.10 ea.
AB	One Hole Coupling	2	.15 ea.
AC	Universal Bracket	2	.10 ea.
AD	Hub Coupling	2	.25 ea.
AE	Spiral Spring	1	.05 ea.
AF	Small Hook	2	.15 doz.
AG	Large Hook	2	.25 doz.
AH	Small Triangle	2	.25 doz.
AI	Large Triangle	2	.05 ea.
AJ	Paper Erector Flag	1	3 for .05
AK	Pile Driver Weight	1	.25 ea.
AL	Collar formed one side	2	.10 doz.
AM	Special Pulley—Metal	3	.05 ea.
AN	Pointer	1	.10 ea.
AQ	Sheave Pulley	3	.05 ea.
AR	8 Hole Strip	2	.10 doz.
AS	2⅞ in. Axle Rod	2	.03 ea.
AT	4 in. Axle Rod	2	.04 ea.
AU	Mast Step	1	.10 ea.
AV	7 Hole Strip Bracket	2	2 for .05
AW	Foot Block	2	.15 ea.
AX	19¾ in. Axle Rod	2	.20 ea.
AY	Bull Ring	3	.50 ea.
AZ	Bull Wheel Plate	3	.25 ea.
BA	B. W. Cntr (with Hub) 3 & 5		.25 ea.
BB	Segment Plate	2	.15 ea.
B2	Wood Handle Screw Driver	4	.15 ea.
BC	Left Fender	5	.35 ea.
BD	Right Fender	5	.35 ea.
BE	6 in. Slotted Angle Strip	1	.50 doz.
BF	Ratchet	1	.10 ea.
BG	Truck Body	5	1.00 ea.
BH	Solid Collar	2	2 for .05
BI	6 in. Flat Beam Girder	1	6 for .50
BJ	12 in. Flat Beam Girder	1	6 for .75
BK	8-32 Wing Nut	2	.25 doz.
BL	Small Washer	2	.05 doz.
BM	Clam Shell Scoop (new)	4	2.50 ea.
BN	Regular Turret Plate	5	.15 ea.
BO	Reverse Switch Attachment	2	.50 ea.
BP	Tip Bucket	4	2.50 ea.
BQ	Resistance Wire (not illustrated)		.10 ea.
BR	Open Slot Angle	2	.25 doz.
BT	Pierced Disc	3	.10 ea.
BV	Chain Bucket (large)	4	.15 ea.

Trade No.	Name of Part	Page	Price
BW	Chain Bucket (small)	4	.10 ea.
BX	Reflector	2	.10 ea.
BY	11 Hole Fibre Strip	2	.05 ea.
BZ	Boiler Plate	4	6 for .50
CA	Signal Arm	1	.10 ea.
CB	Wrench	4	.05 ea.
CC	Cab Top B (with large hole)	4	.25 ea.
CD	Cab Top A (without large hole)	4	.25 ea.
CE	(Discontinued—see R)		
CF	Brass Brush	2	2 for .05
CG	Miniature Light Bulb	2	.10 ea.
CH	Right Angle	2	.10 doz.
CI	Large Brass Segment	2	3 for .10
CJ	36 Tooth Gear	3	.20 ea.
CK	Coil Magnet Wire	2	.25 ea.
CL	Small Rubber Tire	1	.10 ea.
CM	Fibre Disc with Hub	3	.10 ea.
CN	Brass Segment (small)	2	2 for .05
CO	Miniature Socket	2	.15 ea.
CP	Fibre Washer	2	.10 doz.
CQ	Slot Coupling	2	.15 ea.
CR	Spec. Tur. Plate with Hub	5	.15 ea.
CS	Wheel Segment	1	.15 ea.
CT	Large Flanged Wheel	3	.25 ea.
CU	Bell	1	.10 ea.
CV	(Discontinued)		
CW	(Discontinued)		
CX	1 in. Axle Rod	2	.01 ea.
CY	5 in. Axle Rod	2	.05 ea.
CZ	7 in. Axle Rod	2	.07 ea.
DA	10 in. Axle Rod	2	.10 ea.
DB	Motor Pulley	3	.10 ea.
DC	Propeller Blade	1	2 for .10
DD	Hood & Radiator	5	.75 ea.
DE	Steering Column	5	.10 ea.
DF	Tie Rod	5	.10 ea.
DG	Drag Link	5	.05 ea.
DH	Steering Knuckle	5	.15 ea.
DI	Front Axle	5	.10 ea.
DJ	Rear Axle	5	.15 ea.
DK	Flat Spring	5	.10 ea.
DL	Bumper	5	.15 ea.
DM	Disc Wheel	3	.25 ea.
DN	Bearing Right Angle	2	2 for .05
DO	Steering Wheel with Hub	3	.15 ea.
DP	12 in. Slotted Angle Strip	1	6 for .50
DQ	Special Large Base Plate (28 holes)	6	.50 ea.
DR	Large Rubber Tire	3	.15 ea.
DS	Cotter Pin	1	.05 doz.
DT	1-hole Set Screw Coupling	2	2 for .15
DU	¼ in. Diam. Axle 8½ in.	2	2 for .25
DV	6 in. Curved Beam Girder	1	6 for .75
DW	Attachment Plug—not illustrated		.15 ea.
DX	Twisted Cord (not illustrated)		.05 ft.
DY	Bushing	5	2 for .05
DZ	Tackle Block	3	.15 ea.

Trade No.	Name of Part	Page	Price
EA	Discontinued—See E. W.		
EB	¼ in. Collar	2	.05 ea.
EC	Giant Axle—29 in. long 5/16 in. diam.	2	.50 ea.
ED	Three Drum Hoist	4	3.50 ea.
EE	Double Angle Bracket	2	.05 ea.
EF	Brush for P58 Motor	2	.05 ea.
EG	Brush Spring for P58 Motor	2	.05 ea.
EH	Gear Box Bracket	2	.05 ea.
EI	Standard Gear Box Side Pl.	4	.15 ea.
EJ	Gear Box Base	6	.20 ea.
EK	Plain Drum	3	.25 ea.
EL	Brake Drum	3	.25 ea.
EM	Universal Car Truck	2	.05 ea.
EN	¼ in. Special Pulley	3	.10 ea.
EO	6 in. Dup. Flat Base Plate	6	.15 ea.
EP	Flat Pulley	3	.10 ea.
EU	3 in. Dup. Flat Base Plate	6	.10 ea.
EW	12 in. Duplex F. B. Plate	6	.50 ea.
EX	Big Channel Girder 12 in.	1	6 for .50
EY	Big Channel Girder 6 in.	1	.05 ea.
EZ	6 in. Curved B. C. Girder	1	.05 ea.
*FA	1¾ in. x 8-32 Screw	2	.15 doz.
FB	Cam	3	.15 ea.
FC	Machine Frame Right	6	.25 ea.
FD	Hinged Loop	2	2 for .05
FJ	Rack	3	.25 ea.
FK	Machine Frame Left	6	.25 ea.
FL	Helical Gear	3	.25 ea.
FM	Cone Pulley	3	.50 ea.
FN	Small Spiral Spring	1	2 for .05
FO	Double Angle Base Plate	6	.05 ea.
FP	Small Disc Wheel	3	.10 ea.
FQ	Double Angle Bracket	2	.35 doz.

NOTE

*N21 Nut used with screws S51, S52, S62, S57, FA.
*N11 Nut used with screw S14.
*P1133 Nut used with screw S3
*N1 Nut used with screw S3.
*S11 Set Screw used with pulleys, couplings, etc.

ERECTOR SEPARATE PARTS PRICES (Continued)

Trade No.	Name of Part	Page	Price
FW	Slotted Crank	2	$ .10 ea.
FX	Quarter Gear	3	.15 ea.
FY	Universal Ball	1	.20 ea.
FZ	Internal Gear	3	.15 ea.
GA	6x8 Duplex Flat Base Plate	6	.35 ea.
GR	Flat Belt	1	.10 ea.
GS	Eccentric	3	.10 ea.
GT	Flat Pulley with Hub	3	.10 ea.
GU	Eccentric Loop	2	.10 ea.
GV	Disc Wheel	3	.10 ea.
GW	Wood Wheel with Hub	3	.05 ea.
GX	8 Hole Double Angle Bracket	2	.10 doz.
GY	Metal Erector Tray	6	1.00 ea.
HA	Rear Axle Housing	5	.15 ea.
*S52	½ in. x 8-32 Screw	2	.10 doz.
HR	Wood Screw	2	.10 doz.

For illustrated Zeppelin parts, see Section 5A in Manual.

Trade No.	Name of Part	Page	Price
HD	Gondola		$ .25 ea.
HE	Tail		.25 ea.
HF	Butt End Plate		.10 ea.
HG	Nose Cap		.25 ea.
HI	Gondola Strut		.30 doz.
HJ	Propeller		.10 ea.
HK	5 inch Girder Formed		.50 doz.
HL	Rudder—Right		.10 ea.
HM	Rudder—Left		.10 ea.
HN	Stabilizers		.10 ea.
HO	Cover for Zeppeli.		2.00 ea.
HP	6 inch Ring		.20 ea.
HQ	Zeppelin Support Rod		.25 ea.
HR	Wood Screw		.10 doz.
HS	Propeller Rod, 3 in.		.05 ea.
HT	Ceiling Support		.30 ea.
HV	Revolving Contact Unit		1.00 ea.
HW	Ball Race		.20 ea.
HX	Bearing Washer		2 for .05
HY	Hub		.15 ea.
HZ	Stationary Contact Unit, with Cord and Plug		1.00 ea.
IA	Swivel Unit Completely Assembled		2.50 ea.
IB	Propeller Rod, 2 in.		.04 ea.
P-61	High Speed Motor		6.00 ea.
B.A.X.	Bull Wheel Center, ¼ in. Hub		.25 ea.
MJ	Electro Magnet with Cord	2	.60 ea.
MG	Radiator Hood	5	.10 ea.
LX	Steering Column Bracket	5	.05 ea.
MI	Front Axle Unit	5	.25 ea.
LV	3 in. Disc Wheel, red	3	.20 ea.
MH	3 in. Disc Wheel, Nickel Rim	3	.25 ea.
MD	New large Base Plate	6	.10 ea.
MC	Small Base Plate	6	.05 ea.
ME	Flat Plate	6	.05 ea.
MF	Flat Plate	6	.05 ea.
MA	New Radiator	5	.15 ea.
MB	18½ in. Angle Girder	1	.15 ea.

REGULAR ERECTOR MANUALS

No. 1	Erector Manual	.25 ea.
No. 3	Erector Manual	.25 ea.
No. 4	Erector Manual	.25 ea.
No. 6	Erector Manual	.25 ea.
No. 7	Erector Manual	.25 ea.
No. 7½	Erector Manual	.50 ea.
No. 8	Locomotive Manual	.25 ea.
No. 8½	Locomotive Manual	.50 ea.
No. 9	Erector Manual	.75 ea.
No. 10	Erector Manual	1.00 ea.

ERECTOR ACCESSORY MANUALS

No. A	Locomotive Manual	.25 ea.
No. 5	Erector Electrical Set Manual	.25 ea.
	Fun with your Motor Manual	.25 ea.

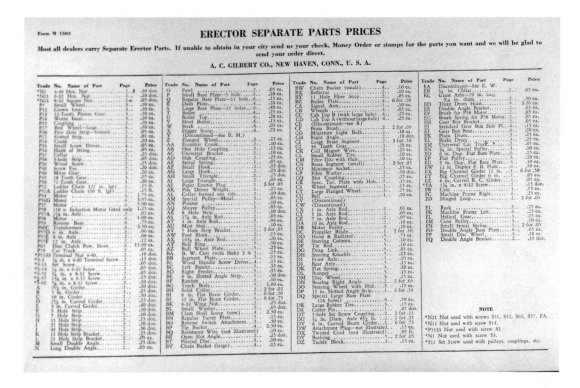

Separate Parts Prices for 1933

Right: Boilers from 1934 came with a gold background decal that had been used since 1928. Left: Later ones came with the same red-lettered decal used on the cab of the Hudson locomotive.

The black background oval outer lid label was introduced in mid-1933. Sometime in the mid-1934, it gave way to the yellow background label used into the 1950s.

	Gd	VG	Exc	Inv	Org

No. A — The Mile-A-Minute No. A Erector

Built 14 models. Accessory set containing only the Hudson locomotive parts and a few regular Erector parts. Came in a wood box 22¾" x 10¾" x 5½", finished in red with black corners, brass side grips and corner trim, suitcase catches, and recessed lid with a large, full-color inside lid label picturing the Erector Hudson locomotive. Two-layer set with removable metal parts tray; sold for $12.95.

	Gd	VG	Exc	Inv	Org
Early version (with rectangular decal)	680	1020	1700	+320	+430
Late version (with circle label)	760	1140	1900	+360	+540

THE 1934 ERECTOR LINE

The old saying, "You can't keep a good man down," certainly described A. C. Gilbert as he moved his company into 1934. The previous year had been an awful one for his business, with sales at very low levels and a substantial net loss to show for the year's efforts. But in spite of those difficulties, Gilbert continued to reshape and rebuild the Erector line.

Seven different sets were offered in 1934: two in cardboard boxes and five in metal boxes. Although one less set appeared in the catalog this year than in 1933, the number of metal boxed sets was greatly expanded. Once again, No. 10 from 1932 was included in the price list, but not in the catalog. And the price of this wonderful monster was reduced from $69.75 to $50.00. Imagine, a "fire sale" on the most gigantic Erector Set of all time!

Two new parts joined the Erector System. The (MM) Wrench replaced the old (CB) Wrench, after a year with no wrench included in the main line of sets, although Hudson sets from 1933 did contain an (LU) Offset Wrench. Sets No. 4 and above came with the (MM) Wrench.

Also new this year was the (LW) Rubber Tire, and it came with the two sets that contained the truck parts. Clearly, Gilbert felt that the truck and automotive models should have rubber tires, as did the White truck model of the Classic Period. The (LW) tires were designed to be used with the (LV) 3" Disc Wheels, Red; these wheels and tires are discussed at length later in this chapter.

Two parts were modified in 1934, and the changes here are most interesting. First, there were two variations of the label used on the boiler this year. The early version came with the gold oval decal used since boilers were first produced with decals in 1928. The later version came with the same red-lettered decal used on the cab of the Erector Hudson, a single line that read, "Erector." This variation is most likely due to simple economics. Toward the end of 1934 (when the variation occurred), Gilbert must have had plans for the changes that would take place in the 1935 line, and one of these changes was a switch to nickel-plated boilers with silver labels (not decals). So when the supply of oval decals ran out, instead of ordering more, the Hudson cab decals were used.

The second modification affected the (AS) 3" Axle Rod. Beginning now, it was known as the (AS) 2⅞" Axle Rod. The reason for this minor change is most interesting. This axle was used on the gearbox, which came assembled and packed in the set boxes. Because of the new metal boxes, this axle had to be shortened slightly to fit into the compartments.

Finally, there were some changes in the parts can. It came three different ways in 1934. There were cans with a powder blue body and lid, as in 1933. But others came with a powder blue body and nickel lid or a royal blue body and nickel lid. This last variation is rare.

Cardboard Box Sets

Only two cardboard sets were available in 1934: Nos. 1 and 3. The No. 1 differed slightly from last year's offering, because the (FP) Small Disc Wheels were eliminated. The (P7) Small Wheels were included, along with the (FP)s last year, but now all models were illustrated with the (P7)s. The models pictured for No. 1 in the instruction manual were changed accordingly. Set No. 3 was unchanged from 1933, although the price increased from $2.00 to $2.50. Set No. 4 was repackaged in a metal box in 1934.

Metal Box Sets

Two special features characterize the metal box sets. First, this was the last year that the entire lineup of metal boxed sets was produced with the colorful cardboard parts displays attached to the inside of the lids. (The exception to this was a series of special sets produced for and sold through Sears, Roebuck & Co.) Second, the outside lid label was modified about halfway through the year. The early label used on these sets was the same circle label with a black background that Gilbert had introduced in 1933 for the metal box sets. On the later 1934 sets, the color was changed to yellow, thus creating two versions of each of the 1934 box sets. The black background label sets are much more desirable because their labels have a unique appearance and were used for such a limited time.

The smallest of the metal box sets was No. 4, which Gilbert still called The Famous No. 4. Its newly created metal box measured 16" x 8" x 3" and was painted red. It had no dividers, but came with a lower green cardboard insert that created a compartment on the right-hand side of the box that housed the (P58) Motor and Gearbox. The lid parts display cardboard was yellow with black lettering and trim. The contents of this set were identical to No. 4 from 1933, which came in a cardboard box, but it now included a newly designed small parts box. That container was the same size and shape as before, but its color was mustard yellow and the black lettering read, "Parts Box The World's Greatest Toy." The price of No. 4 increased from $3.95 in 1933 to $5.00.

Next in the lineup was No. 6, still known as The Super 6 and packaged in an 18" x 10" x 3" green box. The trim, lettering, and arrangement of the parts mounted on the insert remained the same as in 1933, but the background of the inside lid cardboard parts display insert had been changed from blue to yellow. This set, which sold for $5.95 the previous year, was now $7.50.

Some confusion occurs when dealing with No. 7. It was still called The Sensational No. 7 and came in a 20" x 12" x 3" box painted red. But the contents were reduced from last year, as all the truck parts had been deleted. The set had the same inside lid display insert, but fewer parts were mounted on it and the positions of the parts had been changed. Likewise, the lower-level green insert was still used, but the parts positions had been altered here as well. There were some new models created for this set, mainly cranes that featured the (MJ) Electro Magnet, and the instruction manual was modified accordingly. Although the contents were reduced, the price remained $10.00.

If you are wondering where the truck parts went, you will find them in a set that was brand new to the 1934 line, No. 7½, named "The Automotive Set." Describing this set as brand new is only partially correct. What was new this year was the box. It measured 22" x 13" x 3" and was painted a dark shade of powder blue. There was a metal divider along each side of the box that formed compartments in which the motor, boiler, electro magnet, parts cans, and assembled gearbox were packed. A green wood block held the parts cans snug against the lid when the box was closed. There were the usual latches and handle and brass corner trim. This box was hinged across the back instead of on the sides. Jointed lid support strips connected the lid to the box body and held the lid upright when the lid was open.

What was not brand new about No. 7½ was the parts that came in it. They were virtually identical to those in No. 7 from 1933. It was the same set, just packed in a larger box! There was one addition to the 1934 set; No. 7½ came with the new (LW) Rubber Tires. There was a cardboard parts display insert mounted on the inside of the lid; the same as the one used in No. 7 from 1933. The parts were even mounted in the same positions as in 1933. The 1934 instruction manual was changed as a new section was added for No. 7½, but the models pictured were the same as those for No. 7 from 1933. Although No. 7½ was a virtual copy of the latter (just in a bigger box), it was priced $5.00 higher at $15.00.

The new box for The Automotive Set was much too big for the parts included in it. The appearance of the set is fine when the cardboard insert is in place as it tends to fill things up, but when the parts are stored with no cardboard insert, the set seems half gone. This box was really sort of a transition box, and Gilbert designed it with the 1935 changes already in mind.

Without a doubt, the greatest accomplishment Gilbert made in 1934, and one of his greatest ever, was the creation of No. 8, named "The World's Champion No. 8 Erector." The Hudson locomotive and tender were the only Classic Period models to survive the ravages of the Great Depression, and No. 8 was the set that was redesigned to feature this model.

A new, very large metal box was created to hold this set. It measured 24" x 14" x 4" and was as large as the metal box sets would ever be. Painted the same shade of powder blue as the box for No. 7½, this box looked slightly different, as it was given a crackle finish. It came with a brass handle, latches, and corner trim, and had a removable metal parts display tray that was also finished in crackle powder blue. Except for the color, this tray was identical to the one used in the Classic Period wood box No. 7.

Inside the box, metal dividers formed four compartments for parts storage, and there were strips welded in place to support the parts tray. As with No. 7½, there were rear-mounted hinges on this box and jointed strips held the lid upright while the box was open. The inside of the lid was covered with a large cardboard parts display insert that was blue with black and white trim. In the center was a black-and-white picture of two boys and the Hudson crossing a bridge made of Erector. This same picture (but much larger and in brighter colors) was used on the inside of the lid of No. 10 in 1931 and 1932.

Some of the packing techniques in this set are most interesting. The Hudson locomotive's frame and the six large drive wheels came assembled, and a second tray of parts was created using the (S) Base Plates. Six metal cans contained the small parts, and the track came assembled, even though the rails and ties could be taken apart. The contents of this set were identical to those of the wood box No. 8½ from 1933, but with the addition of the (LW) Rubber Tires.

Set No. 8 came with two instruction manuals. The first was identical to the manual packed with No. 7½ and illustrated all the models that could be built with the regular

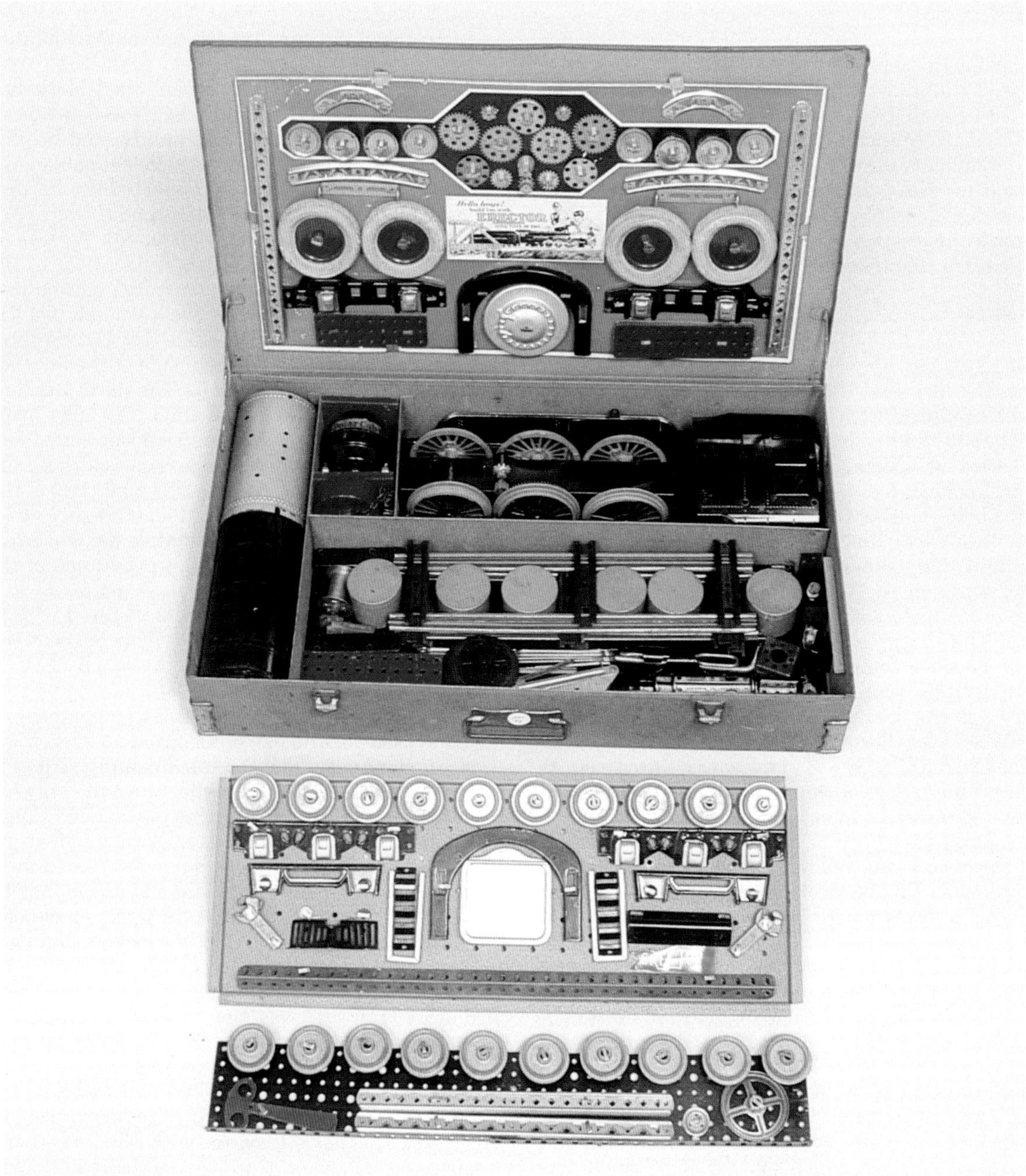

Beginning in 1934 and continuing through 1937, the Erector Hudson locomotive and tender sets came in a huge metal box. The No. 8 was modified in each of those four years. The powder blue metal tray was unique to the version from 1934.

Erector parts. The second manual pictured the Hudson locomotive and tender on the cover and was labeled No. 8. It contained the instructions for assembling those two models as well as other special ones that could be built with parts in No. 8. The presence of two manuals continued (with appropriate set number changes) in the Hudson sets until that model was discontinued in 1938.

Surprisingly, the price of this wonderful set was $25.00, the same as that of No. 8½ from the previous year. It was the only set in the lineup with neither a price increase nor a contents reduction. The No. 8 from 1934 is the most difficult of the metal box Hudson sets to find.

An Aside: The (MH) And (LV) Wheels And The (LW) Rubber Tires

When Gilbert modified the Erector System at the beginning of the Transition Period, he created a new 3"-diameter wheel, but with variations. Later he added a rubber tire for this wheel. These variations and changes can be confusing, so I will try to clarify the matter here.

In 1933, Gilbert created two versions of this wheel: (LV) 3" Disc Wheel, Red, and (MH) 3" Disc Wheel, Nickel Rim. The (LV)s were less expensive to produce because they were simply red-painted steel. The (MH)s cost more to make because

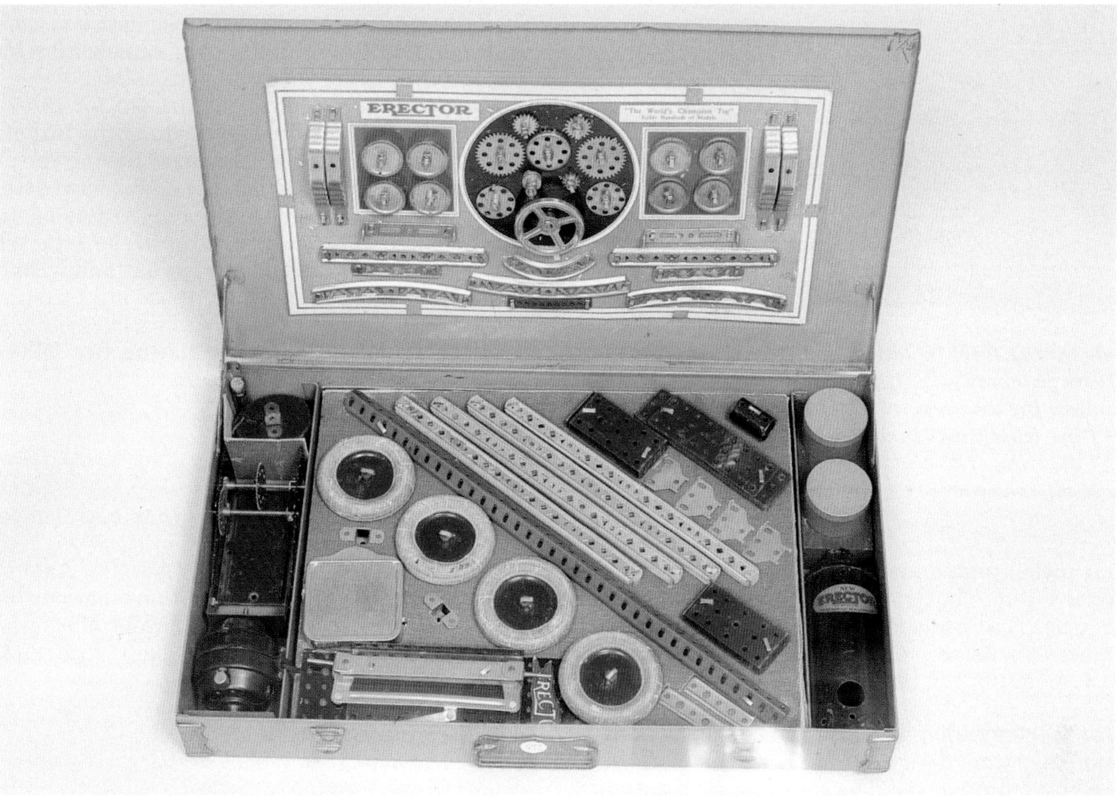

Set No. 7½ came in a large, powder blue box in 1934. With the exception of the (LV) Wheels and (LW) Tires, its contents were identical to those in No. 7 from 1933.

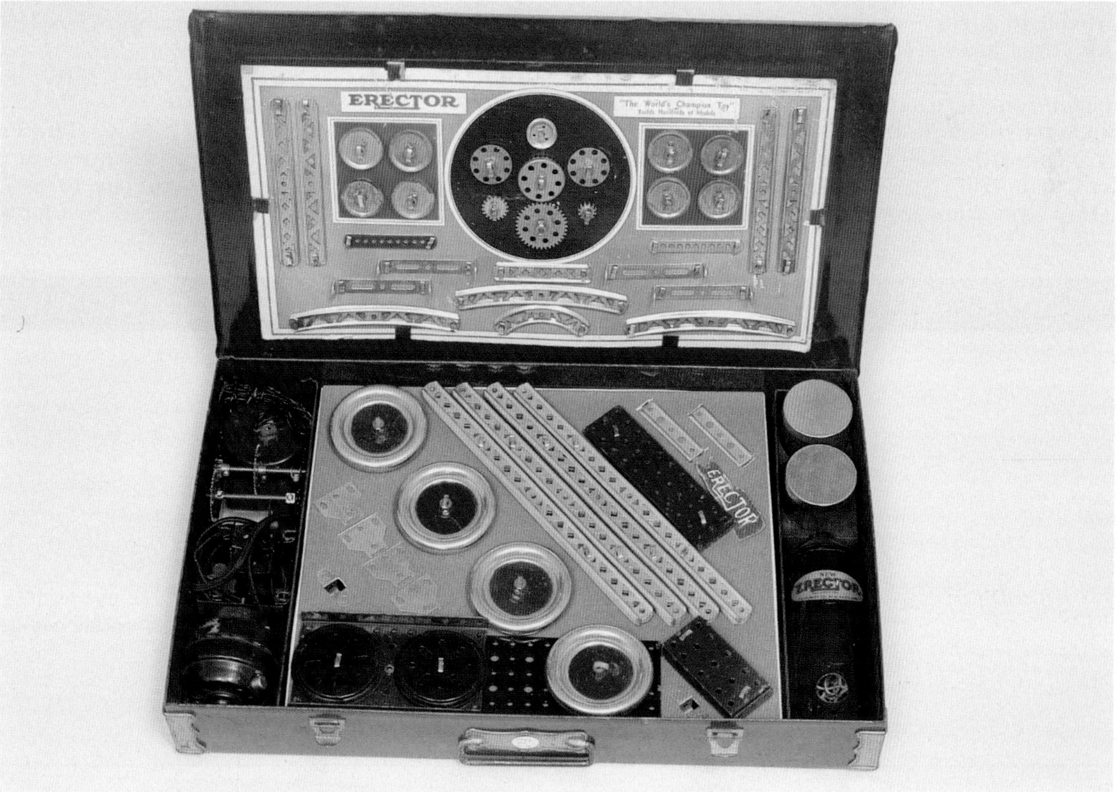

Although still billed in the catalog as "The Sensational No. 7" and packed in the same size box, No. 7 from 1934 had changed since 1933. Gilbert eliminated the specialized parts for building truck and automobiles.

The disc wheels that Gilbert included in different sets (beginning in 1934) can be confusing. Left: The (LV) 3" Disc Wheel, Red, which came in the smallest sets. Middle: The (MH) 3" Disc Wheel, Nickel Rim, which was included in one midrange set. Right: The (LV) with the (LW) Rubber Tire, which was packed in only the most expensive sets.

they were first nickel-plated and then only a center "hubcap" was painted red. The latter looked more realistic, especially for truck and automotive models, so they were used in the more expensive sets. In 1933, the (LV) wheels came in Nos. 3, 4, and 6; the (MH)s were included in Nos. 7, 8, and 8½.

Then in 1934 Gilbert added the (LW) Rubber Tires to the Erector System. They were designed to be used only with the solid red (LV) wheels, since it would be aesthetically pointless to use them over the nickel-rimmed (MH) wheels. An (LV) wheel with an (LW) tire was the most realistic truck tire of all. But this was also the most expensive combination to produce, so these parts were added to only the most expensive sets. In 1934 the (LV)s alone were used in Nos. 3, 4, and 6. The (MH)s were used only in No. 7. And the combination of (LV) wheels and (LW) tires was were included in Nos. 7½ and 8.

In 1935, the (LV) wheels and (LW) tires were again part of the Erector System, but were included only in the top-of-the-line Hudson locomotive set. All the other sets, except for the very smallest, came with (MH) wheels from this point forward. The next year, 1936, was the last one that the (LV) wheels and (LW) tires were part of the system, and they were included in the Hudson locomotive set for only part of the year. The early No. 10½ sets came with (LV)s and (LW)s; the late No. 10½ sets came with (MH)s.

Sadly, the chemical formula used for the rubber in the (LW) tires was not able to withstand the test of time. Unlike the (DR) Large Rubber Tires used during the Classic Period for the White Truck model, the (LW)s have deteriorated horribly over the years. Usually only traces of these tires are left on the (LV) wheels found in large sets. When the tires are intact, they tend to be dried out and wrinkled. Even so, regardless of their condition, these are rare parts.

Erector System Modifications for 1934

I. New Parts
(LW) Rubber Tire
(MM) Wrench

II. Modified Parts
(T) Boiler, with gold oval decal (early) or red-lettered "Erector" decal (late)
(AS) 3" Axle Rods became (AS) 2⅞" Axle Rods
( ) Parts Cans. Three variations: powder blue body with matching lid (as in 1933), powder blue body with nickel-plated lid, and royal blue body with nickel-plated lid (the scarcest)

III. Eliminated Parts
(FP) Small Disc Wheel

Listings of 1934 Erector Sets

	Gd	VG	Exc	Inv	Org

NO. 1 **The Dandy Beginner's Set**
Built 50 models. Came in a cardboard box 13½" x 9½" x 1"; sold for $2.00.

	Gd	VG	Exc	Inv	Org
	30	50	80	+15	+20

NO. 4 **The Famous No. 4**
Built more than 100 models and featured battery-operated (P58) Motor. Came in a red metal box 16" x 8" x 3", with a parts display on the inside of the lid; sold for $5.00.

SETS IN THE ERECTOR SYSTEM 1933–34

	Box Size	1933	1934
Cardboard Box Sets		No. 1	No. 1
		No. 3	No. 3
		No. 4	
Metal Box Sets	16" x 8" x 3"	N/A	No. 4, red
	18" x 10" x 3"	No. 6, green	No. 6, green
	20" x 12" x 3"	No. 7, red	No. 7, red
	22" x 13" x 3"	N/A	No. 7½, powder blue
	24" x 14" x 4"	N/A	No. 8, crackle powder blue
Wood Box Sets	23" x 11" x 6"	No. A	N/A
	26" x 11" x 6"	No. 8	N/A
	30" x 11" x 6"	No. 8½	N/A

As the picture of metal box Erector Sets develops over this and subsequent chapters, you will notice that not many types of boxes were used. But the set that each box contained changed over the years, as did the set number, color of the box, and elements of the box construction. This chart traces these changes and should make clear the evolution of the metal boxes.

	Gd	VG	Exc	Inv	Org
Early version (with black background lid label)	100	150	250	+50	+65
Late version (with yellow background lid label)	80	120	200	+40	+50

NO. 6 **The Super 6**

Built more than 125 models and featured 110-volt (P56G) Motor and Boiler. Came in a green metal box 18" x 10" x 3" with parts display on inside of lid; sold for $7.50.

	Gd	VG	Exc	Inv	Org
Early version (with black background lid label)	120	180	300	+60	+75
Late version (with yellow background lid label)	100	150	250	+50	+65

NO. 7 **The Sensational No. 7**

Built more than 150 models and featured (MJ) Electro Magnet. Came in a red metal box 20" x 12" x 3" with brass corner trim and parts display on inside of lid; sold for $10.00.

	Gd	VG	Exc	Inv	Org
Early version (with black background lid label)	180	270	450	+90	+110
Late version (with yellow background lid label)	140	210	350	+70	+90

NO. 7½ **The Automotive Set**

Built more than 180 models and featured automotive parts. Came in a powder blue metal box 22" x 13" x 3" with brass corner trim and parts display on inside of lid; sold for $15.00.

	Gd	VG	Exc	Inv	Org
Early version (with black background lid label)	240	360	600	+120	+150
Late version (with yellow background lid label)	200	300	500	+100	+125

NO. 8 **The World's Champion No. 8 Erector**

Built 210 models, including all models from No. 7½, and contained parts for the Hudson locomotive and tender. Came in a powder blue crackle-finish metal box 24" x 14" x 4", with brass corner trim and inside lid parts display. Multiple-layer set with removable metal parts tray; sold for $25.00.

	Gd	VG	Exc	Inv	Org
Early version (with black background lid label)	1280	1920	3400	+680	+850
Late version (with yellow background lid label)	1200	1800	3200	+640	+800

THE 1935 ERECTOR LINE

In the evolution of the Erector System, 1935 was a key year. Gilbert added important new parts that had an impact on nearly all the sets. These additions included special architectural parts that created a radical new concept of model building. The metal boxes were re-engineered because a new method of packaging and display had been invented. The entire Erector line got a new numbering system, and several new models were created. These modifications were common to virtually the entire line, so they deserve comment before I describe individual sets.

It may be hard to believe, but the addition of a single component to the system in 1935 not only caused a virtual redesigning of most of the larger Erector models and the rewriting of the instruction manual but also led to a totally new method of packaging and display for the line of sets. What part promoted so much change? The (MN) 12" Base Plate.

This new part replaced and improved upon the old (S) Large Base Plate. The (MN) was slightly larger than its predecessor and was made from a lighter-gauge steel, so it was less costly to produce. As a result, Gilbert found it economically feasible to include these new base plates in all but the smallest sets. In the past, the (S) base plates were included in only the most expensive sets. The (MN) was a versatile part; it was just the right size to build a base for many of the

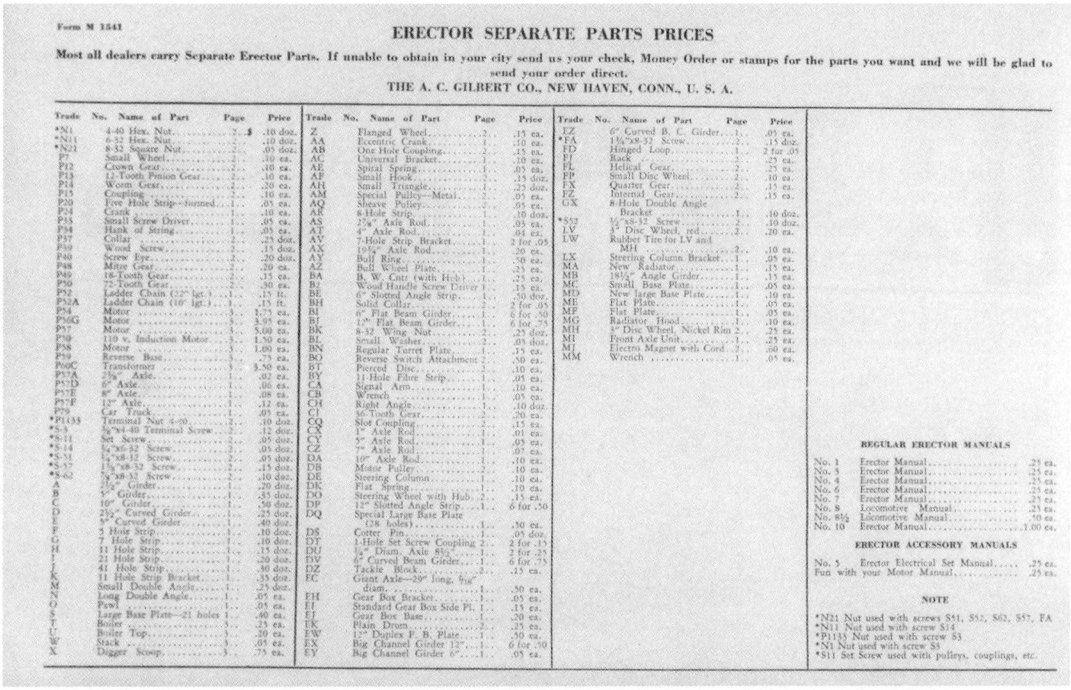

Form M 1541

ERECTOR SEPARATE PARTS PRICES

Most all dealers carry Separate Erector Parts. If unable to obtain in your city send us your check, Money Order or stamps for the parts you want and we will be glad to send your order direct.

THE A. C. GILBERT CO., NEW HAVEN, CONN., U. S. A.

Trade No.	Name of Part	Page	Price
*N1	4-40 Hex. Nut	2	$ .10 doz.
*N11	6-32 Hex. Nut	2	.10 doz.
*N21	8-32 Square Nut	2	.05 doz.
P7	Small Wheel	2	.10 ea.
P12	Crown Gear	2	.10 ea.
P13	12-Tooth Pinion Gear	2	.10 ea.
P14	Worm Gear	2	.20 ea.
P15	Coupling	2	.10 ea.
P20	Five Hole Strip—formed	1	.05 ea.
P24	Crank	1	.10 ea.
P33	Small Screw Driver	1	.05 ea.
P34	Hank of String	1	.05 ea.
P37	Collar	2	.25 doz.
P39	Wood Screw	3	.15 doz.
P40	Screw Eye	2	.20 doz.
P48	Mitre Gear	2	.20 ea.
P49	18-Tooth Gear	2	.15 ea.
P50	72-Tooth Gear	2	.30 ea.
P52	Ladder Chain (22" lgt.)	1	.15 ft.
P52A	Ladder Chain (10" lgt.)	1	.15 ft.
P54	Motor	3	1.75 ea.
P56G	Motor	3	3.95 ea.
P57	Motor	3	5.00 ea.
P59	110 v. Induction Motor	3	1.50 ea.
P58	Motor	3	1.00 ea.
P59	Reverse Base	3	.75 ea.
P60C	Transformer	3	3.50 ea.
P37A	2⅞" Axle	1	.02 ea.
P37D	6" Axle	1	.06 ea.
P37E	8" Axle	1	.08 ea.
P37F	12" Axle	1	.12 ea.
P79	Car Truck	1	.05 ea.
*P1133	Terminal Nut 4-40	2	.10 doz.
*S-3	⅜"x4-40 Terminal Screw	2	.12 doz.
*S-11	Set Screw	2	.05 doz.
*S-14	¼"x6-32 Screw	2	.05 doz.
*S-51	¼"x8-32 Screw	2	.05 doz.
*S-57	1⅝"x8-32 Screw	2	.15 doz.
*S-62	⅞"x8-32 Screw	2	.10 doz.
A	2½" Girder	1	.20 doz.
B	5" Girder	1	.35 doz.
C	10" Girder	1	.50 doz.
D	2½" Curved Girder	1	.25 doz.
E	5" Curved Girder	1	.40 doz.
F	5 Hole Strip	1	.10 doz.
G	7 Hole Strip	1	.10 doz.
H	11 Hole Strip	1	.15 doz.
I	21 Hole Strip	1	.20 doz.
J	41 Hole Strip	1	.30 doz.
K	11 Hole Strip Bracket	1	.35 doz.
M	Small Double Angle	1	.25 doz.
N	Long Double Angle	1	.05 ea.
O	Pawl	1	.05 ea.
S	Large Base Plate—21 holes	1	.40 ea.
T	Boiler	3	.25 ea.
U	Boiler Top	3	.20 ea.
W	Stack	3	.05 ea.
X	Digger Scoop	3	.75 ea.

Trade No.	Name of Part	Page	Price
Z	Flanged Wheel	2	.15 ea.
AA	Eccentric Crank	1	.10 ea.
AB	One Hole Coupling	2	.15 ea.
AC	Universal Bracket	1	.10 ea.
AE	Spiral Spring	1	.05 ea.
AF	Small Hook	2	.15 doz.
AH	Small Triangle	1	.25 doz.
AM	Special Pulley—Metal	2	.05 ea.
AQ	Sheave Pulley	2	.05 ea.
AR	8-Hole Strip	1	.10 doz.
AS	2⅞" Axle Rod	1	.03 ea.
AT	4" Axle Rod	1	.04 ea.
AV	7-Hole Strip Bracket	1	2 for .05
AX	19¾" Axle Rod	1	.20 ea.
AY	Bull Ring	1	.50 ea.
AZ	Bull Wheel Plate	1	.25 ea.
BA	B. W. Cntr (with Hub)	1	.25 ea.
B2	Wood Handle Screw Driver	1	.15 ea.
BE	6" Slotted Angle Strip	1	.50 doz.
BH	Solid Collar	2	2 for .05
BI	6" Flat Beam Girder	1	6 for .50
BJ	12" Flat Beam Girder	1	6 for .75
BK	8-32 Wing Nut	2	.25 doz.
BL	Small Washer	2	.05 doz.
BN	Regular Turret Plate	1	.15 ea.
BO	Reverse Switch Attachment	2	.50 ea.
BT	Pierced Disc	2	.10 ea.
BY	11-Hole Fibre Strip	1	.05 ea.
CA	Signal Arm	1	.10 ea.
CB	Wrench	1	.05 ea.
CH	Right Angle	1	.10 doz.
CI	36-Tooth Gear	2	.20 ea.
CQ	Slot Coupling	2	.15 ea.
CX	1" Axle Rod	1	.01 ea.
CY	5" Axle Rod	1	.05 ea.
CZ	7" Axle Rod	1	.07 ea.
DA	10" Axle Rod	1	.10 ea.
DB	Motor Pulley	2	.10 ea.
DE	Steering Column	1	.10 ea.
DK	Flat Spring	1	.10 ea.
DO	Steering Wheel with Hub	2	.15 ea.
DP	12" Slotted Angle Strip	1	6 for .50
DQ	Special Large Base Plate (28 holes)	1	.50 ea.
DS	Cotter Pin	1	.05 doz.
DT	1-Hole Set Screw Coupling	2	2 for .15
DU	¼" Diam. Axle 8½"	1	2 for .25
DV	6" Curved Beam Girder	1	6 for .75
DZ	Tackle Block	2	.15 ea.
EC	Giant Axle—29" long, 5/16" diam.	1	.50 ea.
EH	Gear Box Bracket	1	.05 ea.
EI	Standard Gear Box Side Pl.	1	.15 ea.
EJ	Gear Box Base	1	.20 ea.
EK	Plain Drum	2	.25 ea.
EW	12" Duplex F. B. Plate	1	.50 ea.
EX	Big Channel Girder 12"	1	6 for .50
EY	Big Channel Girder 6"	1	.05 ea.

Trade No.	Name of Part	Page	Price
EZ	6" Curved B. C. Girder	1	.05 ea.
*FA	1¼"x8-32 Screw	2	.15 doz.
FD	Hinged Loop	1	2 for .05
FJ	Rack	2	.25 ea.
FL	Helical Gear	2	.25 ea.
FP	Small Disc Wheel	2	.10 ea.
FX	Quarter Gear	2	.15 ea.
FZ	Internal Gear	2	.15 ea.
GX	8-Hole Double Angle Bracket	1	.10 doz.
*S52	½"x8-32 Screw	2	.10 doz.
LV	3" Disc Wheel, red	2	.20 ea.
LW	Rubber Tire for LV and MH	2	.10 ea.
LX	Steering Column Bracket	1	.05 ea.
MA	New Radiator	1	.15 ea.
MB	18½" Angle Girder	1	.15 ea.
MC	Small Base Plate	1	.05 ea.
MD	New large Base Plate	1	.10 ea.
ME	Flat Plate	1	.05 ea.
MF	Flat Plate	1	.05 ea.
MG	Radiator Hood	1	.10 ea.
MH	3" Disc Wheel, Nickel Rim	2	.25 ea.
MI	Front Axle Unit	1	.25 ea.
MJ	Electro Magnet with Cord	2	.60 ea.
MM	Wrench	1	.05 ea.

REGULAR ERECTOR MANUALS

No. 1	Erector Manual	.25 ea.
No. 3	Erector Manual	.25 ea.
No. 4	Erector Manual	.25 ea.
No. 6	Erector Manual	.25 ea.
No. 7	Erector Manual	.25 ea.
No. 8	Locomotive Manual	.25 ea.
No. 8½	Locomotive Manual	.50 ea.
No. 10	Erector Manual	1.00 ea.

ERECTOR ACCESSORY MANUALS

No. 5	Erector Electrical Set Manual	.25 ea.
Fun with your Motor Manual		.25 ea.

NOTE

*N21 Nut used with screws S51, S52, S62, S57, FA
*N11 Nut used with screw S14
*P1133 Nut used with screw S3
*N1 Nut used with screw S3
*S11 Set Screw used with pulleys, couplings, etc.

Separate Parts Prices for 1934

1934 CONTENTS LIST

Set No.		1	3	4	6	7	7½	8
P 7	SMALL WHEEL	4	4	4	4	4	4	4
P12	CROWN GEAR	0	0	1	1	1	1	1
P13	12 TOOTH PINION GEAR	0	0	2	2	2	2	2
P13A	12 TOOTH PINION (SPECIAL)	0	0	0	0	0	0	1
P14	WORM GEAR	0	0	1	1	1	1	1
P15	COUPLING	0	0	1	1	1	1	4
P20	5 HOLE STRIP—FORMED	0	0	0	2	2	4	4
P24	CRANK	1	1	1	2	2	2	2
P33	SMALL SCREW DRIVER	1	1	1	1	1	1	1
P34	HANK OF STRING	0	1	1	1	1	1	2
P37	COLLAR	1	4	6	8	8	10	10
P48	MITRE GEAR	0	0	0	0	0	0	2
P49	18 TOOTH GEAR	0	0	1	1	1	2	2
P50A	72 TOOTH GEAR (HUDSON)	0	0	0	0	0	0	1
P52	LADDER CHAIN	0	0	0	0	0	1	1
P56G	MOTOR	0	0	0	1	1	1	1
P57A	2⅛" AXLE ROD	1	1	1	1	1	1	3
P57D	6" AXLE ROD	0	1	1	1	2	2	2
P58	MOTOR	0	0	1	0	0	0	0
P79	CAR TRUCK	4	4	4	4	4	4	4
A	2½" GIRDER	4	4	4	4	4	4	4
B	5" GIRDER	4	4	8	8	12	12	12
C	10" GIRDER	4	8	12	16	48	48	48
D	2½" CURVED GIRDER	4	4	4	4	4	4	4
E	5" CURVED GIRDER	0	2	4	4	13	13	13
F	5 HOLE STRIP	0	0	2	2	2	3	3
G	7 HOLE STRIP	0	0	2	2	2	4	4
H	11 HOLE STRIP	0	0	4	4	4	4	4
I	21 HOLE STRIP	0	0	2	2	4	6	6
J	41 HOLE STRIP	0	0	0	0	2	2	2
M	SMALL DOUBLE ANGLE	0	0	2	2	6	6	6
N	LONG DOUBLE ANGLE	2	4	4	4	4	4	4
O	PAWL	0	0	1	1	2	4	4
S	LARGE BASE PLATE—21 HOLE	0	0	0	0	2	2	2
T	BOILER	0	0	0	1	1	1	1
U	BOILER TOP	0	0	0	1	1	1	1
W	STACK	0	0	0	3	3	3	3
Z	FLANGED WHEEL	0	0	0	4	4	4	4
AA	ECCENTRIC CRANK	0	0	0	0	0	0	4
AC	UNIVERSAL BRACKET	0	0	0	0	0	0	1
AE	SPIRAL SPRING	0	0	0	0	1	1	1
AF	SMALL HOOK	1	1	1	1	1	1	2
AJ	PAPER ERECTOR FLAG	0	0	1	1	1	1	1
AM	SPECIAL PULLEY—METAL	0	0	0	1	1	2	2
AS	2⅞" AXLE ROD	0	0	2	4	4	4	4
AT	4" AXLE ROD	2	2	2	4	4	4	4
AX	19¾" AXLE ROD	0	0	0	0	0	0	4
BH	SOLID COLLAR	0	0	0	0	2	2	12
BL	SMALL WASHER	6	12	12	12	12	12	20
BN	REGULAR TURRET PLATE	0	0	2	4	4	4	4
BT	PIERCED DISC	1	1	1	2	2	2	2
BY	11 HOLE FIBRE STRIP	0	0	0	0	0	1	1
CH	RIGHT ANGLE	8	12	12	14	24	36	36
CJ	36 TOOTH GEAR	0	0	3	3	3	4	4
CQ	SLOT COUPLING	0	0	0	0	0	0	2
CY	5" AXLE ROD	0	2	2	2	2	2	2

1934 CONTENTS LIST

Set No.		1	3	4	6	7	7½	8
CZ	7" AXLE ROD	0	0	0	0	1	2	2
DB	MOTOR PULLEY	0	0	1	1	1	1	1
DE	STEERING COLUMN	0	0	0	0	0	1	1
DK	FLAT SPRING	0	0	0	0	0	4	4
DO	STEERING WHEEL WITH HUB	0	0	0	0	0	1	1
DS	COTTER PIN	0	0	0	0	0	1	1
DT	ONE SET SCREW COUPLING	0	0	0	0	0	0	6
EH	GEAR BOX BRACKET	0	0	2	2	2	2	2
EI	GEAR BOX SIDE PLATE	0	0	2	2	2	2	2
EJ	GEAR BOX BASE	0	0	1	1	1	1	1
EK	PLAIN DRUM	0	0	0	0	1	1	1
FA	1¾" x 8-32 SCREW	0	0	0	0	0	0	3
FD	HINGED LOOP	0	0	0	0	0	6	6
HF	BUTT ENDPLATE	0	0	0	0	0	0	1
IR	ENGINE FRAME	0	0	0	0	0	0	1
IS	DRIVER WHEEL	0	0	0	0	0	0	6
IT	COACH WHEEL	0	0	0	0	0	0	20
IU	SAND BOX	0	0	0	0	0	0	1
IV	STEAM DOME	0	0	0	0	0	0	1
IW	FEED WATER HEATER	0	0	0	0	0	0	1
IX	BELL	0	0	0	0	0	0	1
IY	BELL HANGER	0	0	0	0	0	0	1
IZ	SMOKE STACK	0	0	0	0	0	0	1
JA	COW CATCHER	0	0	0	0	0	0	1
JC	SMOKE BOX FRONT	0	0	0	0	0	0	1
JD	AXLE BOX	0	0	0	0	0	0	16
JE	PARALLEL ROD	0	0	0	0	0	0	2
JF	MAIN CONNECTING ROD	0	0	0	0	0	0	2
JG	REAR TRUCK FRAME, RIGHT	0	0	0	0	0	0	1
JH	REAR TRUCK FRAME, LEFT	0	0	0	0	0	0	1
JI	FRONT TRUCK FRAME	0	0	0	0	0	0	2
JJ	SMOKE BOX SHELL	0	0	0	0	0	0	1
JK	STEAM CHEST & CYLINDER PLATE	0	0	0	0	0	0	2
JL	STEAM CHEST & CYLINDER BAND	0	0	0	0	0	0	1
JM	STEAM CHEST END	0	0	0	0	0	0	13
JN	CYLINDER END	0	0	0	0	0	0	5
JO	CROSSHEAD GUIDE BAR	0	0	0	0	0	0	2
JP	CROSSHEAD	0	0	0	0	0	0	4
JQ	CROSSHEAD BEARER, RIGHT	0	0	0	0	0	0	1
JR	CROSSHEAD BEARER, LEFT	0	0	0	0	0	0	1
JS	LINK FRAME	0	0	0	0	0	0	2
JT	LINK ROD	0	0	0	0	0	0	2
JU	ROD CLAMP	0	0	0	0	0	0	2
JV	CROSSHEAD LINK	0	0	0	0	0	0	2
JW	COMBINING LEVER	0	0	0	0	0	0	2
JX	VALVE LEVER	0	0	0	0	0	0	4
JY	AIR DRUM SHELL	0	0	0	0	0	0	4
JZ	JACKET	0	0	0	0	0	0	1
KA	STEAM PIPE CASING	0	0	0	0	0	0	2
KB	MAIN BOILER	0	0	0	0	0	0	1
KC	BOILER FIRE BOX	0	0	0	0	0	0	1
KD	FIRE BOX FRONT	0	0	0	0	0	0	1
KE	BOILER BACKHEAD	0	0	0	0	0	0	1
KF	FIRING DECK	0	0	0	0	0	0	1

1934 CONTENTS LIST

Set No.		1	3	4	6	7	7½	8
KG	ASH PAN	0	0	0	0	0	0	1
KH	CAB	0	0	0	0	0	0	1
KI	CAB END	0	0	0	0	0	0	2
KJ	DRAW CASING	0	0	0	0	0	0	1
KK	FIRING DECK PLATE	0	0	0	0	0	0	1
KL	FRONT RUNNING BOARD, RIGHT	0	0	0	0	0	0	1
KM	FRONT RUNNING BOARD, LEFT	0	0	0	0	0	0	1
KN	REAR RUNNING BOARD	0	0	0	0	0	0	2
KO	RUNNING BOARD STEP	0	0	0	0	0	0	2
KP	FRONT BUMPER PLATE STEP	0	0	0	0	0	0	1
KQ	APRON	0	0	0	0	0	0	1
KR	M.C.B. COUPLING	0	0	0	0	0	0	3
KS	COUPLING PIN LIFTER	0	0	0	0	0	0	3
KT	¼" AXLE 3 5/32" LONG	0	0	0	0	0	0	5
KU	¼" AXLE 3⅝" LONG	0	0	0	0	0	0	8
KV	HEADLIGHT	0	0	0	0	0	0	1
KW	TRUCK FRAME	0	0	0	0	0	0	4
KX	TRUCK BOLSTER	0	0	0	0	0	0	2
KZ	TENDER BASE STEP	0	0	0	0	0	0	1
LA	TENDER SIDE PLATE	0	0	0	0	0	0	2
LB	TENDER BACK PLATE	0	0	0	0	0	0	2
LC	CORNER PLATE	0	0	0	0	0	0	4
LD	FRONT FUEL BOARD	0	0	0	0	0	0	1
LE	SIDE FUEL BOARD	0	0	0	0	0	0	2
LF	BACK FUEL BOARD WITH DECK	0	0	0	0	0	0	1
LG	FUEL SLIDE	0	0	0	0	0	0	1
LH	TENDER STEP	0	0	0	0	0	0	4
LI	COUPLING YOKE	0	0	0	0	0	0	2
LJ	TANK HANDLE	0	0	0	0	0	0	4
LK	TENDER STEP ANGLE	0	0	0	0	0	0	4
LL	REAR TIE FRAME	0	0	0	0	0	0	2
LP	RAILROAD TIE	0	0	0	0	0	0	12
LS	JACK	0	0	0	0	0	0	2
LT	MOTOR SUPPORT BRACKET	0	0	0	0	0	0	2
LU	OFFSET WRENCH	0	0	0	0	0	0	2
LV	3" DISC WHEEL, RED	0	4	4	4	0	4	4
LW	RUBBER TIRE	0	0	0	0	0	4	4
LX	STEERING COLUMN BRACKET	0	0	0	0	0	1	1
MA	NEW RADIATOR	0	0	0	0	0	1	1
MB	18½" ANGLE GIRDER	0	0	0	0	0	4	4
MC	SMALL BASE PLATE	2	2	2	2	2	4	4
MD	NEW LARGE BASE PLATE	1	1	1	1	1	1	1
ME	FLAT PLATE	0	0	0	0	0	4	4
MF	FLAT PLATE	0	2	4	4	8	11	11
MG	RADIATOR HOOD	0	0	0	0	0	1	1
MH	3" DISC WHEEL, NICKEL RIM	0	0	0	0	4	0	0
MI	FRONT AXLE UNIT	0	0	0	0	0	1	1
MJ	ELECTRO MAGNET WITH CORD	0	0	0	0	1	1	1
ML	RAILROAD RAIL	0	0	0	0	0	0	8
MM	WRENCH	0	0	1	1	1	1	1
S51	¼" x 8-32 SCREW	20	35	48	88	114	125	250
S52	½" x 8-32 SCREW	0	0	0	0	0	0	28
S57	1⅜" x 8-32 SCREW	0	0	0	4	4	4	12
S62	⅞" x 8-32 SCREW	3	6	6	6	24	24	56
N21	8-32 SQUARE NUT	23	45	54	100	150	175	354

To give Erector engineers opportunities to create architectural models, Gilbert developed "skyscraper panels" in 1935. All but the smallest sets included a sampling, which used special snap rivets and a rivet extractor.

new and improved 1935 models. The hole pattern in the (MN) was "duplex"; that is, it featured an alternating pattern of large and small holes.

The other major change that occurred as a result of the new (MN) Base Plate was a modification in the packaging and display of the metal box sets. For, in addition to the many uses these base plates had in model building, they made excellent parts display trays. So beginning in 1935 and continuing through 1962, (MN) Base Plates were clipped together to form trays with a variety of other parts attached to them with paper fasteners. Each of the different metal boxes was re-engineered and modified on the inside with ledges and/or brackets to accommodate this new display technique.

The change in the appearance of these metal box sets went even further. Since two layers of parts could now be packed in the bottom of the box using a cardboard insert under the (MN) trays, there was no need for the inside lid cardboard parts display used in 1933 and 1934. So in 1935 Gilbert dropped that practice in all but the largest set. In place of the inside lid display each of the metal box sets came with a large, colorful inside lid label.

The wave of creativity continued on in 1935 with the creation of the Skyscraper parts. To incorporate architectural models into the Erector System, Gilbert developed a new concept in model building with the creation of lithographed cardboard building panels. They pictured the exterior of commercial buildings and were designed to be attached to a frame made of regular Erector angle girders. These new parts are known as "skyscraper panels" because Gilbert called the special set created to feature them the Skyscraper Set.

There were seven different designs of skyscraper panels, ranging in size from 3" x 6" to 6" x 6". Both sides of each panel were lithographed, which enhanced their versatility. One side pictured sections of buildings made from concrete, the other side pictured buildings made of brick. The instruction manual illustrated models of factories, office buildings, stores, and skyscrapers. The panels were attached to the Erector frame with (MT) Snap Rivets, which popped in to hold the panels in place. To pop out the rivets, Gilbert offered a special tool, the (MU) Rivet Extractor.

Many other new parts were created for the 1935 line, including two electric motors. The (A52) Induction Motor was a 110-volt motor, and it replaced the (P58) Motor, which was missing from the line this year. This was the first time since the inception of the Erector System that a battery-powered motor had not been offered in a set. Along with the (A52) came the (MP) 24 Tooth Gear, designed exclusively for the new induction motor. Used only in No. 4½, the (A52) so resembled the old (P58) in shape and size that Gilbert did not even bother to change the illustrations in the instruction manual.

Also in 1935, the more expensive sets featured the new 110-volt (P51) Electric Engine in place of the old (P56G) Motor (deleted this year). Gilbert called this new creation an electric engine instead of just a motor, because it was a motor and a gearbox. Along with the (P51) came two parts designed to be used with it: the (MQ) 27 Tooth Worm Gear and (MS) Compression Spring.

Another new part was the (MO) 3" Angle Girder. Gilbert returned the (BE) 6" Angle Girder and (DP) 12" Angle Girder to the Erector System as well; these parts were made

The (A52) Induction Motor (right) replaced the (P58) battery-powered motor in 1935. The (A52) was included in only the smallest of the metal box sets, and it so resembled the (P58) that Gilbert did not bother to upgrade the instruction manuals.

Gilbert continued to refine the Erector System in 1935 by adding new motors, base plates, and other parts as well as giving the boiler a new look.

Beginning in 1935, a variation of the outer lid label appeared (right). Both of these labels were used on the metal box sets through 1958.

of a heavier-gauge steel than during the Classic Period. With the existing (MB) 18½" Angle Girder, this made for a very complete series. Finally, there were the (MV) Flat Car Truck, a modification of the (P79) Car Truck, and (MR) Drum with Gear, which replaced the (EK) Plain Drum (deleted).

In addition, several old parts missing since the end of the Classic Period were reintroduced this year. They included the (AA) Eccentric Crank, (CA) Signal Arm, (CR) Special Turret Plate, (CS) Wheel Segment, and the whole series of Big Channel Girders–(EX), (EY), and (EZ)–which were now nickel-plated instead of painted red. Also, all the large axle rods–(P57E0, (P57F), and (DA)–were returned to the system. Clearly Erector was on the rebound.

Gilbert modified many of the parts used in 1935. For example, the (P79) Car Truck came with eight holes instead of seven, which made for greater versatility. It was painted red now and matched the new (MV) Flat Car Truck. The (T) Boiler was nickel-plated instead of painted black, and it came with a new label that had a silver background. A new look was also given to the (U) Boiler Top, which was painted red instead of black.

Beginning in 1935, all base plates, including the (MN), were painted blue. This certainly gave a different look to models built with those parts. All the base plates were manufactured from the same gauge of steel now, so the (MC)s and (MD)s were considerably lighter than versions from 1934. Also, the finish on the housing for the (MJ) Electro Magnet was changed from red paint to nickel-plating.

Another part modified at this point was the (CJ) 36 Tooth Gear. In the past, it had been produced with eight holes. Now it came with four holes and four slots, stamped in an alternating pattern. This change was made because the (CJ) was also used with the new (MR) Drum With Gear, and the slots were necessary to secure the drum to the gear.

Once more, Gilbert changed the look of the parts can. In 1934 it had a blue body with a nickel-plated lid. Now that lid went with a body painted dark red.

One alteration that affected the entire lineup related to the numbering system. Gilbert decided to append "½" to the number of each set. Set No. 1 from 1934 became No. 1½, and so forth. This change was peculiar, to say the least. In the past, the "½" designation was used when a new set was added to the line and the size of the new set dictated that it be numbered between two existing sets. Such was the case in 1926, when No. 7½ was created. It was larger than No. 7 yet smaller than No. 8. But there was no reason to add "½" to every set number in 1935. Perhaps Gilbert liked the way these new numbers looked or sounded. Or maybe he thought the new designation made the product appear more complex and sophisticated. Whatever the reason, he must have been pleased because Gilbert carried on this numbering anomaly for more than 20 years.

As a final note, a curious variation related to the outer lid label used on the metal box sets. It now contained the words, "MADE IN U.S.A. PRINTED IN U.S.A." Some sets came with labels identical to those used in late 1934 and lacked this wording. But about an equal number of sets came with the new label variation, which included the extra text. Most interesting is that both variations were used simultaneously (and with equal frequency) until these labels were abandoned in the late 1950s.

Cardboard Box Sets

Three different sets were offered in cardboard boxes. Two were extensions of 1934 sets; the third, known as "The

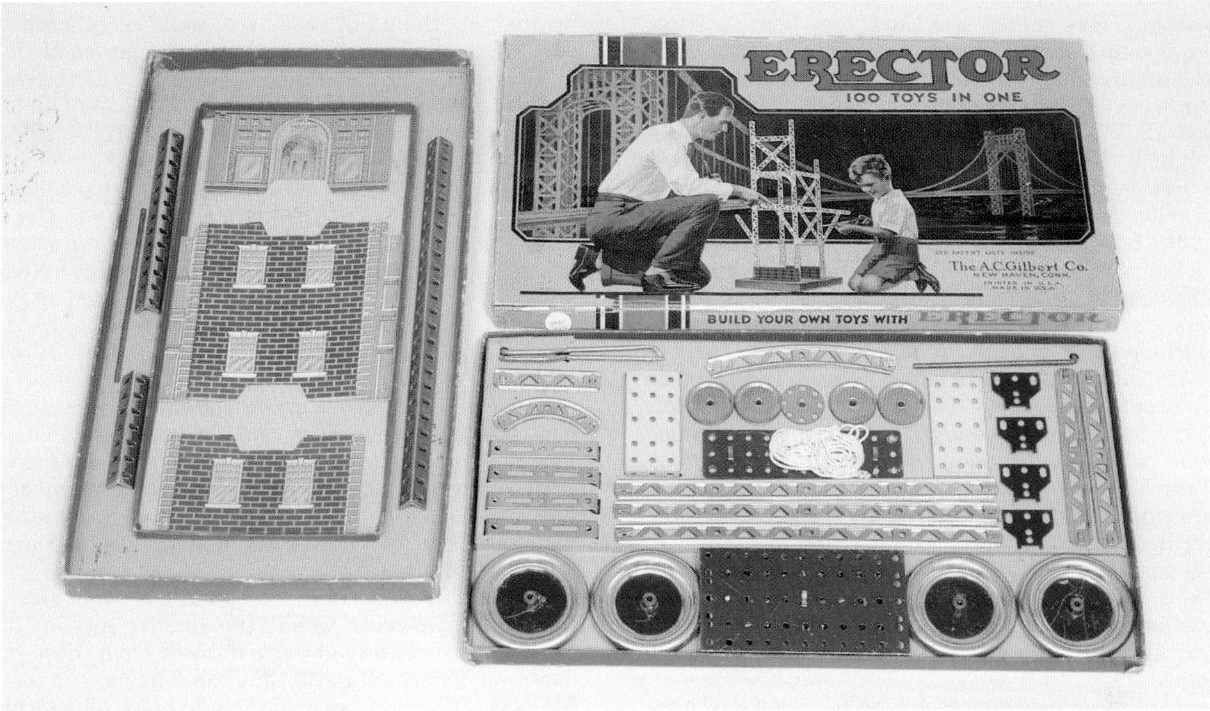

Note the unusual packing arrangement for No. 3½ from 1935. Under the removable cardboard parts display tray was a unique cardboard insert glued to the bottom of the box that contained the skyscraper panels.

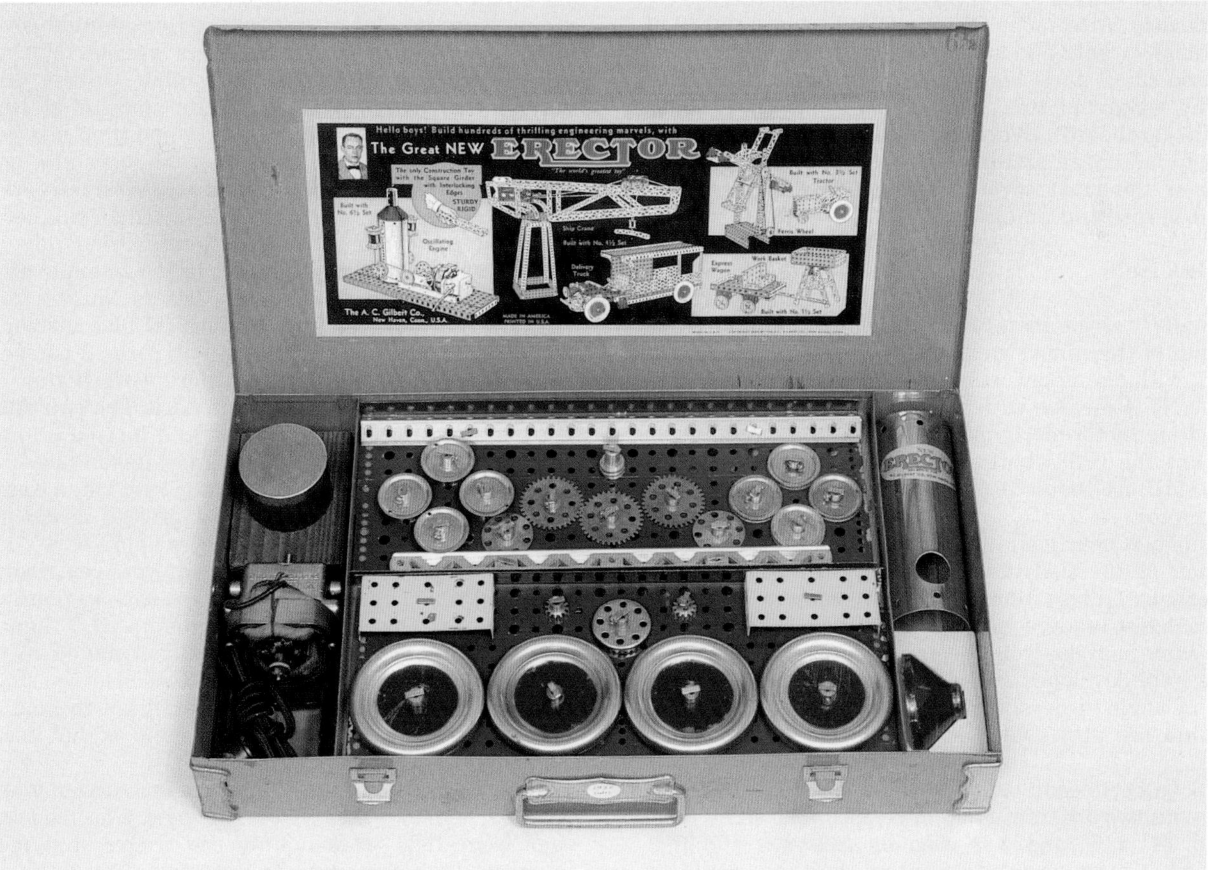

Still packed in a green metal box, this No. 6½ from 1935 is a favorite of collectors. It was the smallest set to come with the (P51) Electric Engine.

Skyscraper Set," was totally new and very special. First came No. 1½, which was slightly upgraded from No. 1 from 1934 by the inclusion of (MF) 1" x 5" Base Plates. The color of cardboard used for the parts display insert was changed on this and all 1935 sets. It had been green, but now was mustard yellow. Beginning in 1935 and continuing until 1949, the first page of the coverless instruction manual was printed in color.

Set No. 3½ had essentially the same contents as No. 3 from 1934, but with one major difference. For only this year, Gilbert added some of the new skyscraper panels to all the regular sets, starting with No. 3½. Only 14 skyscraper panels were included, just enough to build a few of the smaller buildings. Undoubtedly, Gilbert added them as a teaser or sampler to promote the sale of The Erector Skyscraper Set. Set No. 3½ was really a two-layer set, as the skyscraper panels came packed in a unique cardboard insert glued to bottom of the box under the regular insert.

The third cardboard box set was No. S, called "The Erector Skyscraper Set." Although billed as an accessory set, it was a complete set. This wonderful new toy was packed in the same 10¼" x 18¼" x 1" box as No. 3½. The picture on the box lid was unique to No. S. The background was done in orange-red, and it illustrated a city of skyscrapers built with Erector.

The Erector Skyscraper Set came with 64 cardboard panels, more than the number packed in the regular line. And No. S was the only set that contained all seven of the different styles of panels that were produced. The twenty-four-page instruction manual had a cover similar to the box lid. It also had an orange-red background and pictured skyscraper models. Also included was a generous number of angle girders, twenty-one-hole strips, and two of the mustard-colored small parts boxes full of nuts, bolts, and snap rivets. The weight of this set was too great for it to be packed in cardboard. Over time, the stress on the box caused it to fall apart, and few sets have survived. The No. S is one of the most coveted sets to Erector collectors because it is rare and unique.

Metal Box Sets

The smallest of the metal box sets was No. 4½. It came in a red box of the same size as the one used for No. 4 from 1934 and, with one noteworthy exception, had similar contents. The No. 4½ came with a new type of 110-volt motor, an induction motor designated (A52) that was slightly larger than the (P58) battery motor it replaced. A new gear, the (MP) 24 Tooth Gear, was created to be used with the new motor.

Oddly enough nearly all the models illustrated in the No. 4½ section of the instruction manual still pictured the (P58). Perhaps Gilbert thought the two motors looked so similar that few readers would notice. Most of the models were the same as those from the previous year, though some new ones were developed and others modified to reflect the addition of angle girders, turret plates, and the new base plates. This set also contained a mustard-colored small parts box.

In 1935, Gilbert began using inner lid labels on the metal box sets, with two different types developed. The small label measured 14" x 6" and was used on Nos. 4½ and 6½. Pictured on it were seven different models that could be built with the small and midrange sets. The big label was used on the larger sets. Because Gilbert designed the new labels to be used on sets of different sizes, no number was printed on them. Instead, the number of each set was rubber-stamped inside the lid at the upper right.

Next in the lineup came No. 6½. It was packed in the same size green box as No. 6 from 1934, but Gilbert added brass corner trim to dress up this set in 1935. Although the basic assortment of parts was similar to the previous year's No. 6, this set was upgraded with the new base plates, angle girders, and new (P51) Electric Engine. As in the set from 1934, there was one parts can, and it was mounted in a green wood base. The inside lid label used for No. 4½ was found on No. 6½; it pictured a variety of models that could be built with the small and midrange sets.

The No. 6½ section in the instruction manual was changed, of course. But most of the changes reflected improvements in No. 6 models from 1934, using the new base plates, angle girders, and electric engine. The Walking Beam Engine, although first illustrated in the previous instruction manual, was redesigned using many of the new parts. Gilbert featured this model when promoting its midrange sets in later years, and it first appeared in its familiar form in 1935.

Set No. 7½ came in a red box of the same size as No. 7 from 1934. However, unlike the smaller sets in this year's lineup, the inventory of parts differed from those in its predecessor. Two small parts cans came in No. 7½; as with No. 6½, a green wood base held them in place. The second of the new labels graced the inside of the lid on No. 7½. Larger than the new label used on Nos. 4½ and 6½, it measured 17" x 9" and pictured the two newly developed models: the Ferris Wheel and the Refrigeration Plant (known later as the Giant Power Plant). These two models were featured for many years in advertising, instruction manual covers, and other promotional literature. This version of the Ferris Wheel, perhaps more than any other Gilbert developed, became the most recognized Erector model of all time.

Although a few models were retained from last year's No. 7½ section of the instruction manual, more new ones were added, and this entire section was virtually rewritten. Several important models were invented for this set in 1935, including the Ferris Wheel and the Bascule Bridge.

The most heavily modified set in the lineup was No. 8½. It came packed in the same size box as No. 7½ from 1934, but now that box was finished in royal blue instead of powder blue. Inside, metal dividers still formed compartments on each side. But now the dividers were higher and had angular slits cut at the front and back. The two (MB) Angle Girders fit between the dividers and formed a support for the parts display trays made of (MN) Base Plates.

The No. 8½ was a highly upgraded set when compared to No. 7½ from 1934. It featured a greater assortment and larger quantity of parts. Also, a host of old parts, discontinued at the end of the Classic Period, were reintroduced this year, and they showed up in this set. Among them were the Big Channel Girders, Wheel Segments, and Signal Arms. Most of these parts were originally included in only the largest Classic Period sets. There were also two small parts cans in this set, along with a wood base to hold them in place. The inside lid label was the same as that used on No. 7½ from this year.

As with the No. 7½ section of the instruction manual, the No. 8½ section was a virtual rewrite. The models carried over from 1934 were mainly the trucks, and most were improved with new parts. Two important models were introduced: the Giant Power Plant (called the Refrigeration Plant on the inside lid label for a few years) and the Dutch Windmill. There were new models of engines that featured

SETS IN THE ERECTOR SYSTEM 1933–35

	Box Size	1933	1934	1935
Cardboard Box Sets		No. 1	No. 1	No. 1½
		No. 3	No. 3	No. 3½
		No. 4		No. 5
Metal Box Sets	16" x 8" x 3"	N/A	No. 4, red	No. 4½, red
	18" x 10" x 3"	No. 6, green	No. 6, green	No. 6½, green
	20" x 12" x 3"	No. 7, red	No. 7, red	No. 7½, red
	22" x 13" x 3"	N/A	No. 7½, powder blue	No. 8½, royal blue
	24" x 14" x 4"	N/A	No. 8, crackle powder blue	No. 9½, crackle powder blue

the reintroduced giant flywheel made of the wheel segments.

The top-of-the-line Hudson locomotive and tender set was No. 9½ in 1935, and it enjoyed the same broad increase in parts as did No. 8½. Set No. 9½ was packed in the same large, powder blue box with crackle finish as was No. 8 from 1934, but with one major change. Instead of the metal parts display tray used the previous year, it contained a large parts display tray constructed of six (MN) Base Plates. The metal strips that had been welded to the inside of the box to hold the old tray were deleted, as the new tray rested on the parts beneath it. The No. 9½ was the only set that retained the inside lid cardboard parts display in 1935 and still contained the (LV) wheels and (LW) tires. Like the Hudson set from 1934, No. 9½ came with two instruction manuals.

Another important change occurred with the Hudson locomotive, as Gilbert deleted the red "ERECTOR" decal from the sides of the cab. Sometimes collectors have worried that someone had removed the decals from their Erector Hudson. Take heart! In 1935 and thereafter this is how it came.

An Aside: Developing a New Engine

In 1935 Gilbert made a radical improvement in the way Erector models were powered, when he developed the (P51) Electric Engine. He called it an engine and not a motor because, for the first time, the motor and the gearbox were a single, combined unit. The (P51) was included in the larger sets from 1935 through 1937, and during this three-year period it was modified in several ways.

The (P51), the first Erector electric engine, came with a nickel-plated motor housing and a cast, white-metal gearbox painted red. In 1935, there were two versions of this engine. One with a reversing toggle switch mounted on the rear of the motor housing came in the largest sets (Nos. 8½ and 9½). A less expensive version with no reversing switch was included in the midrange sets (Nos. 6½ and 7½). There was only an empty hole on the rear of the motor housing. This practice of including the reversing version in only the two largest sets continued through 1936. A year later, however, Gilbert packed the reversing version in the midrange sets as well, perhaps because this engine was soon to be replaced.

When the (P51) Electric Engine was invented, two other parts were added to the Erector System: the (MQ) 27 Tooth Worm Wheel and (MS) Compression Spring, both created especially for the (P51). The second modification for the (P51) involved the worm wheel. In 1935 and 1936, the worm wheel was a separate part. It was made of paper, impregnated with resin, and had a hub and set screw. But in 1937, this part was dropped as the gear box on the engine was modified. Instead, a brass worm wheel (gear) lacking a hub and set screw was mounted on an axle that was part of the gear box.

Another Aside: Cleaning Out the Storeroom

At the same time engineers were developing the (P51), others at Gilbert were talking about how to use up parts from many years earlier. The Classic Period had ended in 1932, and with its end, all but one of the elaborate models associated with that era had been discontinued (the exception was the Hudson locomotive and tender). All the same, leftover parts surely survived, notably those designed to build a single model such as the White truck or the Zeppelin. Gilbert continued to offer Nos. 9 and 10 from 1932 (at least in the price list) in 1933 and 1934, presumably to dispose of leftover inventory.

But there is evidence that Gilbert went even further. Shown here is a most unusual set, a Zeppelin set that dates from no earlier than 1935. This date can be established because on the rudder is a type of Erector label (with a silver background) introduced in 1935. In addition, this set contains nickel-plated big channel girders and a mustard-colored small parts box, which strengthens the view that it came from the mid-1930s. Finally, it was packed in a cardboard box of an unusual size (20½" x 13" x 2½"). Although the length and width were identical to the box used for the Erector Airplane Set in 1932, this Zeppelin box was not as deep. The label on the outside of the lid is identical to the one used on the Classic Period Zeppelin set, but it lacks a number and some of the lettering has been removed. This unusual Zeppelin set is unnumbered and uncataloged.

While the origin of this set is not clearly established, I believe Gilbert created it to dispose of discontinued inventory. Most likely, these sets were made up until the supply of all the leftover Zeppelin parts was exhausted. Then these special sets were sold to one large retailer, such as Sears, Roebuck & Co., where they were disposed of, probably at bargain prices. Logic suggests Gilbert followed the same procedure to liquidate other Classic Period model parts, such as those for the White truck, but such sets have yet to be reported. Anyone having knowledge of such sets should contact the author or publisher.

Erector System Modifications For 1935

I. New Parts

(P51) Electric Engine
(A52) Induction Motor
(MN) 12" Base Plate, painted blue with duplex holes
(MO) 3" Angle Girder

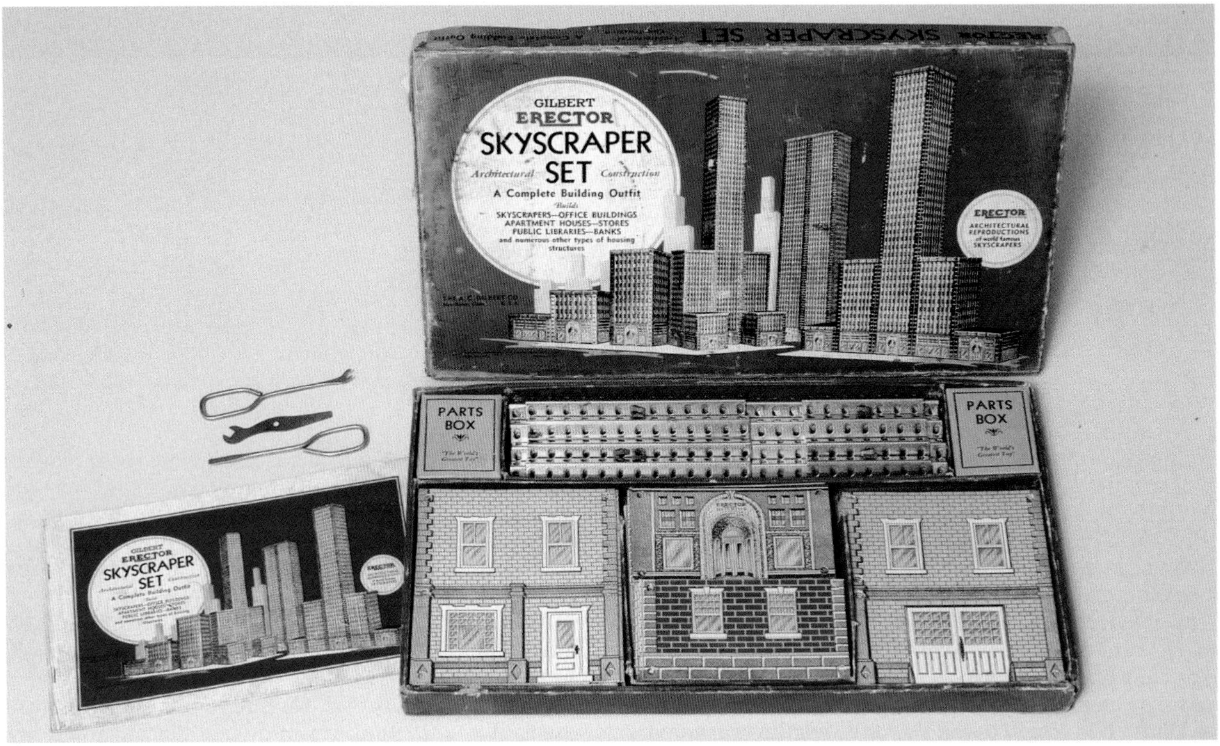

The Skyscaper Set, among the scarcest and most coveted Erector Sets, was offered from 1935 through 1937. It contained more and different panels than were packed in regular Erector sets.

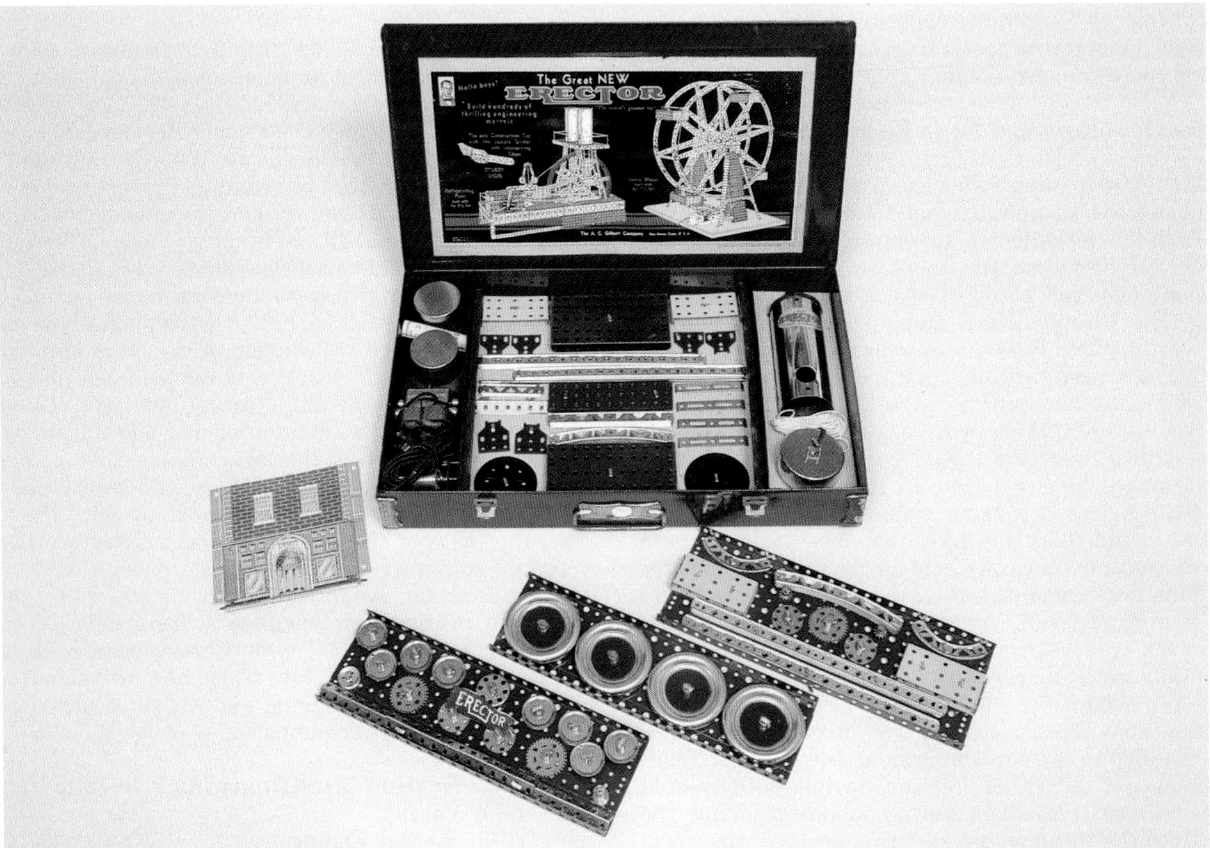

Set No. 7½ from 1935 was the first to feature the Ferris Wheel. With minor modifications, it evolved into No. 8½, a mainstay of the line during Gilbert's Renaissance Period.

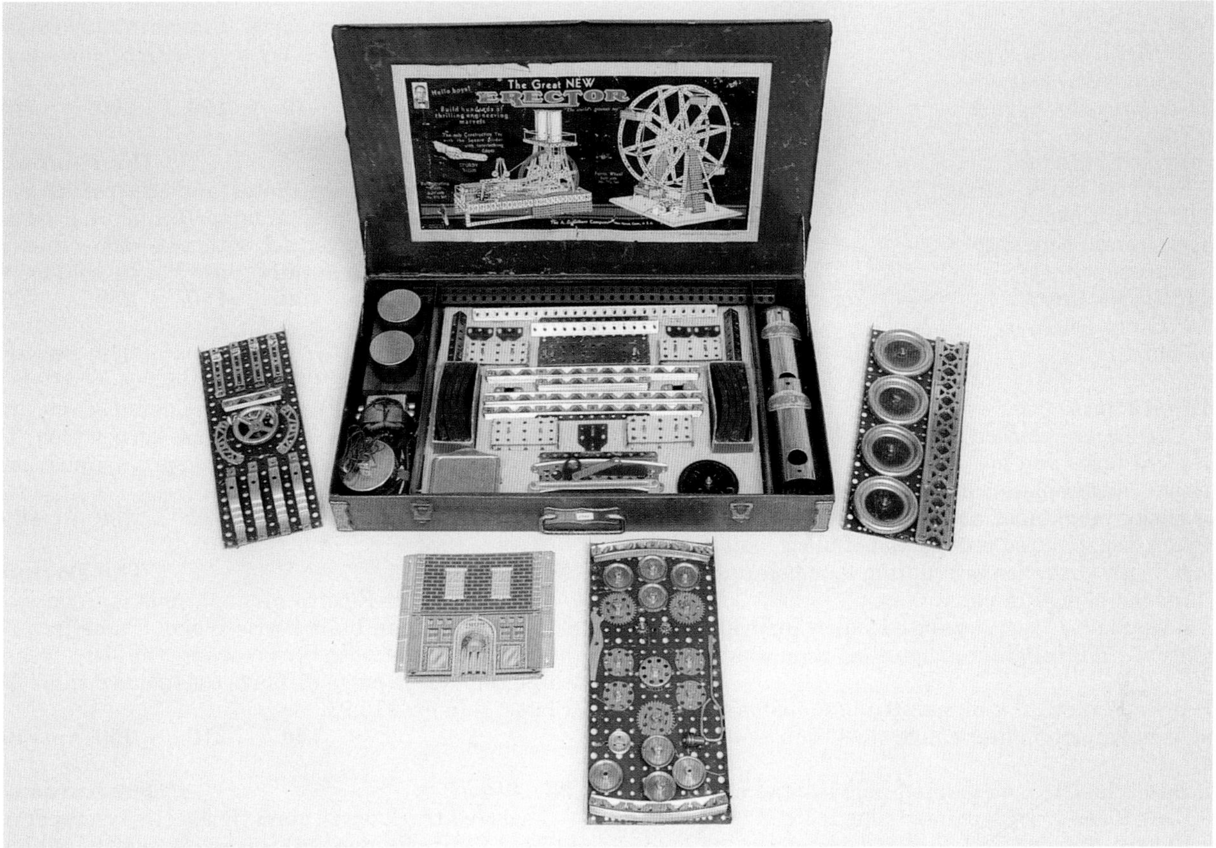

The version of The Automotive Set (No. 8½) from 1935 featured a new number, a royal blue box, and many new parts and models.

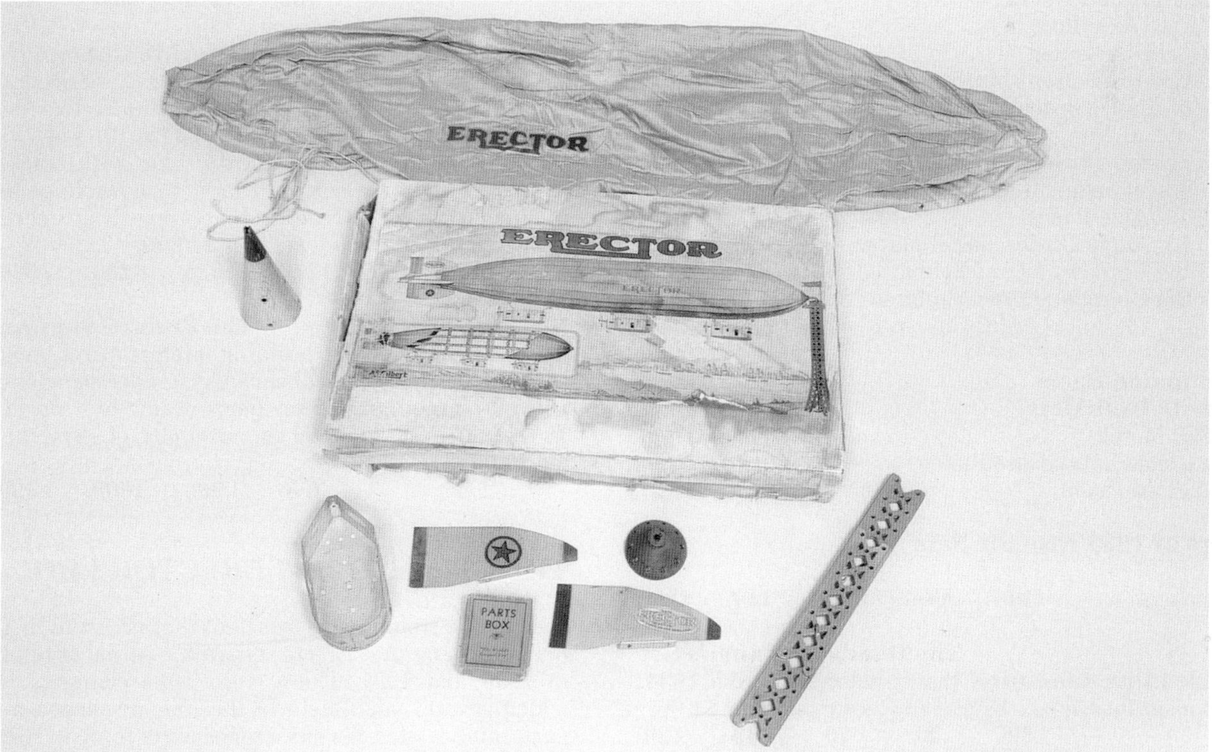

This uncataloged Zeppelin Set from around 1935 was neither numbered nor cataloged. It represented an attempt by Gilbert to dispose of stock left from the Classic Period.

(MP) 24 Tooth Gear
(MQ) 27 Tooth Worm Wheel
(MR) Drum with Gear
(MS) Compression Spring
(MT) Snap Rivet
(MU) Rivet Extractor
(MV) Flat Car Truck, painted red
(NA) 3" Main Entrance
(NB) 3" Ground Entrance
(NC) 3" Upper Story
(ND) 6" Upper Story
(NF) 6" Office Entrance
(NG) Roof

II. Modified Parts

(P79) Car Truck, painted red instead of nickel-plated; given eight holes and not seven
(T) Boiler, nickel-plated instead of painted black; has silver background label, not gold background decal
(U) Boiler Top, painted red instead of black
(CJ) 36 Tooth Gear, has alternating four holes and four slots instead of eight holes
(MC) Base Plate 1" x 2½", painted yellow instead of red; made from a much lighter-gauge steel than was used in 1934
(MD) Base Plate 2½" x 5", painted blue instead of red; made from a much lighter-gauge steel than was used in 1934
(ME) Base Plate 1" x 4", painted blue instead of red
(MF) Base Plate 1" x 5", painted blue instead of red
(MJ) Electro Magnet, nickel-plated instead of painted red
( ) Parts Can, body painted dark red, not blue, with nickel-plated lid

III. Reintroduced Parts

(P57E) 8" Axle Rod
(P57F) 12" Axle Rod
(AA) Eccentric Crank, with two holes
(BE) 6" Angle Girder, nickel-plated
(CA) Signal Arm, painted red
(CR) Special Turret Plate with Hub, painted black
(CS) Wheel Segment, painted red
(DA) 10" Axle Rod
(DP) 12" Angle Girder, nickel-plated
(EX) Big Channel 12", nickel-plated
(EY) Big Channel 6", nickel-plated
(EZ) Big Channel Girder Curved 6", nickel-plated

IV. Eliminated Parts

(P49) 18 Tooth Gear
(P56G) Motor
(S) 21 Hole Large Base Plate
(EK) Plain Drum

Listings of 1935 Erector Sets

	Gd	VG	Exc	Inv	Org

NO. 1½ — The Dandy Beginner's Set

Upgraded with more parts than predecessor from 1934. Came in a cardboard box 13½" x 9½" x ¾"; sold for $1.00.

	Gd	VG	Exc	Inv	Org
	30	40	70	+15	+20

NO. 3½ — The Set With The Big Red Wheels

Upgraded with more parts than predecessor from 1934, including skyscraper parts. Came in a cardboard box 18¼" x 10¼" x 1¼"; two-layer set with removable parts display tray; sold for $5.95.

	Gd	VG	Exc	Inv	Org
	80	120	200	+40	+50

NO. 4½ — The Famous No. 4½

Featured (MN) Base Plates and skyscraper parts; only set to have (A52) induction motor. Came in a red metal box 16" x 8" x 3"; two-layer set with two removable parts displays constructed from (MN) Base Plates; sold for $5.95.

	Gd	VG	Exc	Inv	Org
	100	150	250	+50	+65

NO. 6½ — The Super No. 6½

Featured modified (T) Boiler and new (P51) Electric Engine and built Walking Beam Engine. Came in a green metal box 18" x 10" x 3" with brass corner trim. Two-layer set with two removable parts displays constructed from (MN) Base Plates; sold for $6.95.

	Gd	VG	Exc	Inv	Org
	120	180	300	+60	+75

NO. 7½ — The Engineer's Set

Featured (MJ) Electro Magnet, hoisting drum, and skyscraper parts and built Ferris Wheel. Came in a red metal box 20" x 12" x 3" with brass corner trim. Two-layer set with three removable parts displays constructed from (MN) Base Plates; sold for $15.95.

	Gd	VG	Exc	Inv	Org
	140	210	350	+70	+90

NO. 8½ — The Automotive Set

Featured truck parts, giant flywheel, skyscraper parts, and (P51) Electric Engine with reversing switch and built Giant Power Plant. Came in a royal blue metal box 22" x 13" x 3" with brass corner trim. Two-layer set with three removable parts displays constructed from (MN) Base Plates; sold for $15.95.

	Gd	VG	Exc	Inv	Org
	180	270	450	+90	+110

NO. 9½ — The World's Champion No. 9½

Featured all parts from No. 8½ and those needed to build Hudson locomotive and tender; included two instruction manuals. Came in a metal box 24" x 14" x 4" with brass corner trim; box painted powder blue with crackle finish. Two-layer set with one very large removable parts display constructed from (MN) Base Plates; cardboard parts display clipped on inside of lid; sold for $25.00.

	Gd	VG	Exc	Inv	Org
	1280	1920	3200	+640	+800

No. S — The Erector Skyscraper Set

Specialized set for building architectural models; featured full range of cardboard skyscraper panels and parts as well as regular Erector parts. Came in a cardboard box 18¼" x 10¼" x 1¼"; lid pictured city of skyscrapers; sold for $3.50.

	Gd	VG	Exc	Inv	Org
	640	960	1600	+320	+400

THE 1936 AND 1937 ERECTOR LINE

After the tremendous overhaul that occurred in 1935, it is not surprising that Erector enjoyed a period of relative quiet in 1936 and 1937. There were some changes, as Gilbert added several small sets to the line, developed a few new parts, and deleted the skyscraper parts from all regular sets. Because of the increase in cardboard box sets, most of the metal box sets came with a new, higher number. But compared to the previous year, these changes were minor.

1935 CONTENTS LIST

Set No.		1½	3½	4½	6½	7½	8½	9½	S
P7	SMALL WHEEL	4	4	4	4	4	4	4	0
P12	CROWN GEAR	0	0	1	1	1	1	1	0
P13	12 TOOTH PINION GEAR, ⅛"	0	0	2	2	2	2	2	0
P13A	12 TOOTH PINION (SPECIAL)	0	0	0	0	0	0	1	0
P14	WORM GEAR	0	0	1	1	1	1	1	0
P15	COUPLING	0	0	1	1	1	2	8	0
P20	5 HOLE STRIP—FORMED	0	0	0	2	2	8	8	0
P24	CRANK	1	1	1	1	1	1	1	0
P33	SMALL SCREW DRIVER	1	1	1	1	1	1	1	1
P34	HANK OF STRING	0	1	1	1	1	1	1	0
P37	COLLAR	2	4	6	7	9	18	18	0
P48	MITRE GEAR	0	0	0	0	0	2	2	0
P49	18 TOOTH GEAR	0	0	1	0	0	0	2	0
P50A	72 TOOTH GEAR (HUDSON)	0	0	0	0	0	0	1	0
P51	ELECTRIC ENGINE	0	0	0	1	1	1	1	0
P52	LADDER CHAIN	0	0	0	0	0	0	1	0
P57A	2⅛" AXLE	1	1	1	1	1	1	4	0
P57D	6" AXLE	0	1	0	0	0	0	1	0
P57E	8" AXLE	0	0	0	0	0	2	2	0
P57F	12" AXLE	0	0	0	0	1	2	2	0
P79	CAR TRUCK	4	4	4	4	4	4	4	0
A52	INDUCTION MOTOR	0	0	1	0	0	0	0	0
A	2½" GIRDER	4	4	4	4	4	4	4	0
B	5" GIRDER	4	4	8	10	12	12	12	0
C	10" GIRDER	4	8	12	14	36	36	36	0
D	2½" CURVED GIRDER	4	4	4	4	4	4	4	0
E	5" CURVED GIRDER	0	2	4	4	26	26	26	0
F	5 HOLE STRIP	0	0	2	2	2	4	4	0
G	7 HOLE STRIP	0	0	2	2	2	6	8	0
H	11 HOLE STRIP	0	0	4	4	4	6	7	0
I	21 HOLE STRIP	0	0	2	2	4	18	18	22
J	41 HOLE STRIP	0	0	0	0	2	2	2	0
K	11 HOLE STRIP BRACKET	0	0	0	0	0	0	4	0
M	SMALL DOUBLE ANGLE	0	0	2	2	6	6	6	0
N	LONG DOUBLE ANGLE	2	4	4	4	4	4	4	0
O	PAWL	0	0	1	2	2	2	6	0
T	BOILER	0	0	0	1	1	2	2	0
U	BOILER TOP	0	0	0	1	1	1	1	0
W	STACK	0	0	0	3	3	3	3	0
Z	FLANGED WHEEL 1 5/16" DIA.	0	0	0	4	4	4	4	0
AA	ECCENTRIC CRANK	0	0	0	0	0	6	6	0
AC	UNIVERSAL BRACKET	0	0	0	0	0	0	1	0
AE	SPIRAL SPRING	0	0	0	0	0	0	2	0
AF	SMALL HOOK	1	1	1	1	1	1	3	0
AJ	PAPER ERECTOR FLAG	0	0	1	1	1	1	1	0
AM	SPECIAL PULLEY	0	0	0	0	1	1	2	0
AS	2⅞" AXLE	0	0	2	3	3	4	4	0
AT	4" AXLE	2	2	2	2	2	2	4	0
AX	19¾" AXLE	0	0	0	0	0	0	4	0
BE	6" ANGLE GIRDER	0	4	4	4	4	4	4	12
BH	SOLID COLLAR	0	0	0	0	0	2	12	0
BL	SMALL WASHER	8	12	12	12	12	12	30	12

1935 CONTENTS LIST

Set No.		1½	3½	4½	6½	7½	8½	9½	S
BN	REGULAR TURRET PLATE	0	0	2	4	4	4	4	0
BT	PIERCED DISC	1	1	1	2	4	4	4	0
BY	11 HOLE FIBRE STRIP	0	0	0	0	0	1	1	0
CA	SIGNAL ARM	0	0	0	0	0	2	2	0
CH	RIGHT ANGLE	8	12	14	14	30	42	42	0
CJ	36 TOOTH GEAR	0	0	3	3	3	3	3	0
CQ	SLOT COUPLING	0	0	0	0	0	0	2	0
CR	SPECIAL TURRET PLATE WITH HUB	0	0	0	0	0	2	2	0
CS	WHEEL SEGMENT	0	0	0	0	0	8	8	0
CY	5" AXLE	0	2	0	0	0	0	0	0
CZ	7" AXLE	0	0	2	2	3	3	4	0
DA	10" AXLE	0	0	0	0	0	0	1	0
DB	MOTOR PULLEY	0	0	1	1	1	1	1	0
DE	STEERING COLUMN	0	0	0	0	0	1	1	0
DK	FLAT SPRING	0	0	0	0	0	4	4	0
DO	STEERING WHEEL WITH HUB	0	0	0	0	0	1	1	0
DP	12" ANGLE GIRDER	0	0	4	4	4	4	4	36
DS	COTTER PIN	0	0	0	0	0	1	1	0
DT	ONE SET SCREW COUPLING	0	0	0	0	0	0	6	0
EH	GEAR BOX BRACKET	0	0	2	0	0	0	0	0
EI	STD. GEAR BOX SIDE PLATE	0	0	2	2	2	2	2	0
EJ	GEAR BOX BASE	0	0	1	0	0	0	0	0
EX	BIG CHANNEL GIRDER 12"	0	0	0	0	0	8	8	0
EY	BIG CHANNEL GIRDER 6"	0	0	0	0	0	4	4	0
EZ	BIG CHAN. GIRDER CURVED 6"	0	0	0	0	0	2	2	0
FA	1¾ x 8-32 SCREW	0	0	0	0	0	12	12	0
FD	HINGED LOOP	0	0	0	0	0	2	10	0
HF	BUTT ENDPLATE	0	0	0	0	0	0	1	0
IR	ENGINE FRAME	0	0	0	0	0	0	1	0
IS	DRIVER WHEEL	0	0	0	0	0	0	6	0
IT	COACH WHEEL	0	0	0	0	0	0	20	0
IU	SAND BOX	0	0	0	0	0	0	1	0
IV	STEAM DOME	0	0	0	0	0	0	1	0
IW	FEED WATER HEATER	0	0	0	0	0	0	1	0
IX	BELL	0	0	0	0	0	0	1	0
IY	BELL HANGER	0	0	0	0	0	0	1	0
IZ	SMOKE STACK	0	0	0	0	0	0	1	0
JA	COW CATCHER	0	0	0	0	0	0	1	0
JC	SMOKE BOX FRONT	0	0	0	0	0	0	1	0
JD	AXLE BOX	0	0	0	0	0	0	16	0
JE	PARALLEL ROD	0	0	0	0	0	0	2	0
JF	MAIN CONNECTING ROD	0	0	0	0	0	0	2	0
JG	REAR TRUCK FRAME, RIGHT	0	0	0	0	0	0	1	0
JH	REAR TRUCK FRAME, LEFT	0	0	0	0	0	0	1	0
JI	FRONT TRUCK FRAME	0	0	0	0	0	0	2	0
JJ	SMOKE BOX SHELL	0	0	0	0	0	0	1	0
JK	STEAM CHEST & CYLINDER PLATE	0	0	0	0	0	0	2	0

1935 CONTENTS LIST

Set No.		1½	3½	4½	6½	7½	8½	9½	S
JL	STEAM CHEST & CYLINDER BAND	0	0	0	0	0	0	1	0
JM	STEAM CHEST END	0	0	0	0	0	0	13	0
JN	CYLINDER END	0	0	0	0	0	0	5	0
JO	CROSSHEAD GUIDE BAR	0	0	0	0	0	0	2	0
JP	CROSSHEAD	0	0	0	0	0	0	4	0
JQ	CROSSHEAD BEARER, RIGHT	0	0	0	0	0	0	1	0
JR	CROSSHEAD BEARER, LEFT	0	0	0	0	0	0	1	0
JS	LINK FRAME	0	0	0	0	0	0	2	0
JT	LINK ROD	0	0	0	0	0	0	2	0
JU	ROD CLAMP	0	0	0	0	0	0	2	0
JV	CROSSHEAD LINK	0	0	0	0	0	0	2	0
JW	COMBINING LEVER	0	0	0	0	0	0	2	0
JX	VALVE LEVER	0	0	0	0	0	0	4	0
JY	AIR DRUM SHELL	0	0	0	0	0	0	4	0
JZ	JACKET	0	0	0	0	0	0	1	0
KA	STEAM PIPE CASING	0	0	0	0	0	0	2	0
KB	MAIN BOILER	0	0	0	0	0	0	1	0
KC	BOILER FIRE BOX	0	0	0	0	0	0	1	0
KD	FIRE BOX FRONT	0	0	0	0	0	0	1	0
KE	BOILER BACKHEAD	0	0	0	0	0	0	1	0
KF	FIRING DECK	0	0	0	0	0	0	1	0
KG	ASH PAN	0	0	0	0	0	0	1	0
KH	CAB	0	0	0	0	0	0	1	0
KI	CAB END	0	0	0	0	0	0	2	0
KJ	DRAW CASING	0	0	0	0	0	0	1	0
KK	FIRING DECK PLATE	0	0	0	0	0	0	1	0
KL	FRONT RUNNING BOARD RIGHT	0	0	0	0	0	0	1	0
KM	FRONT RUNNING BOARD LEFT	0	0	0	0	0	0	1	0
KN	REAR RUNNING BOARD	0	0	0	0	0	0	2	0
KO	RUNNING BOARD STEP	0	0	0	0	0	0	2	0
KP	FRONT BUMPER PLATE STEP	0	0	0	0	0	0	1	0
KQ	APRON	0	0	0	0	0	0	1	0
KR	M.C.B. COUPLING	0	0	0	0	0	0	3	0
KS	COUPLING PIN LIFTER	0	0	0	0	0	0	3	0
KT	¼" AXLE 3⁵⁄₃₂" LONG	0	0	0	0	0	0	5	0
KU	¼" AXLE 3⅝" LONG	0	0	0	0	0	0	8	0
KV	HEADLIGHT	0	0	0	0	0	0	1	0
KW	TRUCK FRAME	0	0	0	0	0	0	4	0
KX	TRUCK BOLSTER	0	0	0	0	0	0	2	0
KZ	TENDER BASE STEP	0	0	0	0	0	0	1	0
LA	TENDER SIDE PLATE	0	0	0	0	0	0	2	0
LB	TENDER BACK PLATE	0	0	0	0	0	0	2	0
LC	CORNER PLATE	0	0	0	0	0	0	4	0
LD	FRONT FUEL BOARD	0	0	0	0	0	0	1	0
LE	SIDE FUEL BOARD	0	0	0	0	0	0	2	0
LF	BACK FUEL BOARD WITH DECK	0	0	0	0	0	0	1	0
LG	FUEL SLIDE	0	0	0	0	0	0	1	0
LH	TENDER STEP	0	0	0	0	0	0	4	0
LI	COUPLING YOKE	0	0	0	0	0	0	2	0

1935 CONTENTS LIST

Set No.		1½	3½	4½	6½	7½	8½	9½	S
LJ	TANK HANDLE	0	0	0	0	0	0	4	0
LK	TENDER STEP ANGLE	0	0	0	0	0	0	4	0
LL	REAR TIE FRAME	0	0	0	0	0	0	2	0
LO	TRACK SECTION	0	0	0	0	0	0	8	0
LP	RAILROAD TIE	0	0	0	0	0	0	12	0
LS	JACK	0	0	0	0	0	0	2	0
LT	MOTOR SUPPORT BRACKET	0	0	0	0	0	0	2	0
LU	OFFSET WRENCH	0	0	0	0	0	0	2	0
LV	3" DISC WHEEL, RED	0	0	0	0	0	0	4	0
LW	RUBBER TIRE FOR LV	0	0	0	0	0	0	4	0
LX	STEERING COLUMN BRACKET	0	0	0	0	0	1	1	0
MA	RADIATOR	0	0	0	0	0	1	1	0
MB	18½" ANGLE GIRDER	0	0	0	0	0	2	2	0
MC	BASE PLATE 1" x 2½"	2	2	2	2	8	8	8	0
MD	BASE PLATE 2½" x 5"	1	1	1	1	4	8	8	0
ME	BASE PLATE 1" x 4"	0	0	0	0	0	4	4	0
MF	BASE PLATE 1" x 5"	2	2	4	4	8	9	12	0
MG	RADIATOR HOOD	0	0	0	0	0	1	1	0
MH	LARGE 3" DISC WHEEL	0	4	4	4	4	4	0	0
MI	FRONT AXLE UNIT	0	0	0	0	0	1	1	0
MJ	ELECTRO MAGNET WITH CORD	0	0	0	0	1	1	1	0
MM	WRENCH	0	0	1	1	1	1	1	1
MN	12" BASE PLATE	0	0	4	4	6	6	6	0
MO	3" ANGLE GIRDER	0	4	4	4	4	4	4	8
MP	24 TOOTH GEAR	0	0	1	0	0	0	0	0
MQ	27 TOOTH WORM WHEEL	0	0	0	1	1	1	1	0
MR	DRUM WITH GEAR	0	0	0	0	1	1	1	0
MS	COMPRESSION SPRING	0	0	0	1	1	1	1	0
MT	SNAP RIVET	0	36	36	36	36	36	36	240
MU	RIVET EXTRACTOR	0	1	1	1	1	1	1	1
MV	FLAT CAR TRUCK	0	0	0	0	4	4	4	0
NA	3" MAIN ENTRANCE	0	2	2	2	2	2	2	5
NB	3" GROUND FLOOR	0	2	2	2	2	2	2	5
NC	3" UPPER STORY	0	4	4	4	4	4	4	10
ND	6" UPPER STORY	0	4	4	4	4	4	4	10
NE	6" GARAGE ENTRANCE	0	0	0	0	0	0	0	14
NF	6" OFFICE ENTRANCE	0	0	0	0	0	0	0	14
NG	ROOF	0	2	2	2	2	2	2	6
N21	8-32 SQUARE NUT	25	45	68	100	134	240	350	62
S51	¼" x 8-32 SCREW	21	35	60	90	114	180	255	62
S52	½" x 8-32 SCREW	0	0	2	2	2	4	28	0
S57	1⅜" x 8-32 SCREW	0	0	0	3	4	4	12	0
S62	⅞" x 8-32 SCREW	3	6	8	8	18	20	56	0

Form M 1541

ERECTOR SEPARATE PARTS PRICES

Most all dealers carry Separate Erector Parts. If unable to obtain in your city send us your check, Money Order or stamps for the parts you want and we will be glad to send your order direct.

THE A. C. GILBERT CO., NEW HAVEN, CONN., U. S. A.

Trade No.	Name of Part	Page	Price
*N21	8-32 Square Nut	2	.05 doz.
P7	Small Wheel	2	.10 ea.
P12	Crown Gear	2	.10 ea.
P13	12-Tooth Pinion Gear	2	.10 ea.
P14	Worm Gear	2	.20 ea.
P15	Coupling	2	.10 ea.
P20	Five Hole Strip—formed	1	.05 ea.
P24	Crank	1	.10 ea.
P33	Small Screw Driver	1	.05 ea.
P34	Hank of String	1	.05 ea.
P37	Collar	2	.25 doz.
P39	Wood Screw	2	.15 doz.
P40	Screw Eye	2	.20 doz.
P48	Mitre Gear	2	.20 ea.
P49	18-Tooth Gear	2	.15 ea.
P50	72-Tooth Gear	2	.30 ea.
P52	Ladder Chain	1	.15 ft.
P51	Electric Engine Reversing	3	3.95 ea.
P54	Motor, 6-14 volts	3	1.75 ea.
P56G	Motor, 110v. A.C. or D.C.		2.9[illegible]
P58	Motor, 6-14 volts	3	1.[illegible] ea.
P59	Reverse Base	3	.75 ea.
A52	Ind. Motor with Side Plates—110v. A.C. only	3	2.50 ea.
P57A	2⅛" Axle	1	.02 ea.
P57D	6" Axle	1	.06 ea.
P57E	8" Axle	1	.08 ea.
P57F	12" Axle	1	.12 ea.
P79	Car Truck	1	.05 ea.
*S11	Set Screw	2	.05 doz.
*S51	¼"x8-32 Screw	2	.05 doz.
*S52	½"x8-32 Screw	2	.10 doz.
*S57	1⅛"x8-32 Screw	2	.15 doz.
*S62	⅞"x8-32 Screw	2	.10 doz.
*FA	1¼"x8-32 Screw	2	.15 doz.
A	2½" Girder	1	.20 doz.
B	5" Girder	1	.35 doz.
C	10" Girder	1	.50 doz.
D	2½" Curved Girder	1	.25 doz.
E	5" Curved Girder	1	.40 doz.
F	5 Hole Strip	1	.10 doz.
G	7 Hole Strip	1	.10 doz.
H	11 Hole Strip	1	.15 doz.
I	21 Hole Strip	1	.20 doz.
J	41 Hole Strip	1	.30 doz.
K	11 Hole Strip Bracket	1	.35 doz.
M	Small Double Angle	1	.25 doz.
N	Long Double Angle	1	.05 ea.
O	Pawl	1	.05 ea.
S	Large Base Plate—21 holes	1	.40 ea.
T	Boiler	3	.25 ea.
U	Boiler Top	3	.20 ea.
W	Stack	3	.05 ea.
X	Digger Scoop	3	.75 ea.
Z	Flanged Wheel	2	.15 ea.
AA	Eccentric Crank	1	.10 ea.
AB	One Hole Coupling	2	.15 ea.
AC	Universal Bracket	1	.10 ea.
AE	Spiral Spring	1	.05 ea.
AF	Small Hook	2	.15 doz.
AH	Small Triangle	1	.25 doz.
AM	Special Pulley—Metal	2	.05 ea.
AQ	Sheave Pulley	2	.05 ea.
AR	8-Hole Strip	1	.10 doz.
AS	2⅞" Axle Rod	1	.03 ea.
AT	4" Axle Rod	1	.04 ea.
AV	7-Hole Strip Bracket	1	2 for .05
AX	19¾" Axle Rod	1	.20 ea.
AY	Bull Ring	1	.50 ea.
AZ	Bull Wheel Plate	1	.25 ea.
BA	B. W. Cntr (with Hub)	1	.25 ea.
B2	Wood Handle Screw Driver	1	.15 ea.
BE	6" Slotted Angle Strip	1	.50 doz.
BH	Solid Collar	2	2 for .05
BI	6" Flat Beam Girder	1	6 for .50
BJ	12" Flat Beam Girder	1	6 for .75
BK	8-32 Wing Nut	2	.25 doz.
BL	Small Washer	2	.05 doz.
BN	Regular Turret Plate	3	.15 ea.
BO	Reverse Switch Attachment	2	.50 ea.
BT	Pierced Disc	2	.10 ea.
BY	11-Hole Fibre Strip	1	.05 ea.
CA	Signal Arm	1	.10 ea.
CH	Right Angle	1	.10 doz.
CI	36-Tooth Gear	2	.20 ea.
CQ	Slot Coupling	2	.15 ea.
CX	1" Axle Rod	1	.01 ea.
CY	5" Axle Rod	1	.05 ea.
CZ	7" Axle Rod	1	.07 ea.
DA	10" Axle Rod	1	.10 ea.
DB	Motor Pulley	2	.10 ea.
DE	Steering Column	1	.10 ea.
DK	Flat Spring	1	.10 ea.
DO	Steering Wheel with Hub	2	.15 ea.
DP	12" Slotted Angle Strip	1	6 for .50
DQ	Special Large Base Plate (28 holes)	1	.50 ea.
DS	Cotter Pin	1	.05 doz.
DT	1-Hole Set Screw Coupling	2	2 for .15
DU	¼" Diam. Axle 8½"	1	2 for .25
DV	6" Curved Beam Girder	1	6 for .75
DZ	Tackle Block	2	.15 ea.
EC	Giant Axle—29" long, $\frac{5}{16}$" diam.	1	.50 ea.
EH	Gear Box Bracket	1	.05 ea.
EI	Standard Gear Box Side Pl.	1	.15 ea.
EJ	Gear Box Base	1	.20 ea.
EK	Plain Drum	2	.25 ea.
EW	12" Duplex F. B. Plate	1	.50 ea.
EX	Big Channel Girder 12"	1	6 for .50
EY	Big Channel Girder 6"	1	.05 ea.
EZ	6" Curved B. C. Girder	1	.05 ea.
FD	Hinged Loop	1	2 for .05
FJ	Rack	2	.25 ea.
FL	Helical Gear	2	.25 ea.
FP	Small Disc Wheel	2	.10 ea.
FX	Quarter Gear	2	.15 ea.
FZ	Internal Gear	2	.15 ea.
GX	8-Hole Double Angle Bracket	1	.10 doz.
LV	3" Disc Wheel, red	2	.20 ea.
LW	Rubber Tire for LV and MH	2	.10 ea.
LX	Steering Column Bracket	1	.05 ea.
MA	New Radiator	1	.15 ea.
MB	18½" Angle Girder	1	.15 ea.
MC	Base Plate 1"x2½"	1	.05 ea.
MD	Base Plate 2½"x5"	1	.10 ea.
ME	Flat Plate 1"x4"	1	.05 ea.
MF	Flat Plate 1"x5"	1	.05 ea.
MG	Radiator Hood	1	.10 ea.
MH	3" Disc Wheel, Nickel Rim	2	.25 ea.
MI	Front Axle Unit	1	.25 ea.
MJ	Electro Magnet with Cord	2	.60 ea.
MM	Wrench	1	.05 ea.
MN	12" Base Plate	1	.40 ea.
MO	3" Angle Girder	1	.75 doz.
MP	24 Tooth Gear	2	.20 ea.
MQ	27 Tooth Worm Wheel	2	.15 ea.
MR	Drum with Gear	2	.35 ea.
MS	Compression Spring	1	.05 ea.
MT	Snap Rivet	2	.10 doz.
MU	Rivet Extractor	1	.05 ea.
MV	Flat Car Truck	1	.05 ea.
NA	3" Main Entrance	3	2 for .05
NB	3" Ground Floor	3	2 for .05
NC	3" Upper Story	3	2 for .05
ND	6" Upper Story	3	.05 ea.
NE	6" Garage Entrance	3	.05 ea.
NF	6" Office Entrance	3	.05 ea.
NG	Roof	3	.05 ea.
CR	Special Turret plate with hub	1	.15 ea.
CS	Wheel Segment	1	.15 ea.

REGULAR ERECTOR MANUALS

No. 1	Erector Manual	.15 ea.
No. 3	Erector Manual	.15 ea.
No. 4	Erector Manual	.25 ea.
No. 6	Erector Manual	.25 ea.
No. 7	Erector Manual	.25 ea.
No. 8	Locomotive Manual	.25 ea.
No. 1½	Erector Manual	.15 ea.
No. 3½	Erector Manual	.15 ea.
No. 4½	Erector Manual	.25 ea.
No. 6½	Erector Manual	.25 ea.
No. 7½	Erector Manual	.35 ea.
No. 8½	Erector Manual	.35 ea.
No. 9½	Locomotive Manual	.25 ea.

ERECTOR ACCESSORY MANUALS

No. 5	Erector Electrical Set Manual	.25 ea.
Fun with your Motor Manual		.25 ea.

NOTE

*N21 Nut used with screws S51, S52, S62, S57, FA

*S11 Set Screw used with pulleys, couplings, etc.

Separate Parts Prices for 1935

Some modifications occurred in the Erector System, and two new parts were added. Gilbert introduced the (MW) Nut Holder in 1936 and included it in No. 4½ and larger sets. This was a welcome addition for builders, as it allowed them to hold nuts in places where fingers could not go. This first version of the (MW) had a ⅝" metal flap at the end that made it easier to grasp.

The (P7) ⅞" Pulley first appeared in 1937, and the designation of this part can be confusing. Since the invention of Erector in 1913, almost every set had 1⅛"-diameter pulley wheels designated as (P7). In 1937, Gilbert developed a pulley with a ⅞" diameter. For unknown reasons, he designated this new part as (P7) and referred to the old pulley as (P7A). Although this change does not appear in the separate parts section until 1938, it did occur in 1937 and affected sets from that year. Sets from No. 1½ through No. 7½ came with the (P7) Pulley. The larger sets, from No. 8½ through No. 10½, came with the larger (P7A) Pulley.

Several other notable changes occurred in 1936. The (P58) Motor returned to the line after a one-year absence. It came in No. 4½. Starting this year, the (CR) Special Turret Plate was painted blue and not black. And, for this year only, the (MA) Radiator was painted black (at least in some sets) instead of being nickel-plated. It was finished this way when it was packed in the Gilbert-Meccano sets at the end of the Classic Period. Perhaps some leftovers were being used.

Cardboard Box Sets

In 1936, the line of cardboard box sets increased from three to five. Except for the deletion of the skyscraper parts, Nos. 1½ and 3½ ran unchanged from the previous year. The No. S, The Erector Skyscraper Set, also was unchanged. But No. 2½ was new, and it included the (MH) Disc Wheels. Gilbert named it "The Apprentice Set" and priced it midway between Nos. 1½ and 3½.

The second new cardboard box set was No. 4½. Other than not having skyscraper panels and coming with a (P58) battery motor instead of an (A52) 110-volt induction motor, its contents were identical to those in No. 4½ from 1935. The No. 4½ from 1935 had been packed in a metal box. This same set was available in 1936 as No. 5½.

The No. 4½ from 1936 was the first cardboard box set to have a hinged lid. To hold the lid upright when the box was open, Gilbert strung two pieces of red cord through holes in the lid and the box body. The inner lid label from the large metal box sets was used on No. 4½; it pictured the Ferris Wheel and the Refrigeration Plant. Although the small label could have been used, Gilbert added the large one because it fit better. The No. 4½ was a two-layer set with a removable cardboard parts tray; two (MN) Base Plates with parts clipped in place rested in it. The rest of the packaging was complicated. Below the removable tray was a cardboard insert with more parts. On the left side another high insert displayed the angle girders; on the right were cardboard boxes for the motor and assembled gearbox. A mustard yellow parts box was included.

Set No. S was available unchanged from 1935 and then dropped after 1937. Meanwhile, Gilbert added a sixth cardboard box set to the lineup, No. SA, called "The Skyscraper Accessory Set." It differed from No. S, though the latter was called an accessory set when introduced in 1935. However, No. S was a complete set because it contained everything, including the regular Erector parts, required to build the skyscraper models. By contrast, No. SA was an accessory set. It had only the skyscraper panels and snap rivets and lacked angle girders and strips from a regular set, so it could not build anything. This set was never pictured in the catalog and only mentioned in the price list (where it sold for a mere 50 cents).

Today, Nos. S and SA are rare and valuable items. Gilbert offered the latter only in 1937, which was the final year for

***Right:** Beginning in 1933, Gilbert used wooden holders to secure the parts cans, with the lids pressed firmly against the box lid so they would not spill during shipment. **Left:** An interesting change occurred in 1937, when the firm began constructing the parts can holders from cardboard.*

skyscraper parts of any kind. Most likely, the company created this inexpensive set to help dispose of the remaining skyscraper panel inventories.

Metal Box Sets

The 1936 and 1937 metal box sets were basically the same as those created in 1935, though they lacked skyscraper parts. Still, due to the expansion of cardboard box sets in the lineup, Gilbert changed the numbering system. Most sets were given a one-digit increase in number.

The No. 5½, the smallest of the metal box sets, was identical to No. 4½ from 1935. Except for having an (A52) 110-volt motor in place of a (P58) battery motor, the contents of No. 5½ did not differ from those of No. 4½ from 1936. Meanwhile, the small inside lid label for this set was modified because of the new numbering system. Various models were illustrated on this label and the number of the set that could build each model was listed. Since the numbering system was altered the label had to be updated. Set No. 7½ also used this small label. A similar change occurred with the large label used on Nos. 4½, 8½, and 9½.

For some unknown reason, Gilbert chose not to designate any set from 1936 as No. 6½; therefore, next in the lineup came No. 7½, which was a carryover of No. 6½ from 1935.

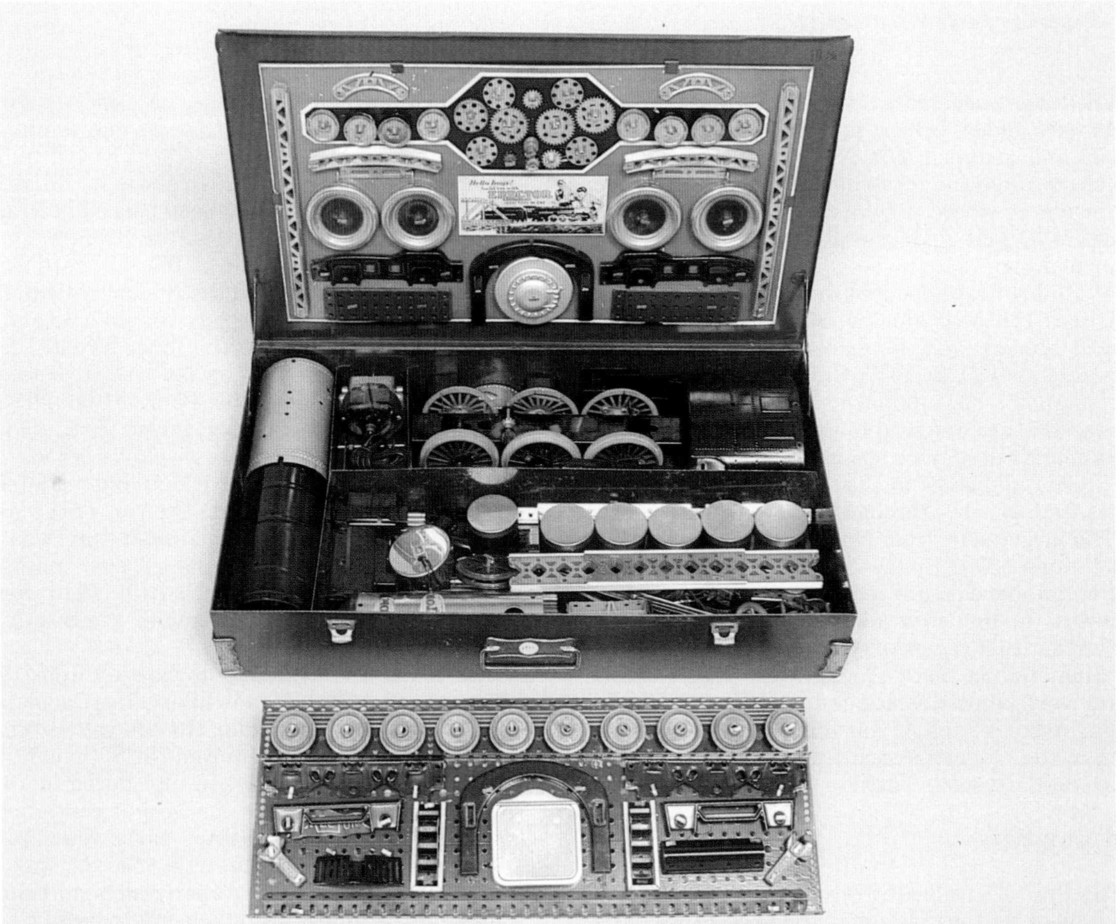

Gilbert offered the Erector Hudson for the last time in 1937 as No. 10½. It contained all the regular parts from No. 9½, along with the train parts. Set No. 10½ was packed in a royal blue box, a color unique to the metal box Hudson set series.

SETS IN THE ERECTOR SYSTEM 1933–37

	Box Size	1933	1934	1935	1936–37
Cardboard Box Sets		No. 1 No. 3 No. 4	No. 1 No. 3	No. 1½ No. 3½ No. 5	No. 1½ No. 2½ No. 3½ Nos. 5 and 5A
Metal Box Sets	16" x 8" x 3"	N/A	No. 4, red	No. 4½, red	No. 5½, red
	18" x 10" x 3"	No. 6, green	No. 6, green	No. 6½, green	No. 7½, royal blue
	20" x 12" x 3"	No. 7, red	No. 7, red	No. 7½, red	No. 8½, red
	27" x 13" x 3"	N/A	No. 7½, powder blue	No. 8½ royal blue	No. 9½ royal blue
	24" x 14" x 4"	N/A	No. 8, crackle powder blue	No. 9½, crackle powder blue	No. 10½, crackle powder blue in 1937 royal blue

The latter came in a green set box, as did the earliest version of the No. 7½ from 1936. But the color of the box was quickly changed to royal blue, and most of the 1936 sets are found that way. The Walking Beam Engine was this set's featured model.

Set No. 8½ came in the same red metal box as did last year's No. 7½ and, except for skyscraper parts, was identical to it. In 1936 and 1937, this set featured the Ferris Wheel and the Bascule Bridge. Also, The Automotive Set was designated No. 9½, despite being the same as No. 8½ from 1935. An interesting change occurred in the packaging of No. 9½ in 1937. In the past, Gilbert had included a green wood base for the small parts cans that held them tight against the lid so they would not come open during transport. Now the base was made of green cardboard.

Set No. 10½, the top-of-the-line Hudson, was a carryover of No. 9½ from 1935. The 1936 version came in a powder blue box with a crackle finish. Beginning in 1937, however, the box was royal blue. Also, the (LV) Disc Wheels with (LW) Rubber Tires were replaced with (MH) Disc Wheels late in 1936.

Some noteworthy changes in the Hudson parts occurred in 1936–37. Earlier, in 1935, Gilbert had deleted the Erector decal from the cab of the engine. Then the following year, he left off the New York Central decal from the sides of the tender. Since Gilbert planned to drop the Hudson after 1937, he likely decided not to order more decals when existing stocks ran out.

Erector System Modifications For 1936 and 1937

I. New Parts

(P7) ⅞" Pulley (1937)
(MW) Nut Holder (1936)

II. Modified Parts

(CR) Special Turret Plate with hub, painted blue instead of black (1936)
(LA) Tender Side Plate, with New York Central decal deleted
(MA) Radiator, painted black instead of nickel-plated in some sets from 1936; the next year it was nickel-plated instead of painted black for all sets

III. Eliminated Parts

(LV) 3" Disc Wheel, Red (late 1936)
(LW) Rubber Tire for LV (late 1936)
(MQ) 27 Tooth Worm Wheel (1937)

Listings of 1936 And 1937 Erector Sets

	Gd	VG	Exc	Inv	Org

NO. 1 — The Dandy Beginner's Set

Came in a cardboard box 13½" x 10¼" x ¾"; sold for $1.00 in 1936 and 1937.

	Gd	VG	Exc	Inv	Org
	30	40	70	+15	+20

NO. 2½ — The Apprentice Set

Featured (MH) Disc Wheels. Came in a cardboard box 18¼" x 10¼" x ¾"; sold for $2.25 in 1936 and $2.50 in 1937.

	Gd	VG	Exc	Inv	Org
	35	50	80	+20	+25

NO. 3½ — The Intermediate Set

Featured (MN) Base Plates and angle girders. Came in a cardboard box 18¼" x 10¼" x 1¼"; two-layer set with removable cardboard parts display tray; sold for $3.00 in 1936 and $3.50 in 1937.

	Gd	VG	Exc	Inv	Org
	40	55	90	+25	+30

NO. 4½ — The Famous No. 4½

Featured battery-operated (P58) Motor and (MN) Base Plates. Came in a cardboard box 18¼" x 10¼" x 2½" with a hinged lid; two-layer set with removable cardboard parts display tray; sold for $5.00 in 1936 and 1937.

	Gd	VG	Exc	Inv	Org
	60	90	150	+30	+40

NO. 5½ — The Super No. 5½

Identical contents as No. 4½ except for (A52) 110-volt induction motor instead of (P58) battery motor. Came in a red metal box 16" x 8" x 3"; two-layer set with two removable parts displays constructed from (MN) Base Plates; sold for $6.95 in 1936 and 1937.

	Gd	VG	Exc	Inv	Org
	60	90	150	+30	+40

NO. 7½ — The Electric Engine Set

Featured (T) Boiler and (P51) Electric Engine and built Walking Beam Engine. Came in a royal blue metal box 18" x 10" x 3" with brass corner trim; earliest version from 1936 was painted green. Two-layer set with two removable parts displays constructed from (MN) Base Plates; sold for $10.00 in 1936 and 1937.

	Gd	VG	Exc	Inv	Org
	70	105	175	+35	+45

	Gd	VG	Exc	Inv	Org

NO. 8½ The Engineer's Set

Featured (MJ) Electro Magnet and hoisting drum and built Ferris Wheel. Came in a red metal box 20" x 12" x 3" with brass corner trim; two-layer set with three removable parts displays constructed from (MN) Base Plates; sold for $12.50 in 1936 and $12.95 in 1937.

	Gd	VG	Exc	Inv	Org
	90	**130**	**225**	**+45**	**+55**

NO. 9½ The Automotive Set

Featured truck parts, giant flywheel, and (P51) Electric Engine with reversing switch and built Giant Power Plant. Came in a royal blue metal box 22" x 13" x 3" with brass corner trim; two-layer set with three removable parts displays constructed from (MN) Base Plates; sold for $16.95 in 1936 and $17.95 in 1937.

	Gd	VG	Exc	Inv	Org
	140	**210**	**350**	**+70**	**+90**

NO. 10½ The World's Champion No. 10½

Featured all parts from No. 9½ and those needed to build Hudson locomotive and tender; included two instruction manuals. Came in a metal box 24" x 14" x 4" with brass corner trim; box painted powder blue with crackle finish in 1936 and royal blue in 1937. Two-layer set with one very large removable parts display constructed from (MN) Base Plates; cardboard parts display clipped on inside of lid; sold for $25.00 in 1936 and $27.50 in 1937.

	Gd	VG	Exc	Inv	Org
	1280	**1920**	**3200**	**+640**	**+800**

No. S The Erector Skyscraper Set

Specialized set for building architectural models; featured full range of cardboard skyscraper panels and parts as well as regular Erector parts. Came in a cardboard box 18¼" x 10¼" x 1¼"; lid pictured city of skyscrapers; sold for $2.50 in 1936 and 1937.

	Gd	VG	Exc	Inv	Org
	640	**960**	**1600**	**+320**	**+400**

No. SA The Skyscraper Accessory Set

Specialized accessory set designed for use only with a regular Erector Set for building architectural models; featured full range of cardboard skyscraper panels and rivets but no regular Erector parts. Came in a cardboard box of unknown size; lid pictured city of skyscrapers; sold for 50 cents in 1937.

	Gd	VG	Exc	Inv	Org
	400	**600**	**1000**	**+200**	**+250**

1936–37 CONTENTS LIST

Set No.		1½	2½	3½	4½	5½	7½	8½	9½	10½	S	SA[1]
P7[2]	SMALL WHEEL	4	4	4	4	4	4	4	4	4	0	0
P12	CROWN GEAR	0	0	0	1	1	1	1	1	1	0	0
P13	12 TOOTH PINION GEAR, ⅛"	0	0	0	2	2	2	2	2	2	0	0
P13A	12 TOOTH PINION (SPECIAL)	0	0	0	0	0	0	0	0	1	0	0
P14	WORM GEAR	0	0	0	1	1	1	1	1	1	0	0
P15	COUPLING	0	0	0	1	1	1	2	2	8	0	0
P20	5 HOLE STRIP —FORMED	0	0	0	0	0	2	2	8	8	0	0
P24	CRANK	1	1	1	1	1	1	1	1	1	0	0
P33	SMALL SCREW DRIVER	1	1	1	1	1	1	1	1	1	1	0
P34	HANK OF STRING	0	1	1	1	1	1	1	1	1	0	0
P37	COLLAR	2	4	4	6	6	7	9	18	18	0	0
P48	MITRE GEAR	0	0	0	0	0	0	0	2	2	0	0
P49	18 TOOTH GEAR	0	0	0	1	0	0	0	0	2	0	0
P50A	72 TOOTH GEAR (HUDSON)	0	0	0	0	0	0	0	0	1	0	0
P51[3]	ELECTRIC ENGINE	0	0	0	0	0	1	1	1	1	0	0
P52	LADDER CHAIN	0	0	0	0	0	0	0	0	1	0	0
P57A	2⅛" AXLE	1	1	1	1	1	1	1	1	4	0	0
P57D	6" AXLE	0	1	2	0	0	0	0	0	1	0	0
P57E	8" AXLE	0	0	0	0	0	0	0	2	2	0	0
P57F	12" AXLE	0	0	0	0	0	0	1	2	2	0	0
P58	MOTOR	0	0	0	1	0	0	0	0	0	0	0
P79	CAR TRUCK	4	4	4	4	4	4	4	4	4	0	0
A52	INDUCTION MOTOR	0	0	0	0	1	0	0	0	0	0	0
A	2½" GIRDER	4	4	4	4	4	4	4	4	4	0	0
B	5" GIRDER	4	4	4	8	8	10	12	12	12	0	0
C	10" GIRDER	4	8	8	12	12	14	36	36	36	0	0
D	2½" CURVED GIRDER	4	4	4	4	4	4	4	4	4	0	0
E	5" CURVED GIRDER	0	2	2	4	4	4	26	26	26	0	0
F	5 HOLE STRIP	0	0	0	2	2	2	2	4	4	0	0
G	7 HOLE STRIP	0	0	0	2	2	2	2	6	8	0	0
H	11 HOLE STRIP	0	0	0	4	4	4	4	6	7	0	0
I	21 HOLE STRIP	0	0	0	2	2	2	4	18	18	22	0
J	41 HOLE STRIP	0	0	0	0	0	0	2	2	2	0	0
K	11 HOLE STRIP BRACKET	0	0	0	0	0	0	0	0	4	0	0
M	SMALL DOUBLE ANGLE	0	0	0	2	2	2	6	6	6	0	0
N	LONG DOUBLE ANGLE	2	4	4	4	4	4	4	4	4	0	0
O	PAWL	0	0	0	1	1	2	2	2	6	0	0
T	BOILER	0	0	0	0	0	1	1	2	2	0	0
U	BOILER TOP	0	0	0	0	0	1	1	1	1	0	0
W	STACK	0	0	0	0	0	3	3	3	3	0	0
Z	FLANGED WHEEL. 15⁄16" DIA	0	0	0	0	0	4	4	4	4	0	0
AA	ECCENTRIC CRANK	0	0	0	0	0	0	0	6	6	0	0
AC	UNIVERSAL BRACKET	0	0	0	0	0	0	0	1	0	0	0
AE	SPIRAL SPRING	0	0	0	0	0	0	0	0	2	0	0
AF	SMALL HOOK	1	1	1	1	1	1	1	1	3	0	0
AJ	PAPER ERECTOR FLAG	0	0	0	1	1	1	1	1	1	0	0
AM	SPECIAL PULLEY	0	0	0	0	0	0	1	1	2	0	0
AS	2⅞" AXLE	0	0	0	2	2	3	3	4	4	0	0
AT	4" AXLE	2	2	2	2	2	2	2	2	4	0	0
AX	19¾" AXLE	0	0	0	0	0	0	0	0	4	0	0
BE	6" ANGLE GIRDER	0	0	4	4	4	4	4	4	4	12	0

1936–37 CONTENTS LIST

Set No.		1½	2½	3½	4½	5½	7½	8½	9½	10½	S	SA[1]
BH	SOLID COLLAR	0	0	0	0	0	0	0	2	12	0	0
BL	SMALL WASHER	8	12	12	12	12	12	12	12	30	12	0
BN	REGULAR TURRET PLATE	0	0	0	2	2	4	4	4	4	0	0
BT	PIERCED DISC	1	1	1	1	1	2	4	4	4	0	0
BY	11 HOLE FIBRE STRIP	0	0	0	0	0	0	0	1	1	0	0
CA	SIGNAL ARM	0	0	0	0	0	0	0	2	2	0	0
CH	RIGHT ANGLE	8	12	12	14	14	14	30	42	42	0	0
CJ	36 TOOTH GEAR	0	0	0	3	3	3	3	3	3	0	0
CQ	SLOT COUPLING	0	0	0	0	0	0	0	0	2	0	0
CR	SPECIAL TURRET PLATE WITH HUB	0	0	0	0	0	0	0	2	2	0	0
CS	WHEEL SEGMENT	0	0	0	0	0	0	0	8	8	0	0
CY	5" AXLE	0	2	2	0	0	0	0	0	0	0	0
CZ	7" AXLE	0	0	0	2	2	2	3	3	4	0	0
DA	10" AXLE	0	0	0	0	0	0	0	0	1	0	0
DB	MOTOR PULLEY	0	0	0	1	1	1	1	1	1	0	0
DE	STEERING COLUMN	0	0	0	0	0	0	0	1	1	0	0
DK	FLAT SPRING	0	0	0	0	0	0	0	4	4	0	0
DO	STEERING WHEEL WITH HUB	0	0	0	0	0	0	0	1	1	0	0
DP	12" ANGLE GIRDER	0	0	4	4	4	4	4	4	4	36	0
DS	COTTER PIN	0	0	0	0	0	0	0	1	1	0	0
DT	ONE SET SCREW COUPLING	0	0	0	0	0	0	0	0	6	0	0
EH	GEAR BOX BRACKET	0	0	0	2	2	0	0	0	0	0	0
EI	STD. GEAR BOX SIDE PLATE	0	0	0	2	2	2	2	2	2	0	0
EJ	GEAR BOX BASE	0	0	0	1	1	0	0	0	0	0	0
EX	BIG CHANNEL GIRDER 12"	0	0	0	0	0	0	0	8	8	0	0
EY	BIG CHANNEL GIRDER 6"	0	0	0	0	0	0	0	4	4	0	0
EZ	BIG CHAN. GIRDER CURVED 6"	0	0	0	0	0	0	0	2	2	0	0
FA	1¾" x 8-32 SCREW	0	0	0	0	0	0	0	12	12	0	0
FD	HINGED LOOP	0	0	0	0	0	0	0	2	10	0	0
HF	BUTT ENDPLATE	0	0	0	0	0	0	0	0	1	0	0
IR	ENGINE FRAME	0	0	0	0	0	0	0	0	1	0	0
IS	DRIVER WHEEL	0	0	0	0	0	0	0	0	6	0	0
IT	COACH WHEEL	0	0	0	0	0	0	0	0	20	0	0
IU	SAND BOX	0	0	0	0	0	0	0	0	1	0	0
IV	STEAM DOME	0	0	0	0	0	0	0	0	1	0	0
IW	FEED WATER HEATER	0	0	0	0	0	0	0	0	1	0	0
IX	BELL	0	0	0	0	0	0	0	0	1	0	0
IY	BELL HANGER	0	0	0	0	0	0	0	0	1	0	0
IZ	SMOKE STACK	0	0	0	0	0	0	0	0	1	0	0
JA	COW CATCHER	0	0	0	0	0	0	0	0	1	0	0
JC	SMOKE BOX FRONT	0	0	0	0	0	0	0	0	1	0	0
JD	AXLE BOX	0	0	0	0	0	0	0	0	16	0	0
JE	PARALLEL ROD	0	0	0	0	0	0	0	0	2	0	0
JF	MAIN CONNECTING ROD	0	0	0	0	0	0	0	0	2	0	0
JG	REAR TRUCK FRAME, RIGHT	0	0	0	0	0	0	0	0	1	0	0
JH	REAR TRUCK FRAME, LEFT	0	0	0	0	0	0	0	0	1	0	0
JI	FRONT TRUCK FRAME	0	0	0	0	0	0	0	0	2	0	0
JJ	SMOKE BOX SHELL	0	0	0	0	0	0	0	0	1	0	0

1936–37 CONTENTS LIST

Set No.		1½	2½	3½	4½	5½	7½	8½	9½	10½	S	SA[1]
JK	STEAM CHEST & CYLINDER PLATE	0	0	0	0	0	0	0	0	2	0	0
JL	STEAM CHEST & CYLINDER BAND	0	0	0	0	0	0	0	0	1	0	0
JM	STEAM CHEST END	0	0	0	0	0	0	0	0	13	0	0
JN	CYLINDER END	0	0	0	0	0	0	0	0	5	0	0
JO	CROSSHEAD GUIDE BAR	0	0	0	0	0	0	0	0	2	0	0
JP	CROSSHEAD	0	0	0	0	0	0	0	0	4	0	0
JQ	CROSSHEAD BEARER, RIGHT	0	0	0	0	0	0	0	0	1	0	0
JR	CROSSHEAD BEARER, LEFT	0	0	0	0	0	0	0	0	1	0	0
JS	LINK FRAME	0	0	0	0	0	0	0	0	2	0	0
JT	LINK ROD	0	0	0	0	0	0	0	0	2	0	0
JU	ROD CLAMP	0	0	0	0	0	0	0	0	2	0	0
JV	CROSSHEAD LINK	0	0	0	0	0	0	0	0	2	0	0
JW	COMBINING LEVER	0	0	0	0	0	0	0	0	2	0	0
JX	VALVE LEVER	0	0	0	0	0	0	0	0	4	0	0
JY	AIR DRUM SHELL	0	0	0	0	0	0	0	0	4	0	0
JZ	JACKET	0	0	0	0	0	0	0	0	1	0	0
KA	STEAM PIPE CASING	0	0	0	0	0	0	0	0	2	0	0
KB	MAIN BOILER	0	0	0	0	0	0	0	0	1	0	0
KC	BOILER FIRE BOX	0	0	0	0	0	0	0	0	1	0	0
KD	FIRE BOX FRONT	0	0	0	0	0	0	0	0	1	0	0
KE	BOILER BACKHEAD	0	0	0	0	0	0	0	0	1	0	0
KF	FIRING DECK	0	0	0	0	0	0	0	0	1	0	0
KG	ASH PAN	0	0	0	0	0	0	0	0	1	0	0
KH	CAB	0	0	0	0	0	0	0	0	1	0	0
KI	CAB END	0	0	0	0	0	0	0	0	2	0	0
KJ	DRAW CASING	0	0	0	0	0	0	0	0	1	0	0
KK	FIRING DECK PLATE	0	0	0	0	0	0	0	0	1	0	0
KL	FRONT RUNNING BOARD, RIGHT	0	0	0	0	0	0	0	0	1	0	0
KM	FRONT RUNNING BOARD, LEFT	0	0	0	0	0	0	0	0	1	0	0
KN	REAR RUNNING BOARD	0	0	0	0	0	0	0	0	2	0	0
KO	RUNNING BOARD STEP	0	0	0	0	0	0	0	0	2	0	0
KP	FRONT BUMPER PLATE STEP	0	0	0	0	0	0	0	0	1	0	0
KQ	APRON	0	0	0	0	0	0	0	0	1	0	0
KR	M.C.B. COUPLING	0	0	0	0	0	0	0	0	3	0	0
KS	COUPLING PIN LIFTER	0	0	0	0	0	0	0	0	3	0	0
KT	¼ INCH AXLE 35⁄32 INCH LONG	0	0	0	0	0	0	0	0	5	0	0
KU	¼ INCH AXLE 3⅝ INCH LONG	0	0	0	0	0	0	0	0	8	0	0
KV	HEADLIGHT	0	0	0	0	0	0	0	0	1	0	0
KW	TRUCK FRAME	0	0	0	0	0	0	0	0	4	0	0
KX	TRUCK BOLSTER	0	0	0	0	0	0	0	0	2	0	0
KZ	TENDER BASE STEP	0	0	0	0	0	0	0	0	1	0	0
LA	TENDER SIDE PLATE	0	0	0	0	0	0	0	0	2	0	0
LB	TENDER BACK PLATE	0	0	0	0	0	0	0	0	2	0	0
LC	CORNER PLATE	0	0	0	0	0	0	0	0	4	0	0
LD	FRONT FUEL BOARD	0	0	0	0	0	0	0	0	1	0	0
LE	SIDE FUEL BOARD	0	0	0	0	0	0	0	0	2	0	0
LF	BACK FUEL BOARD WITH DECK	0	0	0	0	0	0	0	0	1	0	0
LG	FUEL SLIDE	0	0	0	0	0	0	0	0	1	0	0

1936–37 CONTENTS LIST

Set No.		1½	2½	3½	4½	5½	7½	8½	9½	10½	S	SA[1]
LH	TENDER STEP	0	0	0	0	0	0	0	0	4	0	0
LI	COUPLING YOKE	0	0	0	0	0	0	0	0	2	0	0
LJ	TANK HANDLE	0	0	0	0	0	0	0	0	4	0	0
LK	TENDER STEP ANGLE	0	0	0	0	0	0	0	0	4	0	0
LL	REAR TIE FRAME	0	0	0	0	0	0	0	0	2	0	0
LO	TRACK SECTION	0	0	0	0	0	0	0	0	8	0	0
LP	RAILROAD TIE	0	0	0	0	0	0	0	0	12	0	0
LS	JACK	0	0	0	0	0	0	0	0	2	0	0
LT	MOTOR SUPPORT BRACKET	0	0	0	0	0	0	0	0	2	0	0
LU	OFFSET WRENCH	0	0	0	0	0	0	0	0	2	0	0
LV[4]	3" DISC WHEEL, RED	0	0	0	0	0	0	0	0	4	0	0
LW[4]	RUBBER TIRE	0	0	0	0	0	0	0	0	4	0	0
LX	STEERING COLUMN BRACKET	0	0	0	0	0	0	0	1	1	0	0
MA	RADIATOR	0	0	0	0	0	0	0	1	1	0	0
MB	18½" ANGLE GIRDER	0	0	0	0	0	0	0	2	2	0	0
MC	BASE PLATE 1" x 2½"	2	2	2	2	2	2	8	8	8	0	0
MD	BASE PLATE 2½" x 5"	1	1	1	1	1	1	4	4	4	0	0
ME	BASE PLATE 1" x 4"	0	0	0	0	0	0	0	4	4	0	0
MF	BASE PLATE 1" x 5"	2	2	4	4	4	4	8	9	12	0	0
MG	RADIATOR HOOD	0	0	0	0	0	0	0	1	1	0	0
MH	LARGE 3" DISC WHEEL	0	4	4	4	4	4	4	4	4	0	0
MI	FRONT AXLE UNIT	0	0	0	0	0	0	0	1	1	0	0
MJ	ELECTRO MAGNET WITH CORD	0	0	0	0	0	0	1	1	1	0	0
MM	WRENCH	0	0	0	1	1	1	1	1	1	1	0
MN	12" BASE PLATE	0	0	2	4	4	4	6	6	6	0	0
MO	3" ANGLE GIRDER	0	0	4	4	4	4	4	4	4	8	0
MP	24 TOOTH GEAR	0	0	0	1	1	0	0	0	0	0	0
MQ[3]	27 TOOTH WORM WHEEL	0	0	0	0	0	1	1	1	1	0	0
MR	DRUM WITH GEAR	0	0	0	0	0	0	1	1	1	0	0
MS	COMPRESSION SPRING	0	0	0	0	0	1	1	1	1	0	0
MT	SNAP RIVET	0	0	0	0	0	0	0	0	0	240	240
MU	RIVET EXTRACTOR	0	0	0	0	0	0	0	0	0	1	1
MV	FLAT CAR TRUCK	0	0	0	0	0	0	4	4	4	0	0
MW	NUT HOLDER	0	0	0	1	1	1	1	1	1	0	0
NA	3" MAIN ENTRANCE	0	0	0	0	0	0	0	0	0	5	5
NB	3" GROUND FLOOR	0	0	0	0	0	0	0	0	0	5	5
NC	3" UPPER STORY	0	0	0	0	0	0	0	0	0	10	10
ND	6" UPPER STORY	0	0	0	0	0	0	0	0	0	10	10
NE	6" GARAGE ENTRANCE	0	0	0	0	0	0	0	0	0	14	14
NF	6" OFFICE ENTRANCE	0	0	0	0	0	0	0	0	0	14	14
NG	ROOF	0	0	0	0	0	0	0	0	0	6	6
N21	8-32 SQUARE NUT	25	45	60	68	68	100	134	240	350	62	0
S51	¼" x 8-32 SCREW	21	35	50	60	60	90	114	180	255	62	0
S52	½" x 8-32 SCREW	0	0	0	2	2	2	2	4	28	0	0
S57	1⅜" x 8-32 SCREW	0	0	0	0	0	3	4	4	12	0	0
S62	⅞" x 8-32 SCREW	3	6	6	8	8	8	18	20	56	0	0

1. Skyscraper Accessory Set No. SA cataloged in 1937 only.

2. The (P7) ⅞" pulley was new in 1937 (but not listed in the Separate Parts Section until 1938), and these pulleys were included in Sets No. 1½ through 7½. The (P7A) 1⅛" pulleys were included in Sets No. 8½ through 10½.

3. In 1937 the (P51) motor was modified and the (MQ) worm wheel was eliminated.

4. The (LV) wheels and (LW) tires were eliminated late in 1936 and replaced with (MH) wheels in Set No. 10½.

Form M 1541

ERECTOR SEPARATE PARTS PRICES

KINDLY ENCLOSE CHECK, MONEY ORDER OR STAMPS WITH YOUR ORDER FOR PARTS

THE A. C. GILBERT CO., NEW HAVEN, CONN., U. S. A.

Trade	No.	Name of Part	Page	Price
*N21		8-32 Square Nut	2	.05 doz.
P7		Small Wheel	2	.10 ea.
P12		Crown Gear	2	.10 ea.
P13		12-Tooth Pinion Gear	2	.10 ea.
P14		Worm Gear	2	.20 ea.
P15		Coupling	2	.10 ea.
P20		Five Hole Strip—formed	1	.05 ea.
P24		Crank	1	.10 ea.
P33		Small Screw Driver	1	.05 ea.
P34		Hank of String	1	.05 ea.
P37		Collar	2	.25 doz.
P39		Wood Screw	2	.15 doz.
P40		Screw Eye	2	.20 doz.
P48		Mitre Gear	2	.20 ea.
P49		18-Tooth Gear	2	.15 ea.
P50		72-Tooth Gear	2	.30 ea.
P52		Ladder Chain	1	.15 ft.
P51		Electric Engine Reversing	3	3.95 ea.
P54		Motor, 6-14 volts	3	1.75 ea.
P56G		Motor, 110v. A.C. or D.C.		2.95 ea.
P58		Motor, 6-14 volts	3	1.00 ea.
P59		Reverse Base (for P58 only)	3	.75 ea.
A52		Ind. Motor with Side Plates—110v. A.C. only	3	2.50 ea.
P57A		2⅛" Axle	1	.02 ea.
P57D		6" Axle	1	.06 ea.
P57E		8" Axle	1	.08 ea.
P57F		12" Axle	1	.12 ea.
P79		Car Truck	1	.05 ea.
*S11		Set Screw	2	.05 doz.
*S51		¼"x8-32 Screw	2	.05 doz.
*S52		½"x8-32 Screw	2	.10 doz.
*S57		1⅛"x8-32 Screw	2	.15 doz.
*S62		⅞"x8-32 Screw	2	.10 doz.
*FA		1¾"x8-32 Screw	2	.15 doz.
A		2½" Girder	1	.20 doz.
B		5" Girder	1	.35 doz.
C		10" Girder	1	.50 doz.
D		2½" Curved Girder	1	.25 doz.
E		5" Curved Girder	1	.40 doz.
F		5 Hole Strip	1	.10 doz.
G		7 Hole Strip	1	.10 doz.
H		11 Hole Strip	1	.15 doz.
I		21 Hole Strip	1	.20 doz.
J		41 Hole Strip	1	.30 doz.
K		11 Hole Strip Bracket	1	.35 doz.
M		Small Double Angle	1	.25 doz.
N		Long Double Angle	1	.05 ea.
O		Pawl	1	.05 ea.
S		Large Base Plate—21 holes	1	.40 ea.
T		Boiler	3	.25 ea.
U		Boiler Top	3	.20 ea.
W		Stack	3	.05 ea.
X		Digger Scoop	3	.75 ea.

Trade	No.	Name of Part	Page	Price
Z		Flanged Wheel	2	.15 ea.
AA		Eccentric Crank	1	.10 ea.
AB		One Hole Coupling	2	.15 ea.
AC		Universal Bracket	1	.10 ea.
AE		Spiral Spring	1	.05 ea.
AF		Small Hook	2	.15 doz.
AH		Small Triangle	1	.25 doz.
AM		Special Pulley—Metal	2	.05 ea.
AQ		Sheave Pulley	2	.05 ea.
AR		8-Hole Strip	1	.10 doz.
AS		2⅞" Axle Rod	1	.03 ea.
AT		4" Axle Rod	1	.04 ea.
AV		7-Hole Strip Bracket	1	2 for .05
AX		19¾" Axle Rod	1	.20 ea.
AZ		Bull Wheel Plate	1	.25 ea.
BA		B. W. Cntr (with Hub)	1	.25 ea.
B2		Wood Handle Screw Driver	1	.15 ea.
BE		6" Slotted Angle Strip	1	.50 doz.
BH		Solid Collar	2	2 for .05
BI		6" Flat Beam Girder	1	6 for .50
BJ		12" Flat Beam Girder	1	6 for .75
BK		8-32 Wing Nut	2	.25 doz.
BL		Small Washer	2	.05 doz.
BN		Regular Turret Plate	3	.15 ea.
BO	P58	Reverse Switch Attachment	2	.50 ea.
BT		Pierced Disc	2	.10 ea.
BY		11-Hole Fibre Strip	1	.05 ea.
CA		Signal Arm	1	.10 ea.
CH		Right Angle	1	.10 doz.
CI		36-Tooth Gear	2	.20 ea.
CQ		Slot Coupling	2	.15 ea.
CX		1" Axle Rod	1	.01 ea.
CY		5" Axle Rod	1	.05 ea.
CZ		7" Axle Rod	1	.07 ea.
DA		10" Axle Rod	1	.10 ea.
DB		Motor Pulley	2	.10 ea.
DE		Steering Column	1	.10 ea.
DK		Flat Spring	1	.10 ea.
DO		Steering Wheel with Hub	2	.15 ea.
DP		12" Slotted Angle Strip	1	6 for .50
DQ		Special Large Base Plate (28 holes)	1	.50 ea.
DS		Cotter Pin	1	.05 doz.
DT		1-Hole Set Screw Coupling	2	2 for .15
DU		¼" Diam. Axle 8½"	1	2 for .25
DV		6" Curved Beam Girder	1	6 for .75
DZ		Tackle Block	2	.15 ea.
EC		Giant Axle—29" long, 5/16" diam.	1	.50 ea.
EH		Gear Box Bracket	1	.05 ea.
EI		Standard Gear Box Side Pl.	1	.15 ea.
EJ		Gear Box Base	1	.20 ea.
EK		Plain Drum	2	.25 ea.
EW		12" Duplex F. B. Plate	1	.50 ea.
EX		Big Channel Girder 12"	1	6 for .50
EY		Big Channel Girder 6"	1	.05 ea.

Trade	No.	Name of Part	Page	Price
EZ		6" Curved B. C. Girder	1	.05 ea.
FD		Hinged Loop	1	2 for .05
FJ		Rack	2	.25 ea.
FL		Helical Gear	2	.25 ea.
GV		Small Disc Wheel	2	.10 ea.
FX		Quarter Gear	2	.15 ea.
FZ		Internal Gear	2	.15 ea.
GX		8-Hole Double Angle Bracket	1	.10 doz.
LV		3" Disc Wheel, red	2	.20 ea.
LW		Rubber Tire for LV and MH	2	.10 ea.
LX		Steering Column Bracket	1	.05 ea.
MA		New Radiator	1	.15 ea.
MB		18½" Angle Girder	1	.15 ea.
MC		Base Plate 1"x2½"	1	.05 ea.
MD		Base Plate 2½"x5"	1	.10 ea.
ME		Flat Plate 1"x4"	1	.05 ea.
MF		Flat Plate 1"x5"	1	.05 ea.
MG		Radiator Hood	1	.10 ea.
MH		3" Disc Wheel, Nickel Rim	2	.25 ea.
MI		Front Axle Unit	1	.25 ea.
MJ		Electro Magnet with Cord	2	.60 ea.
MM		Wrench	1	.05 ea.
MN		12" Base Plate	1	.40 ea.
MO		3" Angle Girder	1	.75 doz.
MP		24 Tooth Gear	2	.20 ea.
MQ		24 Tooth Worm Wheel	2	.15 ea.
MR		Drum with Gear	2	.35 ea.
MS		Compression Spring	1	.05 ea.
MT		Snap Rivet	2	.10 doz.
MU		Rivet Extractor	1	.05 ea.
MV		Flat Car Truck	1	.05 ea.
NA		3" Main Entrance	3	2 for .05
NB		3" Ground Floor	3	2 for .05
NC		3" Upper Story	3	2 for .05
ND		6" Upper Story	3	.05 ea.
NE		6" Garage Entrance	3	.05 ea.
NF		6" Office Entrance	3	.05 ea.
NG		Roof	3	.05 ea.
CR		Special Turret plate with hub	1	.15 ea.
CS		Wheel Segment	1	.15 ea.
MW		Nut Holder	1	.10 ea.

ERECTOR HOW TO MAKE 'EM BOOKS

No. 1	Erector How to Make 'Em Book	.15 ea.
No. 3	Erector How to Make 'Em Book	.15 ea.
No. 4	Erector How to Make 'Em Book	.25 ea.
No. 6	Erector How to Make 'Em Book	.25 ea.
No. 7	Erector How to Make 'Em Book	.25 ea.
No. 8	Erector How to Make 'Em Book	.25 ea.
No. 1½	Erector How to Make 'Em Book	.15 ea.
No. 2½	Erector How to Make 'Em Book	.15 ea.
No. 3½	Erector How to Make 'Em Book	.15 ea.
No. 4½	Erector How to Make 'Em Book	.25 ea.
No. 5½	Erector How to Make 'Em Book	.25 ea.
No. 7½	Erector How to Make 'Em Book	.25 ea.
No. 8½	Erector How to Make 'Em Book	.35 ea.
No. 9½	Erector How to Make 'Em Book	.35 ea.
	Locomotive How to Make 'Em Book	.25 ea.

REGULAR ERECTOR MANUALS

No. 1	Erector Manual	.15 ea.
No. 3	Erector Manual	.15 ea.
No. 4	Erector Manual	.25 ea.
No. 6	Erector Manual	.25 ea.
No. 7	Erector Manual	.25 ea.
No. 8	Locomotive Manual	.25 ea.
No. 1½	Erector Manual	.15 ea.
No. 3½	Erector Manual	.15 ea.
No. 4½	Erector Manual	.25 ea.
No. 6½	Erector Manual	.25 ea.
No. 7½	Erector Manual	.35 ea.
No. 8½	Erector Manual	.35 ea.
No. 9½	Locomotive Manual	.25 ea.

ERECTOR ACCESSORY MANUALS

No. 5	Erector Electrical Set Manual	.25 ea.
	Fun with your Motor Manual	.25 ea.

NOTE

*N21 Nut used with screws S51, S52, S62, S57, FA

*S11 Set Screw used with pulleys, couplings, etc.

Separate Parts Prices for early 1936

Form M 1541

ERECTOR SEPARATE PARTS PRICES

KINDLY ENCLOSE CHECK, MONEY ORDER OR STAMPS WITH YOUR ORDER FOR PARTS

THE A. C. GILBERT CO., NEW HAVEN, CONN., U. S. A.

Trade	No.	Name of Part	Page	Price
*N21		8-32 Square Nut	2	.05 doz.
P7		Small Wheel	2	.10 ea.
P12		Crown Gear	2	.10 ea.
P13		12-Tooth Pinion Gear	2	.10 ea.
P14		Worm Gear	2	.20 ea.
P15		Coupling	2	.10 ea.
P20		Five Hole Strip—formed	1	.05 ea.
P24		Crank	1	.10 ea.
P33		Small Screw Driver	1	.05 ea.
P34		Hank of String	1	.05 ea.
P37		Collar	2	.25 doz.
P39		Wood Screw	2	.15 doz.
P40		Screw Eye	2	.20 doz.
P48		Mitre Gear	2	.20 ea.
P49		18-Tooth Gear	2	.15 ea.
P50		72-Tooth Gear	2	.30 ea.
P52		Ladder Chain	1	.15 ft.
P51		Electric Engine Reversing	3	3.95 ea.
P54		Motor, 6-14 volts	3	1.75 ea.
P56G		Motor, 110v. A.C. or D.C.		2.95 ea.
P58		Motor, 6-14 volts	3	1.00 ea.
P59		Reverse Base (for P58 only)	3	.75 ea.
A52		Ind. Motor with Side Plates—110v. A.C. only	3	2.50 ea.
P57A		2⅛" Axle	1	.02 ea.
P57D		6" Axle	1	.06 ea.
P57E		8" Axle	1	.08 ea.
P57F		12" Axle	1	.12 ea.
P79		Car Truck	1	.05 ea.
*S11		Set Screw	2	.05 doz.
*S51		¼"x8-32 Screw	2	.05 doz.
*S52		½"x8-32 Screw	2	.10 doz.
*S57		1⅛"x8-32 Screw	2	.15 doz.
*S62		⅞"x8-32 Screw	2	.10 doz.
*FA		1¾"x8-32 Screw	2	.15 doz.
A		2½" Girder	1	.20 doz.
B		5" Girder	1	.35 doz.
C		10" Girder	1	.50 doz.
D		2½" Curved Girder	1	.25 doz.
E		5" Curved Girder	1	.40 doz.
F		5 Hole Strip	1	.10 doz.
G		7 Hole Strip	1	.10 doz.
H		11 Hole Strip	1	.15 doz.
I		21 Hole Strip	1	.20 doz.
J		41 Hole Strip	1	.30 doz.
K		11 Hole Strip Bracket	1	.35 doz.
M		Small Double Angle	1	.25 doz.
N		Long Double Angle	1	.05 ea.
O		Pawl	1	.05 ea.
S		Large Base Plate—21 holes	1	.40 ea.
T		Boiler	3	.25 ea.
U		Boiler Top	3	.20 ea.
W		Stack	3	.05 ea.
X		Digger Scoop	3	.75 ea.

Trade	No.	Name of Part	Page	Price
Z		Flanged Wheel	2	.15 ea.
AA		Eccentric Crank	1	.10 ea.
AB		One Hole Coupling	2	.15 ea.
AC		Universal Bracket	1	.10 ea.
AE		Spiral Spring	1	.05 ea.
AF		Small Hook	2	.15 doz.
AH		Small Triangle	1	.25 doz.
AM		Special Pulley—Metal	2	.05 ea.
AQ		Sheave Pulley	2	.05 ea.
AR		8-Hole Strip	1	.10 doz.
AS		2⅞" Axle Rod	1	.03 ea.
AT		4" Axle Rod	1	.04 ea.
AV		7-Hole Strip Bracket	1	2 for .05
AX		19¾" Axle Rod	1	.20 ea.
AZ		Bull Wheel Plate	1	.25 ea.
BA		B. W. Cntr (with Hub)	1	.25 ea.
B2		Wood Handle Screw Driver	1	.15 ea.
BE		6" Slotted Angle Strip	1	.50 doz.
BH		Solid Collar	2	2 for .05
BI		6" Flat Beam Girder	1	6 for .50
BJ		12" Flat Beam Girder	1	6 for .75
BK		8-32 Wing Nut	2	.25 doz.
BL		Small Washer	2	.05 doz.
BN		Regular Turret Plate	3	.15 ea.
BO	P58	Reverse Switch Attachment	2	.50 ea.
BT		Pierced Disc	2	.10 ea.
BY		11-Hole Fibre Strip	1	.05 ea.
CA		Signal Arm	1	.10 ea.
CH		Right Angle	1	.10 doz.
CI		36-Tooth Gear	2	.20 ea.
CQ		Slot Coupling	2	.15 ea.
CX		1" Axle Rod	1	.01 ea.
CY		5" Axle Rod	1	.05 ea.
CZ		7" Axle Rod	1	.07 ea.
DA		10" Axle Rod	1	.10 ea.
DB		Motor Pulley	2	.10 ea.
DE		Steering Column	1	.10 ea.
DK		Flat Spring	1	.10 ea.
DO		Steering Wheel with Hub	2	.15 ea.
DP		12" Slotted Angle Strip	1	6 for .50
DQ		Special Large Base Plate (28 holes)	1	.50 ea.
DS		Cotter Pin	1	.05 doz.
DT		1-Hole Set Screw Coupling	2	2 for .15
DU		¼" Diam. Axle 8½"	1	2 for .25
DV		6" Curved Beam Girder	1	6 for .75
DZ		Tackle Block	2	.15 ea.
EC		Giant Axle—29" long, 5/16" diam.	1	.50 ea.
EH		Gear Box Bracket	1	.05 ea.
EI		Standard Gear Box Side Pl.	1	.15 ea.
EJ		Gear Box Base	1	.20 ea.
EK		Plain Drum	2	.25 ea.
EW		12" Duplex F. B. Plate	1	.50 ea.
EX		Big Channel Girder 12"	1	6 for .50
EY		Big Channel Girder 6"	1	.05 ea.

Trade	No.	Name of Part	Page	Price
EZ		6" Curved B. C. Girder	1	.05 ea.
FD		Hinged Loop	1	2 for .05
FJ		Rack	2	.25 ea.
FL		Helical Gear	2	.25 ea.
GV		Small Disc Wheel	2	.10 ea.
FX		Quarter Gear	2	.15 ea.
FZ		Internal Gear	2	.15 ea.
GX		8-Hole Double Angle Bracket	1	.10 doz.
LV		3" Disc Wheel, red	2	.20 ea.
LW		Rubber Tire for LV and MH	2	.10 ea.
LX		Steering Column Bracket	1	.05 ea.
MA		New Radiator	1	.15 ea.
MB		18½" Angle Girder	1	.15 ea.
MC		Base Plate 1"x2½"	1	.05 ea.
MD		Base Plate 2½"x5"	1	.10 ea.
ME		Flat Plate 1"x4"	1	.05 ea.
MF		Flat Plate 1"x5"	1	.05 ea.
MG		Radiator Hood	1	.10 ea.
MH		3" Disc Wheel, Nickel Rim	2	.25 ea.
MI		Front Axle Unit	1	.25 ea.
MJ		Electro Magnet with Cord	2	.60 ea.
MM		Wrench	1	.05 ea.
MN		12" Base Plate	1	.40 ea.
MO		3" Angle Girder	1	.75 doz.
MP		24 Tooth Gear	2	.20 ea.
MQ		24 Tooth Worm Wheel	2	.15 ea.
MR		Drum with Gear	2	.35 ea.
MS		Compression Spring	1	.05 ea.
MT		Snap Rivet	2	.10 doz.
MU		Rivet Extractor	1	.05 ea.
MV		Flat Car Truck	1	.05 ea.
NA		3" Main Entrance	3	2 for .05
NB		3" Ground Floor	3	2 for .05
NC		3" Upper Story	3	2 for .05
ND		6" Upper Story	3	.05 ea.
NE		6" Garage Entrance	3	.05 ea.
NF		6" Office Entrance	3	.05 ea.
NG		Roof	3	.05 ea.
CR		Special Turret plate with hub	1	.15 ea.
CS		Wheel Segment	1	.15 ea.
MW		Nut Holder	1	.10 ea.

ERECTOR HOW TO MAKE 'EM BOOKS

No. 1	Erector How to Make 'Em Book	.15 ea.
No. 3	Erector How to Make 'Em Book	.15 ea.
No. 4	Erector How to Make 'Em Book	.25 ea.
No. 6	Erector How to Make 'Em Book	.25 ea.
No. 7	Erector How to Make 'Em Book	.25 ea.
No. 8	Erector How to Make 'Em Book	.25 ea.
No. 1½	Erector How to Make 'Em Book	.15 ea.
No. 2½	Erector How to Make 'Em Book	.15 ea.
No. 3½	Erector How to Make 'Em Book	.15 ea.
No. 4½	Erector How to Make 'Em Book	.25 ea.
No. 5½	Erector How to Make 'Em Book	.25 ea.
No. 7½	Erector How to Make 'Em Book	.25 ea.
No. 8½	Erector How to Make 'Em Book	.35 ea.
No. 9½	Erector How to Make 'Em Book	.35 ea.
	Locomotive How to Make 'Em Book	.25 ea.

ERECTOR ACCESSORY MANUALS

No. 5	Erector Electrical Set Manual	.25 ea.
	Fun with your Motor Manual	.25 ea.

NOTE

*N21 Nut used with screws S51, S52, S62, S57, FA

*S11 Set Screw used with pulleys, couplings, etc.

Separate Parts Prices for late 1936

Form M 1541

ERECTOR SEPARATE PARTS PRICES

KINDLY ENCLOSE CHECK, MONEY ORDER OR STAMPS WITH YOUR ORDER FOR PARTS

THE A. C. GILBERT CO., NEW HAVEN, CONN., U. S. A.

Trade No.	Name of Part	Page	Price
*N21	8-32 Square Nut	2	.05 doz.
P7	Small Wheel	2	.10 ea.
P12	Crown Gear	2	.10 ea.
P13	12-Tooth Pinion Gear	2	.10 ea.
P14	Worm Gear	2	.20 ea.
P15	Coupling	2	.10 ea.
P20	Five Hole Strip—formed	1	.05 ea.
P24	Crank	1	.10 ea.
P33	Small Screw Driver	1	.05 ea.
P34	Hank of String	1	.05 ea.
P37	Collar	2	.25 doz.
P39	Wood Screw	2	.15 doz.
P40	Screw Eye	2	.20 doz.
P48	Mitre Gear	2	.20 ea.
P49	18-Tooth Gear	2	.15 ea.
P50	72-Tooth Gear	2	.30 ea.
P52	Ladder Chain	1	.15 ft.
P51	Electric Engine Reversing	3	3.95 ea.
P54	Motor, 6-14 volts	3	1.75 ea.
P56G	Motor, 110v. A.C. or D.C.	3	2.95 ea.
P58	Motor, 6-14 volts	3	1.00 ea.
P59	Reverse Base (for P58 only)	3	.75 ea.
A52	Ind. Motor with Side Plates—110v. A.C. only	3	2.50 ea.
P57A	2⅛" Axle	1	.02 ea.
P57D	6" Axle	1	.06 ea.
P57E	8" Axle	1	.08 ea.
P57F	12" Axle	1	.12 ea.
P79	Car Truck	1	.05 ea.
*S11	Set Screw	2	.05 doz.
*S51	¼"x8-32 Screw	2	.05 doz.
*S52	½"x8-32 Screw	2	.10 doz.
*S57	1⅛"x8-32 Screw	2	.15 doz.
*S62	⅞"x8-32 Screw	2	.10 doz.
*FA	1¼"x8-32 Screw	2	.15 doz.
A	2½" Girder	1	.20 doz.
B	5" Girder	1	.35 doz.
C	10" Girder	1	.50 doz.
D	2½" Curved Girder	1	.25 doz.
E	5" Curved Girder	1	.40 doz.
F	5 Hole Strip	1	.10 doz.
G	7 Hole Strip	1	.10 doz.
H	11 Hole Strip	1	.15 doz.
I	21 Hole Strip	1	.20 doz.
J	41 Hole Strip	1	.30 doz.
K	11 Hole Strip Bracket	1	.35 doz.
M	Small Double Angle	1	.25 doz.
N	Long Double Angle	1	.05 ea.
O	Pawl	1	.05 ea.
S	Large Base Plate—21 holes	1	.40 ea.
T	Boiler	3	.25 ea.
U	Boiler Top	3	.20 ea.
W	Stack	3	.05 ea.
Z	Flanged Wheel	2	.15 ea.
AA	Eccentric Crank	1	.10 ea.
AB	One Hole Coupling	2	.15 ea.
AC	Universal Bracket	1	.10 ea.
AE	Spiral Spring	1	.05 ea.

Trade No.	Name of Part	Page	Price
AF	Small Hook	2	.15 doz.
AH	Small Triangle	1	.25 doz.
AM	Special Pulley—Metal	2	.05 ea.
AQ	Sheave Pulley	2	.05 ea.
AS	2⅞" Axle Rod	1	.03 ea.
AT	4" Axle Rod	1	.04 ea.
AX	19¾" Axle Rod	1	.20 ea.
AZ	Bull Wheel Plate	1	.25 ea.
BA	B. W. Cntr. (with Hub)	1	.25 ea.
B2	Wood Handle Screw Driver	1	.15 ea.
BE	6" Slotted Angle Strip	1	.50 doz.
BH	Solid Collar	2	2 for .05
BK	8-32 Wing Nut	2	.25 doz.
BL	Small Washer	2	.05 doz.
BN	Regular Turret Plate	3	.15 ea.
BO P58	Reverse Switch Attachment	2	.50 ea.
BT	Pierced Disc	2	.10 ea.
BY	11-Hole Fibre Strip	1	.05 ea.
CA	Signal Arm	1	.10 ea.
CH	Right Angle	1	.10 doz.
CJ	36-Tooth Gear	2	.20 ea.
CO	Slot Coupling	2	.15 ea.
CR	Special Turret plate with hub	1	.15 ea.
CS	Wheel Segment	1	.15 ea.
CX	1" Axle Rod	1	.01 ea.
CY	5" Axle Rod	1	.05 ea.
CZ	7" Axle Rod	1	.07 ea.
DA	10" Axle Rod	1	.10 ea.
DB	Motor Pulley	2	.10 ea.
DE	Steering Column	1	.10 ea.
DK	Flat Spring	1	.10 ea.
DO	Steering Wheel with Hub	2	.15 ea.
DP	12" Slotted Angle Strip	1	6 for .50
DQ	Special Large Base Plate (28 holes)	1	.50 ea.
DS	Cotter Pin	1	.05 doz.
DT	1-Hole Set Screw Coupling	2	2 for .15
DU	¼" Diam. Axle 8½"	1	2 for .25
DZ	Tackle Block	2	.15 ea.
EC	Giant Axle—29" long, 5/16" diam.	1	.50 ea.
EH	Gear Box Bracket	1	.05 ea.
EI	Standard Gear Box Side Pl.	1	.15 ea.
EJ	Gear Box Base	1	.20 ea.
EX	Big Channel Girder 12"	1	6 for .50
EY	Big Channel Girder 6"	1	.05 ea.
EZ	6" Curved B. C. Girder	1	.05 ea.
FD	Hinged Loop	1	2 for .05
FJ	Rack	2	.25 ea.
FI	Helical Gear	2	.25 ea.
GV	Small Disc Wheel	2	.10 ea.
LV	3" Disc Wheel, red	2	.20 ea.
LX	Steering Column Bracket	1	.05 ea.
MA	New Radiator	1	.15 ea.
MB	18½" Angle Girder	1	.15 ea.
MC	Base Plate 1"x2½"	1	.05 ea.
MD	Base Plate 2½"x5"	1	.10 ea.

Trade No.	Name of Part	Page	Price
ME	Flat Plate 1"x4"	1	.05 ea.
MF	Flat Plate 1"x5"	1	.05 ea.
MG	Radiator Hood	1	.10 ea.
MH	3" Disc Wheel, Nickel Rim	2	.25 ea.
MI	Front Axle Unit	1	.25 ea.
MJ	Electro Magnet with Cord	2	.60 ea.
MM	Wrench	1	.05 ea.
MN	12" Base Plate	1	.40 ea.
MO	3" Angle Girder	1	.75 doz.
MP	24 Tooth Gear	2	.20 ea.
MR	Drum with Gear	2	.35 ea.
MS	Compression Spring	1	.05 ea.
MT	Snap Rivet	2	.10 doz.
MU	Rivet Extractor	1	.05 ea.
MV	Flat Car Truck	1	.05 ea.
MW	Nut Holder	1	.10 ea.
NA	3" Main Entrance	3	2 for .05
NB	3" Ground Floor	3	2 for .05
NC	3" Upper Story	3	2 for .05
ND	6" Upper Story	3	.05 ea.
NE	6" Garage Entrance	3	.05 ea.
NF	6" Office Entrance	3	.05 ea.
NG	Roof	3	.05 ea.

NOTE

*N21 Nut used with screws S51, S52, S62, S57, FA

*S11 Set Screw used with pulleys, couplings, etc.

REPLACEMENT MANUALS

Same as copy included in sets.

ERECTOR HOW TO MAKE 'EM BOOKS

No. 1	Erector How to Make 'Em Book	.15 ea.
No. 3	Erector How to Make 'Em Book	.15 ea.
No. 4	Erector How to Make 'Em Book	.25 ea.
No. 6	Erector How to Make 'Em Book	.25 ea.
No. 7	Erector How to Make 'Em Book	.25 ea.
No. 8	Erector How to Make 'Em Book	.25 ea.
No. 1½	Erector How to Make 'Em Book	.15 ea.
No. 2½	Erector How to Make 'Em Book	.15 ea.
No. 3½	Erector How to Make 'Em Book	.15 ea.
No. 4½	Erector How to Make 'Em Book	.25 ea.
No. 5½	Erector How to Make 'Em Book	.25 ea.
No. 7½	Erector How to Make 'Em Book	.25 ea.
No. 8½	Erector How to Make 'Em Book	.35 ea.
No. 9½	Erector How to Make 'Em Book	.35 ea.
	Locomotive How to Make 'Em Book	.25 ea.

Separate Parts Prices for 1937

2

LATE TRANSITION PERIOD AND WORLD WAR II: 1938–45

THE 1938 AND 1939 ERECTOR LINE

In retrospect, 1938 turned out to be a very dynamic year in the evolution of Erector. Gilbert developed and added a substantial number of new parts, including a greatly improved electric engine. The company used new packaging techniques to dress up the sets and created a wonderful new top-of-the-line set that featured an electric train. Since so many of the changes that occurred in 1938 were due to the new parts, I will first discuss them and their significance.

One of the most recognized Erector components of all time was introduced in 1938: the (MX) House. Looking more like a watchman's shanty than a house, it was made of three pieces of lightweight, lithographed tin. The earliest version had windows punched in the doors and a roof that measured 2¾" along the peak. It was included in No. 4½ and larger sets.

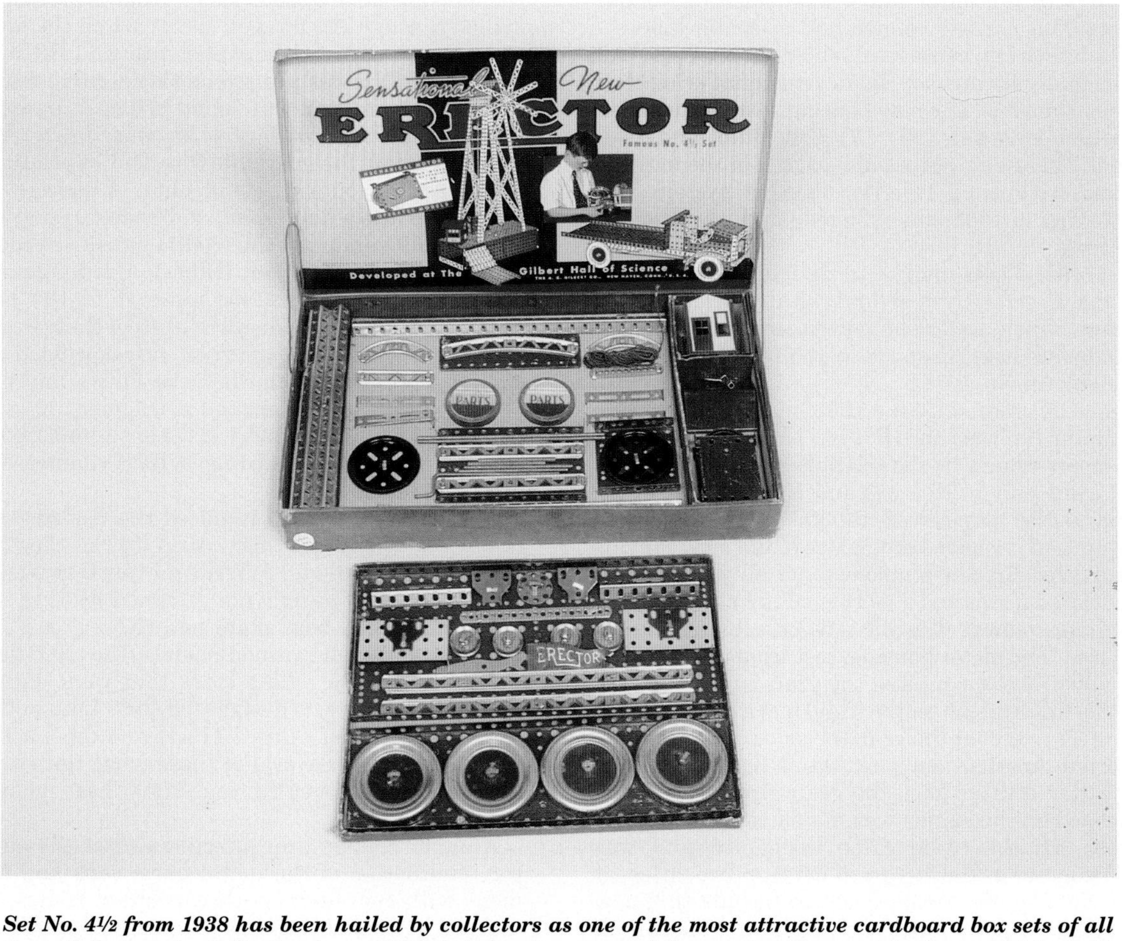

Set No. 4½ from 1938 has been hailed by collectors as one of the most attractive cardboard box sets of all time. It featured a full-color inner lid label showing some of the outstanding models that could be built with this set.

Without question, 1938 was a prolific year in the evolution of the Erector System. These parts were introduced then and became Erector standards for many years: (MX) House, (A48) Mechanical Motor, and the lighting system.

Also making their first appearance in 1938 were two "general purpose" parts. The (MY) 2½" x 2½" Base Plate complemented the existing series of base plates and was included in all sets beginning with No. 4½. The (MZ) Bearing Block, primarily used with the miter gears, was added to No. 6½ and larger sets. This earliest version had no center hole.

The 1938 advertising campaign hailed Erector as "All Electric," principally because of the development of electric lights for various models. The new lighting system consisted of the (NH) Lamp Socket, (NI) 1½ Volt Bulb, and (NJ) Battery Holder. These new parts came packed in the four top sets, beginning with No. 7½. (The lighting system was included in No. 7½ in 1938 and 1939 only and was dropped from it in 1940.)

An old part with a new name and designation was reintroduced to the Erector System in 1938. It was the (NL) Bolster Bracket, which used to be known as the (K) 11 Hole Strip Bracket before being dropped in 1933. Back five years later, it came only in No. 10½.

Two motors were created for the 1938 line. One, the (A48) Mechanical Motor replaced the (P58) in No. 4½. The (A48), a clockwork motor wound by the (K48) Key, was finished in royal blue. It came only in Nos. 4½ and 10½.

The second motor introduced in 1938 was the (A49) Electric Engine, and it was to become one of the most famous and best recognized Erector components of all time. With a completely enclosed motor and a more sophisticated gearbox, it was a real improvement over the (P51) Electrical Engine, which it replaced. The motor housing, cast from white metal, was painted silver-blue for most of the year; but a very rare variation of this first version on the (A49) had a nickel-plated motor housing. Throughout the year, the sides of the gearbox were painted red. Another new part, the (NK) Ratchet, was included with the (A49) to keep the gears from slipping on certain models when the engine was in neutral.

The gearbox for the (A49) came assembled and was attached to the motor at the factory. It came in two different ways. In Set No. 6½, the smallest set to include this new engine, the gearbox had a single driving gear that ran off the motor. The rest of the gearbox was mostly empty, with lots of holes for axles that could be used with the gears packed in the set.

In No. 7½ and larger sets, however, the gearbox contained a series of gears that formed a transmission ("like an automobile," A. C. Gilbert said) that produced two forward speeds, two reverse speeds, and a neutral position. A gearshift protruded from the gearbox, and a special blue wooden handle was included for use on it. The handle was packed separately in a parts can because the box lid could not be closed when the handle was mounted on the gearshift. This handle was never given a part name or designation, but was part of all sets with an electric engine until 1962.

In the separate parts section of the instruction manual, Gilbert listed the (A49B) Electric Engine Conversion Unit. This four-speed gearbox was available to upgrade the less sophisticated engine that came in No. 6½. This option continued until 1948, when all (A49) engines were given a four-speed gearbox.

The (A49) was introduced in 1938 and used (with one interruption) in the larger sets through 1962. During this engine's twenty-six-year history, it was continually modified and improved. Here I begin to trace the evolution of this highly successful Erector component.

The earliest version came with a cast motor housing painted silver-blue or nickel-plated and a gearbox whose sides were painted red. There were sixteen vertical vent holes on the housing, and the screw holes at the bottom of the housing were closed; that is, the screw holes were holes drilled through the flanges (feet) cast on the motor housing. A decal was used on the motor core, and ERECTOR ELECTRIC ENGINE was printed on this decal in red. In the gearbox, the worm gear was made of paper impregnated with resin while the secondary gears were brass. As the engine was operating, the gearshift was held in position by a series of depressions on a gearshift plate. A springy steel "finger" would slip into a depression and keep the gearshift in place.

The 1939 version of the (A49) engine was identical to the prior version, except that Gilbert added a guard to prevent little fingers from getting pinched in the gearbox. This guard was simply a thin strip of steel that covered the most dangerous spot on the gearbox. It was welded to one side of the gearbox. These guards were flimsy and easily broken off, but when this happened a fragment always remained where the weld was made. It is easy to mistake a 1939 version with a broken guard for a 1938 version, except for the weld fragment.

Also in 1938, Gilbert replaced the Hudson with a brand-new top-of-the-line set. He called it "The Electric Train Set" because it featured an American Flyer O gauge electric train engine. Six new parts were designed for this set. The (NM) 10" x 2" flanged base plate and (NN) 1" x 2" flanged base plate were used in railroad models. The (NO) flanged wheels were used on the rolling stock that went with the locomotive. The engine was designated (NP) Locomotive, the track as (NQ) Section of Curved Track, and the track clip as (NR) Track Terminal. Several of these parts underwent interesting modification over the years, and these modifications will be discussed later.

A major change that affected almost the entire line was the elimination of the metal parts cans and their replacement with containers with cardboard bodies. The cylinder and the bottom of these containers were cardboard, and the lids were metal. The lid was first plated in nickel and then a round paper label was affixed in its center. This label was done in red and yellow and read "Parts." The volume of the container could easily and economically be varied by adjusting the depth of the cylinder, and there were three different sizes of these containers: 1", 1⅜", and 1⅝" high. The small container was used in No. 4½, the middle one in Nos. 6½ and 7½, and the large size in Nos. 8½, 9½, and 10½. This practice (with some variation) continued throughout the Transition Period.

In 1939, two major components were modified in interesting ways. These changes occurred late in the year and affected the (MH) Large 3" Disc Wheel and (MN) 12" Base Plate. Ever since the (MH) was introduced in 1933, it had been formed from a single piece of steel, with a red hubcap painted in the center (and a brass hub and set screw, of course). But now, the design was different. The hubcap was formed from a second piece of steel, a disk painted red, and attached to the wheel at the hub. This "two piece construction" continued into the 1950s.

The (MN) Base Plate was changed about the same time. Since being introduced in 1935, it always had been produced with "Duplex Standardization"; that is, alternating small and large holes. Gilbert had developed this idea during the Classic Period, when axles came in different diameters. Large axles fit the large holes, and standard axles fit the small ones. So why, in 1935, Gilbert chose to produce the (MN) with the duplex hole pattern, long after large diameter axles had been eliminated, is a mystery. No other base plate (or part) used that pattern.

Late in 1939 things changed, and the duplex standardization was dropped. The (MN) Base Plate came with all small holes. (An even greater mystery is why Gilbert again made this part with the duplex pattern in 1942 and kept using it until the end of traditional Erector in 1962. Maybe he just liked the way it looked.)

Cardboard Box Sets

Gilbert offered only four cardboard box Erector Sets in 1938 and 1939, as both No. S and No. SA, the Skyscraper sets, were dropped. Set Nos. 1½, 2½, and 3½ were unchanged from 1937, but No. 4½ was totally redesigned. The most significant aspect of No. 4½ was its being the only cardboard box set to contain the (A48) Mechanical Motor.

The No. 4½ section of the instruction manual was rewritten to illustrate the models that could be built with this new motor. Included, among others, was an updated truck (the key model of this set). The manual also featured a windmill, airplane, and walking beam engine. All of these models used the clockwork motor. This section of the manual was twelve pages long, and included only with the No. 4½. The instruction manuals for all the larger sets, which didn't include the clockwork motor, came with a No. 4½ section that was only four pages long because none of the clockwork models were illustrated! This anomaly was specific to No. 4½, and it continued well into the 1950s. Set No. 10½ was the exception, as it did contain the (A48) motor and full No. 4½ instruction manual section.

The packaging of No. 4½ was also different, beginning in 1938. It was still in the same size box, but a new label adorned the inside of the lid. This colorful label featured the truck and windmill models. It was a real improvement over the prior label, borrowed from the large metal box sets, primarily because it was the right size to fill the lid. This new inner lid label ranks as one of the most attractive pieces of Erector artwork.

The (A49) Electric Engine also was introduced in 1938. Left: The first version lacked a gearbox guard. Right: The one from 1939 came with a guard.

Also modified in No. 4½ were the cardboard insert and the arrangement of parts. The (MX) House and (A48) Motor were packed in a compartment on the left side. Two of the new parts containers were included in this set. They were only 1" deep, making them the smallest container produced. The set still came with a removable cardboard parts display tray. This version of No. 4½, which was produced through 1942, is one of the finest display sets of all time.

Metal Box Sets

The first set in the metal box lineup did not belong there at all. It was No. 5½, which was offered for the last time this year, clearly to dispose of excess inventory from 1937. The leftover Gilbert was getting rid of in No. 5½ was the (A52) induction motor. Since this motor came only in No. 5½ and was being dropped from the system, he was forced to continue this set until the supply of motors was exhausted. Set No. 6½ was new this year; it was the set Gilbert really wanted to

Gilbert redesigned the parts cans in 1938. Now they had cardboard bodies and came in three different sizes.

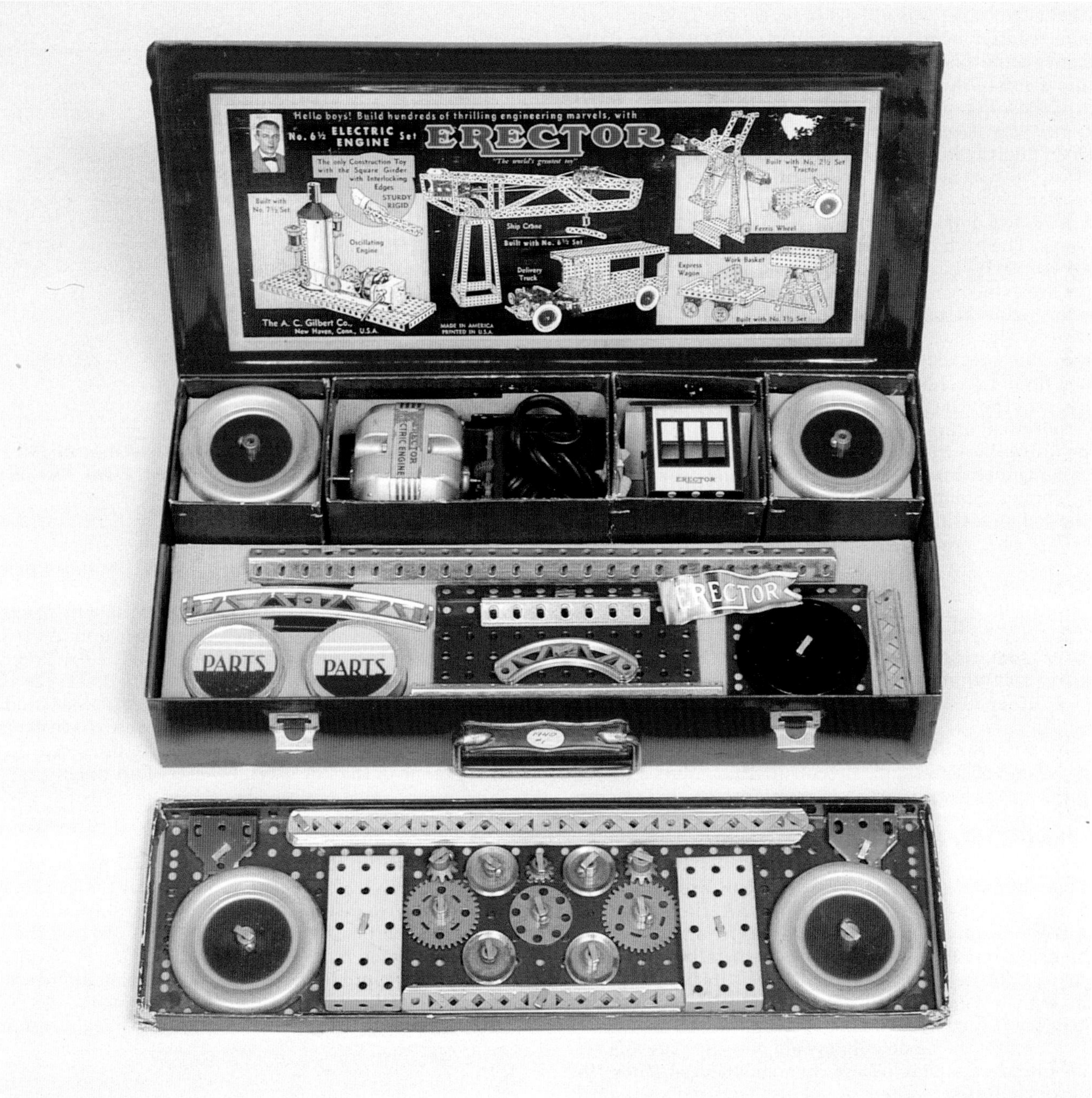

In 1938, No. 6½ was the smallest set to contain the new Electric Engine. Note the complicated assortment of cardboard inserts used for packing this set.

pack in the No. 5½ size box. This was the only time two regular-line sets were offered in a metal box of the same size during the same year.

As mentioned above, Set No. 6½ was back in the line in 1938, though it bore little resemblance to its 1935 ancestor. It featured the (A49) Electric Engine, and was the smallest set to have this new component. This set came packed in the same size red box as Set No. 5½, but the box construction was modified. The metal brackets used to support the display tray made from (MN) base plates in Set No. 5½ was eliminated, as this set came with a whole new look.

Set No. 6½ had a rather complex packing arrangement. Across the back of the box were four cardboard boxes: a long one to hold the motor and three small ones. One of the latter contained the house; the other two each contained one (MH) wheel mounted on a cardboard insert that otherwise filled this box. In front of this row of boxes was a large, lower-level cardboard display insert. Among other parts, it held two of the new parts containers. Set No. 6½ used the middle-size cylinders (1⅜" deep), which were used in No. 7½ as well. On top of the lower insert was a removable cardboard tray where more parts were displayed on (MN) Base Plates trays. All of these cardboard packaging pieces except the lower insert were finished in royal blue.

The inner lid label used on No. 6½ is another anomaly. In the 1938 Erector catalog, the label pictured on this set was new and clearly designed for Nos. 6½ and 7½. It had a yellow background and featured only two models: the Airplane Ride (erroneously titled the Merry Go Round on the label) built with No. 6½ and the Walking Beam Engine built with No. 7½. This new label was used on No. 7½, but though No. 6½ was pictured in the catalogs with this label through 1942, it never came this way!

Actually, the inner lid label used on No. 6½ was a modification of the old No. 5½ label. All the same models were pictured, but the set numbers that built the models were updated. Where the text on the old version of this label read, "The Great New Erector," the new version had an overlay lettered "No. 6½ Electric Engine Set," where "The Great New" used to be. This overlay was made on the master plate prior to the printing of the labels, but the work was shoddy and the overlay clearly shows. By using this overlay, Gilbert made the label specific to No. 6½. Oddly, through 1942 this label pictured the (P51) Electric Engine, which was deleted after 1937.

Most of the models for No. 6½ were upgrades of those found in the old No. 5½, but they were built around the new (A49) Electric Engine. These models included the Builder's Hoist, Lift Bridge, and Hoisting Crane. But the most important model and the one that would be the featured one for this set for many years was the Airplane Ride. All in all, this addition to the 1938 line was quite a set for the modest price of $7.95.

Set No. 7½ for 1938 and 1939, still packed in the royal blue metal box, was an extension of last year's set with some accommodations made for the new parts. Brand new was the lighting system, and several new models were illustrated in the instruction manual to feature the new parts, such as headlights for trucks, lights over machinery, and lights inside the (MX) House.

This set was the smallest to have the (A49) Electric Engine complete with the new gearbox. Surprisingly, no new models were developed to take advantage of the forward and reverse feature the new engine offered. Indeed, with the exception of the lighting system models, most models illustrated in the No. 7½ section of the instruction manual (which tended to be steam engines) were the same as had been shown in 1937, though they now were built with the (A49).

Some changes had been made in the appearance of the No. 7½. Because the (MX) House (packed in a blue cardboard

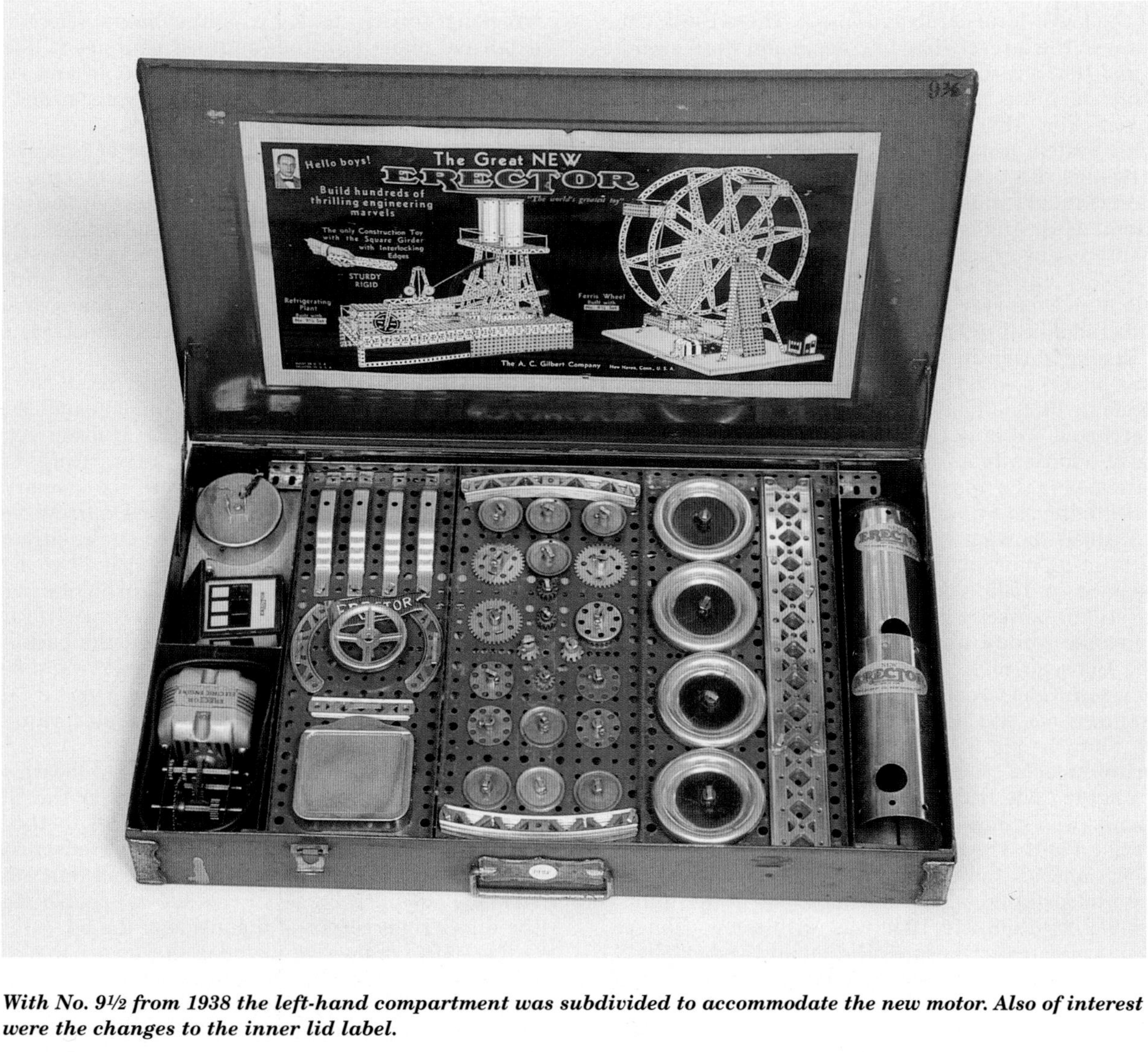

With No. 9½ from 1938 the left-hand compartment was subdivided to accommodate the new motor. Also of interest were the changes to the inner lid label.

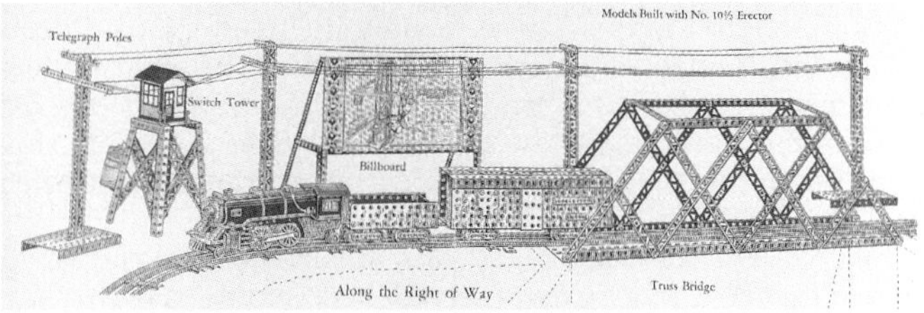

The instruction manual for No. 10½ featured a foldout page that illustrated the railroad-related models that could be built with this colossal set.

box) was placed in the left side compartment, the new 1⅜" parts containers were moved to the middle of the lower-level insert. Gilbert also added the new inner lid label, which pictured the Airplane Ride and Walking Beam Engine models. This label would continue to grace the inside lid of No. 7½ (and eventually No. 6½) well into the 1950s.

The version of No. 8½ available in 1938 and 1939 was an extension of the one offered in 1937, with the addition of the appropriate new parts. As with No. 7½, the (MX) House was packed in a blue cardboard box located in the left-side compartment and the new parts containers were moved to the center of the lower-level cardboard insert. These containers were, however, the largest size (1⅝" deep) and were used in Nos. 9½ and 10½ as well. The insert on the right side, which housed the boiler, was modified to hold the lighting system parts as well. The (MR) Drum with gear was dropped from the Erector System this year; No. 8½ was the smallest set affected by this deletion. Substituted for the (MR) in the instruction manual's illustrations was a drum made from a (CJ) 36 Tooth Gear and two (Z) Flanged Wheels.

Many interesting changes were made on the inner lid label of No. 8½ during 1938. The label pictured the Giant Power Plant and the Ferris Wheel, and the early sets came with a label identical to the 1937, but with the new (A49) Electric Engine shown instead of the old (P51). The (MX) House was pictured with the Ferris Wheel.

Sometime in 1938, a more dramatic inner lid label modification occurred. Prior to that year, each of the metal box sets had, in addition to an inner lid label, a black number rubber-stamped in the upper right corner of the inside of the lid to indicate the set's number. But Gilbert eliminated this number, instead showing it on the insert. However, he did not want to spend much money on this change. The inner lid label designed in 1935, which already had been modified this year, still fit perfectly with Nos. 8½ and 9½. So Gilbert created another overlay, similar to the one used for the label of No. 6½. Consequently, "No. 8½ All Electric" appeared on the label where "The Great New" used to be.

At the same time, text in two other areas on the label was modified. First, in place of "Builds Hundreds of Thrilling Engineering Models," it read "Electric Lights / Reversing Electric Engine / Electric Hoist." Second, the Giant Power Plant finally was called by its "new" name and not the Refrigeration Plant. The printing for all these changes was poorly done, and all the overlay work clearly shows. This otherwise wonderful lid label looks like a patchwork quilt.

Set No. 9½ for 1938 and 1939 was, with a few changes, similar to its precursor. One modification involved subdividing the left-hand compartment by adding a second metal divider. The compartment in the front held the (A49) Electric Engine, and the one in the rear contained the (MX) House and a cardboard insert on which to mount the electro magnet and lighting system.

Set No. 9½ had the very same progression of inner lid label changes as did No. 8½, with one additional twist. About halfway through 1938, when Gilbert dropped the rubber-stamping and began designating set numbers on the labels, he discovered another way to save a little money. Set No. 9½ got exactly the same label as did No. 8½, but glued over the section of the label lettered "No 8½" was a similar one that read "No. 9½."

THE ELECTRIC TRAIN SET OF 1938

A. C. Gilbert acquired the American Flyer line of electric trains in 1937, and he wasted no time in forming a marriage of this wonderful toy with Erector by including a locomotive in a new, top-of-the-line set a year later. Known as "The Electric Train Set," No. 10½ replaced the Hudson locomotive set as the premiere one. This was a set with a theme—to build railroad cars, accessories, and other related items out of Erector parts—and thereby create an Erector Railroad to go with the American Flyer electric locomotive.

The instruction manual for The Electric Train Set came with a newly developed section that was specific to railroad models. It illustrated plans for a tender, gondola, boxcar, wrecking derrick, tank car, and caboose. There were also extensive plans for other railroad equipment, including a functional coal station, working turntable and roadhouse, station, railroad signal, switch tower, water tower, and telegraph poles to place alongside the track.

The telegraph pole models hold a bit of irony, because in his autobiography, *The Man Who Lives in Paradise*, A. C. Gilbert reports that the original idea for the creation of Erector came to him while riding on the New York, New Haven & Hartford Railroad and watching workers construct a telegraph and gantry system from steel girders. Who would have guessed that twenty-seven years later the toy that was inspired by this sight would illustrate the same principle in miniature?

Many interesting modifications occurred in No. 10½ during its five-year history. The 1938 version came in the same huge royal blue box as did the 1937 Hudson set, but the dividers in the interior of the box were rearranged to accommodate the new contents. There were six compartments in the front of the box, including two long narrow ones in the center. Six pieces of track were packed on the edge in the forward-most of these long compartments, and two more pieces of track were packed flat under the train engine in the other. The remaining four pieces of track were packed under the lower-level cardboard insert that filled the back section of the box. Mounted in the lower-level insert were four of the new, large parts containers. Above this insert a large parts display, constructed of six (MN) Base Plates, rested on left- and right-side brackets.

As with the 1937 Hudson set, a large cardboard parts display insert was fastened to the inside of the lid of The Electric Train Set's box. It was identical to the previous year's insert with the same picture of the Hudson locomotive and tender in the center. Unlike the trend that affected the smaller sets, the number for this set was rubber-stamped on the upper right corner of the inside of the lid.

The (NP) Locomotive included in this set was a no. 3315 left over from the 1937 American Flyer line. It is possible that other 1937 vintage locomotives may show up in this set, as Gilbert was not one to waste anything. Readers with knowledge of other locomotives in this set should contact the publisher or author. The (NQ) Section of Curved Track was also taken straight from the current Flyer line, and at this point the track ties had no flange.

It is fascinating that the (NO) 3/4" Flanged Wheels used to build the railroad cars were taken from Meccano. The American right to Meccano had come under Gilbert's control in the late 1920s, and these flanged wheels were originally a part in the Meccano system (no. 20b). In the very early 1938 Electric Train Sets, the (NO)s had a Meccano screw (tapped differently than Erector), and "Meccano" was stamped on each wheel. Imagine the indignity that Gilbert felt including a Meccano part in his premiere Erector Set. Before the end of the year the "Meccano" was deleted and the wheels were tapped for a regular Erector screw.

THE ELECTRIC TRAIN SET OF 1939

For 1939, Gilbert made some changes in the Electric Train Set. First, the inner lid cardboard display insert was updated, with the picture in the center illustrating an electric train and freight cars made from Erector. The old Hudson was gone. The new insert was labeled in the upper left-hand corner: "No. 10½ Electric Train Set," and the rubber-stamping was eliminated.

Perhaps the key improvement was the inclusion of a transformer. Gilbert selected a No. 5 50-watt model from the Flyer line; the metal dividers on the inside of the box were slightly rearranged so the transformer would fit. The compartment used for the (MX) House in 1938 was widened, and along with the transformer, a blue wood block was housed there. The block kept the transformer in place during shipment. With the addition of the transformer, the set was much more complete. Now the (MX) House was packed in the lower cardboard insert. In order for the house to fit there, the roof was not attached.

Of even greater interest was the new locomotive that came with the 1939 set. It was a no. 420 steam engine with copper trim, taken straight from the American Flyer line. Two versions of this locomotives were designed, differing only in that one had a weight for extra traction. Gilbert chose the nonweighted version for Erector.

Two other 1939 variations are worth noting. First, the (NO) Wheels were given a wider flange. Now the cars they built were less likely to jump the track. Second, the track in this set was changed. About half way through the year, the ties came with rolled flanges, and the track was higher. Each tie had four holes so it could be attached to a board. Gilbert made the same modification to the track in the regular American Flyer line.

Erector System Modifications for 1938

I. New Parts

(P13B) 12 Tooth Pinion Gear, 7/32", brass
(A48) Mechanical Motor, painted blue
(A49) Electric Engine, 110-volt, housing painted silver-blue, gearbox painted red
(K48) Mechanical Motor Key, nickel-plated
(MX) House, with cutout windows in the doors and a 2¾" roof
(MZ) Bearing Block, painted red, no center hole
(NH) Lamp Socket Unit, with detachable wire
(NI) Bulb, 1½ volts
(NJ) Battery Holder, nickel-plated
(NK) Ratchet, nickel-plated
(NL) Bolster Bracket, nickel-plated
(NM) 10" x 2" Flanged Plate, painted blue
(NN) 1" x 2" Flanged Plate, painted blue
(NO) Flanged Wheel, ¾" diameter, narrow flange
(NP) Locomotive, American Flyer O gauge no. 3315
(NQ) Section of Curved Track, O gauge, no flanges on ties
(NR) Track Terminal

II. Modified Parts

( ) Parts Containers, came in three sizes: 1", 1⅜", and 1⅝" deep, with cardboard bodies and bottoms, nickel-plated metal lids, and paper labels

III. Eliminated Parts

(P13A) 12 Tooth Pinion (Special)
(P14) Worm Gear
(P49) 18 Tooth Gear
(P50A) 72 Tooth Gear
(P51) Electric Engine, 110 Volt
(P52) Ladder Chain
(P58) Motor, 6-14 Volts
(K) 11 Hole Strip Bracket
(AC) Universal Bracket
(AX) 19¾" Axle Rod
(CQ) Slot Coupling
(DT) One Set Screw Coupling
(EH) Gear Box Bracket
(EJ) Gear Box Base
(HF) Butt End Plate
(LU) Offset Wrench, dropped from parts list but still included in No. 10½
(MR) Drum with Gear
(MS) Compression Spring
(MT) Snap Rivet
(MU) Rivet Extractor
(NA) 3" Main Entrance
(NB) 3" Ground Entrance
(NC) 3" Upper Story
(ND) 6" Upper Story
(NE) 6" Garage Entrance
(NF) 6" Office Entrance
(NG) Roof
( ) All parts specific to the Hudson locomotive and tender

Erector System Modifications for 1939

I. New Parts

(No. 5) Transformer

II. Modified Parts

(A49) Electric Engine, guard strip added
(MH) 3" Disc Wheels, two piece construction with separate hubcap painted red and secured to nickel-plated wheel by hub in the center. Also, curve around side of the tire was reduced (occurred well into 1939)
(MN) 12" Base Plate, with "duplex" hole arrangement (alternating large and small holes) replaced with nonduplex hole pattern of all small holes (occurred well into 1939)
(NP) Locomotive, American Flyer O gauge no. 420, nickel-trimmed
(NO) Flanged wheels, ¾" diameter, wide flanges
(NQ) Section of Curved Track, O gauge, rolled flanges on ties

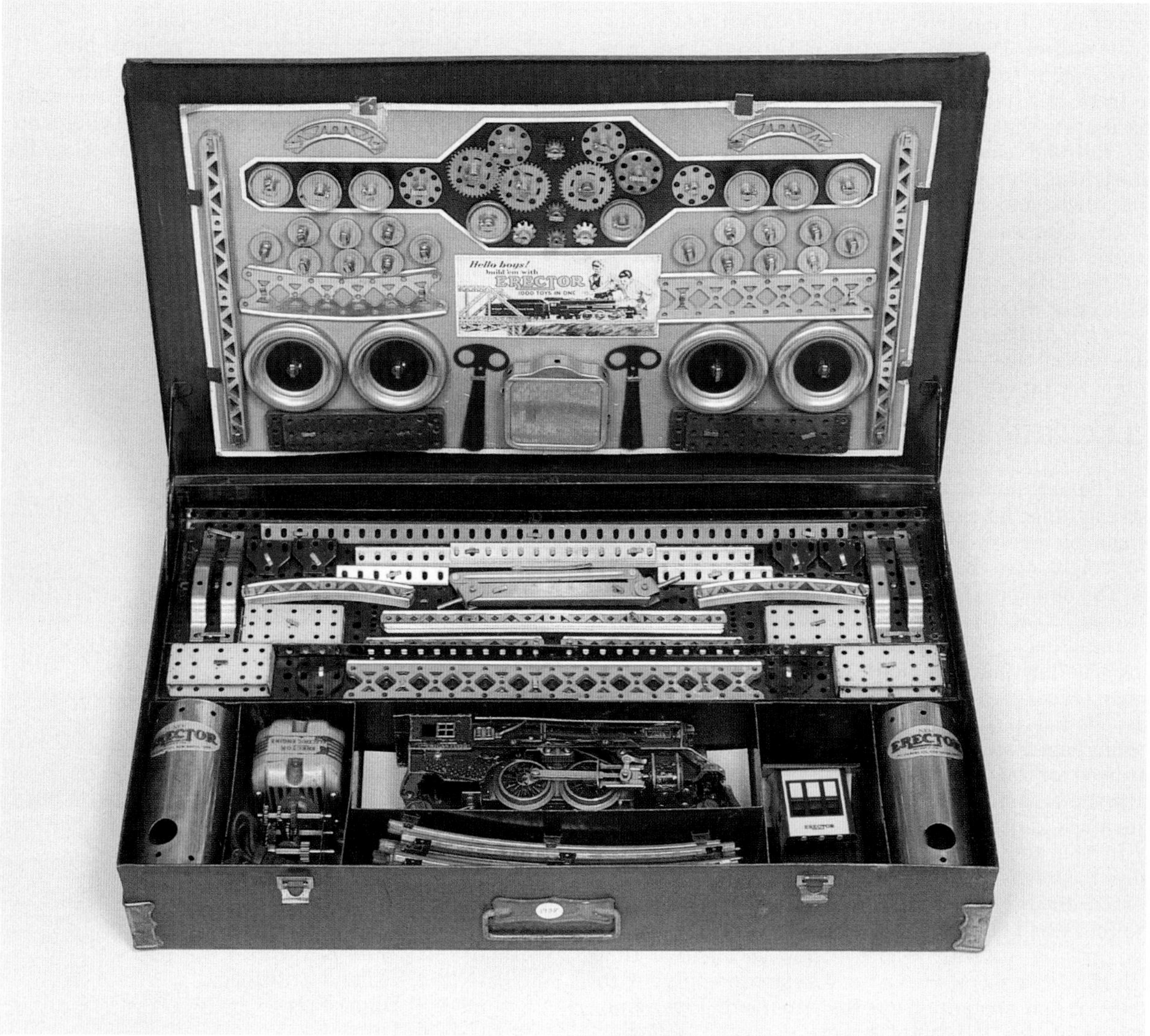

Set No. 10½ replaced the Hudson set at the top of the Erector line in 1938. The first version is unique, as it contained an American Flyer No. 3315 O gauge locomotive but no transformer.

SETS IN THE ERECTOR SYSTEM 1935–39

	Box Size	1935	1936–37	1938–39
Cardboard Box Sets		No. 1½	No. 1½	No. 1½
		No. 3½	No. 2½	No. 2½
		No. S	No. 3½	No. 3½
			Nos. S and SA	No. 4½
Metal Box Sets	16" x 8" x 3"	No. 4½, red	No. 5½, red	No. 6½, red[2]
	18" x 10" x 3"	No. 6½, green	No. 7½, royal blue	No. 7½ royal blue
	20" x 12" x 3"	No. 7½, red	No. 8½, red	No. 8½, red
	22" x 13" x 3"	No. 8½, royal blue	No. 9½, royal blue	No. 9½, royal blue
	24" x 14" x 4"	No. 9½, powder blue	No. 10½, blue[1]	No. 10½, royal blue

1. Powder blue in 1936; royal blue in 1937.
2. Set No. 5½ also offered in this box in 1938.

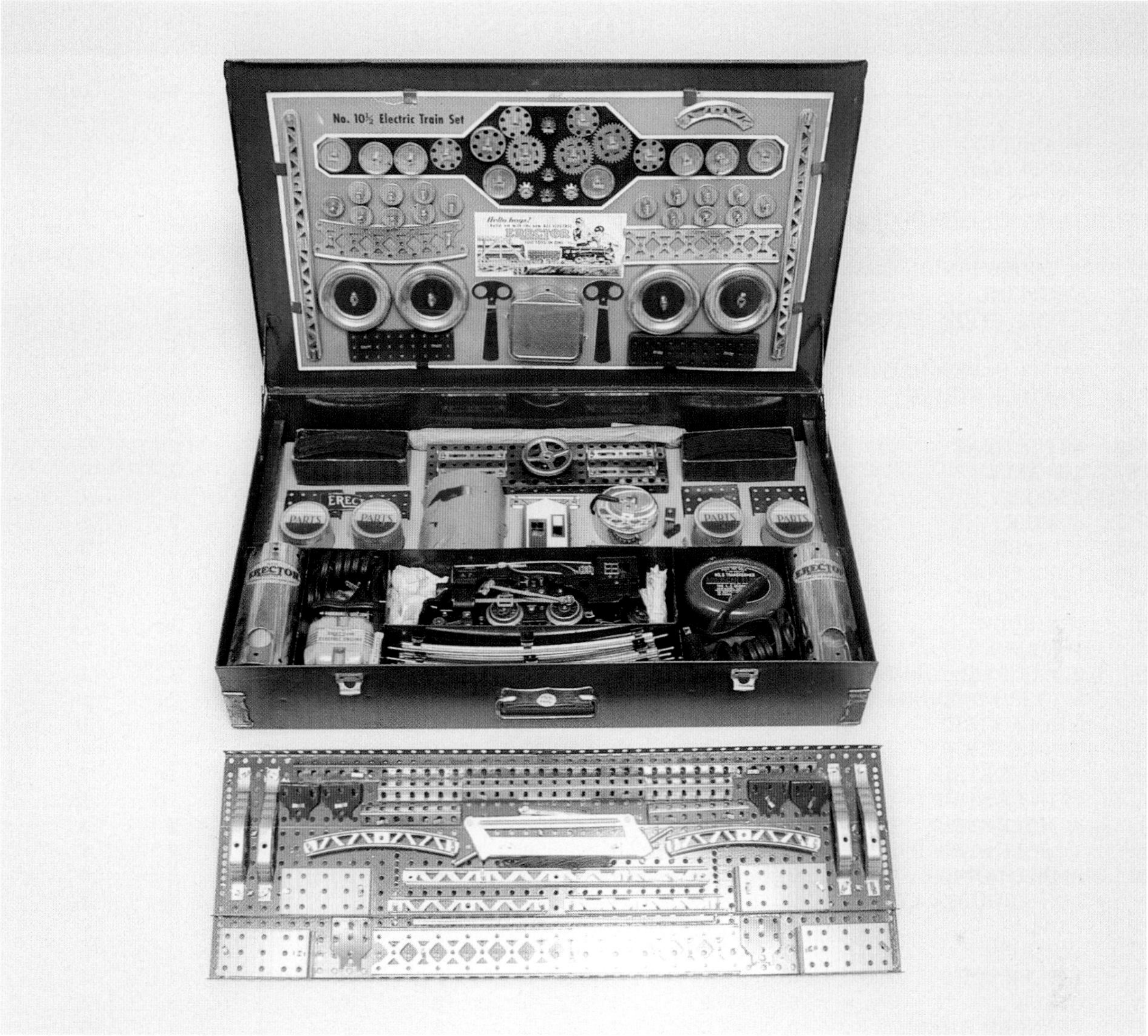

In 1939 Gilbert improved The Electric Train Set by including a transformer. Other modifications included the substitution of a copper-trimmed No. 420 O gauge locomotive for the No. 3315 used in 1938.

II. Eliminated Parts

(A52) Induction Motor
(MP) 24 Tooth Gear

Listings of 1938 and 1939 Erector Sets

NO. 1½ — The Dandy Beginner's Set

Came in a cardboard box 13½" x 10¼" x ¾"; sold for $1.00 in 1938 and 1939.

Gd	VG	Exc	Inv	Org
30	40	70	+15	+20

NO. 2½ — The Apprentice Set

Featured the (MH) Disc Wheels. Came in a cardboard box 18¼" x 10¼" x ¾"; sold for $2.50 in 1938 and 1939.

Gd	VG	Exc	Inv	Org
35	50	80	+20	+25

NO. 3½ — The Intermediate Set

Featured the (MN) Base Plates and angle girders. Came in a cardboard box 18¼" x 10¼" x 1¼"; two-layer set with removable cardboard parts display tray; sold for $3.50 in 1938 and 1939.

Gd	VG	Exc	Inv	Org
40	55	90	+25	+30

NO. 4½ — The Famous No. 4½

Featured the (A48) Mechanical Motor and (MN) 12" Base Plates, and (MX) House and built truck with (A48); model pictured on inside lid label. Came in a cardboard box 18¼" x 10¼" x 2½" with a hinged lid; two-layer set with removable cardboard parts display tray; sold for $5.00 in 1938 and 1939.

Gd	VG	Exc	Inv	Org
80	120	200	+40	+50

NO. 5½ — The Super No. 5½

Identical contents as No. 4½ from 1937. Came in a red

1938–39 CONTENTS LIST

Set No.		1½	2½	3½	4½	6½	7½	8½	9½	10½[1]
P7	⅞" PULLEY	4	4	4	4	4	4	0	0	0
P7A	1⅛" PULLEY	0	0	0	0	0	0	4	4	4
P12	CROWN GEAR	0	0	0	0	0	0	0	1	1
P13	12 TOOTH PINION GEAR, ⅛"	0	0	0	0	1	2	2	2	2
P13B	12 TOOTH PINION GEAR,	0	0	0	0	0	1	1	1	1
P15	COUPLING	0	0	0	1	1	1	2	2	2
P20	5 HOLE STRIP—FORMED	0	0	0	0	0	2	2	8	8
P24	CRANK	1	1	1	1	1	1	1	1	1
P33	SMALL SCREW DRIVER	1	1	1	1	1	1	1	1	1
P34	HANK OF STRING	0	1	1	1	1	1	1	1	1
P37	COLLAR	2	4	4	5	6	7	9	18	18
P48	MITRE GEAR	0	0	0	0	2	2	2	2	2
P57A	2⅛" AXLE	1	1	1	1	1	1	1	2	8
P57D	6" AXLE	0	1	2	0	0	0	0	0	2
P57E	8" AXLE	0	0	0	0	0	0	0	2	2
P57F	12" AXLE	0	0	0	0	0	0	1	2	2
P79	CAR TRUCK	4	4	4	4	4	4	4	4	4
A	2½" GIRDER	4	4	4	4	4	4	4	4	4
B	5" GIRDER	4	4	4	8	12	12	12	12	12
C	10" GIRDER	4	8	8	8	14	14	36	36	36
D	2½" CURVED GIRDER	4	4	4	4	4	4	4	4	4
E	5" CURVED GIRDER	0	2	2	2	4	4	26	26	26
F	5 HOLE STRIP	0	0	0	2	2	2	2	2	16
G	7 HOLE STRIP	0	0	0	2	2	2	2	2	8
H	11 HOLE STRIP	0	0	0	4	4	4	4	4	7
I	21 HOLE STRIP	0	0	0	2	2	2	4	18	18
J	41 HOLE STRIP	0	0	0	0	0	0	2	2	4
K	11 HOLE STRIP BRACKET	0	0	0	0	0	0	0	0	4
M	SMALL DOUBLE ANGLE	0	0	0	0	0	2	6	6	6
N	LONG DOUBLE ANGLE	2	4	4	4	4	4	4	4	4
O	PAWL	0	0	0	0	1	2	2	6	6
T	BOILER	0	0	0	0	0	1	1	2	2
U	BOILER TOP	0	0	0	0	0	1	1	1	1
W	STACK	0	0	0	0	0	3	3	3	3
Z	FLANGED WHEEL, 15⁄16" DIA	0	0	0	0	0	4	4	4	4
AA	ECCENTRIC CRANK	0	0	0	0	0	0	0	6	6
AE	SPIRAL SPRING	0	0	0	0	0	0	0	0	2
AF	SMALL HOOK	1	1	1	1	1	1	1	1	1
AJ	PAPER ERECTOR FLAG	0	0	0	1	1	1	1	1	1
AM	SPECIAL PULLEY	0	0	0	0	0	0	1	1	1
AS	2⅞" AXLE	0	0	0	2	2	3	3	4	4
AT	4" AXLE	2	2	2	2	2	2	2	2	2
BE	6" ANGLE GIRDER	0	0	4	4	4	4	4	4	4
BH	SOLID COLLAR	0	0	0	0	0	0	0	2	2
BL	SMALL WASHER	8	12	12	12	12	12	12	12	17
BN	REGULAR TURRET PLATE	0	0	0	2	2	4	4	4	4
BT	PIERCED DISC	1	1	1	1	2	2	4	4	4
BY	11 HOLE FIBRE STRIP	0	0	0	0	0	0	1	1	1
CA	SIGNAL ARM	0	0	0	0	0	0	0	2	2
CH	RIGHT ANGLE	8	12	12	14	14	14	30	42	42
CJ	36 TOOTH GEAR	0	0	0	0	2	3	3	3	3
CR	SPECIAL TURRET PLATE WITH HUB	0	0	0	0	0	0	0	2	2
CS	WHEEL SEGMENT	0	0	0	0	0	0	0	8	8
CY	5" AXLE	0	2	2	0	0	0	0	0	0
CZ	7" AXLE	0	0	0	2	2	2	3	3	3
DB	MOTOR PULLEY	0	0	0	1	1	1	1	1	1
DE	STEERING COLUMN	0	0	0	0	0	0	0	1	1
DK	FLAT SPRING	0	0	0	0	0	0	0	4	4

1938–39 CONTENTS LIST

Set No.		1½	2½	3½	4½	6½	7½	8½	9½	10½[1]
DO	STEERING WHEEL WITH HUB	0	0	0	0	0	0	0	1	1
DP	12" ANGLE GIRDER	0	0	4	4	4	4	4	4	4
DS	COTTER PIN	0	0	0	0	0	0	0	1	1
EI	STD. GEAR BOX SIDE PLATE	0	0	0	0	2	2	2	2	2
EX	BIG CHANNEL GIRDER 12"	0	0	0	0	0	0	0	8	8
EY	BIG CHANNEL GIRDER 6"	0	0	0	0	0	0	0	4	4
EZ	BIG CHAN. GIRDER CURVED 6"	0	0	0	0	0	0	0	2	2
FA	1¾" x 8-32 SCREW	0	0	0	0	0	0	0	12	12
FD	HINGED LOOP	0	0	0	0	0	0	0	2	2
LX	STEERING COLUMN BRACKET	0	0	0	0	0	0	0	1	1
MA	RADIATOR	0	0	0	0	0	0	0	1	1
MB	18½" ANGLE GIRDER	0	0	0	0	0	0	0	2	2
MC	BASE PLATE 1" x 2½"	2	2	2	2	2	2	8	8	8
MD	BASE PLATE 2½" x 5"	1	1	1	1	1	1	4	4	4
ME	BASE PLATE 1" x 4"	0	0	0	0	0	0	0	4	4
MF	BASE PLATE 1" x 5"	2	2	4	4	4	4	8	9	12
MG	RADIATOR HOOD	0	0	0	0	0	0	0	1	1
MH	LARGE 3" DISC WHEEL	0	4	4	4	4	4	4	4	4
MI	FRONT AXLE UNIT	0	0	0	0	0	0	0	1	1
MJ	ELECTRO MAGNET WITH CORD	0	0	0	0	0	0	1	1	1
MM	WRENCH	0	0	0	1	1	1	1	1	1
MN	12" BASE PLATE	0	0	2	2	4	4	6	6	6
MO	3" ANGLE GIRDER	0	0	4	4	4	4	4	4	4
MV	FLAT CAR TRUCK	0	0	0	0	0	2	4	4	4
MW	NUT HOLDER	0	0	0	1	1	1	1	1	1
MX	HOUSE	0	0	0	1	1	1	1	1	1
MY	2½" x 2½" BASE PLATE	0	0	0	1	1	1	1	1	1
MZ	BEARING BLOCK	0	0	0	0	1	1	1	1	1
NH	LAMP SOCKET UNIT	0	0	0	0	0	2	2	2	2
NI	BULB, 1½ VOLT	0	0	0	0	0	2	2	2	2
NJ	BATTERY HOLDER	0	0	0	0	0	1	1	1	1
NK	RATCHET	0	0	0	0	0	2	2	2	2
NL	BOLSTER BRACKET0	0	0	0	0	0	0	0	4	
NM	10" x 2" FLANGED PLATE	0	0	0	0	0	0	0	0	2
NN	1" x 2" FLANGED PLATE	0	0	0	0	0	0	0	0	5
NO	FLANGED WHEEL, ¾" DIA.	0	0	0	0	0	0	0	0	16
NP	LOCOMOTIVE—O GAUGE	0	0	0	0	0	0	0	0	1
NQ	SECTION OF CURVED TRACK	0	0	0	0	0	0	0	0	12
NR	TRACK TERMINAL	0	0	0	0	0	0	0	0	1
A48	MECHANICAL MOTOR	0	0	0	1	0	0	0	0	1
K48	KEY FOR MECH. MOTOR	0	0	0	1	0	0	0	0	1
A49	ELECTRIC ENGINE	0	0	0	0	1	1	1	1	1
A52	INDUCTION MOTOR	0	0	0	0	0	0	0	0	0
NO. 5	TRANSFORMER[2]	0	0	0	0	0	0	0	0	1
N21	8-32 SQUARE NUT	25	45	60	88	93	93	169	240	350
S51	¼" x 8-32 SCREW	21	35	50	80	84	84	162	206	255
S52	½" x 8-32 SCREW	0	0	0	0	4	4	4	4	4
S57	1⅜" x 8-32 SCREW	0	0	0	0	0	4	4	4	4
S62	⅞" x 8-32 SCREW	3	6	6	8	8	8	18	20	20

1. Set No. 10½ also contained an offset wrench.

2. 1938 Set No. 10½ did not contain a transformer.

Form M 1541-A

ERECTOR SEPARATE PARTS PRICES

KINDLY ENCLOSE CHECK, MONEY ORDER OR STAMPS WITH YOUR ORDER FOR PARTS

THE A. C. GILBERT CO., NEW HAVEN, CONN., U. S. A.

Trade	No.	Name of Part	Page	Price
*N21		8-32 Square Nut	2	.05 doz.
P7		Small Wheel, ⅞" Dia.	2	.10 ea.
P7A		Small Wheel, 1⅛" Dia.	2	.10 ea.
P12		Crown Gear	2	.10 ea.
P13		12-Tooth Pinion Gear, ⅛"	2	.10 ea.
P13B		12-Tooth Pinion Gear, 7/32"	2	.10 ea.
P14		Worm Gear	2	.20 ea.
P15		Coupling	2	.10 ea.
P20		Five Hole Strip—formed	1	.05 ea.
P24		Crank	1	.10 ea.
P33		Small Screw Driver	1	.05 ea.
P34		Hank of String	1	.05 ea.
P37		Collar	2	.25 doz.
P39		Wood Screw	2	.15 doz.
P40		Screw Eye	2	.20 doz.
P48		Mitre Gear	2	.20 ea.
P49		18-Tooth Gear	2	.15 ea.
P50		72-Tooth Gear	2	.30 ea.
P52		Ladder Chain	1	.15 ft.
P51		Electric Engine Reversing 110v. A.C. or D.C.	3	3.95 ea.
P54		Motor, 6-14 volts	3	1.75 ea.
P56G		Motor, 110v. A.C. or D.C.	3	2.95 ea.
P58		Motor, 6-14 volts	3	1.00 ea.
P59		Reverse Base (for P58 only)	3	.75 ea.
A48		Mechanical Motor	3	1.00 ea.
K48		Mechanical Motor Key	3	.20 ea.
A49		Electric Engine, 110v. A.C. only	3	3.95 ea.
A49B		Electric Engine Conversion Unit	3	1.25 ea.
P57A		2⅛" Axle	1	.02 ea.
P57D		6" Axle	1	.06 ea.
P57E		8" Axle	1	.08 ea.
P57F		12" Axle	1	.12 ea.
P79		Car Truck	1	.05 ea.
*S11		Set Screw	2	.05 doz.
*S51		¼"x8-32 Screw	2	.05 doz.
*S52		½"x8-32 Screw	2	.10 doz.
*S57		1⅛"x8-32 Screw	2	.15 doz.
*S62		⅞"x8-32 Screw	2	.10 doz.
*FA		1¾"x8-32 Screw	2	.15 doz.
A		2½" Girder	1	.20 doz.
B		5" Girder	1	.35 doz.
C		10" Girder	1	.50 doz.
D		2½" Curved Girder	1	.25 doz.
E		5" Curved Girder	1	.40 doz.
F		5 Hole Strip	1	.10 doz.
G		7 Hole Strip	1	.10 doz.
H		11 Hole Strip	1	.15 doz.
I		21 Hole Strip	1	.20 doz.
J		41 Hole Strip	1	.30 doz.
K		11 Hole Strip Bracket	1	.35 doz.
M		Small Double Angle	1	.25 doz.
N		Long Double Angle	1	.05 ea.
O		Pawl	1	.05 ea.
S		Large Base Plate—21 holes	1	.40 ea.

Trade	No.	Name of Part	Page	Price
T		Boiler	3	.25 ea.
U		Boiler Top	3	.20 ea.
W		Stack	3	.05 ea.
Z		Flanged Wheel, 13/16" Dia.	2	.15 ea.
AA		Eccentric Crank	1	.10 ea.
AB		One Hole Coupling	2	.15 ea.
AC		Universal Bracket	1	.10 ea.
AE		Spiral Spring	1	.05 ea.
AF		Small Hook	2	.15 doz.
AH		Small Triangle	1	.25 doz.
AM		Special Pulley—Metal	2	.05 ea.
AQ		Sheave Pulley	2	.05 ea.
AS		2⅞" Axle Rod	1	.03 ea.
AT		4" Axle Rod	1	.04 ea.
AX		19¾" Axle Rod	1	.20 ea.
BE		6" Angle Girder	1	.50 doz.
BH		Solid Collar	2	2 for .05
BK		8-32 Wing Nut	2	.25 doz.
BL		Small Washer	2	.05 doz.
BN		Regular Turret Plate	3	.15 ea.
BO	P58	Reverse Switch Attachment	2	.50 ea.
BT		Pierced Disc	2	.10 ea.
BY		11-Hole Fibre Strip	1	.05 ea.
CA		Signal Arm	1	.10 ea.
CH		Right Angle	1	.10 doz.
CJ		36-Tooth Gear	2	.20 ea.
CQ		Slot Coupling	2	.15 ea.
CR		Special Turret plate with hub	3	.15 ea.
CS		Wheel Segment	3	.15 ea.
CX		1" Axle Rod	1	.01 ea.
CY		5" Axle Rod	1	.05 ea.
CZ		7" Axle Rod	1	.07 ea.
DA		10" Axle Rod	1	.10 ea.
DB		Motor Pulley	2	.10 ea.
DE		Steering Column	1	.10 ea.
DK		Flat Spring	1	.10 ea.
DO		Steering Wheel with Hub	2	.15 ea.
DP		12" Angle Girder	1	6 for .50
DS		Cotter Pin	1	.05 doz.
DT		1-Hole Set Screw Coupling	2	2 for .15
DU		¼" Diam. Axle 8½"	1	2 for .25
DZ		Tackle Block	2	.15 ea.
EC		Giant Axle—29" long, 5/16" diam.	1	.50 ea.
EH		Gear Box Bracket	1	.05 ea.
EI		Standard Gear Box Side Pl.	1	.15 ea.
EJ		Gear Box Base	1	.20 ea.
EX		Big Channel Girder 12"	1	6 for .50
EY		Big Channel Girder 6"	1	.05 ea.
EZ		6" Curved B. C. Girder	1	.05 ea.
FD		Hinged Loop	1	2 for .05
FJ		Rack	2	.25 ea.
FL		Helical Gear	2	.25 ea.
GV		Small Disc Wheel	2	.10 ea.
LV		3" Disc Wheel, red	2	.20 ea.
LX		Steering Column Bracket	1	.05 ea.

Trade	No.	Name of Part	Page	Price
MA		Radiator	1	.15 ea.
MB		18½" Angle Girder	1	.15 ea.
MC		Base Plate 1"x2½"	1	.05 ea.
MD		Base Plate 2½"x5"	1	.10 ea.
ME		Flat Plate 1"x4"	1	.05 ea.
MF		Flat Plate 1"x5"	1	.05 ea.
MG		Radiator Hood	1	.10 ea.
MH		3" Disc Wheel, Nickel Rim	2	.25 ea.
MI		Front Axle Unit	1	.25 ea.
MJ		Electro Magnet with Cord	2	.60 ea.
MM		Wrench	1	.05 ea.
MN		12" Base Plate	1	.40 ea.
MO		3" Angle Girder	1	.30 doz.
MP		24 Tooth Gear	2	.20 ea.
MR		Drum with Gear	2	.35 ea.
MS		Compression Spring	1	.05 ea.
MT		Snap Rivet	2	.10 doz.
MU		Rivet Extractor	1	.05 ea.
MV		Flat Car Truck	1	.05 ea.
MW		Nut Holder	1	.10 ea.
MX		House	3	.35 ea.
MY		2½"x2½" Base Plate	1	.05 ea.
MZ		Bearing Block	1	.10 ea.
NA		3" Main Entrance	3	2 for .05
NB		3" Ground Floor	3	2 for .05
NC		3" Upper Story	3	2 for .05
ND		6" Upper Story	3	.05 ea.
NE		6" Garage Entrance	3	.05 ea.
NF		6" Office Entrance	3	.05 ea.
NG		Roof	3	.05 ea.
NH		Lamp Socket Unit	2	.15 ea.
NI		Bulb—1½ Volt	2	.05 ea.
NJ		Battery Holder	2	.15 ea.
NK		Ratchet	1	.05 ea.
NL		Bolster Bracket	1	2 for .05
NM		10"x2" Flange Plate	1	.40 ea.
NN		1"x2" Flange Plate	1	.05 ea.
NO		Flanged Wheel, ¾" Dia.	2	.15 ea.
NP		Locomotive—O Gauge		8.50 ea.
NQ		Section of Curved Track—O Gauge—(12 Sections per circle)		.20 ea.
NR		Track Terminal		.20 ea.

NOTE

*N21 Nut used with screws S51, S52, S62, S57, FA

*S11 Set Screw used with pulleys, couplings, etc.

ERECTOR HOW TO MAKE 'EM BOOKS

Same as copy included in sets.

No. 1	Erector How to Make 'Em Book	.15 ea.
No. 3	Erector How to Make 'Em Book	.15 ea.
No. 4	Erector How to Make 'Em Book	.25 ea.
No. 6	Erector How to Make 'Em Book	.25 ea.
No. 7	Erector How to Make 'Em Book	.25 ea.
No. 8	Erector How to Make 'Em Book	.25 ea.
No. 1½	Erector How to Make 'Em Book	.15 ea.
No. 2½	Erector How to Make 'Em Book	.15 ea.
No. 3½	Erector How to Make 'Em Book	.15 ea.
No. 4½	Erector How to Make 'Em Book	.25 ea.
No. 5½	Erector How to Make 'Em Book	.25 ea.
No. 7½	Erector How to Make 'Em Book	.25 ea.
No. 8½	Erector How to Make 'Em Book	.35 ea.
No. 9½	Erector How to Make 'Em Book	.35 ea.
No. 10½	Erector How to Make 'Em Book	.35 ea.

Separate Parts Prices for 1938

Form M 1541-A

ERECTOR SEPARATE PARTS PRICES

KINDLY ENCLOSE CHECK, MONEY ORDER OR STAMPS WITH YOUR ORDER FOR PARTS

THE A. C. GILBERT CO., NEW HAVEN, CONN., U. S. A.

Trade	No.	Name of Part	Page	Price
*N21		8-32 Square Nut	2	.05 doz.
P7		Small Wheel, ⅞" Dia.	2	.10 ea.
P7A		Small Wheel, 1⅛" Dia.	2	.10 ea.
P12		Crown Gear	2	.10 ea.
P13		12-Tooth Pinion Gear, ⅛"	2	.10 ea.
P13B		12-Tooth Pinion Gear, 7/32"	2	.10 ea.
P14		Worm Gear	2	.20 ea.
P15		Coupling	2	.10 ea.
P20		Five Hole Strip—formed	1	.05 ea.
P24		Crank	1	.10 ea.
P33		Small Screw Driver	1	.05 ea.
P34		Hank of String	1	.05 ea.
P37		Collar	2	.25 doz.
P39		Wood Screw	2	.15 doz.
P40		Screw Eye	2	.20 doz.
P48		Mitre Gear	2	.20 ea.
P49		18-Tooth Gear	2	.15 ea.
P50		72-Tooth Gear	2	.30 ea.
P52		Ladder Chain	1	.15 ft.
P51		Electric Engine Reversing 110v. A.C. or D.C.	3	3.95 ea.
P56G		Motor, 110v. A.C. or D.C.	3	2.95 ea.
P58		Motor, 6-14 volts	3	1.00 ea.
P59		Reverse Base (for P58 only)	3	.75 ea.
A48		Mechanical Motor	3	1.00 ea.
K48		Mechanical Motor Key	3	.20 ea.
A49		Electric Engine, 110v. A.C. only	3	3.95 ea.
A49B		Electric Engine Conversion Unit	3	1.25 ea.
P57A		2⅛" Axle	1	.02 ea.
P57D		6" Axle	1	.06 ea.
P57E		8" Axle	1	.08 ea.
P57F		12" Axle	1	.12 ea.
P79		Car Truck	1	.05 ea.
*S11		Set Screw	2	.05 doz.
*S51		¼"x8-32 Screw	2	.05 doz.
*S52		½"x8-32 Screw	2	.10 doz.
*S57		1⅛"x8-32 Screw	2	.15 doz.
*S62		⅞"x8-32 Screw	2	.10 doz.
*FA		1¾"x8-32 Screw	2	.15 doz.
A		2½" Girder	1	.20 doz.
B		5" Girder	1	.35 doz.
C		10" Girder	1	.50 doz.
D		2½" Curved Girder	1	.25 doz.
E		5" Curved Girder	1	.40 doz.
F		5 Hole Strip	1	.10 doz.
G		7 Hole Strip	1	.10 doz.
H		11 Hole Strip	1	.15 doz.
I		21 Hole Strip	1	.20 doz.
J		41 Hole Strip	1	.30 doz.
K		11 Hole Strip Bracket	1	.35 doz.
M		Small Double Angle	1	.25 doz.
N		Long Double Angle	1	.05 ea.
O		Pawl	1	.05 ea.
S		Large Base Plate—21 holes	1	.40 ea.

Trade	No.	Name of Part	Page	Price
T		Boiler	3	.25 ea.
U		Boiler Top	3	.20 ea.
W		Stack	3	.05 ea.
Z		Flanged Wheel, 13/16" Dia.	2	.15 ea.
AA		Eccentric Crank	1	.10 ea.
AC		Universal Bracket	1	.10 ea.
AE		Spiral Spring	1	.05 ea.
AF		Small Hook	2	.15 doz.
AM		Special Pulley—Metal	2	.05 ea.
AQ		Sheave Pulley	2	.05 ea.
AS		2⅞" Axle Rod	1	.03 ea.
AT		4" Axle Rod	1	.04 ea.
AX		19¾" Axle Rod	1	.20 ea.
BE		6" Angle Girder	1	.50 doz.
BH		Solid Collar	2	2 for .05
BK		8-32 Wing Nut	2	.25 doz.
BL		Small Washer	2	.05 doz.
BN		Regular Turret Plate	3	15 ea.
BT		Pierced Disc	2	.10 ea.
BY		11-Hole Fibre Strip	1	.05 ea.
CA		Signal Arm	1	.10 ea.
CH		Right Angle	1	.10 doz.
CJ		36-Tooth Gear	2	.20 ea.
CQ		Slot Coupling	2	.15 ea.
CR		Special Turret plate with hub	3	.15 ea.
CS		Wheel Segment	3	.15 ea.
CX		1" Axle Rod	1	.01 ea.
CY		5" Axle Rod	1	.05 ea.
CZ		7" Axle Rod	1	.07 ea.
DA		10" Axle Rod	1	.10 ea.
DB		Motor Pulley	2	.10 ea.
DE		Steering Column	1	.10 ea.
DK		Flat Spring	1	.10 ea.
DO		Steering Wheel with Hub	2	.15 ea.
DP		12" Angle Girder	1	6 for .50
DS		Cotter Pin	1	.05 doz.
DT		1-Hole Set Screw Coupling	2	2 for .15
DU		¼" Diam. Axle 8½"	1	2 for .25
DZ		Tackle Block	2	.15 ea.
EH		Gear Box Bracket	1	.05 ea.
EI		Standard Gear Box Side Pl.	1	.15 ea.
EJ		Gear Box Base	1	.20 ea.
EX		Big Channel Girder 12"	1	6 for .50
EY		Big Channel Girder 6"	1	.05 ea.
EZ		6" Curved B. C. Girder	1	.05 ea.
FD		Hinged Loop	1	2 for .05
GV		Small Disc Wheel	2	.10 ea.
LV		3" Disc Wheel, red	2	.20 ea.
LX		Steering Column Bracket	1	.05 ea.

Trade	No.	Name of Part	Page	Price
MA		Radiator	1	.15 ea.
MB		18½" Angle Girder	1	.15 ea.
MC		Base Plate 1"x2½"	1	.05 ea.
MD		Base Plate 2½"x5"	1	.10 ea.
ME		Flat Plate 1"x4"	1	.05 ea.
MF		Flat Plate 1"x5"	1	.05 ea.
MG		Radiator Hood	1	.10 ea.
MH		3" Disc Wheel, Nickel Rim	2	.25 ea.
MI		Front Axle Unit	1	.25 ea.
MJ		Electro Magnet with Cord	2	.60 ea.
MM		Wrench	1	.05 ea.
MN		12" Base Plate	1	.40 ea.
MO		3" Angle Girder	1	.30 doz.
MP		24 Tooth Gear	2	.20 ea.
MR		Drum with Gear	2	.35 ea.
MS		Compression Spring	1	.05 ea.
MT		Snap Rivet	2	.10 doz.
MU		Rivet Extractor	1	.05 ea.
MV		Flat Car Truck	1	.05 ea.
MW		Nut Holder	1	.10 ea.
MX		House	3	.35 ea.
MY		2½"x2½" Base Plate	1	.05 ea.
MZ		Bearing Block	1	.10 ea.
NA		3" Main Entrance	3	2 for .05
NB		3" Ground Floor	3	2 for .05
NC		3" Upper Story	3	2 for .05
ND		6" Upper Story	3	.05 ea.
NE		6" Garage Entrance	3	.05 ea.
NF		6" Office Entrance	3	.05 ea.
NG		Roof	3	.05 ea.
NH		Lamp Socket Unit	2	.15 ea.
NI		Bulb—1½ Volt	2	.05 ea.
NJ		Battery Holder	2	.15 ea.
NK		Ratchet	1	.05 ea.
NL		Bolster Bracket	1	2 for .05
NM		10"x2" Flange Plate	1	.40 ea.
NN		1"x2" Flange Plate	1	.05 ea.
NO		Flanged Wheel, ¾" Dia.	2	.15 ea.
NP		Locomotive—O Gauge		8.50 ea.
NQ		Section of Curved Track—O Gauge—(12 Sections per circle)		.20 ea.
NR		Track Terminal		.20 ea.

NOTE

*N21 Nut used with screws S51, S52, S62, S57, FA

*S11 Set Screw used with pulleys, couplings, etc.

ERECTOR HOW TO MAKE 'EM BOOKS

Same as copy included in sets.

No. 1	Erector How to Make 'Em Book	.15 ea.
No. 3	Erector How to Make 'Em Book	.15 ea.
No. 4	Erector How to Make 'Em Book	.25 ea.
No. 6	Erector How to Make 'Em Book	.25 ea.
No. 7	Erector How to Make 'Em Book	.25 ea.
No. 8	Erector How to Make 'Em Book	.25 ea.
No. 1½	Erector How to Make 'Em Book	.15 ea.
No. 2½	Erector How to Make 'Em Book	.15 ea.
No. 3½	Erector How to Make 'Em Book	.15 ea.
No. 4½	Erector How to Make 'Em Book	.25 ea.
No. 5½	Erector How to Make 'Em Book	.25 ea.
No. 7½	Erector How to Make 'Em Book	.25 ea.
No. 8½	Erector How to Make 'Em Book	.35 ea.
No. 9½	Erector How to Make 'Em Book	.35 ea.
No. 10½	Erector How to Make 'Em Book	.35 ea.

Separate Parts Prices for 1939

metal box 16" x 8" x 3"; two-layer set with two removable parts displays constructed from (MN) Base Plates; sold for $6.95 in 1938 and deleted in 1939.

Gd	VG	Exc	Inv	Org
60	90	150	+30	+40

NO. 6½ **The Sensational No. 6½**

Featured the (A49) Electric Engine without gearbox and built Airplane Ride. Came in a red metal box 16" x 8" x 3"; two-layer set with removable parts display tray; sold for $7.95 in 1938 and 1939.

Gd	VG	Exc	Inv	Org
40	60	100	+20	+25

NO. 7½ **The Electric Engine Set**

Featured the (T) Boiler, (A49) Electric Engine with gearbox, and lighting parts system and built Walking Beam Engine. Came in a royal blue metal box 18" x 10" x 3" with brass corner trim; two-layer set with two removable parts displays constructed from (MN) Base Plates; sold for $10.00 in 1938 and 1939.

Gd	VG	Exc	Inv	Org
70	100	170	+35	+45

NO. 8½ **The Engineer's Set**

Featured the (MJ) Electro Magnet and lighting system parts and built Ferris Wheel. Came in a red metal box 20" x 12" x 3" with brass corner trim; two-layer set with three removable parts displays constructed from (MN) Base Plates; sold for $12.95 in 1938 and 1939.

Gd	VG	Exc	Inv	Org
80	120	200	+40	+50

NO. 9½ **The Automotive Set**

Featured the truck parts and giant flywheel and built Giant Power Plant. Came in a royal blue metal box 22" x 13" x 3" with brass corner trim; two-layer set with three removable parts displays constructed from (MN) Base Plates; sold for $17.95 in 1938 and 1939.

Gd	VG	Exc	Inv	Org
125	195	300	+65	+80

NO. 10½ **The Electric Train Set**

Featured American Flyer O gauge electric locomotive, track, flanged wheels, and flanged plates for building railroad models (theme of set). Came in a royal blue metal box 24" x 14" x 4" with brass corner trim; two-layer set with one very large removable parts display constructed from (MN) Base Plates; cardboard parts display clipped on inside of lid; sold without transformer for $27.50 in 1938 and $29.95 with transformer in 1939.

	Gd	VG	Exc	Inv	Org
1938 version	900	1325	2200	+440	+550
1939 version	800	1200	2000	+400	+500

THE 1940, 1941, AND 1942 ERECTOR LINE

After seemingly taking a year off in 1939, A. C. Gilbert's Erector engineers were back to work in 1940, inventing new parts and models for the system. They made many changes, but these modifications affected only the four top sets: Nos. 7½, 8½, 9½, and 10½. The smaller ones were not altered.

With No. 7½, Gilbert deleted the electrical system parts. Apparently he decided that these parts belonged only in the more expensive sets. Missing were the (NH) Lamp Socket Unit, (NI) Bulb, and (NJ) Battery Holder.

The modifications that occurred in No. 8½ were more positive. First, a major new part was added to this and the larger sets, the (NV) Whistle. Rather complicated, it was designed to be attached to the rear housing of the (A49) Electric Engine. A (P13) Pinion Gear was mounted to the high speed shaft of the motor, so when someone pulled the handle of the (NV) Whistle, a brass strip came in contact with the moving gear and produced the whistle sound. It sounded more like a scream than a whistle, but for Gilbert's first attempt at an audio Erector accessory, it was not bad. A second label was added to the inside of the lid to promote this new part. It read, "First set with the whistle" in black letters on a yellow background.

The whistle was mounted on the (A49) at the factory, and the engine was modified in 1940 with extra screw holes tapped in the rear motor housing to accommodate it. The Electric Engines made between 1940 and 1942 are most easily identified by these extra screw holes. A second blue wooden handle, identical to the one used on the engine's gear shift, was added for use with the whistle. Part of the latter's mechanism included a spring and an adjustment screw that limited the movement of the brass plate.

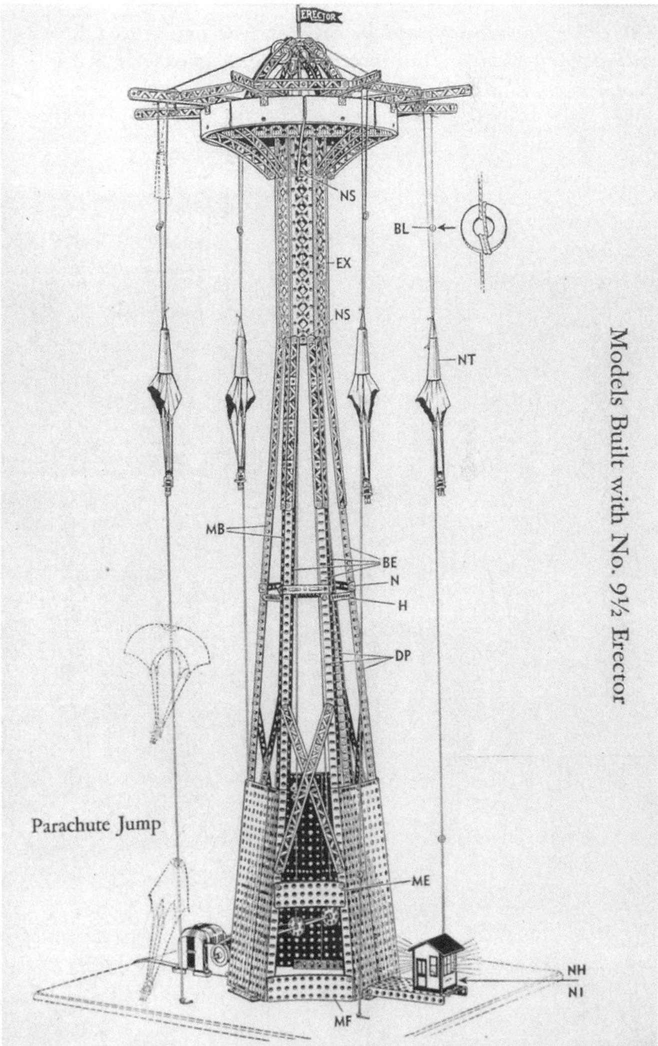

The 1940–48 version of the Parachute Jump, a 5-foot extravaganza inspired by a ride at the New York World's Fair of 1939–40. The parachutes were raised to the top of the model with (NT) Cones.

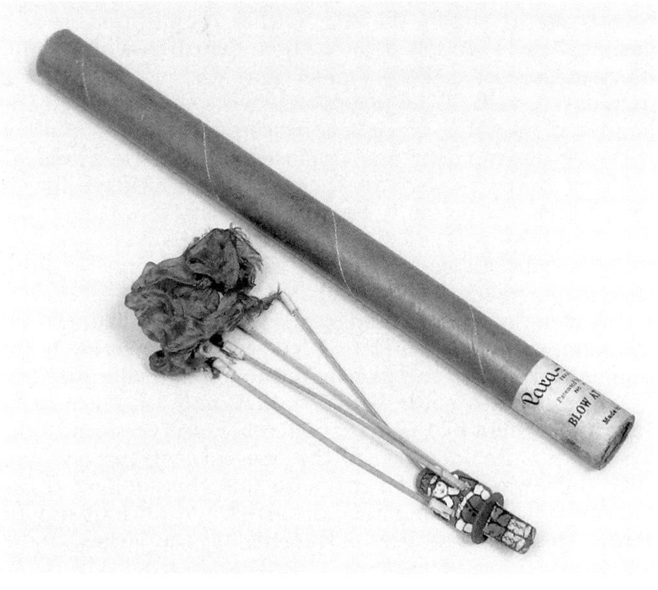

The (NU) Parachute used in Erector Sets originated in a toy called Para-Shooter that another, unidentified firm made.

Over the years, these springs had a tendency to come loose.

The second innovation that occurred in No. 8½ and the larger sets was an improved (MJ) Electro Magnet. Since its introduction in 1933, this part had been bulky, measuring 2¾" in diameter. The casing was wide open at the bottom, and the magnetic core was fully exposed. While the (MJ) worked well, it was not particularly authentic in appearance or scale. The new version was smaller (1⅜" in diameter), making it more realistic and accurate in appearance with a sculptured casing and fully enclosed core. The electro magnet was one of the most popular components in the Erector System; with only a few minor changes, the 1940 version continued to be used in the larger sets well into the 1960s.

History is a retrospective science. Manufacturers like Gilbert made decisions and exercised creativity, and these actions determined the fate of their business. Historical perspective often clarifies the validity of a decision. In 1940, such creativity was employed and such a decision was made, and history has judged it very much correct. The result was the unveiling of the Parachute Jump, undoubtedly one of the most important models in modern Erector history. Inspired by the Parachute Jump Ride at the 1939 World's Fair in New York, this model stood 5 feet high. It was the tallest and most sophisticated Erector model of the period. In 1940, the sets that were upgraded with the parts to build

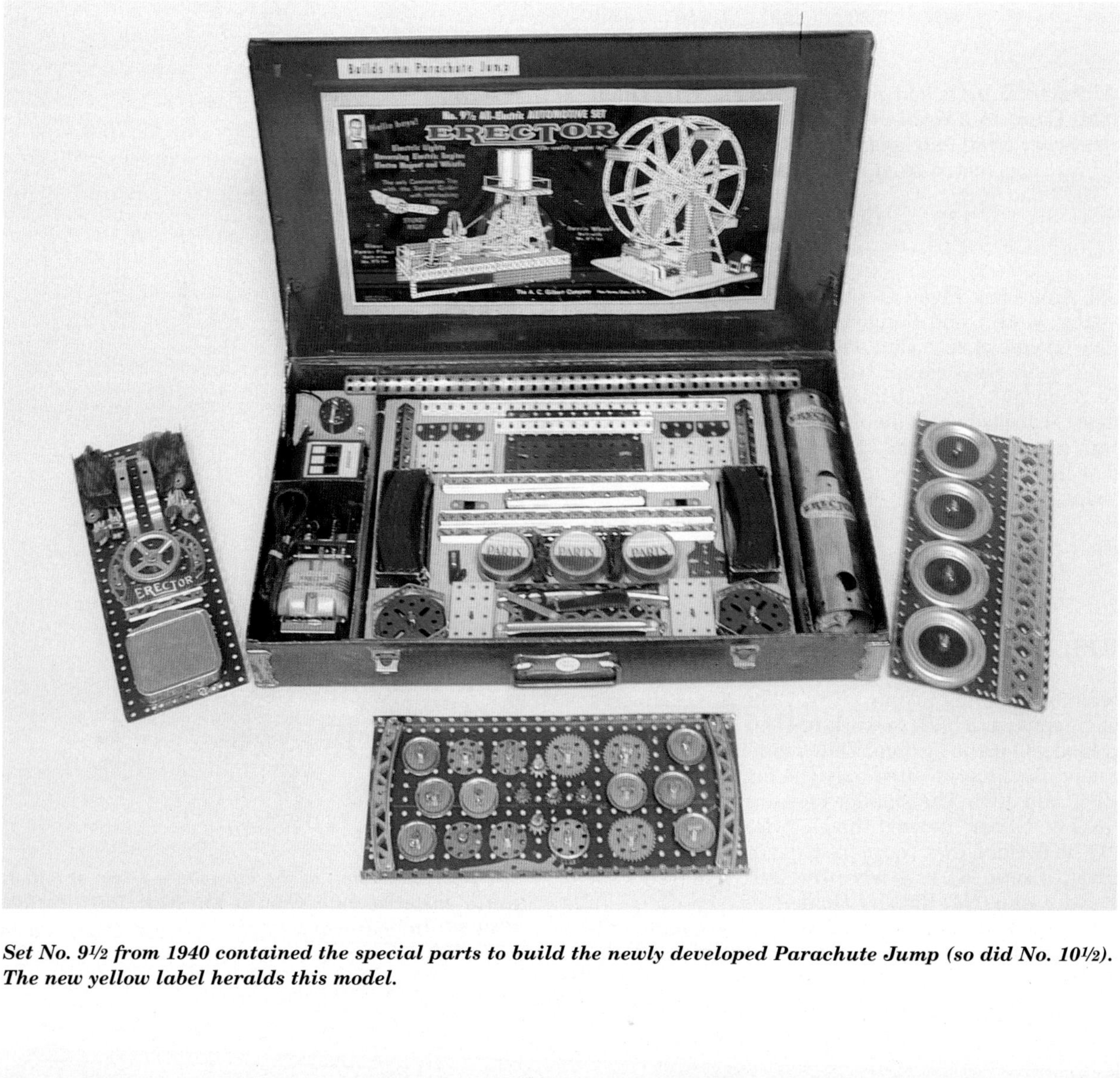

Set No. 9½ from 1940 contained the special parts to build the newly developed Parachute Jump (so did No. 10½). The new yellow label heralds this model.

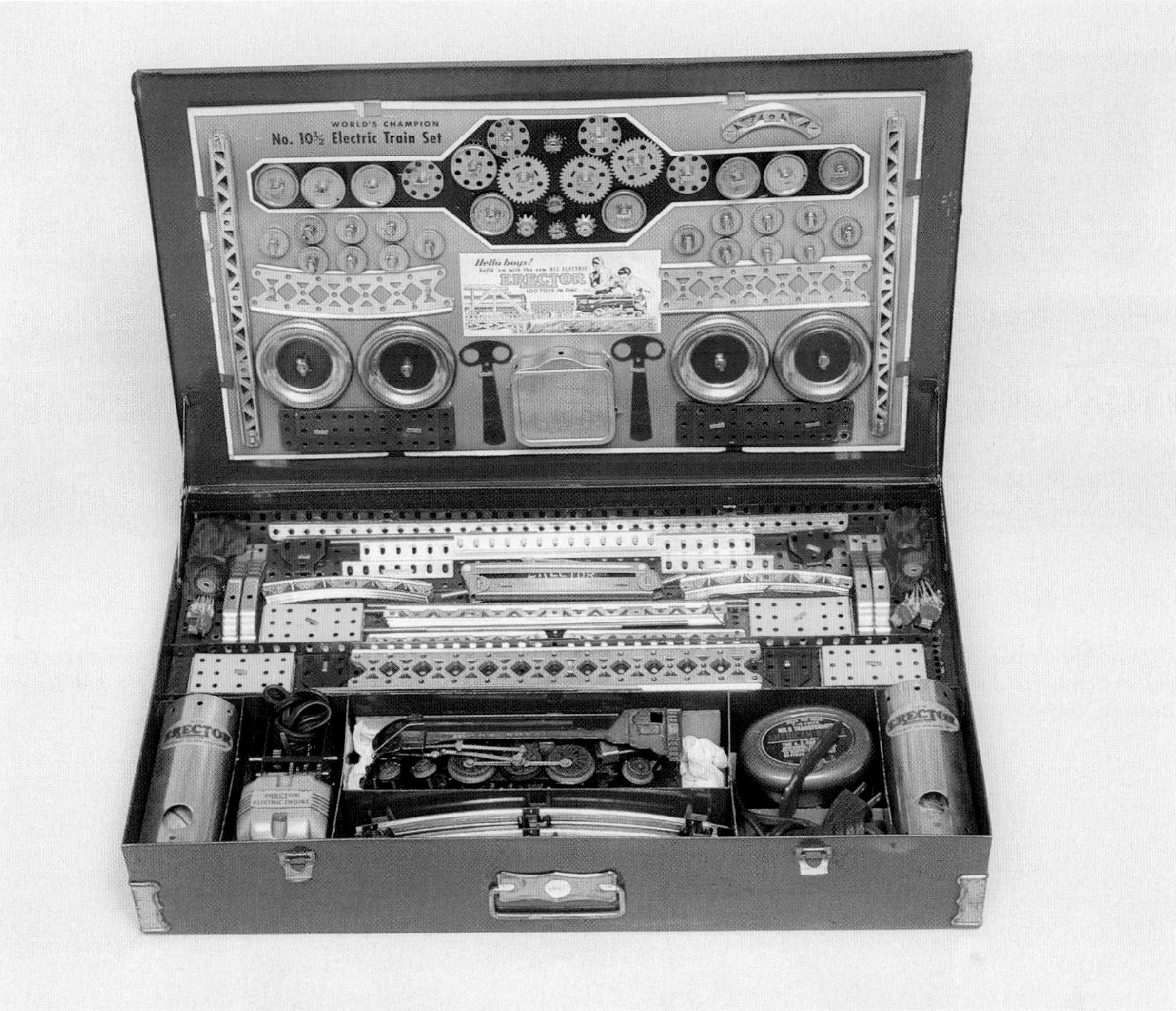

In the version of No. 10½ from 1941, Gilbert substituted an American Flyer No. 556 Royal Blue steam engine for the nickel-trimmed No. 420 used in 1940. The inside lid parts display was modified to include "World's Champion" in mid-1940.

this impressive model were Nos. 9½ (The Automotive Set) and 10½ (The Electric Train Set).

In addition to some increases in the supply of existing Erector parts, three new parts specific to the Parachute Jump were included in Nos. 9½ and 10½. First, there was the (NS) 41 Hole Strip Formed; two of them (formed into a hexagon) supported the (EX) Big Channel Girders at the top of the tower. Next, there was the (NT) Cone; four of them lifted the parachutes to the top of the tower. The early sets came with cones painted yellow, but these quickly gave way to the more common blue-painted versions. In 1942, a limited number of sets came with red cones. Finally, there was the (NU) Parachute, and each set contained four of them. Most parachutes from 1940 came with red silk, but there are examples with white silk from this period. In no case were the colors ever mixed in a set. The struts for these parachutes were made of wood.

Gilbert Co. did not produce these parachutes. The firm had discovered them in a toy known as the Para-Shooter (patented March 10, 1931, manufacturer unknown). This simple toy consisted of a green cardboard tube about ½" in diameter with a parachute in it. Blowing through the tube "shot" a parachute into the air and then it floated to the ground. I imagine Gilbert knew about the Para-Shooter and probably liked it. When he saw the Parachute Jump at the World's Fair, he put the two together and my favorite Erector model was conceived.

Some interesting changes occurred in No. 9½ in 1940. As a result of adding the parachute jump parts, a third parts can was added to the set and the packing arrangement of both the lower-level insert and the display trays was slightly altered. Also, a second label was added to the inside of the lid to promote this great new model. Placed above the large label, it measured 6½" x ¾". It stated, "Builds the Parachute Jump," in bold black letters on a yellow background.

Finally, 1940 brought another change to the inside label used on Nos. 8½ and 9½. In 1939, a small overlay label that read, "No. 9½," was pasted over the No. 8½ when the label was used in the No. 9½. The result was a label that read, "No. 9½ All Electric." Now an overlay label was used that covered all the unwanted script and read, "No. 9½ All Electric Automotive Set."

Different American Flyer O gauge locomotives were used in The Electric Train Set. Top left: No. 3315 in 1938. Top right: Copper-trimmed No. 420 in 1939. Bottom left: Nickel-trimmed No. 420 in 1940. Bottom right: No. 556 Royal Blue in 1941–42.

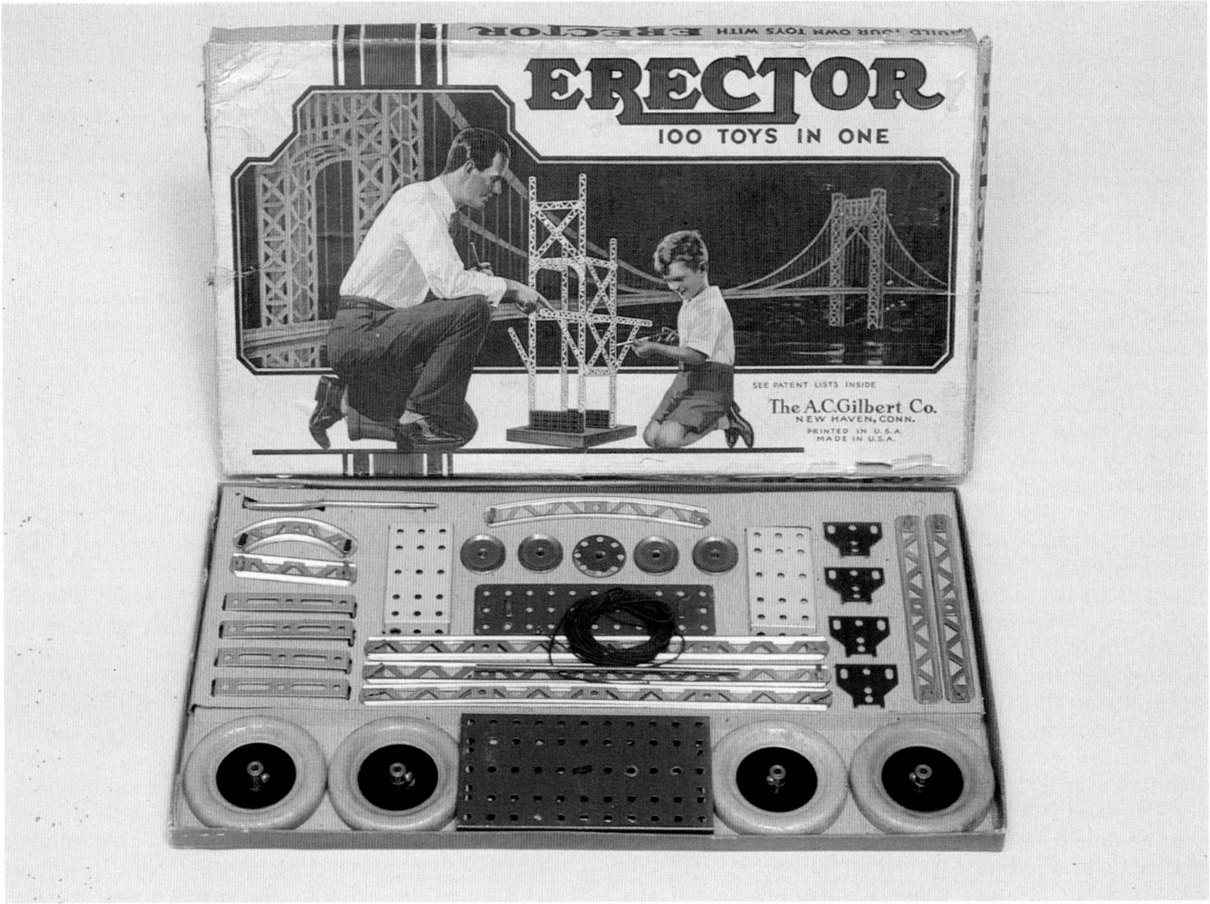

Parts in No. 3½ also differed in appearance in 1942.

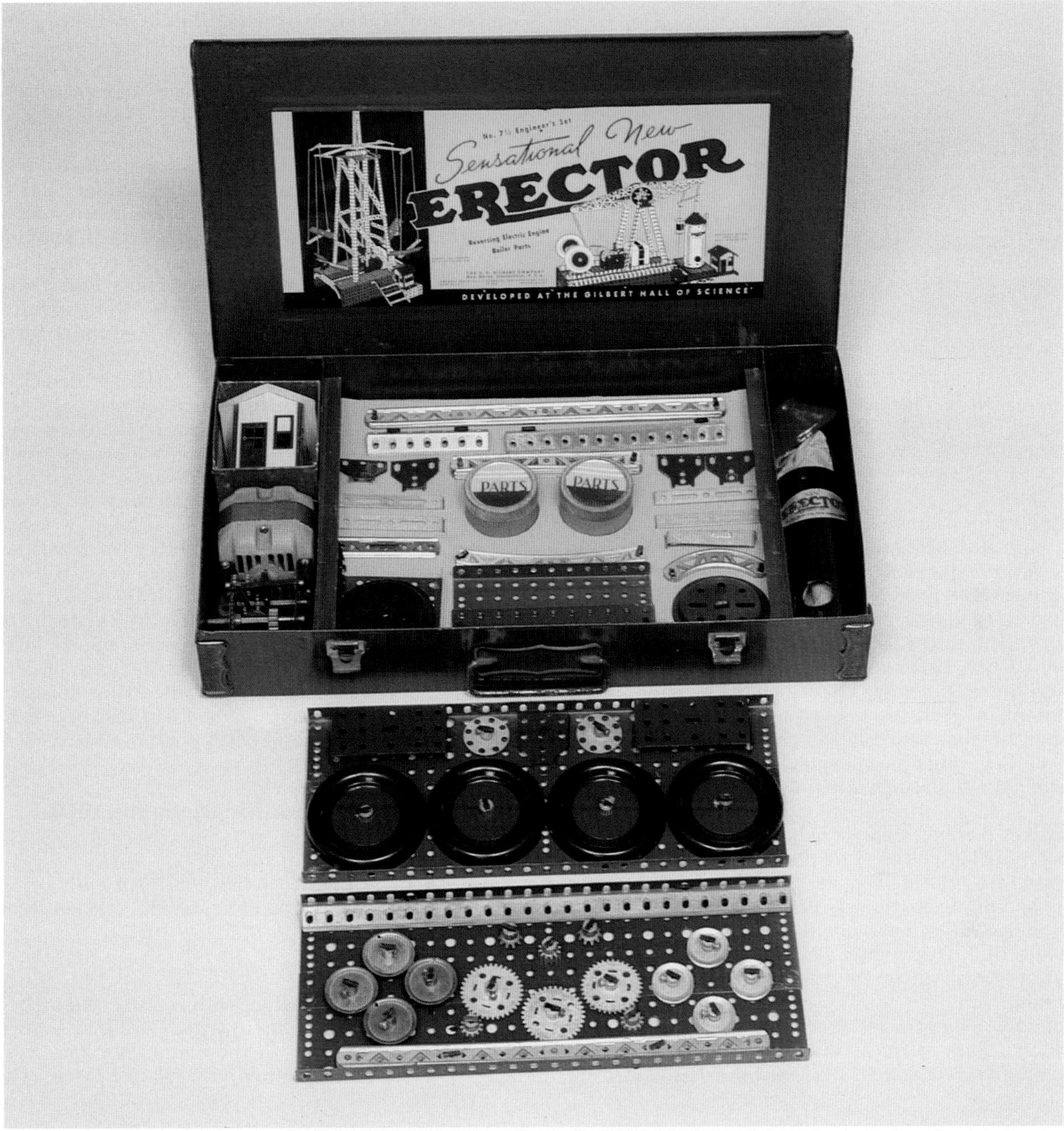

Note the zinc-plating on the pulleys and gears included in No. 7½ from 1942. These parts were mixed with brass-plated flanged wheels.

Set No. 10½, known as "The Electric Train Set," also evolved in 1940. Once again, the inside lid parts display cardboard was modified, with "World's Champion" added on the top left corner. This created a third variation of the insert.

Another key change related to the (NP) Locomotive included with No. 10½. Gilbert was still using an American Flyer no. 420 locomotive, but the plating on all the trim pieces of the 1940 version was changed from copper to nickel. By now, this engine had been dropped from the American Flyer line; in 1940, it was available only in No. 10½. This makes the nickel-trimmed no. 420 engine difficult to find. Also, Gilbert included a traction weight in these 1940 locomotives.

A notable variation occurred on the (NQ) Section of Curved Track in these sets. In 1939, each track tie had four screw holes. Now there were only two.

One last noteworthy change in 1940 had to do with the parts containers. In 1939, Gilbert produced them in three sizes. A year later, however, only two were available, as the middle-sized container (1⅜" deep) was dropped. The large, 1⅝" container was used in all the large sets, beginning with No. 6½.

The only set that was modified in 1941 was No. 10½, the Electric Train Set. This year, an American Flyer O gauge no. 556 Royal Blue locomotive was substituted for the nickel-trimmed no. 420. Gilbert's choice of this locomotive was likely a last-minute decision.

Left: The first version of the (NV) Whistle came in the large sets from 1940 and 1941. Right: The second, simpler version was used in 1942 and 1946.

According to an original contents inventory list for this 1941 set (part of the collection of the late Peter Jugle), the American Flyer O gauge no. 565 Atlantic locomotive was to be used. But it had a third rail pickup in the tender. Because Gilbert had no plans (or room in the set box) to include a tender in this set, the no. 556 Royal Blue was used instead.

Without a doubt, 1942 was a wild year at Erector Square. While there were no changes in either the Erector lineup or the contents of sets, there was vast experimentation in the platings, finishes, and colors of parts. Although some of the changes to painted parts carried over to postwar sets, the experiments in platings and finishes was most specific to 1942.

Two distinct finishes were introduced to parts that were traditionally nickel-plated: zinc-plating and a gunmetal black patina. Zinc-plating was not entirely new to Erector, as Gilbert had used zinc to plate certain parts, mainly pulleys and pierced discs, back in the mid-1920s. Zinc-plated parts have a dull, frosty, gray-white appearance. But the black patina finish given to some parts in 1942 was uniquely new.

Interestingly, not all the affected parts were zinc-plated or finished with a black patina all the time. Nickel-plated parts were also produced for sets in 1942, and finishes were even mixed within a particular set. But all identical parts always had the same finish. For example, in a given set, all the (A) 2½" Girders might have been plated with zinc, and the (B) 5½" girders may have been plated with nickel. But there were no sets with half the (A) 2½" Girders plated in zinc and half plated in nickel.

Still other noteworthy modifications occurred in 1942. The (P13) Pinion Gear ⅛" and the (P13B) Pinion Gear 7⁄32" were made of white metal instead of brass so they matched the miter gears, which had been made of white metal since the 1920s. The (AM) Special Pulleys were replaced with brass (AQ) Sheave Pulleys, which were reintroduced after a ten-year absence. The (MN) Base Plates were again produced with the duplex hole configuration. And the axles were finished in black instead of gray.

Gilbert redesigned the (NV) Whistle for a short period in 1942. The new design was much simpler, with the sound produced by a strip of steel contacting the revolving gear. In the original design, a thin brass diaphragm produced the sound. This new whistle was less costly to produce but the result was clearly less than satisfactory as it was quickly shelved. Curiously, these modified whistles, which are quite scarce always seem to show up with a black patina finish.

There was also a significant change in the construction of the box for No. 9½. Since this 22" x 13" x 3" container was introduced in 1934, it used three hinges to secure the lid at the back and a jointed strap on each side to hold the lid upright when the box was open. Now a hinge on each side of the box brought the same results. This design was not entirely new; the same method of construction had been used on the small metal boxes shortly after their introduction in 1933.

Erector System Modifications for 1940

I. New Parts

(NS) 41 Hole Strip, formed
(NT) Cone, painted yellow (early) or blue
(NU) Parachute, red or white silk, wooden struts
(NV) Whistle

II. Modified Parts

(A49) Electric Engine, with screw holes tapped on the rear motor housing to attach whistle. Two different decals were used on the motor core: one with all-red lettering and the other with red and black lettering

SETS IN THE ERECTOR SYSTEM 1936–42

	Box Size	1936–37	1938–39	1940–42
Cardboard Box Sets		No. 1½	No. 1½	No. 1½
		No. 2½	No. 2½	No. 2½
		No. 3½	No. 3½	No. 3½
		Nos. 5 and 5A	No. 4½	No. 4½
Metal Box Sets	16" x 8" x 3"	No. 5½, red	No. 6½, red	No. 6½, red
	18" x 10" x 3"	No. 7½, royal blue	No. 7½ royal blue	No. 7½, royal blue
	20" x 12" x 3"	No. 8½, red	No. 8½, red	No. 8½, red
	22" x 13" x 3"	No. 9½, royal blue	No. 9½, royal blue	No. 9½, royal blue[2]
	24" x 14" x 4"	No. 10½, blue[1]	No. 10½, royal blue	No. 10½, royal blue[2]

1. Powder blue in 1936; royal blue in 1937.
2. Parachute Jump parts added.

(MJ) Electro Magnet, smaller and more authentic, painted red
(NP) Locomotive, nickel-trimmed and not copper American Flyer O gauge no. 420
(NQ) Section of Curved Track, two screw holes in the ties instead of four

III. Eliminated Parts
( ) 1⅜" Parts Container

Erector System Modifications for 1941

I. Modified Parts
(NP) Locomotive, American Flyer O gauge no. 556 Royal Blue substituted for nickel-trimmed no. 420

II. Parts with Noteworthy Colors or Finishes
(T) Boiler, painted black or nickel-plated
(MH) Large 3" Disc Wheel, black-painted tire and red-painted hubcap or nickel-plated tire and red-painted hubcap

Erector System Modifications for 1942

I. Reintroduced Parts
(AQ) Sheave Pulley, brass

II. Modified Parts
(P13) 12 Tooth Pinion Gear, ½", made of white metal instead of brass
(P13B) 12 tooth Pinion Gear, 7/32", made of white metal instead of brass
(P57D) 6" Axle, finished in black instead of gray
(P57E) 8" Axle, finished in black instead of gray
(P57F) 12" Axle, finished in black instead of gray
(AS) 2⅞" Axle, finished in black instead of gray
(AT) 4" Axle, finished in black instead of gray
(CY) 5" Axle, finished in black instead of gray
(CZ) 7" Axle, finished in black instead of gray
(MN) 12" Base Plate, duplex hole arrangement replaced nonduplex pattern
(NV) Whistle, temporarily redesigned

III. Eliminated Parts
(AM) Special Pulley

IV. Parts Plated with Nickel or Zinc
All (regular) Girders: (A), (B), (C), (D), (E)
All strips: (F), (G), (H), (I), (J), (O)
Angle Girders: (BE), (DP), (MO)
All Big Channel Girders: (EX), (EY), (EZ)
(DK) Flat Spring
(DO) Steering Wheel
(MA) Radiator
(NJ) Battery Holder
(NK) Ratchet
(NV) Whistle

V. Parts Plated with Brass or Zinc
(P7) ⅞" Pulley
(P7A) 1⅛" Pulley
(Z) Flanged Wheel, 15/16" diameter
(CJ) 36 Tooth Gear

VI. Parts Plated with Nickel or Finished with a Black Patina
(N) Long Double Angle
(MB) 18½" Angle Girder
(MW) Nut Holder
(NV) Whistle
( ) Lids for Parts Cans
( ) Paper clips for fastening parts in place; a black patina finish was also used in place of brass-plating on corner trim plates for the metal boxes on some sets

VII. Parts Painted in New Colors
All (regular) Girders: (A), (B), (C), (D), and (E), painted yellow or plated with nickel or zinc
(A49) Electric Engine, motor housing painted gray or silver-blue
(BN) Regular Turret Plate, painted black or red
(CR) Special Turret Plate, painted black or blue
(CS) Wheel Segment, painted blue or red
(DP) 12" Angle Girder, painted blue or yellow or plated with nickel or zinc
(MB) 18½" Angle Girder, painted blue or finished with black patina
(MC) Base Plate 1" x 2½", painted green, red, or yellow
(ME) Base Plate 1" x 4", painted blue or red
(MF) Base Plate 1" x 5", painted blue or red
(MH) Large 3" Disc Wheel, black-painted tire and red-painted hubcap, zinc-plated tire and black-painted hubcap, or nickel-plated tire and red-painted hubcap
(NT) Cone, painted blue or red

Listings of 1940, 1941, and 1942 Erector Sets

	Gd	VG	Exc	Inv	Org

NO. 1½ — The Dandy Beginner's Set
Came in a cardboard box 13½" x 10¼" x ¾"; sold for $1.00 in 1940, 1941, and 1942.

	Gd	VG	Exc	Inv	Org
NO. 1½	30	40	70	+15	+20

NO. 2½ — The Apprentice Set
Featured the (MH) Disc Wheels. Came in a cardboard box 18¼" x 10¼" x ¾"; sold for $2.50 in 1940 and $2.75 in 1941 and 1942.

	Gd	VG	Exc	Inv	Org
NO. 2½	35	50	80	+20	+25

NO. 3½ — The Intermediate Set
Featured the (MN) Base Plates and angle girders. Came in a cardboard box 18¼" x 10¼" x 1¼"; two-layer set with removable cardboard parts display tray; sold for $3.50 in 1940 and $3.75 in 1941 and 1942.

	Gd	VG	Exc	Inv	Org
NO. 3½	40	55	90	+25	+30

NO. 4½ — The Famous No. 4½
Featured the (A48) Mechanical Motor and (MN) 12" Base Plates, and (MX) House and built truck with (A48); model pictured on inside lid label. Came in a cardboard box 18¼" x 10¼" x 2½" with a hinged lid; two-layer set with removable cardboard parts display tray; sold for $5.00 in 1940, 1941, and 1942.

	Gd	VG	Exc	Inv	Org
NO. 4½	80	120	200	+40	+50

NO. 6½ — The Sensational No. 6½
Featured the (A49) Electric Engine without gearbox and built Airplane Ride. Came in a red metal box 16" x 8" x 3"; two-layer set with removable parts display tray; sold for $7.95 in 1940 and $8.50 in 1941 and 1942.

	Gd	VG	Exc	Inv	Org
NO. 6½	40	60	100	+20	+25

1940–42 CONTENTS LIST

Set No.		1½	2½	3½	4½	6½	7½	8½	9½	10½[1]
P7	⅞" PULLEY	4	4	4	4	4	4	0	0	0
P7A	1⅛" PULLEY	0	0	0	0	0	0	4	4	4
P12	CROWN GEAR	0	0	0	0	0	0	0	1	1
P13	12 TOOTH PINION GEAR, ⅛"	0	0	0	0	1	2	2	2	2
P13B	12 TOOTH PINION GEAR, 7⁄32"	0	0	0	0	0	1	1	1	1
P15	COUPLING	0	0	0	1	1	1	2	2	2
P20	5 HOLE STRIP—FORMED	0	0	0	0	0	2	2	8	8
P24	CRANK	1	1	1	1	1	1	1	1	1
P33	SMALL SCREW DRIVER	1	1	1	1	1	1	1	1	1
P34	HANK OF STRING	0	1	1	1	1	1	1	1	1
P37	COLLAR	2	4	4	5	6	7	9	18	18
P48	MITRE GEAR	0	0	0	0	2	2	2	2	2
P57A	2⅛" AXLE	1	1	1	1	1	1	1	2	8
P57D	6" AXLE	0	1	2	0	0	0	0	0	2
P57E	8" AXLE	0	0	0	0	0	0	0	2	2
P57F	12" AXLE	0	0	0	0	0	0	1	2	2
P79	CAR TRUCK	4	4	4	4	4	4	4	4	4
A	2½" GIRDER	4	4	4	4	4	4	4	4	4
B	5" GIRDER	4	4	4	8	12	12	12	12	12
C	10" GIRDER	4	8	8	8	14	14	36	36	36
D	2½" CURVED GIRDER	4	4	4	4	4	4	4	4	4
E	5" CURVED GIRDER	0	2	2	2	4	4	26	26	26
F	5 HOLE STRIP	0	0	0	2	2	2	2	2	16
G	7 HOLE STRIP	0	0	0	2	2	2	2	2	8
H	11 HOLE STRIP	0	0	0	4	4	4	4	4	7
I	21 HOLE STRIP	0	0	0	2	2	2	4	18	18
J	41 HOLE STRIP	0	0	0	0	0	0	2	2	4
M	SMALL DOUBLE ANGLE	0	0	0	0	0	2	6	6	8
N	LONG DOUBLE ANGLE	2	4	4	4	4	4	4	4	4
O	PAWL	0	0	0	0	1	2	2	6	6
T	BOILER	0	0	0	0	0	1	1	2	2
U	BOILER TOP	0	0	0	0	0	1	1	1	1
W	STACK	0	0	0	0	0	3	3	3	3
Z	FLANGED WHEEL 15⁄16" DIA	0	0	0	0	0	4	4	4	4
AA	ECCENTRIC CRANK	0	0	0	0	0	0	0	6	6
AE	SPIRAL SPRING	0	0	0	0	0	0	0	0	2
AF	SMALL HOOK	1	1	1	1	1	1	1	1	1
AJ	PAPER ERECTOR FLAG	0	0	0	1	1	1	1	1	1
AM	SPECIAL PULLEY (1940–1941)	0	0	0	0	0	0	0	4	4
AQ	SHEAVE PULLEY (1942)	0	0	0	0	0	0	0	4	4
AS	2⅞" AXLE	0	0	0	2	2	3	3	4	4
AT	4" AXLE	2	2	2	2	2	2	2	2	2
BE	6" ANGLE GIRDER	0	0	4	4	4	4	4	4	4
BH	SOLID COLLAR	0	0	0	0	0	0	0	2	2
BL	SMALL WASHER	8	12	12	12	12	12	12	14	17
BN	REGULAR TURRET PLATE	0	0	0	2	2	4	4	4	4
BT	PIERCED DISC	1	1	1	1	2	2	4	4	4
BY	11 HOLE FIBRE STRIP	0	0	0	0	0	0	1	1	1
CA	SIGNAL ARM	0	0	0	0	0	0	0	2	2
CH	RIGHT ANGLE	8	12	12	14	14	14	30	42	42
CJ	36 TOOTH GEAR	0	0	0	0	2	3	3	3	3
CR	SPECIAL TURRET PLATE WITH HUB	0	0	0	0	0	0	0	2	2
CS	WHEEL SEGMENT	0	0	0	0	0	0	0	8	8
CY	5" AXLE	0	2	2	0	0	0	0	0	0
CZ	7" AXLE	0	0	0	2	2	2	3	3	3
DB	MOTOR PULLEY	0	0	0	1	1	1	1	1	1
DE	STEERING COLUMN	0	0	0	0	0	0	0	1	1
DK	FLAT SPRING	0	0	0	0	0	0	0	4	4

1940–42 CONTENTS LIST

SSet No.		1½	2½	3½	4½	6½	7½	8½	9½	10½[1]
DO	STEERING WHEEL WITH HUB	0	0	0	0	0	0	0	1	1
DP	12" ANGLE GIRDER	0	0	4	4	4	4	4	4	4
DS	COTTER PIN	0	0	0	0	0	0	0	1	1
EI	STD. GEAR BOX SIDE PLATE	0	0	0	0	2	2	2	2	2
EX	BIG CHANNEL GIRDER 12"	0	0	0	0	0	0	0	8	8
EY	BIG CHANNEL GIRDER 6"	0	0	0	0	0	0	0	4	4
EZ	BIG CHAN. GIRDER CURVED 6"	0	0	0	0	0	0	0	2	2
FA	1¾" x 8-32 SCREW	0	0	0	0	0	0	0	12	12
FD	HINGED LOOP	0	0	0	0	0	0	0	2	2
LX	STEERING COLUMN BRACKET	0	0	0	0	0	0	0	1	1
MA	RADIATOR	0	0	0	0	0	0	0	1	1
MB	18½" ANGLE GIRDER	0	0	0	0	0	0	0	2	2
MC	BASE PLATE 1" x 2½"	2	2	2	2	2	2	8	8	8
MD	BASE PLATE 2½" x 5"	1	1	1	1	1	1	4	4	4
ME	BASE PLATE 1" x 4"	0	0	0	0	0	0	0	4	4
MF	BASE PLATE 1" x 5"	2	2	4	4	4	4	8	9	12
MG	RADIATOR HOOD	0	0	0	0	0	0	0	1	1
MH	LARGE 3" DISC WHEEL	0	4	4	4	4	4	4	4	4
MI	FRONT AXLE UNIT	0	0	0	0	0	0	0	1	1
MJ	ELECTRO MAGNET WITH CORD	0	0	0	0	0	0	1	1	1
MM	WRENCH	0	0	0	1	1	1	1	1	1
MN	12" BASE PLATE	0	0	2	2	4	4	6	6	6
MO	3" ANGLE GIRDER	0	0	4	4	4	4	4	4	4
MV	FLAT CAR TRUCK	0	0	0	0	0	2	4	4	4
MW	NUT HOLDER	0	0	0	1	1	1	1	1	1
MX	HOUSE	0	0	0	1	1	1	1	1	1
MY	2½" x 2½" BASE PLATE	0	0	0	1	1	1	1	1	1
MZ	BEARING BLOCK	0	0	0	0	1	1	1	1	1
NH	LAMP SOCKET UNIT	0	0	0	0	0	0	2	2	2
NI	BULB, 1½ VOLT	0	0	0	0	0	0	2	2	2
NJ	BATTERY HOLDER	0	0	0	0	0	0	1	1	1
NK	RATCHET	0	0	0	0	0	2	2	2	2
NL	BOLSTER BRACKET	0	0	0	0	0	0	0	0	4
NM	10" x 2" FLANGED PLATE	0	0	0	0	0	0	0	0	2
NN	1" x 2" FLANGED PLATE	0	0	0	0	0	0	0	0	5
NO	FLANGED WHEEL, ¾" DIA.	0	0	0	0	0	0	0	0	16
NP	LOCOMOTIVE—O GAUGE	0	0	0	0	0	0	0	0	1
NQ	SECTION OF CURVED TRACK	0	0	0	0	0	0	0	0	12
NR	TRACK TERMINAL	0	0	0	0	0	0	0	0	1
NS	41 HOLE STRIP FORMED	0	0	0	0	0	0	0	2	2
NT	CONE	0	0	0	0	0	0	0	4	4
NU	PARACHUTE	0	0	0	0	0	0	0	4	4
NV	WHISTLE	0	0	0	0	0	0	1	1	1
A48	MECHANICAL MOTOR	0	0	0	1	0	0	0	0	1
K48	KEY FOR MECH. MOTOR	0	0	0	1	0	0	0	0	1
A49	ELECTRIC ENGINE	0	0	0	0	1	1	1	1	1
NO. 5	TRANSFORMER	0	0	0	0	0	0	0	0	1
N21	8-32 SQUARE NUT	25	45	60	88	93	93	169	254	350
S51	¼" x 8-32 SCREW	21	35	50	80	84	84	162	206	255
S52	½" x 8-32 SCREW	0	0	0	0	4	4	4	4	4
S57	1⅜" x 8-32 SCREW	0	0	0	0	0	4	4	4	4
S62	⅞" x 8-32 SCREW	3	6	6	8	8	8	18	20	20

1. Set No. 10½ also contained an offset wrench.

ERECTOR SEPARATE PARTS PRICES

KINDLY ENCLOSE CHECK, MONEY ORDER OR STAMPS WITH YOUR ORDER FOR PARTS

THE A. C. GILBERT CO., NEW HAVEN, CONN., U. S. A.

Trade No.	Name of Part	Page	Price
*N21	8-32 Square Nut	3	.05 doz.
P7	Small Wheel, 7/8" Dia.	2	.10 ea.
P7A	Small Wheel, 1 1/8" Dia.	2	.10 ea.
P12	Crown Gear	2	.10 ea.
P13	12-Tooth Pinion Gear, 1/8"	2	.10 ea.
P13B	12-Tooth Pinion Gear, 7/32"	2	.10 ea.
P14	Worm Gear	2	.20 ea.
P15	Coupling	2	.10 ea.
P20	Five Hole Strip—formed	2	.05 ea.
P24	Crank	2	.10 ea.
P33	Small Screw Driver	3	.05 ea.
P34	Hank of String	3	.05 ea.
P37	Collar	2	.25 doz.
P48	Mitre Gear	2	.20 ea.
P49	18-Tooth Gear	2	.15 ea.
P50	72-Tooth Gear	2	.30 ea.
P52	Ladder Chain	3	.15/ft
P51	Electric Engine Reversing 110v. A.C. or D.C.	3	3.95 ea.
No. 5	Transformer	3	2.50 ea.
P56G	Motor, 110v. A.C. or D.C.	3	2.95 ea.
P58	Motor, 6-14 volts	3	1.00 ea.
P59	Reverse Base (for P58 only)	3	.75 ea.
A48	Mechanical Motor	3	1.00 ea.
K48	Mechanical Motor Key	3	.20 ea.
A49	Electric Engine, 110v. A.C. only	3	3.95 ea.
A49B	Electric Engine Conversion Unit	3	1.25 ea.
P57A	2 1/8" Axle	2	.02 ea.
P57D	6" Axle	2	.06 ea.
P57E	8" Axle	2	.08 ea.
P57F	12" Axle	2	.12 ea.
P79	Car Truck	2	.05 ea.
*S11	Set Srew	3	.05 doz.
*S51	1/4"x8-32 Screw	3	.05 doz.
*S52	1/2"x8-32 Screw	3	.10 doz.
*S57	1 3/8"x8-32 Screw	3	.15 doz.
*S62	7/8"x8-32 Screw	3	.10 doz.
*FA	1 3/4"x8-32 Screw	3	.15 doz.
A	2 1/2" Girder	2	.20 doz.
B	5" Girder	2	.35 doz.
C	10" Girder	2	.50 doz.
D	2 1/2" Curved Girder	2	.25 doz.
E	5" Curved Girder	2	.40 doz.
F	5 Hole Strip	2	.10 doz.
G	7 Hole Strip	2	.10 doz.
H	11 Hole Strip	2	.15 doz.
I	21 Hole Strip	2	.20 doz.
J	41 Hole Strip	2	.30 doz.
K	11 Hole Strip Bracket	2	.35 doz.
M	Small Double Angle	2	.25 doz.
N	Long Double Angle	2	.05 ea.
O	Pawl	2	.05 ea.
S	Large Base Plate—21 holes	2	.40 ea.
T	Boiler	3	.25 ea.
U	Boiler Top	3	.20 ea.

Trade No.	Name of Part	Page	Price
W	Stack	3	.05 ea.
Z	Flanged Wheel, 15/16" Dia.	2	.15 ea.
AA	Eccentric Crank	2	.10 ea.
AC	Universal Bracket	2	.10 ea.
AE	Spiral Spring	3	.05 ea.
AF	Small Hook	2	.15 doz.
AM	Special Pulley—Metal	2	.05 ea.
AQ	Sheave Pulley	2	.05 ea.
AS	2 7/8" Axle Rod	2	.03 ea.
AT	4" Axle Rod	2	.04 ea.
AX	19 3/4" Axle Rod	2	.20 ea.
BE	6" Angle Girder	2	.50 doz.
BH	Solid Collar	2	2 for .05
BL	Small Washer	2	.05 doz.
BN	Regular Turret Plate	3	.15 ea.
BT	Pierced Disc	2	.10 ea.
BY	11-Hole Fibre Strip	2	.05 ea.
CA	Signal Arm	3	.10 ea.
CH	Right Angle	2	.10 doz.
CJ	36-Tooth Gear	2	.20 ea.
CR	Special Turret plate with hub	3	.15 ea.
CS	Wheel Segment	3	.15 ea.
CX	1" Axle Rod	2	.01 ea.
CY	5" Axle Rod	2	.05 ea.
CZ	7" Axle Rod	2	.07 ea.
DA	10" Axle Rod	2	.10 ea.
DB	Motor Pulley	2	.10 ea.
DE	Steering Column	3	.10 ea.
DK	Flat Spring	3	.10 ea.
DO	Steering Wheel with Hub	2	.15 ea.
DP	12" Angle Girder	2	6 for .50
DS	Cotter Pin	3	.05 doz.
DT	1-Hole Set Screw Coupling	2	2 for .15
DZ	Tackle Block	2	.15 ea.
EH	Gear Box Bracket	2	.05 ea.
EI	Standard Gear Box Side Pl.	2	.15 ea.
EJ	Gear Box Base	2	.20 ea.
EX	Big Channel Girder 12"	2	6 for .50
EY	Big Channel Girder 6"	2	.05 ea.
EZ	6" Curved B. C. Girder	2	.05 ea.
FD	Hinged Loop	2	2 for .05
GV	Thin Disc Wheel Nickel Rim	2	.10 ea.
GW	Thin Disc Wheel—Red	2	.10 ea.
LV	3" Disc Wheel, red	2	.20 ea.
LX	Steering Column Bracket	3	.05 ea.
MA	Radiator	3	.15 ea.
MB	18 1/2" Angle Girder	2	.15 ea.
MC	Base Plate 1"x2 1/2"	2	.05 ea.
MD	Base Plate 2 1/2"x5"	2	.10 ea.
ME	Flat Plate 1"x4"	2	.05 ea.

Trade No.	Name of Part	Page	Price
MF	Flat Plate 1"x5"	2	.05 ea.
MG	Radiator Hood	3	.10 ea.
MH	3" Disc Wheel, Nickel Rim	2	.25 ea.
MI	Front Axle Unit	3	.25 ea.
MJ	Electro Magnet with Cord	3	.60 ea.
MM	Wrench	3	.05 ea.
MN	12" Base Plate	2	.40 ea.
MO	3" Angle Girder	2	.30 doz.
MP	24-Tooth Gear	2	.20 ea.
MR	Drum with Gear	2	.35 ea.
MS	Compression Spring	3	.05 ea.
MV	Flat Car Truck	2	.05 ea.
MW	Nut Holder	3	.10 ea.
MX	House	3	.35 ea.
MY	2 1/2"x2 1/2" Base Plate	2	.05 ea.
MZ	Bearing Block	2	.10 ea.
NH	Lamp Socket Unit	3	.15 ea.
NI	Bulb—1 1/2 Volt	3	.05 ea.
NJ	Battery Holder	3	.15 ea.
NK	Ratchet	2	.05 ea.
NL	Bolster Bracket	2	2 for .05
NM	10"x2" Flange Plate	2	.40 ea.
NN	1"x2" Flange Plate	2	.05 ea.
NO	Flanged Wheel, 3/4" Dia.	2	.15 ea.
NP	Locomotive—O Gauge	3	8.50 ea.
NQ	Section of Curved Track—O Gauge—(12 Sections per circle)	3	.20 ea.
NR	Track Terminal	3	.20 ea.
NS	41-Hole Strip—formed	2	.05 ea.
NT	Cone	3	.10 ea.
NU	Parachute	3	.25 ea.
NV	Whistle (Note—P13 gear required.)	3	.75 ea.

ERECTOR HOW TO MAKE 'EM BOOKS

Same as copy included in sets.

No. 1	Erector How to Make 'Em Book	.15 ea.
No. 3	Erector How to Make 'Em Book	.15 ea.
No. 4	Erector How to Make 'Em Book	.25 ea.
No. 6	Erector How to Make 'Em Book	.25 ea.
No. 7	Erector How to Make 'Em Book	.25 ea.
No. 8	Erector How to Make 'Em Book	.25 ea.
No. 9	Erector How to Make 'Em Book	.35 ea.

NOTE

*N21 Nut used with screws S51, S52, S62, S57, FA

*S11 Set Screw used with pulleys, couplings, etc.

HOW TO MAKE 'EM BOOKS
Showing features in 9 big sets

Books

No. 1½ DANDY BEGINNER'S SET. Builds battleship, wagon, trucks, jib crane, etc. .15 ea.

No. 2½ THE APPRENTICE SET. With red wheels, etc. Builds ferris wheel, drawbridge, elevator, cranes, etc. .15 ea.

No. 3½ INTERMEDIATE SET. With new big base plates, angle girders, big wheels, etc. Builds derrick, walking beam engine, lift bridge, snow remover, trucks, etc. .15 ea.

No. 4½ THE FAMOUS NO. 4½. Powerful mechanical motor operates models. No wires, batteries or transformer necessary. Builds horizontal engine, windmill, trip hammer, trucks, etc. Miniature house for bridge tender, ticket seller, watchman, etc. .25 ea.

No. 6½ THE SENSATIONAL 6½. Induction motored electric engine with gears, pinions, pulleys, etc. Operates on 110 volts A.C. only. Builds windmill pump, lift bridge, airplane beacon, pile driver, Airplane ride, etc. .25 ea.

No. 7½ THE ENGINEER'S SET. 110 volt Electric Engine with gear shift. Operates two movements, each of which can be independently started, stopped or reversed. Boiler parts. Builds Walking Beam, Steam, Marine, Hoisting and Oscillating Engines, Compressors, Trucks, etc. .35 ea.

No. 8½ THE ALL-ELECTRIC SET. 110 volt Reversing Electric Engine, Whistle, Lifting Magnet, Electric lights illuminate models. Builds Bascule Bridge, Ferris Wheel, Oil Drilling Rig, Magnetic Cranes, Derricks, etc. .35 ea.

No. 9½ AUTOMOTIVE SET Electric engine, chassis parts, big channel girders, giant fly wheel segment, etc. Builds automobiles, trucks, giant power plant, elevator, mammoth walking beam engine, parachute jump, etc. .35 ea.

No. 10½ WORLD'S CHAMPION ELECTRIC TRAIN SET. Features completely assembled electric locomotive with circle of track. Additional equipment builds tender, freight cars, turntable and a host of other fine models including all those built with the above sets.... .35 ea.

Separate Parts Prices for early 1940

ERECTOR SEPARATE PARTS PRICES

KINDLY ENCLOSE CHECK, MONEY ORDER OR STAMPS WITH YOUR ORDER FOR PARTS

THE A. C. GILBERT CO., NEW HAVEN, CONN., U. S. A.

Trade No.	Name of Part	Page	Price
*N21	8-32 Square Nut	3	.05 doz.
P7	Small Wheel, 7/8" Dia.	2	.10 ea.
P7A	Small Wheel, 1 1/8" Dia.	2	.10 ea.
P12	Crown Gear	2	.10 ea.
P13	12-Tooth Pinion Gear, 1/8"	2	.10 ea.
P13B	12-Tooth Pinion Gear, 7/32"	2	.10 ea.
P14	Worm Gear	2	.20 ea.
P15	Coupling	2	.10 ea.
P20	Five Hole Strip—formed	2	.05 ea.
P24	Crank	2	.10 ea.
P33	Small Screw Driver	3	.05 ea.
P34	Hank of String	3	.05 ea.
P37	Collar	2	.25 doz.
P48	Mitre Gear	2	.20 ea.
P49	18-Tooth Gear	2	.15 ea.
P50	72-Tooth Gear	2	.30 ea.
P52	Ladder Chain	3	.15/ft
P51	Electric Engine Reversing 110v. A.C. or D.C.	3	3.95 ea.
No. 5	Transformer	3	2.50 ea.
P56G	Motor, 110v. A.C. or D.C.	3	2.95 ea.
P58	Motor, 6-14 volts	3	1.00 ea.
P59	Reverse Base (for P58 only)	3	.75 ea.
A48	Mechanical Motor	3	1.00 ea.
K48	Mechanical Motor Key	3	.20 ea.
P57A	2 1/8" Axle	2	.02 ea.
P57D	6" Axle	2	.06 ea.
P57E	8" Axle	2	.08 ea.
P57F	12" Axle	2	.12 ea.
P79	Car Truck	2	.05 ea.
*S11	Set Srew	3	.05 doz.
*S51	1/4"x8-32 Screw	3	.05 doz.
*S52	1/2"x8-32 Screw	3	.10 doz.
*S57	1 3/8"x8-32 Screw	3	.15 doz.
*S62	7/8"x8-32 Screw	3	.10 doz.
*FA	1 3/4"x8-32 Screw	3	.15 doz.
A	2 1/2" Girder	2	.20 doz.
B	5" Girder	2	.35 doz.
C	10" Girder	2	.50 doz.
D	2 1/2" Curved Girder	2	.25 doz.
E	5" Curved Girder	2	.40 doz.
F	5 Hole Strip	2	.10 doz.
G	7 Hole Strip	2	.10 doz.
H	11 Hole Strip	2	.15 doz.
I	21 Hole Strip	2	.20 doz.
J	41 Hole Strip	2	.30 doz.
K	11 Hole Strip Bracket	2	.35 doz.
M	Small Double Angle	2	.25 doz.
N	Long Double Angle	2	.05 ea.
O	Pawl	2	.05 ea.
S	Large Base Plate—21 holes	2	.40 ea.
T	Boiler	3	.25 ea.
U	Boiler Top	3	.20 ea.

Trade No.	Name of Part	Page	Price
W	Stack	3	.05 ea.
Z	Flanged Wheel, 15/16" Dia.	2	.15 ea.
AA	Eccentric Crank	2	.10 ea.
AC	Universal Bracket	2	.10 ea.
AE	Spiral Spring	3	.05 ea.
AF	Small Hook	2	.15 doz.
AM	Special Pulley—Metal	2	.05 ea.
AQ	Sheave Pulley	2	.05 ea.
AS	2 7/8" Axle Rod	2	.03 ea.
AT	4" Axle Rod	2	.04 ea.
AX	19 3/4" Axle Rod	2	.20 ea.
BE	6" Angle Girder	2	.50 doz.
BH	Solid Collar	2	2 for .05
BL	Small Washer	2	.05 doz.
BN	Regular Turret Plate	3	.15 ea.
BT	Pierced Disc	2	.10 ea.
BY	11-Hole Fibre Strip	2	.05 ea.
CA	Signal Arm	3	.10 ea.
CH	Right Angle	2	.10 doz.
CJ	36-Tooth Gear	2	.20 ea.
CR	Special Turret plate with hub	3	.15 ea.
CS	Wheel Segment	3	.15 ea.
CX	1" Axle Rod	2	.01 ea.
CY	5" Axle Rod	2	.05 ea.
CZ	7" Axle Rod	2	.07 ea.
DA	10" Axle Rod	2	.10 ea.
DB	Motor Pulley	2	.10 ea.
DE	Steering Column	3	.10 ea.
DK	Flat Spring	3	.10 ea.
DO	Steering Wheel with Hub	2	.15 ea.
DP	12" Angle Girder	2	6 for .50
DS	Cotter Pin	3	.05 doz.
DT	1-Hole Set Screw Coupling	2	2 for .15
DZ	Tackle Block	2	.15 ea.
EH	Gear Box Bracket	2	.05 ea.
EI	Standard Gear Box Side Pl.	2	.15 ea.
EJ	Gear Box Base	2	.20 ea.
EX	Big Channel Girder 12"	2	6 for .50
EY	Big Channel Girder 6"	2	.05 ea.
EZ	6" Curved B. C. Girder	2	.05 ea.
FD	Hinged Loop	2	2 for .05
GV	Thin Disc Wheel Nickel Rim	2	.10 ea.
GW	Thin Disc Wheel—Red	2	.10 ea.
LV	3" Disc Wheel, red	2	.20 ea.
LX	Steering Column Bracket	3	.05 ea.
MA	Radiator	3	.15 ea.
MB	18 1/2" Angle Girder	2	.15 ea.
MC	Base Plate 1"x2 1/2"	2	.05 ea.
MD	Base Plate 2 1/2"x5"	2	.10 ea.
ME	Flat Plate 1"x4"	2	.05 ea.

Trade No.	Name of Part	Page	Price
MF	Flat Plate 1"x5"	2	.05 ea.
MG	Radiator Hood	3	.10 ea.
MH	3" Disc Wheel, Nickel Rim	2	.25 ea.
MI	Front Axle Unit	3	.25 ea.
MJ	Electro Magnet with Cord	3	.60 ea.
MM	Wrench	3	.05 ea.
MN	12" Base Plate	2	.40 ea.
MO	3" Angle Girder	2	.30 doz.
MP	24-Tooth Gear	2	.20 ea.
MR	Drum with Gear	2	.35 ea.
MS	Compression Spring	3	.05 ea.
MV	Flat Car Truck	2	.05 ea.
MW	Nut Holder	3	.10 ea.
MX	House	3	.35 ea.
MY	2 1/2"x2 1/2" Base Plate	2	.05 ea.
MZ	Bearing Block	2	.10 ea.
NH	Lamp Socket Unit	3	.15 ea.
NI	Bulb—1 1/2 Volt	3	.05 ea.
NJ	Battery Holder	3	.15 ea.
NK	Ratchet	2	.05 ea.
NL	Bolster Bracket	2	2 for .05
NM	10"x2" Flange Plate	2	.40 ea.
NN	1"x2" Flange Plate	2	.05 ea.
NO	Flanged Wheel, 3/4" Dia.	2	.15 ea.
NP	Locomotive—O Gauge	3	8.50 ea.
NQ	Section of Curved Track—O Gauge—(12 Sections per circle)	3	.20 ea.
NR	Track Terminal	3	.20 ea.
NS	41-Hole Strip—formed	2	.05 ea.
NT	Cone	3	.10 ea.
NU	Parachute	3	.25 ea.
NV	Whistle (Note—P13 gear required.)	3	.75 ea.
A49	Electric Engine, gear shift 110v. A.C. only	3	$3.95 ea.
A49-A	Electric Eng., no gear shift.		3.00 ea.
A49-B	Elec. Eng., conversion unit Converts A49-A to A49.	3	1.25 ea.
A49-C	A49 E.E. with Whistle		4.50 ea.

ERECTOR HOW TO MAKE 'EM BOOKS

Same as copy included in sets.

No. 1	Erector How to Make 'Em Book	.15 ea.
No. 3	Erector How to Make 'Em Book	.15 ea.
No. 4	Erector How to Make 'Em Book	.25 ea.
No. 6	Erector How to Make 'Em Book	.25 ea.
No. 7	Erector How to Make 'Em Book	.25 ea.
No. 8	Erector How to Make 'Em Book	.25 ea.
No. 9	Erector How to Make 'Em Book	.35 ea.

NOTE

*N21 Nut used with screws S51, S52, S62, S57, FA

*S11 Set Screw used with pulleys, couplings, etc.

HOW TO MAKE 'EM BOOKS
Showing features in 9 big sets

Books

No. 1½ DANDY BEGINNER'S SET. Builds battleship, wagon, trucks, jib crane, etc. .15 ea.

No. 2½ THE APPRENTICE SET. With red wheels, etc. Builds ferris wheel, drawbridge, elevator, cranes, etc. .15 ea.

No. 3½ INTERMEDIATE SET. With new big base plates, angle girders, big wheels, etc. Builds derrick, walking beam engine, lift bridge, snow remover, trucks, etc. .15 ea.

No. 4½ THE FAMOUS NO. 4½. Powerful mechanical motor operates models. No wires, batteries or transformer necessary. Builds horizontal engine, windmill, trip hammer, trucks, etc. Miniature house for bridge tender, ticket seller, watchman, etc. .25 ea.

No. 6½ THE SENSATIONAL 6½. Induction motored electric engine with gears, pinions, pulleys, etc. Operates on 110 volts A.C. only. Builds windmill pump, lift bridge, airplane beacon, pile driver, Airplane ride, etc. .25 ea.

No. 7½ THE ENGINEER'S SET. 110 volt Electric Engine with gear shift. Operates two movements, each of which can be independently started, stopped or reversed. Boiler parts. Builds Walking Beam, Steam, Marine, Hoisting and Oscillating Engines, Compressors, Trucks, etc. .35 ea.

No. 8½ THE ALL-ELECTRIC SET. 110 volt Reversing Electric Engine, Whistle, Lifting Magnet, Electric lights illuminate models. Builds Bascule Bridge, Ferris Wheel, Oil Drilling Rig, Magnetic Cranes, Derricks, etc. .35 ea.

No. 9½ AUTOMOTIVE SET Electric engine, chassis parts, big channel girders, giant fly wheel segment, etc. Builds automobiles, trucks, giant power plant, elevator, mammoth walking beam engine, parachute jump, etc. .35 ea.

No. 10½ WORLD'S CHAMPION ELECTRIC TRAIN SET. Features completely assembled electric locomotive with circle of track. Additional equipment builds tender, freight cars, turntable and a host of other fine models including all those built with the above sets.... .35 ea.

Separate Parts Prices for late 1940

ERECTOR SEPARATE PARTS PRICES

KINDLY ENCLOSE CHECK, MONEY ORDER OR STAMPS WITH YOUR ORDER FOR PARTS

THE A. C. GILBERT CO., NEW HAVEN, CONN., U. S. A.

Trade No.	Name of Part	Page	Price
*N21	8-32 Square Nut	3	.05 doz.
P7	Small Wheel, ⅞" Dia.	2	.10 ea.
P7A	Small Wheel, 1⅛" Dia.	2	.10 ea.
P12	Crown Gear	2	.10 ea.
P13	12-Tooth Pinion Gear, ⅛"	2	.10 ea.
P13B	12-Tooth Pinion Gear, 7/32"	2	.10 ea.
P14	Worm Gear	2	.20 ea.
P15	Coupling	2	.10 ea.
P20	Five Hole Strip—formed	2	.05 ea.
P24	Crank	2	.10 ea.
P33	Small Screw Driver	3	.05 ea.
P34	Hank of String	3	.05 ea.
P37	Collar	2	.25 doz.
P48	Mitre Gear	2	.20 ea.
P49	18-Tooth Gear	2	.15 ea.
P52	Ladder Chain	3	.15/ft
P51	Electric Engine Reversing 110v. A.C. or D.C.	3	3.95 ea.
No. 5	Transformer	3	2.50 ea.
P56G	Motor, 110v. A.C. or D.C.	3	2.95 ea.
P58	Motor, 6-14 volts	3	1.00 ea.
P59	Reverse Base (for P58 only)	3	.75 ea.
A48	Mechanical Motor	3	1.00 ea.
K48	Mechanical Motor Key	3	.20 ea.
P57A	2⅛" Axle	2	.02 ea.
P57D	6" Axle	2	.06 ea.
P57E	8" Axle	2	.08 ea.
P57F	12" Axle	2	.12 ea.
P79	Car Truck	2	.05 ea.
*S11	Set Srew	3	.05 doz.
*S51	¼"x8-32 Screw	3	.05 doz.
*S52	½"x8-32 Screw	3	.10 doz.
*S57	1⅛"x8-32 Screw	3	.15 doz.
*S62	⅞"x8-32 Screw	3	.10 doz.
*FA	1¼"x8-32 Screw	3	.15 doz.
A	2½" Girder	2	.20 doz.
B	5" Girder	2	.35 doz.
C	10" Girder	2	.50 doz.
D	2½" Curved Girder	2	.25 doz.
E	5" Curved Girder	2	.40 doz.
F	5 Hole Strip	2	.10 doz.
G	7 Hole Strip	2	.10 doz.
H	11 Hole Strip	2	.15 doz.
I	21 Hole Strip	2	.20 doz.
J	41 Hole Strip	2	.30 doz.
K	11 Hole Strip Bracket	2	.35 doz.
M	Small Double Angle	2	.25 doz.
N	Long Double Angle	2	.05 ea.
O	Pawl	2	.05 ea.
S	Large Base Plate—21 holes	2	.40 ea.
T	Boiler	3	.25 ea.
U	Boiler Top	3	.20 ea.

Trade No.	Name of Part	Page	Price
W	Stack	3	.05 ea.
Z	Flanged Wheel, 15/16" Dia.	2	.15 ea.
AA	Eccentric Crank	2	.10 ea.
AC	Universal Bracket	2	.10 ea.
AE	Spiral Spring	3	.05 ea.
AF	Small Hook	2	.15 doz.
AM	Special Pulley—Metal	2	.05 ea.
AQ	Sheave Pulley	2	.05 ea.
AS	2⅞" Axle Rod	2	.03 ea.
AT	4" Axle Rod	2	.04 ea.
AX	19¾" Axle Rod	2	.20 ea.
BE	6" Angle Girder	2	.50 doz.
BH	Solid Collar	2	2 for .05
BL	Small Washer	2	.05 doz.
BN	Regular Turret Plate	3	.15 ea.
BT	Pierced Disc	2	.10 ea.
BY	11-Hole Fibre Strip	2	.05 ea.
CA	Signal Arm	3	.10 ea.
CH	Right Angle	2	.10 doz.
CJ	36-Tooth Gear	2	.20 ea.
CR	Special Turret plate with hub	3	.15 ea.
CS	Wheel Segment	3	.15 ea.
CX	1" Axle Rod	2	.01 ea.
CY	5" Axle Rod	2	.05 ea.
CZ	7" Axle Rod	2	.07 ea.
DA	10" Axle Rod	2	.10 ea.
DB	Motor Pulley	2	.10 ea.
DE	Steering Column	3	.10 ea.
DK	Flat Spring	3	.10 ea.
DO	Steering Wheel with Hub	2	.15 ea.
DP	12" Angle Girder	2	6 for .50
DS	Cotter Pin	3	.05 doz.
DT	1-Hole Set Screw Coupling	2	2 for .15
DZ	Tackle Block	2	.15 ea.
EH	Gear Box Bracket	2	.05 ea.
EI	Standard Gear Box Side Pl.	2	.15 ea.
EJ	Gear Box Base	2	.20 ea.
EX	Big Channel Girder 12"	2	6 for .50
EY	Big Channel Girder 6"	2	.05 ea.
EZ	6" Curved B. C. Girder	2	.05 ea.
FD	Hinged Loop	2	2 for .05
GV	Thin Disc Wheel Nickel Rim	2	.10 ea.
GW	Thin Disc Wheel—Red	2	.10 ea.
LV	3" Disc Wheel, red	2	.20 ea.
LX	Steering Column Bracket	3	.05 ea.
MA	Radiator	3	.15 ea.
MB	18½" Angle Girder	2	.15 ea.
MC	Base Plate 1"x2½"	2	.05 ea.
MD	Base Plate 2½"x5"	2	.10 ea.
ME	Flat Plate 1"x4"	2	.05 ea.

Trade No.	Name of Part	Page	Price
MF	Flat Plate 1"x5"	2	.05 ea.
MG	Radiator Hood	3	.10 ea.
MH	3" Disc Wheel, Nickel Rim	2	.25 ea.
MI	Front Axle Unit	3	.25 ea.
MJ	Electro Magnet with Cord	3	.60 ea.
MM	Wrench	3	.05 ea.
MN	12" Base Plate	2	.40 ea.
MO	3" Angle Girder	2	.30 doz.
MR	Drum with Gear	2	.35 ea.
MS	Compression Spring	3	.05 ea.
MV	Flat Car Truck	2	.05 ea.
MW	Nut Holder	3	.10 ea.
MX	House	3	.35 ea.
MY	2½"x2½" Base Plate	2	.05 ea.
MZ	Bearing Block	2	.10 ea.
NH	Lamp Socket Unit	3	.15 ea.
NI	Bulb—1½ Volt	3	.05 ea.
NJ	Battery Holder	3	.15 ea.
NK	Ratchet	2	.05 ea.
NL	Bolster Bracket	2	2 for .05
NM	10"x2" Flange Plate	2	.40 ea.
NN	1"x2" Flange Plate	2	.05 ea.
NO	Flanged Wheel, ¾" Dia.	2	.15 ea.
NP	Locomotive—O Gauge	3	8.50 ea.
NQ	Section of Curved Track—O Gauge—(12 Sections per circle)	3	.20 ea.
NR	Track Terminal	3	.20 ea.
NS	41-Hole Strip—formed	2	.05 ea.
NT	Cone	3	.10 ea.
NU	Parachute	3	.25 ea.
NV	Whistle (Note—P13 gear required.)	3	.75 ea.
A49	Electric Engine, gear shift 110v. A.C. only	3	$3.95 ea.
A49-A	Electric Eng., no gear shift.		3.00 ea.
A49-B	Elec. Eng., conversion unit Converts A49-A to A49.	3	1.25 ea.
A49-C	A49 E.E. with Whistle		4.50 ea.

ERECTOR HOW TO MAKE 'EM BOOKS

Same as copy included in sets.

No. 1	Erector How to Make 'Em Book	.15 ea.
No. 3	Erector How to Make 'Em Book	.15 ea.
No. 4	Erector How to Make 'Em Book	.25 ea.
No. 6	Erector How to Make 'Em Book	.25 ea.
No. 7	Erector How to Make 'Em Book	.25 ea.
No. 8	Erector How to Make 'Em Book	.25 ea.
No. 9	Erector How to Make 'Em Book	.35 ea.

NOTE

*N21 Nut used with screws S51, S52, S62, S57, FA
*S11 Set Screw used with pulleys, couplings, etc.

HOW TO MAKE 'EM BOOKS
Showing features in 9 big sets

Books

No. 1½ DANDY BEGINNER'S SET. Builds battleship, wagon, trucks, jib crane, etc. .15 ea.

No. 2½ THE APPRENTICE SET. With red wheels, etc. Builds ferris wheel, drawbridge, elevator, cranes, etc. .15 ea.

No. 3½ INTERMEDIATE SET. With new big base plates, angle girders, big wheels, etc. Builds derrick, walking beam engine, lift bridge, snow remover, trucks, etc. .15 ea.

No. 4½ THE FAMOUS NO. 4½. Powerful mechanical motor operates models. No wires, batteries or transformer necessary. Builds horizontal engine, windmill, trip hammer, trucks, etc. Miniature house for bridge tender, ticket seller, watchman, etc. .25 ea.

No. 6½ THE SENSATIONAL 6½. Induction motored electric engine with gears, pinions, pulleys, etc. Operates on 110 volts A.C. only. Builds windmill pump, lift bridge, airplane beacon, pile driver, Airplane ride, etc. .25 ea.

No. 7½ THE ENGINEER'S SET. 110 volt Electric Engine with gear shift. Operates two movements, each of which can be independently started, stopped or reversed. Boiler parts. Builds Walking Beam, Steam, Marine, Hoisting and Oscillating Engines, Compressors, Trucks, etc. .35 ea.

No. 8½ THE ALL-ELECTRIC SET. 110 volt Reversing Electric Engine, Whistle, Lifting Magnet, Electric lights illuminate models. Builds Bascule Bridge, Ferris Wheel, Oil Drilling Rig, Magnetic Cranes, Derricks, etc. .35 ea.

No. 9½ AUTOMOTIVE SET Electric engine, chassis parts, big channel girders, giant fly wheel segment, etc. Builds automobiles, trucks, giant power plant, elevator, mammoth walking beam engine, parachute jump, etc. .35 ea.

No. 10½ WORLD'S CHAMPION ELECTRIC TRAIN SET. Features completely assembled electric locomotive with circle of track. Additional equipment builds tender, freight cars, turntable and a host of other fine models including all those built with the above sets.... .35 ea.

Separate Parts Prices for 1941 and early 1942

ERECTOR SEPARATE PARTS PRICES

KINDLY ENCLOSE CHECK, MONEY ORDER OR STAMPS WITH YOUR ORDER FOR PART

THE A. C. GILBERT CO., NEW HAVEN, CONN., U. S. A.

Trade No.	Name of Part	Page	Price
*N21	8-32 Square Nut	3	.05 doz.
P7	Small Wheel, ⅞" Dia.	2	.10 ea.
P7A	Small Wheel, 1⅛" Dia.	2	.10 ea.
P12	Crown Gear	2	.10 ea.
P13	12-Tooth Pinion Gear, ⅛"	2	.10 ea.
P13B	12-Tooth Pinion Gear, 7/32"	2	.10 ea.
P14	Worm Gear	2	.20 ea.
P15	Coupling	2	.10 ea.
P20	Five Hole Strip—formed	2	.05 ea.
P24	Crank	2	.10 ea.
P33	Small Screw Driver	3	.05 ea.
P34	Hank of String	3	.05 ea.
P37	Collar	2	.25 doz.
P48	Mitre Gear	2	.20 ea.
P49	18-Tooth Gear	2	.15 ea.
P52	Ladder Chain	3	.15/ft
P51	Electric Engine Reversing 110v. A.C. or D.C.	3	3.95 ea.
No. 5	Transformer	3	2.50 ea.
P56G	Motor, 110v. A.C. or D.C.	3	2.95 ea.
P58	Motor, 6-14 volts	3	1.00 ea.
P59	Reverse Base (for P58 only)	3	.75 ea.
A48	Mechanical Motor	3	1.00 ea.
K48	Mechanical Motor Key	3	.20 ea.
P57A	2⅛" Axle	2	.02 ea.
P57D	6" Axle	2	.06 ea.
P57E	8" Axle	2	.08 ea.
P57F	12" Axle	2	.12 ea.
P79	Car Truck	2	.05 ea.
*S11	Set Srew	3	.05 doz.
*S51	¼"x8-32 Screw	3	.05 doz.
*S52	½"x8-32 Screw	3	.10 doz.
*S57	1⅛"x8-32 Screw	3	.15 doz.
*S62	⅞"x8-32 Screw	3	.10 doz.
*FA	1¼"x8-32 Screw	3	.15 doz.
A	2½" Girder	2	.20 doz.
B	5" Girder	2	.35 doz.
C	10" Girder	2	.50 doz.
D	2½" Curved Girder	2	.25 doz.
E	5" Curved Girder	2	.40 doz.
F	5 Hole Strip	2	.10 doz.
G	7 Hole Strip	2	.10 doz.
H	11 Hole Strip	2	.15 doz.
I	21 Hole Strip	2	.20 doz.
J	41 Hole Strip	2	.30 doz.
K	11 Hole Strip Bracket	2	.35 doz.
M	Small Double Angle	2	.25 doz.
N	Long Double Angle	2	.05 ea.
O	Pawl	2	.05 ea.
S	Large Base Plate—21 holes	2	.40 ea.
T	Boiler	3	.25 ea.
U	Boiler Top	3	.20 ea.

Trade No.	Name of Part	Page	Price
W	Stack	3	.05 ea.
Z	Flanged Wheel, 15/16" Dia.	2	.15 ea.
AA	Eccentric Crank	2	.10 ea.
AC	Universal Bracket	2	.10 ea.
AE	Spiral Spring	3	.05 ea.
AF	Small Hook	2	.15 doz.
AM	Special Pulley—Metal	2	.05 ea.
AQ	Sheave Pulley	2	.05 ea.
AS	2⅞" Axle Rod	2	.03 ea.
AT	4" Axle Rod	2	.04 ea.
AX	19¾" Axle Rod	2	.20 ea.
BE	6" Angle Girder	2	.50 doz.
BH	Solid Collar	2	2 for .05
BL	Smali Washer	2	.05 doz.
BN	Regular Turret Plate	3	.15 ea.
BT	Pierced Disc	2	.10 ea.
BY	11-Hole Fibre Strip	2	.05 ea.
CA	Signal Arm	3	.10 ea.
CH	Right Angle	2	.10 doz.
CJ	36-Tooth Gear	2	.20 ea.
CR	Special Turret plate with hub	3	.15 ea.
CS	Wheel Segment	3	.15 ea.
CX	1" Axle Rod	2	.01 ea.
CY	5" Axle Rod	2	.05 ea.
CZ	7" Axle Rod	2	.07 ea.
DA	10" Axle Rod	2	.10 ea.
DB	Motor Pulley	2	.10 ea.
DE	Steering Column	3	.10 ea.
DK	Flat Spring	3	.10 ea.
DO	Steering Wheel with Hub	2	.15 ea.
DP	12" Angle Girder	2	6 for .50
DS	Cotter Pin	3	.05 doz.
DT	1-Hole Set Screw Coupling	2	2 for .15
DZ	Tackle Block	2	.15 ea.
EH	Gear Box Bracket	2	.05 ea.
EI	Standard Gear Box Side Pl.	2	.15 ea.
EJ	Gear Box Base	2	.20 ea.
EX	Big Channel Girder 12"	2	6 for .50
EY	Big Channel Girder 6"	2	.05 ea.
EZ	6" Curved B. C. Girder	2	.05 ea.
FD	Hinged Loop	2	2 for .05
GV	Thin Disc Wheel Nickel Rim	2	.10 ea.
GW	Thin Disc Wheel—Red	2	.10 ea.
LV	3" Disc Wheel, red	2	.20 ea.
LX	Steering Column Bracket	3	.05 ea.
MA	Radiator	3	.15 ea.
MB	18½" Angle Girder	2	.15 ea.
MC	Base Plate 1"x2½"	2	.05 ea.
MD	Base Plate 2½"x5"	2	.10 ea.
ME	Flat Plate 1"x4"	2	.05 ea.

Trade No.	Name of Part	Page	Price
MF	Flat Plate 1"x5"	2	.05 ea.
MG	Radiator Hood	3	.10 ea.
MH	3" Disc Wheel, Nickel Rim	2	.25 ea.
MI	Front Axle Unit	3	.25 ea.
MJ	Electro Magnet with Cord	3	.60 ea.
MM	Wrench	3	.05 ea.
MN	12" Base Plate	2	.40 ea.
MO	3" Angle Girder	2	.30 doz.
MR	Drum with Gear	2	.35 ea.
MS	Compression Spring	3	.05 ea.
MV	Flat Car Truck	2	.05 ea.
MW	Nut Holder	3	.10 ea.
MX	House	3	.35 ea.
MY	2½"x2½" Base Plate	2	.05 ea.
MZ	Bearing Block	2	.10 ea.
NH	Lamp Socket Unit	3	.15 ea.
NI	Bulb—1½ Volt	3	.05 ea.
NJ	Battery Holder	3	.15 ea.
NK	Ratchet	2	.05 ea.
NL	Bolster Bracket	2	2 for .05
NM	10"x2" Flange Plate	2	.40 ea.
NN	1"x2" Flange Plate	2	.05 ea.
NO	Flanged Wheel, ¾" Dia.	2	.15 ea.
NP	Locomotive—O Gauge	3	8.50 ea.
NQ	Section of Curved Track—O Gauge—(12 Sections per circle)	3	.20 ea.
NR	Track Terminal	3	.20 ea.
NS	41-Hole Strip—formed	2	.05 ea.
NT	Cone	3	.10 ea.
NU	Parachute	3	.25 ea.
NV	Whistle (Note—P13 gear required.)	3	.75 ea.
A49	Electric Engine, gear shift 110v. A.C. only	3	$3.95 ea.
A49-A	Electric Eng., no gear shift.		3.00 ea.
A49-B	Elec. Eng., conversion unit Converts A49-A to A49.	3	1.25 ea.
A49-C	A49 E.E. with Whistle		4.50 ea.

ERECTOR HOW TO MAKE 'EM BOOKS

Same as copy included in sets.

No. 1	Erector How to Make 'Em Book	.15 ea.
No. 3	Erector How to Make 'Em Book	.15 ea.
No. 4	Erector How to Make 'Em Book	.25 ea.
No. 6	Erector How to Make 'Em Book	.25 ea.
No. 7	Erector How to Make 'Em Book	.25 ea.
No. 8	Erector How to Make 'Em Book	.25 ea.
No. 9	Erector How to Make 'Em Book	.35 ea.

NOTE

*N21 Nut used with screws S51, S52, S62, S57, FA
*S11 Set Screw used with pulleys, couplings, etc.

ERECTOR
HOW TO MAKE 'EM BOOKS
Same as copy included in Sets

		Pri
No. 1½	Erector How to Make 'Em Book	.15
No. 2½	Erector How to Make 'Em Book	.15
No. 3½	Erector How to Make 'Em Book	.15
No. 4½	Erector How to Make 'Em Book	.25
No. 6½	Erector How to Make 'Em Book	.25
No. 7½	Erector How to Make 'Em Book	.35
No. 8½	Erector How to Make 'Em Book	.35
No. 9½	Erector How to Make 'Em Book	.35
No. 10½	Erector How to Make 'Em Book	.35

No. 9½ AUTOMOTIVE SET Electric engine, chassis parts, big channel girders, giant fly wheel segment, etc. Builds automobiles, trucks, giant power plant, elevator, mammoth walking beam engine, parachute jump, etc. .35

No. 10½ WORLD'S CHAMPION ELECTRIC TRAIN SET. Features completely assembled electric locomotive with circle of track. Additional equipment builds tender, freight cars, turntable and a host of other fine models including all those built with the above sets.... .35

Separate Parts Prices for late 1942 and early 1946

	Gd	VG	Exc	Inv	Org

NO. 7½ **The Electric Engine Set**

Featured the (T) Boiler, (A49) Electric Engine with gearbox and built Walking Beam Engine. Came in a royal blue metal box 18" x 10" x 3" with brass corner trim; two-layer set with two removable parts displays constructed from (MN) Base Plates; sold for $10.00 in 1940 and $10.50 in 1941 and 1942.

	Gd	VG	Exc	Inv	Org
	70	**100**	**170**	**+35**	**+45**

NO. 8½ **The Engineer's Set**

Featured the (MJ) Electro Magnet, (NV) Whistle, and lighting system parts and built Ferris Wheel. Came in a red metal box 20" x 12" x 3" with brass corner trim; two-layer set with three removable parts displays constructed from (MN) Base Plates; sold for $12.95 in 1940 and $13.50 in 1941 and 1942.

	Gd	VG	Exc	Inv	Org
	80	**120**	**200**	**+40**	**+50**

NO. 9½ **The Automotive Set**

Featured the truck parts, giant flywheel, and new parts to build Parachute Jump as well as Giant Power Plant. Came in a royal blue metal box 22" x 13" x 3" with brass corner trim; two-layer set with three removable parts displays constructed from (MN) Base Plates; sold for $18.95 in 1940 and $19.95 in 1941 and 1942.

	Gd	VG	Exc	Inv	Org
	160	**240**	**400**	**+80**	**+100**

NO. 10½ **Electric Train Set**

Featured American Flyer O gauge electric locomotive, transformer, track, flanged wheels, and flanged plates for building railroad models (theme of set); also had new parts to build Parachute Jump. Came in a royal blue metal box 24" x 14" x 4" with brass corner trim; two-layer set with one very large removable parts display constructed from (MN) Base Plates; cardboard parts display clipped on inside of lid; sold for $32.50 in 1940 and $35.00 in 1941 and 1942.

	Gd	VG	Exc	Inv	Org
	900	**1325**	**2200**	**+440**	**+550**

THE WORLD WAR II ERECTOR JUNIOR LINE

World War II affected virtually every manufacturer in the country, and The A. C. Gilbert Company was no exception. Steel, the most basic ingredient in the production of Erector Sets, began to be rationed in 1942. There were no metal Erector Sets produced throughout the duration of the war, as steel became a commodity critical to the war effort.

While the vast majority of the factory at Erector Square was given over to the production of war materiel, thanks to the unquenchable creativity of A. C. Gilbert an Erector line was available during the war. Since it was not possible to produce sets from metal, Gilbert looked for another material to use—and he chose wood! He went so far as to make this sound like an advantage in the 1943 advertising campaign when he likened these sets to the famous Mosquito Bomber, which he also made of wood.

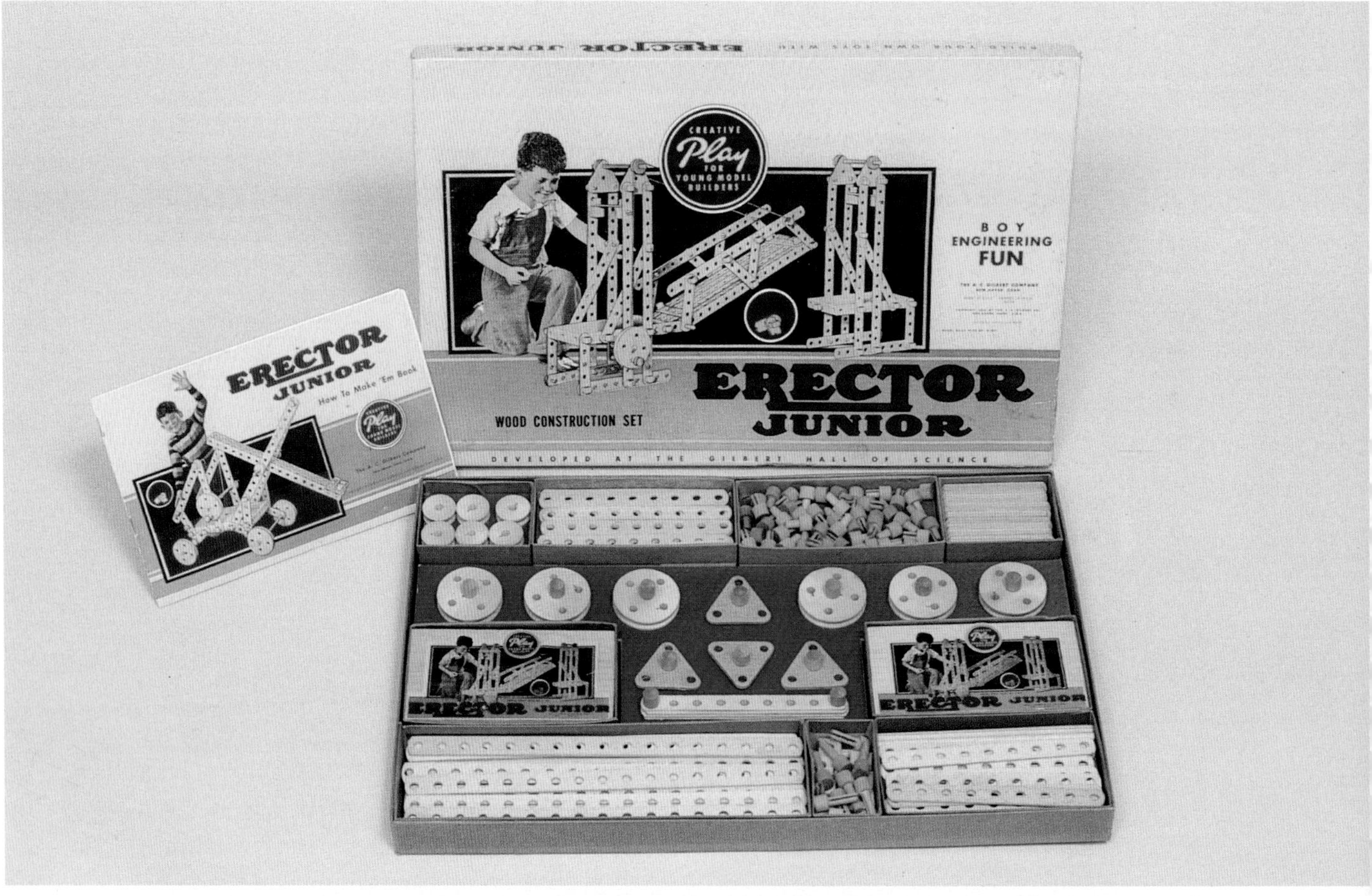

Since Gilbert could not use steel to manufacture Erector during the war, the company offered Erector Junior made from wood. Here is No. 5 from 1945, one of these prized sets.

The new series of sets was called Erector Junior. This building system was composed of strips (straight girders in three different sizes), base blocks, wheels, pulleys, axles, and a few other parts, all made of wood. Far less sophisticated than regular Erector components, construction was accomplished by assembling these parts with wooden pins.

Erector Junior was packed in brightly lithographed cardboard boxes, and it came in three different sizes. Set No. 1 came in a box that measured 12⅜" x 8⅝" x 1⅜"; No. 3 was packed in an 18" x 10" x 1¼" box; and No. 5, the largest set in the series, came in a box that measured 20½" x 13⅝" x 1¼". Each of these sets had blue cardboard inserts; the two larger ones also had internal compartments to hold the smaller parts.

Since there were no metal paper fasteners owing to the lack of steel, wooden pins held the parts in place on the inserts. This led to some interesting anomalies in the contents of these sets. The pins came in two different sizes, with the large ones used to hold parts to the cardboard insert. The number of large pins in each set was more a function of packaging requirements than construction needs. That is why there were more long pins in Nos. 1 and 3 than in No. 5. More were needed to hold the parts in place on the cardboard inserts of these smaller sets.

Gilbert produced Erector Junior from 1943 through 1947, with some interesting modifications occurring along the way. These changes were made in 1945, creating an early and a late version of the sets. The first of these modifications, and the most apparent, related to the (J-1) Base Block. In 1943 and 1944, it was an unadorned wood block. In 1945, however, trying to enliven these sets, Gilbert included a colorful lithographed label that covered one side of the Base Block. The scene on this label was identical to the one on the box lid that showed a young boy in coveralls with the Erector Junior version of the Bascule Bridge. Oddly, this label covered one of the holes in the Base Block. If you are fortunate enough to find one of these sets, you will be even luckier if the original owner did not discover this hole. If he did, there will be a hole in the middle of this lovely label.

The other parts affected by the 1945 modifications were the (J-2) 17 Hole Angle, (J-11) Short Pin, (J-12) Long Pin, (J-14) Crank Pin, and (J-15) Splicer. Actually, the (J-2) 17 Hole Angle, an angle girder, was replaced by the (J-2) 17 Hole Square Girder at this point. The Square Girder served the same purpose, but was less costly to produce. The pins were redesigned with heads that were sturdier and easier to grip, and the Splicer was dropped. The latter was designed to attach two of the strips (girders) end to end to produce a very long strip. But none of the models illustrated in the instruction manual called for long strips or the splicer, so in 1945 it was dropped.

Erector Junior sets are scarce for two reasons. First, they were fragile. When the wooden pin was inserted through the wooden strip (girder), the strip tended to split along the grain. When too many strips were split, the set was likely discarded. Second, Tinkertoy already had a firm grip on the wooden construction toy market, so I doubt that many of these Erector Sets were sold in the first place. They were discontinued in 1947.

Listings of 1943–47 Erector Junior Sets

	Gd	VG	Exc	Inv	Org

NO. 1

Featured the (J-1) Base Block, large wheels, and three sizes of strips. Came in a cardboard box 12⅜" x 8⅝" x 1⅜" with four-color label; sold for $1.95.

	Gd	VG	Exc	Inv	Org
	60	**90**	**150**	**+30**	**+40**

NO. 3

Featured the (J-2) 17 Hole Angle in 1943–44 and (J-2) 17 Hole Square Girder in 1945–47. Came in a cardboard box 18" x 10" x 1¼" with four-color label; sold for $3.50.

	Gd	VG	Exc	Inv	Org
	90	**135**	**225**	**+45**	**+60**

NO. 5

Featured the Gusset and Cube Pin. Came in a cardboard box 20½" x 13⅜" x 1¼" with four-color label; sold for $5.95.

	Gd	VG	Exc	Inv	Org
	120	**180**	**300**	**+60**	**+75**

ERECTOR JR. CONTENTS LIST

Set No.		1	3	5
J-1	BASE BLOCK	1	1	3
J-2	17 HOLE ANGLE (1943–44)	0	2	4
J-2	17 HOLE SQUARE GIRDER (1945–47)	0	2	4
J-3	17 HOLE STRIP	4	8	16
J-4	9 HOLE STRIP	10	16	24
J-5	5 HOLE STRIP	8	16	28
J-6	2¼" WHEEL	4	5	6
J-7	COLLAR-PULLEY	4	4	8
J-8	5¼" AXLE	2	4	4
J-9	6¼" AXLE	0	0	2
J-10	KEY	12	12	12
J-11	SHORT PIN	2	12	48
J-12[1]	LONG PIN	20	32	16
J-13	CUBE PIN	0	0	8
J-14	CRANK PIN	0	2	2
J-15	SPLICER (1943–44)	0	2	4
J-16	GUSSET	0	0	4
J-6-A	2¼" WHEEL (NO HOLES)	0	0	0

1. Anomaly due to packing requirements.

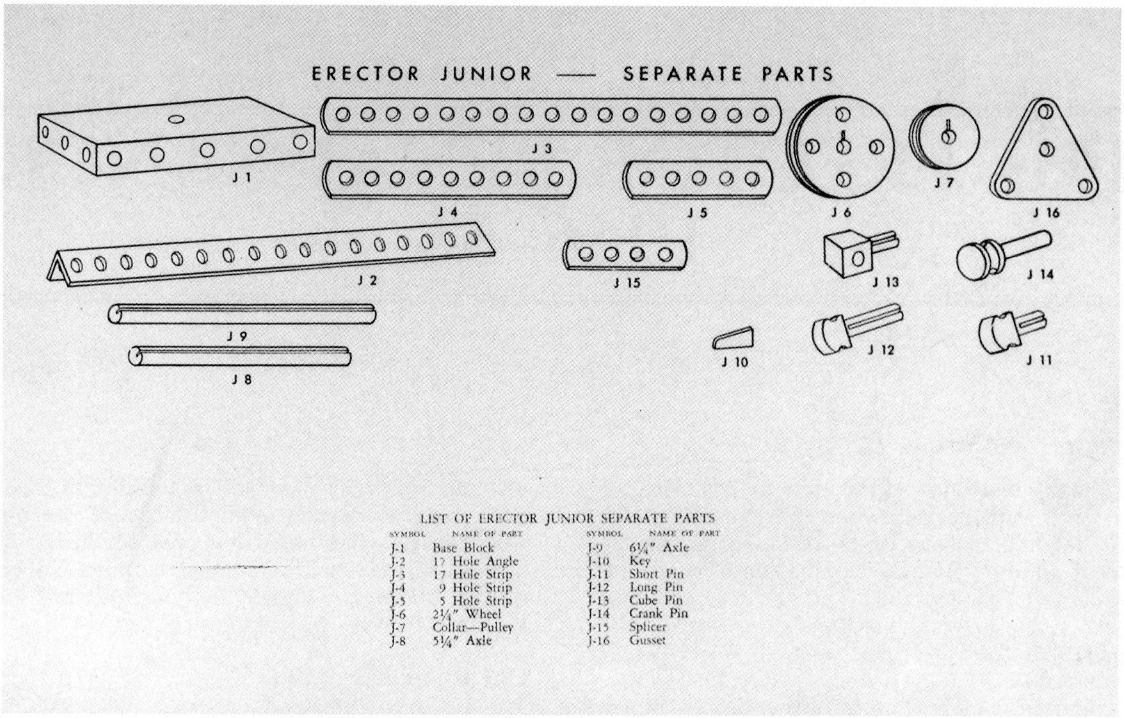

Separate Parts Prices for Erector Junior from 1943–44

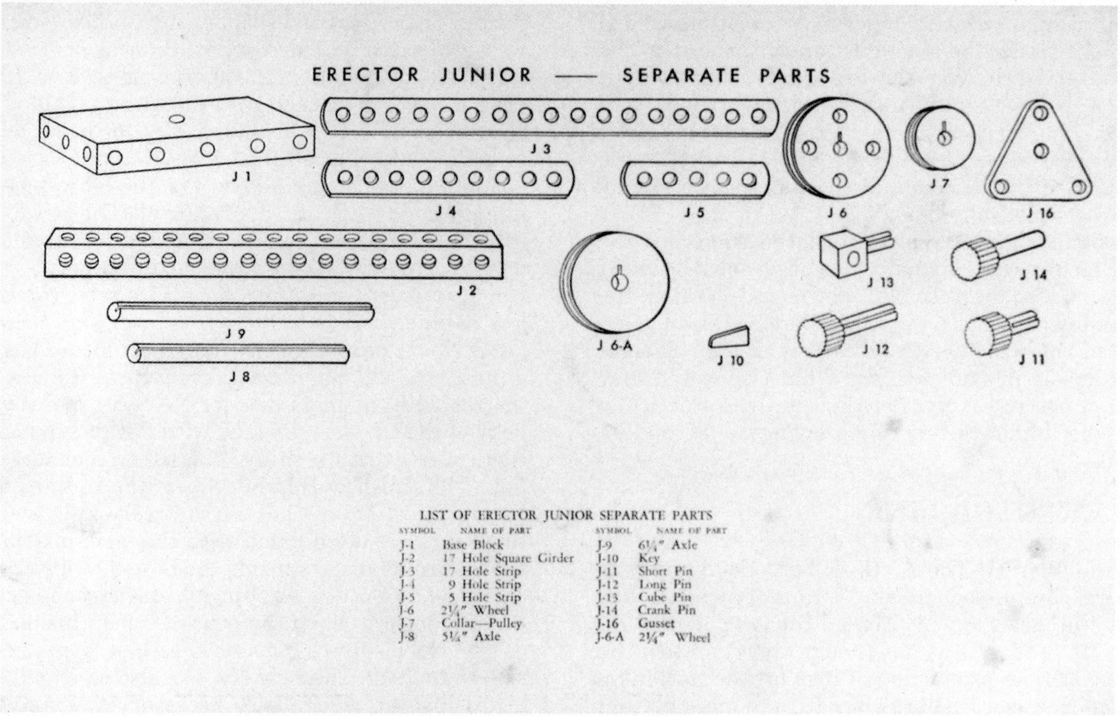

Separate Parts Prices for Erector Junior from 1945–47

3

THE ERECTOR RENAISSANCE: 1946–56

When taking the broadest view of the history of the Erector System, there were two periods when this wonderful toy reached great heights. In both cases, these extraordinary levels of success resulted from a combination of good economic conditions and a good product. The first apex occurred during the late 1920s in what has become known as the Classic Period (1924–32). The second followed World War II and will be referred to the Renaissance Period (1946–56).

Even though the economic climate of the United States was favorable, the success that Erector enjoyed during the Classic period was clearly the result of the ambition and creativity of the man at the helm, A. C. Gilbert. The splendid extravagance of his product, with detailed models of trucks, zeppelins, and locomotives in magnificent sets that weighed up to 150 pounds mirrored a country enjoying growth and prosperity.

While the first high point was driven by creativity aided by good economic times, the second reversed this order. The sets created after World War II were excellent in content and proportion, and several new and exciting models were developed. But the driving force that spurred Erector's Renaissance Period was a force beyond Gilbert's control, one that has controlled the direction of the American economy since 1945. It was the Baby Boom.

Gilbert probably did not realize it at the time, but the success of Erector was virtually assured for the next decade. Returning soldiers settled down and created the largest pool of toy customers the world had ever seen; even better, many of these soldiers had been reared on Erector and Gilbert's irresistible advertising. What else would they buy their son, if not an Erector Set? Erector was practically a standard issue item for every boy growing up in the late 1940s and '50s.

THE 1946 ERECTOR LINE

During World War II, The A. C. Gilbert Company was almost totally committed to the manufacture of war materiel for the government. When the war ended in September of 1945, there was not enough time to retool the plant to the peacetime production of toys for the upcoming holiday season. However, 1946 saw a return to more normal times, and Erector Sets began to roll off the Gilbert production lines once again.

Prior to the war, Gilbert offered Erector in nine sizes. Set Nos. 1½ through 4½ came in cardboard boxes, and Nos. 6½ through 10½ were packed in metal boxes. It is not surprising that, after the disruption caused by the war, the 1946 offering was more modest. Six different sized sets were available, in addition to three sizes of Erector Junior, the wooden sets that had been created during the war. But because of the low level of steel supplies, Gilbert was forced to pack all but the largest sets in cardboard this year. Only the top two sets came in metal boxes.

Cardboard Box Sets

Only two of the cardboard box sets from 1942 were carried over into 1946: Nos. 2½ and 4½. Set No. 2½ was identical to the 1942 offering, and No. 4½ featured a change in packaging. In 1942, its box had come with a hinged lid inside of which a beautifully lithographed label pictured a truck model. Gilbert deleted both the hinge and the picture in 1946. Instead, the lid lifted off and was unadorned on the inside. The cardboard display inserts for Nos. 2½ and 4½ were the same mustard yellow color as before the war.

Set No. 6½ came in cardboard as well in 1946, the first time it was not packed in a metal box. This new container measured 16" x 8" x 3" and, except for being a bit deeper to accommodate the (A49) Electric Engine, was similar to the box for No. 4½. And like No. 4½, the lid was neither hinged nor adorned with an inside label. The cardboard display inserts were a new color, with Gilbert introducing flat blue ones at this time. Over the next few years, the company would convert the inserts for all its sets from mustard yellow to blue.

Set No. 7½ was also packed in a cardboard box in 1946, and a most unusual box it was! It measured 20¾" x 13½" x 3½" (bigger than the metal box for No. 8½), and it was blue. The body of the box was finished with flat blue paper, and the lid was covered with a shiny blue paper that looks almost like foil. (The finish of this lid paper was so hard that the oval Erector label did not adhere to it very well, and examples of these sets are often found with the label missing.) The cardboard display inserts inside the box were also blue.

The lid on No. 7½ was hinged, and cords on each side of the lid supported it when the box was open. Inside the lid was a colorful label—the same one that had been used on No. 7½ sets from 1942. The new No. 7½ also came with many cardboard inserts, which were necessary to make the box look fuller. (The box provided far more volume than was needed for the parts it contained.) When all the parts are placed in the box without inserts, the box is less than half full.

Set No. 7½ from 1946 (as well as the different No. 7½ from 1947) is fairly difficult to find. For that reason, along with its unusual appearance, it has become a favorite of collectors.

Set No. 4½ was somewhat downgraded for 1946. A lift-off lid replaced the hinged version, and the wonderful full-color inner lid label was eliminated.

Metal Box Sets

Gilbert offered only two sets in metal boxes. The No. 8½, which came in a red-painted box, was virtually unchanged from 1942. It featured the Bascule Bridge and the Ferris Wheel. The cardboard display inserts were mustard yellow.

Also carried over from 1942 was No. 9½, whose box still was painted royal blue. This set featured the Giant Power Plant and the Parachute Jump models. The cardboard inserts were mustard yellow. Like No. 8½, this set is almost indistinguishable from the 1942 version. Surprisingly, this set was not pictured or promoted in the 1946 Erector catalog.

The most conspicuous deletion from the lineup was No. 10½. There were probably two reasons why this wonderful set was dropped. First, while the top-of-the-line sets were always the most expensive, they were not necessarily the most profitable to produce and sell. Because of the extravagance of these big sets, they were priced out of most consumers' budgets. When Gilbert converted his factory back to toy production, he surely had this in mind.

The second reason for the demise of The Electric Train Set is ultimately more profound. The most important event that occurred in the Gilbert toy family after World War II was the creation of American Flyer S gauge trains to replace the prewar O gauge line. More than anything else, the conversion to S gauge caused No. 10½ to disappear from the Erector roster.

In the old O gauge system, the electric motor that powered the train was housed in the locomotive and a third rail collector under the engine completed the circuit through a system of three-rail track. Each locomotive could be operated by itself. But the new S gauge system featured more realistic two-rail track. Now each locomotive was attached to a tender, which was needed to supply current to the motor. The locomotive could no longer operate on its own.

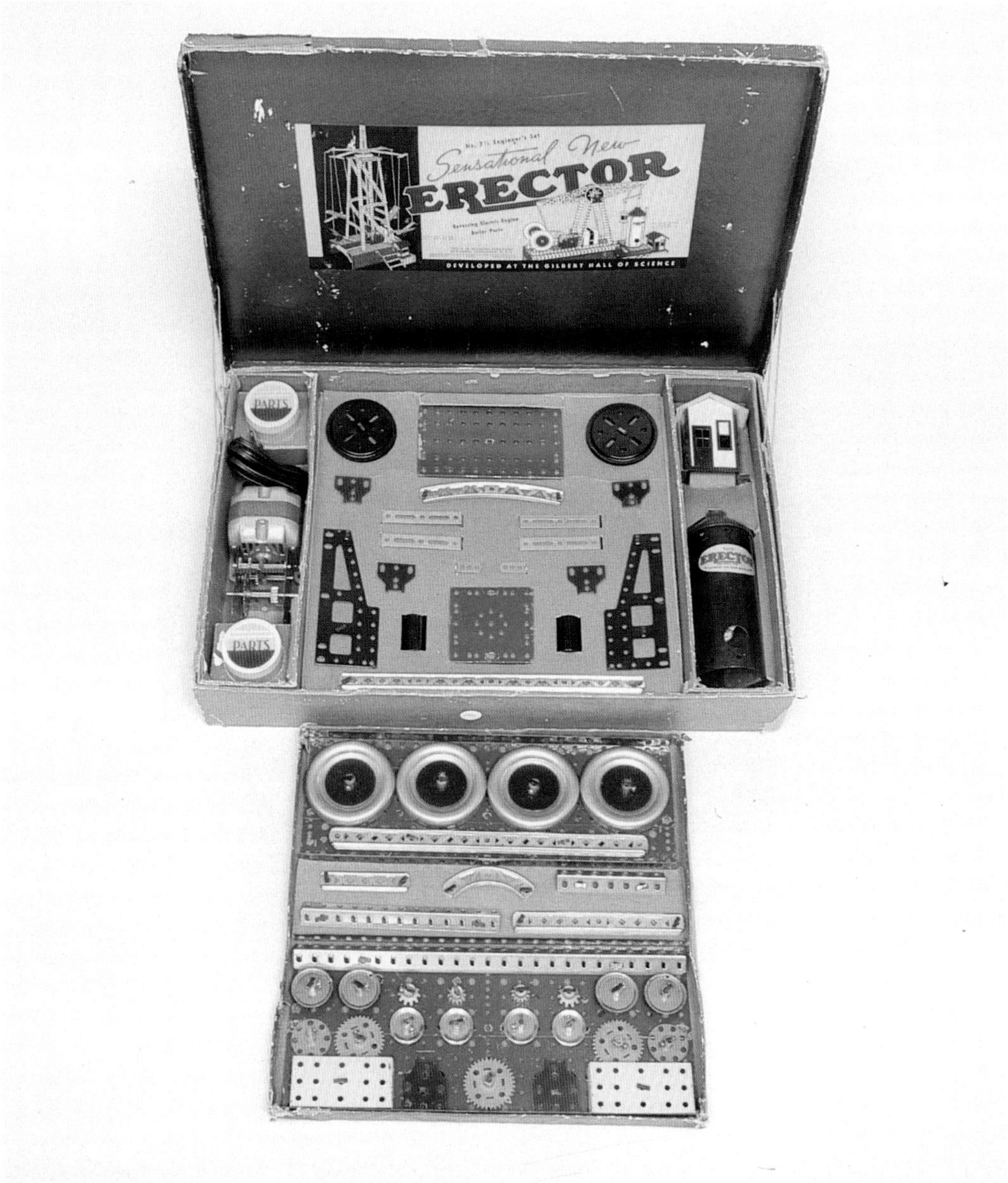

Steel was in short supply after the war, and Gilbert was forced to pack even the larger sets in cardboard boxes. Set No. 7½ was most unusual, with a complicated arrangement of cardboard display inserts in 1946.

This is an important distinction, because, though there was room in the No. 10½ box for a locomotive, there was not for a locomotive and a tender! In retrospect, the development of S gauge trains might have been a boon to the model railroading community; it was not so for Erector Set fans. It caused the elimination of one of the greatest sets of all time.

An Aside: The 1946, 1947, and 1948 Catalogs

Erector collectors have long been aware of inaccuracies in the Gilbert catalogs. Pictures of sets were used year after year, long after changes were made in the sets. Box sizes and other descriptive material were misstated. There are examples of set descriptions placed under the wrong pictures. But the catalogs from 1946, 1947, and 1948 are the worst of all. Apparently Gilbert was more concerned with selling sets than preserving a historical record for us. I share the frustration of trying to make sense out of the discrepancies between what I've read and what I've seen. I hope the information presented here will help.

Erector System Modifications for 1946

During 1942, especially the early part of that year, Gilbert did a lot of experimenting with the finish and color of Erector parts. Zinc replaced nickel as the plating medium for some of the girders, strips, and other unpainted parts. A black patina finish showed up on parts can lids, paper fasteners, and even the corner trim of the metal set boxes. For parts that were painted, the color selected for the finish was hardly traditional.

But these trends ended after the war. Unpainted parts

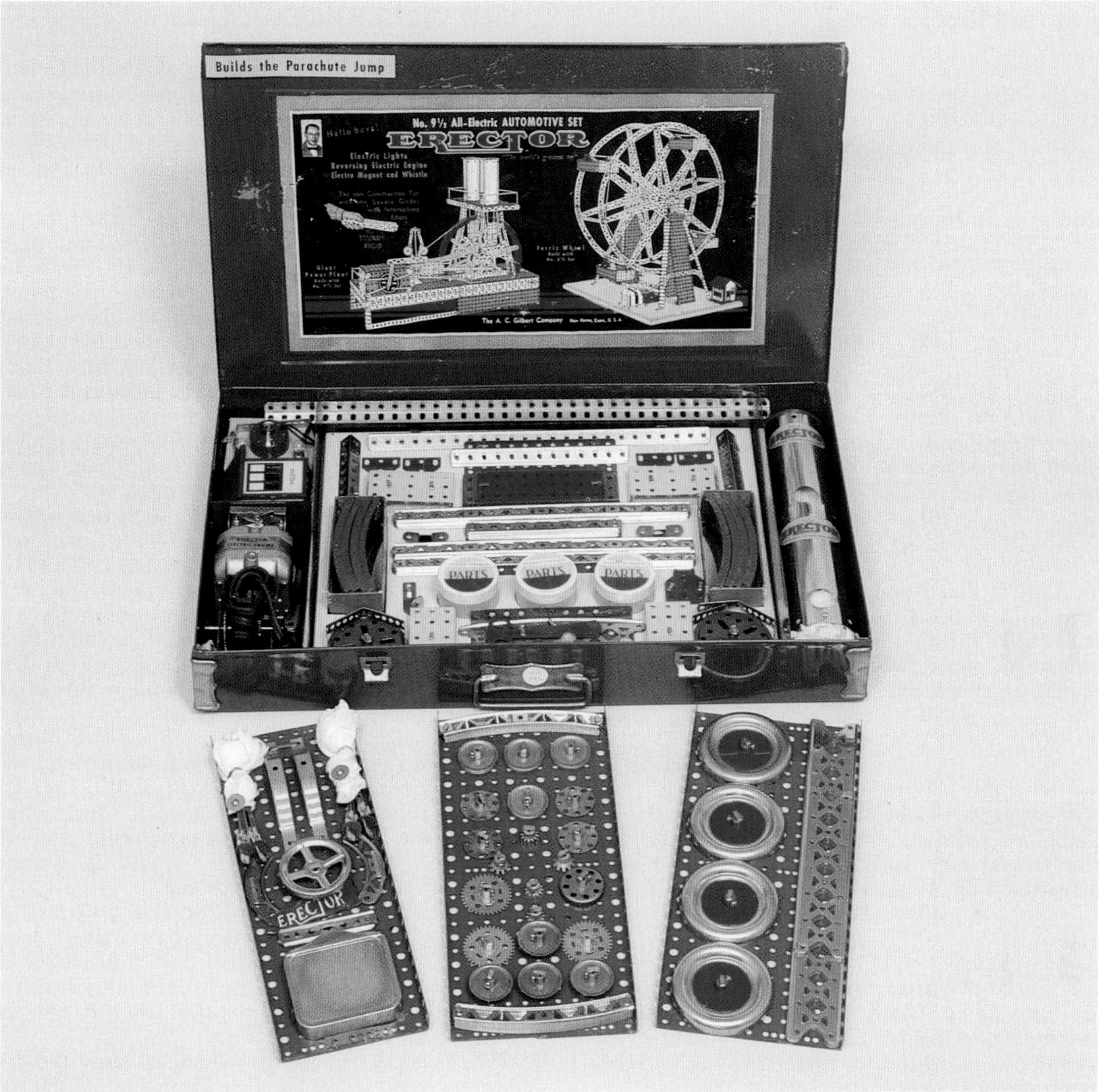

Set No. 9½ from 1946 was the only one to come in a royal blue box after the war. Beginning in 1947, the box for this set, like all the other metal boxes, was painted red.

again were nickel-plated, and the pulleys, gears, and small wheels were washed in brass as before. Most of the painted parts were finished in their usual colors.

I. Noteworthy Paint Colors and Finishes

(T) Boiler, painted black or nickel-plated
(BN) Regular Turret Plate, painted black
(CR) Special Turret Plate, painted blue
(CS) Wheel Segment, painted blue
(MB) 18½" Angle Girder, painted blue or nickel-plated
(MC) Base Plate 1" x 2½", painted yellow or red
(MD) Base Plate 2½" x 5", painted blue
(ME) Base Plate 1" x 4", painted blue or red
(MF) Base Plate 1" x 5", painted blue
(MH) Large 3" Disc Wheel, nickel-plated tire with red-painted hubcap
(NT) Cone, painted blue
(A49) Electric Engine, with motor housing painted silver-blue. All red lettering or black and red lettering on decal. The engine in all sets except No. 6½ came with a full gearbox
( ) Parts Cans, with label pasted on lids painted creamy white instead of nickel-plated; cans came with cardboard bottoms. (The creamy white paint on these lids is the best way to distinguish 1946 sets from 1942 ones.)

II. Eliminated Parts

(NN) 1" x 2" Flanged Plate
(NO) Flanged Wheel, ¾" diameter
(NP) Locomotive, O gauge
(NQ) Section of Curved Track
(NR) Track Terminal
(No. 5) Transformer

Listings of 1946 Erector Sets

NO. 2½ **The Apprentice Set**

Featured the (MH) Disc Wheels. Came in a cardboard box 18" x 10" x ¾"; sold for $3.00.

Gd	VG	Exc	Inv	Org
35	50	80	+20	+25

NO. 4½ **The Famous No. 4½**

Featured the (A48) Mechanical Motor and (MN) 12" Base Plates, and (MX) House and built truck with (A48). Came in a cardboard box 18" x 10" x 2⅜" with a lift-off lid; two-layer set with removable cardboard parts display tray; sold for $6.50.

Gd	VG	Exc	Inv	Org
40	60	100	+20	+25

NO. 6½ **The Sensational No. 6½**

Featured the (A49) Electric Engine without gearbox and built Airplane Ride. Came in a cardboard box 18" x 10" x 3" with a lift-off lid; two-layer set with removable cardboard parts display tray; sold for $9.75.

Gd	VG	Exc	Inv	Org
40	60	100	+20	+25

NO. 7½ **The Engineer's Set**

Featured the (T) Boiler and (A49) Electric Engine with gearbox and built Walking Beam Engine. Came in a blue cardboard box 20¾" x 13¾" x 3½" with a hinged lid covered with shiny blue foil paper; two-layer set with two removable cardboard parts display tray; sold for $12.50.

Gd	VG	Exc	Inv	Org
120	180	300	+60	+80

NO. 8½ **The All-Electric Set**

Featured the (MJ) Electro Magnet, (NV) Whistle, and lighting system parts and built Ferris Wheel and Bascule Bridge. Came in a red metal box 20" x 12" x 3" with brass corner trim; two-layer set with three removable parts displays constructed from (MN) Base Plates; sold for $16.95.

Gd	VG	Exc	Inv	Org
80	120	200	+40	+50

NO. 9½ **The Automotive Set**

Featured the truck parts, giant flywheel, and parts to build Parachute Jump, Giant Power Plant, and trucks. Came in a royal blue metal box 22" x 13" x 3" with brass corner trim; two-layer set with three removable parts displays constructed from (MN) Base Plates; sold for $25.00.

Gd	VG	Exc	Inv	Org
160	240	400	+80	+100

THE 1947 ERECTOR LINE

The year 1947 witnessed substantial changes in the Erector System. While the line of sets continued unchanged from 1946, significant changes did occur in the materials used to manufacture the parts. Also, Gilbert made modifications in the packaging of the metal box sets, and redesigned and improved certain parts.

Although steel was available in limited quantities in 1946, the massive labor strikes that occurred in 1947 and beyond had a devastating impact on the entire industrial community. The A. C. Gilbert Company was no exception, and the result was the most noteworthy characteristic of the 1947 line: the introduction of massive quantities of aluminum parts. Nearly half of the Erector parts that had traditionally been made of steel were fabricated in aluminum during the next several years. Even so, not all parts in all sets ever were totally aluminum. Whenever a limited supply of steel became available, it was used. Then, whatever else was needed was produced in aluminum.

The 1947 sets seem to have the highest concentration of aluminum parts ever (compared to those from the following three years), and these parts proved to be less than satisfactory. This soft metal was too easily bent, and the finish on the base plates was dull and unattractive. Over the next several years, Gilbert might have used an alloy, because the quality of these aluminum parts improved. The finish became brighter, and the parts became harder and more resistant to bending.

Several parts, including the (MJ) Electro Magnet, were redesigned and improved. The 1940–46 version had a small, recessed circular plate on the bottom. The 1947 one had a larger plate that extended to a point which matched the depth of the housing. Now this plate could come in contact with the objects it was supposed to pick up, and the performance of the magnet was improved.

The (NH) Lamp Socket Unit also was also modified. Previously, the socket and lamp base contact were each a separate piece, and they were held together by an (N21) Nut. But from this point forward, the lamp socket unit was produced as a single piece, and the nut was no longer required to hold it together.

The (MX) House was also changed. Until this time, windows were cut out of the door. From now on, the doors were solid and had no window. This change was made to reduce

The (MJ) Electro Magnet was redesigned in 1947, with a larger core plate (right). Performance was improved because the plate made better contact with the "load."

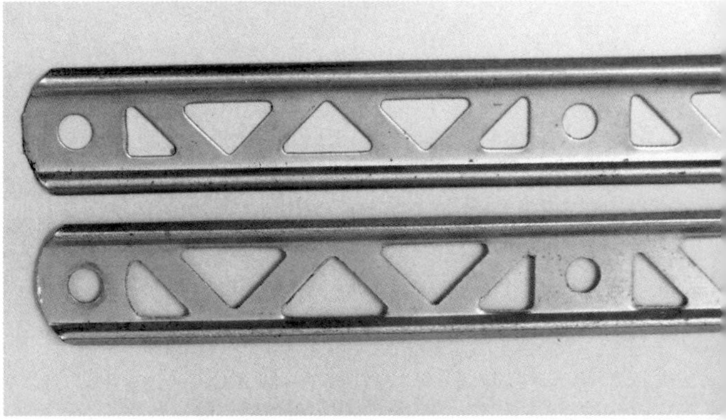

Note the difference in the hole pattern for the (C) 10" Girders prior to 1947 (bottom) and after (top). During 1947 and later, the old pattern occasionally showed up, even mixed in with girders having the new pattern.

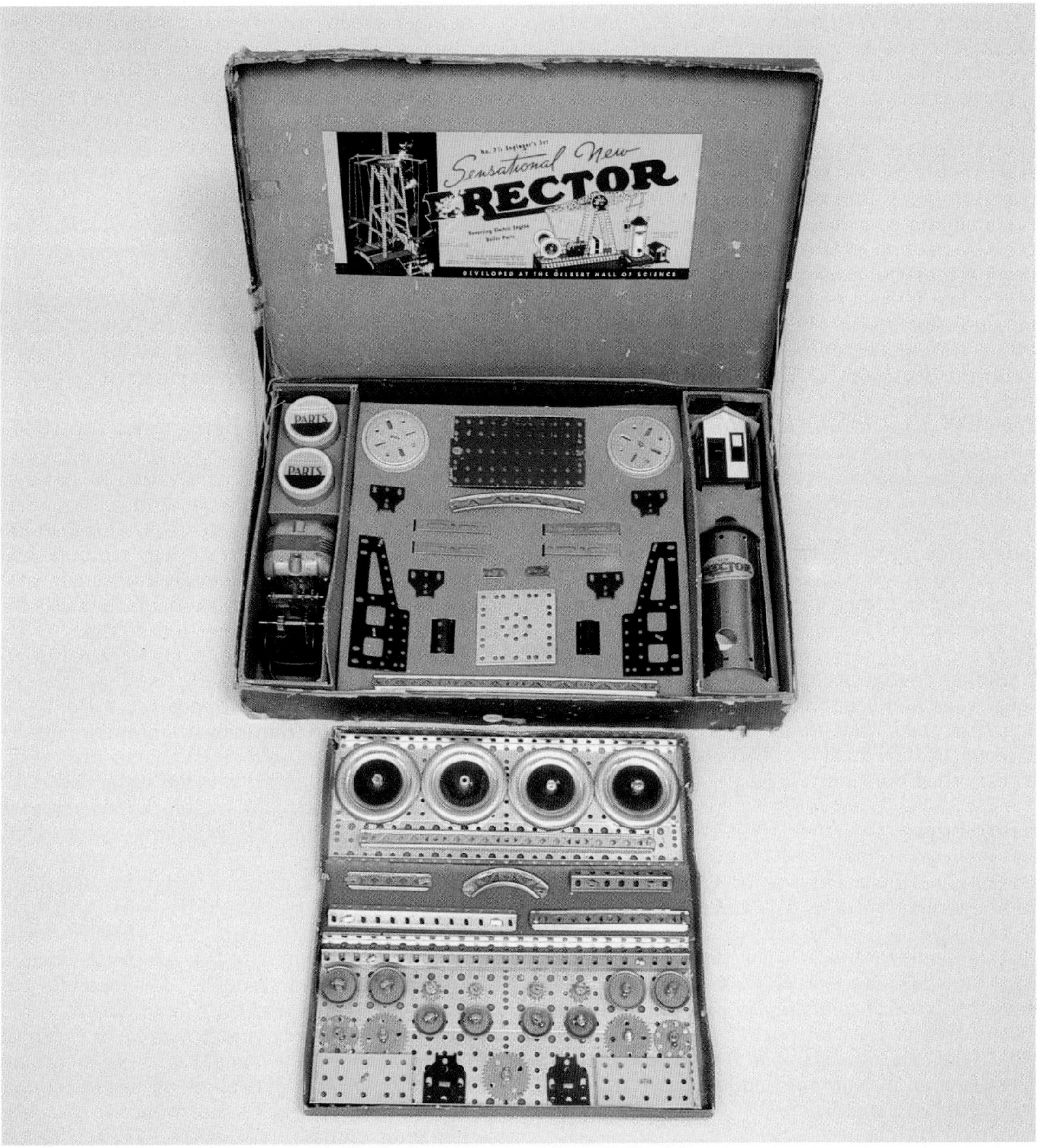

Although still packed in a cardboard box, No. 7½ from 1947 differed from the 1946 version. The color of the box and the packing arrangement were altered.

the steps in producing the house and thereby save money.

There was also a distinct change in the (C) 10" Girders. If you hold one of these girders vertically and look at the first triangular hole punched in the girder (the one under the screw hole), you will see that the edge of the triangle is curved or straight. All the 10" angle girders produced prior to 1947 had curved edges. Nearly all the 10" girders produced in 1947 and thereafter came with straight edges. (Very infrequently the old-style girders show up in sets from after 1947. Perhaps old dies were put into use when production requirements were high.)

Several other parts had interesting changes in 1947. The (CJ) 36 Tooth Gear was made with four slots (in addition to four screw holes) prior to this point. The slots were added to this gear back in 1935, when it was used on the (MR) Drum with Gear. But Gilbert dropped that part in 1938. Apparently it took the firm another nine years to stop stamping out the slots.

Two other parts were given new screw holes. The (MZ) Bearing Block had a hole added in its center. This new hole seemed to have no purpose in model building, but it did allow the bearing block to be clipped to a parts display for packing. The (MA) Radiator was given two new screw holes on the lower flange.

Yet another change occurred when the radius of the (EZ) Six Inch Curved Big Channel Girder was reduced. The reason for this modification remains a mystery. Is it possible that the plans for the Merry-Go-Round (introduced in 1949) were already on the drawing board? The platform for this extraordinary model required nine of these girders formed in a circle. If so, Gilbert still got it wrong, as the radius is too large, and the circle is imperfectly formed.

Further, 1947 saw a new design in the (K48) Key for the Mechanical Motor. The design was simplified, and a notch was stamped in the side of the key to fit a (N21) Nut. The key could now serve as an extra wrench, in addition to winding the motor.

Gilbert also modified the (A49) Electric Engine. First, a new casting was created for the motor housing. The old version had twelve vent holes on each side; the new one came with four. Also, the motor core decals with red and black lettering were gone by the end of 1946, and only all red letter decals were used. A major improvement in the durability of these decals was made. Gilbert had been using them around the motor core since the creation of the (A49) in 1938. But these decals were fragile and prone to getting chipped. (I suspect that after the decals got nicked, a lot of boys rubbed off the remainder to improve the motor's appearance. That would explain why so many motors show up with no decal.) Gilbert began to place a piece of silvery protective tape over the motor core, and the decal was placed on top of the tape. These decals still have a tendency to come off, and many engines show up with only the silver tape left.

The last modification on the (A49) was the elimination of the screw holes in the motor housing. In prior years, these screw holes were used to attach the (NV) Whistle. But the whistle was dropped in 1947 and so were the extra screw holes.

Finally, yet another change occurred with the parts cans. Since 1938, these cans had been made with cardboard bodies and bottoms. Now, the bottoms were made of metal. Also, in place of the paper PARTS label that had been used on the lid, Gilbert lithographed the same design.

Cardboard Box Sets

The lineup of cardboard box sets was basically a continuation of the 1946 line. Set Nos. 2½, 4½, and 6½ were available as before, only laced with aluminum parts.

Set No. 7½ had some interesting cosmetic changes. In 1946 it came in a blue box; now the color was changed to red (almost burgundy). The cardboard display packing was also modified. In 1946 each of the two parts cans had its own cardboard holder. One can was packed in front of the motor, and the other can behind it. Now one double holder secured both parts cans behind the motor.

Metal Box Sets

As in 1946, Nos. 8½ and 9½ were the only sets offered in metal boxes. But both were modified in interesting ways. When Gilbert introduced metal box sets for Erector, the larger ones were adorned with brass (plated) corner trim. This decoration was eliminated in 1947. Early versions of No. 8½ do show up with corner trim, but by the end of the year it was gone.

Set No. 8½ also changed appearance on the inside. The large inner label that pictured the Giant Power Plant and the Ferris Wheel models had been printed in four colors (red, blue, yellow, and green). Now, presumably to save money, the same label was printed using only red and yellow. Also modified was the yellow strip label that appeared above the large label on the inside of the lid. In the past it read, "First Set With The Whistle." Because Gilbert dropped the whistle in 1947, the text was changed to "Builds Giant Ferris Wheel." Mustard yellow display inserts were used to pack this set.

Set No. 9½ underwent similar modifications. But by far the most significant change that occurred with it related to the color of the box; it was painted bright red instead of royal blue as in the past. Back in the mid-1930s, Gilbert had painted the metal boxes assorted colors, such as red, green, and blue. But beginning now and until the advent of lithographed boxes in 1958, all the metal box sets were painted red. The box for No. 9½ came without brass corner trim.

Like No. 8½, the version of No. 9½ from 1947 used the large, two-color inner label introduced this year. As in the past, a strip was pasted on this label that covered the lettering which read, "No. 8½ All Electric Set." This strip read, "No. 9½ All Electric Automotive Set." The yellow strip label (above the large label) was changed as well. Previously, it had read, "Builds The Parachute Jump." Now the text was "Builds The Parachute Jump—5 Feet High." The display inserts used in this set were mustard yellow.

Erector System Modifications for 1947

The most significant modification in 1947 was the forced introduction of aluminum parts, and there is no consistency as to which parts were made of aluminum at any given time. It is interesting to note that other metals occasionally were substituted for steel, although not nearly as often as aluminum. Some brass nuts show up in small sets, and brass sheave pulleys appear from time to time.

Several of the aluminum parts were painted, but this generally proved unsatisfactory, because the paint did not adhere well to it and chipped off with the slightest flex, bend, or pressure from a nut tightening on a bolt. The (MN) Base Plate was painted blue in some early sets, but the flaw was quickly seen and it was left unpainted for most of 1947 and thereafter. Only the car truck, flat car truck, and wheel segments were painted year after year through the aluminum period.

Also worthy of mention was the deletion of the (NV) Whistle from the two metal box sets. Although it was not a particularly effective part, the whistle was Gilbert's first attempt to add sound to the Erector System. At the least, this part foreshadowed the development of the Erector Whistle Kit (1950) and the Sound Effects Kit (1958).

One final anomaly that occurred in these 1947 sets was the appearance of hexagonal nuts. As mentioned, they were made of brass, but also show up in aluminum. At no other time in the history of Erector were the (N21) Nuts anything other than square.

I. Noteworthy Parts Colors and Finishes

(P79) Car Truck, steel or aluminum painted red
(A) 2½" Girder, nickel-plated steel or aluminum
(D) 2½" Curved Girder, nickel-plated steel or aluminum
(N21) 8-32 Nut, square steel or hexagonal brass or aluminum
(S51) ¼" x 8-32 Screw, nickel-plated steel or aluminum
(S62) ⅞" x 8-32 Screw, nickel-plated steel or aluminum
(T) Boiler, steel nickel-plated or painted black
(W) Stack, steel painted black or aluminum
(AQ) Sheave Pulley, steel or brass
(BE) 6" Angle Girder, nickel-plated steel or aluminum
(BN) Regular Turret Plate, steel painted black or aluminum
(CR) Special Turret Plate, steel painted blue or aluminum
(CS) Wheel Segment, steel or aluminum painted red
(DK) Flat Spring, nickel-plated steel or aluminum
(EI) Gear Box Side Plate, steel painted black or aluminum

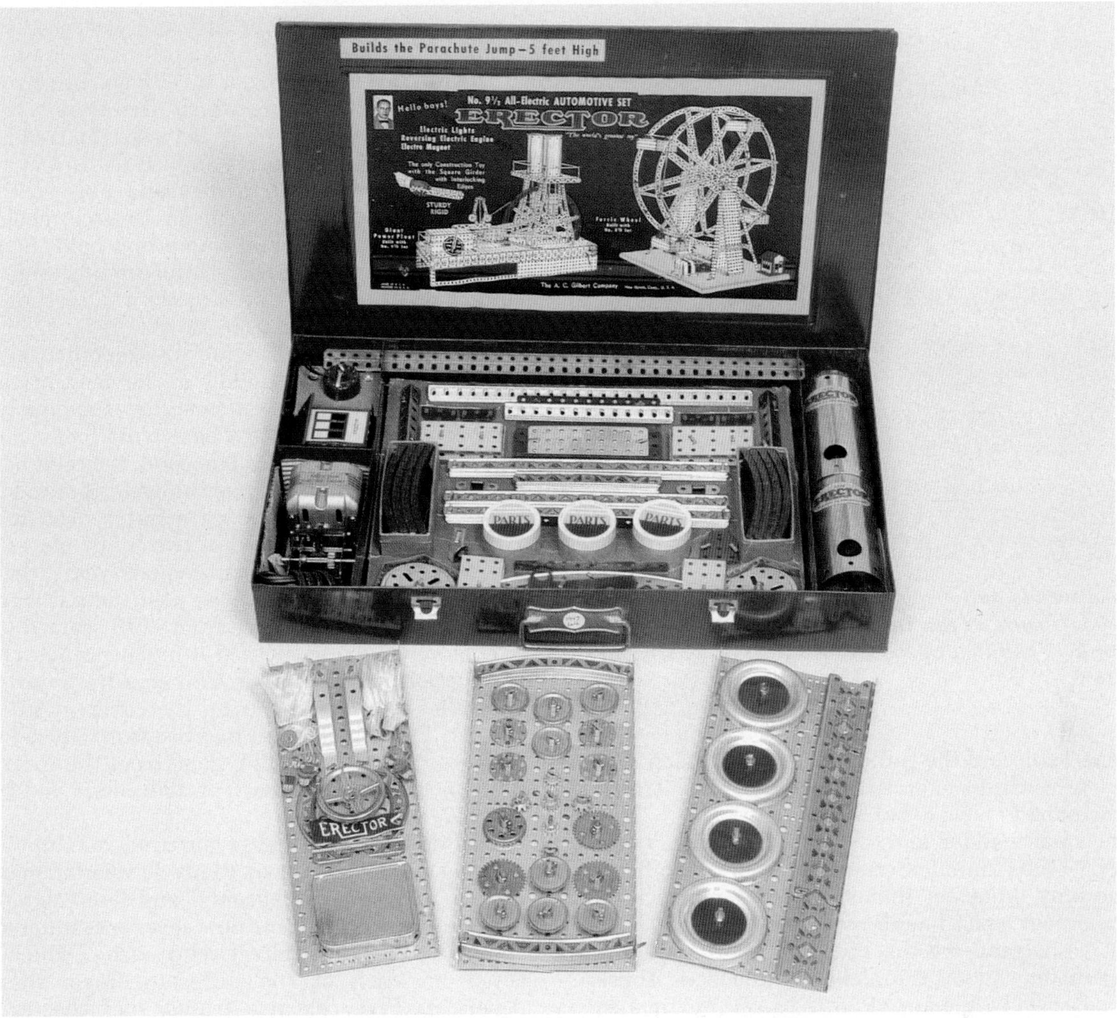

Beginning in 1947, all the metal box sets were painted red. Note the profusion of aluminum parts this year in No. 9½.

(MR) Radiator, nickel-plated steel or aluminum
(MB) 18½" Angle Girder, steel nickel-plated or painted blue
(MC) Base Plate 1" x 2½", steel painted yellow or aluminum
(MD) Base Plate 2½" x 5", steel painted blue or aluminum
(ME) Base Plate 1" x 4", steel painted blue or aluminum
(MF) Base Plate 1" x 5", steel painted blue or aluminum
(MG) Radiator Hood, steel painted red or aluminum
(MH) Large 3" Disc Wheel, aluminum with steel hubcap painted red
(MN) 12" Base Plate, aluminum unpainted or painted blue
(MO) 3" Angle Girder, nickel-plated steel or aluminum
(MV) Flat Car Truck, steel or aluminum painted red
(MY) Base Plate, 2½" x 2½", steel painted blue or aluminum

II. Modified Parts

(A49) Electric Engine, four-vent hole motor housing, silver tape under decal, screw holes (for mounting whistle) eliminated
(C) 10" Girder, new hole pattern
(K48) Key for Mechanical Motor, new design
(CJ) 36 Tooth Gear, slots eliminated
(EZ) 6" Curved Big Channel Girder, radius reduced
(MA) Radiator, two screw holes added
(MJ) Electro Magnet, core plate enlarged and extended
(MX) House, door windows eliminated
(MZ) Bearing Block, center hole added
(NH) Lamp Socket Unit, one-piece construction
( ) Parts Can, metal bottoms and lithographed lids

III. Eliminated Parts

(NV) Whistle

THE 1948 ERECTOR LINE

The system evolved further in 1948. While there were minor modifications in parts and packaging, the big news was the creation of No. 12½, known as "The Remote Control Set." This top-of-the-line item came in a metal box the same size as the one that had held The Electric Train Set, though now it was painted red. Several new parts were included, most of which, especially the remote control motor and control box, were created for the Mysterious Walking Giant, the featured model. Other new parts, such as the Treads, were

The addition of treads and a remote-control motor spurred a host of new models such as the Tank. This model is a factory-built store display exhibited at the Gilbert Hall of Science in Washington, D. C.

featured on the Tank and the Bulldozer models, which also used the remote control motor. An American Flyer transformer was included to power that motor.

Of all the new parts added to the Erector System in 1948, all but the (NZ) Wood Handle Screwdriver were specific to No. 12½. The only other set that shared the new screwdriver with a brown wood handle was No. 9½. The (NW) Clip and Belt Unit (renamed the Tread in 1949) and (NX) Tread Pulleys made wonderful tanks and bulldozers. These models were powered by the new (P55) 7-15 Volt Motor, also known as the Remote Control Motor. It also powered the new Walking Giant, with the new (OA) 18 Volt Bulbs used for that model's eyes. The (2B) Transformer came straight from the American Flyer line and was used with the new motor and bulbs.

The (NW) was made, not by Gilbert, but by a competitor, Louis Marx & Company, which used it as a tread for a toy tractor. The main difference between the treads Marx made for its tractor and those it supplied Gilbert was that the latter came with special fittings and pins so they could be installed and removed from an Erector model. The Marx treads came with a metal clamp that held them in place on a more permanent basis. (Interestingly, the Marx metal clamps occasionally showed up with the treads in early versions of No. 12½ from 1948.)

The (A49) Electric Engine was modified again in 1948, sometime around the middle of the year. First, the casting for the motor housing was modified. Previously, the flanges used to bolt the motor to a base plate had come with holes; now they had slots instead. Second, the color of the lettering on the motor core decal was changed from red to black.

For this year only, the parachutes needed to build the Parachute Jump consisted of two "half" pieces of silk sewn together. In previous and subsequent years, they were a single piece of silk. While in the past the parachutes came as white or red sets, all those from 1948 seemed to be red.

This year also witnessed a much needed change in the instruction manual cover. The sets from early 1948 came with the manuals featuring the cover picturing the Coal Loader. This illustration had been introduced in 1925. Not only was that loader long gone from the instruction manual, but the parts with which to build it had been dropped in 1927.

The new manual cover pictured a "Happy-Faced Boy" viewing the Giant Power Plant. It was far more appealing, with a dark blue background and four-color printing. The back outside page of this new cover was unique to 1948 and 1949. There were six blue circles, each of which illustrated a toy from each of the different lines: chemistry sets, American Flyer electric trains, tool chests, puzzle sets, magic outfits, and microscopes. All and all, this new instruction manual cover (M2645, copyrighted 1948) was a major improvement in the appearance of Erector.

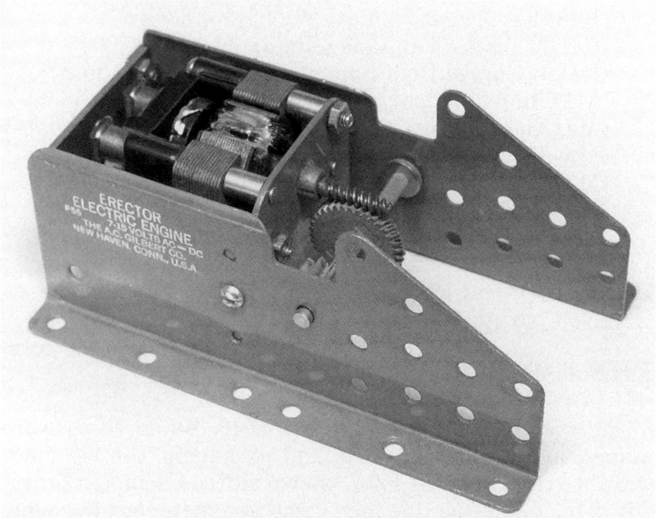

The (P55) Remote Control Motor, introduced in 1948, was packed in only the top-of-the-line No. 12½. Its core originated in the American Flyer line.

Cardboard Box Sets

Gilbert offered three different sets in cardboard boxes. Set Nos. 2½ and 4½ ran unchanged from 1947, with the exception of the cardboard display inserts, which went from mustard yellow to blue. Set No. 6½ also came with blue inserts, along with some other changes. Since the creation of the (A49) Electric Engine in 1938, Gilbert had included a stripped down version in No. 6½, as most of the gears in the gearbox as well as the gear shift had been left out to reduce costs. Starting in 1948, No. 6½ came with the same version of the Electric Engine as all the other sets.

Metal Box Sets

Four different sets were available in metal boxes, including No. 7½ again. But the steel supply still posed a problem, so Gilbert compromised when upgrading this set from a cardboard to metal container. While the body of the box was made of steel, the lid was aluminum. This same change was made in the No. 8½. These sets are fairly easy to spot, because paint did not adhere well to the aluminum, and many of the surviving sets show up with flaking on their lids.

The large inside label was also modified on No. 7½. In 1947, the label for Nos. 8½ and 9½ had changed from four

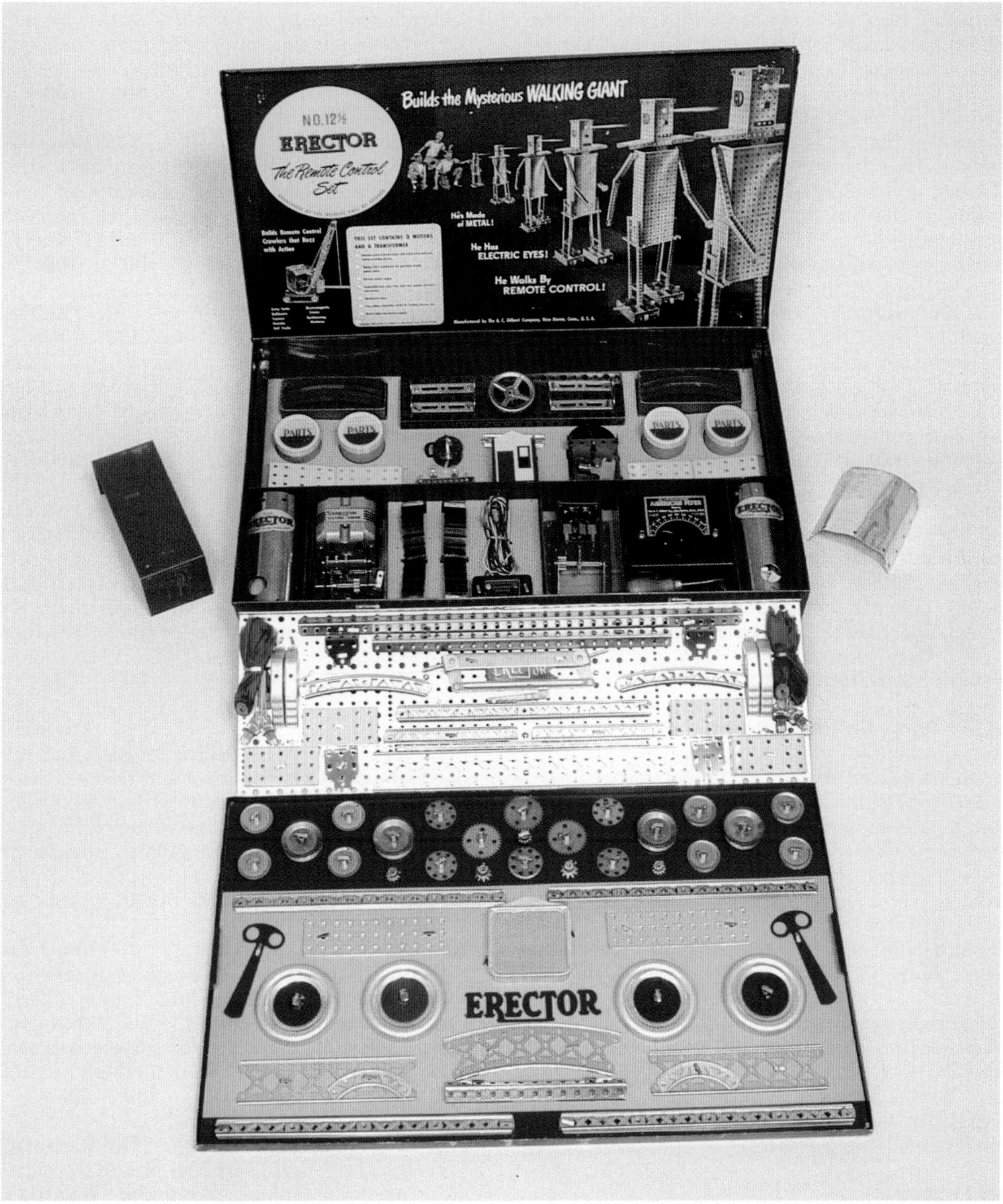

The new No. 12½, the top-of-the-line set for 1948, came with a lift-out parts display tray that covered the entire top layer of the box. This tray was unique to the 1948 version of this spectacular set.

colors to two. Now this same modification was made on the label for No. 7½. The color of the cardboard parts display inserts in this and No. 8½ was changed from mustard yellow to blue.

Set No. 9½ was offered again, and it was similar to the version from 1947. The color of the cardboard display inserts was changed from mustard yellow to blue, and the wood handle screwdriver was substituted for the wire one. Also, the red parachutes in this set consisted of two pieces of silk sewn together.

The new member of the Erector family, No. 12½, was a magnificent addition. Packed in the 24" x 14" x 4" metal box that had housed the Hudson locomotive and tender and The Electric Train Set in years past, it was finished in bright red and had a heavy cardboard label on the inside of the lid. The lid pictured the Mysterious Walking Giant, the featured model.

The No. 12½ had a unique parts display tray that covered the top layer of the box. The tray was made of aluminum, which was easily bent, and many of these fragile trays were damaged and discarded over the years. Inside the tray was a large, red and yellow parts display insert with "Erector" in large red letters. Many of the parts were clipped to the insert with paper fasteners.

Gd VG Exc Inv Org

Under the display tray, the body of the box was divided into six small compartments in the front and a large one in the rear for parts storage. There was a variety of cardboard parts displays in these compartments, whose inserts were mustard yellow. There were also brackets welded to the side of the box so another display tray would fit over the large rear compartment. This display tray was constructed from (MN) Base Plates; a red-painted steel support (known to Erector collectors as the "bridge") that kept the (MN) display tray from sagging.

Four parts cans were included in this set, and even they were special and unique to this year. The parts cans for the other sets from 1948 were 1¾" deep; these were 2" deep.

Also included in No. 12½ was the (A48) Mechanical Motor, and its inclusion had an interesting impact on the instruction manual. This clockwork motor was featured in No. 4½, but no other larger set. So most of the No. 4½ section of the instruction manual—the pages that picture the (A48) motor models—was deleted in the larger sets except for No. 12½. It is the only other set to include these models in the instruction manual.

Finally, No. 12½ contained two (NM) 10" x 2" Flanged Plates. They were designed for the Electric Train Set and were dropped when that set was discontinued in 1942. Since no model in the instruction manual used these plates, Gilbert most likely included them to get rid of old inventory.

Erector System Modifications for 1948

I. Noteworthy Parts Colors and Finishes

(N21) Nut, square brass
(T) Boiler, nickel-plated steel
(CR) Special Turret Plate, steel or aluminum painted black
(MB) 18½" Angle Girder, nickel-plated steel

II. New Parts

(P55) 7-15 Volt Motor
(NW) Belt and Clip Unit
(NX) Tread Pulley
(NY) 3⅛" Axle
(NZ) Wood Handle Screwdriver
(OA) 18 Volt Bulb
(OB) Tread Pin
(OC) Single Wire & Plug Unit
(OD) Control Box with Wires
(2B) Transformer

III. Modified Parts

(A49) Electric Engine, all engines in every set came with a complete gearbox and gearshift. In the middle of the year, flanges on the motor housing were made with slots instead of holes, and the lettering on the core decal was changed from red to black
(NU) Parachute, two-piece sewn red silk

Listings of 1947 and 1948 Erector Sets

NO. 2½ — The Apprentice Set

Featured the (MH) Disc Wheels. Came in a cardboard box 18" x 10" x ¾"; sold for $3.00 in 1947 and 1948.

35 50 80 +20 +25

NO. 4½ — The Famous No. 4½

Featured the (A48) Mechanical Motor and (MN) 12" Base Plates, and (MX) House and built truck with (A48). Came in a cardboard box 18" x 10" x 2⅜" with a lift-off lid; two-layer set with removable cardboard parts display tray; sold for $6.50 in 1947 and $6.95 in 1948.

40 60 100 +20 +25

NO. 6½ — The Sensational No. 6½

Featured the (A49) Electric Engine with gearshift and built Airplane Ride. Came in a cardboard box 18" x 10" x 3" with a lift-off lid; two-layer set with removable cardboard parts display tray; sold for $9.75 in 1947 and $10.00 in 1948.

40 60 100 +20 +25

NO. 7½ (1947) — The Engineer's Set

Featured the (T) Boiler and (A49) Electric Engine with gearbox and built Walking Beam Engine. Came in a maroon cardboard box 20¾" x 13¾" x 3½" with a hinged lid; two-layer set with removable cardboard parts display tray; sold for $12.50.

120 180 300 +60 +80

NO. 7½ (1948) — The Engineer's Set

Featured the (T) Boiler and (A49) Electric Engine with gearbox and built Walking Beam Engine. Came in a red metal box 18" x 10" x 3" with a steel body and steel or aluminum lid; two-layer set with two removable cardboard parts display trays constructed from (MN) Base Plates; sold for $15.00.

50 70 120 +25 +30

NO. 8½ — The All-Electric Set

Featured the (MJ) Electro Magnet and lighting system parts and built Ferris Wheel and Bascule Bridge. Came in a red metal box 20" x 12" x 3" with steel or aluminum lid in 1948; two-layer set with three removable parts display trays constructed from (MN) Base Plates; sold for $16.95 in 1947 and $19.95 in 1948.

75 110 180 +40 +45

NO. 9½ — The Automotive Set

Featured the truck parts, giant flywheel, and parts to build Parachute Jump, Giant Power Plant, and trucks. Came in a red metal box 22" x 13" x 3"; two-layer set with three removable parts display trays constructed from (MN) Base Plates; sold for $25.00 in 1947 and $27.50 in 1948.

140 210 350 +70 +90

NO. 12½ (1948) — The Remote Control Set

Featured the (P55) 7-15 Volt Motor, (2B) Transformer, and other parts for building Mysterious Walking Giant as well as treads and tread pulleys for building Tank and Bulldozer. Came in a red metal box 24" x 14" x 4"; three-layer set with two removable parts trays; top one made of aluminum and covered inside of box, with red and yellow parts display insert; lower one constructed from (MN) Base Plates; sold for $50.00.

480 720 1200 +240 +300

THE 1949 ERECTOR LINE

Still another key year in the evolution of Erector was 1949, one filled with creativity and invention. Junior Erector, a completely new type of Erector (not to be confused with Erector Junior) was created. New sets were added to the regular line, and a new series of accessory sets was launched. Important new models were developed, and

ERECTOR SEPARATE PARTS PRICES

KINDLY ENCLOSE CHECK, MONEY ORDER OR STAMPS WITH YOUR ORDER FOR PARTS

THE A. C. GILBERT CO., NEW HAVEN, CONN., U. S. A.

Trade No.	Name of Part	Page	Price
*N21	8-32 Square Nut	3	.05 doz.
P7	Small Wheel, 7/8" Dia.	2	.10 ea.
P7A	Small Wheel, 1 1/8" Dia.	2	.10 ea.
P12	Crown Gear	2	.10 ea.
P13	12-Tooth Pinion Gear, 1/8"	2	.10 ea.
P13B	12-Tooth Pinion Gear, 7/32"	2	.10 ea.
P14	Worm Gear	2	.20 ea.
P15	Coupling	2	.10 ea.
P20	Five Hole Strip—formed	2	.05 ea.
P24	Crank	2	.10 ea.
P33	Small Screw Driver	3	.05 ea.
P34	Hank of String	3	.05 ea.
P37	Collar	2	.25 doz.
P48	Mitre Gear	2	.20 ea.
P49	18-Tooth Gear	2	.15 ea.
P52	Ladder Chain	3	.15/ft
P51	Electric Engine Reversing 110v. A.C. or D.C.	3	3.95 ea.
No. 5	Transformer	3	2.50 ea.
P56G	Motor, 110v. A.C. or D.C.	3	2.95 ea.
P58	Motor, 6-14 volts	3	1.00 ea.
P59	Reverse Base (for P58 only)	3	.75 ea.
A48	Mechanical Motor	3	1.00 ea.
K48	Mechanical Motor Key	3	.20 ea.
P57A	2 1/8" Axle	2	.02 ea.
P57D	6" Axle	2	.06 ea.
P57E	8" Axle	2	.08 ea.
P57F	12" Axle	2	.12 ea.
P79	Car Truck	2	.05 ea.
*S11	Set Srew	3	.05 doz.
*S51	1/4"x8-32 Screw	3	.05 doz.
*S52	1/2"x8-32 Screw	3	.10 doz.
*S57	1 3/8"x8-32 Screw	3	.15 doz.
*S62	7/8"x8-32 Screw	3	.10 doz.
*FA	1 1/4"x8-32 Screw	3	.15 doz.
A	2 1/2" Girder	2	.20 doz.
B	5" Girder	2	.35 doz.
C	10" Girder	2	.50 doz.
D	2 1/2" Curved Girder	2	.25 doz.
E	5" Curved Girder	2	.40 doz.
F	5 Hole Strip	2	.10 doz.
G	7 Hole Strip	2	.10 doz.
H	11 Hole Strip	2	.15 doz.
I	21 Hole Strip	2	.20 doz.
J	41 Hole Strip	2	.30 doz.
K	11 Hole Strip Bracket	2	.35 doz.
M	Small Double Angle	2	.25 doz.
N	Long Double Angle	2	.05 ea.
O	Pawl	2	.05 ea.
S	Large Base Plate—21 holes	2	.40 ea.
T	Boiler	3	.25 ea.
U	Boiler Top	3	.20 ea.

Trade No.	Name of Part	Page	Price
W	Stack	3	.05 ea.
Z	Flanged Wheel, 15/16" Dia.	2	.15 ea.
AA	Eccentric Crank	2	.10 ea.
AC	Universal Bracket	2	.10 ea.
AE	Spiral Spring	3	.05 ea.
AF	Small Hook	2	.15 doz.
AM	Special Pulley—Metal	2	.05 ea.
AQ	Sheave Pulley	2	.05 ea.
AS	2 7/8" Axle Rod	2	.03 ea.
AT	4" Axle Rod	2	.04 ea.
AX	19 3/4" Axle Rod	2	.20 ea.
BE	6" Angle Girder	2	.50 doz.
BH	Solid Collar	2	2 for .05
BL	Small Washer	2	.05 doz.
BN	Regular Turret Plate	3	.15 ea.
BT	Pierced Disc	2	.10 ea.
BY	11-Hole Fibre Strip	2	.05 ea.
CA	Signal Arm	3	.10 ea.
CH	Right Angle	2	.10 doz.
CJ	36-Tooth Gear	2	.20 ea.
CR	Special Turret plate with hub	3	.15 ea.
CS	Wheel Segment	3	.15 ea.
CX	1" Axle Rod	2	.01 ea.
CY	5" Axle Rod	2	.05 ea.
CZ	7" Axle Rod	2	.07 ea.
DA	10" Axle Rod	2	.10 ea.
DB	Motor Pulley	2	.10 ea.
DE	Steering Column	3	.10 ea.
DK	Flat Spring	3	.10 ea.
DO	Steering Wheel with Hub	2	.15 ea.
DP	12" Angle Girder	2	6 for .50
DS	Cotter Pin	3	.05 doz.
DT	1-Hole Set Screw Coupling	2	2 for .15
DZ	Tackle Block	2	.15 ea.
EH	Gear Box Bracket	2	.05 ea.
EI	Standard Gear Box Side Pl.	2	.15 ea.
EJ	Gear Box Base	2	.20 ea.
EX	Big Channel Girder 12"	2	6 for .50
EY	Big Channel Girder 6"	2	.05 ea.
EZ	6" Curved B. C. Girder	2	.05 ea.
FD	Hinged Loop	2	2 for .05
GV	Thin Disc Wheel Nickel Rim	2	.10 ea.
GW	Thin Disc Wheel—Red	2	.10 ea.
LV	3" Disc Wheel, red	2	.20 ea.
LX	Steering Column Bracket	3	.05 ea.
MA	Radiator	3	.15 ea.
MB	18 1/2" Angle Girder	2	.15 ea.
MC	Base Plate 1"x2 1/2"	2	.05 ea.
MD	Base Plate 2 1/2"x5"	2	.10 ea.
ME	Flat Plate 1"x4"	2	.05 ea.

Trade No.	Name of Part	Page	Price
MF	Flat Plate 1"x5"	2	.05 ea.
MG	Radiator Hood	3	.10 ea.
MH	3" Disc Wheel, Nickel Rim	2	.25 ea.
MI	Front Axle Unit	3	.25 ea.
MJ	Electro Magnet with Cord	3	.60 ea.
MM	Wrench	3	.05 ea.
MN	12" Base Plate	2	.40 ea.
MO	3" Angle Girder	2	.30 doz.
MR	Drum with Gear	2	.35 ea.
MS	Compression Spring	3	.05 ea.
MV	Flat Car Truck	2	.05 ea.
MW	Nut Holder	3	.10 ea.
MX	House	3	.35 ea.
MY	2 1/2"x2 1/2" Base Plate	2	.05 ea.
MZ	Bearing Block	2	.10 ea.
NH	Lamp Socket Unit	3	.15 ea.
NI	Bulb—1 1/2 Volt	3	.05 ea.
NJ	Battery Holder	3	.15 ea.
NK	Ratchet	2	.05 ea.
NL	Bolster Bracket	2	2 for .05
NM	10"x2" Flange Plate	2	.40 ea.
NN	1"x2" Flange Plate	2	.05 ea.
NO	Flanged Wheel, 3/4" Dia.	2	.15 ea.
NP	Locomotive—O Gauge	3	8.50 ea.
NQ	Section of Curved Track—O Gauge—(12 Sections per circle)	3	.20 ea.
NR	Track Terminal	3	.20 ea.
NS	41-Hole Strip—formed	2	.05 ea.
NT	Cone	3	.10 ea.
NU	Parachute	3	.25 ea.
NV	Whistle (Note—P13 gear required.)	3	.75 ea.
A49	Electric Engine, gear shift 110v. A.C. only	3	$3.95 ea.
A49-A	Electric Eng., no gear shift.		3.00 ea.
A49-B	Elec. Eng., conversion unit Converts A49-A to A49.	3	1.25 ea.
A49-C	A49 E.E. with Whistle		4.50 ea.

ERECTOR HOW TO MAKE 'EM BOOKS

Same as copy included in sets.

No. 1	Erector How to Make 'Em Book	.15 ea.
No. 3	Erector How to Make 'Em Book	.15 ea.
No. 4	Erector How to Make 'Em Book	.25 ea.
No. 6	Erector How to Make 'Em Book	.25 ea.
No. 7	Erector How to Make 'Em Book	.25 ea.
No. 8	Erector How to Make 'Em Book	.25 ea.
No. 9	Erector How to Make 'Em Book	.35 ea.

NOTE

*N21 Nut used with screws S51, S52, S62, S57, FA

*S11 Set Screw used with pulleys, couplings, etc.

ERECTOR HOW TO MAKE 'EM BOOKS

Same as copy included in Sets

		Price
No. 1 1/2	Erector How to Make 'Em Book	.15 ea
No. 2 1/2	Erector How to Make 'Em Book	.15 ea
No. 3 1/2	Erector How to Make 'Em Book	.15 ea
No. 4 1/2	Erector How to Make 'Em Book	.25 ea
No. 6 1/2	Erector How to Make 'Em Book	.25 ea
No. 7 1/2	Erector How to Make 'Em Book	.35 ea
No. 8 1/2	Erector How to Make 'Em Book	.35 ea
No. 9 1/2	Erector How to Make 'Em Book	.35 ea
No. 10 1/2	Erector How to Make 'Em Book	.35 ea

No. 9 1/2 AUTOMOTIVE SET
Electric engine, chassis parts, big channel girders, giant fly wheel segment, etc. Builds automobiles, trucks, giant power plant, elevator, mammoth walking beam engine, parachute jump, etc. .35

No. 10 1/2 WORLD'S CHAMPION ELECTRIC TRAIN SET.
Features completely assembled electric locomotive with circle of track. Additional equipment builds tender, freight cars, turntable and a host of other fine models including all those built with the above sets.... .35

Separate Parts Prices for late 1946 and early 1947

ERECTOR SEPARATE PARTS PRICES

KINDLY ENCLOSE CHECK, MONEY ORDER OR STAMPS WITH YOUR ORDER FOR PARTS

THE A. C. GILBERT CO., NEW HAVEN, CONN., U. S. A.

Trade No.	Name of Part	Page	Price
*N21	8-32 Square Nut	3	.05 doz.
P7	Small Wheel, 7/8" Dia.	2	.10 ea.
P7A	Small Wheel, 1 1/8" Dia.	2	.10 ea.
P12	Crown Gear	2	.10 ea.
P13	12-Tooth Pinion Gear, 1/8"	2	.10 ea.
P13B	12-Tooth Pinion Gear, 7/32"	2	.10 ea.
P14	Worm Gear	2	.20 ea.
P15	Coupling	2	.10 ea.
P20	Five Hole Strip—formed	2	.05 ea.
P24	Crank	2	.10 ea.
P33	Small Screw Driver	3	.05 ea.
P34	Hank of String	3	.05 ea.
P37	Collar	2	.25 doz.
P48	Mitre Gear	2	.20 ea.
P49	18-Tooth Gear	2	.15 ea.
P52	Ladder Chain	3	.15/ft
P51	Electric Engine Reversing 110v. A.C. or D.C.	3	3.95 ea.
No. 5	Transformer	3	2.50 ea.
P56G	Motor, 110v. A.C. or D.C.	3	2.95 ea.
P58	Motor, 6-14 volts	3	1.00 ea.
P59	Reverse Base (for P58 only)	3	.75 ea.
A48	Mechanical Motor	3	1.00 ea.
K48	Mechanical Motor Key	3	.20 ea.
P57A	2 1/8" Axle	2	.02 ea.
P57D	6" Axle	2	.06 ea.
P57E	8" Axle	2	.08 ea.
P57F	12" Axle	2	.12 ea.
P79	Car Truck	2	.05 ea.
*S11	Set Srew	3	.05 doz.
*S51	1/4"x8-32 Screw	3	.05 doz.
*S52	1/2"x8-32 Screw	3	.10 doz.
*S57	1 3/8"x8-32 Screw	3	.15 doz.
*S62	7/8"x8-32 Screw	3	.10 doz.
*FA	1 1/4"x8-32 Screw	3	.15 doz.
A	2 1/2" Girder	2	.20 doz.
B	5" Girder	2	.35 doz.
C	10" Girder	2	.50 doz.
D	2 1/2" Curved Girder	2	.25 doz.
E	5" Curved Girder	2	.40 doz.
F	5 Hole Strip	2	.10 doz.
G	7 Hole Strip	2	.10 doz.
H	11 Hole Strip	2	.15 doz.
I	21 Hole Strip	2	.20 doz.
J	41 Hole Strip	2	.30 doz.
K	11 Hole Strip Bracket	2	.35 doz.
M	Small Double Angle	2	.25 doz.
N	Long Double Angle	2	.05 ea.
O	Pawl	2	.05 ea.
S	Large Base Plate—21 holes	2	.40 ea.
T	Boiler	3	.25 ea.
U	Boiler Top	3	.20 ea.

Trade No.	Name of Part	Page	Price
W	Stack	3	.05 ea.
Z	Flanged Wheel, 15/16" Dia.	2	.15 ea.
AA	Eccentric Crank	2	.10 ea.
AC	Universal Bracket	2	.10 ea.
AE	Spiral Spring	3	.05 ea.
AF	Small Hook	2	.15 doz.
AM	Special Pulley—Metal	2	.05 ea.
AQ	Sheave Pulley	2	.05 ea.
AS	2 7/8" Axle Rod	2	.03 ea.
AT	4" Axle Rod	2	.04 ea.
AX	19 3/4" Axle Rod	2	.20 ea.
BE	6" Angle Girder	2	.50 doz.
BH	Solid Collar	2	2 for .05
BL	Small Washer	2	.05 doz.
BN	Regular Turret Plate	3	.15 ea.
BT	Pierced Disc	2	.10 ea.
BY	11-Hole Fibre Strip	2	.05 ea.
CA	Signal Arm	3	.10 ea.
CH	Right Angle	2	.10 doz.
CJ	36-Tooth Gear	2	.20 ea.
CR	Special Turret plate with hub	3	.15 ea.
CS	Wheel Segment	3	.15 ea.
CX	1" Axle Rod	2	.01 ea.
CY	5" Axle Rod	2	.05 ea.
CZ	7" Axle Rod	2	.07 ea.
DA	10" Axle Rod	2	.10 ea.
DB	Motor Pulley	2	.10 ea.
DE	Steering Column	3	.10 ea.
DK	Flat Spring	3	.10 ea.
DO	Steering Wheel with Hub	2	.15 ea.
DP	12" Angle Girder	2	6 for .50
DS	Cotter Pin	3	.05 doz.
DT	1-Hole Set Screw Coupling	2	2 for .15
DZ	Tackle Block	2	.15 ea.
EH	Gear Box Bracket	2	.05 ea.
EI	Standard Gear Box Side Pl.	2	.15 ea.
EJ	Gear Box Base	2	.20 ea.
EX	Big Channel Girder 12"	2	6 for .50
EY	Big Channel Girder 6"	2	.05 ea.
EZ	6" Curved B. C. Girder	2	.05 ea.
FD	Hinged Loop	2	2 for .05
GV	Thin Disc Wheel Nickel Rim	2	.10 ea.
GW	Thin Disc Wheel—Red	2	.10 ea.
LV	3" Disc Wheel, red	2	.20 ea.
LX	Steering Column Bracket	3	.05 ea.
MA	Radiator	3	.15 ea.
MB	18 1/2" Angle Girder	2	.15 ea.
MC	Base Plate 1"x2 1/2"	2	.05 ea.
MD	Base Plate 2 1/2"x5"	2	.10 ea.
ME	Flat Plate 1"x4"	2	.05 ea.

Trade No.	Name of Part	Page	Price
MF	Flat Plate 1"x5"	2	.05 ea.
MG	Radiator Hood	3	.10 ea.
MH	3" Disc Wheel, Nickel Rim	2	.25 ea.
MI	Front Axle Unit	3	.25 ea.
MJ	Electro Magnet with Cord	3	.60 ea.
MM	Wrench	3	.05 ea.
MN	12" Base Plate	2	.40 ea.
MO	3" Angle Girder	2	.30 doz.
MR	Drum with Gear	2	.35 ea.
MS	Compression Spring	3	.05 ea.
MV	Flat Car Truck	2	.05 ea.
MW	Nut Holder	3	.10 ea.
MX	House	3	.35 ea.
MY	2 1/2"x2 1/2" Base Plate	2	.05 ea.
MZ	Bearing Block	2	.10 ea.
NH	Lamp Socket Unit	3	.15 ea.
NI	Bulb—1 1/2 Volt	3	.05 ea.
NJ	Battery Holder	3	.15 ea.
NK	Ratchet	2	.05 ea.
NL	Bolster Bracket	2	2 for .05
NM	10"x2" Flange Plate	2	.40 ea.
NN	1"x2" Flange Plate	2	.05 ea.
NO	Flanged Wheel, 3/4" Dia.	2	.15 ea.
NP	Locomotive—O Gauge	3	8.50 ea.
NQ	Section of Curved Track—O Gauge—(12 Sections per circle)	3	.20 ea.
NR	Track Terminal	3	.20 ea.
NS	41-Hole Strip—formed	2	.05 ea.
NT	Cone	3	.10 ea.
NU	Parachute	3	.25 ea.
A49	Electric Engine, gear shift 110v. A.C. only	3	$3.95 ea.
A49-A	Electric Eng., no gear shift.		3.00 ea.
A49-B	Elec. Eng., conversion unit Converts A49-A to A49.	3	1.25 ea.

ERECTOR HOW TO MAKE 'EM BOOKS

Same as copy included in sets.

No. 1	Erector How to Make 'Em Book	.15 ea.
No. 3	Erector How to Make 'Em Book	.15 ea.
No. 4	Erector How to Make 'Em Book	.25 ea.
No. 6	Erector How to Make 'Em Book	.25 ea.
No. 7	Erector How to Make 'Em Book	.25 ea.
No. 8	Erector How to Make 'Em Book	.25 ea.
No. 9	Erector How to Make 'Em Book	.35 ea.

NOTE

*N21 Nut used with screws S51, S52, S62, S57, FA

*S11 Set Screw used with pulleys, couplings, etc.

ERECTOR HOW TO MAKE 'EM BOOKS

Same as copy included in Sets

		Price
No. 1 1/2	Erector How to Make 'Em Book	.15 ea
No. 2 1/2	Erector How to Make 'Em Book	.15 ea
No. 3 1/2	Erector How to Make 'Em Book	.15 ea
No. 4 1/2	Erector How to Make 'Em Book	.25 ea
No. 6 1/2	Erector How to Make 'Em Book	.25 ea
No. 7 1/2	Erector How to Make 'Em Book	.35 ea
No. 8 1/2	Erector How to Make 'Em Book	.35 ea
No. 9 1/2	Erector How to Make 'Em Book	.35 ea
No. 10 1/2	Erector How to Make 'Em Book	.35 ea

No. 9 1/2 AUTOMOTIVE SET
Electric engine, chassis parts, big channel girders, giant fly wheel segment, etc. Builds automobiles, trucks, giant power plant, elevator, mammoth walking beam engine, parachute jump, etc. .35

No. 10 1/2 WORLD'S CHAMPION ELECTRIC TRAIN SET.
Features completely assembled electric locomotive with circle of track. Additional equipment builds tender, freight cars, turntable and a host of other fine models including all those built with the above sets.... .35

Separate Parts Prices for late 1947

1946–48 CONTENTS LIST

Part No.	Description	2½	4½	6½	7½	8½	9½	12½[1]
P7	7/8" Pulley	4	4	4	4	0	0	0
P7A	1 1/8" PULLEY	0	0	0	0	4	4	4
P12	CROWN GEAR	0	0	0	0	0	1	1
P13	12 TOOTH PINION GEAR, 1/8"	0	0	1	2	2	2	2
P13B	12 TOOTH PINION GEAR, 7/23"	0	0	0	1	1	1	1
P15	COUPLING	0	1	1	1	2	2	2
P20	5 HOLE STRIP—FORMED	0	0	0	2	2	8	8
P24	CRANK	1	1	1	1	1	1	2
P33	SMALL SCREW DRIVER	1	1	1	1	1	1	0
P34	HANK OF STRING	1	1	1	1	1	1	1
P37	COLLAR	4	5	6	7	9	18	18
P48	MITRE GEAR	0	0	2	2	2	2	2
P55[2]	7-15 VOLT ERECTOR MOTOR	0	0	0	0	0	0	1
P57A	2 1/8" AXLE	1	1	1	1	1	4	8
P57D	6" AXLE	1	0	0	0	0	0	1
P57E	8" AXLE	0	0	0	0	0	2	2
P57F	12" AXLE	0	0	0	0	1	2	2
P79	CAR TRUCK	4	4	4	4	4	4	4
A	2½" GIRDER	4	4	4	4	4	4	4
B	5" GIRDER	4	8	12	12	12	12	12
C	10" GIRDER	8	8	14	14	36	36	36
D	2½" CURVED GIRDER	4	4	4	4	4	4	4
E	5" CURVED GIRDER	2	2	4	4	26	26	26
F	5 HOLE STRIP	0	2	2	2	2	2	16
G	7 HOLE STRIP	0	2	2	2	2	2	8
H	11 HOLE STRIP	0	4	4	4	4	4	7
I	21 HOLE STRIP	0	2	2	2	4	18	18
J	41 HOLE STRIP	0	0	0	0	2	2	4
M	SMALL DOUBLE ANGLE	0	0	0	2	6	6	6
N	LONG DOUBLE ANGLE	4	4	4	4	4	4	4
O	PAWL	0	0	1	2	2	6	6
T	BOILER	0	0	0	1	1	2	2
U	BOILER TOP	0	0	0	1	1	1	2
W	STACK	0	0	0	3	3	3	3
Z	FLANGED WHEEL 15/16" DIA.	0	0	0	4	4	4	4
AA	ECCENTRIC CRANK	0	0	0	0	0	6	6
AE	SPIRAL SPRING	0	0	0	0	0	0	2
AF	SMALL HOOK	1	1	1	1	1	1	1
AJ	PAPER ERECTOR FLAG	0	1	1	1	1	1	1
AQ	SHEAVE PULLEY	0	0	0	0	1	4	5

Part No.	Description	2½	4½	6½	7½	8½	9½	12½[1]
AS	2 7/8" AXLE	0	2	2	3	3	4	4
AT	4" AXLE	2	2	2	2	2	2	2
BE	6" ANGLE GIRDER	0	4	4	4	4	4	4
BH	SOLID COLLAR	0	0	0	0	0	2	2
BL	SMALL WASHER	12	12	12	12	12	14	17
BN	REGULAR TURRET PLATE	0	2	2	4	4	4	4
BT	PIERCED DISC	1	1	2	2	4	4	4
BY	11 HOLE FIBRE STRIP	0	0	0	0	1	1	1
CA	SIGNAL ARM	0	0	0	0	0	2	2
CH	RIGHT ANGLE	12	14	14	14	30	42	42
CJ	36 TOOTH GEAR	0	0	2	3	3	3	3
CR	SPECIAL TURRET PLATE WITH HUB	0	0	0	0	0	2	2
CS	WHEEL SEGMENT	0	0	0	0	0	8	8
CY	5" AXLE	2	0	0	0	0	0	0
CZ	7" AXLE	0	2	2	2	3	3	3
DA	10" AXLE ROD	0	0	0	0	0	0	2
DB	MOTOR PULLEY	0	1	1	1	1	1	1
DE	STEERING COLUMN	0	0	0	0	0	1	1
DK	FLAT SPRING	0	0	0	0	0	4	4
DO	STEERING WHEEL WITH HUB	0	0	0	0	0	1	1
DP	12" ANGLE GIRDER	0	4	4	4	4	4	4
DS	COTTER PIN	0	0	0	0	0	1	1
EI	STD. GEAR BOX SIDE PLATE	0	0	2	2	2	2	2
EX	BIG CHANNEL GIRDER 12"	0	0	0	0	0	8	8
EY	BIG CHANNEL GIRDER 6"	0	0	0	0	0	4	4
EZ	BIG CHAN.GIRDER CURVED 6"	0	0	0	0	0	2	2
FA	1¾" x 8-32 SCREW	0	0	0	0	0	12	12
FD	HINGED LOOP	0	0	0	0	0	2	2
LX	STEERING COLUMN BRACKET	0	0	0	0	0	1	1
MA	RADIATOR	0	0	0	0	0	1	1
MB	18½" ANGLE GIRDER	0	0	0	0	0	2	2
MC	BASE PLATE 1" x 2½"	2	2	2	2	8	8	8
MD	BASE PLATE 2½" x 5"	1	1	1	1	4	4	4
ME	BASE PLATE 1" x 4"	0	0	0	0	0	4	4
MF	BASE PLATE 1" x 5"	2	4	4	4	8	9	12
MG	RADIATOR HOOD	0	0	0	0	0	1	1

1946–48 CONTENTS LIST

Set No. Part No.	Description	2½	4½	6½	7½	8½	9½	12½[1]
		Pieces Per Set						
MH	LARGE 3" DISC WHEEL	4	4	4	4	4	4	4
MI	FRONT AXLE UNIT	0	0	0	0	0	1	1
MJ	ELECTRO MAGNET WITH CORD	0	0	0	0	1	1	1
MM	WRENCH	0	1	1	1	1	1	1
MN	12" BASE PLATE	0	4	4	4	6	6	6
MO	3" ANGLE GIRDER	0	4	4	4	4	4	4
MV	FLAT CAR TRUCK	0	0	0	2	4	4	4
MW	NUT HOLDER	0	1	1	1	1	1	1
MX	HOUSE	0	1	1	1	1	1	1
MY	2½" x 2½" BASE PLATE	0	1	1	1	1	1	1
MZ	BEARING BLOCK	0	0	1	1	1	1	1
NH	LAMP SOCKET UNIT	0	0	0	0	2	2	2
NI	BULB, 1½ VOLT	0	0	0	0	2	2	2
NJ	BATTERY HOLDER	0	0	0	0	1	1	1
NK	RATCHET	0	0	0	2	2	2	2
NL	BOLSTER BRACKET	0	0	0	0	0	0	4
NM	10" x 2" FLANGED PLATE	0	0	0	0	0	0	2
NS	41 HOLE STRIP—FORMED	0	0	0	0	0	2	2
NT	CONE	0	0	0	0	0	4	4
NU	PARACHUTE	0	0	0	0	0	4	4
NW[2]	BELT AND CLIP UNIT	0	0	0	0	0	0	2

Set No. Part No.	Description	2½	4½	6½	7½	8½	9½	12½[1]
		Pieces Per Set						
NX[2]	TREAD PULLEY	0	0	0	0	0	0	4
NY[2]	3⅛" AXLE ROD	0	0	0	0	0	0	1
NZ[2]	WOOD HANDLE SCREWDRIVER	0	0	0	0	0	1	1
OA[2]	BULB—18 VOLT	0	0	0	0	0	0	2
OB[2]	TREAD PIN	0	0	0	0	0	0	2
OC[2]	SINGLE WIRE AND PLUG UNIT	0	0	0	0	0	0	1
OD[2]	CONTROL BOX WITH WIRES	0	0	0	0	0	0	1
A48	MECHANICAL MOTOR	0	1	0	0	0	0	1
K48	KEY FOR MECH. MOTOR	0	1	0	0	0	0	1
A49	ELECTRIC ENGINE	0	0	1	1	1	1	1
2-B[2]	TRANSFORMER	0	0	0	0	0	0	1
N21	8-32 SQUARE NUT	45	88	93	93	169	254	350
S51	¼" x 8-32 SCREW	35	80	84	84	162	206	255
S52	½" x 8-32 SCREW	0	0	4	4	4	4	4
S57	1⅜" x 8-32 SCREW	0	0	0	4	4	4	4
S62	⅞" x 8-32 SCREW	6	8	8	8	18	20	20

1. Set No. 12½ was first available in 1948; Set No. 12½ also contained an offset wrench.

2. These parts were first available in 1948.

ERECTOR SEPARATE PARTS PRICES

KINDLY ENCLOSE CHECK, MONEY ORDER OR STAMPS WITH YOUR ORDER FOR PARTS

THE A. C. GILBERT CO., NEW HAVEN, CONN., U. S. A.

Trade No.	Name of Part	Page	Price
*N21	8-32 Square Nut	3	.10 doz.
P7	Small Wheel, ⅞" Dia.	2	.10 ea.
P7A	Small Wheel, 1⅛" Dia.	2	.10 ea.
P12	Crown Gear	2	.15 ea.
P13	12-Tooth Pinion Gear, ⅛"	2	.10 ea.
P13B	12-Tooth Pinion Gear, 3/32"	2	.10 ea.
P15	Coupling	2	.10 ea.
P20	Five Hole Strip—formed	2	.10 ea.
P24	Crank	2	.10 ea.
P33	Small Screw Driver	3	.10 ea.
P34	Hank of String	3	.10 ea.
P37	Collar	2	.25 doz.
P48	Mitre Gear	2	.20 ea.
P57A	2⅞" Axle	2	.02 ea.
P57D	6" Axle	2	.06 ea.
P57E	8" Axle	2	.08 ea.
P57F	12" Axle	2	.12 ea.
P79	Car Truck	2	.05 ea.
*S11	Set Screw	3	.05 doz.
*S51	¼" x 8-32 Screw	3	.10 doz.
*S52	½" x 8-32 Screw	3	.10 doz.
*S57	1⅜" x 8-32 Screw	3	.15 doz.
*S62	⅞" x 8-32 Screw	3	.10 doz.
*FA	1¼" x 8-32 Screw	3	.15 doz.
A	2½" Girder	2	.20 doz.
B	5" Girder	2	.35 doz.
C	10" Girder	2	.50 doz.
D	2½" Curved Girder	2	.25 doz.
E	5" Curved Girder	2	.40 doz.
F	5 Hole Strip	2	.10 doz.
G	7 Hole Strip	2	.10 doz.
H	11 Hole Strip	2	.15 doz.
I	21 Hole Strip	2	.20 doz.
J	41 Hole Strip	2	.50 doz.
M	Small Double Angle	2	.25 doz.
N	Long Double Angle	2	.05 ea.
O	Pawl	2	.05 ea.
S	Large Base Plate—21 holes	2	.40 ea.
T	Boiler	3	.30 ea.
U	Boiler Top	3	.20 ea.
W	Stack	3	.05 ea.
Z	Flanged Wheel 1 5/16" Dia.	2	.15 ea.
AA	Eccentric Crank	2	.10 ea.
AE	Spiral Spring	3	.05 ea.
AF	Small Hook	2	.15 doz.
AM	Special Pulley—Metal	2	.05 ea.
AQ	Sheave Pulley	2	.05 ea.
AS	2⅞" Axle Rod	2	.03 ea.
AT	4" Axle Rod	2	.04 ea.
BE	6" Angle Girder	2	.50 doz.
BH	Solid Collar	2	2 for .10
BL	Small Washer	2	.05 doz.
BN	Regular Turret Plate	3	.15 ea.
BT	Pierced Disc	2	.10 ea.
BY	11-Hole Fibre Strip	2	.05 ea.
CA	Signal Arm	3	.10 ea.
CH	Right Angle	2	.10 doz.
CJ	36-Tooth Gear	2	.20 ea.
CR	Special Turret Plate with hub	3	.20 ea.
CS	Wheel Segment	3	.15 ea.
CZ	7" Axle Rod	2	.07 ea.
DA	10" Axle Rod	2	.10 ea.
DB	Motor Pulley	2	.10 ea.
DE	Steering Column	3	.15 ea.
DK	Flat Spring	3	.10 ea.
DO	Steering Wheel with Hub	2	.15 ea.
DP	12" Angle Girder	2	6 for .50
DS	Cotter Pin	3	.05 doz.
EI	Standard Gear Box Side Plate	2	.15 ea.
EX	Big Channel Girder 12"	2	6 for .50
EY	Big Channel Girder 6"	2	.05 ea.
EZ	Big Channel Curved Girder 6"	2	.10 ea.
FD	Hinged Loop	2	2 for .10
LX	Steering Column Bracket	3	.10 ea.
MA	Radiator	3	.25 ea.
MB	18½" Angle Girder	2	.25 ea.
MC	Base Plate 1" x 2½"	2	.05 ea.
MD	Base Plate 2½" x 5"	2	.10 ea.
ME	Base Plate 1" x 4"	2	.05 ea.
MF	Base Plate 1" x 5"	2	.05 ea.
MG	Radiator Hood	3	.20 ea.
MH	Nickle Rim, 3" Disc Wheel	2	.25 ea.
MI	Front Axle Unit	3	.45 ea.
MJ	Electro Magnet with Cord	3	1.10 ea.
MM	Wrench	3	.05 ea.
MN	12" Base Plate	2	.40 ea.
MO	3" Angle Girder	2	.30 doz.
MV	Flat Car Truck	2	.05 ea.
MW	Nut Holder	3	.10 ea.
MX	House	3	.35 ea.
MY	2½" x 2½" Base Plate	2	.05 ea.
MZ	Bearing Block	2	.10 ea.
NH	Lamp Socket Unit	3	.20 ea.
NI	Bulb—1½ Volt	3	.10 ea.
NJ	Battery Holder	3	.15 ea.
NK	Ratchet	2	.05 ea.
NL	Bolster Bracket	2	2 for .05
NM	10" x 2" Flange Plate	2	.40 ea.
NS	41 Hole strip—formed	2	.10 ea.
NT	Cone	3	.10 ea.
NU	Parachute	3	.35 ea.
NW	Belt and Clip Unit	3	.25 ea.
NX	Tread Pulley	2	.20 ea.
NY	3⅛" Axle Rod	2	.05 ea.
NZ	Wood Handle Screwdriver	3	.20 ea.
OA	Bulb—18 Volt	3	.20 ea.
OB	Tread Pin	3	.10 ea.
OC	Single Wire and Plug Unit	3	.10 ea.
OD	Control Box with wires	3	1.50 ea.
OE	6" Flexible Coupling	3	.15 ea.
A48	Mechanical Motor	3	1.75 ea.
K48	Key for Mechancal Motor	3	.20 ea.
A49	Electric Engine, gear shift 110v. A.C. only	3	5.95 ea.
A49A	Electric Engine—No Gear Shift	3	4.95 ea.
A49B	Electric Engine Conversion Unit. Convert A49A to A49	3	1.25 ea.
P55	7-15 Volt Erector Motor A.C. or D.C.	3	4.50 ea.
2-B	Transformer with Circuit Breaker	3	7.95 ea.

NOTE

*N21 Nut used with screws S51, S52, S57, S62, FA
*S11 Set Screw used with pulleys, couplings, etc.

ERECTOR
HOW TO MAKE 'EM BOOKS

Same as copy included in Sets

		Price
No. 2½	Erector How To Make 'Em Book	.25 ea.
No. 4½	Erector How To Make 'Em Book	.25 ea.
No. 6½	Erector How To Make 'Em Book	.35 ea.
No. 7½	Erector How To Make 'Em Book	.35 ea.
No. 8½	Erector How To Make 'Em Book	.40 ea.
No. 9½	Erector How To Make 'Em Book	.50 ea.
No. 12½	Erector How To Make 'Em Book	.75 ea.

Separate Parts Prices for 1948

More than any other model, the Ferris Wheel (1935–62) has come to symbolize A. C. Gilbert's Erector sets. This is a factory-built store display model from the early 1950s.

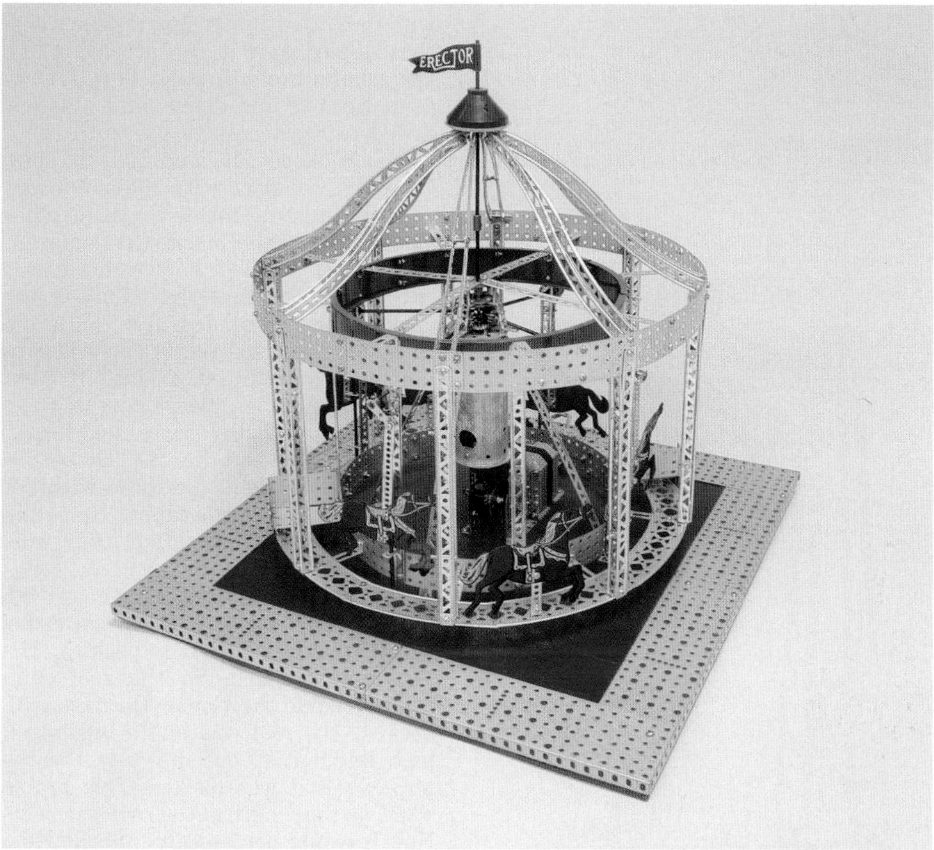

The Merry-Go-Round, developed in 1949, was one of the premiere models of the Renaissance Period. It spurred the creation of one of the finest Erector Sets, the No. 10½ Amusement Park Set.

special parts were added to the Erector System. At the same time, some major models were redesigned and improved.

Junior Erector was a completely new style of Erector with parts made from brightly colored plastic. Gilbert hailed it as "Erector for Small Fry—2 to 6 Years"; this system replaced the wooden Erector Junior line.

There were three additional sets included in the roster in 1949. Set No. 1½, missing since the war, was returned at the bottom of the line. Set No 6½A (in a metal box) was offered in addition to "regular" No. 6½ (in a cardboard box). But most important, an entirely new set, perhaps the best proportioned and most functional of all time, was created: No. 10½ Amusement Park Set.

What really spurred the creation of the Amusement Park Set was the invention of the new Merry-Go-Round model. If the Parachute Jump was the greatest model of the Renaissance Period, the Merry-Go-Round was a close second. It could almost be built with No. 9½; only a handful of parts were needed, in addition to the carousel horses.

I imagine that Gilbert's first thought was to add these new parts to No. 9½. But if he had, he would have had an Automotive Set that also built a Parachute Jump and a Merry-Go-Round. No, something more spectacular was needed here.

In my mind I can picture Gilbert, late one night in his office, sitting in an overstuffed chair, smoking his pipe, and thinking, "This new set will build an airplane ride, a Ferris wheel, a parachute jump ride, and a merry-go-round. Should I still call it the Automotive Set? Or should I give it a new name and number? Aha! I'll name it the No. 10½ Amusement Park Set!"

Set No. 9½ was cataloged, along with No. 10½, and both sets were packed in the same size metal box. But by the end of the year (or more likely, when the inventories were exhausted), No 9½ was dropped.

The Parachute Jump was redesigned in 1949. In the past, the (NT) Cone was used to lift the (NU) Parachute to the top of the tower. Now a new mechanism for this action was created using the (OH) 72 Tooth Gear and (OI) Segment of 72 Tooth Gear. The result was a much more pleasing action with better, free-falling parachutes. The height of this model was also increased from 5 feet to nearly 6. The improved Parachute Jump parts were packed in Nos. 10½ and 12½, but not in the 1949 version of No. 9½.

The Mysterious Walking Giant was also redesigned this year. The (NW) Belt and Clip Units (Treads) were incorporated into the model's feet, as a much improved method of propulsion was developed. And the new (OE) Flexible Couplings were used to make the arms move.

Gilbert produced two different versions of No. 12½ in 1949. In contents, the earlier version was similar to No. 12½ from 1948: neither the Merry-Go-Round parts nor the improved parts for the Parachute Jump were included. However, the later version of No. 12½ did have them.

In addition, 1949 was the most obviously fragmented year in Erector history. While there was always some modification and change throughout most any year, no other year had the remarkable and abrupt improvements as did 1949.

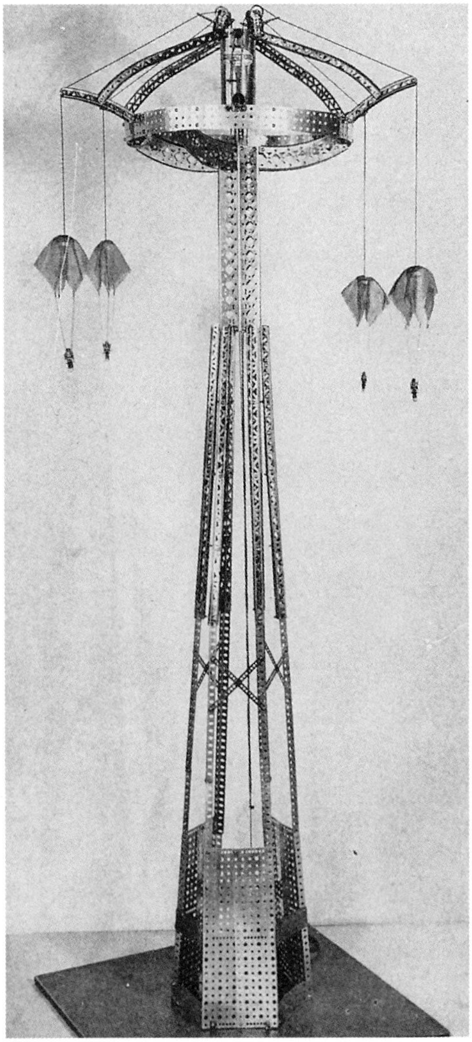

The Parachute Jump was redesigned in 1949. The old cones were replaced with new gears, and the mechanism for raising and releasing the parachutes was much improved. This revised model also stood a foot higher than its predecessor.

Clearly, the creation of the Merry-Go-Round and the improvements in the Parachute Jump occurred in midyear. Not only is this borne out by the existence of two different No. 12½s, but by the literature as well. The *Gilbert Scientific Toys Complete Catalog for 1949* (item no. D1531) makes no mention of the Merry-Go-Round or No. 10½. But *Fun and Thrills* (no. D1536), published later in 1949, heavily promoted both the Merry-Go-Round (included in Nos. 10½ and 12½), and No. 10½, the Amusement Park Set.

Some interesting new parts joined the Erector System in 1949. The (OF) Horse, (OG) 21 Hole Strip Formed, and the (P57JA) 7½" Axle were all designed for use on the Merry-Go-Round. The (OH) 72 Tooth Gear and (OI) Segment of 72 Tooth Gear made the new Parachute Jump mechanism work. But the new part that was given the most hype was the (OE) 6" Flexible Coupling.

Actually, the Flexible Coupling was first included in the parts pages in 1948. But apparently it came along too late to include it in the sets, because 1949 was the first year that it was mentioned in the advertising or packed in the sets. This part was really a flexible axle, and although it was a worthwhile addition to Erector, it didn't deserve all the attention that Gilbert gave it. But according to the 1949 ads, it was a spectacular breakthrough. Part (OE) was included in all sets from No. 6½ and above, and a second (P15) coupling was added to these sets to use with the (OE). The instruction manuals were all modified to show how this Flexible Coupling was used with the motor and various gear trains.

An interesting mystery still exists with the (OF) Horse. The picture of the Merry-Go-Round in the instruction manuals shows carousel horses that are decorated quite differently from the ones that came in the sets. And since the illustration is a photograph, there is reason to believe that these early horses really exist. But none of these mystery horses have surfaced, to date. If anyone has knowledge of these early horses, please contact the author.

Other noteworthy parts modifications include the (MV) Flat Car Truck and the (MX) House. Beginning this year, the Flat Car Truck was produced with two notches in the base (the side opposite the taper). Since these notches served no purpose in model building, they must have aided in the manufacturing process.

The modification made in the (MX) House was even more interesting. When Set No. 12½ was developed in 1948, there was no room in the box to pack the House, at least not with the roof attached. So the roof came unassembled, and packed inside the House. But this still didn't work too well, because the roof was just a bit longer than the house was high, and it stuck out and caught on the cardboard parts display when it was packed. This problem was alleviated in 1949, as the length of the roof was reduced from 2¾" to 2½". Now it would pack nicely into the House and No. 12½.

Finally, the (NU) Parachute was changed again this year. In 1948, the parachutes were made from red silk, and each chute had a seam, as the fabric was sewn. Now the chutes were made from a single piece of fabric again, and the color of the silk was always white.

Gilbert introduced three accessory kits in 1949 that were different from anything he had offered in the past. Accessory sets had been part of the line from the beginning. Between 1913 and 1920, they were available to move a set up one notch (Accessory Set 1A contained the extra parts necessary to make No. 1 into No. 2). In the 1920s, accessory sets came with special parts. The B Accessory Set from 1928 had the special girders and other parts necessary to build the Giant Ferris Wheel. But these accessory sets were complete sets in themselves. Now, for the first time, accessory kits really were accessory! They contained some extra parts or something special to be used with Erector, but the contents of these sets were useless by themselves.

The first of these 1949 accessory kits was No. 1E, named "The Erector Square Girder Kit"; it was intended to supply extra parts. Included in it were twenty (C) 10" Girders, eight (B) 5" Girders, fifteen (S62) ⅞" Screws, and fifteen (N21) Nuts. These parts were packed in a heavy cardboard tube with a metal screw-off cap. The tube was finished in a yellow background with red and black letters. A picture of a hand holding a square girder (reminiscent of the picture used on the set box lids in the 1910s) completed the artwork on the tube of this unusual item.

The second accessory kit introduced in 1949, No. 5, was called "The Erector Illumination Kit," and it offered the addition of colored lights to Erector models. Along with directions on how to add blinking or steady lights to a model, this kit included:

1 (X10073) Commutator
1 (X129) Brush Unit

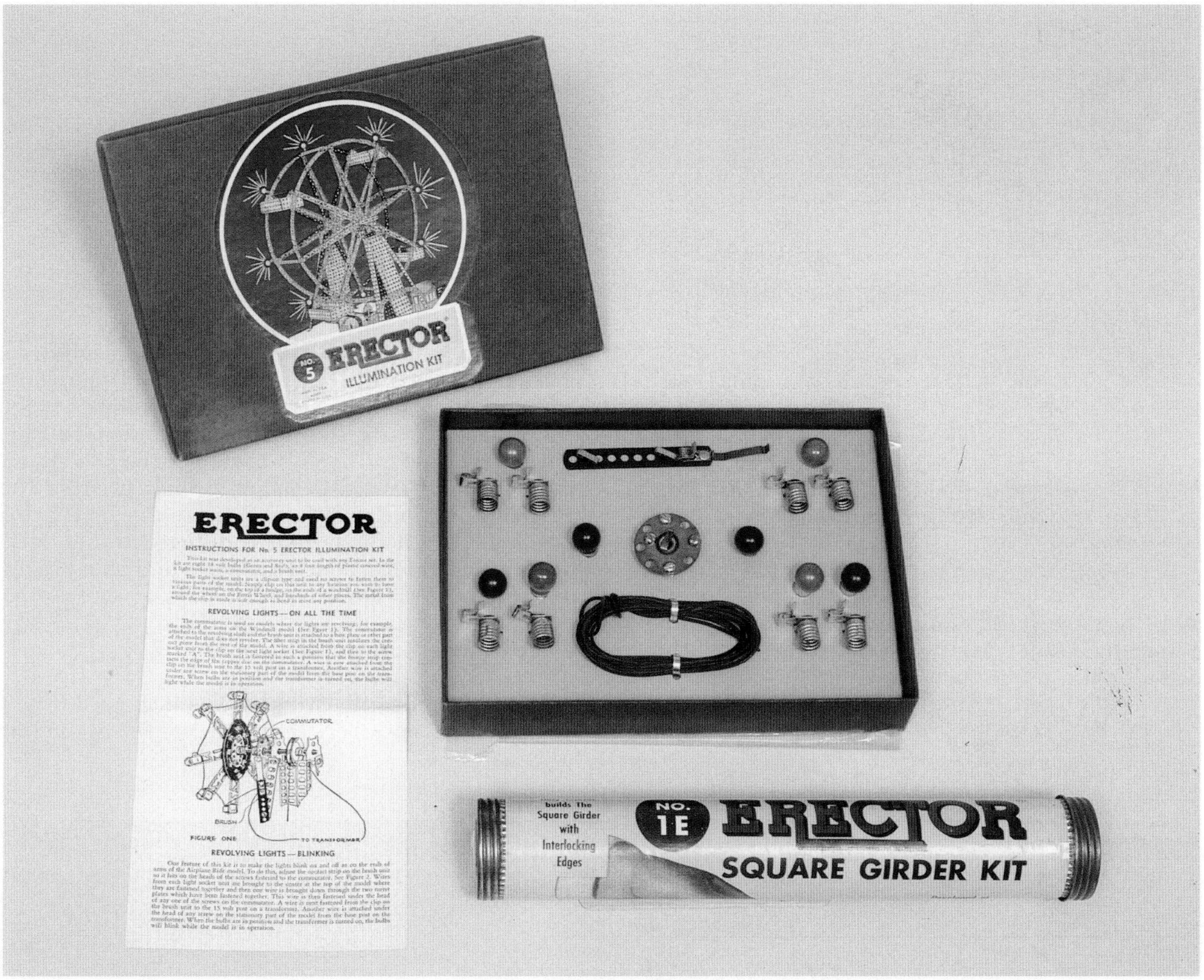

In 1949 Gilbert began to develop a series of accessory kits. The Square Girder Kit (No. 1E) provided additional girders; The Erector Illumination Kit (No. 5) provided colored lights for Erector models.

(X9593-A) Light Socket Assembly
(441) Light Bulb-Red-18 Volts
(443) Light Bulb-Green-18 Volts
(PA10249-AN) 8 Feet of Plastic Covered Wire

This pretty little kit came in an 8¾" x 6¼" x 1½" pale red ardboard box. The label on the lid was the same size and hape as the label used on the outside of the metal box sets, ut the background was blue. Pictured on this label was the rector Ferris Wheel, ablaze with lights. Below the Ferris Vheel, red and black lettering on a yellow background comleted the scene. Inside the box was a yellow cardboard dislay insert with all the parts fastened in place.

During the four years that the No. 5 was offered 1949–52), there were four variations of the commutator. he earliest version was thick and heavy, with eight holes. ach hole was tapped and came with a screw. The second ersion of the commutator was made from a (BT) Pierced isc (with an insulated hub, of course), but with seventeen oles. Four ¼" screws and nuts came with this commutator. he final version of the commutator was similar, but came ith only nine holes.

The final accessory kit offered in 1949 (and only this year) as No. 12½A, known as "The Erector Merry-Go-Round arts Kit." It contained the extra parts to be added to a No.

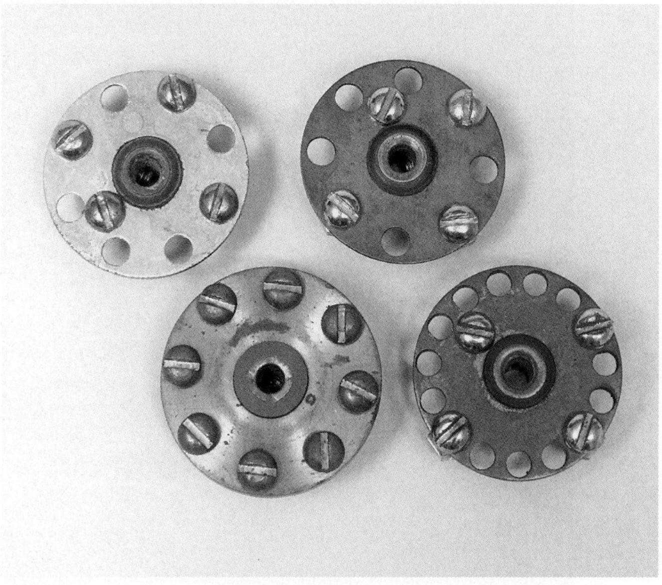

Gilbert offered The Erector Illumination Kit for four years. Going counterclockwise from bottom left, the four variations of the commutator proceed from earliest to latest.

Adding the highly collectible No. 12½A Accessory Kit from 1949 to Nos. 9½ or 12½ from 1948 provided the parts to build the Merry-Go-Round.

12½ from 1948 or early 1949 or a No. 9½ to build the Merry-Go-Round. Besides instructions for building this model, this kit had:

3	(P48) Miter Gear
4	(P57JA) 7½" Axle
12	(C) 10" Girder
12	(N) Long Double Angle
2	(M) Short Double Angle
10	(O) Pawl
7	(EZ) 6" Curved Big Channel Girder
8	(MF) Flat Plate 1" x 5"
6	(OF) Horse
2	(OG) 21 Hole Strip Formed
30	(S51) ¼" Screw
16	(S62) ⅞" Screw
46	(N21) Square Nut

This kit came packed in a plain brown cardboard box that measured 11½" x 4½" x 1¼". A black and white label on the end of the box indicating the kit and number was the only adornment. Clearly, this kit was not intended to generate any visual appeal. The only customers for it were those limited few who wanted to upgrade their existing No. 9½ or 12½ sets. For that reason (and due to the limited time it was available) this accessory kit is difficult to find. Most everyone who bought one added the parts to their existing set and discarded the kit box.

Cardboard Box Sets

The roster of cardboard sets was increased from three to four in 1949, as Gilbert returned No. 1½ to the lineup. Se

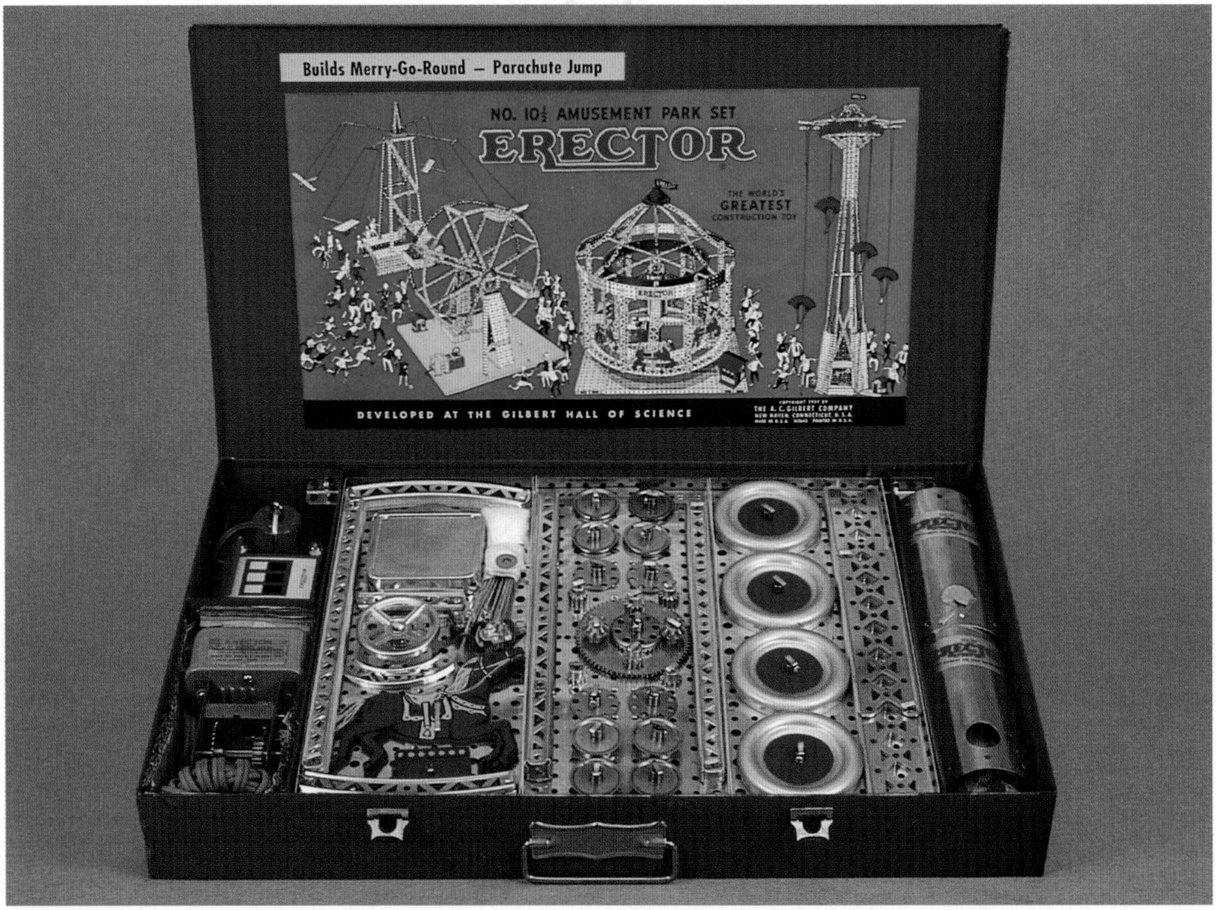

Gilbert introduced "The Amusement Park Set" in 1949. A nearly perfect blend of size, sophistication, and visual appeal makes No. 10½ perhaps the most loved of all Renaissance Period sets.

No. 1½ was identical to its predecessor from 1942 in contents, but the color of the cardboard display insert was changed from mustard yellow to blue.

Set Nos. 2½ and 4½ were not changed this year, but No. 6½ was upgraded to include the new (OE) Flexible Coupling. A second (P15) coupling was added to the inventory for use with the (OE). In addition, the (OE) and a second (P15) were added to all the larger sets.

Metal Box Sets

It's clear that the supply of steel was better this year, as there were two new sets offered in metal boxes. And the aluminum lids from 1948 were replaced with steel lids in the 1949 lineup.

The smallest metal box set for 1949 was No. 6½A, a most unusual designation. It had the same parts as the cardboard boxed No. 6½, but came in a metal box. This was the first time Gilbert had offered the same set in a choice of containers. The version in a metal box cost an extra $2.00.

The prewar No. 6½ box was resurrected for this set. It measured 16" x 8" x 3" and came with a new inner label designed for this set. This label, in black, yellow, and red, pictured the Airplane Ride (the featured model of the set) and promoted the new Flexible Coupling. The cardboard display inserts were blue.

Set Nos. 7½ and 8½ ran with only minor changes, including steel lids. The contents was also upgraded to contain the new (OE) Flexible Coupling.

Set No. 9½ was also cataloged, but only to get rid of leftovers from 1948. No upgrades occurred in this set; it was identical to the previous year's offering.

The most significant development in 1949 was the creation of No. 10½, called "The Amusement Park Set." While it came packed in the same size box as No. 9½, there was a substantial change, namely, the most attractive inner label in Erector history. Printed in three colors (plus black and white), it pictured the Airplane Ride, Ferris Wheel, Parachute Jump, and Merry-Go-Round. An entire amusement park was illustrated, complete with throngs of happy people, eager to get on the rides. This was Gilbert showmanship and creativity at their best!

The inner lid was further adorned with a yellow strip label above the amusement park label. It read "Builds Merry-Go-Round—Parachute Jump." There were four parts cans packed in this wonderful set. And the cardboard parts display inserts were blue.

This was a strange year for No. 12½, because, in addition to some general changes that had occurred since 1948, there were two distinct versions of the set in 1949. The most obvious change occurred with the top parts tray. In 1948, this tray was huge, covering the entire top of the box. But the set was redesigned for 1949, with the tray being only half as large. The depth of the lower-level compartments was also altered to accommodate the new tray. So a tray from 1948 will not fit correctly into a box from 1949 and vice-versa. The new tray came with a cardboard insert covered with shiny silver foil and lacking any printing.

Gilbert also redesigned the Mysterious Walking Giant, featured in No. 12½. The (NW) Treads were incorporated into this model, and the mechanism that moved the arms was modified to include the new (OE) Flexible Coupling. Two of them were required, so two came with the set.

There were four other interesting changes with No. 12½ this year. First, the parts cans for the 1948 version had been extra deep and unique to the set. Now only standard parts

Based on a ride sponsored by Life-Savers candy at the World's Fair of 1939–40, the Parachute Jump is an all-time favorite of Erector enthusiasts. Pictured here is a factory-built store model from the early 1950s.

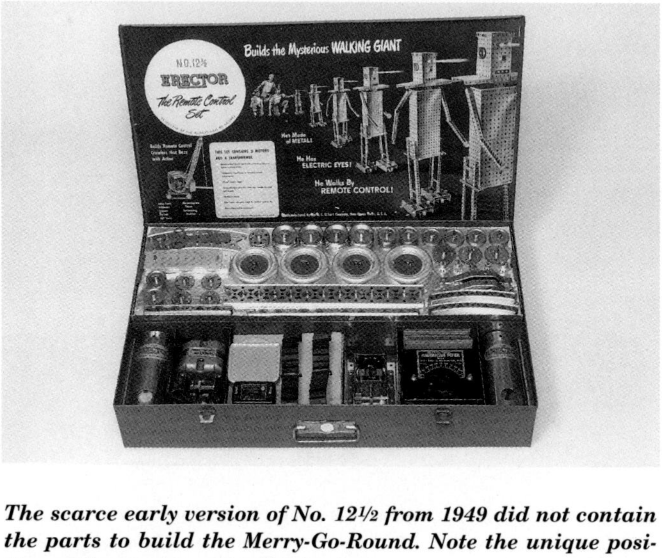

The scarce early version of No. 12½ from 1949 did not contain the parts to build the Merry-Go-Round. Note the unique position of the parts on the display tray.

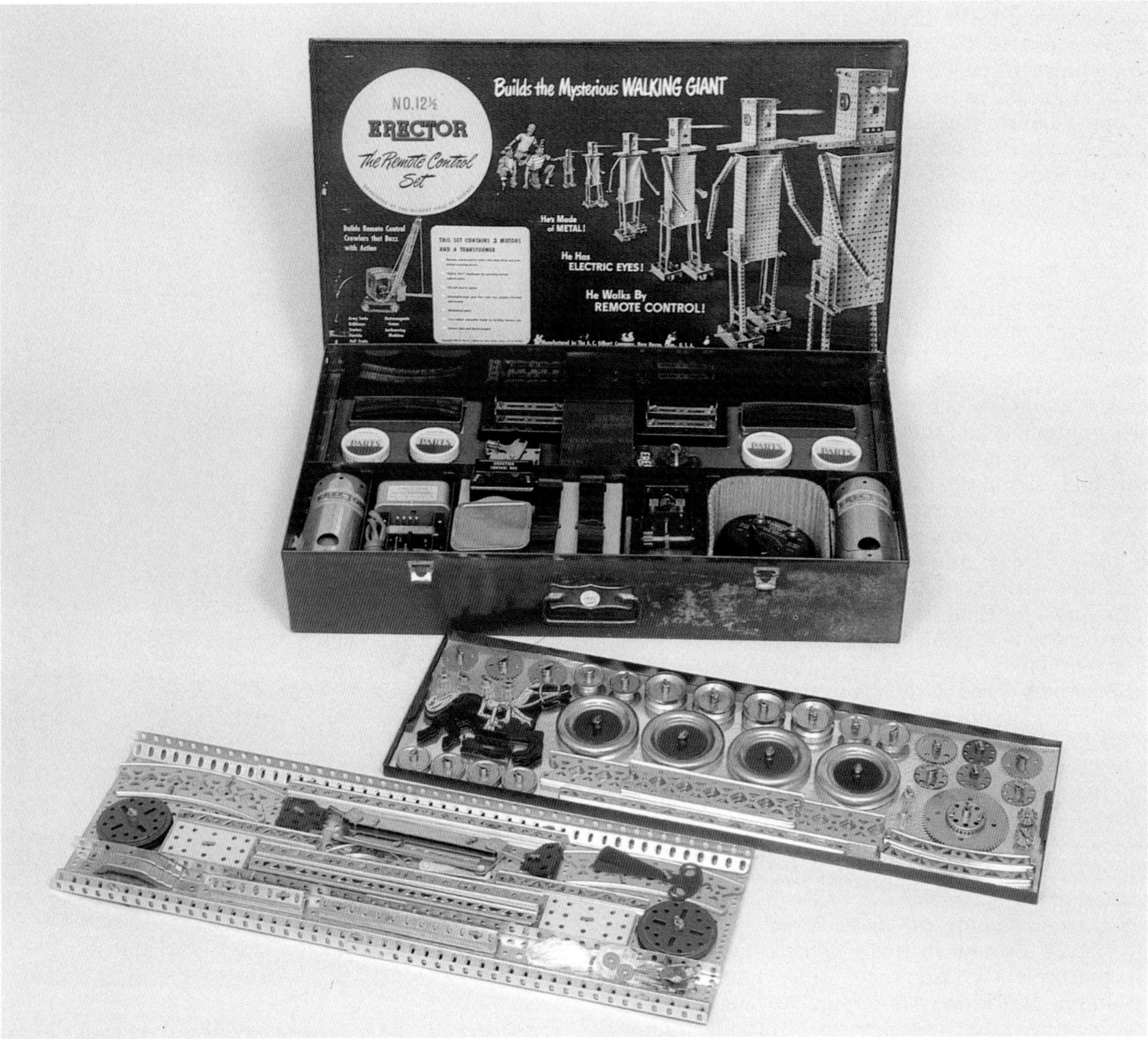

Gilbert made substantial changes to No. 12½ in 1949, but the most apparent was the removable parts display tray, which, as this late version shows, was only half as big as it had been in 1948.

An interesting change occurred with the transformer and control box used with No. 12½ in 1949. Compare the components in the 1948 version (left) with those from the 1949 (right).

cans were used. Second, the 1948 instruction manual had a foldout page that illustrated the Mysterious Walking Giant. When the model was modified, the instructions were changed, and the foldout was eliminated. The third change dealt with the transformer packed in the set. Last year, an American Flyer (2-B) was used. This year, a less expensive No. 1 came in this set.

The final change affected the control box for the (P55) Remote Control Motor. Last year, it was taken straight out of the American Flyer line, where it had been used to operate model railroad accessories. This 1948 control box was labeled "American Flyer Equipment Control." But now, the control box was redesigned for Erector (although it still paralleled what was offered in the Flyer line) and labeled "Erector Control Box."

There were two distinct versions of No. 12½ in 1949. The early one did not contain the parts for the Merry-Go-Round or new Parachute Jump, while the later version did. But the new parts were added fairly early in the year, because the early version is rare. It can be identified by both the instruction manual (no Merry-Go-Round and old Parachute

Jump) as well as the silver cardboard parts display for the upper tray, for the packing arrangement was different (the Horses, which came only in the late version, were displayed on this insert).

Erector System Modifications for 1949

In terms of parts, 1949 was a fairly stable year. The most significant difference was a much lower usage of aluminum. The only parts that show up in aluminum with any regularity are the (MH) Disc Wheels and the Base Plates. Clearly, the steel supply was better.

The (A49) Electric Engine motor casting was modified again, when the four vent slots were rearranged to form a circle. These vent slots had been vertical and straight before. This change occurred in mid year, as did an interesting change in the (A48) Mechanical Motor. Until now, this clockwork motor had been painted blue. But at this point, it was plated (probably with a brass wash), and the final color was gold. Gold (A48)s are unique to 1949.

Finally, the boiler got a new label, starting in mid-1949. The old label was in the shape of an oval. The new one, with identical printing, was rectangular.

I. Noteworthy Parts Colors and Finishes
(CR) Special Turret Plated, steel painted blue

II. New Parts
(P57JA) 7½" Axle
(OE) 6" Flexible Coupling
(OF) Horse
(OG) 21 Hole Strip Formed
(OH) 72 Tooth Gear
(OI) Segment of 72 Tooth Gear
(No. 1) Transformer

III. Modified Parts
(T) Boiler, rectangular label
(MV) Flat Car Truck, with notches
(MX) House, with roof length reduced from 2¾" to 2½"
(NU) Parachute, with white silk, not sewn
(A48) Mechanical Motor, plated gold color
(A49) Electric Engine, circular vent slots

IV. Deleted Parts
(NT) Cone
(2B) Transformer

Junior Erector

During World War II, when no steel was available for the production of toys, Gilbert created Erector Junior. Far simpler than regular Erector, the parts were made of wood and models were built using pegs. After the war, Gilbert kept Erector Junior in the line and promoted these sets "for the boy who's not old enough to use a screwdriver." Clearly, he was trying to reach a younger market.

But Erector Junior was drab in appearance, and the wooden girders were prone to splitting, which made for unhappy customers. So in 1949 Gilbert decided to redesign this toy with more pizzazz and reliability. He named the result Junior Erector and made it more colorful than its predecessor, with plastic tubes and other parts in bright red,

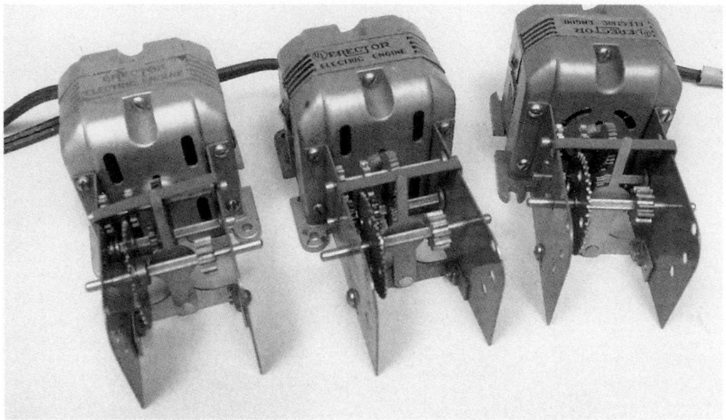

The (A49) Electric Engine continued to evolve after the war. Left: The version from 1947 with red lettering on the core decal. Middle: The version from 1948 with black lettering. Right: The version from 1949 with circular vent holes.

green, blue, yellow, and white. Building was accomplished by connecting a plastic tube to a spindle, called a Connector. These Connectors had small knobs that would fit snugly into the tubes.

The resemblance to Tinker Toys was amazing. Perhaps Gilbert avoided a patent infringement suit because of the way the parts connected. A big deal was made of this in the advertising for Junior Erector: "Unique method of joining Junior Erector parts is based on tests in many children's clinics. These tests prove it is much easier for 2 to 6 year olds to push a hollow tube *onto* a knob than to push a tube *into* a hole."

In any event, Junior Erector was a good product. Building was made easy for young children because the color of the tube also indicated its size. These colorful sets were part of the Gilbert toy family through 1955.

Junior Erector was available in three sizes: Nos. 2, 4, and 10. The smaller sets were single-layer sets, but the impressive No. 10 had a removable parts tray as well as more parts mounted on the inside of the lid.

All three sets were packed in cardboard boxes, with an attractive outer lid label. Printed in four colors (plus black and white), it pictured a Ferris Wheel built from Junior Erector. The promotion on the lid emphasized simplicity and the two-to-six age group. The lid on Nos. 2 and 4 lifted off, but the one on No. 10 was hinged.

Over the seven years Gilbert offered Junior Erector, there were some interesting variations. First, the cardboard parts display inserts came in two different styles: in the early sets (probably until 1953) the cardboard had a wood-grain pattern. The later sets came with plain, silver parts display inserts.

The *How to Make 'Em Book* was changed at about the same time. In the early sets, the instructions came on a large, folded sheet of paper (21" x 20" unfolded). Not only was it awkward to work with, but the illustrations were not in color, so the color of each tube was labeled. The later book was much improved. In addition to a booklet format, the illustrations were in color and much easier for a pre-reader to work with.

The color of rubber used in the Tire and the Lock was at some point changed. The early sets used white rubber, while later ones used gray. The composition of the horse was changed from plastic to heavy paper in 1951, mirroring the change in the regular Erector line.

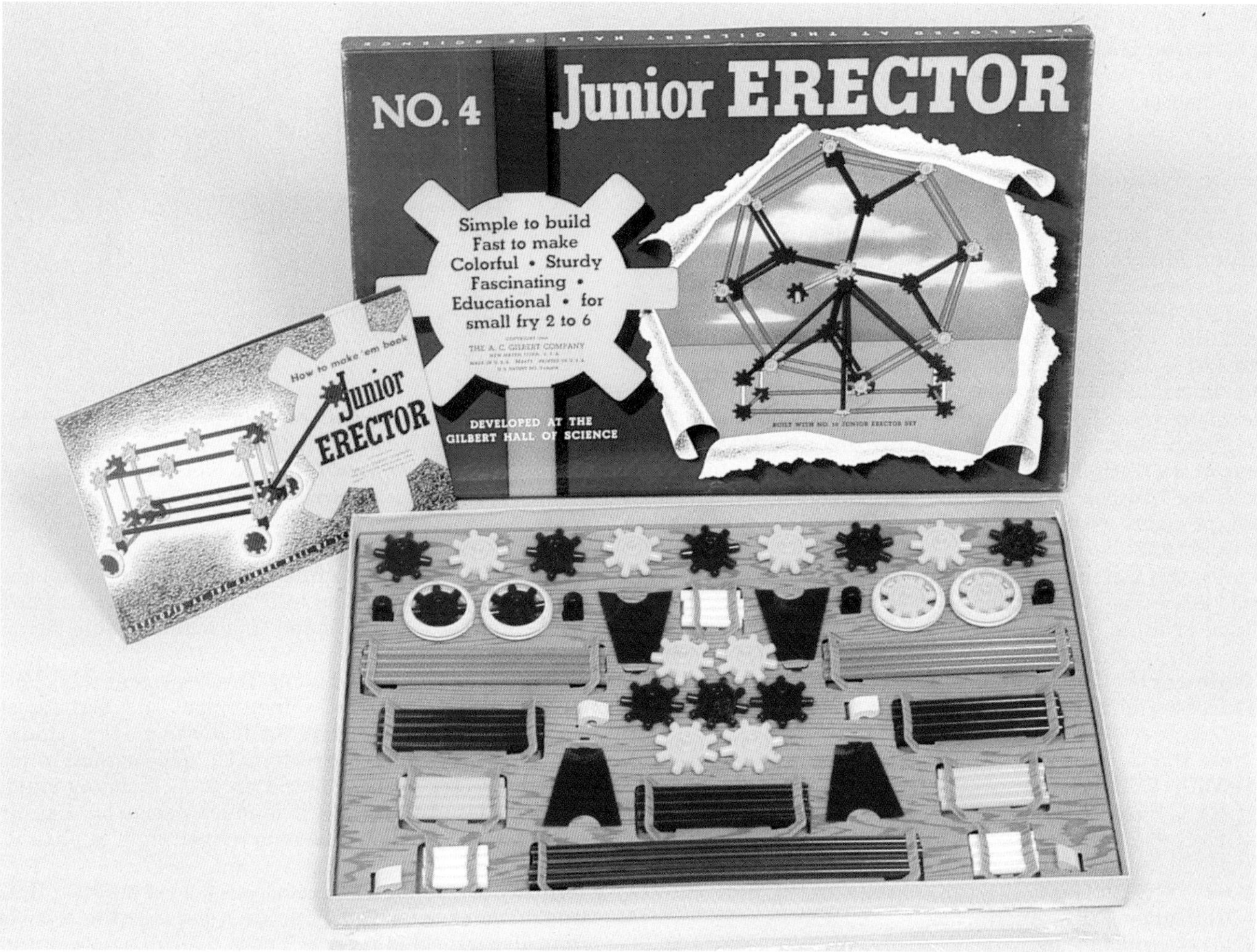

In 1949 Gilbert introduced Junior Erector, including this No. 4, for children too young to build with Erector.

Listings of Junior Erector Sets

NO. 2

Featured five different lengths of tubes and built Windmill and Tricycle. Came in a cardboard box 13½" x 9½" x 1¼"; sold for $1.50 in 1949.

Gd	VG	Exc	Inv	Org
40	**60**	**100**	**+20**	**+25**

NO. 4

Featured five different lengths of tubes as well as Tires and Propeller Blades and built Bridge, Derrick, and Tank. Came in a cardboard box 20½" x 13½" x 1¼"; sold for $3.95 in 1949.

Gd	VG	Exc	Inv	Org
60	**90**	**150**	**+30**	**+40**

NO. 10

Featured the (P10071) Seat and (P4072) Horse and built Ferris Wheel and Merry-Go-Round. Came in a cardboard box 20½" x 13½" x 2½; two-layer set with a removable cardboard parts display tray and additional parts mounted on inside of the lid; sold for $6.95 in 1949.

Gd	VG	Exc	Inv	Org
120	**180**	**300**	**+60**	**+75**

Junior Erector Contents List

	No. 2	No. 4	No. 10
P4067Y Yellow Connector	5	10	24
P4067R Red Connector	5	10	24
P4066B 10" Blue Tube	0	4	22
P4066R 4 29/64" Red Tube	8	12	30
P4066Y 2 13/16" Yellow Tube	4	8	16
P4066W 1 43/64" White Tube	0	12	24
P4070 Tire	0	4	4
P4068 Bearing	2	4	6
P10070 Lock	2	4	6
P4071 Propeller Blade	0	4	4
P10071 Seat	0	0	4
P4072 Horse	0	0	2

THE 1950 ERECTOR LINE

Considering all the innovation that occurred in 1949, it's not surprising that 1950 was a fairly quiet year in Erector evolution. But some of last year's creativity did manage to spill over. While there were no additions (or deletions) from the regular line, two new accessory sets were added to the Erector roster. A new Electric Engine made its first appearance, and the Mitre Gear was improved.

In addition, 1950 saw an increasing availability of steel, as fewer aluminum parts were packed in the sets. Actually, the only parts made from aluminum this year were some of the base plates. The (MD) 2½" x 5" Base Plate shows up in aluminum in the early 1950 sets, but by the end of the year this part was made of steel and painted blue. The

(MF) 1" x 5" Base Plate underwent a similar change, while the (ME) 1" x 4" Base Plate came in steel, painted blue all year long.

The (MN) 12" Base Plate and the (MY) 2½" x 2½" Base Plate also began the year in aluminum, but by year's end they were both made of steel. But when they were done in steel, they were painted silver. These were the first silver base plates, and Gilbert obviously liked what he saw. For all the base plates would be painted silver beginning next year, and would remain so until the demise of traditional Erector in 1962. The (MH) 3" Disc Wheel was produced in steel throughout 1950, but an interesting change occurred with this part at the very end of the year. Since 1939 these wheels had been manufactured with two-piece construction, with the separate "hubcap" section secured to the wheel by the hub in the center. But starting at the end of 1950, Gilbert returned to the one-piece construction method, with the red "hubcap" simply painted on the nickel wheel.

A major improvement took place with the (P48) Mitre Gear this year. These gears were made of white metal that was quite brittle, and the teeth on these gears were easily broken. So now the teeth were reinforced. These improved gears are easy to recognize because of their shape. When viewed from the side, the old gears were Y-shaped; the new gears are shaped like a T.

Two other parts had noteworthy modifications. The (OF) Horse, since its creation in 1949 had been made with only two screw holes. Now a third hole was added, and the hole pattern changed, with an oversized hole in the center. And the (NZ) Wood Handle Screwdriver was also changed. In the past, the wood handle was not colored, but natural brown. Beginning now, the handle was stained red.

Further, 1950 marked the introduction of a new 110-volt electric engine, as the (A47) was created this year. Like the (A49) which it replaced, the (A47) Electric Engine was a combination motor and gearbox. But both the motor and the gearbox were different than their counterparts on the (A49).

This new engine had a motor housing that was made from sheet metal; the (A49) had been made with a cast housing. Most of these new housings were painted gray, scarcer ones were painted silver. And the 1950 version of this motor was rated at 25 watts, and this was indicated on a metal plate, which also noted the engine number. This plate was mounted on the motor housing.

With the (A47) Electric Engine came a new and improved gearbox. First, the thin protective strip which had been welded to the top of the gearbox on the old (A49)s was replaced with a wider steel plate that was pressed into both sides of the gear box. This new plate was far more durable that the strip on the (A49) (which is almost always found broken off today), and more efficient at keeping little fingers out of the gears. Second, this new gearbox had flanges at the bottom, with screw holes. Now there were more places to secure the engine to the model.

In addition, 1950 saw a significant modification in the instruction manual's cover. In the past, the outside of the back cover had promoted the other toy lines, with blue circles on a yellow background. Now the scene was changed, with an American Flyer freight train pictured, amid a group of Erector models. On the inside of the back cover, the promotion was changed from trains to the Erector accessory sets. The cover was still copyrighted 1948 and numbered M2645.

Gilbert expanded the line of accessory kits, with two additions. The first was No. 6, named "The Erector Whistle Kit," differed dramatically from the (NV) Whistle (dropped in 1946). The new whistle came with a blue housing and measured 4" x 1½" x 1½", with rubber-stamped white lettering. The housing was flanged so that it could be attached to the model with which it was used. The mechanism for making the whistle sound was taken straight from the American Flyer line.

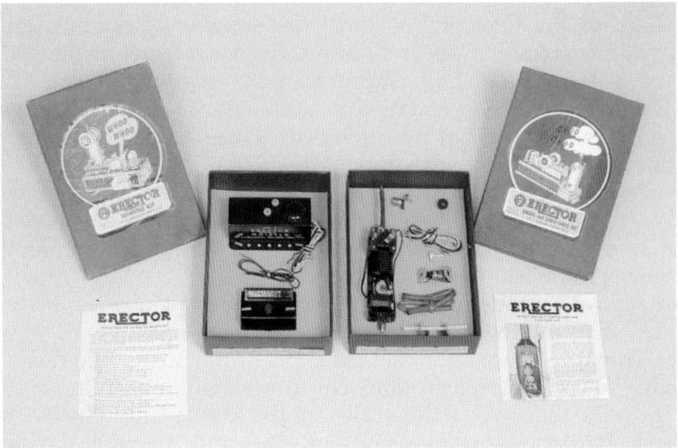

Two more accessory kits joined the line in 1950. Left: The No. 6 Erector Whistle Kit added an element of sound to Erector models. Right: The No. 7 added sound and smoke. Both were spun off from the American Flyer line.

Included in the No. 6 were a whistle unit, plastic control box (labeled "Erector Whistle"), and small coil of wire. The whistle was recommended for use in industrial and train model building, and the instructions came with a long list of different whistle signals and directions for their use. This accessory required a transformer to power it, and the transformer was not included.

The whistle kit was a companion to the No. 5 and packaged similarly. It came in a pale red cardboard box 8¾" x 6¼" x 2", just a bit deeper than the box for the illumination kit. The parts were mounted on a yellow cardboard display insert. The label on the lid was also quite similar to the label on the Illumination kit, but the background color was red, and the picture illustrated a steam engine model, featuring the whistle unit.

The second accessory offered in 1950 (and the third in the series) was No. 7, called "The Erector Smoke and Choo-Choo Kit." Like the whistle, the mechanism for this kit was taken from the American Flyer line and modified for use with Erector. This kit contained the Smoke and Choo-Choo unit, identical to the one used in the train tenders, but mounted to a twenty-one-hole strip (for easy installation in Erector models). Also included in this kit were a coil of rubber tubing (to direct the smoke), "Smoke Cartridge No. 25" (a small gel vial of smoke-making fluid), tiny funnel (to insert the smoke fluid), small section of pipe cleaner, and coil of black and yellow wire. The kit also contained illumination parts: (X9593-A) Light Socket Assembly and (441) Light Bulb-Red-18 Volts.

The history of the Smoke and Choo-Choo unit is interesting. It was developed in 1946 for the more expensive American Flyer locomotives where it was built into the tender. But this was a complicated and expensive mechanism, and it was replaced in 1949 train line with a less sophisticated unit. While it is possible that Gilbert started remanufacturing these units in 1950 just for Erector, it is more likely that there was a large quantity of leftovers from 1948. It may have taken two years for him to discover the adaptability of these units to Erector, but when he did, he added them to the Erector line until the supply was exhausted.

The instruction sheet illustrated ways of mounting and using the smoke and choo-choo unit—usually in the (T) Boiler—and how to wire this accessory to a transformer (required for use but not included). This accessory was recommended for use with steam engine and ship models.

Accessory Set No. 7 was packed in the same size box as No. 6, and the parts were mounted on a yellow cardboard display insert. The label on the lid was similar to Set No. 6 with a red background and the steam engine model, but now there was smoke in the scene, and a "Choo Choo" replaced the "Whoo Whoo."

This line of accessory sets is a most interesting and desirable series to collect. The No. 5 was offered from 1949 through 1952 and is the easiest of the kits to find. The No. 6 was available only in 1950 and 1951 and therefore is the most difficult to locate. The No. 7 ran from 1950 until 1953 (the only one in 1953).

Cardboard Box Sets

Other than the parts modifications noted above, the only significant change in the cardboard box line in 1950 was the elimination of No. 6½. However, No. 6½ still was available in a metal box and cataloged as No. 6½A.

Metal Box Sets

Other than the parts modifications already noted, the only significant change in the metal box line was the elimination of No. 9½.

Erector System Modifications for 1950

I. Noteworthy Parts Colors and Finishes

(AQ) Sheave Pulley, nickel-plated steel
(MD) 2½" x 5" Base Plate, aluminum or blue-painted steel (late in the year)
(ME) 1" x 4" Base Plate, blue-painted steel
(MF) 1" x 5" Base Plate, aluminum or blue painted steel (late)
(MH) 3" Disc Wheel, steel, with two-piece construction (red-painted hubcap on nickel-plated wheel) or one-piece construction (red-painted hubcap on nickel-plated wheel) (late)
(MN) 12" Base Plate, aluminum or silver-painted steel (late)
(MY) 2½" x 2½" Base Plate, aluminum or silver-painted steel (late)
(OF) Horse, with three and not two screw holes
(NZ) Wood Handle Screw Driver, red-stained handle

II. New Parts

(A47) Electric Engine, with gray or silver (scarce) pressed-steel motor housing and 25-watt motor

III. Modified Parts

(P48) Mitre Gear, with reinforced teeth

IV. Eliminated Parts

(A49) Electric Engine

Listings of 1949 and 1950 Erector Sets

	Gd	VG	Exc	Inv	Org

NO. 1½
Came in a cardboard box 13½" x 9¾" x ¾"; sold for $1.75 in 1949 and 1950.

30	40	70	+15	+20

NO. 2½ — The Apprentice Set
Featured the (MH) Disc Wheels. Came in a cardboard box 18" x 10" x 1⅛"; sold for $3.00 in 1949 and 1950.

35	50	80	+20	+25

NO. 4½ — The Famous No. 4½
Featured the (A48) Mechanical Motor and (MN) 12" Base Plates, and (MX) House and built truck with (A48). Came in a cardboard box 18" x 10" x 2⅜" with a lift-off lid; two-layer set with removable cardboard parts display tray; sold for $6.95 in 1949 and 1950.

40	60	100	+20	+25

NO. 6½ (1949) — The Sensational No. 6½
Featured the (A49) Electric Engine and built Airplane Ride. Came in a cardboard box 18" x 10" x 3" with a lift-off lid; two-layer set with removable cardboard parts display tray; sold for $8.95.

40	60	100	+20	+25

NO. 6½ — The Electric Engine Set
Featured the (A49) Electric Engine in 1949 and the (A47) Electric Engine in 1950 and built Airplane Ride. Contents were identical to those of No. 6½ in cardboard box from 1949. Came in a red metal box 16" x 8" x 3"; two-layer set with removable cardboard parts display tray; sold for $10.95 in 1949 and 1950.

40	60	100	+20	+25

NO. 7½ — The Engineer's Set
Featured the (T) Boiler and built Walking Beam Engine. Came in a red metal box 18" x 10" x 3"; two-layer set with

ERECTOR SYSTEM 1942 AND 1946–50

	Box Size	1942	1946–47	1948	1949	1950
Cardboard Box Sets		No. 1½, No. 2½, No. 3½, No. 4½	No. 2½, No. 4½, No. 6½, No. 7½	No. 2½, No. 4½, No. 6½	No. 1½, No. 2½, No. 4½, No. 6½	No. 1½, No. 2½, No. 4½
Metal Box Sets	16" x 8" x 3"	No. 6½				
	18" x 10" x 3"	No. 7½	N/A	No. 7½	No. 7½	No. 7½
	20" x 12" x 3"	No. 8½	No. 8½	No. 8½	No. 8½	No. 8½
	22" x 13" x 3"	No. 9½	No. 9½[1]	No. 9½	No. 9½ & No. 10½	No. 10½
	24" x 14" x 4"	No. 10½	N/A	No. 12½	No. 12½	No. 12½

1. Royal blue box in 1946; red one in 1947.

	Gd	VG	Exc	Inv	Org

two removable parts display trays constructed from (MN) Base Plates; sold for $15.00 in 1949 and 1950.

	Gd	VG	Exc	Inv	Org
	50	70	120	+25	+30

NO. 8½ The All-Electric Set
Featured the (MJ) Electro Magnet and lighting system parts and built Ferris Wheel and Bascule Bridge. Came in a red metal box 20" x 12" x 3"; two-layer set with three removable parts display trays constructed from (MN) Base Plates; sold for $19.95 in 1949 and 1950.

	Gd	VG	Exc	Inv	Org
	75	110	180	+40	+45

NO. 9½ (1949) The Automotive Set
Featured the truck parts, giant flywheel, and parts to build Parachute Jump, Giant Power Plant, and trucks. Came in a red metal box 22" x 13" x 3"; two-layer set with three removable parts display trays constructed from (MN) Base Plates; sold for $25.00.

	Gd	VG	Exc	Inv	Org
	140	210	350	+70	+90

NO. 10½ The Amusement Park Set
Featured the truck parts, giant flywheel, parachutes, and carousal horses and built Parachute Jump, Merry-Go-Round, and other amusement park models as well as Giant Power Plant. Came in a red metal box 22" x 13" x 3"; two-layer set with three removable parts display trays constructed from (MN) Base Plates; sold for $29.50 in 1949 and 1950.

	Gd	VG	Exc	Inv	Org
	160	240	400	+80	+100

NO. 12½ The Remote Control Set
Featured the (P55) 7-15 Volt Motor, (2B) Transformer, and other parts for building Mysterious Walking Giant, as well as treads and tread pulleys for building Tank and Bulldozer. Came in a red metal box 24" x 14" x 4"; three-layer set with two removable parts trays; upper one covered half of inside of box, with silver cardboard parts display insert; lower one constructed from (MN) Base Plates; sold for $50.00 in 1949 and 1950.

	Gd	VG	Exc	Inv	Org
	440	660	1100	+220	+275

NO. IE (1949–50) The Square Girder Kit
Featured extra 5" and 10" straight girders. Came in a heavy cardboard tube 10¾" long x 1¾" in diameter; sold for $1.00 in 1949 and 1950.

	Gd	VG	Exc	Inv	Org
	60	90	150	+35	N/A

NO. 5 (1949–52) The Erector Illumination Kit
Featured red and green light bulbs and hardware for adding them to Erector models. Came in a pale red cardboard box 8¾" x 6¼" x 1½"; sold for $1.95 in 1949–51 and $2.95 in 1952.

	Gd	VG	Exc	Inv	Org
	80	120	200	+40	+50

NO. 6 (1950–51) The Erector Whistle Kit
Featured whistle unit and control box to operate it. Came in a pale red cardboard box 8¾" x 6¼" x 2¼"; sold for $5.95 in 1950 and 1951.

	Gd	VG	Exc	Inv	Org
	100	145	240	+50	+60

NO. 7 (1950–53) The Erector Smoke and Choo-Choo Kit
Featured smoke and choo-choo unit and control box to operate it. Came in a pale red cardboard box 8¾" x 6¼" x 2½"; sold for $5.95 in 1950–52 and $7.95 in 1953.

	Gd	VG	Exc	Inv	Org
	90	130	220	+45	+55

NO. 12½A (1949) The Merry-Go-Round Kit
Featured carousel horses and other parts to build Merry-Go-Round with No. 12½ from 1948 or No. 9½ from 1949. Came in a plain brown cardboard box 11½" x 4½" x 1¼", with black and white label on end; sold for $5.95 in 1950 and 1951.

	Gd	VG	Exc	Inv	Org
	100	145	240	+50	N/A

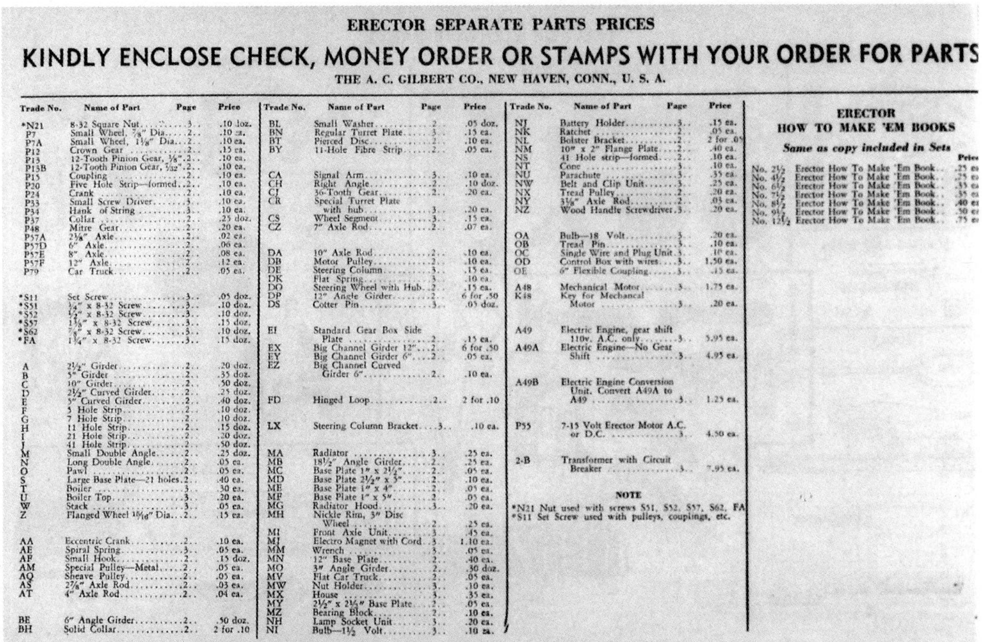

ERECTOR SEPARATE PARTS PRICES

KINDLY ENCLOSE CHECK, MONEY ORDER OR STAMPS WITH YOUR ORDER FOR PARTS

THE A. C. GILBERT CO., NEW HAVEN, CONN., U. S. A.

Trade No.	Name of Part	Page	Price
*N21	8-32 Square Nut	3	.10 doz.
P7	Small Wheel, 7/8" Dia.	2	.10 ea.
P7A	Small Wheel, 1 1/8" Dia.	2	.10 ea.
P12	Crown Gear	2	.15 ea.
P13	12-Tooth Pinion Gear, 1/8"	2	.10 ea.
P13B	12-Tooth Pinion Gear, 5/32"	2	.10 ea.
P15	Coupling	2	.10 ea.
P20	Five Hole Strip—formed	2	.10 ea.
P24	Crank	2	.10 ea.
P33	Small Screw Driver	3	.10 ea.
P34	Hank of String	3	.10 ea.
P37	Collar	2	.25 doz.
P48	Mitre Gear	2	.20 ea.
P57A	2 7/8" Axle	2	.02 ea.
P57D	6" Axle	2	.06 ea.
P57E	8" Axle	2	.08 ea.
P57F	12" Axle	2	.12 ea.
P79	Car Truck	2	.05 ea.
*S11	Set Screw	3	.05 doz.
*S51	1/4" x 8-32 Screw	3	.10 doz.
*S52	1/2" x 8-32 Screw	3	.10 doz.
*S57	1 3/8" x 8-32 Screw	3	.15 doz.
*S62	7/8" x 8-32 Screw	3	.10 doz.
*FA	1 1/4" x 8-32 Screw	3	.15 doz.
A	2½" Girder	2	.20 doz.
B	5" Girder	2	.35 doz.
C	10" Girder	2	.50 doz.
D	2½" Curved Girder	2	.25 doz.
E	5" Curved Girder	2	.40 doz.
F	5 Hole Strip	2	.10 doz.
G	7 Hole Strip	2	.10 doz.
H	11 Hole Strip	2	.15 doz.
I	21 Hole Strip	2	.20 doz.
J	41 Hole Strip	2	.50 doz.
M	Small Double Angle	2	.25 doz.
N	Long Double Angle	2	.05 ea.
O	Pawl	2	.05 ea.
S	Large Base Plate—21 holes	2	.40 ea.
T	Boiler	3	.30 ea.
U	Boiler Top	3	.20 ea.
W	Stack	3	.05 ea.
Z	Flanged Wheel 15/16" Dia.	2	.15 ea.
AA	Eccentric Crank	2	.10 ea.
AE	Spiral Spring	3	.05 ea.
AF	Small Hook	2	.15 doz.
AM	Special Pulley—Metal	2	.05 ea.
AQ	Sheave Pulley	2	.05 ea.
AS	2 7/8" Axle Rod	2	.03 ea.
AT	4" Axle Rod	2	.04 ea.
BE	6" Angle Girder	2	.50 doz.
BH	Solid Collar	2	2 for .10

Trade No.	Name of Part	Page	Price
BL	Small Washer	2	.05 doz.
BN	Regular Turret Plate	3	.15 ea.
BT	Pierced Disc	2	.10 ea.
BY	11-Hole Fibre Strip	2	.05 ea.
CA	Signal Arm	3	.10 ea.
CH	Right Angle	2	.10 doz.
CJ	36-Tooth Gear	2	.20 ea.
CR	Special Turret Plate with hub	3	.20 ea.
CS	Wheel Segment	3	.15 ea.
CZ	7" Axle Rod	2	.07 ea.
DA	10" Axle Rod	2	.10 ea.
DB	Motor Pulley	2	.10 ea.
DE	Steering Column	3	.15 ea.
DK	Flat Spring	3	.10 ea.
DO	Steering Wheel with Hub	2	.15 ea.
DP	12" Angle Girder	2	6 for .50
DS	Cotter Pin	3	.05 doz.
EI	Standard Gear Box Side Plate	2	.15 ea.
EX	Big Channel Girder 12"	2	6 for .50
EY	Big Channel Girder 6"	2	.05 ea.
EZ	Big Channel Curved Girder 6"	2	.10 ea.
FD	Hinged Loop	2	2 for .10
LX	Steering Column Bracket	3	.10 ea.
MA	Radiator	3	.25 ea.
MB	18½" Angle Girder	2	.25 ea.
MC	Base Plate 1" x 2½"	2	.05 ea.
MD	Base Plate 2½" x 5"	2	.10 ea.
ME	Base Plate 1" x 4"	2	.05 ea.
MF	Base Plate 1" x 5"	2	.05 ea.
MG	Radiator Hood	3	.20 ea.
MH	Nickle Rim, 3" Disc Wheel	2	.25 ea.
MI	Front Axle Unit	3	.45 ea.
MJ	Electro Magnet with Cord	3	1.10 ea.
MM	Wrench	3	.05 ea.
MN	12" Base Plate	2	.40 ea.
MO	3" Angle Girder	2	.30 doz.
MV	Flat Car Truck	2	.05 ea.
MW	Nut Holder	3	.10 ea.
MX	House	3	.35 ea.
MY	2½" x 2½" Base Plate	2	.05 ea.
MZ	Bearing Block	2	.10 ea.
NH	Lamp Socket Unit	3	.20 ea.
NI	Bulb—1½ Volt	3	.10 ea.

Trade No.	Name of Part	Page	Price
NJ	Battery Holder	3	.15 ea.
NK	Ratchet	2	.05 ea.
NL	Bolster Bracket	2	2 for .05
NM	10" x 2" Flange Plate	2	.40 ea.
NS	41 Hole strip—formed	2	.10 ea.
NT	Cone	3	.10 ea.
NU	Parachute	3	.35 ea.
NW	Belt and Clip Unit	3	.25 ea.
NX	Tread Pulley	2	.20 ea.
NY	3 1/8" Axle Rod	2	.05 ea.
NZ	Wood Handle Screwdriver	3	.20 ea.
OA	Bulb—18 Volt	3	.20 ea.
OB	Tread Pin	3	.10 ea.
OC	Single Wire and Plug Unit	3	.10 ea.
OD	Control Box with wires	3	1.50 ea.
OE	6" Flexible Coupling	3	.15 ea.
A48	Mechanical Motor	3	1.75 ea.
K48	Key for Mechancal Motor	3	.20 ea.
A49	Electric Engine, gear shift 110v. A.C. only	3	5.95 ea.
A49A	Electric Engine—No Gear Shift	3	4.95 ea.
A49B	Electric Engine Conversion Unit. Convert A49A to A49	3	1.25 ea.
P55	7-15 Volt Erector Motor A.C. or D.C.	3	4.50 ea.
2-B	Transformer with Circuit Breaker	3	7.95 ea.

NOTE

*N21 Nut used with screws S51, S52, S57, S62, FA
*S11 Set Screw used with pulleys, couplings, etc.

ERECTOR
HOW TO MAKE 'EM BOOKS
Same as copy included in Sets

		Price
No. 2½	Erector How To Make 'Em Book	.25 ea.
No. 4½	Erector How To Make 'Em Book	.25 ea.
No. 6½	Erector How To Make 'Em Book	.35 ea.
No. 7½	Erector How To Make 'Em Book	.35 ea.
No. 8½	Erector How To Make 'Em Book	.40 ea.
No. 9½	Erector How To Make 'Em Book	.50 ea.
No. 12½	Erector How To Make 'Em Book	.75 ea.

Separate Parts Prices for early 1949

1949–50 CONTENTS LIST

Set No.		1½	2½	4½	6½[1]	7½	8½	9½[2]	10½	12½[3]
P7	⅞" PULLEY	4	4	4	4	4	0	0	0	0
P7A	1⅛" PULLEY	0	0	0	0	0	4	4	4	4
P12	CROWN GEAR	0	0	0	0	0	0	1	1	1
P13	12 TOOTH PINION GEAR, ⅛"	0	0	0	1	2	2	2	2	2
P13B	12 TOOTH PINION GEAR, 7⁄23"	0	0	0	0	1	1	1	4	4
P15	COUPLING	0	0	1	2	2	2	2	2	2
P20	5 HOLE STRIP—FORMED	0	0	0	0	2	2	2	8	8
P24	CRANK	1	1	1	1	1	1	1	1	1
P33	SMALL SCREW DRIVER	1	1	1	1	1	1	0	0	0
P34	HANK OF STRING	0	1	1	1	1	1	1	3	3
P37	COLLAR	2	4	5	6	7	9	18	20	20
P48	MITRE GEAR	0	0	0	2	2	2	2	2	2
P55	7-15 VOLT ERECTOR MOTOR	0	0	0	0	0	0	0	0	1
P57A	2⅛" AXLE	1	1	1	1	1	1	4	1	8
P57D	6" AXLE	0	1	0	0	0	0	0	0	1
P57E	8" AXLE	0	0	0	0	0	0	2	2	2
P57F	12" AXLE	0	0	0	0	0	1	2	2	2
P57JA	7½" AXLE	0	0	0	0	0	0	0	4	4
P79	CAR TRUCK	4	4	4	4	4	4	4	4	4
A	2½" GIRDER	4	4	4	4	4	4	4	4	6
B	5" GIRDER	4	4	8	12	12	12	12	12	12
C	10" GIRDER	4	8	8	14	14	36	36	52	52
D	2½" CURVED GIRDER	4	4	4	4	4	4	4	4	4
E	5" CURVED GIRDER	0	2	2	4	4	26	26	26	26
F	5 HOLE STRIP	0	0	2	2	2	2	2	2	16
G	7 HOLE STRIP	0	0	2	2	2	2	2	6	8
H	11 HOLE STRIP	0	0	4	4	4	4	4	16	16
I	21 HOLE STRIP	0	0	2	2	2	4	18	18	18
J	41 HOLE STRIP	0	0	0	0	0	2	2	2	4
M	SMALL DOUBLE ANGLE	0	0	0	0	2	6	6	24	24
N	LONG DOUBLE ANGLE	2	4	4	4	4	4	4	16	16
O	PAWL	0	0	0	1	2	2	2	16	16
T	BOILER	0	0	0	0	1	1	2	2	2
U	BOILER TOP	0	0	0	0	1	1	1	1	1
W	STACK	0	0	0	0	3	3	3	3	3
Z	FLANGED WHEEL 15⁄16" DIA.	0	0	0	0	4	4	4	4	4
AA	ECCENTRIC CRANK	0	0	0	0	0	0	6	6	6
AE	SPIRAL SPRING	0	0	0	0	0	0	0	0	2
AF	SMALL HOOK	1	1	1	1	1	1	1	1	1
AJ	PAPER ERECTOR FLAG	0	0	1	1	1	1	1	1	1
AQ	SHEAVE PULLEY	0	0	0	0	0	1	4	4	5
AS	2⅞" AXLE	0	0	2	2	3	3	4	4	4
AT	4" AXLE	2	2	2	2	2	2	2	2	4
BE	6" ANGLE GIRDER	0	0	4	4	4	4	4	4	8
BH	SOLID COLLAR	0	0	0	0	0	0	2	2	2

1949–50 CONTENTS LIST

Set No.		1½	2½	4½	6½[1]	7½	8½	9½[2]	10½	12½[3]
BL	SMALL WASHER	8	12	12	12	12	12	12	12	17
BN	REGULAR TURRET PLATE	0	0	2	2	4	4	4	4	4
BT	PIERCED DISC	1	1	1	2	2	4	4	4	4
BY	11 HOLE FIBRE STRIP	0	0	0	0	0	1	1	2	2
CA	SIGNAL ARM	0	0	0	0	0	0	2	2	2
CH	RIGHT ANGLE	8	12	14	14	14	30	42	42	42
CJ	36 TOOTH GEAR	0	0	0	2	3	3	3	3	5
CR	SPECIAL TURRET PLATE WITH HUB	0	0	0	0	0	0	2	2	2
CS	WHEEL SEGMENT	0	0	0	0	0	0	8	8	8
CY	5" AXLE	0	2	0	0	0	0	0	0	0
CZ	7" AXLE	0	0	2	2	2	3	3	4	4
DA	10" AXLE	0	0	0	0	0	0	0	0	2
DB	MOTOR PULLEY	0	0	1	1	1	1	1	1	1
DE	STEERING COLUMN	0	0	0	0	0	0	1	1	1
DK	FLAT SPRING	0	0	0	0	0	0	4	4	4
DO	STEERING WHEEL WITH HUB	0	0	0	0	0	0	1	1	1
DP	12" ANGLE GIRDER	0	0	4	4	4	4	4	4	8
DS	COTTER PIN	0	0	0	0	0	0	1	1	1
EI	STD. GEAR BOX SIDE PLATE	0	0	0	2	2	2	2	2	2
EX	BIG CHANNEL GIRDER 12"	0	0	0	0	0	0	8	8	8
EY	BIG CHANNEL GIRDER 6"	0	0	0	0	0	0	4	8	8
EZ	BIG CHAN. GIRDER CURVED 6"	0	0	0	0	0	0	2	9	9
FA	1¾" x 8-32 SCREW	0	0	0	0	0	0	12	12	12
FD	HINGED LOOP	0	0	0	0	0	0	2	2	2
LX	STEERING COLUMN BRACKET	0	0	0	0	0	0	1	1	1
MA	RADIATOR	0	0	0	0	0	0	1	1	1
MB	18½" ANGLE GIRDER	0	0	0	0	0	0	2	2	2
MC	BASE PLATE 1" x 2½"	2	2	2	2	2	8	8	8	8
MD	BASE PLATE 2½" x 5"	1	1	1	1	1	4	4	4	4
ME	BASE PLATE 1" x 4"	0	0	0	0	0	0	4	4	4
MF	BASE PLATE 1" x 5"	2	2	4	4	4	8	9	21	21
MG	RADIATOR HOOD	0	0	0	0	0	0	1	1	1
MH	LARGE 3" DISC WHEEL	0	4	4	4	4	4	4	4	4
MI	FRONT AXLE UNIT	0	0	0	0	0	0	1	1	1
MJ	ELECTRO MAGNET WITH CORD	0	0	0	0	0	1	1	1	1
MM	WRENCH	0	0	1	1	1	1	1	1	1
MN	12" BASE PLATE	0	0	4	4	4	6	6	6	6
MO	3" ANGLE GIRDER	0	0	4	4	4	4	4	4	8
MV	FLAT CAR TRUCK	0	0	0	0	2	4	4	4	12
MW	NUT HOLDER	0	0	1	1	1	1	1	1	1

1949–50 CONTENTS LIST

Set No.		1½	2½	4½	6½[1]	7½	8½	9½[2]	10½	12½[3]
MX	HOUSE	0	0	1	1	1	1	1	1	1
MY	2½" x 2½" BASE PLATE	0	0	1	1	1	1	1	1	1
MZ	BEARING BLOCK	0	0	0	1	1	1	1	1	1
NH	LAMP SOCKET UNIT	0	0	0	0	0	2	2	2	2
NI	BULB, 1½ VOLT	0	0	0	0	0	2	2	2	2
NJ	BATTERY HOLDER	0	0	0	0	0	1	1	1	1
NK	RATCHET	0	0	0	0	2	2	2	2	2
NL	BOLSTER BRACKET	0	0	0	0	0	0	0	0	4
NM	10" x 2" FLANGED PLATE	0	0	0	0	0	0	0	0	2
NS	41 HOLE STRIP—FORMED	0	0	0	0	0	0	2	2	2
NT	CONE	0	0	0	0	0	0	4	0	0
NU	PARACHUTE	0	0	0	0	0	0	4	4	4
NW	BELT AND CLIP UNIT	0	0	0	0	0	0	0	0	2
NX	TREAD PULLEY	0	0	0	0	0	0	0	0	4
NY	3⅛" AXLE ROD	0	0	0	0	0	0	0	2	2
NZ	WOOD HANDLE SCREWDRIVER	0	0	0	0	0	0	1	1	1
OA	BULB—18 VOLT	0	0	0	0	0	0	0	0	2
OB	TREAD PIN	0	0	0	0	0	0	0	0	2
OC	SINGLE WIRE AND PLUG UNIT	0	0	0	0	0	0	0	0	1
OD	CONTROL BOX WITH WIRES	0	0	0	0	0	0	0	0	1
OE	6" FLEXIBLE COUPLING	0	0	0	1	1	1	1	1	2
OF	HORSE	0	0	0	0	0	0	0	6	6
OG	21 HOLE STRIP—FORMED	0	0	0	0	0	0	0	2	2
OH	72 TOOTH GEAR	0	0	0	0	0	0	0	1	1
OI	SEGMENT OF 72 TOOTH GEAR	0	0	0	0	0	0	0	1	1
A48	MECHANICAL MOTOR	0	0	1	0	0	0	0	0	1
K48	KEY FOR MECH. MOTOR	0	0	1	0	0	0	0	0	1
A47[4]	ELECTRIC ENGINE	0	0	0	1	1	1	1	1	1
NO. 1	TRANSFORMER	0	0	0	0	0	0	0	0	1
N21	8-32 SQUARE NUT	25	45	88	93	93	169	254	271	360
S51	¼" x 8-32 SCREW	21	35	80	84	84	162	206	240	265
S52	½" x 8-32 SCREW	0	0	0	4	4	4	4	8	8
S57	1⅜" x 8-32 SCREW	0	0	0	0	4	4	4	4	4
S62	⅞" x 8-32 SCREW	3	6	8	8	8	18	20	64	64

1. In 1949 Set No. 6½ came in a cardboard box (Set 6½) or a metal box (Set 6½A). The parts contents were identical.
2. Set No. 9½ was available for the last time in 1949.
3. Set No. 12½ also contained an offset wrench.
4. The A47 was substituted for the A49 in mid-1950.

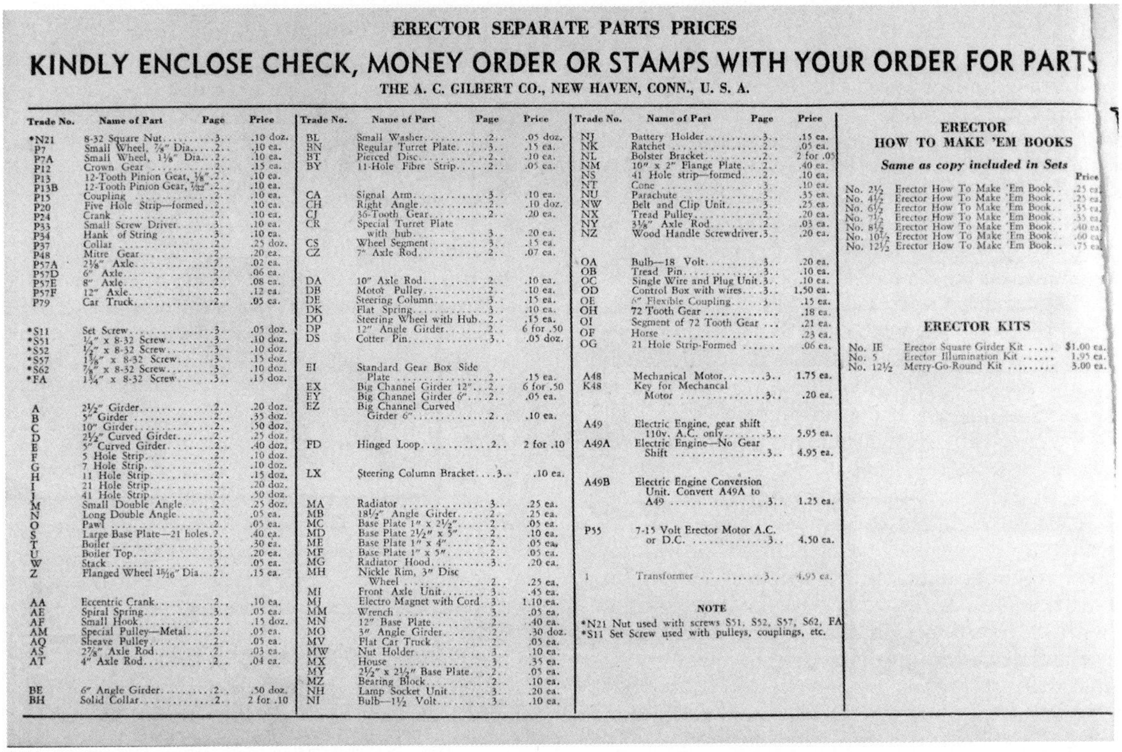

ERECTOR SEPARATE PARTS PRICES

KINDLY ENCLOSE CHECK, MONEY ORDER OR STAMPS WITH YOUR ORDER FOR PARTS

THE A. C. GILBERT CO., NEW HAVEN, CONN., U. S. A.

Trade No.	Name of Part	Page	Price
*N21	8-32 Square Nut	3	.10 doz.
P7	Small Wheel, 7/8" Dia.	2	.10 ea.
P7A	Small Wheel, 1 1/8" Dia.	2	.10 ea.
P12	Crown Gear	2	.15 ea.
P13	12-Tooth Pinion Gear, 1/8"	2	.10 ea.
P13B	12-Tooth Pinion Gear, 7/32"	2	.10 ea.
P15	Coupling	2	.10 ea.
P20	Five Hole Strip—formed	2	.10 ea.
P24	Crank	2	.10 ea.
P33	Small Screw Driver	3	.10 ea.
P34	Hank of String	3	.10 ea.
P37	Collar	2	.25 doz.
P48	Mitre Gear	2	.20 ea.
P57A	2 1/8" Axle	2	.02 ea.
P57D	6" Axle	2	.06 ea.
P57E	8" Axle	2	.08 ea.
P57F	12" Axle	2	.12 ea.
P79	Car Truck	2	.05 ea.
*S11	Set Screw	3	.05 doz.
*S51	1/4" x 8-32 Screw	3	.10 doz.
*S52	1/2" x 8-32 Screw	3	.10 doz.
*S57	1 5/8" x 8-32 Screw	3	.15 doz.
*S62	7/8" x 8-32 Screw	3	.10 doz.
*FA	1 3/4" x 8-32 Screw	3	.15 doz.
A	2½" Girder	2	.20 doz.
B	5" Girder	2	.35 doz.
C	10" Girder	2	.50 doz.
D	2½" Curved Girder	2	.25 doz.
E	5" Curved Girder	2	.40 doz.
F	5 Hole Strip	2	.10 doz.
G	7 Hole Strip	2	.10 doz.
H	11 Hole Strip	2	.15 doz.
I	21 Hole Strip	2	.20 doz.
J	41 Hole Strip	2	.50 doz.
M	Small Double Angle	2	.25 doz.
N	Long Double Angle	2	.05 ea.
O	Pawl	2	.05 ea.
S	Large Base Plate—21 holes	2	.40 ea.
T	Boiler	3	.30 ea.
U	Boiler Top	3	.20 ea.
W	Stack	3	.05 ea.
Z	Flanged Wheel 1 5/16" Dia.	2	.15 ea.
AA	Eccentric Crank	2	.10 ea.
AE	Spiral Spring	3	.05 ea.
AF	Small Hook	2	.15 doz.
AM	Special Pulley—Metal	2	.05 ea.
AQ	Sheave Pulley	2	.05 ea.
AS	2 7/8" Axle Rod	2	.03 ea.
AT	4" Axle Rod	2	.04 ea.
BE	6" Angle Girder	2	.50 doz.
BH	Solid Collar	2	2 for .10

Trade No.	Name of Part	Page	Price
BL	Small Washer	2	.05 doz.
BN	Regular Turret Plate	3	.15 ea.
BT	Pierced Disc	2	.10 ea.
BY	11-Hole Fibre Strip	2	.05 ea.
CA	Signal Arm	3	.10 ea.
CH	Right Angle	2	.10 doz.
CJ	36-Tooth Gear	2	.20 ea.
CR	Special Turret Plate with hub	3	.20 ea.
CS	Wheel Segment	3	.15 ea.
CZ	7" Axle Rod	2	.07 ea.
DA	10" Axle Rod	2	.10 ea.
DB	Motor Pulley	2	.10 ea.
DE	Steering Column	3	.15 ea.
DK	Flat Spring	3	.10 ea.
DO	Steering Wheel with Hub	2	.15 ea.
DP	12" Angle Girder	2	6 for .50
DS	Cotter Pin	3	.05 doz.
EI	Standard Gear Box Side Plate	2	.15 ea.
EX	Big Channel Girder 12"	2	6 for .50
EY	Big Channel Girder 6"	2	.05 ea.
EZ	Big Channel Curved Girder 6"	2	.10 ea.
FD	Hinged Loop	2	2 for .10
LX	Steering Column Bracket	3	.10 ea.
MA	Radiator	3	.25 ea.
MB	18½" Angle Girder	2	.25 ea.
MC	Base Plate 1" x 2½"	2	.05 ea.
MD	Base Plate 2½" x 5"	2	.10 ea.
ME	Base Plate 1" x 4"	2	.05 ea.
MF	Base Plate 1" x 5"	2	.05 ea.
MG	Radiator Hood	3	.20 ea.
MH	Nickle Rim, 3" Disc Wheel	2	.25 ea.
MI	Front Axle Unit	3	.45 ea.
MJ	Electro Magnet with Cord	3	1.10 ea.
MM	Wrench	3	.05 ea.
MN	12" Base Plate	2	.40 ea.
MO	3" Angle Girder	2	.30 doz.
MV	Flat Car Truck	2	.05 ea.
MW	Nut Holder	3	.10 ea.
MX	House	3	.35 ea.
MY	2½" x 2½" Base Plate	2	.05 ea.
MZ	Bearing Block	2	.10 ea.
NH	Lamp Socket Unit	3	.20 ea.
NI	Bulb—1½ Volt	3	.10 ea.

Trade No.	Name of Part	Page	Price
NJ	Battery Holder	3	.15 ea.
NK	Ratchet	2	.05 ea.
NL	Bolster Bracket	2	2 for .05
NM	10" x 2" Flange Plate	2	.40 ea.
NS	41 Hole strip—formed	2	.10 ea.
NT	Cone	3	.10 ea.
NU	Parachute	3	.35 ea.
NW	Belt and Clip Unit	3	.25 ea.
NX	Tread Pulley	2	.20 ea.
NY	3 1/8" Axle Rod	2	.03 ea.
NZ	Wood Handle Screwdriver	3	.20 ea.
OA	Bulb—18 Volt	3	.20 ea.
OB	Tread Pin	3	.10 ea.
OC	Single Wire and Plug Unit	3	.10 ea.
OD	Control Box with wires	3	1.50 ea.
OE	6" Flexible Coupling	3	.15 ea.
OH	72 Tooth Gear		.18 ea.
OI	Segment of 72 Tooth Gear		.21 ea.
OF	Horse		.23 ea.
OG	21 Hole Strip-Formed		.06 ea.
A48	Mechanical Motor	3	1.75 ea.
K48	Key for Mechancal Motor	3	.20 ea.
A49	Electric Engine, gear shift 110v. A.C. only	3	5.95 ea.
A49A	Electric Engine—No Gear Shift	3	4.95 ea.
A49B	Electric Engine Conversion Unit. Convert A49A to A49	3	1.25 ea.
P55	7-15 Volt Erector Motor A.C. or D.C.	3	4.50 ea.
1	Transformer	3	4.95 ea.

NOTE

*N21 Nut used with screws S51, S52, S57, S62, FA

*S11 Set Screw used with pulleys, couplings, etc.

ERECTOR HOW TO MAKE 'EM BOOKS

Same as copy included in Sets

		Price
No. 2½	Erector How To Make 'Em Book	.25 ea.
No. 4½	Erector How To Make 'Em Book	.25 ea.
No. 6½	Erector How To Make 'Em Book	.35 ea.
No. 7½	Erector How To Make 'Em Book	.35 ea.
No. 8½	Erector How To Make 'Em Book	.40 ea.
No. 10½	Erector How To Make 'Em Book	.60 ea.
No. 12½	Erector How To Make 'Em Book	.75 ea.

ERECTOR KITS

No. IE	Erector Square Girder Kit	$1.00 ea.
No. 5	Erector Illumination Kit	1.95 ea.
No. 12½	Merry-Go-Round Kit	3.00 ea.

Separate Parts Prices for late 1949

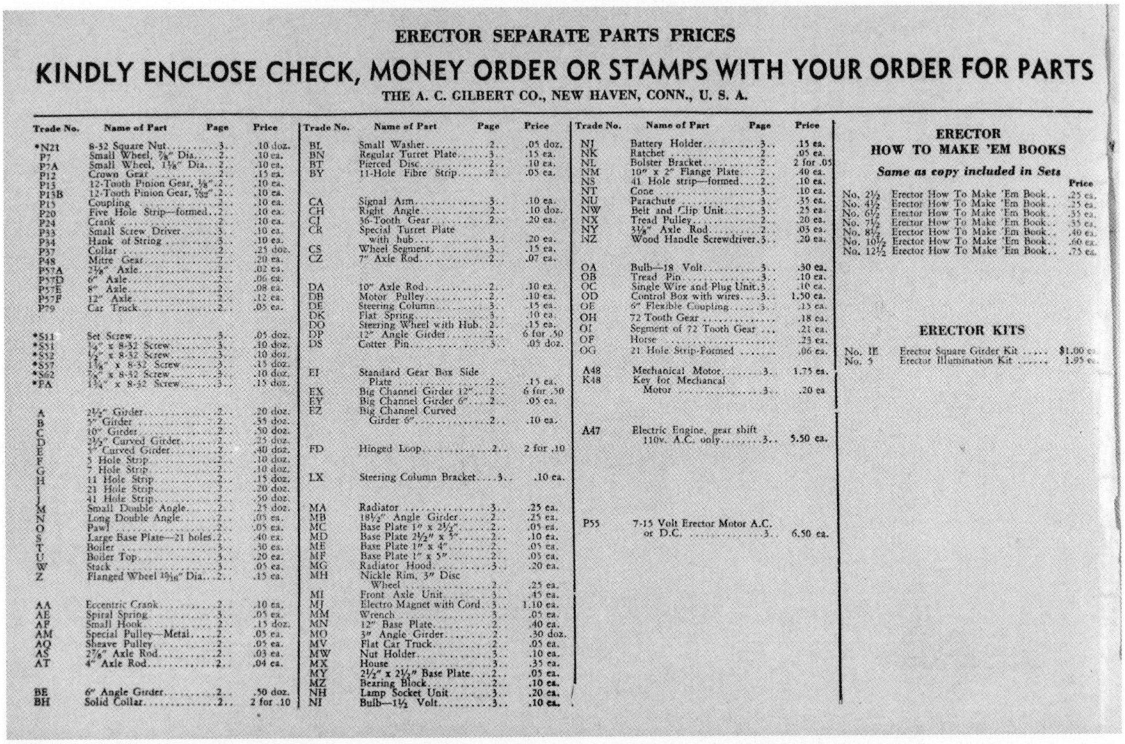

ERECTOR SEPARATE PARTS PRICES

KINDLY ENCLOSE CHECK, MONEY ORDER OR STAMPS WITH YOUR ORDER FOR PARTS

THE A. C. GILBERT CO., NEW HAVEN, CONN., U. S. A.

Trade No.	Name of Part	Page	Price
*N21	8-32 Square Nut	3	.10 doz.
P7	Small Wheel, 7/8" Dia.	2	.10 ea.
P7A	Small Wheel, 1 1/8" Dia.	2	.10 ea.
P12	Crown Gear	2	.15 ea.
P13	12-Tooth Pinion Gear, 1/8"	2	.10 ea.
P13B	12-Tooth Pinion Gear, 7/32"	2	.10 ea.
P15	Coupling	2	.10 ea.
P20	Five Hole Strip—formed	2	.10 ea.
P24	Crank	2	.10 ea.
P33	Small Screw Driver	3	.10 ea.
P34	Hank of String	3	.10 ea.
P37	Collar	2	.25 doz.
P48	Mitre Gear	2	.20 ea.
P57A	2 1/8" Axle	2	.02 ea.
P57D	6" Axle	2	.06 ea.
P57E	8" Axle	2	.08 ea.
P57F	12" Axle	2	.12 ea.
P79	Car Truck	2	.05 ea.
*S11	Set Screw	3	.05 doz.
*S51	1/4" x 8-32 Screw	3	.10 doz.
*S52	1/2" x 8-32 Screw	3	.10 doz.
*S57	1 5/8" x 8-32 Screw	3	.15 doz.
*S62	7/8" x 8-32 Screw	3	.10 doz.
*FA	1 3/4" x 8-32 Screw	3	.15 doz.
A	2½" Girder	2	.20 doz.
B	5" Girder	2	.35 doz.
C	10" Girder	2	.50 doz.
D	2½" Curved Girder	2	.25 doz.
E	5" Curved Girder	2	.40 doz.
F	5 Hole Strip	2	.10 doz.
G	7 Hole Strip	2	.10 doz.
H	11 Hole Strip	2	.15 doz.
I	21 Hole Strip	2	.20 doz.
J	41 Hole Strip	2	.50 doz.
M	Small Double Angle	2	.25 doz.
N	Long Double Angle	2	.05 ea.
O	Pawl	2	.05 ea.
S	Large Base Plate—21 holes	2	.40 ea.
T	Boiler	3	.30 ea.
U	Boiler Top	3	.20 ea.
W	Stack	3	.05 ea.
Z	Flanged Wheel 1 5/16" Dia.	2	.15 ea.
AA	Eccentric Crank	2	.10 ea.
AE	Spiral Spring	3	.05 ea.
AF	Small Hook	2	.15 doz.
AM	Special Pulley—Metal	2	.05 ea.
AQ	Sheave Pulley	2	.05 ea.
AS	2 7/8" Axle Rod	2	.03 ea.
AT	4" Axle Rod	2	.04 ea.
BE	6" Angle Girder	2	.50 doz.
BH	Solid Collar	2	2 for .10

Trade No.	Name of Part	Page	Price
BL	Small Washer	2	.05 doz.
BN	Regular Turret Plate	3	.15 ea.
BT	Pierced Disc	2	.10 ea.
BY	11-Hole Fibre Strip	2	.05 ea.
CA	Signal Arm	3	.10 ea.
CH	Right Angle	2	.10 doz.
CJ	36-Tooth Gear	2	.20 ea.
CR	Special Turret Plate with hub	3	.20 ea.
CS	Wheel Segment	3	.15 ea.
CZ	7" Axle Rod	2	.07 ea.
DA	10" Axle Rod	2	.10 ea.
DB	Motor Pulley	2	.10 ea.
DE	Steering Column	3	.15 ea.
DK	Flat Spring	3	.10 ea.
DO	Steering Wheel with Hub	2	.15 ea.
DP	12" Angle Girder	2	6 for .50
DS	Cotter Pin	3	.05 doz.
EI	Standard Gear Box Side Plate	2	.15 ea.
EX	Big Channel Girder 12"	2	6 for .50
EY	Big Channel Girder 6"	2	.05 ea.
EZ	Big Channel Curved Girder 6"	2	.10 ea.
FD	Hinged Loop	2	2 for .10
LX	Steering Column Bracket	3	.10 ea.
MA	Radiator	3	.25 ea.
MB	18½" Angle Girder	2	.25 ea.
MC	Base Plate 1" x 2½"	2	.05 ea.
MD	Base Plate 2½" x 5"	2	.10 ea.
ME	Base Plate 1" x 4"	2	.05 ea.
MF	Base Plate 1" x 5"	2	.05 ea.
MG	Radiator Hood	3	.20 ea.
MH	Nickle Rim, 3" Disc Wheel	2	.25 ea.
MI	Front Axle Unit	3	.45 ea.
MJ	Electro Magnet with Cord	3	1.10 ea.
MM	Wrench	3	.05 ea.
MN	12" Base Plate	2	.40 ea.
MO	3" Angle Girder	2	.30 doz.
MV	Flat Car Truck	2	.05 ea.
MW	Nut Holder	3	.10 ea.
MX	House	3	.35 ea.
MY	2½" x 2½" Base Plate	2	.05 ea.
MZ	Bearing Block	2	.10 ea.
NH	Lamp Socket Unit	3	.20 ea.
NI	Bulb—1½ Volt	3	.10 ea.

Trade No.	Name of Part	Page	Price
NJ	Battery Holder	3	.15 ea.
NK	Ratchet	2	.05 ea.
NL	Bolster Bracket	2	2 for .05
NM	10" x 2" Flange Plate	2	.40 ea.
NS	41 Hole strip—formed	2	.10 ea.
NT	Cone	3	.10 ea.
NU	Parachute	3	.35 ea.
NW	Belt and Clip Unit	3	.25 ea.
NX	Tread Pulley	2	.20 ea.
NY	3 1/8" Axle Rod	2	.03 ea.
NZ	Wood Handle Screwdriver	3	.20 ea.
OA	Bulb—18 Volt	3	.30 ea.
OB	Tread Pin	3	.10 ea.
OC	Single Wire and Plug Unit	3	.10 ea.
OD	Control Box with wires	3	1.50 ea.
OE	6" Flexible Coupling	3	.15 ea.
OH	72 Tooth Gear		.18 ea.
OI	Segment of 72 Tooth Gear		.21 ea.
OF	Horse		.23 ea.
OG	21 Hole Strip-Formed		.06 ea.
A48	Mechanical Motor	3	1.75 ea.
K48	Key for Mechancal Motor	3	.20 ea.
A47	Electric Engine, gear shift 110v. A.C. only	3	5.50 ea.
P55	7-15 Volt Erector Motor A.C. or D.C.	3	6.50 ea.

ERECTOR HOW TO MAKE 'EM BOOKS

Same as copy included in Sets

		Price
No. 2½	Erector How To Make 'Em Book	.25 ea.
No. 4½	Erector How To Make 'Em Book	.25 ea.
No. 6½	Erector How To Make 'Em Book	.35 ea.
No. 7½	Erector How To Make 'Em Book	.35 ea.
No. 8½	Erector How To Make 'Em Book	.40 ea.
No. 10½	Erector How To Make 'Em Book	.60 ea.
No. 12½	Erector How To Make 'Em Book	.75 ea.

ERECTOR KITS

No. IE	Erector Square Girder Kit	$1.00 ea.
No. 5	Erector Illumination Kit	1.95 ea.

Separate Parts Prices for 1950

THE 1951 ERECTOR LINE

Challenge and innovation marked the year 1951 for The A. C. Gilbert Company. The challenge was caused by a yet another steel shortage, this time resulting from the Korean War. But all his post–World War II experience with this problem had prepared Gilbert to deal with the current shortage more effectively. In the past, when supplies were low, he had used what steel he could get to construct the larger set boxes, and the balance of steel was then used to produce parts. Now he dealt with the shortage by creating some unusual and innovative cardboard boxes for the larger sets, as we shall see when we examine the 1951 line. With the exception of an occasional set with aluminum (MN) Base Plates, there was enough steel for everything else.

There were two significant innovations in the Erector line that had a real impact on the appearance of the models. First, Gilbert began plating parts with cadmium, a finish that would be used through the remainder of the Renaissance Period. Cadmium-plating produced a bright, shiny finish when first applied; over time, however, the finish became frosty, with a satin appearance. (When examining a like-new set with cadmium-plated parts, it is sometimes difficult to distinguish cadmium-plating from nickel-plating. But the frosty-satin finish is easy to spot on parts that were handled.)

The second impact on appearance this year was a new color for nearly all the base plates. In 1950 Gilbert had done some experimenting here, since the (MY) Base Plate was painted silver, as was the (MN) Base Plate when it was not made of aluminum. He must have liked what he saw, for beginning this year and until the end of traditional Erector production in 1962, all the base plates (except for the yellow (MC)s) were painted silver.

A variety of other changes occurred in 1951. Gilbert began experimenting with the (CA) Signal Arm. Since 1925 it had been produced in steel and painted maroon (1925–26) or red (1927–50). But in 1951–52, this part was made of black fiber, the same material as the (BY) 11 Hole Fiber Strip, and painted a dull shade of red. These (CA) Signal Arms were easily broken and seldom found intact.

Also of interest was the modification in the (OH) Horse, which was now made from thin, red cardboard. The pattern for the horse, in black and yellow, was stamped onto the cardboard, then laminated, which gave it a shiny finish. In the past, this part had been made from red plastic. The cardboard horses were more fragile than their plastic counterparts and harder to find in good condition.

There were several notable paint changes, in addition to the new color for the base plates. The "tire" of the (MH) 3" Disc Wheel was painted silver this (and next) year, and occasionally so was the (T) Boiler. But painted boilers are scarce;

Set No. 1½ was the smallest cataloged in 1951. These small sets are difficult to find in good condition today.

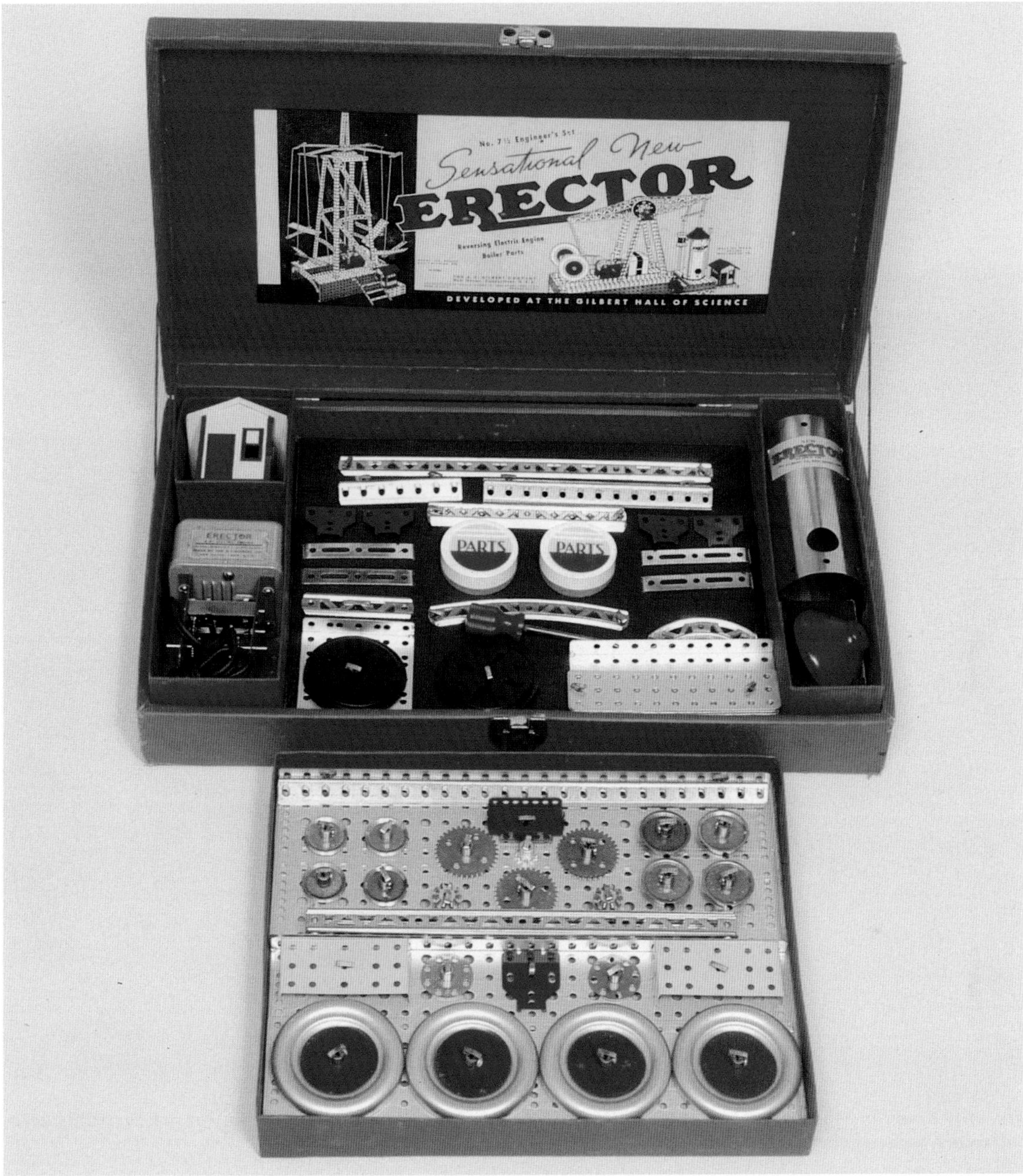

Packed in a cardboard box once again, this 1951 version of No. 7½ was more durable than the 1946–47 version, as the cardboard was much heavier.

most were plated in cadmium. With the passage of aluminum, the (W) Stack, (BN) Turret Plate, and (EL) Gear Box Side Plate were painted black again, and the (MG) Radiator hood was once more painted red.

The (NZ) Plastic Handle Screw Driver replaced the (NZ) Wood Handle Screw Driver. This new tool came with a short handle made of red plastic and was included in Set Nos. 7½ and above.

An anomaly occurred beginning this year with the location of the circular Erector label used on the outside lid of the metal box sets. Since the creation of this label in 1933, it always had been affixed on the left side of the lid. From 1951 through 1959 (when it was dropped), this label was glued to the right side of the lid.

Another interesting modification was a new look for the blue cardboard inserts. The cardboard used for these inserts in prior years was smooth. But now the insert had a mottled finish, and the color was a deeper, more royal blue.

Although the instruction manual retained the same dark blue background with the "Happy-Faced Boy" on the cover, its copyright was updated to 1951 and the number changed to M2950. Also, the first inside page, which had been printed in color since 1935, was changed to black and white. In the past, the instruction manuals for the small sets (Nos. 1½, 2½, and 3½) lacked a cover. The first inside page for the large sets was the outside page for the small ones. Printing it in color helped to dress up the small sets. But beginning in 1951, all sets came with covers, so this colored page was no longer needed.

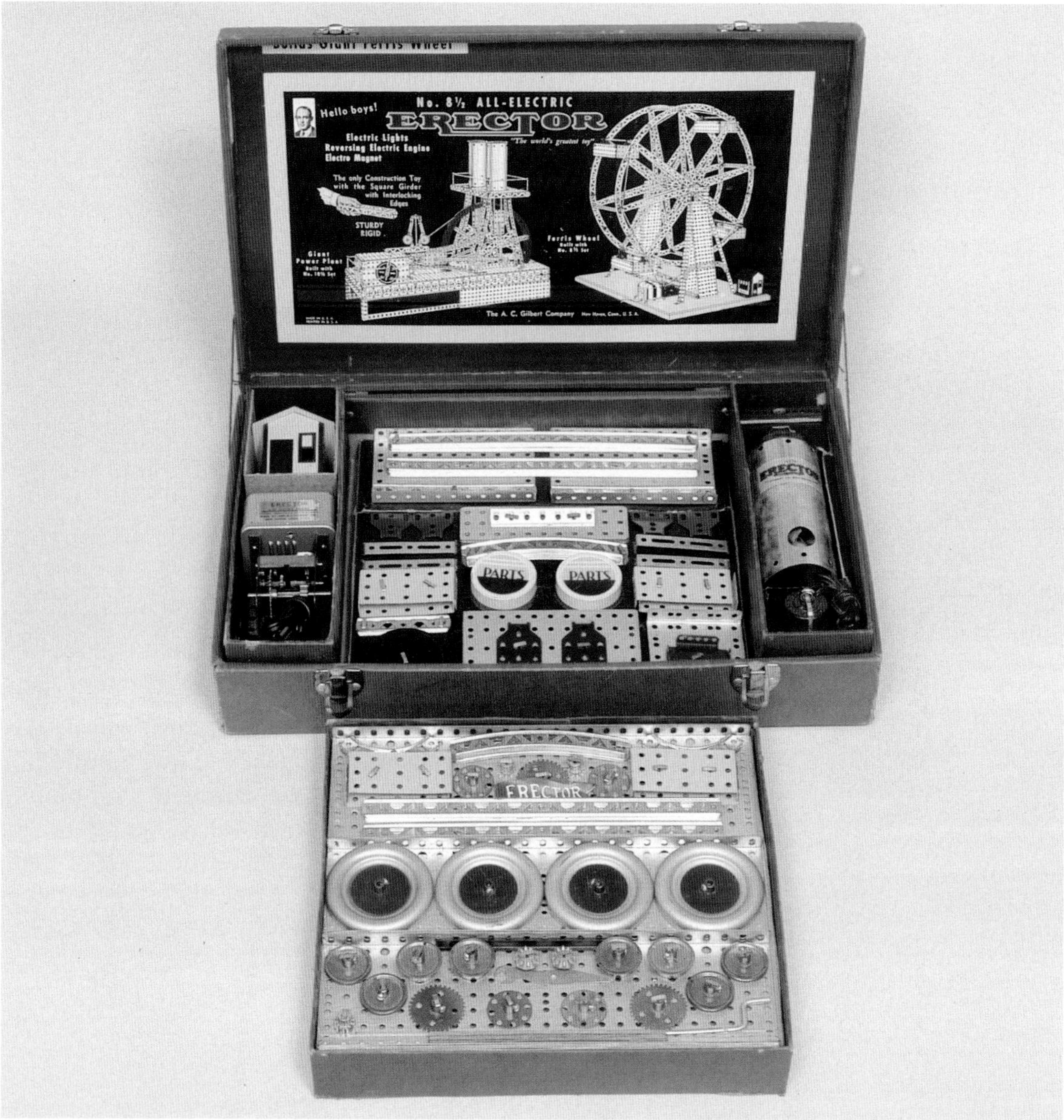

The only time No. 8½ was packed in a cardboard box was 1951–52. This set and No. 7½ are favorites with collectors because they are unique.

There were no additions to the line in 1951, but several deletions occurred, including the No. 1E accessory kit. A sadder loss was No. 12½, an expensive, top-of-the-line set that never sold well. The steel shortage that stemmed from the Korean War very likely caused Gilbert to drop this wonderful set.

Cardboard Box Sets

Steel was in short supply in 1951; the most obvious impact this had on The A. C. Gilbert Company was the greatly expanded number of cardboard box sets. Gilbert had learned from prior experience that aluminum parts were not successful, so he used what steel he could find for Erector parts, and made all but the largest set box out of cardboard.

Set Nos. 1½, 2½, and 4½ were available again. With the exception of the parts modifications already mentioned, they were unchanged from 1950.

Set No. 6½A (the metal box version of No. 6½) was dropped, and No. 6½ (the cardboard box version) was resurrected from 1949 and returned to the line. But there were some significant changes in the 1951 version. The body of the box, which had been covered with blue paper in the past, was now covered with pale red paper. And the lid was now hinged across the back, with a red cords attached between the lid and the box body to hold the lid upright while the set was open. On the inside of the lid, Gilbert used the same label that was used on last year's metal box set. Also, a new cardboard display insert, with a new packing arrangement, was used for the lower level of this set. Now only one parts container was included; in the past there had been two.

But the most remarkable modifications occurred with the next two sets, for their packaging was dramatically different from anything in the past. Set No. 7½ came packed in a newly created cardboard box that measured 19½" x 11" x 3¼". The cardboard used to construct this box was heavy, more than

⅜" thick. Gilbert had never used cardboard like this before. Also, the box was covered with pale red paper—the same paper that was used on the little accessory set boxes.

The lid on No. 7½ was hinged and held in the open position by red cord. A single suit case clasp kept the lid closed. Inside the lid was the standard label for No. 7½, which pictured the Airplane Ride and Walking Beam Engine. There was a cardboard parts display tray, and the box was divided into three sections in the lower level for parts storage.

A similar cardboard box was created for the 1951 version of No. 8½. Measuring 20" x 12" x 4", it was made of the same heavy cardboard and covered with the same pale red paper as No. 7½. The hinged lid was held in the open position with red cord, and it came with two suit case clasps. The inside lid label was the same as was used on the metal box version of this set last year. There was a removable cardboard parts display tray, and the lower level of the set box was divided into three compartments with cardboard dividers.

Set Nos. 7½ and 8½ from 1951 (and 1952) are difficult to find, especially in good condition. Despite the extraordinarily heavy cardboard used in these set boxes, they were just not sturdy enough to handle the weight of the parts, and they tended to disintegrate over time.

Metal Box Sets

With the elimination of No. 12½, the only metal box set in the 1951 line was No. 10½. With the exception of the parts modifications already discussed, it was identical to the offering from 1950.

Erector System Modifications for 1951

I. Noteworthy Parts Colors and Finishes

(P20) 5 Hole Strip Formed, cadmium-plated
(P33) Screw Driver, cadmium-plated
(P37) Collar, cadmium-plated
(A), (B), (C), (D), and (E) Girders, cadmium-plated
(E), (F), (G), (H), (I), and (J) Strips, cadmium-plated
(M) and (N) Double Angles, cadmium-plated
(O) Pawl, cadmium-plated
(T) Boiler, cadmium-plated or painted silver
(W) Stack, painted black
(AA) Eccentric Crank, cadmium-plated
(AF) Small Hook, cadmium-plated
(AQ) Sheave Pulley, cadmium-plated
(BE), (DP), (MB), and (MO), Angle Girders, cadmium-plated
(BL) Small Washer, cadmium-plated
(BN) Regular Turret Plate, painted black
(CH) Right Angle, cadmium-plated
(DK) Flat Spring, cadmium-plated
(DO) Steering Wheel with Hub, cadmium-plated
(DS) Cotter Pin, cadmium-plated
(EL) Gear Box Side Plate, painted black
(EX), (EY), and (EZ) Big Channel Girders, cadmium-plated
(FD) Hinged Loop, cadmium-plated
(LX) Steering Column Bracket, cadmium-plated
(MA) Radiator, cadmium-plated
(MD), (ME), (MF), and (MY) Base Plates, painted silver
(MG) Radiator Hood, painted red
(MH) 3" Disc Wheel, single-piece construction, hub painted red, tire silver
(MI) Front Axle Unit, cadmium-plated
(MM) Wrench, cadmium-plated
(MN) 12" Large Base Plate, painted silver or aluminum
(NJ) Battery Holder, cadmium-plated
(NK) Ratchet, cadmium-plated
(NS) and (OG) Formed Strips, cadmium-plated
(A48) and (K48) Mechanical Motor and Key, cadmium-plated
(S51), (S52), (S57), (S62), and (FA) Screws, cadmium-plated
(N21) Square Nut, cadmium-plated

II. Modified Parts

(CA) Signal Arms, made of fiber, painted dull red
(OG) Horse, laminated cardboard
(NZ) Plastic Handle Screw Driver substituted for (NZ) Wood Handle Screw Driver

III. Eliminated Parts

(NL) Bolster Bracket
(NW) Tread
(NX) Tread Pulley
(OA) 18 Volt Bulb
(OB) Tread Pin
(OC) Single Wire Plug Unit
(OD) Control Box with Wires
(P55) 7-15 Volt Erector Motor
(No. 5) Transformer

THE 1952 ERECTOR LINE

Things were quiet at 1 Erector Square in 1952. While there were modifications in few of the parts, the line of regular sets continued without change, and the only difference in the range of products offered was the elimination of No. 6, The Erector Whistle Kit.

A noteworthy change did occur with No. 10½, the only metal box set in the line. The diameter of the metal rod used to form the box's handle was reduced. It was painful to carry this heavy set by its handle before; now it was torture. The use of a smaller handle was continued on metal box sets from this point forward.

The most significant modification that occurred in 1952 involved the (A47) Electric Engine, and there were really two changes here. First, the motor, which had been rated at 25 watts, was downgraded to 22 watts.

The second change affected the gearbox. In the past, the gearshift was held in one of five positions by a springy metal "finger" that would snap into one of five indentations on a plate that was part of the gearshift lever. Now the finger and indention plate were replaced by five notches in the protective plate. The gearshift lever was stamped with a crimp that would snap into one of the five notches. This prevented the motor from slipping out of gear while the engine was at work.

The change in the motor rating preceded the change in the gearbox design. Examples of 22-watt motors with old-style gearboxes exist, but all the new gearboxes have 22-watt motors.

An interesting new (N21) Square Nut was introduced in 1952. This nut was thinner than the old style of nut, and the corners were clearly rounded. Not all sets came with the new nuts, and the old and new style of nuts were never mixed in a set. (These two styles of nuts continued to be used simultaneously through 1953. In 1954, the early style of square nuts disappeared, and another new style with a convex surface was introduced.)

By 1952 the last vestiges of aluminum parts were gone

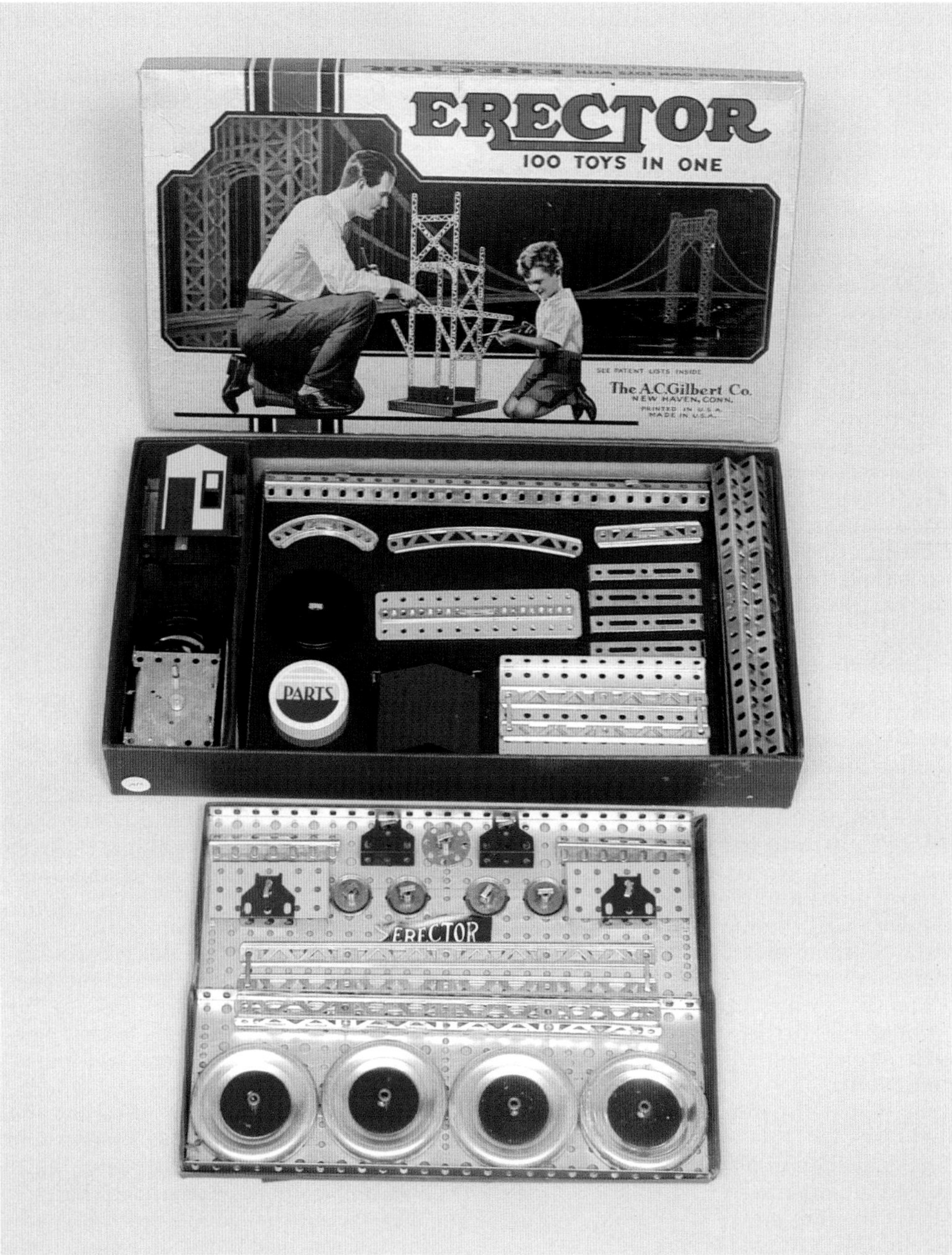

Set No. 4½ from 1952 featured the (A48) Mechanical Motor. The complicated arrangement of cardboard inserts makes for an attractive display.

from the sets, including the (MN) Base Plates, the last part to be produced in this soft metal. Also of interest was the (CR) Special Turret Plate, which was painted silver this year.

Erector System Modifications for 1952

I. Noteworthy Parts Colors and Finishes
(T) Boiler, cadmium-plated
(CR) Special Turret Plate, painted silver
(MN) 12" Large Base Plate, silver-painted steel

II. Modified Parts
(N21) Square Nut, with 90-degree-angle corners (as before) or thinner, with rounded corners
(A47) Electric Engine, rated at 22 watts, with old or new style of gearbox

Listings of 1951 and 1952 Erector Sets

NO. 1½ — The Builder's Set
Came in a cardboard box 13½" x 9¾" x ¾"; sold for $2.00 in 1951 and 1952.

30 40 70 +15 +20

NO. 2½ — The Apprentice Set
Featured the (MH) Disc Wheels. Came in a cardboard box 18" x 10" x 1⅛"; sold for $3.50 in 1951 and 1952.

35 50 80 +20 +25

NO. 4½ The Motorized Set

Featured the (A48) Mechanical Motor and (MN) 12" Base Plates, and (MX) House and built truck with (A48). Came in a cardboard box 18" x 10" x 2⅜" with a lift-off lid; two-layer set with removable cardboard parts display tray; sold for $7.95 in 1951 and 1952.

Gd	VG	Exc	Inv	Org
40	60	100	+20	+25

NO. 6½ The Electric Engine Set

Featured the (A47) Electric Engine and built Airplane Ride. Came in a cardboard box 18" x 10" x 3" with a hinged lid; two-layer set with removable cardboard parts display tray; sold for $12.95 in 1951 and 1952.

Gd	VG	Exc	Inv	Org
40	60	100	+20	+25

NO. 7½ The Engineer's Set

Featured the (T) Boiler and built Walking Beam Engine. Came in a cardboard box 19½" x 11" x 3"; constructed from heavy cardboard, covered with pale red paper, and had a hinged lid. Two-layer set with one removable cardboard parts display tray; sold for $16.95 in 1951 and 1952.

Gd	VG	Exc	Inv	Org
120	180	300	+60	+75

NO. 8½ The All-Electric Set

Featured the (MJ) Electro Magnet and lighting system parts and built Ferris Wheel and Bascule Bridge. Came in a cardboard box 29" x 12" x 4"; constructed from heavy cardboard, covered with pale red paper, and had a hinged lid. Two-layer set with one removable cardboard parts display tray; sold for $22.50 in 1951 and $23.50 in 1952.

Gd	VG	Exc	Inv	Org
140	210	350	+70	+90

NO. 10½ The Amusement Park Set

Featured the truck parts, giant flywheel, parachutes, and carousel horses and built Parachute Jump, Merry-Go-Round, and other amusement park models as well as Giant Power Plant. Came in a red metal box 22" x 13" x 3"; two-layer set with three removable parts display trays constructed from (MN) Base Plates; sold for $35.00 in 1951 and $36.50 in 1952.

Gd	VG	Exc	Inv	Org
160	240	400	+80	+100

THE 1953 ERECTOR LINE

A high point in Erector history begins with 1953, though no sets were added and one (No. 5) was deleted in that year. With wars and labor strikes behind him, Gilbert finally had an adequate supply of steel with which to manufacture his sets with no compromises. Set Nos. 7½ and above came packed in steel boxes from this point forward, and the way was clear for a gradual expansion through the remainder of the Renaissance Period. From a quality standpoint, the sets manufactured between 1953 and 1956 were superb.

Erector continued to evolve in 1953, as a new manufacturing process known as "sintering" was adopted for certain parts. A sintered part is one made from a metallic powder that is subjected to heat and pressure in a mold. This turns the powder into a solid part. Gilbert found this process ideal for small gears and pulleys and the like. So beginning in 1953 and until the end of traditional Erector, the (P7) and (P7A) Pulleys, (P13) and (P13B) 12 Tooth Gears, (Z) Flanged Wheel, (BT) Pierced Disk, and (CJ) 36 Tooth Gear were produced from sintered metal.

Other parts also underwent interesting changes. The (P13) and (P13B) 12 Tooth Gears were redesigned and produced with teeth that tapered to the hub. The (BT) Turret Plate and the (CR) Special Turret Plate were no longer painted, but joined the ranks of cadmium-plated parts.

Plastic continued to invade Erector. In 1951 the first plastic showed up on the handle of the screwdriver. Now other parts were plastic as well. The (U) Boiler Top showed up in plastic this year, and some interesting experimentation occurred over the course of the year. In the earliest version of this 1953 boiler top, the color of the plastic was milky-red, distinctly different from the bright red plastic that would be used by the end of the year. Part way through the year, the color was changed to a dark, burgundy shade of red. Towards the end of 1953, Gilbert settled on the bright red plastic that continued until the end of traditional Erector production. Both of the early versions of the Boiler Top are difficult to find.

Gilbert also continued his experiment with the (CA) Signal Arm, and it was produced in bright red plastic instead of fiber. But these plastic Signal Arms proved to be just as fragile as the ones made of fiber, and few have survived intact.

Major modifications occurred with the (A47) Electric Engine in 1952. Left: The version from 1950–51. Right: The version from 1952–53 with an improved gearbox design.

In 1953 Gilbert began to manufacture gears and wheels from sintered metal. Left: Gear from before 1953. Center: Sintered gear from 1953–54. Right: Sintered gear with thicker hub from 1955–62.

1951–52 CONTENTS LIST

Set No.		1½	2½[1]	4½	6½	7½	8½	10½
P7	⅞" PULLEY	4	4	4	4	4	0	0
P7A	1⅛" PULLEY	0	0	0	0	0	4	4
P12	CROWN GEAR	0	0	0	0	0	0	1
P13	12 TOOTH PINION GEAR, ⅛"	0	0	0	1	1	2	2
P13B	12 TOOTH PINION GEAR, 7⁄23"	0	0	0	0	0	1	4
P15	COUPLING	0	0	1	2	2	2	2
P20	5 HOLE STRIP—FORMED	0	0	0	0	2	2	8
P24	CRANK	1	1	1	1	1	1	1
P33	SMALL SCREW DRIVER	1	1	1	1	0	0	0
P34	HANK OF STRING	0	1	1	1	1	1	3
P37	COLLAR	1	4	5	6	7	9	20
P48	MITRE GEAR	0	0	0	2	2	2	2
P57A	2⅛" AXLE	1	1	1	1	1	1	1
P57D	6" AXLE	0	1	0	0	0	0	0
P57E	8" AXLE	0	0	0	0	0	0	2
P57F	12" AXLE	0	0	0	0	0	1	2
P57JA	7½" AXLE	0	0	0	0	0	0	4
P79	CAR TRUCK	4	4	4	4	4	4	4
A	2½" GIRDER	4	4	4	4	4	4	4
B	5" GIRDER	4	4	8	8	8	12	12
C	10" GIRDER	2	8	8	8	8	36	52
D	2½" CURVED GIRDER	4	4	4	4	4	4	4
E	5" CURVED GIRDER	0	2	2	4	4	26	26
F	5 HOLE STRIP	0	0	2	2	2	2	2
G	7 HOLE STRIP	0	0	2	2	2	2	6
H	11 HOLE STRIP	0	0	4	4	4	4	16
I	21 HOLE STRIP	0	0	2	2	2	4	18
J	41 HOLE STRIP	0	0	0	0	0	2	2
M	SMALL DOUBLE ANGLE	0	0	0	0	2	6	24
N	LONG DOUBLE ANGLE	2	4	4	4	4	4	16
O	PAWL	0	0	0	1	2	2	16
T	BOILER	0	0	0	0	1	1	2
U	BOILER TOP	0	0	0	0	1	1	1
W	STACK	0	0	0	0	3	3	3
Z	FLANGED WHEEL 15⁄16" DIA.	0	0	0	0	4	4	4
AA	ECCENTRIC CRANK	0	0	0	0	0	0	6
AF	SMALL HOOK	1	1	1	1	1	1	1
AJ	PAPER ERECTOR FLAG	0	0	1	1	1	1	1
AQ	SHEAVE PULLEY	0	0	0	0	0	1	4
AS	2⅞" AXLE	0	0	2	2	3	3	4
AT	4" AXLE	2	2	2	2	2	2	2
BE	6" ANGLE GIRDER	0	0	4	4	4	4	4
BH	SOLID COLLAR	0	0	0	0	0	0	2
BL	SMALL WASHER	6	12	12	12	12	12	12
BN	REGULAR TURRET PLATE	0	0	2	2	4	4	4
BT	PIERCED DISC	1	1	1	2	2	4	4
BY	11 HOLE FIBRE STRIP	0	0	0	0	0	2	2
CA	SIGNAL ARM	0	0	0	0	0	0	2
CH	RIGHT ANGLE	8	12	14	14	14	30	42
CJ	36 TOOTH GEAR	0	0	0	2	3	3	3
CR	SPECIAL TURRET PLATE	0	0	0	0	0	0	2
CS	WHEEL SEGMENT WITH HUB	0	0	0	0	0	0	8
CZ	7" AXLE	0	0	2	2	2	4	4

1951–52 CONTENTS LIST

Set No.		1½	2½[1]	4½	6½	7½	8½	10½
DB	MOTOR PULLEY	0	0	1	1	1	1	1
DE	STEERING COLUMN	0	0	0	0	0	0	1
DK	FLAT SPRING	0	0	0	0	0	0	4
DO	STEERING WHEEL WITH HUB	0	0	0	0	0	0	1
DP	12" ANGLE GIRDER	0	0	4	4	4	4	4
DS	COTTER PIN	0	0	0	0	0	0	1
EI	STD. GEAR BOX SIDE PLATE	0	0	0	2	2	2	2
EX	BIG CHANNEL GIRDER 12"	0	0	0	0	0	0	8
EY	BIG CHANNEL GIRDER 6"	0	0	0	0	0	0	4
EZ	BIG CHAN. GIRDER CURVED 6"	0	0	0	0	0	0	9
FA	1¾" x 8-32 SCREW	0	0	0	0	0	0	12
FD	HINGED LOOP	0	0	0	0	0	0	2
LX	STEERING COLUMN BRACKET	0	0	0	0	0	0	1
MA	RADIATOR	0	0	0	0	0	0	1
MB	18½" ANGLE GIRDER	0	0	0	0	0	0	2
MC	BASE PLATE 1" x 2½"	2	2	2	2	2	8	8
MD	BASE PLATE 2½" x 5"	1	1	1	1	1	4	4
ME	BASE PLATE 1" x 4"	0	0	0	0	0	0	4
MF	BASE PLATE 1" x 5"	0	2	4	4	4	8	21
MG	RADIATOR HOOD	0	0	0	0	0	0	1
MH	LARGE 3" DISC WHEEL	0	4	4	4	4	4	4
MI	FRONT AXLE UNIT	0	0	0	0	0	0	1
MJ	ELECTRO MAGNET WITH CORD	0	0	0	0	0	1	1
MM	WRENCH	0	0	1	1	1	1	1
MN	12" BASE PLATE	0	0	4	4	4	6	6
MO	3" ANGLE GIRDER	0	0	4	4	4	4	4
MV	FLAT CAR TRUCK	0	0	0	0	2	4	4
MW	NUT HOLDER	0	0	1	1	1	1	1
MX	HOUSE	0	0	1	1	1	1	1
MY	2½" x 2½" BASE PLATE	0	0	1	1	1	1	1
MZ	BEARING BLOCK	0	0	0	1	1	1	1
NH	LAMP SOCKET UNIT	0	0	0	0	0	2	2
NI	BULB, 1½ VOLT	0	0	0	0	0	2	2
NJ	BATTERY HOLDER	0	0	0	0	0	1	1
NK	RATCHET	0	0	0	0	0	2	2
NS	41 HOLE STRIP—FORMED	0	0	0	0	0	0	2
NU	PARACHUTE	0	0	0	0	0	0	4
NY	3⅛" AXLE ROD	0	0	0	0	0	0	2
NZ	PLASTIC SCREW DRIVER	0	0	0	0	1	1	1
OE	6" FLEXIBLE COUPLING	0	0	0	1	1	1	1
OF	HORSE	0	0	0	0	0	0	6
OG	21 HOLE STRIP FORMED	0	0	0	0	0	0	2
OH	72 TOOTH GEAR	0	0	0	0	0	0	1
OI	SEGMENT OF 72 TOOTH GEAR	0	0	0	0	0	0	1
A48	MECHANICAL MOTOR	0	0	1	0	0	0	0
K48	KEY FOR MECH. MOTOR	0	0	1	0	0	0	0
A47	ELECTRIC ENGINE	0	0	0	1	1	1	1
N21	8-32 SQUARE NUT	23	45	88	93	93	169	271
S51	¼" x 8-32 SCREW	20	35	80	84	84	162	240
S52	½" x 8-32 SCREW	0	0	0	4	4	4	8
S57	1⅜" x 8-32 SCREW	0	0	0	0	4	4	4
S62	⅞" x 8-32 SCREW	3	6	8	8	8	18	64

1. Set No. 2½ also contained two 5" axles.

ERECTOR SEPARATE PARTS PRICES

KINDLY ENCLOSE CHECK, MONEY ORDER OR STAMPS WITH YOUR ORDER FOR PARTS

THE A. C. GILBERT CO., NEW HAVEN, CONN., U. S. A.

Trade No.	Name of Part	Page	Price
*N21	8-32 Square Nut	3	.10 doz.
P7	Small Wheel, 7/8" Dia.	2	.10 ea.
P7A	Small Wheel, 1 1/8" Dia.	2	.10 ea.
P12	Crown Gear	2	.15 ea.
P13	12-Tooth Pinion Gear, 1/8"	2	.10 ea.
P13B	12-Tooth Pinion Gear, 7/32"	2	.10 ea.
P15	Coupling	2	.10 ea.
P20	Five Hole Strip—formed	2	.10 ea.
P24	Crank	2	.10 ea.
P33	Small Screw Driver	3	.10 ea.
P34	Hank of String	3	.10 ea.
P37	Collar	2	.25 doz.
P48	Mitre Gear	2	.20 ea.
P57A	2 1/8" Axle	2	.02 ea.
P57D	6" Axle	2	.06 ea.
P57E	8" Axle	2	.08 ea.
P57F	12" Axle	2	.12 ea.
P79	Car Truck	2	.05 ea.
*S11	Set Screw	3	.05 doz.
*S51	1/4" x 8-32 Screw	3	.10 doz.
*S52	1/2" x 8-32 Screw	3	.10 doz.
*S57	1 3/8" x 8-32 Screw	3	.15 doz.
*S62	7/8" x 8-32 Screw	3	.10 doz.
*FA	1 3/4" x 8-32 Screw	3	.15 doz.
A	2 1/2" Girder	2	.20 doz.
B	5" Girder	2	.35 doz.
C	10" Girder	2	.50 doz.
D	2 1/2" Curved Girder	2	.25 doz.
E	5" Curved Girder	2	.40 doz.
F	5 Hole Strip	2	.10 doz.
G	7 Hole Strip	2	.10 doz.
H	11 Hole Strip	2	.15 doz.
I	21 Hole Strip	2	.20 doz.
J	41 Hole Strip	2	.50 doz.
M	Small Double Angle	2	.25 doz.
N	Long Double Angle	2	.05 ea.
O	Pawl	2	.05 ea.
S	Large Base Plate—21 holes	2	.40 ea.
T	Boiler	3	.30 ea.
U	Boiler Top	3	.20 ea.
W	Stack	3	.05 ea.
Z	Flanged Wheel 15/16" Dia.	2	.15 ea.
AA	Eccentric Crank	2	.10 ea.
AE	Spiral Spring	3	.05 ea.
AF	Small Hook	2	.15 doz.
AM	Special Pulley—Metal	2	.05 ea.
AQ	Sheave Pulley	2	.05 ea.
AS	2 7/8" Axle Rod	2	.03 ea.
AT	4" Axle Rod	2	.04 ea.
BE	6" Angle Girder	2	.50 doz.
BH	Solid Collar	2	2 for .10
BL	Small Washer	2	.05 doz.
BN	Regular Turret Plate	3	.15 ea.
BT	Pierced Disc	2	.10 ea.
BY	11-Hole Fibre Strip	2	.05 ea.
CA	Signal Arm	3	.10 ea.
CH	Right Angle	2	.10 doz.
CJ	36-Tooth Gear	2	.20 ea.
CR	Special Turret Plate with hub	3	.20 ea.
CS	Wheel Segment	3	.15 ea.
CZ	7" Axle Rod	2	.07 ea.
DA	10" Axle Rod	2	.10 ea.
DB	Motor Pulley	2	.10 ea.
DE	Steering Column	3	.15 ea.
DK	Flat Spring	3	.10 ea.
DO	Steering Wheel with Hub	2	.15 ea.
DP	12" Angle Girder	2	6 for .50
DS	Cotter Pin	3	.05 doz.
EI	Standard Gear Box Side Plate	2	.15 ea.
EX	Big Channel Girder 12"	2	6 for .50
EY	Big Channel Girder 6"	2	.05 ea.
EZ	Big Channel Curved Girder 6"	2	.10 ea.
FD	Hinged Loop	2	2 for .10
LX	Steering Column Bracket	3	.10 ea.
MA	Radiator	3	.25 ea.
MB	18 1/2" Angle Girder	2	.25 ea.
MC	Base Plate 1" x 2 1/2"	2	.05 ea.
MD	Base Plate 2 1/2" x 5"	2	.10 ea.
ME	Base Plate 1" x 4"	2	.05 ea.
MF	Base Plate 1" x 5"	2	.05 ea.
MG	Radiator Hood	3	.20 ea.
MH	Nickle Rim, 3" Disc Wheel	2	.25 ea.
MI	Front Axle Unit	3	.45 ea.
MJ	Electro Magnet with Cord	3	1.10 ea.
MM	Wrench	3	.05 ea.
MN	12" Base Plate	2	.40 ea.
MO	3" Angle Girder	2	.30 doz.
MV	Flat Car Truck	2	.05 ea.
MW	Nut Holder	3	.10 ea.
MX	House	3	.35 ea.
MY	2 1/2" x 2 1/2" Base Plate	2	.05 ea.
MZ	Bearing Block	2	.10 ea.
NH	Lamp Socket Unit	3	.20 ea.
NI	Bulb—1 1/2 Volt	3	.10 ea.
NJ	Battery Holder	3	.15 ea.
NK	Ratchet	2	.05 ea.
NL	Bolster Bracket	2	2 for .05
NM	10" x 2" Flange Plate	2	.40 ea.
NS	41 Hole strip—formed	2	.10 ea.
NT	Cone	3	.10 ea.
NU	Parachute	3	.35 ea.
NW	Belt and Clip Unit	3	.25 ea.
NX	Tread Pulley	2	.20 ea.
NY	3 1/8" Axle Rod	2	.03 ea.
NZ	Wood Handle Screwdriver	3	.20 ea.
OA	Bulb—18 Volt	3	.30 ea.
OB	Tread Pin	3	.10 ea.
OC	Single Wire and Plug Unit	3	.10 ea.
OD	Control Box with wires	3	1.50 ea.
[illegible]	[illegible] Coupling	3	.15 ea.
OH	72 Tooth Gear		.18 ea.
OI	Segment of 72 Tooth Gear		.21 ea.
OF	Horse		.23 ea.
OG	21 Hole Strip-Formed		.06 ea.
A48	Mechanical Motor	3	1.75 ea.
K48	Key for Mechancal Motor	3	.20 ea.
A47	Electric Engine, gear shift 110v. A.C. only	3	5.50 ea.
P55	7-15 Volt Erector Motor A.C. or D.C.	3	6.50 ea.
1	Transformer	3	4.95 ea.

NOTE

*N21 Nut used with screws S51, S52, S57, S62, FA
*S11 Set Screw used with pulleys, couplings, etc.

ERECTOR
HOW TO MAKE 'EM BOOKS

Same as copy included in Sets

		Price
No. 2 1/2	Erector How To Make 'Em Book	.25 ea.
No. 4 1/2	Erector How To Make 'Em Book	.25 ea.
No. 6 1/2	Erector How To Make 'Em Book	.35 ea.
No. 7 1/2	Erector How To Make 'Em Book	.35 ea.
No. 8 1/2	Erector How To Make 'Em Book	.40 ea.
No. 10 1/2	Erector How To Make 'Em Book	.60 ea.
No. 12 1/2	Erector How To Make 'Em Book	.75 ea.

ERECTOR KITS

No. IE	Erector Square Girder Kit	$1.00 ea.
No. 5	Erector Illumination Kit	1.95 ea.

Separate Parts Prices for 1951

ERECTOR SEPARATE PARTS PRICES

KINDLY ENCLOSE CHECK, MONEY ORDER OR STAMPS WITH YOUR ORDER FOR PARTS

THE A. C. GILBERT CO., NEW HAVEN, CONN., U. S. A.

Trade No.	Name of Part	Page	Price
*N21	8-32 Square Nut	3	.10 doz.
P7	Small Wheel, 7/8" Dia.	2	.10 ea.
P7A	Small Wheel, 1 1/8" Dia.	2	.10 ea.
P12	Crown Gear	2	.15 ea.
P13	12-Tooth Pinion Gear, 1/8"	2	.10 ea.
P13B	12-Tooth Pinion Gear, 7/32"	2	.10 ea.
P15	Coupling	2	.10 ea.
P20	Five Hole Strip—formed	2	.10 ea.
P24	Crank	2	.10 ea.
P33	Small Screw Driver	3	.10 ea.
P34	Hank of String	3	.10 ea.
P37	Collar	2	.25 doz.
P48	Mitre Gear	2	.20 ea.
P57A	2 1/8" Axle	2	.02 ea.
P57D	6" Axle	2	.06 ea.
P57E	8" Axle	2	.08 ea.
P57F	12" Axle	2	.12 ea.
P79	Car Truck	2	.05 ea.
*S11	Set Screw	3	.05 doz.
*S51	1/4" x 8-32 Screw	3	.10 doz.
*S52	1/2" x 8-32 Screw	3	.10 doz.
*S57	1 3/8" x 8-32 Screw	3	.15 doz.
*S62	7/8" x 8-32 Screw	3	.10 doz.
*FA	1 3/4" x 8-32 Screw	3	.15 doz.
A	2 1/2" Girder	2	.20 doz.
B	5" Girder	2	.35 doz.
C	10" Girder	2	.50 doz.
D	2 1/2" Curved Girder	2	.25 doz.
E	5" Curved Girder	2	.40 doz.
F	5 Hole Strip	2	.10 doz.
G	7 Hole Strip	2	.10 doz.
H	11 Hole Strip	2	.15 doz.
I	21 Hole Strip	2	.20 doz.
J	41 Hole Strip	2	.50 doz.
M	Small Double Angle	2	.25 doz.
N	Long Double Angle	2	.05 ea.
O	Pawl	2	.05 ea.
S	Large Base Plate—21 holes	2	.40 ea.
T	Boiler	3	.30 ea.
U	Boiler Top	3	.20 ea.
W	Stack	3	.05 ea.
Z	Flanged Wheel 15/16" Dia.	2	.15 ea.
AA	Eccentric Crank	2	.10 ea.
AE	Spiral Spring	3	.05 ea.
AF	Small Hook	2	.15 doz.
AM	Special Pulley—Metal	2	.05 ea.
AQ	Sheave Pulley	2	.05 ea.
AS	2 7/8" Axle Rod	2	.03 ea.
AT	4" Axle Rod	2	.04 ea.
BE	6" Angle Girder	2	.50 doz.
BH	Solid Collar	2	2 for .10
BL	Small Washer	2	.05 doz.
BN	Regular Turret Plate	3	.15 ea.
BT	Pierced Disc	2	.10 ea.
BY	11-Hole Fibre Strip	2	.05 ea.
CA	Signal Arm	3	.10 ea.
CH	Right Angle	2	.10 doz.
CJ	36-Tooth Gear	2	.20 ea.
CR	Special Turret Plate with hub	3	.20 ea.
CS	Wheel Segment	3	.15 ea.
CZ	7" Axle Rod	2	.07 ea.
DA	10" Axle Rod	2	.10 ea.
DB	Motor Pulley	2	.10 ea.
DE	Steering Column	3	.15 ea.
DK	Flat Spring	3	.10 ea.
DO	Steering Wheel with Hub	2	.15 ea.
DP	12" Angle Girder	2	6 for .50
DS	Cotter Pin	3	.05 doz.
EI	Standard Gear Box Side Plate	2	.15 ea.
EX	Big Channel Girder 12"	2	6 for .50
EY	Big Channel Girder 6"	2	.05 ea.
EZ	Big Channel Curved Girder 6"	2	.10 ea.
FD	Hinged Loop	2	2 for .10
LX	Steering Column Bracket	3	.10 ea.
MA	Radiator	3	.25 ea.
MB	18 1/2" Angle Girder	2	.25 ea.
MC	Base Plate 1" x 2 1/2"	2	.05 ea.
MD	Base Plate 2 1/2" x 5"	2	.10 ea.
ME	Base Plate 1" x 4"	2	.05 ea.
MF	Base Plate 1" x 5"	2	.05 ea.
MG	Radiator Hood	3	.20 ea.
MH	Nickle Rim, 3" Disc Wheel	2	.25 ea.
MI	Front Axle Unit	3	.45 ea.
MJ	Electro Magnet with Cord	3	1.10 ea.
MM	Wrench	3	.05 ea.
MN	12" Base Plate	2	.40 ea.
MO	3" Angle Girder	2	.30 doz.
MV	Flat Car Truck	2	.05 ea.
MW	Nut Holder	3	.10 ea.
MX	House	3	.35 ea.
MY	2 1/2" x 2 1/2" Base Plate	2	.05 ea.
MZ	Bearing Block	2	.10 ea.
NH	Lamp Socket Unit	3	.20 ea.
NI	Bulb—1 1/2 Volt	3	.10 ea.
NJ	Battery Holder	3	.15 ea.
NK	Ratchet	2	.05 ea.
NL	Bolster Bracket	2	2 for .05
NM	10" x 2" Flange Plate	2	.40 ea.
NS	41 Hole strip—formed	2	.10 ea.
NU	Parachute	3	.35 ea.
NW	Belt and Clip Unit	3	.25 ea.
NX	Tread Pulley	2	.20 ea.
NY	3 1/8" Axle Rod	2	.03 ea.
NZ	Wood Handle Screwdriver	3	.20 ea.
OA	Bulb—18 Volt	3	.30 ea.
OB	Tread Pin	3	.10 ea.
OC	Single Wire and Plug Unit	3	.10 ea.
OD	Control Box with wires	3	1.50 ea.
OE	6" Flexible Coupling	3	.15 ea.
OH	72 Tooth Gear		.18 ea.
OI	Segment of 72 Tooth Gear		.21 ea.
OF	Horse		.23 ea.
OG	21 Hole Strip-Formed		.06 ea.
A48	Mechanical Motor	3	1.75 ea.
K48	Key for Mechanical Motor	3	.20 ea.
A47	Electric Engine, gear shift 110v. A.C. only	3	5.50 ea.
P55	7-15 Volt Erector Motor A.C. or D.C.	3	6.50 ea.
1	Transformer	3	4.95 ea.

NOTE

*N21 Nut used with screws S51, S52, S57, S62, FA
*S11 Set Screw used with pulleys, couplings, etc.

ERECTOR
HOW TO MAKE 'EM BOOKS

Same as copy included in Sets

		Price
No. 2 1/2	Erector How To Make 'Em Book	.25 ea.
No. 4 1/2	Erector How To Make 'Em Book	.25 ea.
No. 6 1/2	Erector How To Make 'Em Book	.35 ea.
No. 7 1/2	Erector How To Make 'Em Book	.35 ea.
No. 8 1/2	Erector How To Make 'Em Book	.40 ea.
No. 10 1/2	Erector How To Make 'Em Book	.60 ea.
No. 12 1/2	Erector How To Make 'Em Book	.75 ea.

ERECTOR KITS

No. IE	Erector Square Girder Kit	$1.00 ea.
No. 5	Erector Illumination Kit	1.95 ea.

Separate Parts Prices for 1952

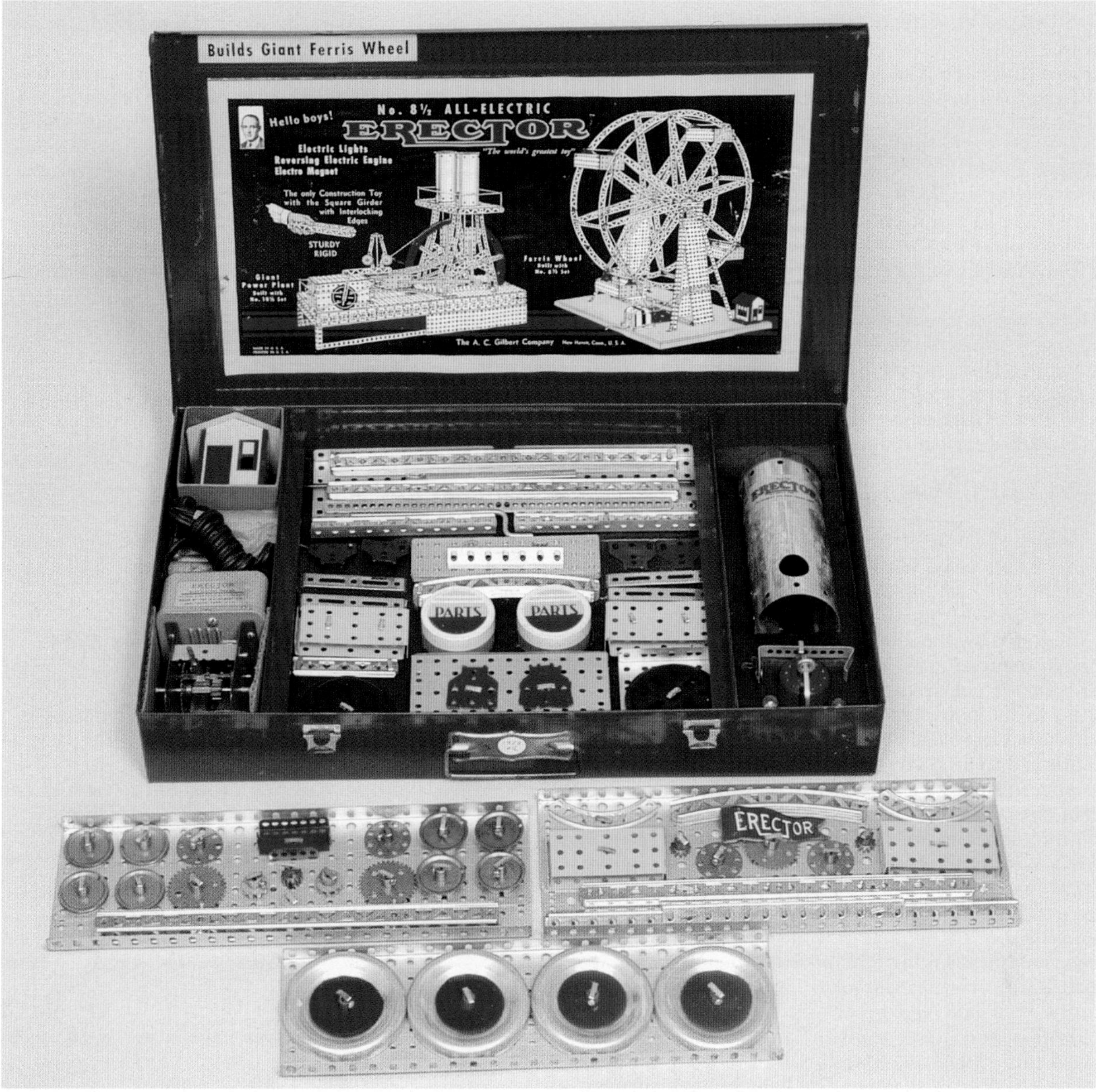

With the steel supply restored, both Nos. 7½ and 8½ (shown here) were packed in metal boxes again in 1953. Set No. 8½ from this period was one of the best sellers of all time.

The final invasion of plastic came with the parachute struts, which were changed from wood to red plastic. Also, all the silks for the parachutes seemed to be white during this period.

The instruction manual underwent a major revision, when the background color of the "Happy-Faced Boy" cover was changed from royal blue to robin's egg blue sometime in the middle of the year. This manual cover was still copyrighted 1951, and the M2950 number was retained. Gilbert even kept the picture of all four accessory kits on the inside back cover page, even though only the No. 7 was offered in 1953.

Cardboard Box Sets

Set Nos. 1½, 2½, 4½, and 6½ were continued in cardboard boxes with no changes other than the modifications mentioned previously.

Metal Box Sets

With an end to the steel shortage, Set Nos. 7½ and 8½ were packed in metal boxes once again. Other than the modifications already described, these sets were identical to those from 1950.

Set No. 10½ was modified in a mystifying way in 1953. Gilbert changed the text on the yellow background label from "Builds The Merry-Go-Round—Parachute Jump" to "Builds The Parachute Jump—5 Feet High." This was a throwback to the label used on the pre-1949 No. 9½, and the old Parachute Jump model. But the current model stood nearly 6 feet high! Anyone who studies Gilbert's advertising knows he was not a man prone to understatement. Why he allowed the premier model of The Amusement Park Set to be described as 12 inches less than its actual height is a puzzle, yet this continued for the rest of the Renaissance Period.

Erector System Modifications for 1953

I. Noteworthy Parts Colors and Finishes
(BT) Turret Plate, cadmium-plated
(CR) Special Turret Plate, cadmium-plated

II. Modified Parts
(P7) 7⁄8" Pulley, sintered
(P7A) 1 1⁄8" Pulley, sintered
(P13) 12 Tooth Gear, 1⁄8", sintered with tapered teeth
(P13B) 12 Tooth Gear, 7⁄23", sintered with tapered teeth
(U) Boiler Top, red-painted steel or creamy red, burgundy red, or bright red plastic
(Z) Flanged Wheel, sintered
(BT) Pierced Disc, sintered
(CA) Signal Arm, bright red plastic
(CJ) 36 Tooth Gear, sintered
(NU) Parachute, with red plastic struts and white silk

THE 1954 ERECTOR LINE

In the history of the Erector System, 1954 was a remarkably unremarkable year! With the exception of the elimination of No. 7, the last of the accessory kits, the lineup remained unchanged from 1953.

There were only two modifications in the parts, though a major change occurred with the reintroduction of the (A49) Electric Engine. It replaced the (A47) in 1954, but the new (A49) is easy to distinguished from its predecessors. First, the improved gearbox developed in 1952 (with the notches in the guard) continued to be used on the new (A49). Also, the cast motor housing was painted a distinctive blue-gray, clearly different from earlier (A49)s. The earliest version of the (A49) from 1954 came with an unusual core decal. As in the past, it was lettered "Erector Electric Engine," but the lettering was thinner and finer than in prior years. This version of the (A49) is scarce, because only a limited number came this way. The majority of the (A49)s came with no core decal at all.

The other modification in 1954 involved the (N21) Square Nut. Since 1952, two versions of this nut had been used concurrently. One had sharp corners, and the other had rounded corners, and it was thinner. The two versions were never mixed in a single set. But starting this year, another version of the Square Nut appeared. It had sharp corners, but one face was convex. The new version replaced the old sharp-cornered nut and was used with the round-corner one through the end of 1955.

A minor change occurred with the cover of the instruction manual cover toward the end of the year. Although there was no difference in the cover, the copyright was updated to 1954 and the number changed to M3279.

Last, 1954 was the year that Gilbert finally took new pictures of the sets for the toy catalog. Through 1953, most of the pictures of the sets used in the catalogs and advertising were taken before the war. Occasionally these old pictures were updated by overlaying a small picture of a new part (perhaps a new motor), but by and large, the 1946–53 catalogs did not accurately represent the sets that were sold. This caused a great deal of frustration for collectors hoping to date a set by matching it to a catalog picture or to use the picture to restore or repack a set.

Cardboard Box Sets

With the exception of the modifications already described, the lineup for 1954 was identical to that from the previous year.

Metal Box Sets

With the exception of the modifications already mentioned, the lineup for 1954 was identical to that from the previous year.

Erector System Modifications for 1954

I. Modified Parts
(A49) Electric Engine, with improved gearbox and blue-gray motor housing. Early version with core decal (rare); late version with no core decal
(N21) Square Nut, with rounded corners or convex face

II. Eliminated Parts
(A47) Electric Engine

Listings of 1953 and 1954 Erector Sets

	Gd	VG	Exc	Inv	Org

NO. 1½ — The Builder's Set
Came in a cardboard box 13½" x 9¾" x ¾"; sold for $2.00 in 1953 and 1954.

	Gd	VG	Exc	Inv	Org
	30	40	70	+15	+20

NO. 2½ — The Apprentice Set
Featured the (MH) Disc Wheels. Came in a cardboard box 18" x 10" x 1⅛"; sold for $3.50 in 1953 and 1954.

	Gd	VG	Exc	Inv	Org
	35	50	80	+20	+25

ERECTOR SYSTEM 1950–56

	Box Size	1950	1951–52	1953–54	1955	1956
Cardboard Box Sets		No. 1½, No. 2½,	No. 1½, No. 2½,	No. 1½, No. 2½,	No. 1½, No. 2½,	No. 1½, No. 2½,
		No. 4½, No. 6½	No. 4½, No. 6½, No. 7½, No. 8½	No. 4½, No. 6½	No. 3½, No. 6½	No. 3½
Metal Box Sets	16" x 8" x 3"	No. 6½A	N/A	N/A	No. 4½	No. 4½
	16" x 10" x 3"	N/A	N/A	N/A	N/A	No. 6½
	18" x 10" x 3"	No. 7½	N/A	No. 7½	No. 7½	No. 7½
	20" x 12" x 3"	No. 8½	N/A	No. 8½	No. 8½	No. 8½
	22" x 13" x 3"	No. 10½	No. 10½	No. 10½	No. 10½	No. 10½
	24" x 14" x 3"	No. 12½	N/A	N/A	N/A	No. 12½

NO. 4½ The Motorized Set

Featured the (A48) Mechanical Motor and (MN) 12" Base Plates, and (MX) House and built truck with (A48). Came in a cardboard box 18" x 10" x 2⅜" with a lift-off lid; two-layer set with removable cardboard parts display tray; sold for $7.95 in 1953 and 1954.

Gd	VG	Exc	Inv	Org
40	60	100	+20	+25

NO. 6½ The Electric Engine Set

Featured the (A47) Electric Engine in 1953 and the (A49) Electric Engine in 1954 and built Airplane Ride. Came in a cardboard box 18" x 10" x 3" with a hinged lid; two-layer set with removable cardboard parts display tray; sold for $12.95 in 1953 and $13.95 in 1954.

Gd	VG	Exc	Inv	Org
40	60	100	+20	+25

NO. 7½ The Engineer's Set

Featured the (T) Boiler and built Walking Beam Engine. Came in a red metal box 18" x 10" x 3"; two-layer set with two removable parts display trays constructed from (MN) Base Plates; sold for $16.95 in 1953 and 1954.

Gd	VG	Exc	Inv	Org
50	70	120	+25	+30

NO. 8½ The All-Electric Set

Featured the (MJ) Electro Magnet and lighting system parts and built Ferris Wheel and Bascule Bridge. Came in a red metal box 20" x 12" x 3"; two-layer set with three removable parts display trays constructed from (MN) Base Plates; sold for $23.50 in 1953 and $24.50 in 1954.

Gd	VG	Exc	Inv	Org
75	110	180	+40	+50

NO. 10½ The Amusement Park Set

Featured the truck parts, giant flywheel, parachutes, and carousel horses and built Parachute Jump, Merry-Go-Round, and other amusement park models as well as Giant Power Plant. Came in a red metal box 22" x 13" x 3"; two-layer set with three removable parts display trays constructed from (MN) Base Plates; sold for $37.50 in 1953 and $39.95 in 1954.

Gd	VG	Exc	Inv	Org
160	240	400	+80	+100

THE 1955 ERECTOR LINE

The tempo of development began to accelerate at The A. C. Gilbert Company in 1955. More of the sets were packed in metal boxes beginning this year, and the roster of sets was expanded, as an old set, No. 3½, was resurrected and returned to the lineup after being gone since 1942.

With 1955 came one of the great anomalies of the Renaissance Period. Since the creation of Erector in 1913, the small sets had been packed in cardboard boxes and the large ones in wood boxes prior to 1933 and metal boxes thereafter. But this year, that was not to be. For No. 4½, which was packed in a cardboard box in 1954, was upgraded to metal in 1955, but No. 6½ still came in cardboard. This is the only time in the history of Erector when such an anomaly existed.

A new feature was added to the large sets: a red light bulb was packed in No. 7½ and above. (Set No. 7½ was also upgraded with a socket and battery holder. Larger sets already contained these parts.) This red bulb was included for use in the (T) Boiler, and Gilbert promoted it to "create the firebox glow in all boiler models." While this new part may be minor, its addition was significant, as this is the first new Erector innovation since 1949. The bulb was never pictured in the separate parts section of the instruction manual and left unrecorded in the separate parts list until 1958, when it was given the odd designation of (P12N677).

ERECTOR SEPARATE PARTS PRICES

KINDLY ENCLOSE CHECK, MONEY ORDER OR STAMPS WITH YOUR ORDER FOR PARTS

THE A. C. GILBERT CO., NEW HAVEN, CONN., U. S. A.

Trade No.	Name of Part	Page	Price
*N21	8-32 Square Nut	3	.10 doz.
P7	Small Wheel, ⅞" Dia.	2	.10 ea.
P7A	Small Wheel, 1⅛" Dia.	2	.10 ea.
P12	Crown Gear	2	.15 ea.
P13	12-Tooth Pinion Gear, ⅛"	2	.10 ea.
P13B	12-Tooth Pinion Gear, 5/32"	2	.10 ea.
P15	Coupling	2	.10 ea.
P20	Five Hole Strip—formed	2	.10 ea.
P24	Crank	2	.10 ea.
P33	Small Screw Driver	3	.10 ea.
P34	Hank of String	3	.10 ea.
P37	Collar	2	.25 doz.
P48	Mitre Gear	2	.20 ea.
P57A	2⅞" Axle	2	.02 ea.
P57D	6" Axle	2	.06 ea.
P57E	8" Axle	2	.08 ea.
P57F	12" Axle	2	.12 ea.
P79	Car Truck	2	.05 ea.
*S11	Set Screw	3	.05 doz.
*S51	¼" x 8-32 Screw	3	.10 doz.
*S52	⅜" x 8-32 Screw	3	.10 doz.
*S57	1⅜" x 8-32 Screw	3	.15 doz.
*S62	⅞" x 8-32 Screw	3	.10 doz.
*FA	1¾" x 8-32 Screw	3	.15 doz.
A	2½" Girder	2	.20 doz.
B	5" Girder	2	.35 doz.
C	10" Girder	2	.50 doz.
D	2½" Curved Girder	2	.25 doz.
E	5" Curved Girder	2	.40 doz.
F	5 Hole Strip	2	.10 doz.
G	7 Hole Strip	2	.10 doz.
H	11 Hole Strip	2	.15 doz.
I	21 Hole Strip	2	.20 doz.
J	41 Hole Strip	2	.50 doz.
M	Small Double Angle	2	.25 doz.
N	Long Double Angle	2	.05 ea.
O	Pawl	2	.05 ea.
S	Large Base Plate—21 holes	2	.40 ea.
T	Boiler	3	.30 ea.
U	Boiler Top	3	.20 ea.
W	Stack	3	.05 ea.
Z	Flanged Wheel 1 5/16" Dia.	2	.15 ea.
AA	Eccentric Crank	2	.10 ea.
AE	Spiral Spring	3	.05 ea.
AF	Small Hook	2	.15 doz.
AM			
AQ	Sheave Pulley	2	.05 ea.
AS	2⅞" Axle Rod	2	.03 ea.
AT	4" Axle Rod	2	.04 ea.
BE	6" Angle Girder	2	.50 doz.
BH	Solid Collar	2	2 for .10
BL	Small Washer	2	.05 doz.
BN	Regular Turret Plate	3	.15 ea.
BT	Pierced Disc	2	.10 ea.
BY	11-Hole Fibre Strip	2	.05 ea.
CA	Signal Arm	3	.10 ea.
CH	Right Angle	2	.10 doz.
CJ	36-Tooth Gear	2	.20 ea.
CR	Special Turret Plate with hub	3	.20 ea.
CS	Wheel Segment	3	.15 ea.
CZ	7" Axle Rod	2	.07 ea.
DA	10" Axle Rod	2	.10 ea.
DB	Motor Pulley	2	.10 ea.
DE	Steering Column	3	.15 ea.
DK	Flat Spring	3	.10 ea.
DO	Steering Wheel with Hub	2	.15 ea.
DP	12" Angle Girder	2	6 for .50
DS	Cotter Pin	3	.05 doz.
EI	Standard Gear Box Side Plate	2	.15 ea.
EX	Big Channel Girder 12"	2	6 for .50
EY	Big Channel Girder 6"	2	.05 ea.
EZ	Big Channel Curved Girder 6"	2	.10 ea.
FD	Hinged Loop	2	2 for .10
LX	Steering Column Bracket	3	.10 ea.
MA	Radiator	3	.25 ea.
MB	18½" Angle Girder	2	.25 ea.
MC	Base Plate 1" x 2½"	2	.05 ea.
MD	Base Plate 2½" x 5"	2	.10 ea.
ME	Base Plate 1" x 4"	2	.05 ea.
MF	Base Plate 1" x 5"	2	.05 ea.
MG	Radiator Hood	3	.20 ea.
MH	Nickle Rim, 3" Disc Wheel	2	.25 ea.
MI	Front Axle Unit	3	.45 ea.
MJ	Electro Magnet with Cord	3	1.10 ea.
MM	Wrench	3	.05 ea.
MN	12" Base Plate	2	.40 ea.
MO	3" Angle Girder	2	.30 doz.
MV	Flat Car Truck	2	.05 ea.
MW	Nut Holder	3	.10 ea.
MX	House	3	.35 ea.
MY	2½" x 2½" Base Plate	2	.05 ea.
MZ	Bearing Block	2	.10 ea.
NH	Lamp Socket Unit	3	.20 ea.
NI	Bulb—1½ Volt	3	.10 ea.
NJ	Battery Holder	3	.15 ea.
NK	Ratchet	2	.05 ea.
NL	Bolster Bracket	2	2 for .05
NM	10" x 2" Flange Plate	2	.40 ea.
NS	41 Hole strip—formed	2	.10 ea.
NU	Parachute	3	.35 ea.
NW	Belt and Clip Unit	3	.25 ea.
NX	Tread Pulley	2	.20 ea.
NY	3⅛" Axle Rod	2	.03 ea.
NZ	Wood Handle Screw-driver	3	.20 ea.
OA	Bulb—18 Volt	3	.30 ea.
OB	Tread Pin	3	.10 ea.
OC	Single Wire and Plug Unit	3	.10 ea.
OD	Control Box with wires	3	1.50 ea.
OE	6" Flexible Coupling	3	.15 ea.
OH	72 Tooth Gear		.18 ea.
OI	Segment of 72 Tooth Gear		.21 ea.
OF	Horse		.23 ea.
OG	21 Hole Strip-Formed		.06 ea.
A48	Mechanical Motor	3	1.75 ea.
K48	Key for Mechanical Motor	3	.20 ea.
A47	Electric Engine, gear shift 110v. A.C. only	3	5.50 ea.
P55	7-15 Volt Erector Motor A.C. or D.C.	3	6.50 ea.
1	Transformer	3	4.95 ea.

NOTE

*N21 Nut used with screws S51, S52, S57, S62, FA
*S11 Set Screw used with pulleys, couplings, etc.

ERECTOR HOW TO MAKE 'EM BOOKS

Same as copy included in Sets

	Price
No. 2½ Erector How To Make 'Em Book	.25 ea.
No. 4½ Erector How To Make 'Em Book	.25 ea.
No. 6½ Erector How To Make 'Em Book	.35 ea.
No. 7½ Erector How To Make 'Em Book	.35 ea.
No. 8½ Erector How To Make 'Em Book	.40 ea.
No. 10½ Erector How To Make 'Em Book	.60 ea.
No. 12½ Erector How To Make 'Em Book	.75 ea.

ERECTOR KITS

No. IE	Erector Square Girder Kit	$1.00 ea.
No. 5	Erector Illumination Kit	1.95 ea.

Separate Parts Prices for early 1953

1953–54 CONTENTS LIST

Set No.		1½	2½[1]	4½	6½	7½	8½	10½
P7	7/8" PULLEY	4	4	4	4	4	0	0
P7A	1 1/8" PULLEY	0	0	0	0	0	4	4
P12	CROWN GEAR	0	0	0	0	0	0	1
P13	12 TOOTH PINION GEAR, 1/8"	0	0	0	1	1	2	2
P13B	12 TOOTH PINION GEAR, 7/23"	0	0	0	0	0	1	4
P15	COUPLING	0	0	1	2	2	2	2
P20	5 HOLE STRIP—FORMED	0	0	0	0	2	2	8
P24	CRANK	1	1	1	1	1	1	1
P33	SMALL SCREW DRIVER	1	1	1	1	0	0	0
P34	HANK OF STRING	0	1	1	1	1	1	3
P37	COLLAR	1	4	5	6	7	9	20
P48	MITRE GEAR	0	0	0	2	2	2	2
P57A	2 1/8" AXLE	1	1	1	1	1	1	1
P57D	6" AXLE	0	1	0	0	0	0	0
P57E	8" AXLE	0	0	0	0	0	0	2
P57F	12" AXLE	0	0	0	0	0	1	2
P57JA	7½" AXLE	0	0	0	0	0	0	4
P79	CAR TRUCK	4	4	4	4	4	4	4
A	2½" GIRDER	4	4	4	4	4	4	4
B	5" GIRDER	4	4	8	8	8	12	12
C	10" GIRDER	2	8	8	8	8	36	52
D	2½" CURVED GIRDER	4	4	4	4	4	4	4
E	5" CURVED GIRDER	0	2	2	4	4	26	26
F	5 HOLE STRIP	0	0	2	2	2	2	2
G	7 HOLE STRIP	0	0	2	2	2	2	6
H	11 HOLE STRIP	0	0	4	4	4	4	16
I	21 HOLE STRIP	0	0	2	2	2	4	18
J	41 HOLE STRIP	0	0	0	0	0	2	2
M	SMALL DOUBLE ANGLE	0	0	0	0	2	6	24
N	LONG DOUBLE ANGLE	2	4	4	4	4	4	16
O	PAWL	0	0	0	1	2	2	16
T	BOILER	0	0	0	0	1	1	2
U	BOILER TOP	0	0	0	0	1	1	1
W	STACK	0	0	0	0	3	3	3
Z	FLANGED WHEEL 15/16" DIA.	0	0	0	0	4	4	4
AA	ECCENTRIC CRANK	0	0	0	0	0	0	6
AF	SMALL HOOK	1	1	1	1	1	1	1
AJ	PAPER ERECTOR FLAG	0	0	1	1	1	1	1
AQ	SHEAVE PULLEY	0	0	0	0	0	1	4
AS	2 7/8" AXLE	0	0	2	2	3	3	4
AT	4" AXLE	2	2	2	2	2	2	2
BE	6" ANGLE GIRDER	0	0	4	4	4	4	4
BH	SOLID COLLAR	0	0	0	0	0	0	2
BL	SMALL WASHER	6	12	12	12	12	12	12
BN	REGULAR TURRET PLATE	0	0	2	2	4	4	4
BT	PIERCED DISC	1	1	1	2	2	4	4
BY	11 HOLE FIBRE STRIP	0	0	0	0	0	2	2
CA	SIGNAL ARM	0	0	0	0	0	0	2
CH	RIGHT ANGLE	8	12	14	14	14	30	42
CJ	36 TOOTH GEAR	0	0	0	2	3	3	3
CR	SPECIAL TURRET PLATE WITH HUB	0	0	0	0	0	0	2
CS	WHEEL SEGMENT	0	0	0	0	0	0	8
CZ	7" AXLE	0	0	2	2	2	4	4
DB	MOTOR PULLEY	0	0	1	1	1	1	1

1953–54 CONTENTS LIST

Set No.		1½	2½[1]	4½	6½	7½	8½	10½
DE	STEERING COLUMN	0	0	0	0	0	0	1
DK	FLAT SPRING	0	0	0	0	0	0	4
DO	STEERING WHEEL WITH HUB	0	0	0	0	0	0	1
DP	12" ANGLE GIRDER	0	0	4	4	4	4	4
DS	COTTER PIN	0	0	0	0	0	0	1
EI	STD. GEAR BOX SIDE PLATE	0	0	0	2	2	2	2
EX	BIG CHANNEL GIRDER 12"	0	0	0	0	0	0	8
EY	BIG CHANNEL GIRDER 6"	0	0	0	0	0	0	4
EZ	BIG CHAN. GIRDER CURVED 6"	0	0	0	0	0	0	9
FA	1¾" x 8-32 SCREW	0	0	0	0	0	0	12
FD	HINGED LOOP	0	0	0	0	0	0	2
LX	STEERING COLUMN BRACKET	0	0	0	0	0	0	1
MA	RADIATOR	0	0	0	0	0	0	1
MB	18½" ANGLE GIRDER	0	0	0	0	0	0	2
MC	BASE PLATE 1" x 2½"	2	2	2	2	2	8	8
MD	BASE PLATE 2½" x 5"	1	1	1	1	1	4	4
ME	BASE PLATE 1" x 4"	0	0	0	0	0	0	4
MF	BASE PLATE 1" x 5"	0	2	4	4	4	8	21
MG	RADIATOR HOOD	0	0	0	0	0	0	1
MH	LARGE 3" DISC WHEEL	0	4	4	4	4	4	4
MI	FRONT AXLE UNIT	0	0	0	0	0	0	1
MJ	ELECTRO MAGNET WITH CORD	0	0	0	0	0	1	1
MM	WRENCH	0	0	1	1	1	1	1
MN	12" BASE PLATE	0	0	4	4	4	6	6
MO	3" ANGLE GIRDER	0	0	4	4	4	4	4
MV	FLAT CAR TRUCK	0	0	0	0	2	4	4
MW	NUT HOLDER	0	0	1	1	1	1	1
MX	HOUSE	0	0	1	1	1	1	1
MY	2½" x 2½" BASE PLATE	0	0	1	1	1	1	1
MZ	BEARING BLOCK	0	0	0	1	1	1	1
NH	LAMP SOCKET UNIT	0	0	0	0	0	2	2
NI	BULB, 1½ VOLT	0	0	0	0	0	2	2
NJ	BATTERY HOLDER	0	0	0	0	0	1	1
NK	RATCHET	0	0	0	0	0	2	2
NS	41 HOLE STRIP FORMED	0	0	0	0	0	0	2
NU	PARACHUTE	0	0	0	0	0	0	4
NY	3½" AXLE ROD	0	0	0	0	0	0	2
NZ	PLASTIC SCREW DRIVER	0	0	0	0	1	1	1
OE	6" FLEXIBLE COUPLING	0	0	0	1	1	1	1
OF	HORSE	0	0	0	0	0	0	6
OG	21 HOLE STRIP—FORMED	0	0	0	0	0	0	2
OH	72 TOOTH GEAR	0	0	0	0	0	0	1
OI	SEGMENT OF 72 TOOTH GEAR	0	0	0	0	0	0	1
A48	MECHANICAL MOTOR	0	0	1	0	0	0	0
K48	KEY FOR MECH. MOTOR	0	0	1	0	0	0	0
A47[2]/ A49	ELECTRIC ENGINE	0	0	0	1	1	1	1
N21	8-32 SQUARE NUT	23	45	88	93	93	169	271
S51	¼" x 8-32 SCREW	20	35	80	84	84	162	240
S52	½" x 8-32 SCREW	0	0	0	4	4	4	8
S57	1⅜" x 8-32 SCREW	0	0	0	0	4	4	4
S62	⅞" x 8-32 SCREW	3	6	8	8	8	18	64

1. Set No. 2½ also contained two 5" axles.
2. Engine was used in 1953, the A49 in 1954.

ERECTOR SEPARATE PARTS PRICES

KINDLY ENCLOSE CHECK, MONEY ORDER OR STAMPS WITH YOUR ORDER FOR PARTS

THE A. C. GILBERT CO., NEW HAVEN, CONN., U. S. A.

Trade No.	Name of Part	Page	Price
*N21	8-32 Square Nut	3	.10 doz.
P7	Small Wheel, ⅞" Dia.	2	.10 ea.
P7A	Small Wheel, 1⅛" Dia.	2	.10 ea.
P12	Crown Gear	2	.15 ea.
P13	12-Tooth Pinion Gear, ⅛"	2	.10 ea.
P13B	12-Tooth Pinion Gear, 7/32"	2	.10 ea.
P15	Coupling	2	.10 ea.
P20	Five Hole Strip—formed	2	.10 ea.
P24	Crank	2	.10 ea.
P33	Small Screw Driver	3	.10 ea.
P34	Hank of String	3	.10 ea.
P37	Collar	2	.25 doz.
P48	Mitre Gear	2	.20 ea.
P57A	2⅛" Axle	2	.02 ea.
P57D	6" Axle	2	.06 ea.
P57E	8" Axle	2	.08 ea.
P57F	12" Axle	2	.12 ea.
P79	Car Truck	2	.05 ea.
*S11	Set Screw	3	.05 doz.
*S51	¼" x 8-32 Screw	3	.10 doz.
*S52	½" x 8-32 Screw	3	.10 doz.
*S57	1⅜" x 8-32 Screw	3	.15 doz.
*S62	⅞" x 8-32 Screw	3	.10 doz.
*FA	1¾" x 8-32 Screw	3	.15 doz.
A	2½" Girder	2	.20 doz.
B	5" Girder	2	.35 doz.
C	10" Girder	2	.50 doz.
D	2½" Curved Girder	2	.25 doz.
E	5" Curved Girder	2	.40 doz.
F	5 Hole Strip	2	.10 doz.
G	7 Hole Strip	2	.10 doz.
H	11 Hole Strip	2	.15 doz.
I	21 Hole Strip	2	.20 doz.
J	41 Hole Strip	2	.50 doz.
M	Small Double Angle	2	.25 doz.
N	Long Double Angle	2	.05 ea.
O	Pawl	2	.05 ea.
S	Large Base Plate—21 holes	2	.40 ea.
T	Boiler	3	.30 ea.
U	Boiler Top	3	.20 ea.
W	Stack	3	.05 ea.
Z	Flanged Wheel 1 5/16" Dia.	2	.15 ea.
AA	Eccentric Crank	2	.10 ea.
AE	Spiral Spring	3	.05 ea.
AF	Small Hook	2	.15 doz.
AQ	Sheave Pulley	2	.05 ea.
AS	2⅞" Axle Rod	2	.03 ea.
AT	4" Axle Rod	2	.04 ea.
BE	6" Angle Girder	2	.50 doz.
BH	Solid Collar	2	2 for .10
BL	Small Washer	2	.05 doz.
BN	Regular Turret Plate	3	.15 ea.
BT	Pierced Disc	2	.10 ea.
BY	11-Hole Fibre Strip	2	.05 ea.
CA	Signal Arm	3	.10 ea.
CH	Right Angle	2	.10 doz.
CI	36-Tooth Gear	2	.20 ea.
CR	Special Turret Plate with hub	3	.20 ea.
CS	Wheel Segment	3	.15 ea.
CZ	7" Axle Rod	2	.07 ea.
DA	10" Axle Rod	2	.10 ea.
DB	Motor Pulley	2	.10 ea.
DE	Steering Column	3	.15 ea.
DK	Flat Spring	3	.10 ea.
DO	Steering Wheel with Hub	2	.15 ea.
DP	12" Angle Girder	2	6 for .50
DS	Cotter Pin	3	.05 doz.
EI	Standard Gear Box Side Plate	2	.15 ea.
EX	Big Channel Girder 12"	2	6 for .50
EY	Big Channel Girder 6"	2	.05 ea.
EZ	Big Channel Curved Girder 6"	2	.10 ea.
FD	Hinged Loop	2	2 for .10
LX	Steering Column Bracket	3	.10 ea.
MA	Radiator	3	.25 ea.
MB	18½" Angle Girder	2	.25 ea.
MC	Base Plate 1" x 2½"	2	.05 ea.
MD	Base Plate 2½" x 5"	2	.10 ea.
ME	Base Plate 1" x 4"	2	.05 ea.
MF	Base Plate 1" x 5"	2	.05 ea.
MG	Radiator Hood	3	.20 ea.
MH	Nickle Rim, 3" Disc Wheel	2	.25 ea.
MI	Front Axle Unit	3	.45 ea.
MJ	Electro Magnet with Cord	3	1.10 ea.
MM	Wrench	3	.05 ea.
MN	12" Base Plate	2	.40 ea.
MO	3" Angle Girder	2	.30 doz.
MV	Flat Car Truck	2	.05 ea.
MW	Nut Holder	3	.10 ea.
MX	House	3	.35 ea.
MY	2½" x 2½" Base Plate	2	.05 ea.
MZ	Bearing Block	2	.10 ea.
NH	Lamp Socket Unit	3	.20 ea.
NI	Bulb—1½ Volt	3	.10 ea.
NJ	Battery Holder	3	.15 ea.
NK	Ratchet	2	.05 ea.
NL	Bolster Bracket	2	2 for .05
NM	10" x 2" Flange Plate	2	.40 ea.
NS	41 Hole strip—formed	2	.10 ea.
NU	Parachute	3	.35 ea.
NW	Belt and Clip Unit	3	.25 ea.
NX	Tread Pulley	2	.20 ea.
NY	3⅛" Axle Rod	2	.03 ea.
NZ	Wood Handle Screw-driver	3	.20 ea.
OA	Bulb—18 Volt	3	.30 ea.
OB	Tread Pin	3	.10 ea.
OC	Single Wire and Plug Unit	3	.10 ea.
OD	Control Box with wires	3	1.50 ea.
OE	6" Flexible Coupling	3	.15 ea.
OH	72 Tooth Gear		.18 ea.
OI	Segment of 72 Tooth Gear		.21 ea.
OF	Horse		.23 ea.
OG	21 Hole Strip-Formed		.06 ea.
A48	Mechanical Motor	3	1.75 ea.
K48	Key for Mechanical Motor	3	.20 ea.
A47	Electric Engine, gear shift 110v. A.C. only	3	5.50 ea.
P55	7-15 Volt Erector Motor A.C. or D.C.	3	6.50 ea.
1	Transformer	3	4.95 ea.

NOTE

*N21 Nut used with screws S51, S52, S57, S62, FA
*S11 Set Screw used with pulleys, couplings, etc.

ERECTOR
HOW TO MAKE 'EM BOOKS

Same as copy included in Sets

	Price
No. 2½ Erector How To Make 'Em Book	.25 ea.
No. 4½ Erector How To Make 'Em Book	.25 ea.
No. 6½ Erector How To Make 'Em Book	.35 ea.
No. 7½ Erector How To Make 'Em Book	.35 ea.
No. 8½ Erector How To Make 'Em Book	.40 ea.
No. 10½ Erector How To Make 'Em Book	.60 ea.
No. 12½ Erector How To Make 'Em Book	.75 ea.

ERECTOR KITS

No. IE	Erector Square Girder Kit	$1.00 ea.
No. 5	Erector Illumination Kit	1.95 ea.

Separate Parts Prices for late 1953

ERECTOR SEPARATE PARTS PRICES

KINDLY ENCLOSE CHECK, MONEY ORDER OR STAMPS WITH YOUR ORDER FOR PARTS

THE A. C. GILBERT CO., NEW HAVEN, CONN., U. S. A.

Part No.	Part Name	Price
N21	8-32 Square Nut	.10 doz.
P7	⅞ Pulley	.10 ea.
P7A	1⅛ Pulley Assy.	.10 ea.
P12	Crown Gear	.15 ea.
P13	12-Tooth Pinion Gears ⅛"	.10 ea.
P13B	12-Tooth Pinion Gear 7/32"	.10 ea.
P15	Coupling	.10 ea.
P20	Five Hole Strip—Formed	.10 ea.
P24	Crank	.10 ea.
P33	Small Screw Driver	.10 ea.
P34	Hank of String	.10 ea.
P37	Collar	.25 doz.
P48	Mitre Gear	.20 ea.
P57A	2⅛" Axle	.05 ea.
P57D	6" Axle	.10 ea.
P57E	8" Axle	.10 ea.
P57F	12" Axle	.15 ea.
P79	Car Truck	.05 ea.
S11	Set Screw	.05 doz.
S51	¼" x 8-32 Screw	.10 doz.
S52	½" x 8-32 Screw	.10 doz.
S57	1⅜" x 8-32 Screw	.15 doz.
S62	⅞" x 8-32 Screw	.10 doz.
FA	1¾" x 8-32 Screw	.15 doz.
A	2½" Girder	.20 doz.
B	5" Girder	.35 doz.
C	10" Girder	.75 doz.
D	2½" Curved Girder	.25 doz.
E	5" Curved Girder	.40 doz.
BT	Pierced Disc	.10 ea.
F	5 Hole Strip	.10 doz.
G	7 Hole Strip	.10 doz.
H	11 Hole Strip	.15 doz.
I	21 Hole Strip	.35 doz.
J	41 Hole Strip	.50 doz.
M	Small Double Angle	.25 doz.
N	Long Double Angle	.05 ea.
O	Pawl	.05 ea.
T	Boiler	.40 ea.
U	Boiler Top	.20 ea.
W	Stack	.05 ea.
Z	Flanged Wheel 1 5/16" Dia.	.15 ea.
AA	Eccentric Crank	.10 ea.
AF	Small Hook	.15 doz.
AQ	Sheave Pulley	.05 ea.
AS	2⅞" Axle Rod	.05 ea.
AT	4" Axle Rod	.05 ea.
BE	6" Angle Girder	.50 doz.
BH	Solid Collar	2 for .10
BL	Small Washer	.05 doz.
BN	Regular Turret Plate	.15 ea.
BY	11 Hole Fibre Strip	.05 ea.
CA	Signal Arm	.10 ea.
CH	Right Angle	.10 doz.
CJ	36-Tooth Gear	.20 ea.
CR	Special Turret Plate with Hub	.20 ea.
CS	Wheel Segment	.15 ea.
CZ	7" Axle Rod	.10 ea.
P57JA	7½" Axle Rod	.05 ea.
P57N	3¼" Axle Rod	.05 ea.
DB	Motor Pulley	.10 ea.
DE	Steering Column	.15 ea.
DK	Flat Spring	.10 ea.
DO	Steering Wheel with Hub	.15 ea.
DP	12" Angle Girder	6 for .50
DS	Cotter Pin	.05 doz.
EI	Standard Gear Box Side Plate	.15 ea.
EX	Big Channel Girder 12"	6 for .65
EY	Big Channel Girder 6"	.10 ea.
EZ	Big Channel Curved Girder 6"	.10 ea.
FD	Hinged Loop	2 for .10
LX	Steering Column Bracket	.10 ea.
MA	Radiator	.25 ea.
MB	18½" Angle Girder	.25 ea.
MC	Base Plate 1" x 2½"	.05 ea.
MD	Base Plate 2½" x 5"	.15 ea.
ME	Base Plate 1" x 4"	.05 ea.
MF	Base Plate 1" x 5"	.05 ea.
MG	Radiator Hood	.20 ea.
MH	Large 3" Disc. Wheel	.25 ea.
MI	Front Axle Unit	.45 ea.
MJ	Electro Magnet with Cord	1.20 ea.
MM	Wrench	.05 ea.
MN	12" Base Plate	.40 ea.
MO	3" Angle Girder	.30 doz.
MV	Flat Car Truck	.05 ea.
MW	Nut Holder	.10 ea.
MX	House	.35 ea.
MZ	Bearing Block	.10 ea.
NH	Lamp Socket Unit	.20 ea.
NI	Bulb—1½ Volt	.10 ea.
NJ	Battery Holder	.15 ea.
NK	Ratchet	.05 ea.
NS	41—Hole Strip—Formed	.10 ea.
NU	Parachute	.40 ea.
NZ	Plastic Screw Driver	.25 ea.
OE	6" Flexible Coupling	.20 ea.
OH	72 Tooth Gear	.25 ea.
OI	Segment of 72 Tooth Gear	.25 ea.
OF	Horse	.25 ea.
OG	21—Hole Strip—Formed	.10 ea.
A48	Mechanical Motor	1.75 ea.
K48	Key for Mechanical Motor	.20 ea.
A49	A49 Electric Engine Gear Shift A.C. Only	5.95 ea.

ERECTOR
HOW TO MAKE 'EM BOOKS

Same as copy included in Sets

	Price
No. 2½ Erector How To Make 'Em Book	.25 ea.
No. 4½ Erector How To Make 'Em Book	.25 ea.
No. 6½ Erector How To Make 'Em Book	.35 ea.
No. 7½ Erector How To Make 'Em Book	.35 ea.
No. 8½ Erector How To Make 'Em Book	.40 ea.
No. 10½ Erector How To Make 'Em Book	.60 ea.

Separate Parts Prices for 1954

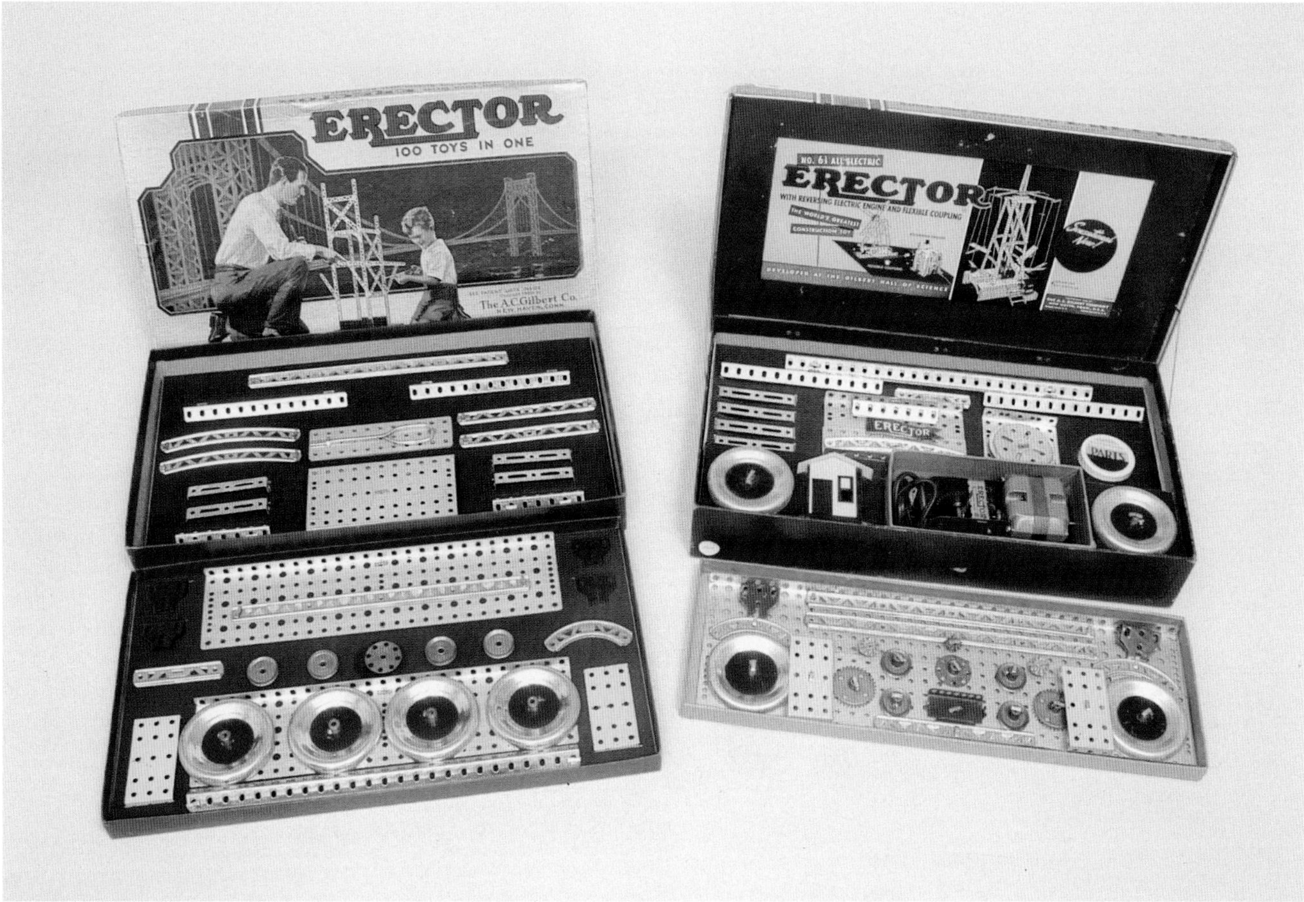

Left: Set No. 3½ was returned to the line in 1955, after a twelve-year absence. Courtesy Dr. Gene Baker. Right: Set No. 6½, although cataloged in a metal box, was packed in cardboard.

A new style of cardboard was used for the parts display inserts beginning in 1955. It was a lighter, brighter shade of blue. Although textured, it was not nearly as mottled as the dark blue cardboard it replaced. All Erector Sets had this new cardboard by 1956.

Only three parts modifications occurred in 1955. First, the (MH) Disc Wheel went from a hub 5/16" in diameter to one that was 3/8". While the difference is small, it is quite noticeable. At the same time, the shade of paint used on the hubcap of this wheel was changed from dark red to bright red.

The second modification involved all the sintered wheels, pulleys, and gears. Since Gilbert had adopted the sintering process in 1953, there had been an ongoing problem. The walls of the hub were too thin and tended to break. To correct this, the company developed new molds, and these parts came with thicker, more durable hubs.

The third change that occurred this year affected the (A49) Electric Engine. From its creation in 1938 through the latter part of 1954, this engine came with a decal on the motor core: "Erector Electric Engine." But these decals had always proved troublesome, as they flaked and peeled off. What remained was less than attractive. So starting in 1954, Gilbert abandoned the idea of a core decal. Most (A49)s from 1954 were made with no core decal or label of any kind.

But Gilbert liked to put the Erector name on the motor, so starting in 1955 he created a paper label that was glued to the gearbox guard. This label had black lettering on a yellow background: "Erector Electric Engine." It was used until 1958, when the same words were embossed into the gearbox guard.

Cardboard Box Sets

Set Nos. 1½ and No. 2½ were available once again. Except for the new parts display insert cardboard, they were identical to those from 1954.

Set No. 3½ was restored to the lineup after a twelve-year absence. Like the prewar version, this set was the smallest set to contain the angle girders and larger base plates, and it featured models built with them. The new No. 3½ was similar in contents to its ancestor, but the "Models built with Set No. 3½" section in the instruction manual was considerably shorter, and many of the prewar models built with this set were not illustrated.

Set No. 6½ was similar to the one from 1954, but the color of paper used to cover the body of the box was changed from pale red to bright red. (The 1955 catalog pictures this set in a metal box, but it would not come that way until 1956.)

Metal Box Sets

Perhaps the best evidence of the ample steel supply that existed in 1955 is the expansion of the number of different sets packed in metal boxes. In 1954, only three sets were

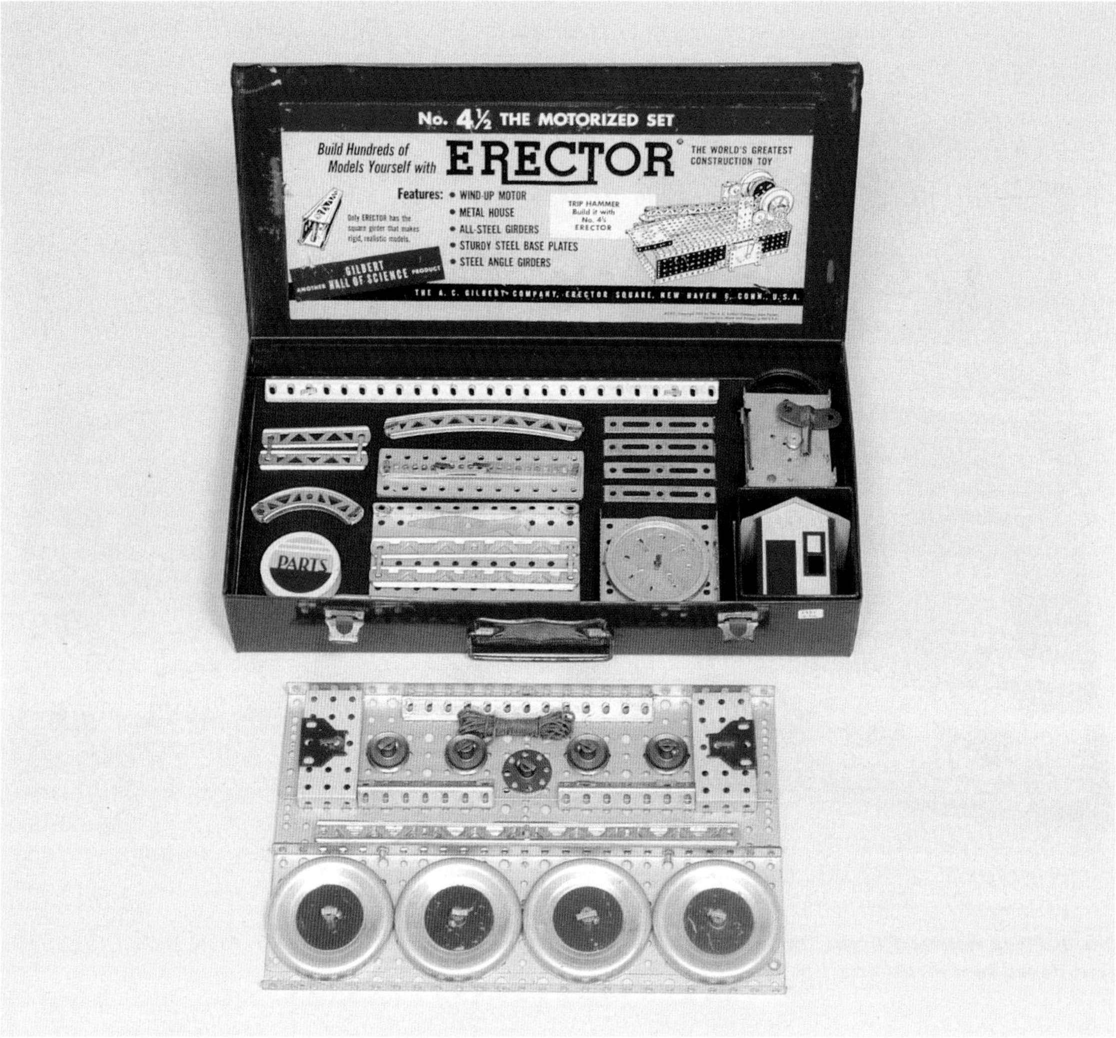

Set No. 4½ from 1955 was upgraded to a metal box that had a new inner lid label. Courtesy Dr. Gene Baker.

offered that way. But starting now, one former cardboard box set was upgraded to a steel container, bringing the metal box set roster to four.

Set No. 4½ was the smallest set packed in a metal box (16" x 8" x 3"). The last time Gilbert had used a box of that size was for No. 6½ in 1949–50. A new inner lid label was created for this new metal box set. Printed in two colors (plus black and white), it had a yellow background and pictured the Trip Hammer. The text on this label listed set features, including the Wind-Up (Mechanical) Motor (A48). There were no changes in contents for this set, compared to last year's cardboard box version, but the price was increased from $7.95 to $9.95.

Set No. 7½ was the smallest set to be upgraded with the red bulb to create a glow in the boiler, and since this set had not contained the lighting system parts since 1940, an (NH) lamp socket unit and (NJ) battery holder came in it. The red bulb and lamp socket were mounted on the same cardboard display unit that held the (U) Boiler Top. Also, a yellow background strip label was added to the inside of the lid; it read, "No. 7½ Engineer's Set."

The red bulb was also added to Set Nos. 8½ and 10½. In No. 8½, it was displayed on the boiler insert, and one of the clear bulbs was packed in a parts can. In No. 10½, the red bulb was added to the Electro Magnet insert. Other than the changes already noted, these sets were identical to those from 1954.

Erector System Modifications for 1955

I. New Parts
( ) Bulb 1.2 Volt (Red), later to be designated (P12N677)

II. Modified Parts
(MH) Disc Wheel, with ⅜"-diameter hub and bright red-painted hubcap
(A49) Electric Engine, with paper label on gearbox guard

THE 1956 ERECTOR LINE

To many collectors, 1956 marks the pinnacle of the Renaissance Period. Set No. 6½ was packed in a metal box this year, thus resolving the anomaly that had occurred in the Erector lineup in 1955 year. But the big news for

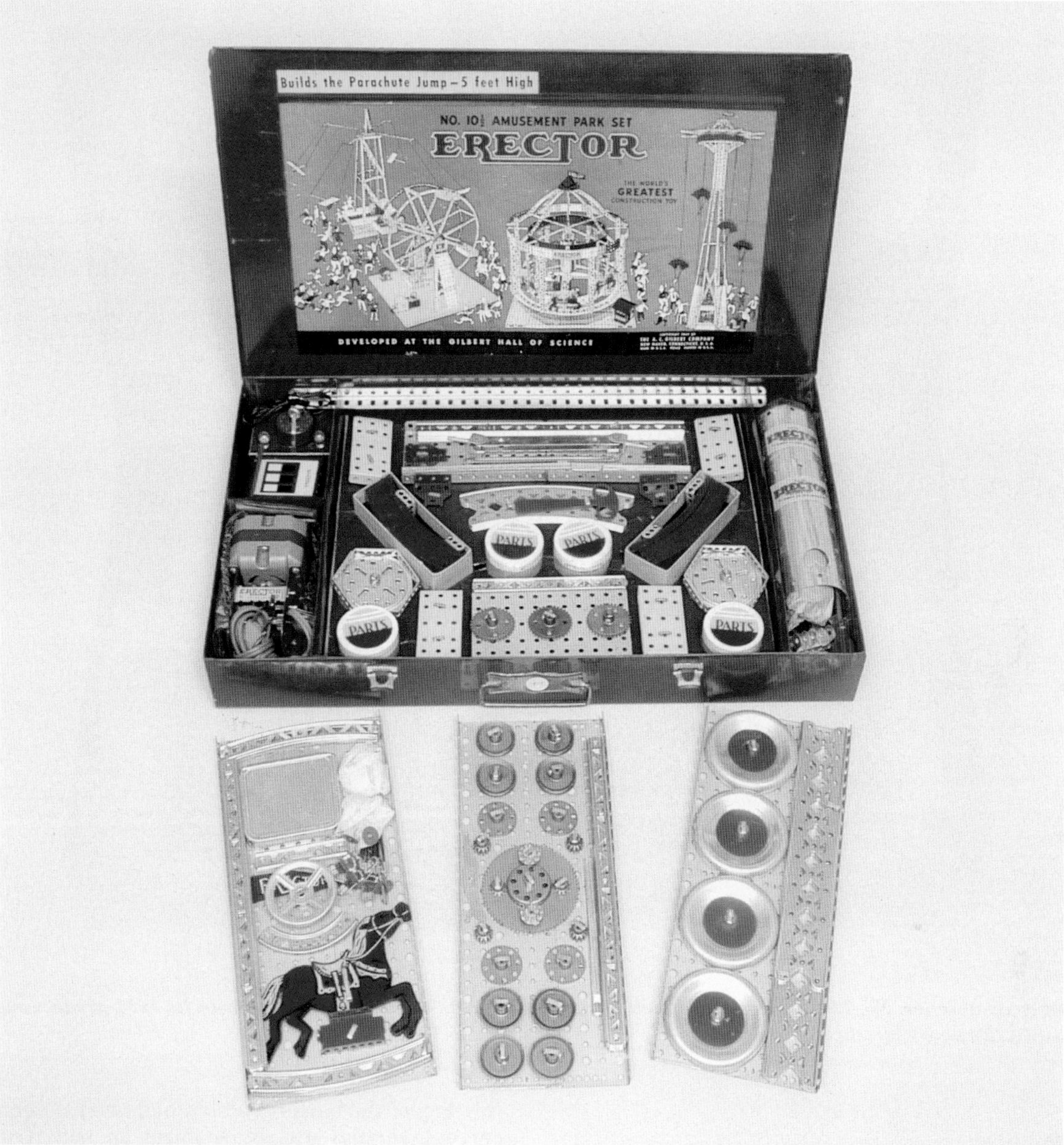

By the mid-1950s, the Erector Sets were highly refined. A good example is No. 10½ from 1955, which is like the one the author received for Christmas when he was eight years old. The Amusement Park Set represents the Renaissance Period at its peak.

1956 was the reintroduction of the top-of-the-line No. 12½.

The new No. 12½ was quite different from the last version of this set, which had been dropped in 1951. While both versions were packed in a 24" x 14" x 4" red metal box, there were major differences in contents, internal box construction, and appearance.

The body of the box for the 1949–50 version of this set had six parts storage compartments across the front, formed from welded steel plates. The remainder of the body was wide open, and a large cardboard parts display insert was used in this space. Above the insert was a parts display tray constructed from six (MN) Base Plates. A removable red steel "bridge" fit over the lower-level cardboard parts display to support the (MN) Base Plate display tray.

The body of the box for the No. 12½ from 1956 was different. Now there were seven parts storage compartments across the front, and a second row of five compartments was added in the center of the box. This left a long, narrow compartment across the back. Most of the middle compartments and the back one were fitted with inserts made from brown corrugated cardboard. These inserts were not typical display inserts, but served more as fillers, so that the parts, which were packed loose in these compartments, would fill them to the top. While parts were not attached to these corrugated inserts, they were sorted, and identical parts were bound together with small rubber bands. This use of rubber bands was unique to this later version of this set.

The 1956 version of No. 12½ differed from the one available from 1949–50 in that it did not use a parts display tray made from (MN) Base Plates. However, like the earlier version, it did come with a removable upper layer parts display tray. While the cardboard insert on

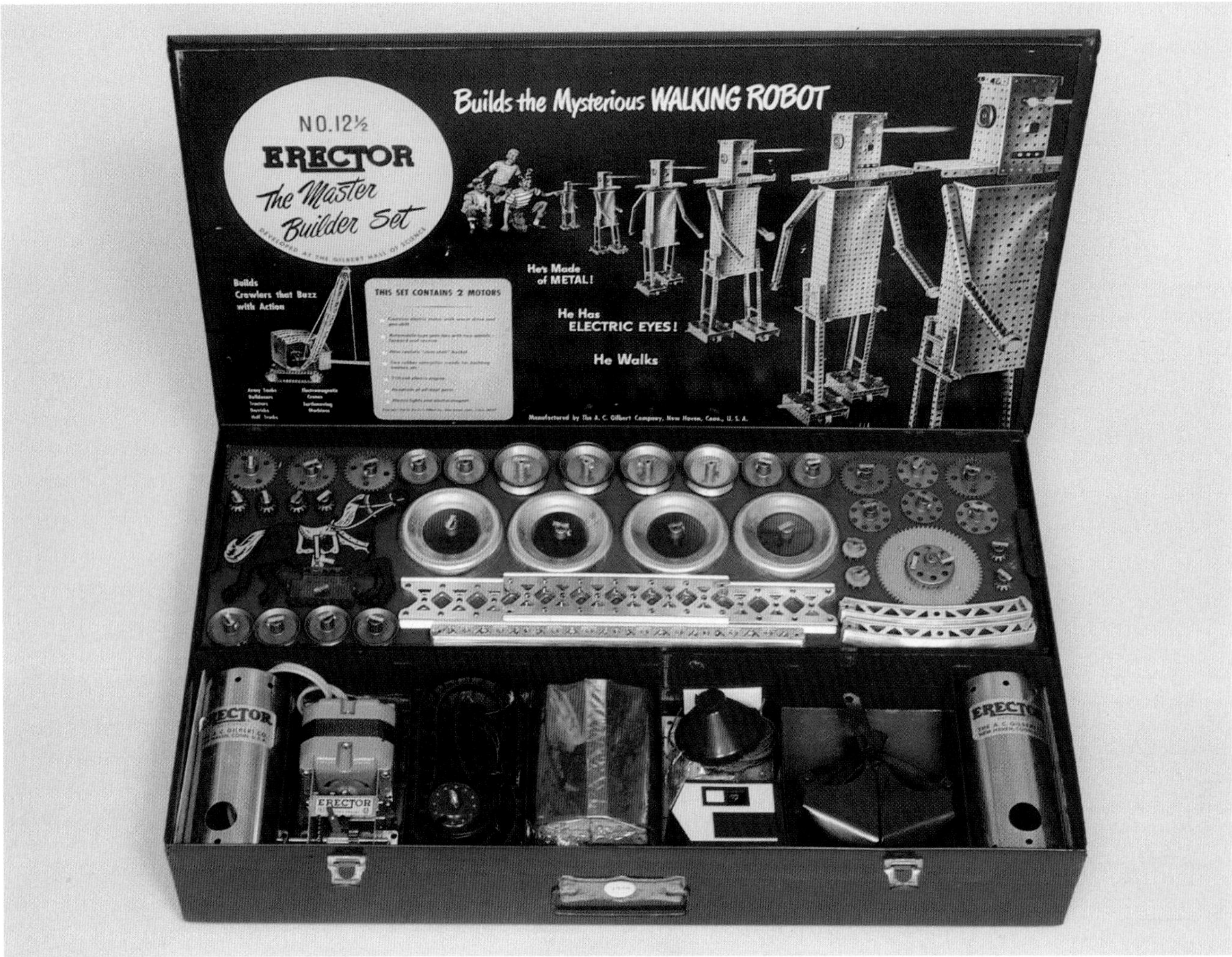

After a four-year absence, No. 12½ was reintroduced into the line in 1956. Vastly different from its 1951 predecessor, the set now contained the new Clamshell Bucket.

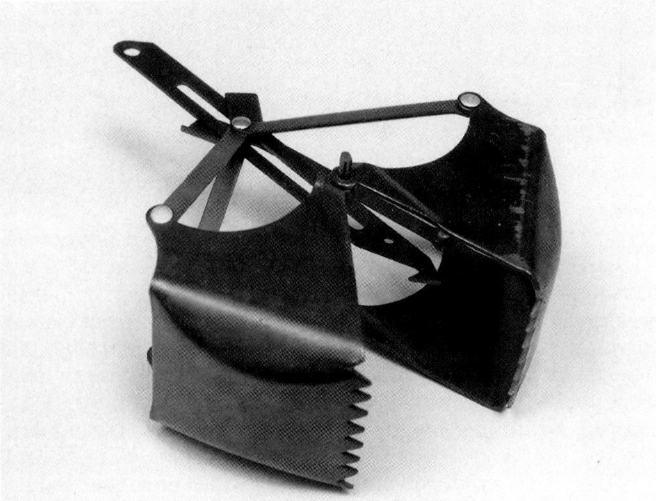

The Clamshell Bucket was included in only the top-of-the-line sets between 1956 and 1962. The most sophisticated part added to the Erector System during the Renaissance Period, it was not manufactured by Gilbert.

the tray of the earlier version had been silver, the insert of current version was blue. Parts on both trays were arranged the same.

Like its predecessor, No. 12½ from 1956 came with a large inner lid label made of heavy cardboard. It looked like the old version and pictured the Mysterious Walking Robot, the same featured model. But there were significant differences in these labels. First, the set name was changed from The Remote Control Set to The Master Builder Set. The latter name influenced the featured model. In 1949–50, it was called the Mysterious Walking Giant. Now it was the Mysterious Walking Robot. (Good! It was clearly a robot from the beginning.) The text on the inner lid label was changed to accurately describe other set features.

While many subtle changes in the contents of the 1949–50 and the 1956 versions of No. 12½ can be gleaned from studying the contents lists, two major modifications deserve comment. First, the (P55) Remote Control Motor and all the supporting paraphernalia, including the (No. 1) Transformer and (OD) Control Box, were not included in the later version. In fact, the Robot, which had been built with these parts in the past, was redesigned to be powered with the (A49) Electric Engine. (This constitutes the third and final version of this excellent model.)

Boiler decals were changed repeatedly during the Renaissance Period. Left: The version from 1950–55. Right: The version from 1956–60.

Second, a wonderful new part, the Clamshell Bucket, was added to the line in 1956, and it came only in No. 12½. The last clamshell included in an Erector Set was the coveted (BM) Clamshell Scoop, packed in only the largest No. 10 sets from the Classic Period. The 1956 version of the Clamshell Bucket was smaller and less sophisticated, but it was better proportioned to Erector models, and went well with the (NW) Treads in building models of construction equipment.

Interestingly, the Clamshell Bucket was not made by Gilbert. This part was produced by Doepke Manufacturing Company, of Rossmoyne, Ohio, a toy firm that used it on an item known as the Mobile Unit Crane. It stands to reason that Gilbert imported this Erector part. The top-of-the-line No. 12½ was expensive and not a big seller. To tool up to make a limited quantity of clamshells, used only in this set, would have cost more than buying them from an outside source.

The clamshell was never pictured in the separate parts section of the instruction manual or listed with the other Erector parts. It was not given a part designation until 1958, when it was denoted on the Separate Parts Order Form as (X14B663) Bucket.

A number of the parts from the 1949–50 version of No. 12½ were reintroduced in 1956. These included the (NL) Bolster Bracket; (NW) Tread, formerly known as the Belt and Clip Unit; (NX) Tread Pulley; and (OB) Tread Pin.

Other parts were modified, such as the label on the (T) Boiler. The size and shape of the label were not changed, but where the one from 1955 read "New Erector," the one from 1956 read "Erector."

Also slightly altered was the (AJ) Paper Erector Flag. Until now, it came ready to use—cut to the proper shape and with a staple in just the right spot so that an axle fit snugly into it to serve as a flagpole. But beginning in 1956, the flag

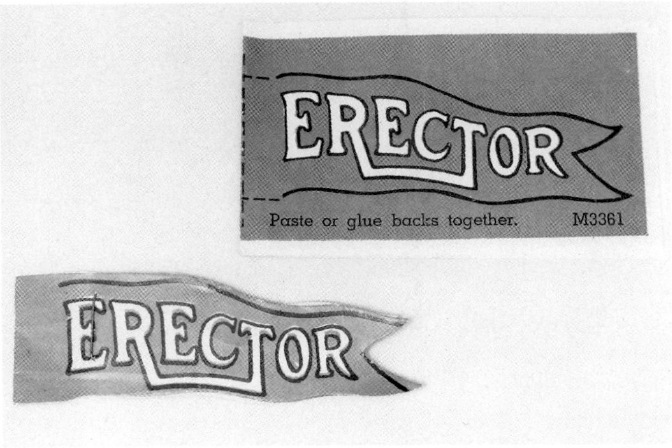

The Erector Flag has been part of the system since the Classic Period, and it always came cut and stapled. But beginning in 1956 a new version appeared that was neither cut nor stapled.

was in the center of a rectangular piece of paper. The set owner had the privilege of cutting out the flag and adding the staple.

Another noteworthy change occurred with the (NZ) Plastic Handle Screw Driver. In the past the plastic handle had been short and squat and made of bright red plastic. Now a new style of screwdriver was used. The handle was longer and narrower and made of translucent yellow plastic. The word "Erector" was molded into the handle with raised letters.

The (NU) Parachute also changed in 1956. Since 1949 the silk fabric used on it had been white. Starting now and lasting until the end of traditional Erector production in 1962, the fabric was bright red.

The designations of the axles was altered, too. The 10" axle, designated (DA) in the past, became (P57K). The old (NY) 3⅛" Axle was designated (P57N), 3¼" Axle. It's actually ⅛" longer, but it was used in all the same places as the (NY). These changes were likely done for convenience so the

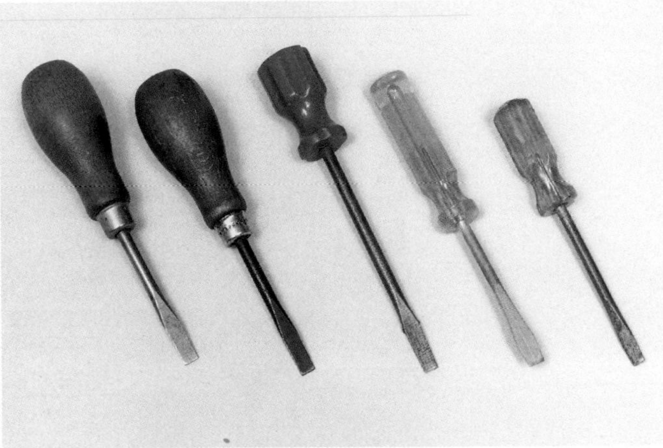

While screwdrivers with wire handles were included in small sets, large sets came with a more substantial tool. Gilbert used a variety of different screwdrivers after the war: (left to right) brown wood handle, 1948; red wood handle, 1949–50; red plastic handle, 1950–55; long yellow plastic handle, 1956–59; and short yellow handle, 1960–62.

Gilbert was constantly refining and redesigning the (A49) Electric Engine: (left to right) scarce early 1954 version, middle and late 1954, 1955, and 1956.

axles could be listed with the others for inventory purposes.

Yet another modification occurred with the (A49) Electric Engine in 1956. The color of the motor housing went from blue-gray to robin's egg blue, and the side plates for the gearbox that had been painted red were cadmium-plated.

Finally, a new look for the parts can bodies appeared. In the past, they had been covered with a pale red paper. Now the color of the paper was changed to bright red in some sets. Not all sets came with the new parts can color, but colors were never mixed in a set. These two variations continued throughout the year.

Cardboard Box Sets

Set Nos. 1½, 2½ and 3½ ran unchanged from 1955. Th cardboard box version of No. 6½ was dropped because thi set now came in a metal box.

Metal Box Sets

Set No. 4½ was continued as the smallest metal box se unchanged from 1955. Meanwhile, No. 6½ was now packe in a brand-new type of metal box. It measured 16" x 10" x 3 and had welded steel brackets on the inside to support th parts trays constructed from (MN) Base Plates.

An interesting variation exists with this set box. The cat alog illustration pictures, and the vast majority of set boxe were produced, with the motor packed on the right side. Bu occasionally a box shows up with the bracket placemen reversed, and the motor packed on the left side. These sets of course, are packed as a mirror image of the typical ones.

Set No. 6½ was a two-layer set, with a lower-level card board parts display insert and two parts display trays con structed from (MN) Base Plates for the upper layer. Th inside lid label was the same one used on the version fron 1955 packed in a cardboard box. It pictured the Airplan Ride and promoted the (OE) 6" Flexible Coupling. With th exception of the modifications already described, the con tents of this set were unchanged from the previous year.

With the exception of changes already noted, Nos. 7½ 8½, and 10½ were identical to the versions offered in 1955

Set No. 12½, called "The Master Builder Set," wa returned to the lineup in 1956. Packed in the mammot 24" x 14" x 4" box through 1959, it remained the top-of-the line set until the demise of traditional Erector in 1962.

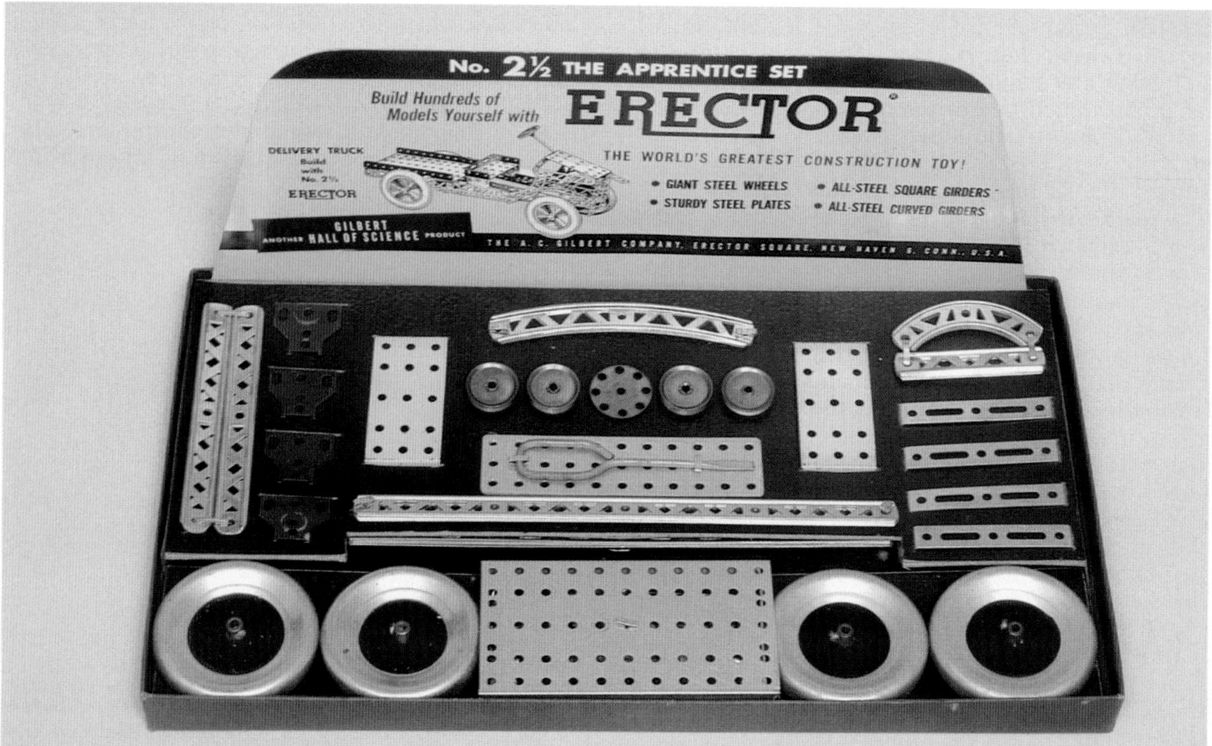

Set No. 2½ from 1956 included a pop-up store display insert to help vendors improve sales.

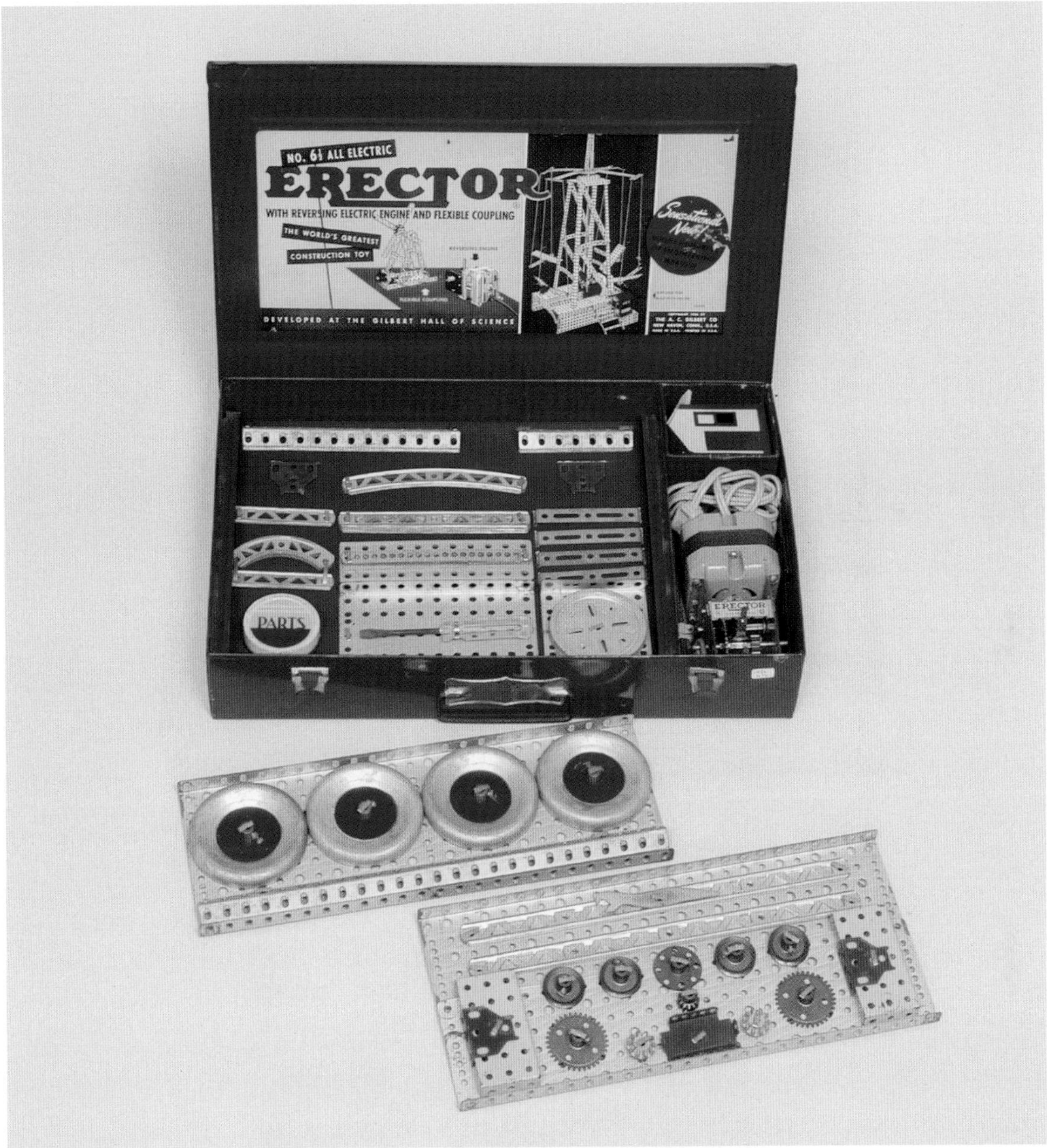

A new box was added to the line in 1956 for No. 6½. Courtesy of Dr. Gene Baker.

Erector System Modifications for 1956

I. New Parts
( ) Clamshell Bucket, no part designation until 1958, then designated (X14B663) Bucket

II. Reintroduced Parts
(NL) Bolster Bracket, cadmium-plated
(NW) Tread
(NX) Tread Pulley
(OB) Tread Pin

III. Modified Parts
(P57K) 10" Axle Rod, substituted for (DA) 10" Axle Rod
(P57N) 3¼" Axle Rod, substituted for (NY) 3⅛" Axle Rod
(T) Boiler, with new label
(AJ) Paper Erector Flag, uncut, no staple
(NU) Parachute, with red silk
(NZ) Plastic Handle Screw Driver, with yellow handle
(A49) Electric Engine, with robin's egg blue motor housing and cadmium-plated gearbox side plates
( ) Parts Cans, with pale red or bright red bodies

Listings of 1955 and 1956 Erector Sets

	Gd	VG	Exc	Inv	Org

NO. 1½ The Builder's Set
Came in a cardboard box 13½" x 9½" x ¾"; sold for $2.00 in 1955 and $2.50 in 1956.

	Gd	VG	Exc	Inv	Org
	30	40	70	+15	+20

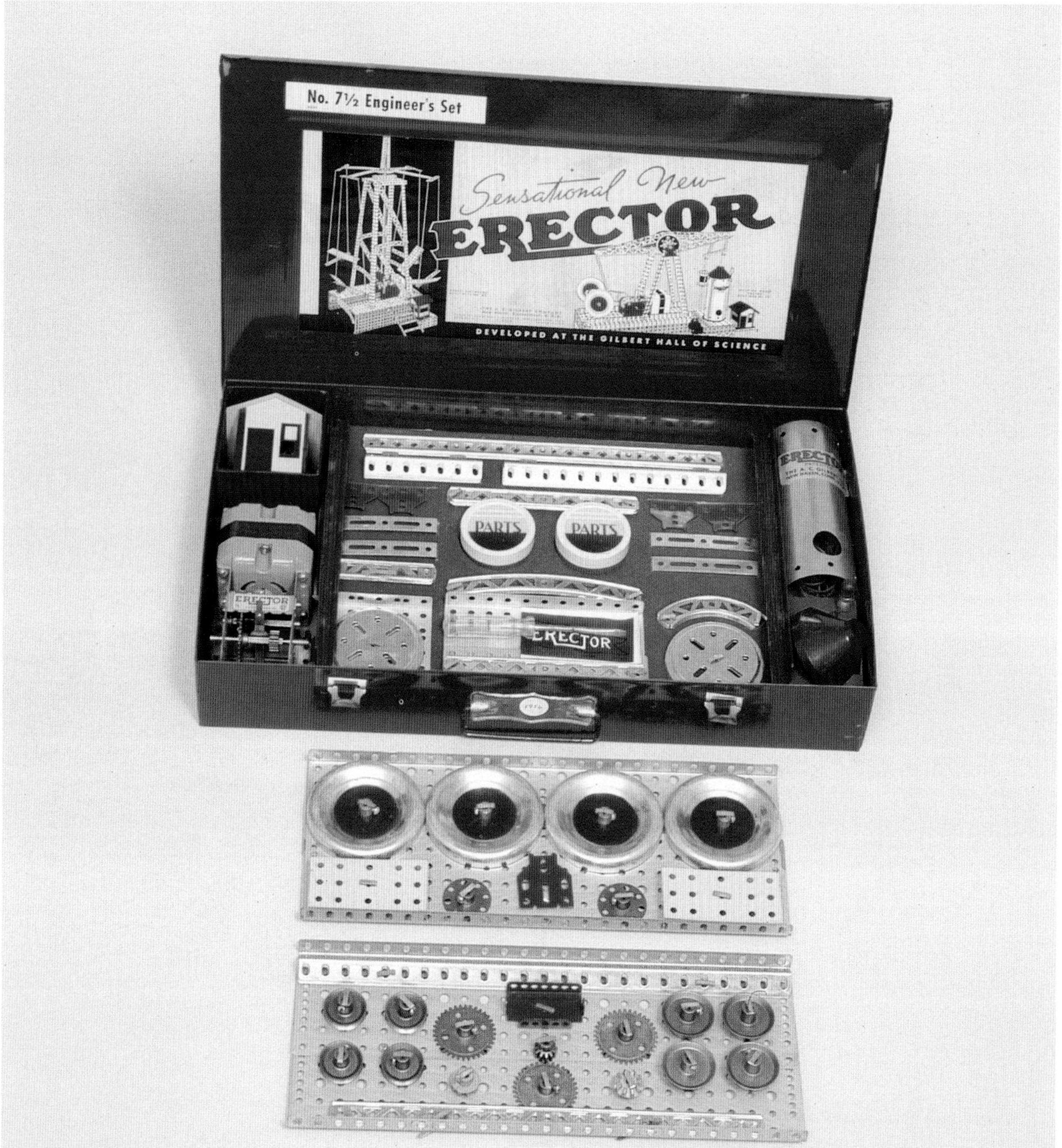

Set. No. 7½ from 1956 was a popular set due largely to its midrange price. The yellow strap label on the lid was unique to that year.

NO. 2½ — The Apprentice Set

Featured the (MH) Disc Wheels. Came in a cardboard box 18" x 10" x 1⅛"; sold for $3.50 in 1955 and $4.50 in 1956.

Gd	VG	Exc	Inv	Org
35	50	80	+20	+25

NO. 3½ — The Professional Set

Featured the angle girders and large base plates. Came in a cardboard box 18" x 10" x 2"; two-layer set with removable cardboard parts display tray; sold for $5.00 in 1955 and $5.95 in 1956.

Gd	VG	Exc	Inv	Org
40	55	90	+20	+25

NO. 4½ — The Motorized Set

Featured the (A48) Mechanical Motor and (MX) House and built truck with (A48). Came in a red metal box 16" x 8" x 3"; two-layer set with two removable parts display trays constructed from (MN) Base Plates; sold for $9.95 in 1955 and $10.95 in 1956.

Gd	VG	Exc	Inv	Org
40	60	100	+20	+25

NO. 6½ (1955) — The Electric Engine Set

Featured the (A49) Electric Engine and built Airplane Ride. Came in a cardboard box 18" x 10" x 3" with a hinged

Gd	VG	Exc	Inv	Org

lid; two-layer set with removable cardboard parts display tray; sold for $14.95.

50	60	100	+20	+25

NO. 6½ (1956) The Electric Engine Set

Featured the (A49) Electric Engine and built Airplane Ride. Came in a red metal box 16" x 10" x 3"; two-layer set with two removable parts display trays constructed from (MN) Base Plates; sold for $16.95.

50	60	100	+20	+25

NO. 7½ The Engineer's Set

Featured the (T) Boiler and Boiler Glow system and built Walking Beam Engine. Came in a red metal box 18" x 10" x 3"; two-layer set with two removable parts display trays constructed from (MN) Base Plates; sold for $17.95 in 1955 and $21.50 in 1956.

50	70	120	+25	+30

NO. 8½ The All-Electric Set

Featured the (MJ) Electro Magnet and lighting system parts and built Ferris Wheel and Bascule Bridge. Came in a red metal box 20" x 12" x 3"; two-layer set with three removable parts display trays constructed from (MN) Base Plates; sold for $24.50 in 1955 and $27.50 in 1956.

75	110	180	+40	+50

NO. 10½ The Amusement Park Set

Featured the truck parts, giant flywheel, parachutes, and carousel horses and built Parachute Jump, Merry-Go-Round, and other amusement park models as well as Giant Power Plant. Came in a red metal box 22" x 13" x 3"; two-layer set with three removable parts display trays constructed from (MN) Base Plates; sold for $39.95 in 1955 and $44.95 in 1956.

160	240	400	+80	+100

NO. 12½ (1956) The Master Builder Set

Featured the Clamshell Bucket and Treads and built the Mysterious Walking Robot and construction equipment. Came in a red metal box 24" x 14" x 3"; two-layer set with removable parts display tray with blue cardboard insert; sold for $65.00.

400	600	1000	+200	+250

1955–56 CONTENTS LIST

Set No.		1½	2½[1]	3½[2]	4½	6½	7½	8½	10½	12½[3]
P7	7/8" PULLEY	4	4	4	4	4	4	0	0	0
P7A	1 1/8" PULLEY	0	0	0	0	0	0	4	4	4
P12	CROWN GEAR	0	0	0	0	0	0	0	1	1
P13	12 PINION GEAR, 1/8"	0	0	0	0	1	1	2	2	2
P13B	12 TOOTH PINION GEAR, 7/23"	0	0	0	0	0	0	1	4	4
P15	COUPLING	0	0	0	1	2	2	2	2	2
P20	5 HOLE STRIP—FORMED	0	0	0	0	0	2	2	8	8
P24	CRANK	1	1	1	1	1	1	1	1	1
P33	SMALL SCREW DRIVER	1	1	1	1	1	0	0	0	0
P34	HANK OF STRING	0	1	1	1	1	1	1	3	3
P37	COLLAR	1	4	4	5	6	7	9	20	20
P48	MITRE GEAR	0	0	0	0	2	2	2	2	2
P57A	2 1/8" AXLE	1	1	1	1	1	1	1	1	8
P57D	6" AXLE	0	1	2	0	0	0	0	0	1
P57E	8" AXLE	0	0	0	0	0	0	0	2	2
P57F	12" AXLE	0	0	0	0	0	0	1	2	2
P57JA	7½" AXLE	0	0	0	0	0	0	0	4	4
P57K	10" AXLE	0	0	0	0	0	0	0	0	2
P57N	3¼" AXLE	0	0	0	0	0	0	0	2	2
P79	CAR TRUCK	4	4	4	4	4	4	4	4	4
A	2½" GIRDER	4	4	4	4	4	4	4	4	6
B	5" GIRDER	4	4	4	8	8	8	12	12	12
C	10" GIRDER	2	8	8	8	8	8	36	52	52
D	2½" CURVED GIRDER	4	4	4	4	4	4	4	4	4
E	5" CURVED GIRDER	0	2	2	2	4	4	26	26	26
F	5 HOLE STRIP	0	0	0	2	2	2	2	2	16
G	7 HOLE STRIP	0	0	0	2	2	2	2	6	8
H	11 HOLE STRIP	0	0	0	4	4	4	4	16	16
I	21 HOLE STRIP	0	0	0	2	2	2	4	18	18
J	41 HOLE STRIP	0	0	0	0	0	0	2	2	4
M	SMALL DOUBLE ANGLE	0	0	0	0	0	2	6	24	24
N	LONG DOUBLE ANGLE	2	4	4	4	4	4	4	16	16
O	PAWL	0	0	0	0	1	2	2	16	16
T	BOILER	0	0	0	0	0	1	1	2	2
U	BOILER TOP	0	0	0	0	0	1	1	1	1
W	STACK	0	0	0	0	0	3	3	3	3
Z	FLANGED WHEEL 15/16" DIA.	0	0	0	0	0	4	4	4	4
AA	ECCENTRIC CRANK	0	0	0	0	0	0	0	6	6
AE	SPRING	0	0	0	0	0	0	0	0	2
AF	SMALL HOOK	1	1	1	1	1	1	1	1	1
AJ	PAPER ERECTOR FLAG	0	0	0	1	1	1	1	1	1
AQ	SHEAVE PULLEY	0	0	0	0	0	0	1	4	5
AS	2 7/8" AXLE	0	0	0	2	2	3	3	4	4
AT	4" AXLE	2	2	2	2	2	2	2	2	4
BE	6" ANGLE GIRDER	0	0	4	4	4	4	4	4	12
BH	SOLID COLLAR	0	0	0	0	0	0	0	2	2
BL	SMALL WASHER	6	12	12	12	12	12	12	12	18

1955–56 CONTENTS LIST

Set No.		1½	2½[1]	3½[2]	4½	6½	7½	8½	10½	12½[3]
BN	REGULAR TURRET PLATE	0	0	0	2	2	4	4	4	4
BT	PIERCED DISC	1	1	1	1	2	2	4	4	4
BY	11 HOLE FIBRE STRIP	0	0	0	0	0	0	2	2	2
CA	SIGNAL ARM	0	0	0	0	0	0	0	2	2
CH	RIGHT ANGLE	8	12	12	14	14	14	30	42	42
CJ	36 TOOTH GEAR	0	0	0	0	2	3	3	3	5
CR	SPECIAL TURRET PLATE WITH HUB	0	0	0	0	0	0	0	2	2
CS	WHEEL SEGMENT	0	0	0	0	0	0	0	8	8
CZ	7" AXLE	0	0	0	2	2	2	4	4	4
DB	MOTOR PULLEY	0	0	0	1	1	1	1	1	2
DE	STEERING COLUMN	0	0	0	0	0	0	0	1	1
DK	FLAT SPRING	0	0	0	0	0	0	0	4	4
DO	STEERING WHEEL WITH HUB	0	0	0	0	0	0	0	1	1
DP	12" ANGLE GIRDER	0	0	4	4	4	4	4	4	6
DS	COTTER PIN	0	0	0	0	0	0	0	1	1
EI	STD. GEAR BOX SIDE PLATE	0	0	0	0	2	2	2	2	2
EX	BIG CHANNEL GIRDER 12"	0	0	0	0	0	0	0	8	8
EY	BIG CHANNEL GIRDER 6"	0	0	0	0	0	0	0	4	8
EZ	BIG CHAN. GIRDER CURVED 6"	0	0	0	0	0	0	0	9	9
FA	1¾" x 8-32 SCREW	0	0	0	0	0	0	0	12	12
FD	HINGED LOOP	0	0	0	0	0	0	0	2	2
LX	STEERING COLUMN BRACKET	0	0	0	0	0	0	0	1	1
MA	RADIATOR	0	0	0	0	0	0	0	1	1
MB	18½" ANGLE GIRDER	0	0	0	0	0	0	0	2	2
MC	BASE PLATE 1" x 2½"	2	2	2	2	2	2	8	8	8
MD	BASE PLATE 2½" x 5"	1	1	1	1	1	1	4	4	4
ME	BASE PLATE 1" x 4"	0	0	0	0	0	0	0	4	4
MF	BASE PLATE 1" x 5"	0	2	4	4	4	4	8	21	21
MG	RADIATOR HOOD	0	0	0	0	0	0	0	1	1
MH	LARGE 3" DISC WHEEL	0	4	4	4	4	4	4	4	4
MI	FRONT AXLE UNIT	0	0	0	0	0	0	0	1	1
MJ	ELECTRO MAGNET	0	0	0	0	0	0	1	1	1
MM	WRENCH WITH CORD	0	0	0	1	1	1	1	1	1
MN	12" BASE PLATE	0	0	2	4	4	4	6	6	6
MO	3" ANGLE GIRDER	0	0	4	4	4	4	4	4	8
MV	FLAT CAR TRUCK	0	0	0	0	0	2	4	4	12
MW	NUT HOLDER	0	0	0	1	1	1	1	1	1
MX	HOUSE	0	0	0	1	1	1	1	1	1
MY	2½" x 2½" BASE PLATE	0	0	0	1	1	1	1	1	1
MZ	BEARING BLOCK	0	0	0	0	1	1	1	1	1

1955–56 CONTENTS LIST

Set No.		1½	2½[1]	3½[2]	4½	6½	7½	8½	10½	12½[3]
NH	LAMP SOCKET UNIT	0	0	0	0	0	1	2	2	2
NI[4]	BULB, 1½ VOLT	0	0	0	0	0	0	2	2	2
NJ	BATTERY HOLDER	0	0	0	0	0	1	1	1	4
NK	RATCHET	0	0	0	0	0	0	2	2	2
NL	BOLSTER BRACKET	0	0	0	0	0	0	0	0	4
NS	41 HOLE STRIP FORMED	0	0	0	0	0	0	0	2	2
NU	PARACHUTE	0	0	0	0	0	0	0	4	4
NW	TREAD	0	0	0	0	0	0	0	0	2
NX	TREAD PULLEY	0	0	0	0	0	0	0	0	4
NZ	PLASTIC SCREW DRIVER	0	0	0	0	0	1	1	1	1
OB	TREAD PIN	0	0	0	0	0	0	0	0	2
OE	6" FLEXIBLE COUPLING	0	0	0	0	1	1	1	1	1
OF	HORSE	0	0	0	0	0	0	0	6	6
OG	21 HOLE STRIP FORMED	0	0	0	0	0	0	0	2	2
OH	72 TOOTH GEAR	0	0	0	0	0	0	0	1	1
OI	SEGMENT OF 72 TOOTH GEAR	0	0	0	0	0	0	0	1	1
CLAM	SHELL BUCKET	0	0	0	0	0	0	0	0	1
A48	MECHANICAL MOTOR	0	0	0	1	0	0	0	0	1
K48	KEY FOR MECH. MOTOR	0	0	0	1	0	0	0	0	1
A49	ELECTRIC ENGINE	0	0	0	0	1	1	1	1	1
N21	8-32 SQUARE NUT	23	45	60	88	93	93	169	271	359
S51	¼" x 8-32 SCREW	20	35	50	80	84	84	162	240	260
S52	½" x 8-32 SCREW	0	0	0	0	4	4	4	8	8
S57	1⅜" x 8-32 SCREW	0	0	0	0	0	4	4	4	4
S62	⅞" x 8-32 SCREW	3	6	6	8	8	8	18	64	64

1. Set No. 2½ contained two 5" axles.

2. Set No. 3½ contained one 5" axle.

3. Set No. 12½ was not produced in 1955. This inventory is for the 1956 version; Set No. 12½ also contained an offset wrench.

4. Beginning in 1955, a third bulb (red) was included in Sets No. 8½, 10½, and 12½ (in 1956). A red bulb was also included in Set No. 7½.

ERECTOR SEPARATE PARTS PRICES

KINDLY ENCLOSE CHECK, MONEY ORDER OR STAMPS WITH YOUR ORDER FOR PARTS

THE A. C. GILBERT CO., NEW HAVEN, CONN., U. S. A.

Part No.	Part Name	Price
N21	8-32 Square Nut	.10 doz.
P7	7/8 Pulley	.10 ea.
P7A	1⅛ Pulley Assy.	.10 ea.
P12	Crown Gear	.15 ea.
P13	12-Tooth Pinion Gears 1/8"	.10 ea.
P13B	12-Tooth Pinion Gear 7/32"	.10 ea.
P15	Coupling	.10 ea.
P20	Five Hole Strip—Formed	.10 ea.
P24	Crank	.10 ea.
P33	Small Screw Driver	.10 ea.
P34	Hank of String	.10 ea.
P37	Collar	.25 doz.
P48	Mitre Gear	.20 ea.
P57A	2⅞" Axle	.05 ea.
P57D	6" Axle	.10 ea.
P57E	8" Axle	.10 ea.
P57F	12" Axle	.15 ea.
P79	Car Truck	.05 ea.
S11	Set Screw	.05 doz.
S51	¼" x 8-32 Screw	.10 doz.
S52	½" x 8-32 Screw	.10 doz.
S57	1⅜" x 8-32 Screw	.15 doz.
S62	7/8" x 8-32 Screw	.10 doz.
FA	1¾" x 8-32 Screw	.15 doz.
A	2½" Girder	.20 doz.
B	5" Girder	.35 doz.
C	10" Girder	.75 doz.
D	2½" Curved Girder	.25 doz.
E	5" Curved Girder	.40 doz.
BT	Pierced Disc	.10 ea.
F	5 Hole Strip	.10 doz.
G	7 Hole Strip	.10 doz.
H	11 Hole Strip	.15 doz.
I	21 Hole Strip	.35 doz.
J	41 Hole Strip	.50 doz.
M	Small Double Angle	.25 doz.
N	Long Double Angle	.05 ea.
O	Pawl	.05 ea.
T	Boiler	.40 ea.
U	Boiler Top	.20 ea.
W	Stack	.05 ea.
Z	Flanged Wheel 1 3/16" Dia.	.15 ea.
AA	Eccentric Crank	.10 ea.
AF	Small Hook	.15 doz.
AQ	Sheave Pulley	.05 ea.
AS	2⅞" Axle Rod	.05 ea.
AT	4" Axle Rod	.05 ea.

Part No.	Part Name	Price
BE	6" Angle Girder	.50 doz.
BH	Solid Collar	2 for .10
BL	Small Washer	.05 doz.
BN	Regular Turret Plate	.15 ea.
BY	11 Hole Fibre Strip	.05 ea.
CA	Signal Arm	.10 ea.
CH	Right Angle	.10 doz.
CJ	36-Tooth Gear	.20 ea.
CR	Special Turret Plate with Hub	.20 ea.
CS	Wheel Segment	.15 ea.
CZ	7" Axle Rod	.10 ea.
P57JA	7½" Axle Rod	.05 ea.
P57N	3¼" Axle Rod	.05 ea.
DB	Motor Pulley	.10 ea.
DE	Steering Column	.15 ea.
DK	Flat Spring	.10 ea.
DO	Steering Wheel with Hub	.15 ea.
DP	12" Angle Girder	6 for .50
DS	Cotter Pin	.05 doz.
EI	Standard Gear Box Side Plate	.15 ea.
EX	Big Channel Girder 12"	6 for .65
EY	Big Channel Girder 6"	.10 ea.
EZ	Big Channel Curved Girder 6"	.10 ea.
FD	Hinged Loop	2 for .10
LX	Steering Column Bracket	.10 ea.
MA	Radiator	.25 ea.
MB	18½" Angle Girder	.25 ea.
MC	Base Plate 1" x 2½"	.05 ea.
MD	Base Plate 2½" x 5"	.15 ea.
ME	Base Plate 1" x 4"	.05 ea.
MF	Base Plate 1" x 5"	.05 ea.
MG	Radiator Hood	.20 ea.
MH	Large 3" Disc. Wheel	.25 ea.
MI	Front Axle Unit	.45 ea.
MJ	Electro Magnet with Cord	1.20 ea.
MM	Wrench	.05 ea.
MN	12" Base Plate	.40 ea.
MO	5" Angle Girder	.30 doz.
MV	Flat Car Truck	.05 ea.

Part No.	Part Name	Price
MW	Nut Holder	.10 ea.
MX	House	.35 ea.
MZ	Bearing Block	.10 ea.
NH	Lamp Socket Unit	.20 ea.
NI	Bulb—1½ Volt	.10 ea.
NJ	Battery Holder	.15 ea.
NK	Ratchet	.05 ea.
NS	41—Hole Strip—Formed	.10 ea.
NU	Parachute	.40 ea.
NZ	Plastic Screw Driver	.25 ea.
OE	6" Flexible Coupling	.20 ea.
OH	72 Tooth Gear	.25 ea.
OI	Segment of 72 Tooth Gear	.25 ea.
OF	Horse	.25 ea.
OG	21--Hole Strip—Formed	.10 ea.
A48	Mechanical Motor	1.75 ea.
K48	Key for Mechanical Motor	.20 ea.
A49	A49 Electric Engine Gear Shift A.C. Only	5.95 ea.

Manufactured Under One Or More Of The Following Patents:

UNITED STATES OF AMERICA

14,250 (Reissue)	1,523,764	1,863,320
	1,526,333	1,868,4.6
1,219,452	1,527,973	1,898,009
1,231,728	1,527,974	1,996,722
1,232,463	1,665,714	(D) 48,675
1,259,616	1,724,470	(D) 48,859
1,260,366	1,732,799	(D) 48,860
1,261,019	1,736 310	(D) 51,277
1,270,812	1,758,887	(D) 51,552
1,271,145	1,760,638	(D) 54,078
1,302,652	1,763,300	(D) 54,205
1,307,094	1,763,302	(D) 54,206
1,323,045	1,777,666	(D) 54,207
1,329,706	1,777,667	(D) 54,208
1,424,720	1,789,868	(D) 54,209
1,426,376	1,789,896	(D) 55,376
1,448,113	1,792,976	(D) 56,136
1,457,361	1,804,926	(D) 73,604
1,457,972	1,804,927	(D) 76,792
1,472,164	1,815,708	(D) 85,427
1,476,294	1,820 660	(D) 85,428
1,476,295	1,820,661	(D) 85,429
1,481,704	1,828,045	
1,492,597	1,860,835	

Other Patents Pending

ERECTOR HOW TO MAKE 'EM BOOKS

Same as copy included in Sets

	Price
No. 2½ Erector How To Make 'Em Book	.25 ea.
No. 4½ Erector How To Make 'Em Book	.25 ea.
No. 6½ Erector How To Make 'Em Book	.35 ea.
No. 7½ Erector How To Make 'Em Book	.35 ea.
No. 8½ Erector How To Make 'Em Book	.40 ea.
No. 10½ Erector How To Make 'Em Book	.60 ea.

FOREIGN PATENTS

Austria
95874 Sept. 15, 1923

Belgium
293536 Feb. 15, 1921

Canada
175575 Mar. 6, 1917
182904 Mar. 12, 1918
203106 Aug. 17, 1920
205335 Nov. 2, 1920
284775 Nov. 13, 1928
284776 Nov. 13, 1928
284777 Nov. 13, 1928
287197 Feb. 12, 1929
287198 Feb. 12, 1929
290387 June 11, 1929
309272 Mar. 10, 1931
313281 July 14, 1931

Germany
382595 July 31, 1923
380882 Sept. 13, 1923

Great Britain
157084 April 30, 1915
105742 April 18, 1916
105743 April 18, 1916
140101 Mar. 11, 1919
140369 Mar. 20, 1919
284728 Feb. 4, 1927
285851 Feb. 23, 1927
289855 May 4, 1927
290220 May 10, 1927
291095 May 24, 1927
307464 July 7, 1930

Japan
68488

Czecko-Slovakja
12677 Dec. 15, 1923

Switzerland
98816 Mar. 31, 1921

France
513535 Nov. 3, 1920
513536 Nov. 3, 1920
532888 Mar. 29, 1921

Others Pending

Licensed Under One Or More Of The Following Patents:

UNITED STATES OF AMERICA

1,079,245	1,202,388	1,412,116
1,161,131	1,242,202	1,412,117
1,164,686	1,242,892	1,454,969
1,166,688	1,289,014	1,454,970
1,171,816	1,293,973	1,614,958
1,193,089	1,355,975	1,619,298
1,196,238	1,361,937	1,812,498

Design Patent 49,308

Separate Parts Prices for 1955–56

4

THE POST-RENAISSANCE DECLINE OF ERECTOR: 1957–62

When did the decline of Erector begin? That is a difficult question to answer, for it involved a variety of issues, including a reduction in quality of the toy, a failure to modernize the models in the instruction manual, as well as changing lifestyles of Erector customers.

The onset of the decline could be dated as early as 1950. For beginning here and over the next eight years, not one new model was added to the instruction manual. During this period the Baby Boomers, the largest sales market in history, were buying Gilbert's premier toy. Yet most of the models being shown had been developed in the 1920s. Steam engines and old-fashioned trucks were not part of the Baby Boomers' world. Gilbert missed a golden opportunity to modernize not the toy, but what it would build.

By the same token, a point as late as 1960 could be selected for the beginning of the end. Things clearly were on the decline, with major deletions from the best sets, substantial reductions in quality, and poor set packaging and visual impact. And television was by then an intimate part of nearly every American household. The impact that this new technology had on life was dramatic. Undoubtedly, the time children spent watching television greatly reduced the time spent on other activities, including Erector construction.

For the purpose of this book, I have chosen 1957 to mark the beginning of the decline. In that year cost-cutting measures invaded Erector, such as the decision to use lighter-gauge steel in the girders and certain set boxes. And the bright red boxes with the yellow oval labels that generations of buyers associated with Erector started to give way to lithographed boxes with artwork of dubious effectiveness. Quality began to decline. But choosing this point in Erector history is certainly arbitrary, for sales remained strong and wonderful innovations such as the sound effects system and new, space-age models still lay in the future.

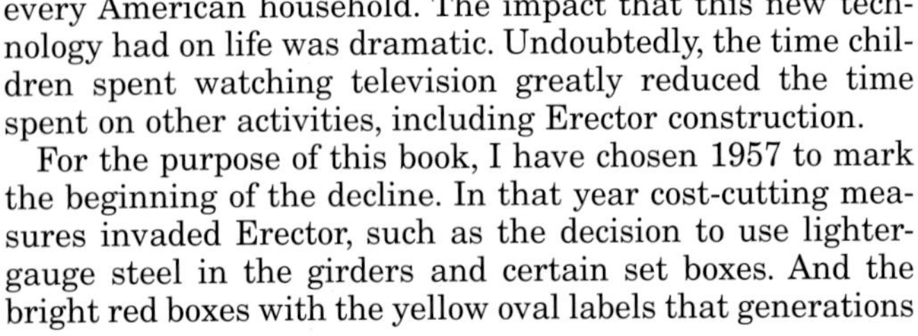

In 1957 Gilbert greatly modified the midrange metal box line with lighter steel and lithography. Left: Set No. 8½ with the early 1957 numbering system. Right: Set No. 10051 with the late 1957 numbering system.

THE 1957 ERECTOR LINE

Major changes occurred in the 1957 lineup. Some changes were made to parts in the Erector System, but the most pronounced development was the appearance of lithography on the midrange metal box sets. Also, cost-cutting measures began creeping into the line, and with them came a reduction in product quality. Finally, a new numbering system was adopted for Gilbert's entire toy line, including Erector.

The introduction of lithography had a huge effect on the visual appearance of Erector. Since metal boxes were first used for Erector Sets back in 1933, each box had been painted in a solid color. An outer lid label was glued to it, and inner lid parts displays gave way to impressive inner lid labels also glued in place.

But in 1957, this changed on all but the top two metal box sets. Now No. 5½ (the smallest metal box set) through No. 8½ came in boxes with lithographed lids. They were done in red and white with black letters, and both the outside and inside of the lid were lithographed. The text included the set's number and name, and additional artwork pictured the featured model from the set.

Concurrent with this major change in appearance was a significant reduction in quality, as the weight of steel used to construct these midrange set boxes was reduced. The old boxes had been solid and ridged. These new ones were light and flimsy.

Another notable modification occurred in 1957, when The A. C. Gilbert Company became computerized and assigned every product a five-digit number. But these new numbers appeared with consistency only in the catalogs. The numbering on the sets themselves was erratic. The cardboard box sets retained their old numbers (Nos. 1½, 2½, and so forth) throughout the year. The midrange metal box sets (Nos. 5½ through 8½) started the year with the old numbers lithographed on the lids, but by the end of the year the five-digit numbers were used. The large metal box sets (Nos. 10½ and 12½) retained their old numbers, along with their heavy-gauge steel containers, throughout the year.

There were also changes in Erector parts. The cost-cutting that led to using lighter-gauge steel on midrange metal boxes spilled over to the whole series of girders (A, B, C, D, and E). Starting now, a new style of girder appeared, made of lighter-gauge steel and plated with tin. Some sets had the new girders, while others had the old style made of heavier steel and plated with cadmium. The two styles were even mixed in some sets, such as new-style 10" Girders (C) and old-style 5" Girders (D). But a particular type of girder was never mixed in a set, such as both old and new 10" (C) girders. Both styles of girders were used through 1959, at which point the heavy-gauge cadmium-plated girders were dropped entirely.

Another change in the system involved the introduction of a new electric motor. The (DC3) was a lightweight 3-volt battery motor, and it replaced the (A48) Mechanical Motor. It came only in Nos. 10041 (No. 5½) and 10091 (No. 12½) as had the old (A48) Mechanical Motor in 1956. The number of No. 4½ from 1956 was changed to No. 5½ in 1957 to denote this change.

The (DC3) was a disappointing substitution. Besides being underpowered, it came in a plastic housing with plastic flanges to attach it to the model. Most of these motors show up today with their "feet" broken off, because when the screw was tightened onto this flange, the plastic tended to crack. The earliest version of the (DC3) had only a clear plastic housing, but by the end of the year, a yellow label with the Erector name and "D.C.-3" was attached to the housing.

Other changes in the system related to the (EI) Gear Box Side Plate, which was cadmium-plated instead of painted black. Also, from this point, only one style of the (N21) Square Nut was used. These nuts were flat with rounded corners.

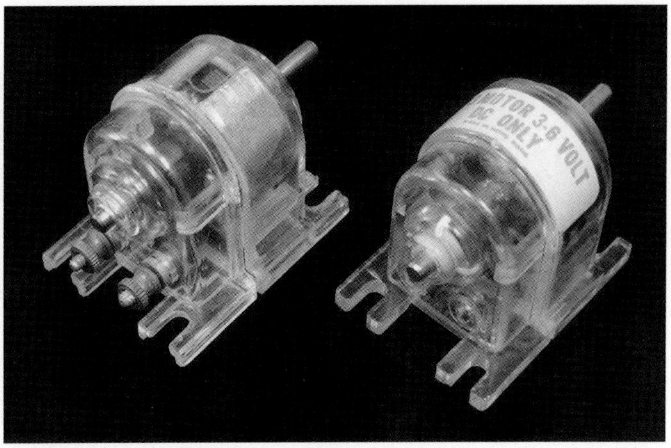

Left: The earliest version of the (DC3) Motor came without a label. Right: The later version is far more common.

Cardboard Box Sets

The number of cardboard box sets in the lineup was expanded from three to five. The smallest was new in 1957 and offered only that year. It was cataloged as No. 16010, but actually designated on the set as No. 100; it came in a 10½" x 9" x ¾" box. Inside the box of this interesting set, parts were mounted to a yellow cardboard insert with clear plastic shrink-wrap. This is the only Erector Set ever packaged in this manner. (According to the catalog, No. 1½ from 1956 was packed with shrink-wrap. But no other Gilbert toys used shrink-wrap prior to 1957, and no examples of this set from 1956 are known to exist.)

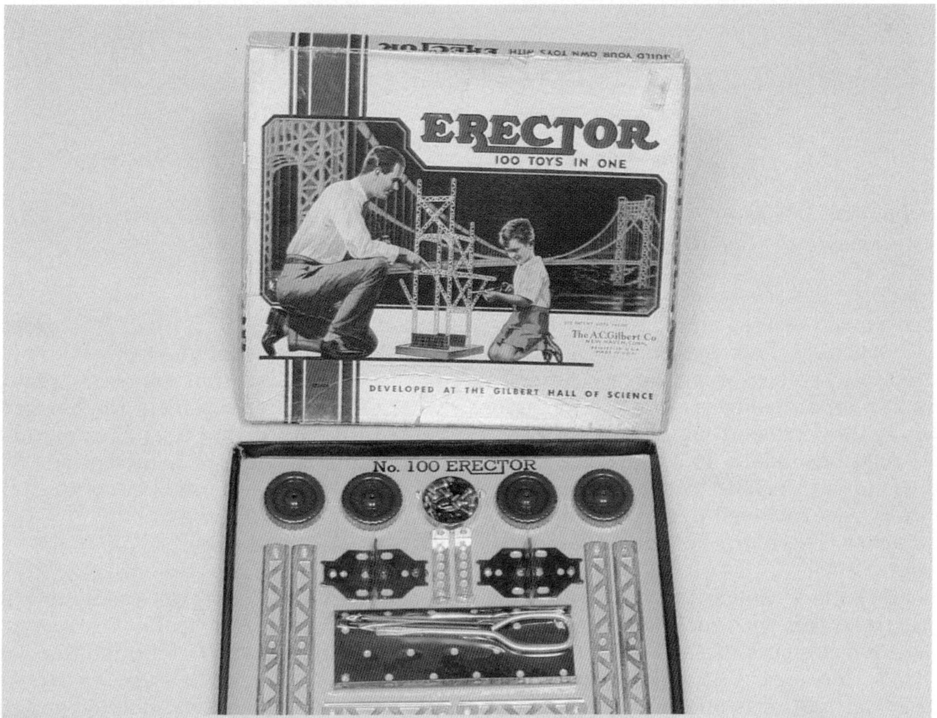

The scarce No. 16010 from 1957, the smallest cataloged set from the Post-Renaissance Period, contained a host of uncataloged parts. Courtesy Dan Yett.

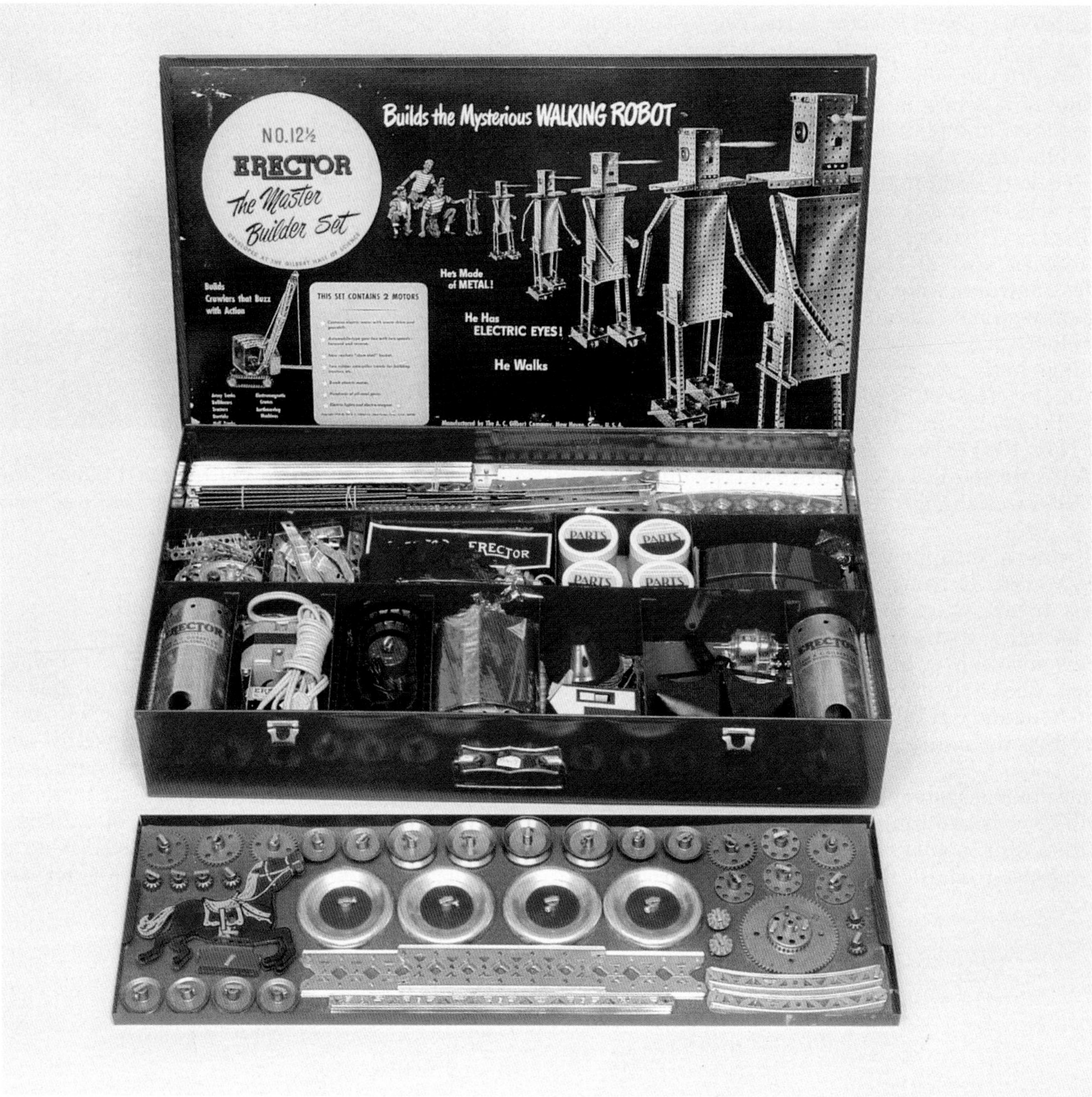

Similar to the 1956 version of The Master Builder Set, No. 12½ (No. 10091) from 1957 came with a (DC3) Motor (mounted with the Clamshell) instead of the old Mechanical Motor.

Also, No. 16010 contained several uncataloged parts found nowhere else. There were four 1½"-diameter blue plastic wheels with "Erector" embossed on them. The set also contained a 5½" x 2" red-painted base plate, a part last used in Nos. 0 and 00 in the 1920s, at which time it was known as (F0) Double Angle Base Plate. Two thin axles also came with No. 16010, along with rubber washers to secure the plastic wheels on them. Also included were two 2" brackets made from Erector strips. These brackets and axles are also uncataloged.

Finally, the few nuts and bolts as well as the washers were packed in a tiny metal parts can with no lid. The shrink-wrap kept them in place for shipping. It seemed as though Gilbert intended to revive the idea of a very inexpensive "stocking stuffer" kind of set with this offering. But apparently these did not sell well, as they were dropped at the end of the year and are difficult to locate.

Set No. 10010, the old No. 1½, was continued in 1957, as were Nos. 10020 (the old No. 2½) and No. 10030 (the old No. 3½). All three sets were produced with the old number on the box through 1957. The fifth cardboard box set was No. 10046, and it is a bit of a curiosity. It was old No. 6½, but in a cardboard box. What makes this set a curiosity is not just that Gilbert offered the old No. 6½ in both a cardboard and a metal box, but that a smaller metal box set, No. 5½, was not available with the same options. The cardboard version of old No. 6½ sold for $2.00 less than the metal box version.

Metal Box Sets

Six metal box sets were available in the 1957 line. The smallest was No. 10041, and it came in the same size box as had No. 4½ in 1956. Actually, the parts and models built with this set were the same as No. 4½ from 1956, except that the (MX) House was deleted and the (DC3) 3 Volt Motor was substituted for the old (A48) Mechanical Motor. For use with the new (DC3) were an (NJ) Battery Holder, some wire, and a second (DB) Motor Pulley.

Set No. 10041, called "The Motorized Set," came in a new lightweight steel box, and the inside and outside of the lid were similarly lithographed. The name and number of this set were listed on the box lid. Early examples were designated "Set No. 5½"; later ones were designated "Set No. 10041." This change occurred midway through the year. Also pictured on the lid was the Airplane Ride, the featured model for this set.

Another curious modification to No. 10041 involved the use of one suitcase catch in place of the two latches used in the past. This was the only set in the line to use this suitcase catch, and it was continued on this size set through 1962.

Set No. 10051 was a continuation of No. 6½ from 1956. It also came in a lightweight lithographed box, with the number and name ("The Electric Engine Set") on the lid. Early examples were designated "Set No. 6½"; later ones were designated "Set No. 10051." Interestingly, the model chosen for the box lid was the Dock Hoist (crane) and not the Airplane Ride, which typically was featured for this set. Because the scaled-down Airplane Ride was used for No. 10041, Gilbert surely did not want to use a similar looking model here.

"The Engineer's Set" was the name used on the box lid for No. 10061, the continuation of No. 7½ from 1956. Like the other midrange metal box sets, this set came in a lightweight lithographed box with "Set No. 7½" on early versions and "Set No. 10061" on later ones. The featured model was the Walking Beam Engine, which was pictured on the lid.

The final set to be modified with lithography and lighter-gauge steel was No. 10071, the continuation of No. 8½ from 1956. Like the other sets in this series, it first came with "Set No. 8½" on the lid and later had "Set No. 10071." Its name, "The All Electric Set," was on the lid, along with a picture of the Ferris Wheel.

The two top sets in the 1957 lineup were spared the lithography and lighter-gauge steel. Except for the modifications to the system already described, No. 10080, as The Amusement Park Set was designated, was identical to the version from 1956. Even the old set number (No. 10½) was used throughout 1957.

Similarly, The Master Builder Set maintained the old numbering system throughout 1957. It always came as No. 12½, even though it was cataloged as No. 10091. And like No. 10041, the new (DC3) motor was substituted for the old (A48) Mechanical Motor, with appropriate changes made in the instruction manual. So it is easy to distinguish this set from its predecessor from 1956.

Erector System Modifications for 1957

I. New Parts

(DC3) 3 Volt Motor, with no housing label (early) or yellow "Erector DC-3" label (late)

II. Eliminated Parts

(A48) Mechanical Motor
(K48) Key for Mechanical Motor

III. Noteworthy Parts Colors and Finishes

(A) 2½" Girder, normal-gauge steel with cadmium-plating or light-gauge steel with tin-plating
(B) 5" Girder, normal-gauge steel with cadmium-plating or light-gauge steel with tin-plating
(C) 10" Girder, normal-gauge steel with cadmium-plating or light-gauge steel with tin-plating
(D) 2½" Curved Girder, normal-gauge steel with cadmium-plating or light-gauge steel with tin-plating
(E) 5" Curved Girder, normal-gauge steel with cadmium-plating or light-gauge steel with tin-plating
(EI) Gear Box Side Plate, cadmium-plated

Listings of 1957 Erector Sets

Gd VG Exc Inv Org

NO. 16010 The Young Builder's Set
Featured many uncataloged parts fastened to yellow insert with shrink-wrap; designated No. 100 on box; came in a cardboard box 10½" x 9" x ¾"; sold for $1.00.
40 60 100 200 (wrap)

NO. 10010 The Builder's Set
Designated No. 1½ on box. Came in a cardboard box 13½" x 9½" x ¾"; sold for $2.50.
30 40 70 +15 +20

NO. 10020 The Apprentice Set
Featured the (MH) Disc Wheels; designated No. 2½ on box. Came in a cardboard box 18" x 10" x 1⅛"; sold for $4.50.
35 50 80 +20 +25

NO. 10030 The Professional Set
Featured the angle girders and large base plates; designated No. 3½ on box. Came in a cardboard box 18" x 10" x 2"; two-layer set with removable cardboard parts display tray; sold for $5.95. **40 55 90 +20 +25**

NO. 10041 The Motorized Set
Featured the (DC3) 3 Volt Motor; designated No. 5½ on box early in year and No. 10041 later. Came in a lithographed metal box 16" x 8" x 3" that pictured scaled-down Airplane Ride. Two-layer set with two removable parts display trays constructed from (MN) Base Plates; sold for $10.95. **40 60 100 +20 +25**

NO. 10046 The Electric Engine Set
Featured the (A49) Electric Engine and built Airplane Ride; designated No. 6½ on box. Came in a cardboard box 18" x 10" x 3"; two-layer set with removable cardboard parts display tray; sold for $15.95.
50 60 100 +20 +25

NO. 10051 The Electric Engine Set
Featured the (A49) Electric Engine and built Airplane Ride; designated No. 6½ on box early in year and No. 10051 later. Came in a lithographed metal box 16" x 10" x 3" that pictured Dock Hoist; two-layer set with two removable parts display trays constructed from (MN) Base Plates; sold for $17.95. **50 60 100 +20 +25**

NO. 10061 The Engineer's Set
Featured the (T) Boiler and built Walking Beam Engine; designated No. 7½ on box early in year and No. 10061 later. Came in a lithographed metal box 18" x 10" x 3" that pictured Walking Beam Engine; two-layer set with two removable parts display trays constructed from (MN) Base Plates; sold for $21.50.
50 70 120 +20 +25

NO. 10071 The All-Electric Set
Featured the (MJ) Electro Magnet and built Ferris Wheel and Bascule Bridge; designated No. 8½ on box early in year and No. 10071 later. Came in a lithographed metal box 20" x 12" x 3" that pictured Ferris Wheel; two-layer set with three removable parts display trays constructed from (MN) Base Plates; sold for $27.95.
75 110 180 +40 +50

1957 CONTENTS LIST

SET NO.		16010[1]	10010	10020[2]	10030[3]	10041	10051[4]	10061	10071	10080	10091[5]
P7	7/8" PULLEY	0	4	4	4	4	4	4	0	0	0
P7A	1 1/8" PULLEY	0	0	0	0	0	0	0	4	4	4
P12	CROWN GEAR	0	0	0	0	0	0	0	0	1	1
P13	12 TOOTH PINION GEAR, 1/8"	0	0	0	0	0	1	1	2	2	2
P13B	12 TOOTH PINION GEAR, 7/23"	0	0	0	0	0	0	0	1	4	4
P15	COUPLING	0	0	0	0	1	2	2	2	2	2
P20	5 HOLE STRIP— FORMED	0	0	0	0	0	0	2	2	8	8
P24	CRANK	0	1	1	1	1	1	1	1	1	1
P33	SMALL SCREW DRIVER	1	1	1	1	1	1	0	0	0	0
P34	HANK OF STRING	0	0	1	1	1	1	1	1	3	3
P37	COLLAR	0	1	4	4	5	6	7	9	20	20
P48	MITRE GEAR	0	0	0	0	0	2	2	2	2	2
P57A	2 1/8" AXLE	0	1	1	1	1	1	1	1	1	8
P57D	6" AXLE	0	0	1	2	0	0	0	0	0	1
P57E	8" AXLE	0	0	0	0	0	0	0	0	2	2
P57F	12" AXLE	0	0	0	0	0	0	0	1	2	2
P57JA	7 1/2" AXLE	0	0	0	0	0	0	0	0	4	4
P57K	10" AXLE	0	0	0	0	0	0	0	0	0	2
P57N	3 1/4" AXLE	0	0	0	0	0	0	0	0	2	2
P79	CAR TRUCK	4	4	4	4	4	4	4	4	4	4
A	2 1/2" GIRDER	4	4	4	4	4	4	4	4	4	6
B	5" GIRDER	4	4	4	4	8	8	8	12	12	12
C	10" GIRDER	0	2	8	8	8	8	8	36	52	52
D	2 1/2" CURVED GIRDER	0	4	4	4	4	4	4	4	4	4
E	5" CURVED GIRDER	0	0	2	2	2	4	4	26	26	26
F	5 HOLE STRIP	0	0	0	0	2	2	2	2	2	16
G	7 HOLE STRIP	0	0	0	0	2	2	2	2	6	8
H	11 HOLE STRIP	0	0	0	0	4	4	4	4	16	16
I	21 HOLE STRIP	0	0	0	0	2	2	2	4	18	18
J	41 HOLE STRIP	0	0	0	0	0	0	0	2	2	4
M	SMALL DOUBLE ANGLE	0	0	0	0	0	0	2	6	24	24
N	LONG DOUBLE ANGLE	0	2	4	4	4	4	4	4	16	16
O	PAWL	0	0	0	0	0	1	2	2	16	16
T	BOILER	0	0	0	0	0	0	1	1	2	2
U	BOILER TOP	0	0	0	0	0	0	1	1	1	1
W	STACK	0	0	0	0	0	0	3	3	3	3
Z	FLANGED WHEEL 15/16" DIA	0	0	0	0	0	0	4	4	4	4
AA	ECCENTRIC CRANK	0	0	0	0	0	0	0	0	6	6
AE	SPRING	0	0	0	0	0	0	0	0	0	2
AF	SMALL HOOK	0	1	1	1	1	1	1	1	1	1
AJ	PAPER ERECTOR FLAG	0	0	0	0	1	1	1	1	1	1
AQ	SHEAVE PULLEY	0	0	0	0	0	0	0	1	4	5
AS	2 7/8" AXLE	2	0	0	0	2	2	3	3	4	4
AT	4" AXLE	0	2	2	2	2	2	2	2	2	4
BE	6" ANGLE GIRDER	0	0	0	4	4	4	4	4	4	12
BH	SOLID COLLAR	0	0	0	0	0	0	0	0	2	2
BL	SMALL WASHER	0	6	12	12	12	12	12	12	12	18

1957 CONTENTS LIST

SET NO.		16010[1]	10010	10020[2]	10030[3]	10041	10051[4]	10061	10071	10080	10091[5]
BN	REGULAR TURRET PLATE	0	0	0	0	2	2	4	4	4	4
BT	PIERCED DISC	0	1	1	1	2	2	2	4	4	4
BY	11 HOLE FIBRE STRIP	0	0	0	0	0	0	0	2	2	2
CA	SIGNAL ARM	0	0	0	0	0	0	0	0	2	2
CH	RIGHT ANGLE	0	8	12	12	14	14	14	30	42	42
CJ	36 TOOTH GEAR	0	0	0	0	0	2	3	3	3	5
CR	SPECIAL TURRET PLATE WITH HUB	0	0	0	0	0	0	0	0	2	2
CS	WHEEL SEGMENT	0	0	0	0	0	0	0	0	8	8
CZ	7" AXLE	0	0	0	0	2	2	2	4	4	4
DB	MOTOR PULLEY	0	0	0	0	2	1	1	1	1	2
DE	STEERING COLUMN	0	0	0	0	0	0	0	0	1	1
DK	FLAT SPRING	0	0	0	0	0	0	0	0	4	4
DO	STEERING WHEEL WITH HUB	0	0	0	0	0	0	0	0	1	1
DP	12" ANGLE GIRDER	0	0	0	4	4	4	4	4	4	6
DS	COTTER PIN	0	0	0	0	0	0	0	0	1	1
EI	STD. GEAR BOX SIDE PLATE	0	0	0	0	0	2	2	2	2	2
EX	BIG CHANNEL GIRDER 12"	0	0	0	0	0	0	0	0	8	8
EY	BIG CHANNEL GIRDER 6"	0	0	0	0	0	0	0	0	4	8
EZ	BIG CHAN. GIRDER CURVED 6"	0	0	0	0	0	0	0	0	9	9
FA	1¾" x 8-32 SCREW	0	0	0	0	0	0	0	0	12	12
FD	HINGED LOOP	0	0	0	0	0	0	0	0	2	2
LX	STEERING COLUMN BRACKET	0	0	0	0	0	0	0	0	1	1
MA	RADIATOR	0	0	0	0	0	0	0	0	1	1
MB	18½" ANGLE GIRDER	0	0	0	0	0	0	0	0	2	2
MC	BASE PLATE 1" x 2½"	0	2	2	2	2	2	2	8	8	8
MD	BASE PLATE 2½" x 5"	0	1	1	1	1	1	1	4	4	4
ME	BASE PLATE 1" x 4"	0	0	0	0	0	0	0	0	4	4
MF	BASE PLATE 1" x 5"	0	0	2	4	4	4	4	8	21	21
MG	RADIATOR HOOD	0	0	0	0	0	0	0	0	1	1
MH	LARGE 3" DISC WHEEL	0	0	4	4	4	4	4	4	4	4
MI	FRONT AXLE UNIT	0	0	0	0	0	0	0	0	1	1
MJ	ELECTRO MAGNET WITH CORD	0	0	0	0	0	0	0	1	1	1
MM	WRENCH	0	0	0	0	1	1	1	1	1	1
MN	12" BASE PLATE	0	0	0	2	2	4	4	6	6	6
MO	3" ANGLE GIRDER	0	0	0	4	4	4	4	4	4	8

1957 CONTENTS LIST

SET NO.		16010[1]	10010	10020[2]	10030[3]	10041	10051[4]	10061	10071	10080	10091[5]
MV	FLAT CAR TRUCK	0	0	0	0	0	0	2	4	4	12
MW	NUT HOLDER	0	0	0	0	1	1	1	1	1	1
MX	HOUSE	0	0	0	0	0	1	1	1	1	1
MY	2½" x 2½" BASE PLATE	0	0	0	0	1	1	1	1	1	1
MZ	BEARING BLOCK	0	0	0	0	0	1	1	1	1	1
NH	LAMP SOCKET UNIT	0	0	0	0	0	0	1	2	2	2
NI	BULB, 1½ VOLT (CLEAR)	0	0	0	0	0	0	0	2	2	2
P12N667	BULB, 1.2 VOLT (RED)	0	0	0	0	0	0	1	1	1	1
NJ	BATTERY HOLDER	0	0	0	0	0	0	1	1	1	4
NK	RATCHET	0	0	0	0	0	0	0	2	2	2
NL	BOLSTER BRACKET	0	0	0	0	0	0	0	0	0	4
NS	41 HOLE STRIP FORMED	0	0	0	0	0	0	0	0	2	2
NU	PARACHUTE	0	0	0	0	0	0	0	0	4	4
NW	TREAD	0	0	0	0	0	0	0	0	0	2
NX	TREAD PULLEY	0	0	0	0	0	0	0	0	0	4
NZ	PLASTIC SCREW DRIVER	0	0	0	0	0	0	1	1	1	1
OB	TREAD PIN	0	0	0	0	0	0	0	0	0	2
OE	6" FLEXIBLE COUPLING	0	0	0	0	0	1	1	1	1	1
OF	HORSE	0	0	0	0	0	0	0	0	6	6
OG	21 HOLE STRIP —FORMED	0	0	0	0	0	0	0	0	2	2
OH	72 TOOTH GEAR	0	0	0	0	0	0	0	0	1	1
OI	SEGMENT OF 72 TOOTH GEAR	0	0	0	0	0	0	0	0	1	1
	CLAM SHELL BUCKET	0	0	0	0	0	0	0	0	0	1
DC3	3 VOLT MOTOR	0	0	0	0	1	0	0	0	0	1
A49	ELECTRIC ENGINE	0	0	0	0	0	1	1	1	1	1
N21	8-32 SQUARE NUT	8	23	45	60	88	93	93	169	271	359
S51	¼" x 8-32 SCREW	8	20	35	50	80	84	84	162	240	260
S52	½" x 8-32 SCREW	0	0	0	0	0	4	4	4	8	8
S57	1⅜" x 8-32 SCREW	0	0	0	0	0	0	4	4	4	4
S62	⅞" x 8-32 SCREW	0	3	6	6	8	8	8	18	64	64

1. Set No. 16010 is unique. Produced only in 1957, it was packaged in shrink-wrap and the cardboard box was designated as Set No. 100. This set also contained uncataloged parts including four blue plastic wheels, four rubber washers, one 5½" x 2" baseplate, two 11 hole strip brackets, and two very thin 3" axles.

2. Set No. 10020 also contained two 5" axles.

3. Set No. 10030 also contained one 5" axle.

4. This is also the inventory for Set No. 10046, which was identical to Set No. 10051, except that it was packed a cardboard (not metal) box.

5. Set No. 10091 also contained an offset wrench.

ERECTOR SEPARATE PARTS PRICES

KINDLY ENCLOSE CHECK, MONEY ORDER or STAMPS with your ORDER for PARTS

THE A. C. GILBERT CO., NEW HAVEN, CONN., U. S. A.

Rev. 10.56

Part No.	Part Name	Price
N21	8-32 Square Nut	.10 doz.
P7	7/8 Pulley	.10 ea.
P7A	1 1/8 Pulley Assy.	.10 ea.
P12	Crown Gear	.15 ea.
P13	12-Tooth Pinion Gears 1/8"	.10 ea.
P13B	12-Tooth Pinion Gear 7/32"	.10 ea.
P15	Coupling	.10 ea.
P20	Five Hole Strip—Formed	.10 ea.
P24	Crank	.10 ea.
P33	Small Screw Driver	.10 ea.
P34	Hank of String	.10 ea.
P37	Collar	.25 doz.
P48	Mitre Gear	.20 ea.
P57A	2 1/8" Axle	.05 ea.
P57D	6" Axle	.10 ea.
P57E	8" Axle	.10 ea.
P57F	12" Axle	.15 ea.
P79	Car Truck	.05 ea.
S11	Set Screw	.05 doz.
S51	1/4" x 8-32 Screw	.10 doz.
S52	1/2" x 8-32 Screw	.10 doz.
S57	1 3/8" x 8-32 Screw	.15 doz.
S62	7/8" x 8-32 Screw	.10 doz.
FA	1 3/4" x 8-32 Screw	.15 doz.
A	2 1/2" Girder	.20 doz.
B	5" Girder	.35 doz.
C	10" Girder	.75 doz.
D	2 1/2" Curved Girder	.25 doz.
E	5" Curved Girder	.40 doz.
BT	Pierced Disc	.10 ea.
F	5 Hole Strip	.10 doz.
G	7 Hole Strip	.10 doz.
H	11 Hole Strip	.15 doz.
I	21 Hole Strip	.35 doz.
J	41 Hole Strip	.50 doz.
M	Small Double Angle	.25 doz.
N	Long Double Angle	.05 ea.
O	Pawl	.05 ea.
T	Boiler	.40 ea.
U	Boiler Top	.20 ea.
W	Stack	.05 ea.
Z	Flanged Wheel 15/16" Dia.	.15 ea.
AA	Eccentric Crank	.10 ea.
AF	Small Hook	.15 doz.
AQ	Sheave Pulley	.05 ea.
AS	2 7/8" Axle Rod	.05 ea.
AT	4" Axle Rod	.05 ea.

Part No.	Part Name	Price
BE	6" Angle Girder	.50 doz.
BH	Solid Collar	2 for .10
BL	Small Washer	.05 doz.
BN	Regular Turret Plate	.15 ea.
BY	11 Hole Fibre Strip	.05 ea.
CA	Signal Arm	.10 ea.
CH	Right Angle	.10 doz.
CJ	36-Tooth Gear	.20 ea.
CR	Special Turret Plate with Hub	.20 ea.
CS	Wheel Segment	.15 ea.
CZ	7" Axle Rod	.10 ea.
P57JA	7 1/2" Axle Rod	.05 ea.
P57N	3 1/4" Axle Rod	.05 ea.
DB	Motor Pulley	.10 ea.
DE	Steering Column	.15 ea.
DK	Flat Spring	.10 ea.
DO	Steering Wheel with Hub	.15 ea.
DP	12" Angle Girder	6 for .50
DS	Cotter Pin	.05 doz.
EI	Standard Gear Box Side Plate	.15 ea.
EX	Big Channel Girder 12"	6 for .65
EY	Big Channel Girder 6"	.10 ea.
EZ	Big Channel Curved Girder 6"	.10 ea.
FD	Hinged Loop	2 for .10
LX	Steering Column Bracket	.10 ea.
MA	Radiator	.25 ea.
MB	18 1/2" Angle Girder	.25 ea.
MC	Base Plate 1" x 2 1/2"	.05 ea.
MD	Base Plate 2 1/2" x 5"	.15 ea.
ME	Base Plate 1" x 4"	.05 ea.
MF	Base Plate 1" x 5"	.05 ea.
MG	Radiator Hood	.20 ea.
MH	Large 3" Disc. Wheel	.25 ea.
MI	Front Axle Unit	.45 ea.
MJ	Electro Magnet with Cord	1.20 ea.
MM	Wrench	.05 ea.
MN	12" Base Plate	.40 ea.
MO	3" Angle Girder	.30 doz.
MV	Flat Car Truck	.05 ea.
MW	Nut Holder	.10 ea.
MX	House	.35 ea.
MY	2 1/2" x 2 1/2" Base Plate	.10 ea.
MZ	Bearing Block	.10 ea.

Part No.	Part Name	Price
NH	Lamp Socket Unit	.20 ea.
NI	Bulb—1 1/2 Volt	.10 ea.
NJ	Battery Holder	.15 ea.
NK	Ratchet	.05 ea.
NS	41—Hole Strip—Formed	.10 ea.
NU	Parachute	.40 ea.
NW	Tread and Clip	1.75 ea.
NX	Tread Pulley	.25 ea.
NZ	Plastic Screw Driver	.25 ea.
OB	Tread Pin	.25 doz.
OE	6" Flexible Coupling	.20 ea.
OH	72 Tooth Gear	.25 ea.
OI	Segment of 72 Tooth Gear	.25 ea.
OF	Horse	.25 ea.
OG	21—Hole Strip—Formed	.10 ea.
DC3	3 volt Motor	2.95 ea.
A49	A49 Electric Engine Gear Shift A.C. Only	7.95 ea.

Manufactured Under One Or More Of The Following Patents:

UNITED STATES OF AMERICA

14,250 (Reissue)	1,523,764	1,863,320
1,219,452	1,526,333	1,868,496
1,231,728	1,527,973	1,898,009
1,232,463	1,527,974	1,996,722
1,259,616	1,665,714	(D) 48,675
1,260,366	1,724,470	(D) 48,859
1,261,019	1,732,799	(D) 48,860
1,270,812	1,736,310	(D) 51,277
1,271,145	1,758,887	(D) 51,552
1,302,652	1,760,638	(D) 54,078
1,307,094	1,763,300	(D) 54,205
1,323,045	1,763,302	(D) 54,206
1,329,706	1,777,666	(D) 54,207
1,424,720	1,777,667	(D) 54,208
1,426,376	1,789,868	(D) 54,209
1,448,113	1,789,896	(D) 55,376
1,457,361	1,792,976	(D) 56,136
1,457,972	1,804,926	(D) 73,604
1,472,164	1,804,927	(D) 76,792
1,476,294	1,815,708	(D) 85,427
1,476,295	1,820,660	(D) 85,428
1,481,704	1,820,661	(D) 85,429
1,492,597	1,828,045	
	1,860,835	

Other Patents Pending

ERECTOR
HOW TO MAKE 'EM BOOKS

Same as copy included in Sets

		Price
No. 2 1/2	Erector How To Make 'Em Book	.25 ea.
No. 5 1/2	Erector How To Make 'Em Book	.25 ea.
No. 6 1/2	Erector How To Make 'Em Book	.35 ea.
No. 7 1/2	Erector How To Make 'Em Book	.35 ea.
No. 8 1/2	Erector How To Make 'Em Book	.40 ea.
No. 10 1/2	Erector How To Make 'Em Book	.60 ea.
No. 12 1/2	Erector How To Make 'Em Book	.75 ea.

FOREIGN PATENTS

Austria
95874 Sept. 15, 1923

Belgium
293536 Feb. 15, 1921

Canada
175575 Mar. 6, 1917
182904 Mar. 12, 1918
203106 Aug. 17, 1920
205335 Nov. 2, 1920
284775 Nov. 13, 1928
284776 Nov. 13, 1928
284777 Nov. 13, 1928
287197 Feb. 12, 1929
287198 Feb. 12, 1929
290387 June 11, 1929
309272 Mar. 10, 1931
313281 July 14, 1931

Czecho-Slovakia
12677 Dec. 15, 1923

France
513535 Nov. 3, 1920
513536 Nov. 3, 1920
532888 Mar. 29, 1921

Germany
382595 July 31, 1923
380882 Sept. 13, 1923

Great Britain
157084 April 30, 1915
105742 April 18, 1916
105743 April 18, 1916
140101 Mar. 11, 1919
140469 Mar. 20, 1919
284728 Feb. 4, 1927
285851 Feb. 23, 1927
289855 May 4, 1927
290220 May 10, 1927
291095 May 24, 1927
307464 July 7, 1930

Japan
68488

Switzerland
98816 Mar. 31, 1921

Others Pending

Licensed Under One or More Of The Following Patents:

UNITED STATES OF AMERICA

1,079,245	1,202,388	1,412,116
1,161,131	1,242,202	1,412,117
1,164,686	1,242,892	1,454,969
1,166,688	1,289,014	1,454,970
1,171,816	1,293,973	1,614,958
1,193,089	1,355,975	1,619,298
1,196,238	1,361,937	1,812,498

Design Patent 49,308

Separate Parts Prices for 1957

	Gd	VG	Exc	Inv	Org

IO. 10081 The Amusement Park Set

Featured the truck parts, giant flywheel, parachutes, and arousel horses and built Parachute Jump, Merry-Go-Round, nd other amusement park models as well as Giant Power lant; designated No. 10½ on box. Came in a red metal box 2" x 13" x 3"; two-layer set with three removable parts dis-lay trays constructed from (MN) Base Plates; sold for 47.50.

	Gd	VG	Exc	Inv	Org
	160	240	400	+80	+100

IO. 10091 The Master Builder Set

Featured the Clamshell Bucket and Treads and built the Iysterious Walking Robot and construction equipment; desig-ated No. 12½ on box. Came in a red metal box 24" x 14" x 3"; vo-layer set with removable parts display tray with blue ardboard insert; sold for $65.00.

	Gd	VG	Exc	Inv	Org
	400	600	1000	+200	+250

'HE 1958 ERECTOR LINE

This year marked the beginning of the last great effort at nnovation and creativity in the line. Great strides were aken to modernize the appearance of Erector and to update ne models. While this effort spilled over into 1959, it would rove insufficient to meet the challenges of a changing mar-etplace. This two-year period represents the final pinnacle r traditional Erector.

The 1958 innovations affected virtually every area of rector production. The instruction manuals were dramati-ally overhauled, with a host of new models based on the pace race and new technologies. These newly designed nanuals were even dressed up with new covers that re-ected the changes. Major parts were created, including the Rocket and the Sound Effects System, and many sets came with new names and numbers. Packaging techniques also changed, with a dramatic impact on the small sets. Not only did a new lid picture appear on the cardboard box sets, but the two smallest sets came packed in a new way.

A look at the 1958 instruction manual shows an impressive number of new Space Age models, with new ones created for almost every set. The cardboard box sets included models of robots, radar scanners, and even a jet bomber. Set No. 10052 (descended from the old No. 6½) included a rocket launcher and beginning this year was aptly renamed "The Rocket Launcher Set." A new robot was created for No. 10062, as was a radar station.

Set No. 10072 (descended from old No. 8½), also came with its own robot, along with a satellite space station. Like almost every other set in the lineup, No. 10082 had a new robot included in this its section of the instruction manual, not to mention a more sophisticated radar scanner. Finally, the instruction manual for No. 10092 was upgraded with an elaborate rocket and launching tower.

A tremendous amount of work went into the preparation of the instruction manual, as nearly forty new models were developed. Models of robots were the primary focus for Erector designers, as seven new models were added to the roster. Erector advertising stated that every set in the lineup built a robot.

New parts were introduced into the Erector System in 1958. In building on the space theme, the (P14A686) Rocket was included in No. 10052 and larger sets. Three variations of this plastic rocket appeared over the next two years, and two of them are specific to 1958. The earliest version had a white body, blue tail fins, and red nose cone. Each piece was cast separately and then assembled into the finished rocket.

By the end of the year, a less costly manufacturing technique was used. Now the entire rocket was cast from a single

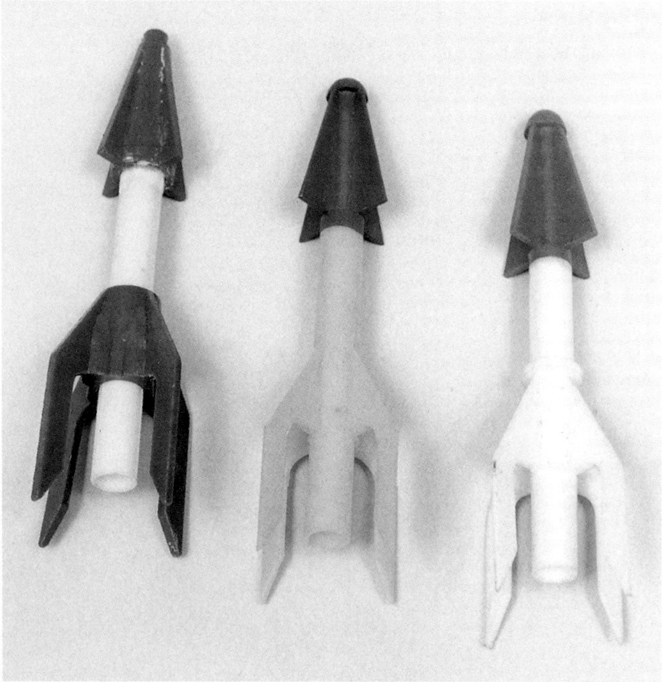

Gilbert used three versions of the Rocket (left to right): red, white, and blue, early 1958; yellow and red, late 1958; and white and red, 1959–62.

The Erector Sound Effects Kit, shown as assembled, contained some of the most fragile (and now scarcest) parts.

piece of yellow plastic, and the nose cone was painted red. (Beginning in 1959 and until the end of traditional Erector production in 1962, the Rocket would be made from white plastic, instead of yellow, creating a third variation of this part.)

These variations mirrored changes in the American Flyer line, where the different rockets were used as a load on a flatcar and rocket launcher car. Not many of these fragile rockets have survived intact, as the tail fins tend to break off when smashed into a box filled with steel parts. The rockets with a yellow body are the most difficult to find, because they were used for the shortest time.

Also new in 1958 was the Erector Sound Effects Kit, and its creation was certainly the most ambitious undertaking of the year. The idea came from the American Flyer line, wher the basic design was used in the Talking Station accessor The Sound Effects Kit was composed of twenty-one differen parts that could be assembled into a tiny phonograph. I 1940 Gilbert created the (NV) Whistle and in the earl 1950s the No. 6 Whistle Kit and No. 7 Smoke and Choo Chc Kit, but this was by far the most extravagant audio Erectc accessory of all time.

The Sound Effects Kit was included in only the top thre sets, Nos. 10072 and above. Set No. 10072 was even rename because of the kit. This set (descended from old No. 8½) sti featured the Ferris Wheel, but once that model was up graded with the Sound Effects parts, the set was rename "The Musical Ferris Wheel Set."

When assembled, the Sound Effects Kit was powered b the (A49) Electric Engine, which, through a series of speci gears, rotated the turntable at 78 rpm. Included in the ki was a small record; one side offered carnival music for us with the amusement park models and the other choo cho sounds for use with steam-engine models. Instructions wer included in the manual for adapting the Sound Effects Ki to the Airplane Ride, Ferris Wheel, Parachute Jump, an Merry-Go-Round. Also, new models featuring this kit wer developed: Record Player, Steam Plant, Twin Cylinder En gine, and Air Compressor.

Two fragile and therefore now rare parts came with th Sound Effects Kit, the (P14A208) Record and (XA14B295 Reproduced Assembly (the speaker). Each underwent a interesting variation. The 1958 version of the Record had carnival barker's voice laid over the sound track of th music. In 1959 the barker's voice was eliminated, so this ver sion of the record contained only music.

The Reproducer Assembly also underwent a noteworth change. In the center of the paper speaker cone, a thin meta strip, (which connected to the needle) pierced the paper. I the earliest version of the assembly, a small drop of clea glue was added here to strengthen the fragile cone Apparently this drop was not sufficient because, from th end of the year until the Sound Effects Kit was discontin ued, a blob of waxy red material was used instead. The re "dot" in the center of the speaker indicates that it was pro duced in late 1958 or 1959.

Also in 1958, the appearance and packaging of the lin changed dramatically, and each and every set was affectec Perhaps the most strikingly different sets were the tw smallest, which came packed in tubes with metal twist-of lids. These containers resembled those used for Tinker Toys The more traditional cardboard box sets were also differen in appearance from their counterparts of 1957, as the boxe were finally updated with the same new picture as was use on the cover of the instruction manuals. The midrange meta box sets were redesigned, with new names and new lithog raphy on the box lids.

Because of the virtually complete overhaul of 1958, all bu one of the sets came with a new number, which for the firs time was printed on every set. Packaging changes occurre inside the sets as well, with new parts layouts and card board parts display insert design. Two new colors of card board inserts, black and pale red, were first used, in additio to the traditional blue.

Several noteworthy modifications occurred with parts i 1958. The (W) Stack, which had been painted black, was nov unpainted but oxidized to a black patina. And the (MN) 3 Disc Wheel, perhaps the most frequently modified part i the Erector System, was changed yet again. Late in the yea

A thin, red cardboard hubcap was used instead of painting the hubcap portion of the wheel red. The cardboard hubcap was glued directly onto the wheel.

An old Erector part was reissued, with the (FP) Small Disc Wheel, last used in 1933, being added. Now, though, it was cadmium-plated instead of painted red and designated FP(X239). Surprisingly, it was used in only one set, No. 10021.

Meanwhile, the (A49) Electric Engine was modified again. In 1957, the motor guard plate came with a small yellow label that read "Erector Electric Engine." Now the same words were embossed directly into the metal motor guard plate. Also, the motor housings on these Electric Engines came in a new color. In 1957, they had been painted robin's egg blue; now they were royal blue. This color is unique to 1958, and collectors prize royal blue examples. (Some of the earliest motor housings from 1958 seem to show up in robin's egg blue. The color of the housing was returned to robin's egg blue in early 1959. There is no way to distinguish an early 1958 robin's egg blue motor housing from the 1959 version.)

An Aside: The Instruction Manuals for 1958

In 1958 the instruction manuals were given an extensive overhaul. Not only were many new space age models created for them, but new styles of manuals were introduced to cut costs.

Gilbert introduced "tube" sets in 1958, and Nos. 10011 and 10021, the smallest ones, were packed in this manner. They did not contain an instruction manual at all. Instead, they had a "blue-print," a large sheet of heavy paper with a dark blue background and various models illustrated in white.

Cardboard box sets and midrange metal box sets came with a traditional instruction manual, but in 1958 they came with a new cover that had a dark blue background and showed two boys building a robot. Jets and rockets were pictured in the background, as was a suspension bridge, and the cover was captioned, "Be An Erector Engineer." It was designated item no. M3934; curiously, the copyright date was 1954, even though it was clearly created in 1958. For Set Nos. 10026 through 10072, this cover replaced the "Happy-Faced Boy" used since 1948.

This new instruction manual cover came in two different variations. The early one had a shiny finish, and the later one had a flat finish. The change occurred early in the year. Another modification occurred in this manual when, later in the year, the "Erector Separate Parts Prices" was deleted.

The list of separate parts prices had been in instruction manuals since 1913, the very beginning of Erector. But it was dropped in 1958 and replaced with a loose sheet of paper titled, "Gilbert Erector Separate Parts Order Form." The earliest version of this form was printed on blue paper and numbered M4210. It was included in all the sets from 1958, even the early ones that still had the "Erector Separate Parts Prices" in the manuals.

This new order form was an improvement over the old price list, as it not only listed all the parts and their prices but also contained postage and mailing instructions. Still, collectors were sorry to see this substitution, because the old separate price list provided the best method of establishing when a set was made.

One final noteworthy change occurred with the 1958 instruction manuals, and it affected the text at the top of each page. In the past, this text identified the set size required to build the models on the page (for example, "Models Built With Set No. 7½"). But now, the set names were substituted for the old numbers.

To save money, Gilbert included a 1957 instruction manual and a now-scarce bonus manual in the two largest sets during the early part of 1958.

Set Nos. 10082 and 10092, the two largest in 1958, had an unusual instruction manual—or should I say manuals? For unlike any of the other sets available this year, they contained a 1957 version of the instruction manual, with a "Happy-Faced Boy" cover and a 1957 Erector Separate Parts Price list as well as an *Erector Bonus Manual*. It would seem that Gilbert had a large supply of leftover 1957 manuals for the two top sets, and the most prudent way to dispose of them was to include them in the sets from 1958, along with the bonus manual.

The *Erector Bonus Manual* was designated item no. M4200, and it is unique to 1958. It contained forty-eight pages and illustrated the new models from No. 10026 and above, including instruction for using the Sound Effects Kit. These manuals had no covers and were made of fragile paper. Few of them have survived intact today.

One final noteworthy item was that 1958 was the year The A. C. Gilbert Company began to publish and include in the sets and other toys a comic book called *Adventures in Science*. This was a thirty-two-page piece done on pulp paper (except for the cover) and was designed to cross-sell among the different toy lines. It told the story of a young man who visited the Gilbert Hall of Science in New York. In doing so it promoted the full range of Gilbert toys.

Tube Sets

Packing sets in tubes was new to Erector in 1958, but certainly not new to the toy industry. Tinker Toys, among others, had been packed this way for decades. But for Gilbert,

Promotional "comic books" were included in Erector Sets and other Gilbert toys:* Adventures in Science *(1958) and* Science Leads the Way *(1959).

this technique offered a new way to cut costs. Sets packed in tubes did not have to be organized. There were no cardboard inserts to produce, and no employee wages had to be spent in clipping parts in place for shipment and display. Anyone who has put a set back in order knows what a time-consuming process this can be.

Two sets were offered in tubes in 1958, Nos. 10011 and 10021. The first, named "The Beginner's Set," came in a tube 11" high and 3½" in diameter with four-color graphics picturing the scene printed on the new instruction manual covers (two boys building a robot). The contents of this set were essentially identical to those in No. 10010 from 1957 (old No. 1½).

"The Young Engineer's Set" was the name given to No. 10021, the larger of the tube sets. Its container was 12" high and 4⅛" in diameter and was similar in appearance to No. 10011. The contents of this set were virtually the same as those in No. 10020 from 1957 (old No. 2½).

Gilbert made the most of this new packaging system, as he incorporated the tube and even its lid into model building. Holes were drilled at the appropriate points in the container, and the instruction blueprint illustrated models that used the tube and lid as integral parts of the model.

Cardboard Box Sets

This was the end of a forty-four-year Erector tradition, for 1958 was the last year sets were packed in cardboard boxes. Only two sets were offered this way, and their containers were completely redesigned and different from anything Gilbert had offered in the past. Clearly, as the 1958 line was developed, there were no thoughts of discontinuing sets packed in cardboard boxes, for significant time and money was spent in the extensive overhaul that occurred here.

First, a new picture graced the lids of the cardboard box sets. It was the same as the one used on the new instruction manuals and showed two boys building the Mysterious Walking Robot.

Modifications inside these boxes were even more dramatic. Gilbert promoted these sets to dealers as "sets designed to sell themselves," and the reason for this was a new feature called a "pop up display card." It was really a new style of cardboard insert that was as large as the full inside of the box. When the lid was removed, the display card was face-down and designed to pop up (open like a book cover) so the set could be displayed. These cards were printed in color and were quite handsome. Not only did they promote the set with pictures of the models that could be built, but they also displayed the instruction manual. It was mounted on this insert with four slots, into which the corners of the manual fit.

Although first promoted in the dealer catalog in 1958, the idea for the pop-up display card was not entirely new. Gilbert had offered similar cardboard display panels to dealers for use in displaying cardboard sets since 1956, and probably even earlier. But the 1958 pop-up display card was the first display panel that was offered in the regular line of cardboard box sets.

The lower level of parts for the cardboard box sets was also redesigned. Instead of a single cardboard display insert as had been used in past years, both of the 1958 sets came with multisectioned inserts that fit into the body of the box. These inserts were made from red, gray, and black cardboard and displayed the parts on a bilevel basis. All the parts were clearly displayed, and even the axles had pop-up holders that fixed them in place.

Set No. 10026, the smaller of the cardboard box sets, measured 18⅛" x 10¼" x 1¼", and the contents of this set were identical to those of No. 10021 (in a tube) with one exception. Set No. 10021 came with (FPX239) Small Disc Wheels and No. 10026 had (MN) Large 3" Disc Wheels.

We can glean some insight into the cost of packaging by comparing the prices of these two sets. Set No. 10021 sold for \$2.98, No. 10026 for \$4.98. Although the wheels in the latter probably cost more to produce, much of the 66 percent increase can be attributed to the labor and materials required to produce this handsome cardboard box and to mount the parts in place. But the container was of little value to the young Erector engineer who played with the set; indeed, the tube was sturdier and therefore more desirable. These factors undoubtedly played a major role in the decision to drop cardboard boxes from the line in 1959.

Set No. 10031 was the larger of the cardboard box sets, and it came packed in a container measuring 20¼" x 13½" x 1¼". Its contents were essentially the same as those of No. 10030 from 1957 (old No. 3½). This set sold for \$7.98, only \$3.00 less than the smallest metal box set.

The two cardboard box sets from 1958 are two of the most extraordinary display sets ever produced by The A. C. Gilbert Company, because of the "pop up display card" and the complex, multicolored, bilevel parts display in the body of the box. Since they were produced for only one year and probably were not big sellers (they were costly for the parts they contained), they are not easy to find. It is especially difficult to locate these sets with their original cardboard inserts, as they were bulky, complicated, and cumbersome. Undoubtedly, most of these inserts were discarded soon after the parts were removed for the first time.

Metal Box Sets

Six metal box sets were offered, and basically they were continuations of items from 1957, though each differed slightly. No. 10041, the smallest set in the metal box line, was the only one to have its number carried over from 1957. It is likely that this number was assigned in error, for this set underwent the same changes as the other sets from

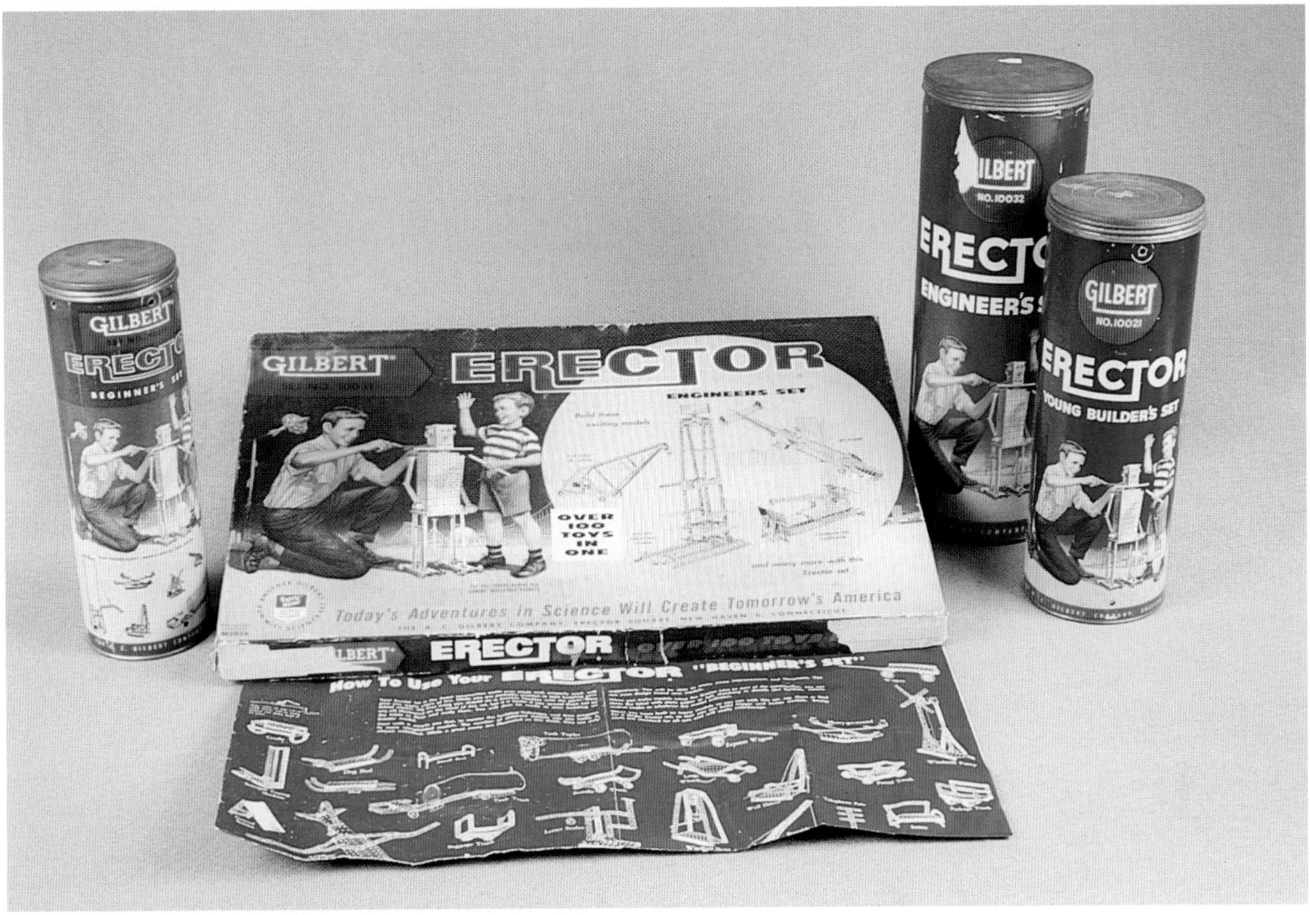

Set No. 10026 and the "tube" set from 1958, which was the last year for cardboard box sets and the first for tube sets. The cardboard box sets from 1958 are the only ones adorned with this kind of artwork.

1958—yet it was the only metal box set to have its designated number end with the digit "1."

Named "The Power Model Set" in 1958, it was essentially equivalent to last year's No. 10041 (old No. 5½) except for the new name and some changes in packaging. The lithography on the box lid still pictured the scaled-down Airplane Ride, but there changes were made in the packing of the parts. The lower-level cardboard parts display insert was blue (as was last year's), but the parts were mounted in different places. And instead of an upper-level parts display constructed from (MN) Base Plates, the 1958 version of this set came with a black cardboard parts tray. The cardboard insert for the (DC-3) Motor was also modified at this point. In the past this insert was made from plain blue cardboard. Now the color of the cardboard was changed to yellow, and it was dressed up with a lightning bolt and the words "Gilbert Powerdome 3 Volt Motor."

Set No. 10052 was next, and it was the most dramatically modified of the metal box sets for 1958. It was basically a continuation of last year's No. 10051 (old No. 6½), but with the addition of the new Rocket. Not only did Gilbert rename this set "The Rocket Launcher Set," but he also redesigned the lithography on the box lid to reflect this change. It was done in brown, red, white, and black, and pictured a boy with the Rocket Launcher. This attractive artwork is unique because it was done in four tones (with more brown than was used on any other set) and because it featured a boy in the scene. All the other sets pictured only models. The lithography of No. 10052 was so different in appearance from the rest of the 1958 lineup that it almost did not fit with the other metal box sets.

Changes occurred inside the box as well. The color of the cardboard used for the lower-level parts display went from blue to pale red. The placement of the parts differed from last year, too. There still were two removable upper-level parts displays, but while one was constructed from (MN) Base Plates (as before), the other was made from black cardboard. All and all, No. 10052 from 1958 was extremely attractive and remains a favorite among collectors.

"The Steam Engine Set" was the new name given to No. 10062, which was essentially the same as No. 10061 from 1957 (old No. 7½) except for the addition of the Rocket. While the number and name were changed, the lithography was the same, and the scene on the box lid pictured the Walking Beam Engine.

Similar changes in packing were made as with the larger metal box sets. The lower-level cardboard parts display was still blue, but the arrangement of parts differed from 1957. Although there still were two removable parts display trays on the upper level, a black cardboard insert was substituted for one of the trays constructed from (MN) Base Plates.

Set No. 10072 replaced the No. 10071 from 1957 (old No. 8½) in the 1958 lineup and had some significant modifications. First, it was the smallest set to contain the new Erector Sound Effects Kit, and that explained its new name, "The Musical Ferris Wheel Set." In addition to the new name

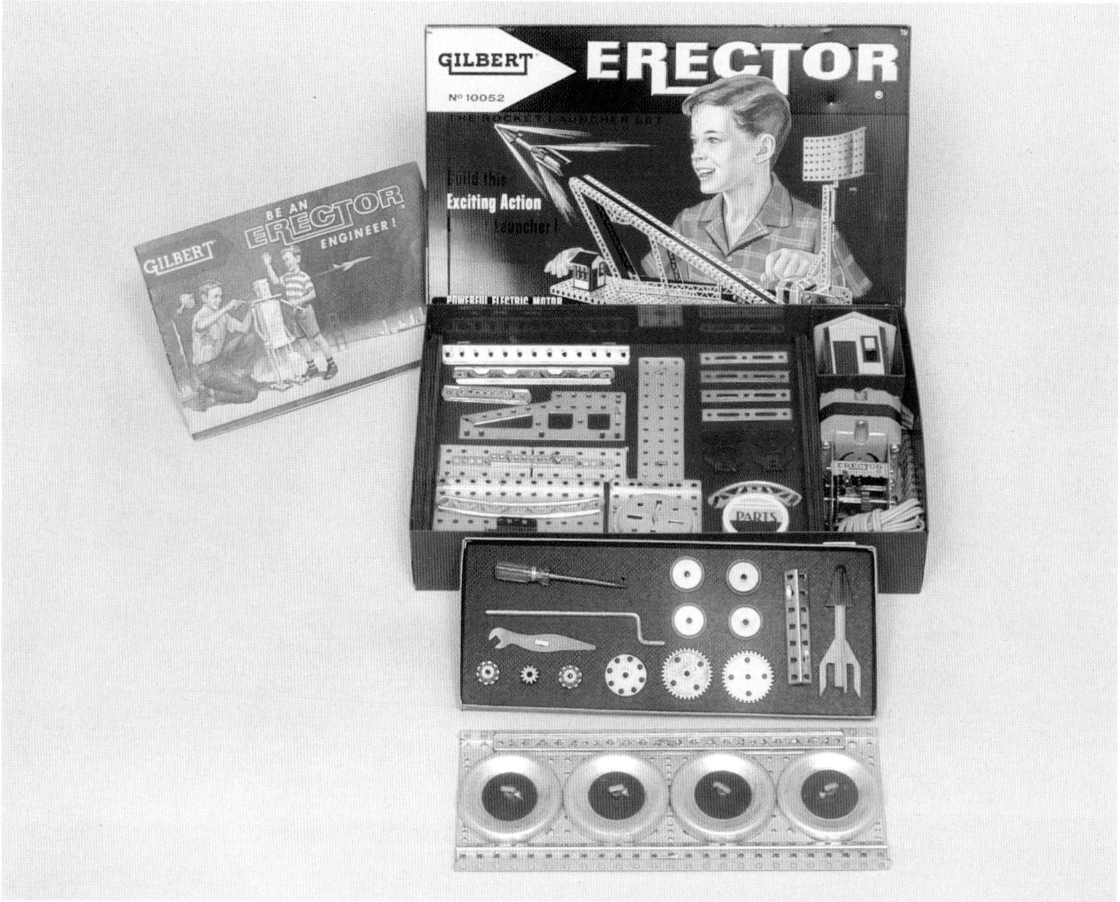

Set No. 10052 from 1958, the earliest version of The Rocket Launcher Set, came in a uniquely lithographed metal box.

and number, there were major changes in packaging and the arrangement of parts.

For No. 10072, the parts of the Sound Effects Kit came in a 5¾" x 5¾" x 2" cardboard box with a yellow cardboard insert labeled "Erector Sound Effects Kit." Many of the kit parts were mounted on this insert; those that were not were packed underneath. When the kit was packed in the front left corner of the center section of the box, there was no room for anything to be packed above it.

There were two distinct versions of the Musical Ferris Wheel set. On one, the center section came with two pale red cardboard parts display inserts, one above the other, with all parts neatly clipped in place. These complicated inserts were difficult to reinstall after they had been removed and are rarely found intact in a set today.

On the other version, the center section cardboard display inserts had one pale red layer (with parts clipped in place) and one pale blue layer (with parts bundled in plastic bags and packed loose). The latter was a less complicated (and less costly) method of packing the set and foreshadowed more changes that would occur in 1959.

Above the lower-level inserts and to the rear of the set, there were two parts display trays constructed from (MN) Base Plates, but they were narrower than in past years, and came with a different arrangement of parts. To the front on these trays and to the right of the Sound Effects Kit was a black cardboard parts display insert on which were mounted the Rocket and various wheels and gears. A final new display insert, packed forward of the boiler, was created for this set. It was pale red and held more gears along with the (W) Stacks.

The Musical Ferris Wheel Set is difficult to find today with the speaker and record intact, and especially difficult to find with all the original cardboard inserts. All the same, it is a favorite among collectors and one of the finest display sets when correctly organized.

The Amusement Park Set was designated No. 10082 in 1958, and it replaced No. 10080 from 1957 (old No. 10½). It had undergone some major alterations. First, Gilbert changed the labels on the inside of the lid. The narrow yellow strip label from prior years was replaced with a new much larger one that measured 1½" x 17½" and read "Contains Exciting New Carnival Sound Effects." The large label with a blue background still pictured the amusement park models, but now read "No. 10082 Amusement Park Set" instead of "No. 10½ Amusement Park Set."

(Many of the early 1958 sets came with two large inside lid labels, one pasted over the other. On several occasions, I was able to peel away the top label, which was numbered 10082. The label underneath was numbered 10½. If you find a "double labeled set," you can be sure it was produced early in the year.)

As with other sets from 1958, changes were made in the packing of No. 10082, but they were not nearly as dramatic.

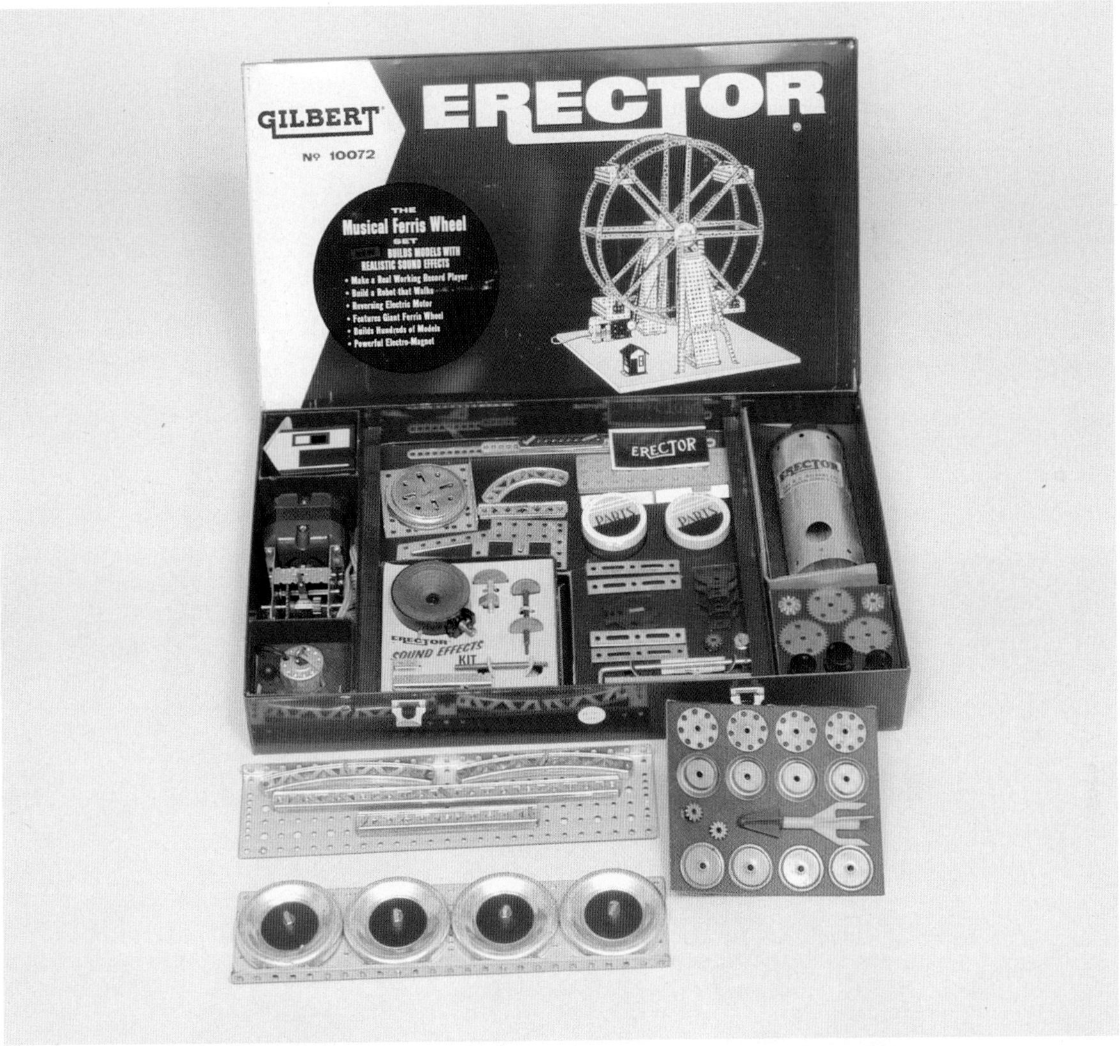

The first version of The Musical Ferris Wheel Set is a favorite among collectors. The complicated arrangement of cardboard display inserts makes No. 10072 from 1958 a superb display set.

The only significant difference was that part of the Sound Effects Kit was displayed in a new yellow cardboard insert, which was mounted on one of the upper-level (MN) Base Plate parts display trays. This insert was similar in appearance to that used in No. 10072, but it was much more shallow. The sound effects parts that were not mounted on this display insert were packed elsewhere in the set.

The 1958 catalog pictures a different packing arrangement for No. 10082, with pale red lower-level inserts and a new arrangement of parts. No examples have surfaced, but anyone knowing about one should contact the author.

Set No. 10092 (The Master Builder Set) was a continuation of No. 10090 from 1957 (old No. 12½). As with The Amusement Park Set, some interesting packing changes were made with it in 1958. First, the color of the cardboard on the parts display tray was changed from blue to black. Second, the arrangement of the parts was modified, with some of the sound effects parts and the Rocket finding their way onto this tray. The rest of the Sound Effects Kit was on a yellow cardboard insert labeled "Erector Sound Effects Kit" and located in one of the forward parts compartments.

Both Nos. 10082 and 10092 still came in heavy-gauge steel boxes painted bright red. While similar to their predecessors from 1957 and earlier, they are very desirable to collectors, who prize them for the Rocket and Sound Effects Kit.

Erector System Modifications for 1958

I. New Parts

(P14A686) Rocket, three-piece construction in red, white, and blue (early) or one-piece construction in red and yellow (late)
(P14B147) Base Plate
(P14A143) Gear Bracket
(P8554A) Turntable
(P14A208) Record
(PA10721) Turntable Bushing
(P99C) Bolster Bracket
(X14884) Sound Parts Assembly
(X14A134) Cam Shaft Assembly
(X14A137) Turntable Shaft Assembly
(X14A139) Lever & Lever Assembly
(XA14B295) Reproducer Assembly
(XA14B269) Needle
(P13A556B) Rubber Coupler

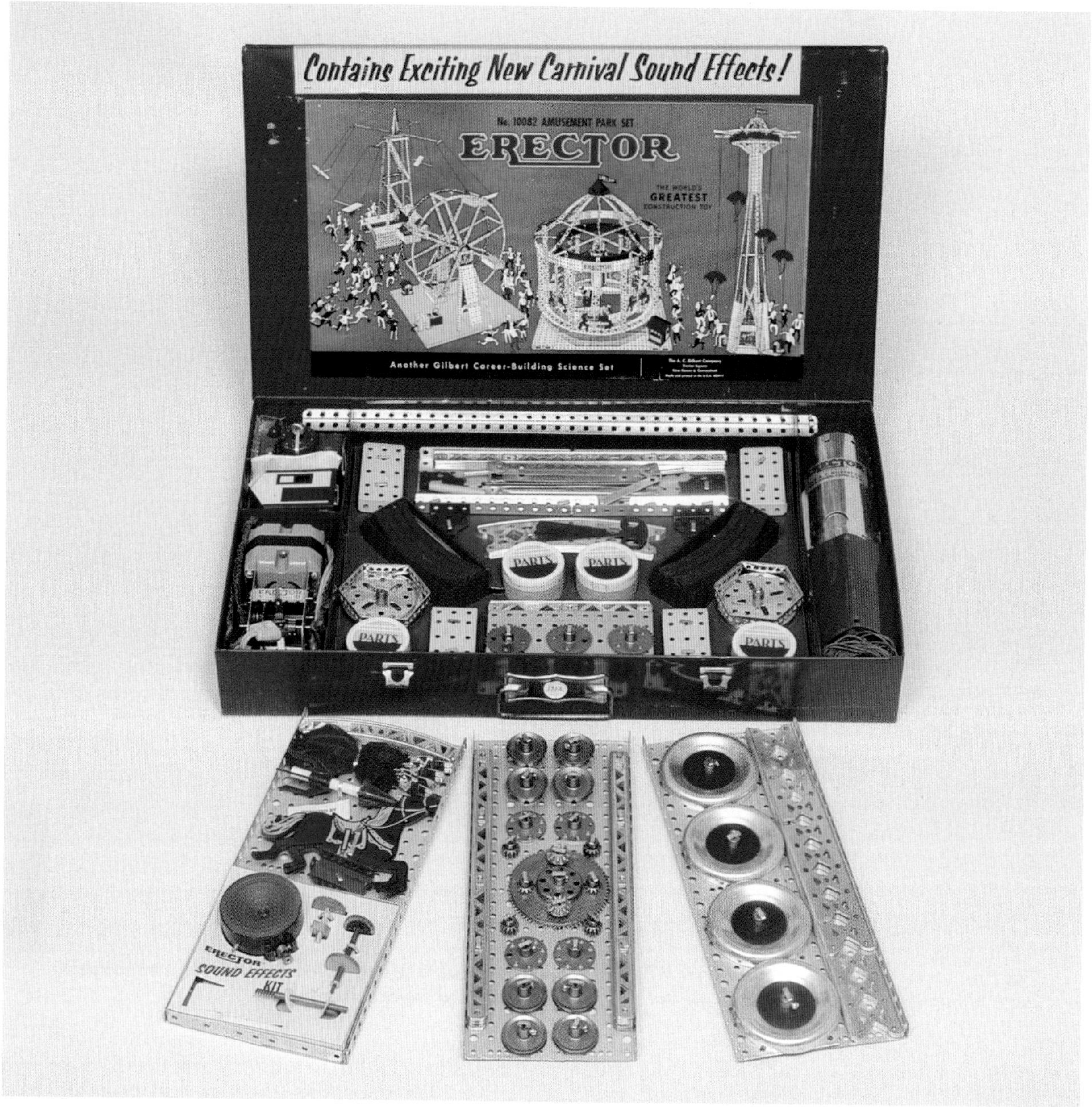

In 1958 the addition of the Sound Effects Kit to No. 10082 (The Amusement Park Set) resulted in a new packing arrangement.

(P14A145) Bracket
(P14A146) Power Shaft
(W1A82) Washer
(W84) Washer
(PA1139) Fiber Washer
(W153) Dished Washer
(PA10721) Adaptor
(N1) Hex Nut

II. Reintroduced Parts
(FPX239) Small Disc Wheel, cadmium-plated

III. Noteworthy Parts Colors and Finishes
(W) Stack, oxidized black
(MN) Large 3" Disc Wheels, with red-painted hubcap (early) or red paper hubcaps (late)
(A49) Electric Engine, with embossed gearbox guard plate and royal blue motor housing

Listings of 1958 Erector Sets

NO. 10011 — The Beginner's Set
Came in a cardboard tube 11" high and 3½" in diameter, with twist-off metal lid; pictured two boys building robot; sold for $1.98.

20 30 50 +10 N/A

NO. 10021 — The Young Builder's Set
Featured the (FP) Disc Wheels. Came in a cardboard tube 12" high and 4½" in diameter, with twist-off metal lid; pictured two boys building robot; sold for $2.98.

25 35 60 +10 N/A

	Gd	VG	Exc	Inv	Org

NO. 10026 The Junior Engineer's Set
Featured the (MN) Disc Wheels. Came in a cardboard box 18⅛" x 10¼" x 1¼", with "pop-up display card"; pictured two boys building robot; sold for $4.98.
30 50 80 +15 +100

NO. 10031 The Engineer's Set
Featured the angle girders and large base plates. Came in a cardboard box 20¼" x 13¼" x 1¼", with "pop-up display card"; pictured two boys building robot; sold for $7.98.
40 60 100 +20 +100

NO. 10041 The Power Model Set
Featured the (DC3) 3 Volt Motor. Came in a lithographed metal box 16" x 8" x 3" that pictured scaled-down Airplane Ride. Two-layer set with removable parts display tray; sold for $10.98. **40 60 100 +20 +25**

NO. 10052 The Rocket Launcher Set
Featured the (A49) Electric Engine and the Rocket and built Rocket Launcher. Came in a four-tone lithographed metal box 16" x 10" x 3" that pictured a boy and Rocket Launcher; two-layer set with two removable parts display trays, one cardboard and other constructed from (MN) Base Plates; sold for $17.98.
50 70 120 +20 +25

NO. 10062 The Steam Engine Set
Featured the (T) Boiler and built Walking Beam Engine. Came in a lithographed metal box 18" x 10" x 3" that pictured Walking Beam Engine; two-layer set with two removable parts display trays, one cardboard and other constructed from (MN) Base Plates; sold for $22.50.
50 70 120 +20 +25

NO. 10072 The Musical Ferris Wheel Set
Featured the (MJ) Electro Magnet and Sound Effects Kit and built Musical Ferris Wheel and Bascule Bridge. Came in a lithographed metal box 20" x 12" x 3" that pictured Ferris Wheel; three-layer set with two cardboard inserts in lower level and three removable parts display trays, one cardboard and two constructed from (MN) Base Plates; sold for $32.98. **120 180 300 +60 +100**

NO. 10082 The Amusement Park Set
Featured the truck parts, giant flywheel, parachutes, carousel horses, and Sound Effects Kit and built Parachute Jump, Merry-Go-Round, and other amusement park models as well as Giant Power Plant. Came in a red metal box 22" x 13" x 3"; two-layer set with three removable parts display trays constructed from (MN) Base Plates; sold for 49.98. **200 300 500 +100 +125**

NO. 10092 The Master Builder Set
Featured the Clamshell Bucket, Treads, and Sound Effects Kit and built the Mysterious Walking Robot and construction equipment. Came in a red metal box 24" x 14" x 3"; two-layer set with removable parts display tray with black cardboard insert; sold for $69.98.
425 625 1100 +200 +250

THE 1959 ERECTOR LINE

Two opposing trends characterized 1959. The first built on the momentum that began in 1958 and focused on improving Erector. It resulted in the addition of exciting new components to the Erector System and interesting new models in the instruction manuals. The second trend reverted to 1957, when cost-cutting invaded, and focused on ways to cut production costs. It resulted in a further cheapening of Erector and the lowering of the visual impact of the midrange sets.

Let us examine the positive changes first. Set No. 10063 and above included the new (TA) Conveyor Belt. This was a

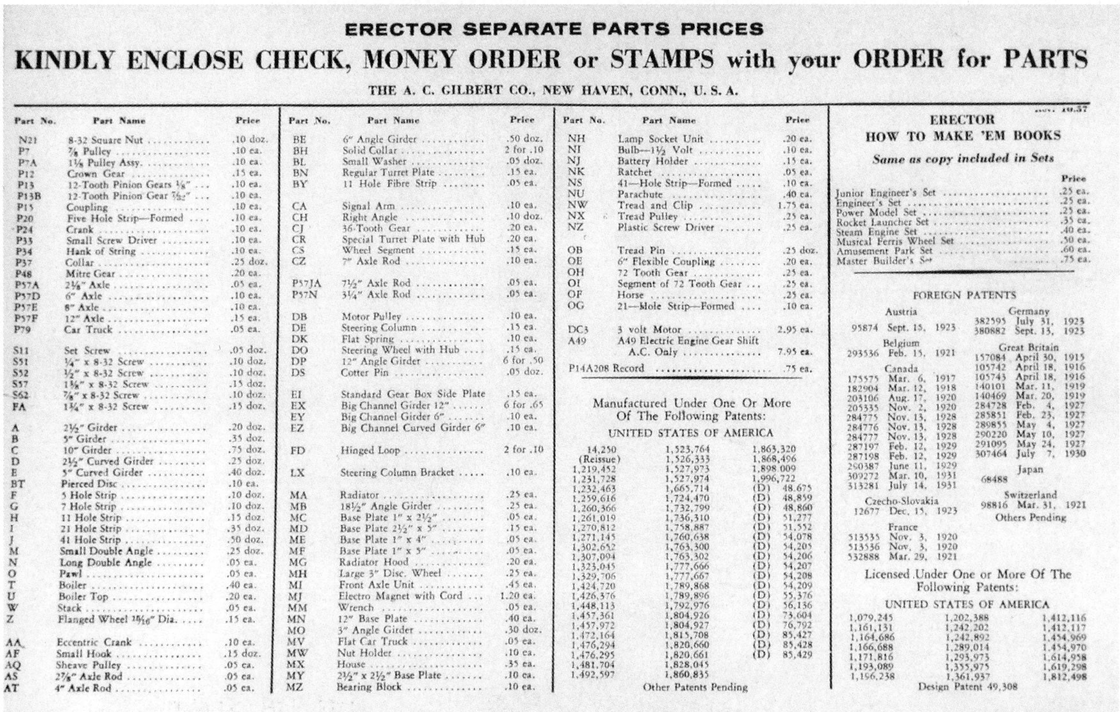

ERECTOR SEPARATE PARTS PRICES

KINDLY ENCLOSE CHECK, MONEY ORDER or STAMPS with your ORDER for PARTS

THE A. C. GILBERT CO., NEW HAVEN, CONN., U. S. A.

Part No.	Part Name	Price
N21	8-32 Square Nut	.10 doz.
P7	⅞ Pulley	.10 ea.
P7A	1⅛ Pulley Assy.	.10 ea.
P12	Crown Gear	.15 ea.
P13	12-Tooth Pinion Gears ⅛"	.10 ea.
P13B	12-Tooth Pinion Gear 7/32"	.10 ea.
P15	Coupling	.10 ea.
P20	Five Hole Strip—Formed	.10 ea.
P24	Crank	.10 ea.
P33	Small Screw Driver	.10 ea.
P34	Hank of String	.10 ea.
P37	Collar	.25 doz.
P48	Mitre Gear	.20 ea.
P57A	2⅛" Axle	.05 ea.
P57D	6" Axle	.10 ea.
P57E	8" Axle	.10 ea.
P57F	12" Axle	.15 ea.
P79	Car Truck	.05 ea.
S11	Set Screw	.05 doz.
S51	¼" x 8-32 Screw	.10 doz.
S52	½" x 8-32 Screw	.10 doz.
S57	1⅛" x 8-32 Screw	.15 doz.
S62	⅞" x 8-32 Screw	.10 doz.
FA	1¾" x 8-32 Screw	.15 doz.
A	2½" Girder	.20 doz.
B	5" Girder	.35 doz.
C	10" Girder	.75 doz.
D	2½" Curved Girder	.25 doz.
E	5" Curved Girder	.40 doz.
BT	Pierced Disc	.10 ea.
F	5 Hole Strip	.10 doz.
G	7 Hole Strip	.10 doz.
H	11 Hole Strip	.15 doz.
I	21 Hole Strip	.35 doz.
J	41 Hole Strip	.50 doz.
M	Small Double Angle	.25 doz.
N	Long Double Angle	.05 ea.
O	Pawl	.05 ea.
T	Boiler	.40 ea.
U	Boiler Top	.20 ea.
W	Stack	.05 ea.
Z	Flanged Wheel 1 5/16" Dia.	.15 ea.
AA	Eccentric Crank	.10 ea.
AF	Small Hook	.15 doz.
AQ	Sheave Pulley	.05 ea.
AS	2⅞" Axle Rod	.05 ea.
AT	4" Axle Rod	.05 ea.

Part No.	Part Name	Price
BE	6" Angle Girder	.50 doz.
BH	Solid Collar	2 for .10
BL	Small Washer	.05 doz.
BN	Regular Turret Plate	.15 ea.
BY	11 Hole Fibre Strip	.05 ea.
CA	Signal Arm	.10 ea.
CH	Right Angle	.10 doz.
CJ	36-Tooth Gear	.20 ea.
CR	Special Turret Plate with Hub	.20 ea.
CS	Wheel Segment	.15 ea.
CZ	7" Axle Rod	.10 ea.
P57JA	7½" Axle Rod	.05 ea.
P57N	3¼" Axle Rod	.05 ea.
DB	Motor Pulley	.10 ea.
DE	Steering Column	.15 ea.
DK	Flat Spring	.10 ea.
DO	Steering Wheel with Hub	.15 ea.
DP	12" Angle Girder	6 for .50
DS	Cotter Pin	.05 doz.
EI	Standard Gear Box Side Plate	.15 ea.
EX	Big Channel Girder 12"	6 for .65
EY	Big Channel Girder 6"	.10 ea.
EZ	Big Channel Curved Girder 6"	.10 ea.
FD	Hinged Loop	2 for .10
LX	Steering Column Bracket	.10 ea.
MA	Radiator	.25 ea.
MB	18½" Angle Girder	.25 ea.
MC	Base Plate 1" x 2½"	.05 ea.
MD	Base Plate 2½" x 5"	.15 ea.
ME	Base Plate 1" x 4"	.05 ea.
MF	Base Plate 1" x 5"	.05 ea.
MG	Radiator Hood	.20 ea.
MH	Large 3" Disc. Wheel	.25 ea.
MI	Front Axle Unit	.45 ea.
MJ	Electro Magnet with Cord	1.20 ea.
MM	Wrench	.05 ea.
MN	12" Base Plate	.40 ea.
MO	3" Angle Girder	.30 doz.
MV	Flat Car Truck	.05 ea.
MW	Nut Holder	.10 ea.
MX	House	.35 ea.
MY	2½" x 2½" Base Plate	.10 ea.
MZ	Bearing Block	.10 ea.

Part No.	Part Name	Price
NH	Lamp Socket Unit	.20 ea.
NI	Bulb—1½ Volt	.10 ea.
NJ	Battery Holder	.15 ea.
NK	Ratchet	.05 ea.
NS	41—Hole Strip—Formed	.10 ea.
NU	Parachute	.40 ea.
NW	Tread and Clip	1.75 ea.
NX	Tread Pulley	.25 ea.
NZ	Plastic Screw Driver	.25 ea.
OB	Tread Pin	.25 doz.
OE	6" Flexible Coupling	.20 ea.
OH	72 Tooth Gear	.25 ea.
OI	Segment of 72 Tooth Gear	.25 ea.
OF	Horse	.25 ea.
OG	21—Hole Strip—Formed	.10 ea.
DC3	3 volt Motor	2.95 ea.
A49	A49 Electric Engine Gear Shift A.C. Only	7.95 ea.
P14A208	Record	.75 ea.

Manufactured Under One Or More Of The Following Patents:

UNITED STATES OF AMERICA

14,250 (Reissue)	1,523,764	1,863,320
1,219,452	1,526,333	1,868,496
1,231,728	1,527,973	1,898 009
1,232,463	1,527,974	1,996,722
1,259,616	1,665,714	(D) 48.675
1,260,366	1,724,470	(D) 48,859
1,261,019	1,732,799	(D) 48,860
1,270,812	1,736,310	(D) 51,277
1,271,145	1,758,887	(D) 51,552
1,302,652	1,760,638	(D) 54,078
1,307,094	1,763,300	(D) 54,205
1,323,045	1,763,302	(D) 54,206
1,329,706	1,777,666	(D) 54,207
1,424,720	1,777,667	(D) 54,208
1,426,376	1,789,868	(D) 54,209
1,448,113	1,789,896	(D) 55,376
1,457,361	1,792,976	(D) 56,136
1,457,972	1,804,926	(D) 73,604
1,472,164	1,804,927	(D) 76,792
1,476,294	1,815,708	(D) 85,427
1,476,295	1,820,660	(D) 85,428
1,481,704	1,820,661	(D) 85,429
1,492,597	1,828,045	
	1,860,835	

Other Patents Pending

ERECTOR
HOW TO MAKE 'EM BOOKS
Same as copy included in Sets

	Price
Junior Engineer's Set	.25 ea.
Engineer's Set	.25 ea.
Power Model Set	.25 ea.
Rocket Launcher Set	.35 ea.
Steam Engine Set	.40 ea.
Musical Ferris Wheel Set	.50 ea.
Amusement Park Set	.60 ea.
Master Builder's Set	.75 ea.

FOREIGN PATENTS

Austria
95874 Sept. 15, 1923

Belgium
293536 Feb. 15, 1921

Canada
175575 Mar. 6, 1917
182904 Mar. 12, 1918
203106 Aug. 17, 1920
205335 Nov. 2, 1920
284775 Nov. 13, 1928
284776 Nov. 13, 1928
284777 Nov. 13, 1928
287197 Feb. 12, 1929
287198 Feb. 12, 1929
290387 June 11, 1929
309272 Mar. 10, 1931
313281 July 14, 1931

Czecho-Slovakia
12677 Dec. 15, 1923

France
513535 Nov. 3, 1920
513536 Nov. 3, 1920
532888 Mar. 29, 1921

Germany
382595 July 31, 1923
380882 Sept. 13, 1923

Great Britain
157084 April 30, 1915
105742 April 18, 1916
105743 April 18, 1916
140101 Mar. 11, 1919
140469 Mar. 20, 1919
284728 Feb. 4, 1927
285851 Feb. 23, 1927
289855 May 4, 1927
290220 May 10, 1927
291095 May 24, 1927
307464 July 7, 1930

Japan
68488

Switzerland
98816 Mar. 31, 1921

Others Pending

Licensed Under One or More Of The Following Patents:

UNITED STATES OF AMERICA

1,079,245	1,202,388	1,412,116
1,161,131	1,242,202	1,412,117
1,164,686	1,242,892	1,454,969
1,166,688	1,289,014	1,454,970
1,171,816	1,293,973	1,614,958
1,193,089	1,355,975	1,619,298
1,196,238	1,361,937	1,812,498

Design Patent 49,308

Separate Parts Prices for 1958

1958 CONTENTS LIST

SET NO.		10011	10021[1]	10026	10031[2]	10041	10052	10062	10072	10082	10092[3]
P7	7⁄8" PULLEY	4	4	4	4	4	4	4	0	0	0
P7A	1 1⁄8" PULLEY	0	0	0	0	0	0	0	4	4	4
P12	CROWN GEAR	0	0	0	0	0	0	0	0	1	1
P13	12 TOOTH PINION GEAR, 1⁄8"	0	0	0	0	0	1	1	2	2	2
P13B	12 TOOTH PINION GEAR, 7⁄23"	0	0	0	0	0	0	0	1	4	4
P15	COUPLING	0	0	0	0	1	2	2	2	2	2
P20	5 HOLE STRIP —FORMED	0	0	0	0	0	0	2	2	8	8
P24	CRANK	1	1	1	1	1	1	1	1	1	1
P33	SMALL SCREW DRIVER	1	1	1	1	1	1	0	0	0	0
P34	HANK OF STRING	0	1	1	1	1	1	1	1	3	3
P37	COLLAR	1	4	4	4	5	6	7	9	20	20
P48	MITRE GEAR	0	0	0	0	0	2	2	2	2	2
P57A	2 1⁄8" AXLE	1	1	1	1	1	1	1	1	1	8
P57D	6" AXLE	0	1	1	2	0	0	0	0	0	1
P57E	8" AXLE	0	0	0	0	0	0	0	0	2	2
P57F	12" AXLE	0	0	0	0	0	0	0	1	2	2
P57JA	7 1⁄2" AXLE	0	0	0	0	0	0	0	0	4	4
P57K	10" AXLE	0	0	0	0	0	0	0	0	0	2
P57N	3 1⁄4" AXLE	0	0	0	0	0	0	0	0	2	2
P79	CAR TRUCK	4	4	4	4	4	4	4	4	4	4
A	2 1⁄2" GIRDER	4	4	4	4	4	4	4	4	4	6
B	5" GIRDER	4	4	4	4	8	8	8	12	12	12
C	10" GIRDER	2	8	8	8	8	8	8	36	52	52
D	2 1⁄2" CURVED GIRDER	4	4	4	4	4	4	4	4	4	4
E	5" CURVED GIRDER	0	2	2	2	2	4	4	26	26	26
F	5 HOLE STRIP	0	0	0	0	2	2	2	2	2	16
G	7 HOLE STRIP	0	0	0	0	2	2	2	2	6	8
H	11 HOLE STRIP	0	0	0	0	4	4	4	4	16	16
I	21 HOLE STRIP	0	0	0	0	2	2	2	4	18	18
J	41 HOLE STRIP	0	0	0	0	0	0	0	2	2	4
M	SMALL DOUBLE ANGLE	0	0	0	0	0	0	2	6	24	24
N	LONG DOUBLE ANGLE	2	4	4	4	4	4	4	4	16	16
O	PAWL	0	0	0	0	0	1	2	2	16	16
T	BOILER	0	0	0	0	0	0	1	1	2	2
U	BOILER TOP	0	0	0	0	0	0	1	1	1	1
W	STACK	0	0	0	0	0	0	3	3	3	3
Z	FLANGED WHEEL 15⁄16" DIA.	0	0	0	0	0	0	4	4	4	4
AA	ECCENTRIC CRANK	0	0	0	0	0	0	0	0	6	6
AE	SPRING	0	0	0	0	0	0	0	0	0	2
AF	SMALL HOOK	1	1	1	1	1	1	1	1	1	1
AJ	PAPER ERECTOR FLAG	0	0	0	0	1	1	1	1	1	1
AQ	SHEAVE PULLEY	0	0	0	0	0	0	0	1	4	5
AS	2 7⁄8" AXLE	0	0	0	0	2	2	3	3	4	4
AT	4" AXLE	2	2	2	2	2	2	2	2	2	4
BE	6" ANGLE GIRDER	0	0	0	4	4	4	4	4	4	12
BH	SOLID COLLAR	0	0	0	0	0	0	0	0	2	2
BL	SMALL WASHER	6	12	12	12	12	12	12	12	12	18
BN	REGULAR TURRET PLATE	0	0	0	0	2	2	4	4	4	4
BT	PIERCED DISC	1	1	1	1	2	2	2	4	4	4
BY	11 HOLE FIBRE STRIP	0	0	0	0	0	0	0	2	2	2
CA	SIGNAL ARM	0	0	0	0	0	0	0	0	2	2
CH	RIGHT ANGLE	8	12	12	12	14	14	14	30	42	42
CJ	36 TOOTH GEAR	0	0	0	0	0	2	3	3	3	5

1958 CONTENTS LIST

SET NO.		10011	10021[1]	10026	10031[2]	10041	10052	10062	10072	10082	10092[3]
CR	SPECIAL TURRET PLATE WITH HUB	0	0	0	0	0	0	0	0	2	2
CS	WHEEL SEGMENT	0	0	0	0	0	0	0	0	8	8
CZ	7" AXLE	0	0	0	0	2	2	2	4	4	4
DB	MOTOR PULLEY	0	0	0	0	2	1	1	1	1	2
DE	STEERING	0	0	0	0	0	0	0	4	1	1
DK	FLAT SPRING	0	0	0	0	0	0	0	0	4	4
DO	STEERING WHEEL WITH HUB	0	0	0	0	0	0	0	0	1	1
DP	12" ANGLE GIRDER	0	0	0	4	4	4	4	4	4	6
DS	COTTER PIN	0	0	0	0	0	0	0	0	1	1
EI	STD. GEAR BOX SIDE PLATE	0	0	0	0	0	2	2	2	2	2
EX	BIG CHANNEL GIRDER 12"	0	0	0	0	0	0	0	0	8	8
EY	BIG CHANNEL GIRDER 6"	0	0	0	0	0	0	0	0	4	8
EZ	BIG CHAN. GIRDER CURVED 6"	0	0	0	0	0	0	0	0	9	9
FA	1¾" x 8-32 SCREW	0	0	0	0	0	0	0	0	12	12
FD	HINGED LOOP	0	0	0	0	0	0	0	0	2	2
FP(X239)	SMALL DISC WHEEL	0	4	0	0	0	0	0	0	0	0
LX	STEERING COLUMN BRACKET	0	0	0	0	0	0	0	0	1	1
MA	RADIATOR	0	0	0	0	0	0	0	0	1	1
MB	18½" ANGLE GIRDER	0	0	0	0	0	0	0	0	2	2
MC	BASE PLATE 1" x 2½"	2	2	2	2	2	2	2	8	8	8
MD	BASE PLATE 2½" x 5"	1	1	1	1	1	1	1	4	4	4
ME	BASE PLATE 1" x 4"	0	0	0	0	0	0	0	0	4	4
MF	BASE PLATE 1" x 5"	0	2	2	4	4	4	4	8	21	21
MG	RADIATOR HOOD	0	0	0	0	0	0	0	0	1	1
MH	LARGE 3" DISC WHEEL	0	0	4	4	4	4	4	4	4	4
MI	FRONT AXLE UNIT	0	0	0	0	0	0	0	0	1	1
MJ	ELECTRO MAGNET WITH CORD	0	0	0	0	0	0	0	1	1	1
MM	WRENCH	0	0	0	0	1	1	1	1	1	1
MN	12" BASE PLATE	0	0	0	2	2	4	4	6	6	6
MO	3" ANGLE GIRDER	0	0	0	4	4	4	4	4	4	8
MV	FLAT CAR TRUCK	0	0	0	0	0	0	2	4	4	12
MW	NUT HOLDER	0	0	0	0	1	1	1	1	1	1
MX	HOUSE	0	0	0	0	0	1	1	1	1	1
MY	2½" x 2½" BASE PLATE	0	0	0	0	1	1	1	1	1	1
MZ	BEARING BLOCK	0	0	0	0	0	1	1	1	1	1
NH	LAMP SOCKET UNIT	0	0	0	0	0	0	1	2	2	2
NI	BULB, 1½ VOLT (CLEAR)	0	0	0	0	0	0	0	2	2	2

1958 CONTENTS LIST

SET NO.		10011	10021[1]	10026	10031[2]	10041	10052	10062	10072	10082	10092[3]
P12N677	BULB, 1.2 VOLT (RED)	0	0	0	0	0	0	1	1	1	1
NJ	BATTERY HOLDER	0	0	0	0	2	0	1	1	1	4
NK	RATCHET	0	0	0	0	0	0	0	2	2	2
NL	BOLSTER BRACKET	0	0	0	0	0	0	0	0	0	4
NS	41 HOLE STRIP —FORMED	0	0	0	0	0	0	0	0	2	2
NU	PARACHUTE	0	0	0	0	0	0	0	0	4	4
NW	TREAD	0	0	0	0	0	0	0	0	0	2
NX	TREAD PULLEY	0	0	0	0	0	0	0	0	0	4
NZ	PLASTIC SCREW DRIVER	0	0	0	0	1	1	1	1	1	1
OB	TREAD PIN	0	0	0	0	0	0	0	0	0	2
OE	6" FLEXIBLE COUPLING	0	0	0	0	0	1	1	1	1	1
OF	HORSE	0	0	0	0	0	0	0	0	6	6
OG	21 HOLE STRIP FORMED	0	0	0	0	0	0	0	0	2	2
OH	72 TOOTH GEAR	0	0	0	0	0	0	0	0	1	1
OI	SEGMENT OF 72 TOOTH GEAR	0	0	0	0	0	0	0	0	1	1
P14A686	ROCKET	0	0	0	0	0	1	1	1	1	1
X14B663	CLAM SHELL BUCKET	0	0	0	0	0	0	0	0	0	1
P14B147	BASE PLATE	0	0	0	0	0	0	0	1	1	1
P14A143	GEAR BRACKET	0	0	0	0	0	0	0	1	1	1
P8554A	TURNTABLE	0	0	0	0	0	0	0	1	1	1
P14A208	RECORD	0	0	0	0	0	0	0	1	1	1
PA10721	TURNTABLE BUSHING	0	0	0	0	0	0	0	1	1	1
P99C	BOLSTER BRACKET	0	0	0	0	0	0	0	1	1	1
X14N884	SOUND PARTS ASSEMBLY	0	0	0	0	0	0	0	1	1	1
X14A134	CAM SHAFT ASSEMBLY	0	0	0	0	0	0	0	1	1	1
X14A137	TURNTABLE SHAFT ASSEMBLY	0	0	0	0	0	0	0	1	1	1
X14A139	LEVER & BRACKET ASSEMBLY	0	0	0	0	0	0	0	1	1	1
XA14B295	REPRODUCER ASSEMBLY	0	0	0	0	0	0	0	1	1	1
XA14B269	NEEDLE	0	0	0	0	0	0	0	1	1	1
P13A566B	RUBBER COUPLER	0	0	0	0	0	0	0	1	1	1
P14A145	BRACKET	0	0	0	0	0	0	0	1	1	1
P14A146	POWER SHAFT	0	0	0	0	0	0	0	1	1	1
W1A82	WASHER	0	0	0	0	0	0	0	7	7	7
W84	WASHER	0	0	0	0	0	0	0	1	1	1
PA1139	FIBER WASHER	0	0	0	0	0	0	0	1	1	1
W153	DISHED WASHER	0	0	0	0	0	0	0	1	1	1
PA10721	ADAPTOR	0	0	0	0	0	0	0	1	1	1
N1	HEX NUT	0	0	0	0	0	0	0	1	1	1
	WOOD SCREWS	0	0	0	0	0	0	0	4	4	4
A49	ELECTRIC ENGINE	0	0	0	0	0	1	1	1	1	1
DC3	3 VOLT MOTOR	0	0	0	0	1	0	0	0	0	1
N21	8-32 SQUARE NUT	23	45	45	60	88	93	93	169	271	359
S51	¼" x 8-32 SCREW	20	35	35	50	80	84	84	162	240	260
S52	½" x 8-32 SCREW	0	0	0	0	0	4	4	4	8	8
S57	1⅜" x 8-32 SCREW	0	0	0	0	0	0	4	4	4	4
S62	⅞" x 8-32 SCREW	3	6	6	6	8	8	10	18	64	64

1. Set no. 10021 also contained two 5" axles.
2. Set no. 10031 also contained one 5" axle.
3. Set No. 10092 also contained an offset wrench.

62"-long and 1½"-wide piece of woven tan cloth. It was designed to be cut to length and formed into a belt, which would be driven by drums constructed from a (W) Stack and two (Z) Flanged Wheels. Extra stacks and flanged wheels were included in the sets for use with the conveyor belt. Four new conveyor models were designed in 1959 for Set No. 10063, and they were excellent, high-action models.

The second innovation for 1959 was the Ball Bearing System, composed of six (TB) Ball Bearings and a (TC) Ball Bearing Retainer Plate. These new parts were included in Nos. 10083 and 10093. The six ball bearings, mounted in the retainer plate, were designed to be sandwiched between two (BN) Turret Plates.

This system was a wonderful addition, as it allowed any heavy model to be rotated smoothly and with minimal friction. Though there were many applications for the ball bearing system throughout the range of existing models, the only model that illustrated its parts was the new Long Range Radar Scanner, built with No. 10083. Apparently, the cost of incorporating the system into the line of existing models and redesigning the illustrations for the instruction manual was too great.

Many other new models were created for the 1959 instruction manual. Some of the finest were the DEW Line Radar, which could be built with No. 10073 (DEW stood for Distant Early Warning, remember?); the Unicyclist, which could be built with No. 10083; and the Electro Magnetic Steel Scrap Loader and the Ship Yard Crane, which could be built with No. 10093. These action-packed models demonstrated the sophistication of the Erector System.

The negative trend that resurfaced in 1959 was one of cutting production costs, and the area it affected was the packaging of the sets. One of the most attractive aspects of Erector, and certainly one of the most appealing to collectors, was that the sets, when new, had always been highly organized. Parts were clipped in place on cardboard inserts or on display trays constructed from large base plates, and everything in each set had its proper place. Organized in this manner, Erector Sets had tremendous visual appeal.

But this forty-four-year tradition was ending. First, no cardboard box sets were offered from this point forward. The three smallest sets (essentially equivalent to old Nos. 1½, 2½, and 3½) were packed in tubes in 1959. Because no time was spent organizing these sets and clipping parts in place, they were much more economical to produce. Set No. 10032 in a tube now sold for $4.98; a year earlier, the equivalent set, No. 10031, had sold for $7.98 in an organized cardboard box.

Packaging changes went even further, affecting the midrange metal box sets (Nos. 10042 through 10073). In the past, these two-layer sets had come with a lower-level cardboard parts display insert, with parts clipped neatly in place. Now, this display insert was replaced with a blue cardboard liner, and the lower-level parts were packed in clear plastic bags. These bags of parts were simply laid on the liner. While production costs were reduced, so was the visual impact.

Other packaging modifications affected these midrange sets. In the past, both the outside and the inside of the lids had been lithographed, and the scene pictured on the inside and outside of the lid was identical. But this changed in 1959.

There actually were two versions of each of the midrange sets. The early ones featured a cardboard insert that covered the entire inside lid. While the inserts differed for each set, all were colorful and filled with text promoting the set. The most interesting feature of these inserts is that they displayed the instruction manual, mounted by way of four slots. The corners of the manual fit into the slots, similar to the "pop up display cards" on cardboard box sets from 1958.

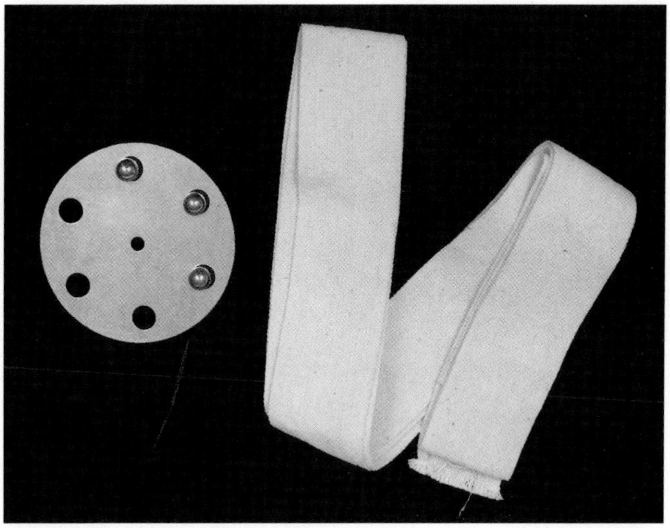

Two well-conceived components joined the Erector System in 1959: the Ball Bearing System (left) and the Conveyor Belt (right).

Toward the end of 1959, the inside lid cardboard inserts gave way to another new method of displaying the manual on the inside of the set lid. The cardboard insert was gone, and the inside of the lid was lithographed again. But the lithography did not match the outside of the lid as was the case in 1958. Instead, it was closer in appearance to the cardboard insert it replaced. The instruction manual was mounted directly onto the lid with paper fasteners! Holes in the manual and the box lid accommodated this change, and the paper fasteners were painted to match the color of the box lid. This method of displaying the instruction manual continued until the end of traditional Erector production in 1962.

An Aside: The Instruction Manuals for 1959

As was true the previous year, 1959 saw many changes in the instruction manuals. The tube sets again came with the "blue print" format of instructions, but now the background color was white, and the drawings of the models were done in blue. Last year, the models were illustrated in white on a blue background.

The remainder of the sets in the line came with traditional instruction manuals, but three different covers were used over the year. The first was a continuation of the cover introduced last year. It pictured two boys building the Mysterious Walking Robot, and the text read "Be An Erector Engineer." This cover was numbered M3934 and copyrighted in 1954.

But fairly early in 1959, this cover was replaced by a new yet similar cover. Numbered M4263 and copyrighted in 1959, it still pictured the two boys with the robot. But the scale was changed, and the boys were made larger and moved from the left side of the cover to the right. The text read "Erector Instruction Manual."

Yet another instruction manual cover appeared just before the end of the year, and this one was entirely new. The boys were playing with a Rocket Launcher, and an Erector Set box, dressed up to look like a factory, completed

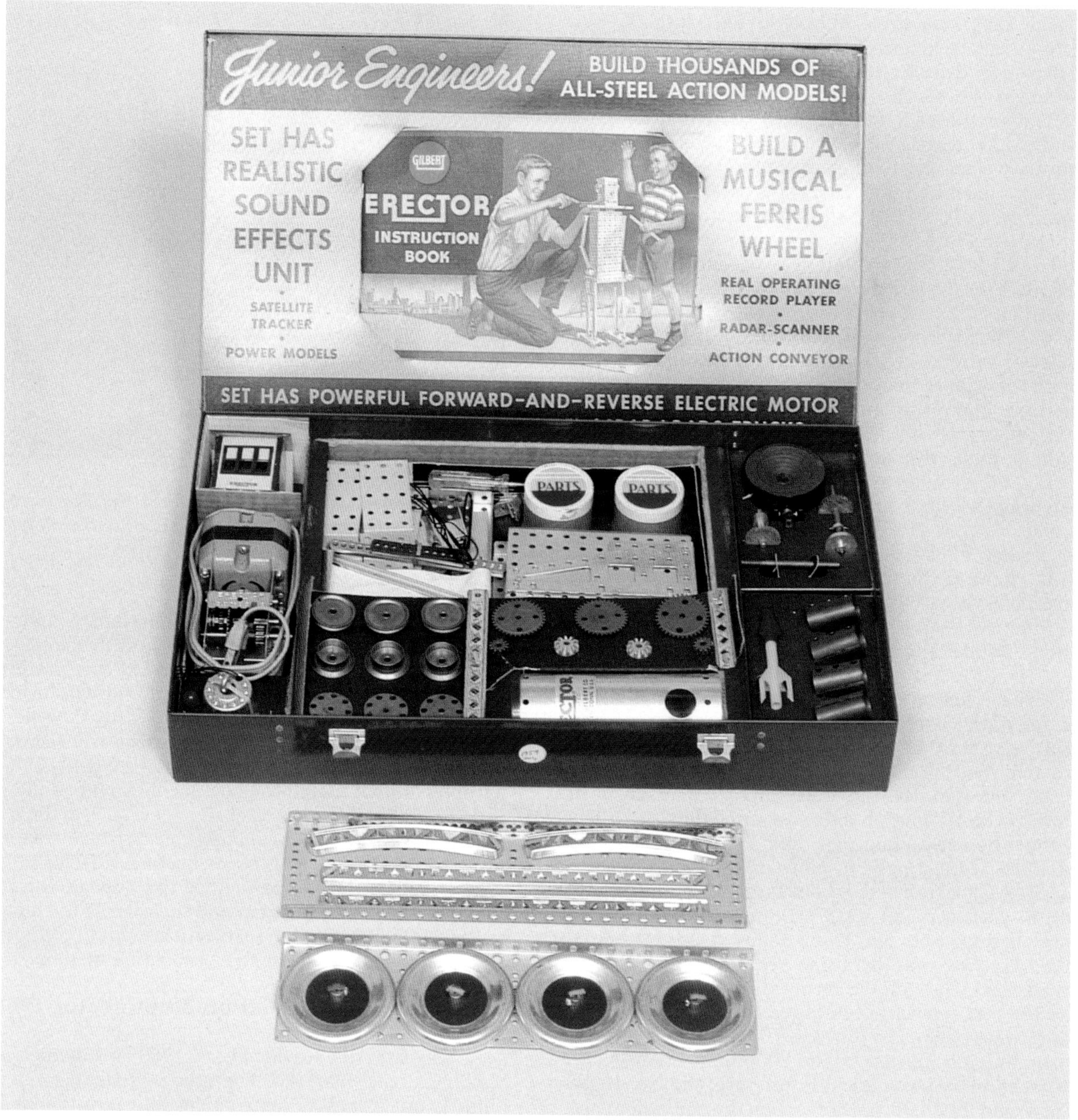

This is the early 1959 version of No. 10073, known as "The Musical Ferris Wheel Set." Note the cardboard display insert, which covers the entire inside lid, and the slots to hold the instruction manual.

the scene. (The sides of the Rocket Launcher set box were decorated like a factory in 1959.) This final cover was numbered M4295 and copyrighted in 1959.

In 1960, the number on the cover that showed the robot was changed from M4263 to M4664, and the number on the cover that pictured the Rocket Launcher was changed from M4295 to M4712. Both covers were used simultaneously through the end of 1961. Although there is no clear pattern, smaller sets tend to show up with M4712, and larger ones with M4664. Even the 1958 cover numbered M3934 occasionally showed up as late as 1960, but only in the largest sets. By 1962, all the metal box set instruction manual covers were M4712, which pictured the Rocket Launcher.

Along with the instruction manuals came new "Gilbert Erector Separate Parts Order Forms." There were two variations during 1959. The first was printed on blue paper and numbered M4287. It was similar to the one from 1958, but included the new 1959 parts. But this order form was used for only a short time and was quickly replaced with M4630. This second, more extensive variation of the order form was printed on yellow paper. Also, a price increase, which affected many of the parts, was made part of M4630, which was used throughout the remaining years of traditional Erector production and discontinued at the end of 1962. After 1960, it was printed on yellow or pale green paper.

An anomaly occurred with the instruction manual for The Amusement Park Set, beginning in 1959 and lasting through 1962. While every other set came with a manual

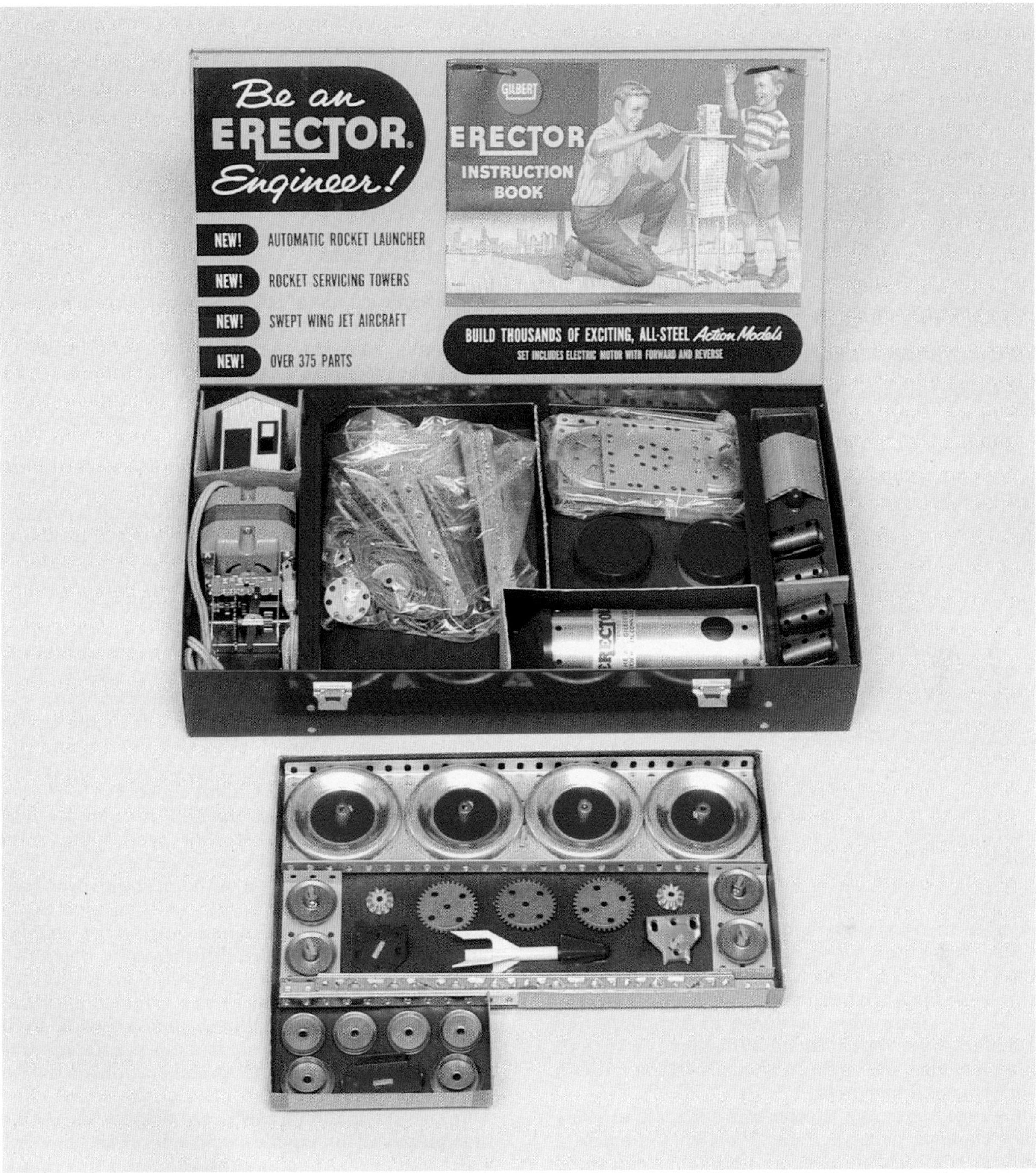

The version of No. 10063 from late 1959 lacked a cardboard display insert in the lid, and its instruction manual was held in place with paper fasteners.

specific to it, The Amusement Park Set came with the same manual as The Master Builder Set. Gilbert produced so few of these large sets that it was less expensive to make one manual for both rather than a specific one for each.

A new comic book was included in the sets. In 1958, *Adventures in Science* was introduced to promote all the toys in the line. The comic book for 1959 was titled *Science Leads The Way*, and, although the story was different, its purpose was the same. This was the last version of this promotional piece, and it was included in all Erector Sets and other Gilbert toys through 1960.

Several noteworthy parts changes occurred in 1959. In some of the midrange metal box sets, the lids for the parts cans were painted red and had no lettering. Also, the (MC) 1" x 2½" Base Plate, which had been made with rounded edges, now had square and sharp ones. The (MJ) Electro Magnet came painted silver and not red as in the past. And the (A49) Electric Engine had the color of its motor housing changed from royal blue back to robin's egg blue. Later in the year, the gearbox was modified. In the past, it had been assembled with nuts and bolts. Beginning now, those parts were replaced with crimped metal tabs that make it

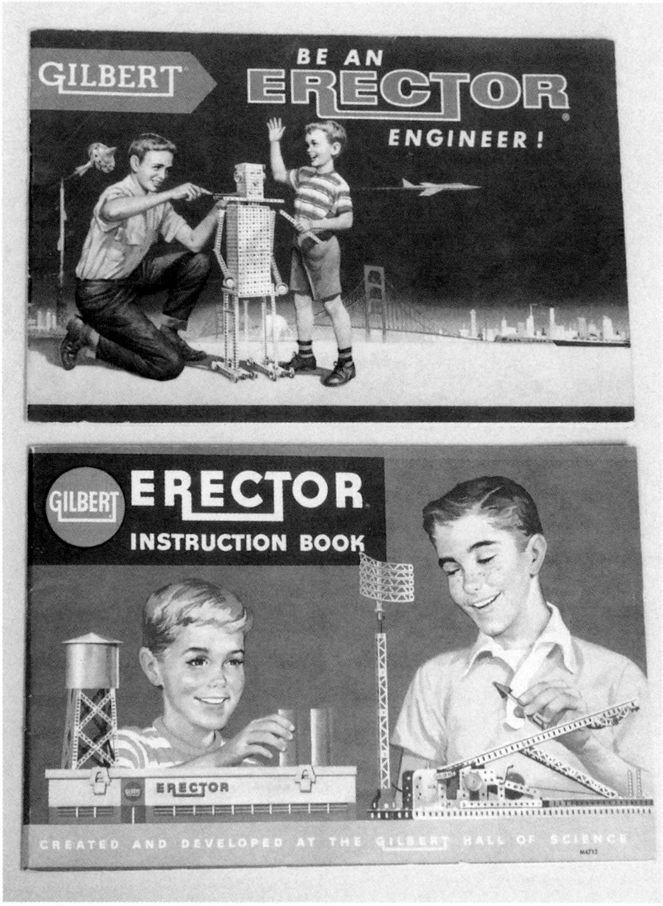

Two new instruction manual covers were introduced in 1959. Top: M4263 appeared early in the year. Bottom: M4295 appeared late.

difficult to open these gearboxes for repair or modification.

Gilbert also introduced a new type of Erector known as "Space Age Erector." This system was composed of plastic parts that were designed to build rocket, aircraft, and spacecraft models. The parts were produced in burgundy and gray, and a black base was included to display the various models. Also included was a sheet of labels (stickers) with military lettering and insignias.

Only one size of Space Age Erector was available in 1959, though that changed next year. Set No. 18000 came in a cardboard box (that also changed in 1960) that measured 18" x 10" x 1". The outside of the lid was done in four colors and pictured models of jets, rockets, and missiles. Inside the box was a yellow cardboard display insert that divided it into three sections. The instruction manual was mounted in the center, and parts were packed on either side. This attractive set apparently was not a big seller, since it is hard to find today.

Tube Sets

By 1959 all the cardboard boxes in the regular Erector line had been replaced with tubes, and now there were three of them. The two smallest sets, Nos. 10011 and 10021, ran unchanged from 1958, except for the instruction sheets. Last year they were printed on blue paper and the models were illustrated in white; this year the paper was white and the drawings were done in blue.

Set No. 10032 was a continuation of No. 10031 from 1958, but now it was packed in a tube that measured 14" high and 5" in diameter. This container was adorned in the same fashion as the two smaller sets, with a picture of two boys building the Mysterious Walking Giant. Unlike the two smaller sets, there were no holes in the tube and no instructions for incorporating the tube into model building.

Metal Box Sets

The same six metal box sets from last year were continued in 1959, but with changes in the set numbers, names, and packaging and—for the larger sets—the inclusion of new parts. The midrange sets, Nos. 10042 through 10073, started the year with a cardboard inner lid insert and finished it with inner lid lithography. With the exception of the multicolored lid inserts for the midrange sets, the color of the upper- and lower-level cardboard inserts used in the metal box sets was blue.

Set No. 10042, the smallest of the metal box sets, and was called "The Automatic Radar Scope Set." New lithography on the outside of the lid pictured a boy playing with the Radar Scope. During the first part of 1959, it came with an inner lid insert printed in red and white on a yellow background. It was a handsome set, the only one with red printing on the lid insert. The inner lid inserts for other midrange sets were printed in blue and white on a yellow background.

Set No. 10053, the Rocket Launcher Set, was a special one. First, the lithography on the outside of the box was completely changed. The colors were different, and the picture was of a boy with a Rocket Launcher. But what really made this set special was that Gilbert chose it to be *the* set to commemorate the 50th anniversary of his venture into the toy business. A unique label that read "50th Anniversary Special" was affixed to the outside of the lid.

Because of the inclusion of the new conveyor belt system, No. 10063 was named "The Action Conveyor Set" in 1959. (Its previous name, "The Steam Engine Set," made it sound old-fashioned.) The outer lid lithography was new and pictured a boy playing with a conveyor model. To build these models, Gilbert added more parts, including a Car Truck, Strips, a Stack, Flanged Wheels, and a Sheave Pulley.

Set No. 10073 was packed in a much different and simpler fashion than last year. The special box for the Erector Sound Effects Kit was gone, and most of the sound effects parts were packed on a blue cardboard display insert that fit into the compartment on the right side of the box (where the boiler had been). A second insert shared this compartment, and on it were mounted the Rocket and Stacks. The upper layer of the center compartment was composed of two parts display trays constructed from (MN) Base Plates and a blue cardboard display insert that fit around the boiler, which was packed in the right front corner of the center compartment. Parts in the lower level came in plastic bags resting on a blue cardboard liner.

Set No. 10073 was upgraded with additional parts, including a Crown Gear, 72 Tooth Gear, and Spring, all for use in building the DEW Line Radar. All the conveyor model parts were also included.

The Amusement Park Set, now designated No. 10083, reached the pinnacle of its development in 1959. For with the addition of the Conveyor Belt and Ball Bearing System, the contents of this set reached a level never to be equaled.

Set No. 18000, Space Age Erector, made its debut in 1959, packed in a cardboard box.

In 1959 Gilbert chose The Rocket Launcher Set to commemorate the 50th anniversary of his toy company. Note the unique label on the box lid of this special version of No. 10053.

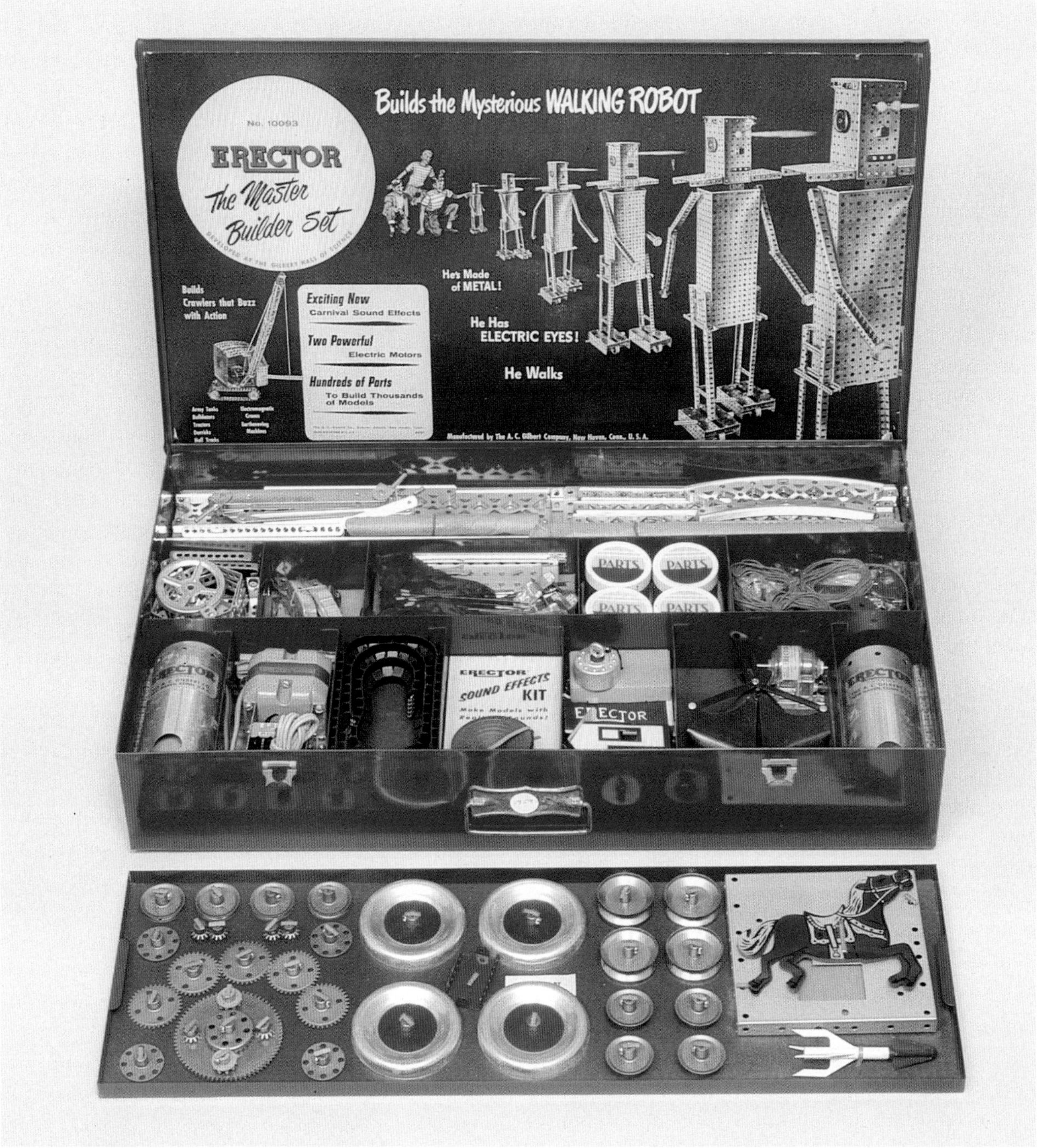

With the addition of the Ball Bearing System and Conveyor Belt, the version of The Master Builder Set from 1959 marked the pinnacle of Erector's evolution after the Classic Period.

Set No. 10083 was still packed in its heavy-gauge steel box, but there were some cosmetic changes. First, the label on the outside of the box was new. Since the early 1930s, metal box sets had been graced by a round label with a caption that read "Erector—the World's Greatest Toy." Since the advent of lithographed boxes for the midrange sets in 1957, the only sets to use this classic label were the two top ones. But now this wonderful label was gone forever, replaced by a 7" x 10½" label that pictured boys building the Mysterious Walking Giant. This was the same scene as was used of the 1958 instruction manual cover.

Set No. 10093 underwent the same outer lid label change as did The Amusement Park Set; like the latter, the contents of The Master Builder Set reached an all-time high. The color of the cardboard parts display insert on the tray was changed from black to blue.

Erector System Modifications for 1959

I. New Parts

(TA) Conveyor Belt, 62"
(TB) Ball Bearing
(TC) Ball Bearing Retainer Plate

SETS IN THE ERECTOR SYSTEM 1956–59

	Box Size	1956	1957	1958	1959
Cardboard Box Sets		No. 1½, No. 2½, No. 3½	No. 100, No. 1½, No. 2½, No. 3½, No. 6½	No. 10026 No. 10031	N/A
Tube Sets		N/A	N/A	No. 10011, No. 10021	No. 10011, No. 10021, No. 10032
Metal Box Sets	16" x 8" x 3"	No. 4½	No. 5½ (10041) Motorized	No. 10041 Power Model	No. 10042 Automatic Radar Scope
	16" x 10" x 3"	No. 6½	No. 6½ (10051) Electric Engine	No. 10052 Rocket Launcher	No. 10053 Rocket Launcher
	18" x 10" x 3"	No. 7½	No. 7½ (10061) Engineer's	No. 10062 Steam Engine	No. 10063 Action Conveyor
	20" x 12" x 3"	No. 8½	No. 8½ (10071) All Electric	No. 10072 Musical Ferris Wheel	No. 10073 Musical Ferris Wheel
	22" x 13" x 3"	No. 10½	No. 10½ (10080) Amusement Park	No. 10082 Amusement Park	No. 10083 Amusement Park
	24" x 14" x 4"	No. 12½	No. 12½ (10091) Master Builder	No. 10092 Master Builder	No. 10093 Master Builder

II. Modified Parts
(MC) 1" x 2½" Base Plate, with sharp, 90-degree corners
(A49) Electric Engine, with permanently assembled gearbox

III. Noteworthy Parts Colors and Finishes
(MJ) Electro Magnet, painted silver
(A49) Electric Engine, with robin's egg blue motor housing
(P14A686) Rocket, with yellow body (early) or white body (late)
( ) Parts Can Lids, painted red and unlettered for the midrange sets

Listings of 1959 Erector Sets

Gd VG Exc Inv Org

NO. 10011 The Beginner's Set
Came in a cardboard tube 11" high and 3½" in diameter, with twist-off metal lid; pictured two boys building robot; sold for $1.98. **20 30 50 +10 N/A**

NO. 10021 The Young Builder's Set
Featured the (FP) Disc Wheels. Came in a cardboard tube 12" high and 4½" in diameter, with twist-off metal lid; pictured two boys building robot; sold for $2.98.
25 35 60 +10 N/A

NO. 10032 The Engineer's Set
Featured the angle girders and large base plates. Came in a cardboard tube 14" high and 5" in diameter, with twist-off metal lid; pictured two boys building robot; sold for $4.89.
30 40 70 +15 N/A

NO. 10042 The Automatic Radar Scope Set
Featured the (DC3) 3 Volt Motor. Came in a lithographed metal box 16" x 8" x 3" that pictured boy playing with Radar Scope. Two-layer set with removable cardboard parts display; early version had inner lid cardboard display insert with manual mounted on insert; late version had lithographed inner lid with manual mounted on lid with paper fasteners; sold for $9.98.
40 60 100 +20 +25

NO. 10052 The Rocket Launcher Set
Featured the (A49) Electric Engine and Rocket and built Rocket Launcher. Came in a lithographed metal box 16" x 10" x 3" that pictured a boy playing with Rocket Launcher and had commemorative label on outer lid announcing this as Gilbert's 50th Anniversary set. Two-layer set with removable cardboard parts display; early version had inner lid cardboard display insert with manual mounted on insert; late version had lithographed inner lid with manual mounted on lid with paper fasteners; sold for $18.95. **60 95 160 +30 +40**

NO. 10063 The Action Conveyor Set
Featured the (T) Boiler and Conveyor Belt and built conveyor models. Came in a lithographed metal box 18" x 10" x 3" that pictured boy playing with conveyor model. Two-layer set with removable cardboard parts display; early version had inner lid cardboard display insert with manual mounted on insert; late version had lithographed inner lid with manual mounted on lid with paper fasteners; sold for $24.98. **50 70 120 +20 +35**

NO. 10073 The Musical Ferris Wheel Set
Featured the (MJ) Electro Magnet and Sound Effects Kit and built Musical Ferris Wheel and Bascule Bridge. Came in a lithographed metal box 20" x 12" x 3" that pictured boy playing with Ferris Wheel. Two-layer set with three removable parts display trays, one cardboard and two constructed from (MN) Base Plates; early version had inner lid cardboard display insert with manual mounted on insert; late version had lithographed inner lid with manual mounted on lid with paper fasteners; sold for $34.98.
120 180 300 +60 +100

NO. 10083 The Amusement Park Set
Featured the truck parts, giant flywheel, parachutes,

1959 CONTENTS LIST

SET NO.		10011	10021[1]	10032[2]	10042	10053	10063	10073	10083	10093[3]
P7	7/8" PULLEY	4	4	4	4	4	4	0	0	0
P7A	1 1/8" PULLEY	0	0	0	0	0	0	4	4	4
P12	CROWN GEAR	0	0	0	0	0	0	1	1	1
P13	12 TOOTH PINION GEAR, 1/8"	0	0	0	0	1	1	2	2	2
P13B	12 TOOTH PINION GEAR, 7/23"	0	0	0	0	0	0	1	4	4
P15	COUPLING	0	0	0	1	2	2	2	2	2
P20	5 HOLE STRIP—FORMED	0	0	0	0	0	2	2	8	8
P24	CRANK	1	1	1	1	1	1	1	1	1
P33	SMALL SCREW DRIVER	1	1	1	1	1	0	0	0	0
P34	HANK OF STRING	0	1	1	1	1	1	1	3	3
P37	COLLAR	1	4	4	5	6	7	9	20	20
P48	MITRE GEAR	0	0	0	0	2	2	2	2	2
P57A	2 1/8" AXLE	1	1	1	1	1	1	1	1	8
P57D	6" AXLE	0	1	2	0	0	0	0	1	1
P57E	8" AXLE	0	0	0	0	0	0	0	2	2
P57F	12" AXLE	0	0	0	0	0	0	1	2	2
P57JA	7 1/2" AXLE	0	0	0	0	0	0	0	4	4
P57K	10" AXLE	0	0	0	0	0	0	0	0	2
P57N	3 1/4" AXLE	0	0	0	0	0	0	0	2	2
P79	CAR TRUCK	4	4	4	4	4	5	5	5	5
A	2 1/2" GIRDER	4	4	4	4	4	4	4	4	6
B	5" GIRDER	4	4	4	8	8	8	12	12	12
C	10" GIRDER	2	8	8	8	8	8	36	52	52
D	2 1/2" CURVED GIRDER	4	4	4	4	4	4	4	4	4
E	5" CURVED GIRDER	0	2	2	2	4	4	26	26	26
F	5 HOLE STRIP	0	0	0	2	2	3	3	3	16
G	7 HOLE STRIP	0	0	0	2	2	2	2	6	8
H	11 HOLE STRIP	0	0	0	4	4	5	5	16	16
I	21 HOLE STRIP	0	0	0	2	2	2	4	18	18
J	41 HOLE STRIP	0	0	0	0	0	0	2	2	4
M	SMALL DOUBLE ANGLE	0	0	0	0	0	2	6	24	24
N	LONG DOUBLE ANGLE	2	4	4	4	4	4	4	16	16
O	PAWL	0	0	0	0	1	2	2	16	16
T	BOILER	0	0	0	0	0	1	1	2	2
U	BOILER TOP	0	0	0	0	0	1	1	1	1
W	STACK	0	0	0	0	0	4	4	4	4
Z	FLANGED WHEEL 15/16" DIA	0	0	00	0	8	8	8	8	
AA	ECCENTRIC CRANK	0	0	0	0	0	0	0	6	6
AE	SPRING	0	0	0	0	0	0	1	1	2
AF	SMALL HOOK	1	1	1	1	1	1	1	1	1
AJ	PAPER ERECTOR FLAG	0	0	0	1	1	1	1	1	1
AQ	SHEAVE PULLEY	0	0	0	0	0	1	1	4	5
AS	2 7/8" AXLE	0	0	0	2	2	3	3	4	4
AT	4" AXLE	2	2	2	2	2	2	2	2	4
BE	6" ANGLE GIRDER	0	0	4	4	4	4	4	4	12
BH	SOLID COLLAR	0	0	0	0	0	0	0	2	2
BL	SMALL WASHER	6	12	12	12	12	12	12	12	18
BN	REGULAR TURRET PLATE	0	0	0	2	2	4	4	4	4
BT	PIERCED DISC	1	1	1	2	2	2	4	4	4
BY	11 HOLE FIBRE STRIP	0	0	0	0	0	0	2	2	2
CA	SIGNAL ARM	0	0	0	0	0	0	0	2	2
CH	RIGHT ANGLE	8	12	12	14	14	14	30	42	42

1959 CONTENTS LIST

SET NO.		10011	10021[1]	10032[2]	10042	10053	10063	10073	10083	10093[3]
CJ	36 TOOTH GEAR	0	0	0	0	2	3	3	3	5
CR	SPECIAL TURRET PLATE WITH HUB	0	0	0	0	0	0	0	2	2
CS	WHEEL SEGMENT	0	0	0	0	0	0	0	8	8
CZ	7" AXLE	0	0	0	2	2	2	4	4	4
DB	MOTOR PULLEY	0	0	0	2	1	1	1	1	2
DE	STEERING COLUMN	0	0	0	0	0	0	4	1	1
DK	FLAT SPRING	0	0	0	0	0	0	0	4	4
DO	STEERING WHEEL WITH HUB	0	0	0	0	0	0	0	1	1
DP	12" ANGLE GIRDER	0	0	4	4	4	4	4	4	6
DS	COTTER PIN	0	0	0	0	0	0	0	1	1
EI	STD. GEAR BOX SIDE PLATE	0	0	0	0	2	2	2	2	2
EX	BIG CHANNEL GIRDER 12"	0	0	0	0	0	0	0	8	8
EY	BIG CHANNEL GIRDER 6"	0	0	0	0	0	0	0	4	8
EZ	BIG CHAN. GIRDER CURVED 6"	0	0	0	0	0	0	0	9	9
FA	1¾" x 8-32 SCREW	0	0	0	0	0	0	0	12	12
FP(X239)	SMALL DISC WHEEL	0	4	0	0	0	0	0	0	0
FD	HINGED LOOP	0	0	0	0	0	0	0	2	2
LX	STEERING COLUMN BRACKET	0	0	0	0	0	0	0	1	1
MA	RADIATOR	0	0	0	0	0	0	0	1	1
MB	18½" ANGLE GIRDER	0	0	0	0	0	0	0	2	2
MC	BASE PLATE 1" x 2½"	2	2	2	2	2	2	8	8	8
MD	BASE PLATE 2½" x 5"	1	1	1	1	1	1	4	4	4
ME	BASE PLATE 1" x 4"	0	0	0	0	0	0	0	4	4
MF	BASE PLATE 1" x 5"	0	2	4	4	4	4	8	21	21
MG	RADIATOR HOOD	0	0	0	0	0	0	0	1	1
MH	LARGE 3" DISC WHEEL	0	0	4	4	4	4	4	4	4
MI	FRONT AXLE UNIT	0	0	0	0	0	0	0	1	1
MJ	ELECTRO MAGNET WITH CORD	0	0	0	0	0	0	1	1	1
MM	WRENCH	0	0	0	1	1	1	1	1	1
MN	12" BASE PLATE	0	0	2	2	4	4	6	6	6
MO	3" ANGLE GIRDER	0	0	4	4	4	4	4	4	8
MV	FLAT CAR TRUCK	0	0	0	0	0	2	4	4	12
MW	NUT HOLDER	0	0	0	1	1	1	1	1	1
MX	HOUSE	0	0	0	0	1	1	1	1	1
MY	2½" x 2½" BASE PLATE	0	0	0	1	1	1	1	1	1
MZ	BEARING BLOCK	0	0	0	0	1	1	1	1	1
NH	LAMP SOCKET UNIT	0	0	0	0	0	1	2	2	2
NI	BULB, 1½ VOLT (CLEAR)	0	0	0	0	0	0	2	2	2
P12N677	BULB, 1.2 VOLT (RED)	0	0	0	0	0	1	1	1	1
NJ	BATTERY HOLDER	0	0	0	2	0	1	1	1	4
NK	RATCHET	0	0	0	0	0	0	2	2	2
NL	BOLSTER BRACKET	0	0	0	0	0	0	0	0	4
NS	41 HOLE STRIP —FORMED	0	0	0	0	0	0	0	2	2
NU	PARACHUTE	0	0	0	0	0	0	0	4	4
NW	TREAD	0	0	0	0	0	0	0	0	2

1959 CONTENTS LIST

SET NO.		10011	10021[1]	10032[2]	10042	10053	10063	10073	10083	10093[3]
NX	TREAD PULLEY	0	0	0	0	0	0	0	0	4
NZ	PLASTIC SCREW DRIVER	0	0	0	1	1	1	1	1	1
OB	TREAD PIN	0	0	0	0	0	0	0	0	2
OE	6" FLEXIBLE COUPLING	0	0	0	0	1	1	1	1	1
OF	HORSE	0	0	0	0	0	0	0	6	6
OG	21 HOLE STRIP—FORMED	0	0	0	0	0	0	0	2	2
OH	72 TOOTH GEAR	0	0	0	0	0	0	1	1	1
OI	SEGMENT OF 72 TOOTH GEAR	0	0	0	0	0	0	0	1	1
TA	CONVEYOR BELT (62")	0	0	0	0	0	1	1	1	1
TB	BALL BEARING	0	0	0	0	0	0	0	6	6
TC	BEARING RETAINER PLATE	0	0	0	0	0	0	0	1	1
P14A686	ROCKET	0	0	0	0	1	1	1	1	1
X14B663	CLAM SHELL BUCKET	0	0	0	0	0	0	0	0	1
P14B147	BASE PLATE	0	0	0	0	0	0	1	1	1
P14A143	GEAR BRACKET	0	0	0	0	0	0	1	1	1
P8554A	TURNTABLE	0	0	0	0	0	0	1	1	1
P14A208	RECORD	0	0	0	0	0	0	1	1	1
PA10721	TURNTABLE BUSHING	0	0	0	0	0	0	1	1	1
P99C	BOLSTER BRACKET	0	0	0	0	0	0	1	1	1
X14N884	SOUND PARTS ASSEMBLY	0	0	0	0	0	0	1	1	1
X14A134	CAM SHAFT ASSEMBLY	0	0	0	0	0	0	1	1	1
X14A137	TURNTABLE SHAFT ASSEMBLY	0	0	0	0	0	0	1	1	1
X14A139	LEVER & BRACKET ASSEMBLY	0	0	0	0	0	0	1	1	1
XA14B295	REPRODUCER ASSEMBLY	0	0	0	0	0	0	1	1	1
XA14B269	NEEDLE	0	0	0	0	0	0	1	1	1
P13A566B	RUBBER COUPLER	0	0	0	0	0	0	1	1	1
P14A145	BRACKET	0	0	0	0	0	0	1	1	1
P14A146	POWER SHAFT	0	0	0	0	0	0	1	1	1
W1A82	WASHER	0	0	0	0	0	0	7	7	7
W84	WASHER	0	0	0	0	0	0	1	1	1
PA1139	FIBER WASHER	0	0	0	0	0	0	1	1	1
W153	DISHED WASHER	0	0	0	0	0	0	1	1	1
PA10721	ADAPTOR	0	0	0	0	0	0	1	1	1
N1	HEX NUT	0	0	0	0	0	0	1	1	1
	WOOD SCREWS	0	0	0	0	0	0	4	4	4
A49	ELECTRIC ENGINE	0	0	0	0	1	1	1	1	1
DC3	3 VOLT MOTOR	0	0	0	1	0	0	0	0	1
N21	8-32 SQUARE NUT	23	45	60	88	93	93	169	271	359
S51	¼" x 8-32 SCREW	20	35	50	80	84	84	162	240	260
S52	½" x 8-32 SCREW	0	0	0	0	4	4	4	8	8
S57	1⅜" x 8-32 SCREW	0	0	0	0	0	4	4	4	4
S62	⅞" x 8-32 SCREW	3	6	6	8	8	10	18	64	64

1. Set No. 10021 also contained two 5" axles.

2. Set No. 10032 also contained one 5" axle.

3. Set No. 10093 also contained an offset wrench.

	Gd	VG	Exc	Inv	Org

carousel horses, Sound Effects Kit, and ball bearing system and built Parachute Jump, Merry-Go-Round, and other amusement park models as well as Giant Power Plant. Came in a red metal box 22" x 13" x 3", with rectangular outer lid label that pictured two boys with robot. Two-layer set with three removable parts display trays constructed from (MN) Base Plates; sold for $49.98.

240 360 600 +120 +150

NO. 10093 The Master Builder Set

Featured the Clamshell Bucket, Treads, Sound Effects Kit, and ball bearing system and built the Mysterious Walking Robot and construction equipment. Came in a red metal box 24" x 14" x 3", with rectangular outer lid label that pictured two boys with robot. Two-layer set with removable parts display tray with blue cardboard insert; sold for $74.98. **480 720 1200 +240 +300**

NO. 18000 The Space Age Erector

Featured plastic parts and built jets, rockets, and space missiles. Came in a cardboard box 18" x 10" x 1", with lid picturing jet plane and other space age models. One-layer set with yellow cardboard insert; sold for $3.98.

80 120 200 +40 +50

THE 1960–61 ERECTOR LINE

Without a doubt, 1960 was a dark year in Erector history, for it marked the beginning of the final demise of the system. The negative, cost-cutting trends that surfaced in 1959 accelerated, and they drastically affected the largest sets, those most coveted by collectors. Included were major changes in packaging and packaging materials, as well as significant reductions in contents.

The first trend saw the introduction of Styrofoam parts trays. Only three sets were affected: The Rocket Launcher Set, The Amusement Park Set, and The Master Builder Set. These trays were designed to fit snugly into the set boxes, and special compartments were formed in the Styrofoam to hold specific parts. The production cost savings was undoubtedly substantial, especially for the two largest sets, which until now had come with parts clipped in place on cardboard display inserts or parts display trays. But the Styrofoam trays were less attractive, and, since parts were not attached to these trays, they rarely stayed in place.

The second negative trend was more drastic (and heart-rending, in the author's opinion), and it affected the two top sets. Until now, the set boxes for The Amusement Park Set and The Master Builder Set were the only ones to escape the cost-cutting measures that occurred in 1957, when the weight of steel used to construct them was reduced, and lithography replaced the highly recognized bright finish and the oval label. Starting in 1960, instead of big red, heavy-gauge steel boxes, these top sets came packed in a "double box": a container formed by riveting together two boxes from smaller sets.

The Amusement Park Set (No. 10084) came in a box formed from two 16" x 10" Rocket Launcher boxes, and The Master Builder Set (No. 10094) came in one assembled from a pair of 18" x 10" Automatic Conveyor boxes. The boxes for the largest sets had double lids that opened on the sides, were lithographed, and pictured featured models on the outside and colorful text on the inside. This new packaging technique reduced manufacturing costs, as it eliminated the need to produce the two most expensive set boxes. But the sets ended up looking cheap next to their predecessors from the previous year.

The third trend was a reduction in components in the system, namely the elimination of parts for the Erector Sound Effects Kit, which was the major accomplishment of the post-Renaissance Period. Although its parts were delicate and somewhat difficult to work with, Erector collectors are fond of them. But the production costs involved with this item (involving twenty-one different parts) were high, and eliminating it from the three top sets (while maintaining or even increasing the set prices) saved money.

Several other parts changes occurred in 1960. An interesting new part was introduced: The (P15B528) Remote Control was a handheld battery pack for use with the (DC3) 3 Volt Motor. Mounted on it were two buttons, so the motor could be operated in forward or reverse. Two sets contained the (DC3): Nos. 10037, which came in a tube, and 10042, which came in a metal box. Surprisingly, only No. 10037 came with the (P15B528); No. 10042 had two (NJ) Battery Holders.

Other parts were modified. The (AQ) Sheave Pulley was made of black plastic instead of steel. The (NZ) Plastic Screw Driver had its 2½" transparent yellow plastic handle reduced to 1¾". A new version of the (MH) Large 3" Disc Wheel was created. Used only in the tube sets, it was completely cadmium-plated, with no red cardboard hubcap.

Another modification occurred with the housing for the (A49) Electric Engine. Now it came with raised letters that read "The A. C. Gilbert Co./New Haven, Conn. U.S.A./A49." This version continued until the end of traditional Erector production in 1962. Also the lids for the parts cans were different. Instead of being lithographed as in the past, they were tin-plated and embossed with "Erector Parts." Finally, starting in 1961 and through 1962, the label on the (T) Boiler was eliminated. In its place, the word "Erector" was printed in red letters.

Space Age Erector

Major revisions were made with Space Age Erector in 1960. When this system was introduced in 1959, only one set was offered, and it came in a cardboard box. Now the line was expanded to four sets, and all came in tubes that were capped with a blue, plastic "nose-cone" that made the container look like a rocket. This nose-cone had a slot so it could serve as a display base for the models. The black plastic display base offered with the set in 1959 was dropped.

Tube Sets

Two major changes occurred in the line of tube sets. First, all but the largest of them came with new artwork and printing on the body of the tube. The dominant colors were brown and white, and the scene for each size was different. These new scenes pictured a boy playing with a simple model that could be built with the parts in the tube. The scene on the old tube had shown the Mysterious Walking Giant, which could be built only with the largest set that Gilbert produced.

The second change was the addition of a new and larger set. Named "The Motorized Remote Control Set," it was designated No. 10037 and came in a tube that was 15¾" high and 5" in diameter. This set really was new and fit between Nos. 10032 (descended from old No. 3½) and 10042

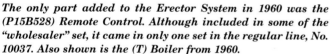

The only part added to the Erector System in 1960 was the (P15B528) Remote Control. Although included in some of the "wholesaler" set, it came in only one set in the regular line, No. 10037. Also shown is the (T) Boiler from 1960.

Space Age Erector was redesigned in 1960 and packed in tubes to make it look like a rocket. The tube sets, like this No. 18030, are easier to find than the ones in the cardboard boxes from 1959.

(descended from old No. 4½). It featured the (DC3) 3 Volt Motor and (P15B528) Remote Control. By far, this was the most sophisticated set ever to be packed in a cardboard tube.

Set No. 10037 was offered in 1960 only, and it probably was a very poor seller. The price of this largest tube set was only $2.00 less than that of the smallest metal box set, and it is likely that most Erector buyers paid the marginal extra amount for the more impressive container the latter featured.

Other than the modifications already mentioned, the tube sets was similar to those from 1959. Set No. 10011 was continued through the end of 1961 with no changes. Set No. 10032 came with modified (MH) Disc Wheels from this point on. These new wheels were plated only and lacked the red cardboard hubcaps.

Metal Box Sets

Six sets were offered in metal boxes in 1960. They were basically a continuation of the 1959 lineup, but each was somehow modified. No. 10042 had its named changed from The Radar Scope Set to "The Radar Scanner Set." Other than the parts modifications already discussed, it was identical to its predecessor from 1959.

The Rocket Launcher Set was more significantly modified. First, since the anniversary year had ended, the commemorative label was removed from the box lid. Second, No. 10053 was the only midrange set to get Styrofoam parts display trays, and there were two of them. When the upper tray was removed, all the parts were readily accessible for easy model building.

Set No. 10063 also had a new name. Called The Action Conveyor Set in 1959, it now was known as "The Automatic Conveyor Set." Other than the parts modifications mentioned above, this set was identical to the 1959 offering.

Because of the deletion of the Erector Sound Effects Kit, last year's Musical Ferris Wheel was not musical anymore. So No. 10073 became No. 10074, now called "The Ferris Wheel Set." Other than the elimination of the sound effects parts and other parts changes previously noted, No. 10074 was similar to its predecessor from 1959. The text on the lid was changed, of course, with the word "musical" deleted. The arrangement of parts differed as well, with a 36 Tooth Gear, Car Trucks, Bearing Block, and a Screw Driver packed

The artwork on No. 10032 and all but the largest tube sets was new in 1960.

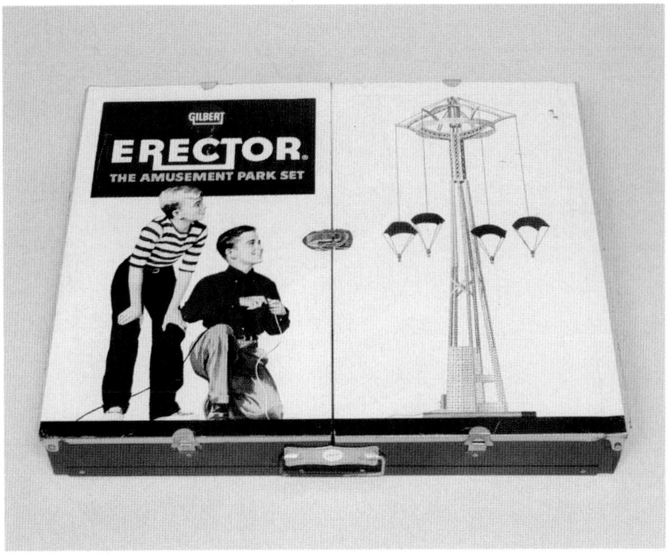

Cost-cutting measures affected even the most expensive sets by 1960. Now No. 10084 (The Amusement Park Set) was packed in a flimsy, double-lidded box.

on the insert that in 1959 had held the sound effects parts.

Set No. 10084 came packed in an entirely new container in 1960. The wonderful 22" x 13" x 3" metal box that had housed this set for over a decade was replaced by a double box, constructed from two No. 10053 size boxes. The new box for The Amusement Park Set measured 20" x 16" x 3" and had a partition down the center where the two smaller boxes were joined. The lid was in two parts and opened down the middle. The outside of the lid was lithographed in red, white, and brown and pictured two boys playing with the Parachute Jump. Incidentally, even though the model had been revised in 1949, the old version had been pictured on the inner lid label of the old set box. But now, after 10 years, Gilbert got it right and pictured the modern model. The inside of the lids were lithographed, and the text promoted the models the set would build.

The inside of the box for No. 10084 was partitioned into two sections, with the left one having two layers of parts. The lower layer was a heavy white cardboard insert with spaces for the motor, parts cans, house, and three parts boxes. The upper one was a Styrofoam parts display tray that held most of the gears, wheels, and pulleys. There were holes in the tray that fit around the motor and house. The right section of the box was subdivided into four compartments by heavy cardboard dividers, with the balance of the parts packed loose there.

Set No. 10094 experienced changes similar to No. 10084. Its double box was made from two No. 10063 size boxes and measured 20" x 18" x 3". The lids opened from the sides and were lithographed in red, white and brown. Pictured was a boy playing with the Mysterious Walking Giant. The inside of the lid was also lithographed, and the text promoted some of the models this set would build.

As with No. 10084, The Master Builder Set was partitioned into two sections where the two boxes were joined. The left side was further subdivided into five compartments by heavy cardboard dividers, and many of the parts were packed loose in these compartments. The right side had two layers of parts. The lower layer was a heavy white cardboard insert with spaces for the motor, parts cans, the Clam Shell, and four parts boxes. The upper one was a Styrofoam parts display tray that held most of the gears, wheels, and pulleys. There were holes in this tray that allowed it to fit around the motor and the Clam Shell.

With the exception of the parts modifications already described, the 1960 line of metal box sets continued through 1961 with only one change. In 1960, both the outside and the inside of the box bodies were painted red. But in 1961, only

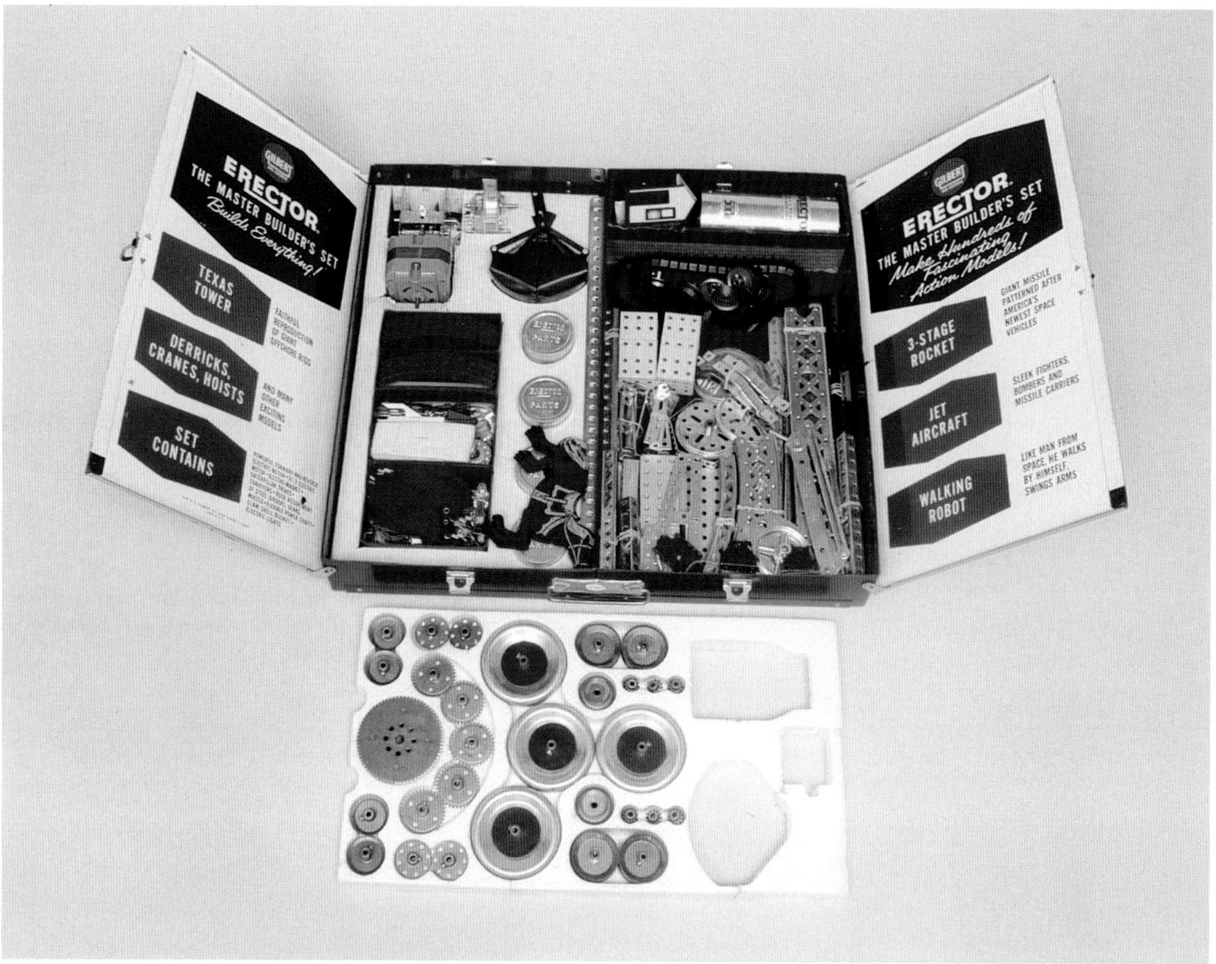

Like The Amusement Park Set, No. 10094 (The Master Builder Set) suffered from Gilbert's cost-cutting measures in 1960. Note the use of Styrofoam display inserts, which began at this point.

the outside was painted; the inside was oxidized with a gold patina finish. Although this modification did not occur at the very beginning of the year, it is one of the best ways to distinguish sets from 1960 from their 1961 counterparts.

Erector System Modifications for 1960

I. New Parts
(P15B528) Remote Control

II. Modified Parts
(AQ) Sheave Pulley, black plastic instead of steel
(MH) Large 3" Disc Wheel, all cadmium-plated with no red cardboard hubcap (small sets only)
(NZ) Plastic Screw Driver, with 1¾" handle
(A49) Electric Engine, with raised lettering on the motor housing
( ) Parts Can Lid, tin-plated with embossed lettering

III. Deleted Parts
( ) All 21 parts specific to the Sound Effects System

Erector System Modifications for 1961

I. Noteworthy Parts Colors and Finishes
(T) Boiler, with painted lettering instead of label

Listings of 1960–61 Erector Sets

Gd VG Exc Inv Org

NO. 1001 The Beginner's Set
Came in a cardboard tube 11" high and 3½" in diameter, with twist-off metal lid; pictured a boy building robot in brown and white; sold for $1.98 in 1960 and 1961.
20 30 50 +10 N/A

NO. 10021 The Young Builder's Set
Featured the (FP) Disc Wheels. Came in a cardboard tube 12" high and 4½" in diameter, with twist-off metal lid; pictured a boy building robot in brown and white; sold for $2.98 in 1960 and 1961.
25 35 60 +10 N/A

NO. 10032 The Engineer's Set
Featured the angle girders and large base plates. Came in a cardboard tube 14" high and 5" in diameter, with twist-off metal lid; pictured a boy with crane in brown and white; sold for $4.98 in 1960 and 1961.
30 40 70 +15 N/A

NO. 10037 (1960) The Motorized Remote Control Set
Featured the (DC3) 3 Volt Motor and (P15B528) Remote

Gd	VG	Exc	Inv	Org

Control. Came in a cardboard tube 15¾" high and 5" in diameter, with twist-off metal lid; pictured two boys building Mysterious Walking Giant with blue background; sold for $7.98.

40	60	100	+20	N/A

NO. 10042 The Automatic Radar Scanner Set
Featured the (DC3) 3 Volt Motor. Came in a lithographed metal box 16" x 8" x 3" that pictured boy playing with Radar Scanner. Two-layer set with removable cardboard parts display tray; sold for $9.98 in 1960 and $10.98 in 1961.

40	60	100	+20	+25

NO. 10053 The Rocket Launcher Set
Featured the (A49) Electric Engine and Rocket and built Rocket Launcher. Came in a lithographed metal box 16" x 10" x 3" that pictured a boy playing with Rocket Launcher. Two-layer set with two Styrofoam parts display trays; sold for $18.98 in 1960 and 1961.

45	65	110	+20	+25

NO. 10063 The Automatic Conveyor Set
Featured the (T) Boiler and Conveyor Belt and built conveyor models. Came in a lithographed metal box 18" x 10" x 3" that pictured boy playing with conveyor model. Two-layer set with removable parts display tray; sold for $24.98 in 1960 and 1961.

50	70	120	+20	+35

NO. 10074 The Ferris Wheel Set
Featured the (MJ) Electro Magnet and built Ferris Wheel and Bascule Bridge. Came in a lithographed metal box 20" x 12" x 3" that pictured boy playing with Ferris Wheel. Two-layer set with three removable parts display trays, one cardboard and two constructed from (MN) Base Plates; sold for $37.98 in 1960 and $34.98 in 1961.

60	85	140	+30	+35

NO. 10084 The Amusement Park Set
Featured the truck parts, giant flywheel, parachutes, carousel horses, and ball bearing system and built Parachute Jump, Merry-Go-Round, and other amusement park models as well as Giant Power Plant. Came in a lithographed metal double box 20" x 16" x 3", with double lids hinged on the sides; outer lids pictured two boys playing with Parachute Jump. Two-layer set in left compartment with removable Styrofoam parts display tray; one-layer set in right compartment with cardboard dividers; sold for 49.98 in 1960 and 1961.

120	180	300	+60	+75

NO. 10094 The Master Builder Set
Featured the Clamshell Bucket, Treads, and ball bearing system and built the Mysterious Walking Giant and construction equipment. Came in a lithographed metal double box 20" x 18" x 3", with double lids hinged on the sides; outer lids pictured boy playing with Mysterious Walking Giant. Two-layer set in right compartment with removable Styrofoam parts display tray; one-layer set in left compartment with cardboard dividers; sold for $74.98 in 1960 and 1961.

320	480	800	+160	+200

NO. 18010 The Space Age Erector
Featured plastic parts and built jets, rockets, and space missiles. Came in a red, white, and blue cardboard tube 9¾" high and 3⅛" in diameter, with plastic "nose-cone" lid; sold for $1.98 in 1960 and 1961.

Gd	VG	Exc	Inv	Org
40	60	100	+20	N/A

NO. 18020 The Space Age Erector
Featured plastic parts and built jets, rockets, and space missiles. Came in a red, white, and blue cardboard tube 11½" high and 3½" in diameter, with plastic "nose-cone" lid; sold for $2.98 in 1960 and 1961.

50	70	120	+25	N/A

NO. 18030 The Space Age Erector
Featured plastic parts and built jets, rockets, and space missiles. Came in a red, white, and blue cardboard tube 14¼" high and 3⅝" in diameter, with plastic "nose-cone" lid; sold for $5.98 in 1960 and $4.98 in 1961.

55	85	140	+30	N/A

NO. 18040 The Space Age Erector
Featured plastic parts and built jets, rockets, and space missiles. Came in a red, white, and blue cardboard tube 17" high and 3⅝" in diameter, with plastic "nose-cone" lid; sold for $7.98 in 1960 and 1961.

80	120	200	+40	N/A

THE 1962 ERECTOR LINE

A great number of changes occurred in the 1962 line, the last of traditional Erector. These changes affected the cardboard container sets, both in the number of sets offered and the way they were packed; the entire line of sets, in terms of set names and numbers; and the instruction manual, with a wealth of new models and a new method of dividing the manual into sections. The 1962 offering represented a last-ditch effort to reduce production costs and increase sales by promoting Erector as a "space-age" toy.

In 1961, Gilbert offered three sets packed in sturdy cardboard tubes with metal twist-off lids. These 1961 sets were essentially a continuation of old Nos. 1½, 2½, and 3½. In 1962, the first disappeared forever, as it was deleted from the line. The remaining two sets came packed in a very different container.

Shaped like a milk carton, these containers were made from a lighter weight of cardboard than were the tube sets from last year. There was no metal lid; they simply folded at the top to open or close. These milk carton containers were obviously less expensive to produce than the heavy cardboard tubes that they replaced, but they looked cheap next to their counterparts from 1961.

Almost every set in the lineup came with a new name in 1962, and the vast majority of these new names focused on space technology. For example, "The Automatic Conveyor Set" became "The Cape Canaveral Set"; "The Ferris Wheel Set" became "The Lunar Drilling Rig Set"; and "The Amusement Park Set" became "The Astronaut Set." In fact, only The Engineer's Set, The Rocket Launcher Set, and The Master Builder Set retained their names.

There also were major (and confusing) modifications in the instruction manual. Prior to 1958, the manuals were divided into sections, one for each size of set (No. 1½ section, No. 2½ section, and so forth). Starting in 1958, the manual was divided in the same way, but set names were used instead of numbers. This made sense and was easily understood. But in 1962, the manual was further divided into 16 numerical sections, and the number of the section and the set

1960–61 CONTENTS LIST

SET NO.		10011	10021[1]	10032[2]	10037	10042	10053	10063	10074	10084	10094
P7	7/8" PULLEY	4	4	4	4	4	4	4	0	0	0
P7A	1 1/8" PULLEY	0	0	0	0	0	0	0	4	4	4
P12	CROWN GEAR	0	0	0	0	0	0	0	1	1	1
P13	12 TOOTH PINION GEAR, 1/8"	0	0	0	0	0	1	1	2	2	2
P13B	12 TOOTH PINION GEAR, 7/23"	0	0	0	0	0	0	0	1	4	4
P15	COUPLING	0	0	0	1	1	2	2	2	2	2
P20	FIVE HOLE STRIP—FORMED	0	0	0	0	0	0	2	2	8	8
P24	CRANK	1	1	1	1	1	1	1	1	1	1
P33	SMALL SCREW DRIVER	1	1	1	1	1	1	0	0	0	0
P34	HANK OF STRING	0	1	1	1	1	1	1	1	3	3
P37	COLLAR	1	4	4	4	5	6	7	9	20	20
P48	MITRE GEAR	0	0	0	0	0	0	2	2	2	2
P57A	2 1/8" AXLE	1	1	1	1	1	1	1	1	1	8
P57D	6" AXLE	0	1	2	2	0	0	0	0	1	1
P57E	8" AXLE	0	0	0	0	0	0	0	0	2	2
P57F	12" AXLE	0	0	0	0	0	0	0	1	2	2
P57JA	7 1/2" AXLE	0	0	0	0	0	0	0	0	4	4
P57K	10" AXLE	0	0	0	0	0	0	0	0	0	2
P57N	3 1/4" AXLE	0	0	0	0	0	0	0	0	2	2
P79	CAR TRUCK	4	4	4	4	4	4	5	5	5	5
A	2 1/2" GIRDER	4	4	4	4	4	4	4	4	4	6
B	5" GIRDER	4	4	4	4	8	8	8	12	12	12
C	10" GIRDER	2	8	8	8	8	8	8	36	52	52
D	2 1/2" CURVED GIRDER	4	4	4	4	4	4	4	4	4	4
E	5" CURVED GIRDER	0	2	2	2	2	4	4	26	26	26
F	5 HOLE STRIP	0	0	0	0	2	2	3	3	3	16
G	7 HOLE STRIP	0	0	0	0	2	2	2	2	6	8
H	11 HOLE STRIP	0	0	0	0	4	4	5	5	16	16
I	21 HOLE STRIP	0	0	0	0	2	2	2	4	18	18
J	41 HOLE STRIP	0	0	0	0	0	0	0	2	2	4
M	SMALL DOUBLE ANGLE	0	0	0	0	0	0	2	6	24	24
N	LONG DOUBLE ANGLE	2	4	4	4	4	4	4	4	16	16
O	PAWL	0	0	0	0	0	1	2	2	16	16
T	BOILER	0	0	0	0	0	0	1	1	2	2
U	BOILER TOP	0	0	0	0	0	0	1	1	1	1
W	STACK	0	0	0	0	0	0	4	4	4	4
Z	FLANGED WHEEL . 15/16" DIA	0	0	0	0	0	0	8	8	8	8
AA	ECCENTRIC CRANK	0	0	0	0	0	0	0	0	6	6
AE	SPRING	0	0	0	0	0	0	0	1	1	2
AF	SMALL HOOK	1	1	1	1	1	1	1	1	1	1
AJ	PAPER ERECTOR FLAG	0	0	0	0	1	1	1	1	1	1
AQ	SHEAVE PULLEY	0	0	0	0	0	0	1	1	4	5
AS	2 7/8" AXLE	0	0	0	0	2	2	3	3	4	4
AT	4" AXLE	2	2	2	2	2	2	2	2	2	4
BE	6" ANGLE GIRDER	0	0	4	4	4	4	4	4	4	12
BH	SOLID COLLAR	0	0	0	0	0	0	0	0	2	2
BL	SMALL WASHER	6	12	12	12	12	12	12	12	12	18

1960–61 CONTENTS LIST

SET NO.		10011	10021[1]	10032[2]	10037	10042	10053	10063	10074	10084	10094
BN	REGULAR TURRET PLATE	0	0	0	0	2	2	4	4	4	4
BT	PIERCED DISC	1	1	1	1	2	2	2	4	4	4
BY	11 HOLE FIBRE STRIP	0	0	0	0	0	0	0	2	2	2
CA	SIGNAL ARM	0	0	0	0	0	0	0	0	2	2
CH	RIGHT ANGLE	8	12	12	12	14	14	14	30	42	42
CJ	36 TOOTH GEAR	0	0	0	0	0	2	3	3	3	5
CR	SPECIAL TURRET PLATE WITH HUB	0	0	0	0	0	0	0	0	2	2
CS	WHEEL SEGMENT	0	0	0	0	0	0	0	0	8	8
CZ	7" AXLE	0	0	0	2	2	2	2	4	4	4
DB	MOTOR PULLEY	0	0	0	2	1	1	1	1	1	2
DE	STEERING COLUMN	0	0	0	0	0	0	0	0	1	1
DK	FLAT SPRING	0	0	0	0	0	0	0	0	4	4
DO	STEERING WHEEL WITH HUB	0	0	0	0	0	0	0	0	1	1
DP	12" ANGLE GIRDER	0	0	4	4	4	4	4	4	4	6
DS	COTTER PIN	0	0	0	0	0	0	0	0	1	1
EI	STD. GEAR BOX SIDE PLATE	0	0	0	0	0	2	2	2	2	2
EX	BIG CHANNEL GIRDER 12"	0	0	0	0	0	0	0	0	8	8
EY	BIG CHANNEL GIRDER 6"	0	0	0	0	0	0	0	0	4	8
EZ	BIG CHAN. GIRDER CURVED 6"	0	0	0	0	0	0	0	0	9	9
FA	1¾" x 8-32 SCREW	0	0	0	0	0	0	0	0	12	12
FP(X239)	SMALL DISC WHEEL	0	4	0	4	0	0	0	0	0	0
FD	HINGED LOOP	0	0	0	0	0	0	0	0	2	2
LX	STEERING COLUMN BRACKET	0	0	0	0	0	0	0	0	1	1
MA	RADIATOR	0	0	0	0	0	0	0	0	1	1
MB	18½" ANGLE GIRDER	0	0	0	0	0	0	0	0	2	2
MC	BASE PLATE 1" x 2½"	2	2	2	2	2	2	2	8	8	8
MD	BASE PLATE 2½" x 5"	1	1	1	1	1	1	1	4	4	4
ME	BASE PLATE 1" x 4"	0	0	0	0	0	0	0	0	4	4
MF	BASE PLATE 1" x 5"	0	2	4	4	4	4	4	8	21	21
MG	RADIATOR HOOD	0	0	0	0	0	0	0	0	1	1
MH	LARGE 3" DISC WHEEL	0	0	4	0	4	4	4	4	4	4
MI	FRONT AXLE UNIT	0	0	0	0	0	0	0	0	1	1
MJ	ELECTRO MAGNET WITH CORD	0	0	0	0	0	0	0	1	1	1
MM	WRENCH	0	0	0	0	1	1	1	1	1	1
MN	12" BASE PLATE	0	0	2	2	2	4	4	6	6	6
MO	3" ANGLE GIRDER	0	0	4	4	4	4	4	4	4	8
MV	FLAT CAR TRUCK	0	0	0	0	0	0	2	4	4	12
MW	NUT HOLDER	0	0	0	0	1	1	1	1	1	1
MX	HOUSE	0	0	0	0	0	0	1	1	1	1
MY	2½" x 2½" BASE PLATE	0	0	0	1	1	1	1	1	1	1

1960–61 CONTENTS LIST

SET NO.		10011	10021[1]	10032[2]	10037	10042	10053	10063	10074	10084	10094
MZ	BEARING BLOCK	0	0	0	0	0	0	1	1	1	1
NH	LAMP SOCKET UNIT	0	0	0	0	0	0	1	2	2	2
NI	BULB, 1½ VOLT (CLEAR)	0	0	0	0	0	0	0	2	2	2
P12N677	BULB, 1.2 VOLT (RED)	0	0	0	0	0	0	1	1	1	1
NJ	BATTERY HOLDER	0	0	0	0	2	0	1	1	1	4
NK	RATCHET	0	0	0	0	0	0	0	2	2	2
NL	BOLSTER BRACKET	0	0	0	0	0	0	0	0	0	4
NS	41 HOLE STRIP—FORMED	0	0	0	0	0	0	0	0	2	2
NU	PARACHUTE	0	0	0	0	0	0	0	0	4	4
NW	TREAD	0	0	0	0	0	0	0	0	0	2
NX	TREAD PULLEY	0	0	0	0	0	0	0	0	0	4
NZ	PLASTIC SCREW DRIVER	0	0	0	0	1	1	1	1	1	1
OB	TREAD PIN	0	0	0	0	0	0	0	0	0	2
OE	6" FLEXIBLE COUPLING	0	0	0	0	0	1	1	1	1	1
OF	HORSE	0	0	0	0	0	0	0	0	6	6
OG	21 HOLE STRIP	0	0	0	0	0	0	0	0	2	2
OH	72 TOOTH GEAR	0	0	0	0	0	0	0	1	1	1
OI	SEGMENT OF 72 TOOTH GEAR	0	0	0	0	0	0	0	0	1	1
TA	CONVEYOR BELT (62")	0	0	0	0	0	0	1	1	1	1
TB	BALL BEARING (62")	0	0	0	0	0	0	0	0	6	6
TC	BEARING RETAINER PLATE	0	0	0	0	0	0	0	0	1	1
P14A686	ROCKET	0	0	0	0	0	1	1	1	1	1
P15B528	REMOTE CONTROL	0	0	0	1	0	0	0	0	0	0
X14B663	CLAM SHELL BUCKET	0	0	0	0	0	0	0	0	0	1
A49	ELECTRIC ENGINE	0	0	0	0	0	1	1	1	1	1
DC3	3 VOLT MOTOR	0	0	0	1	1	0	0	0	0	1
N21	8-32 SQUARE NUT	23	45	60	60	88	93	93	169	271	359
S51	¼" x 8-32 SCREW	20	35	50	50	80	84	84	162	240	260
S52	½" x 8-32 SCREW	0	0	0	0	0	4	4	4	8	8
S57	1⅜" x 8-32 SCREW	0	0	0	0	0	0	4	4	4	4
S62	⅞" x 8-32 SCREW	3	6	6	6	8	8	10	18	64	64

1. Set No. 10021 also contained two 5" axles.

2. Set No. 10032 also contained one 5" axle.

Most of the sets in the metal box line got new names and artwork in 1962 (left to right): The Nos. 10211 Cape Canaveral Set, 10201, 10221 Lunar Drilling Rig Set, and 10201 Rocket Launcher Set.

that built the models from that section were hard to follow.

Section No. 1 of the instruction manual from 1962 was for No. 10161 (The Model Maker's Set). It was identical to the section for The Junior Engineer's Set from 1961 and pictured many models from the old section for Set Nos. 1½ and 2½. (In the very earliest 1962 sets, the section was labeled Section No. 2½ and contained no models from old section No. 1½.)

Section No. 1A was for No. 10171 (The Engineer's Set). It was the same as the section for The Engineer's Set from 1961. Pictured here were many models from old section No. 3½.

Section No. 2 included the nonmotorized models from The Automatic Radar Scanner Set from 1961. Section 2A included the motorized models. Both sections were used in No. 10181 (The Action Helicopter Set), but only No. 2 was used for the larger sets, as they did not contain the (DC3) Motor. Set No. 10094 was the exception to this, as it did have the (DC3) and so used Section 2A.

Section No. 2B was a special one with 10 unique models. It was used only for the Electric Engine Set that was available through Sears, Roebuck & Company and Montgomery Ward as part of the Science Series (see Chapter Five). Consequently, it was not included in the manual for the regular line.

Section No. 3 was for use with No. 10201 (The Rocket Launcher Set). It was identical to the section for the version of that set from 1961, though it did show the redesigned Rocket Launcher.

Section Nos. 4 and 5 were for The Cape Canaveral Set. Together, they were identical to the section for The Automatic Conveyor Set from 1961. Why it was divided into two parts is unknown.

Section Nos. 6, 7, 8, and 9 were for The Lunar Drilling Rig Set. Together, they were identical to The Ferris Wheel Set section of the manual from 1961. The reason for dividing it into four parts is also a mystery.

Section Nos. 10, 11, and 12 were for The Astronaut Set. Together, these three sections were the same as the section for The Amusement Park Set from 1961. And section No. 13 was for No. 10094. It was unchanged from the section for The Master Builder Set from 1961.

Each set came with an instruction manual that was specific to the given set except for the two largest sets. Set Nos. 10231 and 10094 came with two manuals. The first was the same as the manual in No. 10211; the second was equally thick and designated XM-5718. It contained sections 10–13, as well as section 2A, which illustrated the models for the (DC3) Motor. The XM-5718 manuals included with The Astronaut Set had a rubber stamp on the first outside page to indicate that it would not build the models shown in section 2A.

Six new models were added to the Erector roster in 1962, and most were sophisticated, space age models for the larger sets. The illustrations for these new models were included in the sets in a most unusual way. Instead of being part of the instruction manual, they were included as loose instruction flyers printed in blue ink. Several of the sets even took their names from these new models, such as The Action Helicopter and The Lunar Drilling Rig Sets. In addition, The

Almost as a final insult, small sets, such as No. 10171, came in "milk cartons" in 1962. These sets are hard to find, especially in good condition, because the containers were so flimsy.

Cape Canaveral Set boasted the Gantry Service Tower and the Cherry Picker, while The Astronaut Set included the 70 Ton Crane and the Astronaut Trainer models.

Several minor but nonetheless interesting modifications also occurred in 1962, First, the (P79) Car Truck and (MV) Flat Car Truck came painted a new color this year. Instead of red, they were the same shade of yellow as the (MC) 1" x 2½" Base Plate. Also different were the (ME) 1" x 4" Base Plate and (MF) 1" x 5" Base Plate. This year they were plated instead of being painted silver. The plating was grainy, with a galvanized appearance.

Finally, Space Age Erector was dropped in 1962. These sets had been offered in tubes for the last two years, and perhaps the elimination of tube sets from the regular line of Erector made the continuation of this line impractical.

Milk Carton Sets

Two sets came packed in "milk cartons," and they were unique to this year. The cartons were constructed of lightweight cream-colored cardboard, with red and blue lettering and trim. The models pictured on the cartons were printed in shades of gray. The top of each carton was fashioned into a carrying handle (which is almost always torn or missing when these sets turn up).

The smaller of the two was No. 10161, known as "The Model Maker's Set." In content, it was equivalent to The Young Builder's Set from 1961 and evolved from old No. 2½. The carton measured 4" x 4" x 13½" and pictured the featured Elevated Crane.

Set No. 10171, the larger of the milk carton sets, was called "The Engineer's Set." It contained the same parts as The Engineer's Set from 1961, and its origins can be traced back to old No. 3½. Packed in a carton that measured 5" x 5" x 16½", it pictured the Rocket Gantry.

Both of the milk carton sets came with a "blue print": a large instruction sheet that illustrated the models. These sets are hard to find, especially in good condition. Their flimsy containers have not withstood the test of time.

Metal Box Sets

Six sets were offered in metal boxes, and while they were identical in contents to those in the line from 1961, all but the largest box came with new lithography. The text and trim on each lid was done in red and blue on a white background, and the models were pictured in shades of gray.

The Action Helicopter Set illustrated the new Action Helicopter, and the Rocket Launcher Set pictured the redesigned Rocket Launcher. As before, it came with Styrofoam parts display trays. The Cape Canaveral Set pictured the Rocket Gantry and Cherry Picker Astronaut Crane, both new this year.

The Lunar Drilling Rig Set pictured the new Lunar Drilling Rig, along with a small illustration of the Ferris Wheel, the previously featured model for this set. The Astronaut Set featured two new models, the Astronaut Trainer (a centrifuge) and the 70 Ton Crane. A small rendition of the Parachute Jump was used on this box lid. The Master Builder Set was the only metal box set in the 1962 lineup that was not changed. It still pictured the boy and the Mysterious Walking Giant.

Erector System Modifications for 1962

I. Noteworthy Parts Colors and Finishes

(P79) Car truck, painted yellow
(ME) 1" x 4" Base Plate, with "galvanized" plating
(MF) 1" x 5" Base Plate, with "galvanized" plating
(MV) Flat Car Truck, painted yellow

Listings of 1962 Erector Sets

	Gd	VG	Exc	Inv	Org

NO. 10161 The Model Maker's Set

Featured the (FP) Disc Wheels. Came in a "milk carton" 4" x 4" x 13½" that pictured Elevated Crane; sold for $2.98.

	Gd	VG	Exc	Inv	Org
	25	35	60	+10	N/A

NO. 10171 The Engineer's Set

Featured the angle girders and large base plates. Came in a "milk carton" 5" x 5" x 16½" that pictured Rocket Gantry; sold for $4.98.

	Gd	VG	Exc	Inv	Org
	30	40	70	+15	N/A

NO. 10181 The Action Helicopter Set

Featured the (DC3) 3 Volt Motor. Came in a lithographed metal box 16" x 8" x 3" that pictured Action Helicopter. Two-layer set with removable cardboard parts display tray; sold for $10.98.

	Gd	VG	Exc	Inv	Org
	40	60	100	+20	+25

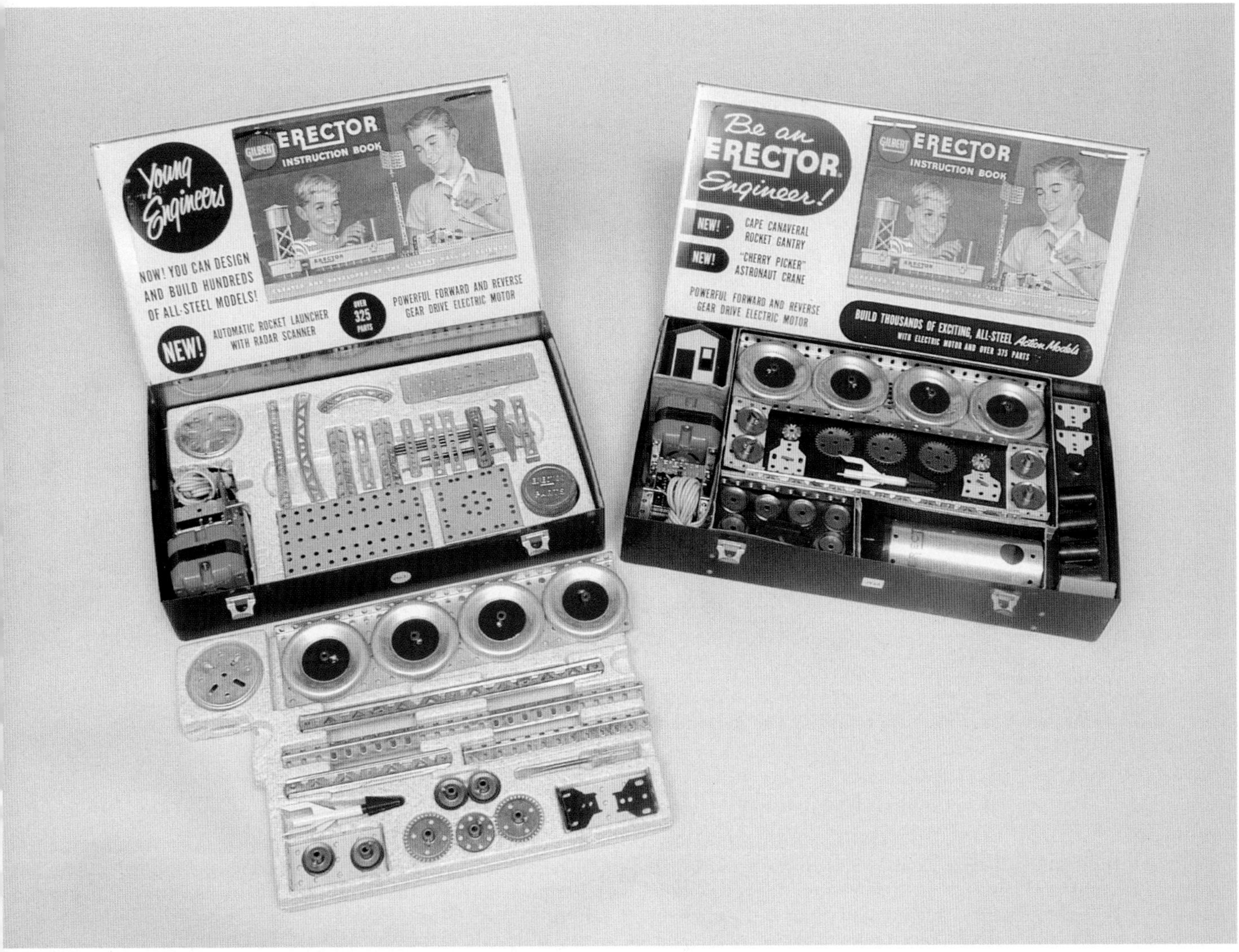

This picture of Nos. 10201 and 10211 shows that not all the sets from 1962 used Styrofoam parts displays.

SETS IN THE ERECTOR SYSTEM 1959–62

	Box Size	1959	1960	1961	1962
Tube Sets		No. 10011, No. 10021, No. 10032	No. 10011, No. 10021, No. 10032, No. 10037	No. 10011, No. 10021, No. 10032	N/A
Milk Carton		N/A	N/A	N/A	No. 10161, No. 10171
Metal Box Sets	16" x 8" x 3"	No. 10042 Automatic Radar Scope	No. 10042 Automatic Radar Scanner	No. 10042 Automatic Radar Scanner	No. 10181 Action Helicopter
	16" x 10" x 3"	No. 10053 Rocket Launcher	No. 10053 Rocket Launcher	No. 10053 Rocket Launcher	No. 10201 Rocket Launcher
	18" x 10" x 3"	No. 10063 Action Conveyor	No. 10063 Automatic Conveyor	No. 10063 Automatic Conveyor	No. 10211 Cape Canaveral
	20" x 12" x 3"	No. 10073 Musical Ferris Wheel	No. 10074 Ferris Wheel	No. 10074 Ferris Wheel	No. 10221 Lunar Drilling Rig
	20" x 16" x 3" Double Box	N/A	No. 10084 Amusement Park	No. 10084 Amusement Park	No. 10231 Astronaut
	20" x 18" x 3" Double Box	N/A	No. 10094 Master Builder	No. 10094 Master Builder	No. 10094 Master Builder

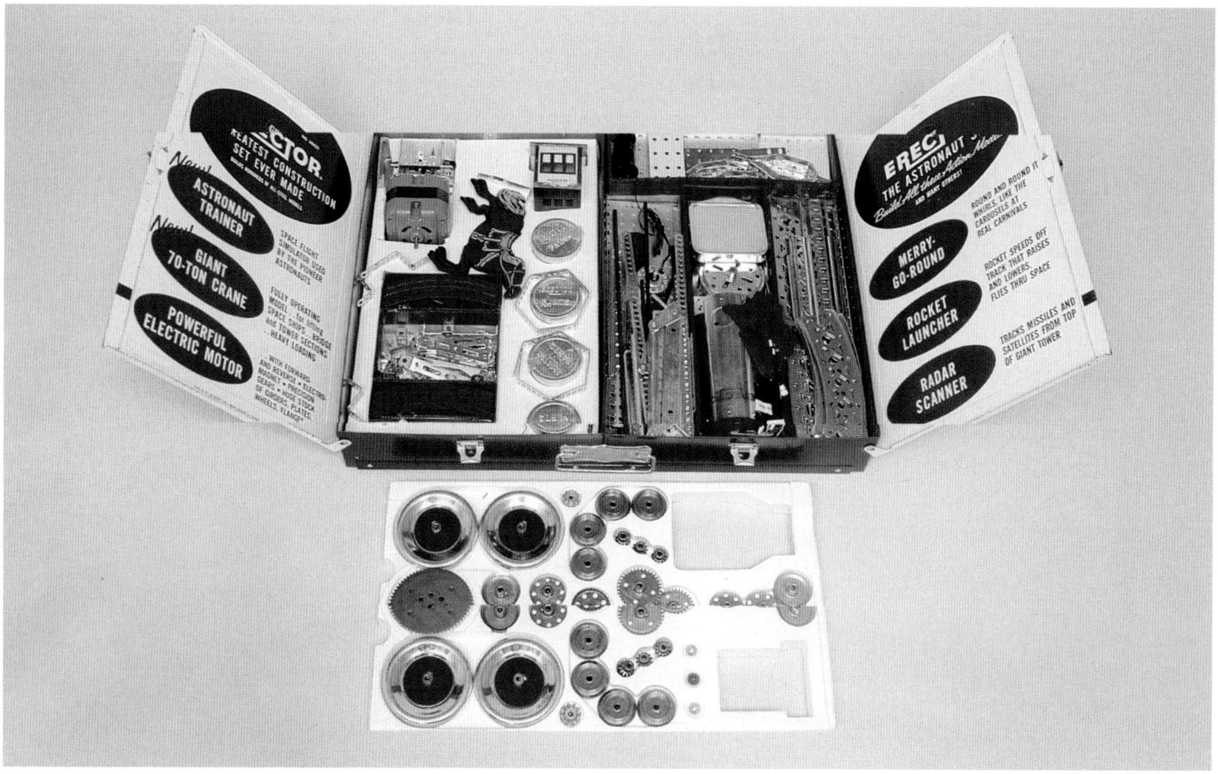

The Amusement Park Set was renamed The Astronaut Set in 1962, its last year of production.

	Gd	VG	Exc	Inv	Org

NO. 10201 The Rocket Launcher Set
Featured the (A49) Electric Engine and Rocket and built Rocket Launcher. Came in a lithographed metal box 16" x 10" x 3" that pictured redesigned Rocket Launcher. Two-layer set with two Styrofoam parts display trays; sold for $19.98. **45 65 110 +20 +25**

NO. 10211 The Cape Canaveral Set
Featured the (T) Boiler and Conveyor Belt and built Rocket Gantry, Cherry Picker, and conveyor models. Came in a lithographed metal box 18" x 10" x 3" that pictured Rocket Gantry and Cherry Picker. Two-layer set with removable cardboard parts display tray; sold for $24.98.
60 85 140 +35 +45

NO. 10221 The Lunar Drilling Rig Set
Featured the (MJ) Electro Magnet and built Ferris Wheel and Lunar Drilling Rig. Came in a lithographed metal box 20" x 12" x 3" that pictured Lunar Drilling Rig. Two-layer set with three removable parts display trays, one cardboard and two constructed from (MN) Base Plates; sold for $37.98.
60 85 140 +30 +35

	Gd	VG	Exc	Inv	Org

NO. 10231 The Astronaut Set
Featured the truck parts, giant flywheel, parachutes, and carousel horses and built Parachute Jump, Merry-Go-Round, and Giant Power Plant. Came in a lithographed metal double box 20" x 16" x 3", with double lids hinged on the sides; outer lid label pictured Astronaut Train and 70 Ton Crane. Two-layer set in left compartment with removable Styrofoam parts display tray; one-layer set in right compartment with cardboard dividers; sold for 49.98.
120 180 300 +60 +75

NO. 10094 The Master Builder Set
Featured the Clamshell Bucket and Treads and built the Mysterious Walking Giant and construction equipment. Came in a lithographed metal double box 20" x 18" x 3", with double lids hinged on the sides; outer lid pictured boy playing with Mysterious Walking Giant. Two-layer set in right compartment with removable Styrofoam parts display tray; one-layer set in left compartment with cardboard dividers; sold for $74.98.
320 480 800 +160 +200

1962 CONTENTS LIST

SET NO.		10161	10171	10181	10201	10211	10221	10231	10094
P7	7⁄8" PULLEY	4	4	4	4	4	0	0	0
P7A	1 1⁄8" PULLEY	0	0	0	0	0	4	4	4
P12	CROWN GEAR	0	0	0	0	0	1	1	1
P13	12 TOOTH PINION GEAR, 1⁄8"	0	0	0	1	1	2	2	2
P13B	12 TOOTH PINION GEAR, 7⁄23"	0	0	0	0	0	1	4	4
P15	COUPLING	0	0	1	2	2	2	2	2
P20	5 HOLE STRIP—FORMED	0	0	0	0	2	2	8	8
P24	CRANK	1	1	1	1	1	1	1	1
P33	SMALL SCREW DRIVER	1	1	1	1	0	0	0	0
P34	HANK OF STRING	1	1	1	1	1	1	3	3
P37	COLLAR	4	4	5	6	7	9	20	20
P48	MITRE GEAR	0	0	0	0	2	2	2	2
P57A	2 1⁄8" AXLE	1	1	1	1	1	1	1	8
P57D	6" AXLE	1	2	0	0	0	0	1	1
P57E	8" AXLE	0	0	0	0	0	0	2	2
P57F	12" AXLE	0	0	0	0	0	1	2	2
P57JA	7 1⁄2" AXLE	0	0	0	0	0	0	4	4
P57K	10" AXLE	0	0	0	0	0	0	0	2
P57N	3 1⁄4" AXLE	0	0	0	0	0	0	2	2
P79	CAR TRUCK	4	4	4	4	5	5	5	5
A	2 1⁄2" GIRDER	4	4	4	4	4	4	4	6
B	5" GIRDER	4	4	8	8	8	12	12	12
C	10" GIRDER	8	8	8	8	8	36	52	52
D	2 1⁄2" CURVED GIRDER	4	4	4	4	4	4	4	4
E	5" CURVED GIRDER	2	2	2	4	4	26	26	26
F	5 HOLE STRIP	0	0	2	2	3	3	3	16
G	7 HOLE STRIP	0	0	2	2	2	2	6	8
H	11 HOLE STRIP	0	0	4	4	5	5	16	16
I	21 HOLE STRIP	0	0	2	2	2	4	18	18
J	41 HOLE STRIP	0	0	0	0	0	2	2	4
M	SMALL DOUBLE ANGLE	0	0	0	0	2	6	24	24
N	LONG DOUBLE ANGLE	4	4	4	4	4	4	16	16
O	PAWL	0	0	0	1	2	2	16	16
T	BOILER	0	0	0	0	1	1	2	2
U	BOILER TOP	0	0	0	0	1	1	1	1
W	STACK	0	0	0	0	4	4	4	4
Z	FLANGED WHEEL 15⁄16" DIA.	0	0	0	0	8	8	8	8
AA	ECCENTRIC CRANK	0	0	0	0	0	0	6	6
AE	SPRING	0	0	0	0	0	1	1	2
AF	SMALL HOOK	1	1	1	1	1	1	1	1
AJ	PAPER ERECTOR FLAG	0	0	1	1	1	1	1	1
AQ	SHEAVE PULLEY	0	0	0	0	1	1	4	5
AS	2 7⁄8" AXLE	0	0	2	2	3	3	4	4
AT	4" AXLE	2	2	2	2	2	2	2	4
BE	6" ANGLE GIRDER	0	4	4	4	4	4	4	12
BH	SOLID COLLAR	0	0	0	0	0	0	2	2

1962 CONTENTS LIST

SET NO.		10161	10171	10181	10201	10211	10221	10231	10094
BL	SMALL WASHER	12	12	12	12	12	12	12	18
BN	REGULAR TURRET PLATE	0	0	2	2	4	4	4	4
BT	PIERCED DISC	1	1	2	2	2	4	4	4
BY	11 HOLE FIBRE STRIP	0	0	0	0	0	2	2	2
CA	SIGNAL ARM	0	0	0	0	0	0	2	2
CH	RIGHT ANGLE	12	12	14	14	14	30	42	42
CJ	36 TOOTH GEAR	0	0	0	2	3	3	3	5
CR	SPECIAL TURRET PLATE WITH HUB	0	0	0	0	0	0	2	2
CS	WHEEL SEGMENT	0	0	0	0	0	0	8	8
CZ	7" AXLE	0	0	2	2	2	4	4	4
DB	MOTOR PULLEY	0	0	1	1	1	1	1	2
DE	STEERING COLUMN	0	0	0	0	0	0	1	1
DK	FLAT SPRING	0	0	0	0	0	0	4	4
DO	STEERING WHEEL WITH HUB	0	0	0	0	0	0	1	1
DP	12" ANGLE GIRDER	0	4	4	4	4	4	4	6
DS	COTTER PIN	0	0	0	0	0	0	1	1
EI	STD. GEAR BOX SIDE PLATE	0	0	0	2	2	2	2	2
EX	BIG CHANNEL GIRDER 12"	0	0	0	0	0	0	8	8
EY	BIG CHANNEL GIRDER 6"	0	0	0	0	0	0	4	8
EZ	BIG CHAN. GIRDER CURVED 6"	0	0	0	0	0	0	9	9
FA	1¾" x 8-32 SCREW	0	0	0	0	0	0	12	12
FP(X239)	SMALL DISC WHEEL	4	0	0	0	0	0	0	0
FD	HINGED LOOP	0	0	0	0	0	0	2	2
LX	STEERING COLUMN BRACKET	0	0	0	0	0	0	1	1
MA	RADIATOR	0	0	0	0	0	0	1	1
MB	18½" ANGLE GIRDER	0	0	0	0	0	0	2	2
MC	BASE PLATE 1" x 2½"	2	2	2	2	2	8	8	8
MD	BASE PLATE 2½" x 5"	1	1	1	1	1	4	4	4
ME	BASE PLATE 1" x 4"	0	0	0	0	0	0	4	4
MF	BASE PLATE 1" x 5"	2	4	4	4	4	8	21	21
MG	RADIATOR HOOD	0	0	0	0	0	0	1	1
MH	LARGE 3" DISC WHEEL	0	4	4	4	4	4	4	4
MI	FRONT AXLE UNIT	0	0	0	0	0	0	1	1
MJ	ELECTRO MAGNET WITH CORD	0	0	0	0	0	1	1	1
MM	WRENCH	0	0	1	1	1	1	1	1
MN	12" BASE PLATE	0	2	2	4	4	6	6	6
MO	3" ANGLE GIRDER	0	4	4	4	4	4	4	8
MV	FLAT CAR TRUCK	0	0	0	0	2	4	4	12
MW	NUT HOLDER	0	0	1	1	1	1	1	1
MX	HOUSE	0	0	0	0	1	1	1	1
MY	2½" x 2½" BASE PLATE	0	0	1	1	1	1	1	1
MZ	BEARING BLOCK	0	0	0	0	1	1	1	1
NH	LAMP SOCKET UNIT	0	0	0	0	1	2	2	2
NI	BULB, 1½ VOLT (CLEAR)	0	0	0	0	0	2	2	2
P12N677	BULB, 1.2 VOLT (RED)	0	0	0	0	1	1	1	1
NJ	BATTERY HOLDER	0	0	2	0	1	1	1	4

1962 CONTENTS LIST

SET NO.		10161	10171	10181	10201	10211	10221	10231	10094
NK	RATCHET	0	0	0	0	0	2	2	2
NL	BOLSTER BRACKET	0	0	0	0	0	0	0	4
NS	41 HOLE STRIP—FORMED	0	0	0	0	0	0	2	2
NU	PARACHUTE	0	0	0	0	0	0	4	4
NW	TREAD	0	0	0	0	0	0	0	2
NX	TREAD PULLEY	0	0	0	0	0	0	0	4
NZ	PLASTIC SCREW DRIVER	0	0	1	1	1	1	1	1
OB	TREAD PIN	0	0	0	0	0	0	0	2
OE	6" FLEXIBLE COUPLING	0	0	0	1	1	1	1	1
OF	HORSE	0	0	0	0	0	0	6	6
OG	21 HOLE STRIP—FORMED	0	0	0	0	0	0	2	2
OH	72 TOOTH GEAR	0	0	0	0	0	1	1	1
OI	SEGMENT OF 72 TOOTH GEAR	0	0	0	0	0	0	1	1
TA	CONVEYOR BELT (62")	0	0	0	0	1	1	1	1
TB	BALL BEARING	0	0	0	0	0	0	6	6
TC	BEARING RETAINER PLATE	0	0	0	0	0	0	1	1
P14A686	ROCKET	0	0	0	1	1	1	1	1
X14B663	CLAM SHELL BUCKET	0	0	0	0	0	0	0	1
A49	ELECTRIC ENGINE	0	0	0	1	1	1	1	1
DC3	3 VOLT MOTOR	0	0	1	0	0	0	0	1
N21	8-32 SQUARE NUT	45	60	88	93	93	169	271	359
S51	1/4" x 8-32 SCREW	35	50	80	84	84	162	240	260
S52	1/2" x 8-32 SCREW	0	0	0	4	4	4	8	8
S57	1 3/8" x 8-32 SCREW	0	0	0	0	4	4	4	4
S62	7/8" x 8-32 SCREW	6	6	8	8	10	18	64	64

5

SPECIAL ERECTOR SETS FOR AMERICAN WHOLESALERS

During the Classic Period, Gilbert developed a marketing arrangement with a variety of major retail operations, including retail chain stores and mail-order houses. Among these retailers were Montgomery Ward, J. C. Penney, and Sears, Roebuck & Company. Gilbert dubbed these special customers his "wholesalers."

With the end of the Classic Period in 1933, this special marketing arrangement was put on hold, though not for long. Two years later, in 1935, Gilbert again created "Wholesale Sets" for Sears, Ward, and possibly other customers that have not yet been documented. Because Sears was undoubtedly Gilbert's largest wholesale customer and because so many Sears catalogs have survived to provide documentation, Erector collectors typically refer to these special items as "Sears Sets." I will follow this custom here while repeating that Sears was not the only major retailer for whom Gilbert made special sets.

As was the practice during the Classic Period, the Erector Sets sold through Sears beginning in 1935 were not the same as those available in the regular line. Sears liked to offer items in its catalog at "marked-down" prices. By making these sets a little different (usually by including fewer parts than regular sets of similar size), Sears could sell them at a marked-down price. While this may have angered some of the retail dealers selling the standard Erector line at full price, the issue was probably a minor one. Sears primarily did business with rural America, where people ordered by mail through the catalog because no retail store was located near them. Most likely, therefore, regular retailers did not think the marked-down sets available from Sears hurt their sales.

When Gilbert downsized Erector in 1933, the entire line was virtually recreated from scratch. The cardboard box sets were given a new lid label, and the contents of all the sets were modified. But the most radical and striking development was the creation of metal set boxes with cardboard parts displays clipped to the inside of the lids. The line of these sets was expanded in 1934, but in 1935 the cardboard inner lid parts displays gave way to inner lid labels as Gilbert continued to develop the regular Erector line.

What is so unique and endearing about the sets designed for Sears from 1935 through 1942 is that they were basically a continuation of the 1933–34 line, with single-digit set numbers and cardboard inside lid parts displays for the metal box sets. Of course, certain features clearly distinguish them from their 1933–34 ancestors. First, the "Erector Separate Parts Prices" list in the instruction manuals for the Sears sets was constantly updated and always corresponded to the separate parts price list in the regular line manuals. By using the separate parts price lists printed in this book, you can date a given set. Second, as Gilbert modified parts for the regular line, the same changes appear in the Sears sets.

THE 1935 SEARS ERECTOR LINE

Sears, Roebuck & Company offered five sets in the 1935 catalog. Set Nos. 1 and 3 were packed in cardboard boxes; Nos. 4, 6, and 7 came in metal boxes. All of these sets were essentially identical to those offered in the regular Erector line for 1934, except the color of the box for Set. No. 6 was changed from green to red on occasion. Red boxes are rare. None was the same as those offered in the regular line for 1935.

These Sears sets from 1935 can be distinguished from the regular 1934 line in several ways. First, the (MC) and (MD) base plates were made of a lighter-gauge steel in 1935 than in 1934. This change was made in the regular line and carried over into the Sears sets. However, the (MC), (MD), (ME), and (MF) base plates were painted red, as in 1934, instead of yellow and blue as was the regular line in 1935. Second, the (CJ) 36 Tooth Gear came with four slots and four holes, which mirrored the modification that occurred in the regular line in 1935.

It is interesting that several parts were not modified to match changes in the regular line. For example, the boilers in Sears sets were painted black, while those in the regular line were nickel-plated. However, the boiler decal with a silver background replaced the one with a gold background for both lines in 1935. The (MH) Disc Wheel for all but The Automotive Set (and later The Giant Power Plant Set) was painted solid red in Sears sets, as were the Disc Wheels in 1934. Also, the (P79) Car Truck was nickel-plated in the Sears sets and not painted red as in the regular line. Although the cardboard used for the lower-level insert was changed from green to mustard in the regular line in 1935, green cardboard continued to be used for the lower-level insert in Sears sets through 1942.

Listings of 1935 Sears Erector Sets

	Gd	VG	Exc	Inv	Org

NO. 1 **The Beginner's Set**

Built 50 models. Came in a cardboard box 12½" x 8¾" x ⅝"; sold for 79 cents.

	Gd	VG	Exc	Inv	Org
	30	50	80	+15	+20

NO. 3 The Big Girder Set

Built 75 models and featured the large wheels. Came in a cardboard box 18¼" x 10¼" x 1"; sold for $1.98.

Gd	VG	Exc	Inv	Org
40	60	100	+20	+25

NO. 4 The Battery Motor Erector

Built 100 models and featured battery-operated (P58) Motor. Came in a red metal box 16" x 8" x 3", with a cardboard parts display on the inside of the lid; sold for $3.98.

Gd	VG	Exc	Inv	Org
60	90	150	+30	+45

NO. 6 The 110 Volt Electric Motor Set

Built 125 models and featured 110-volt (P56G) Motor and (T) Boiler. Came in a red or green metal box 18" x 10" x 3" with brass corner trim and parts display on inside of lid; sold for $5.98.

Gd	VG	Exc	Inv	Org
100	150	250	+50	+65

NO. 7 The Electric Lifting Magnet Set

Built 160 models and featured crane models built with (MJ) Electro Magnet. Came in a red metal box 20" x 12" x 3" with brass corner trim and parts display on inside of lid; sold for $7.98.

Gd	VG	Exc	Inv	Org
140	210	350	+70	+90

The 1936–42 Sears Erector Line

The line of sets produced for Sears, Roebuck & Company was refined in 1936. From this point until 1942, the sets in the line remained fairly consistent. Three sets were offered in cardboard boxes: Nos. 1 and 3, which were identical to their predecessors from 1935, and No. 4. In 1935, No. 4 had been packed in a metal box (as in 1934); from 1936 through 1942, however, from this point forward it was packed in a cardboard box with a lid apron that extended to the bottom of the box (as in 1933).

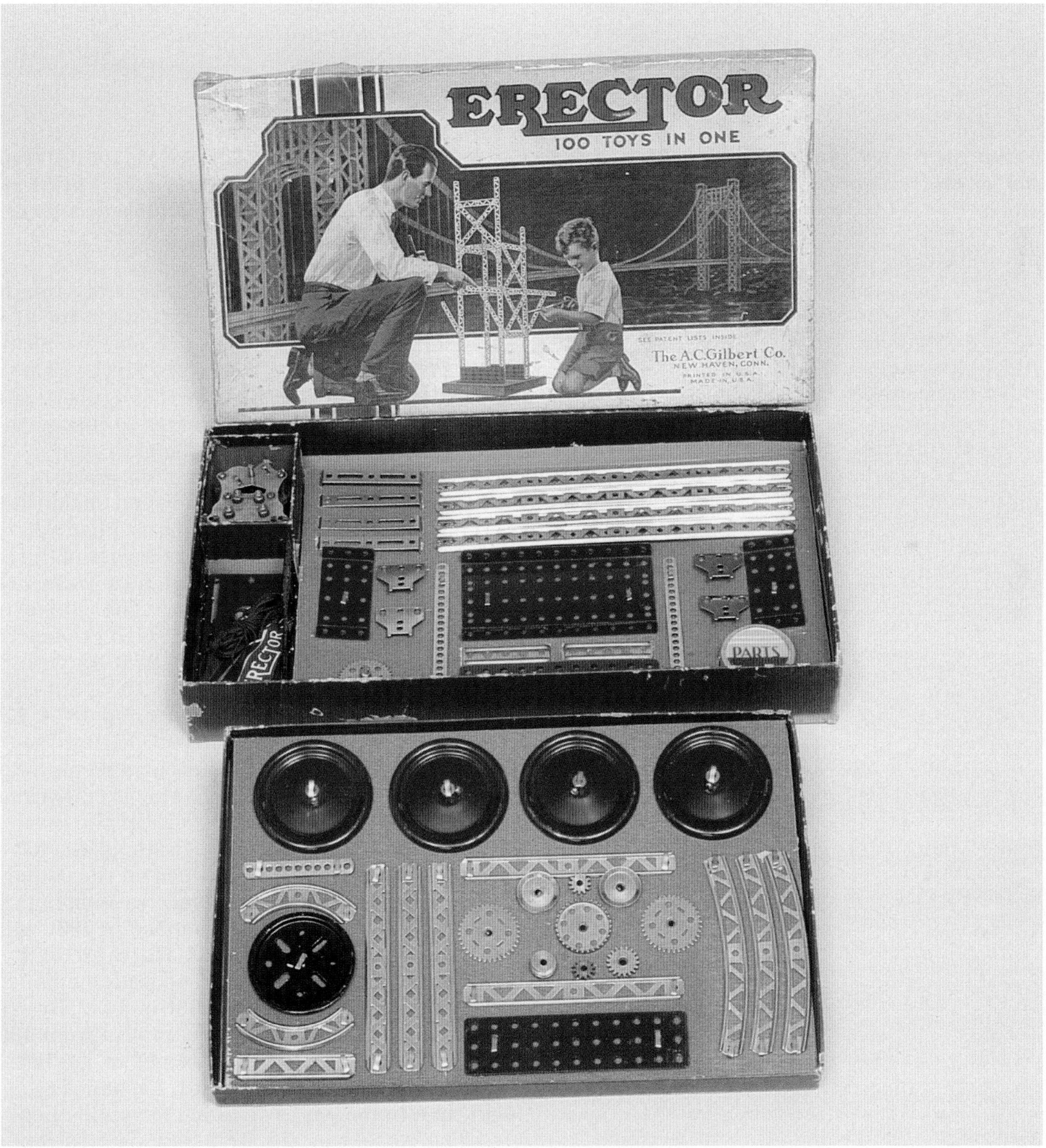

Sears Set No. 4 from 1942. This special line of sets mirrored the regular Erector line offered in the early 1930s. The apron on the lid extended to the bottom of the box (as in 1933), a practice long abandoned in the regular line.

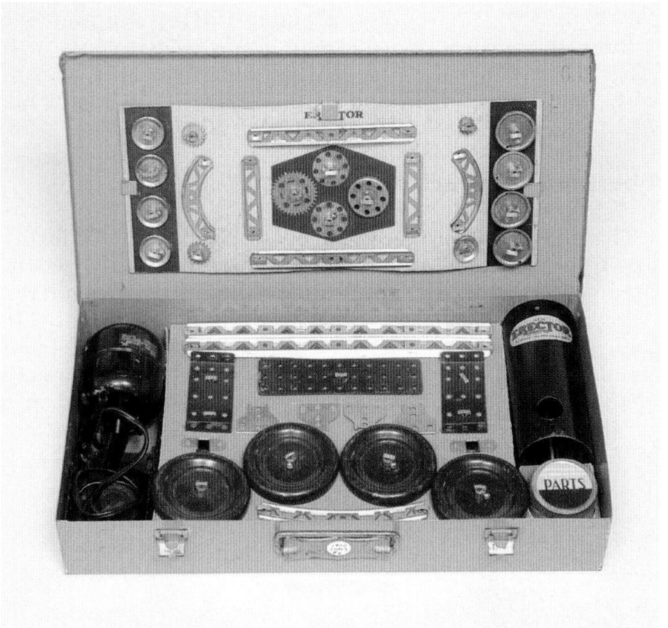

The box for Sears Set No. 6 from 1940 measured 17" x 9" x 3". The size and color of this unique container make this set a favorite of collectors.

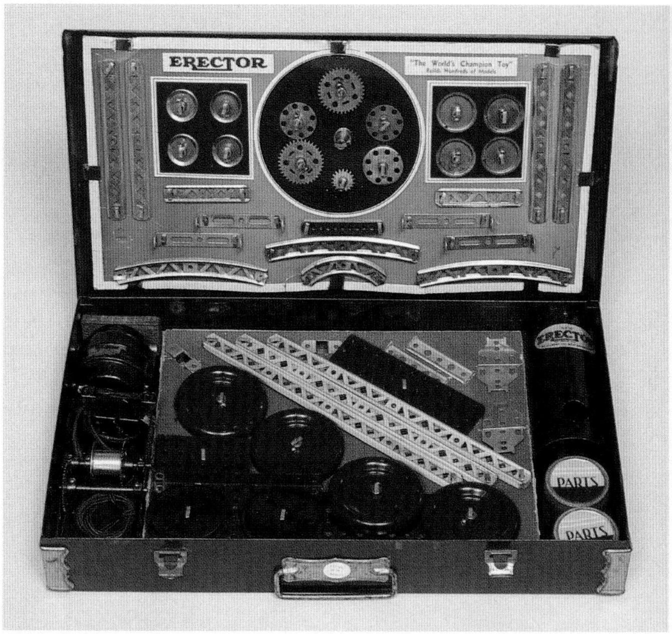

While the contents of Sears Set No. 7 from 1940 (including the inner lid parts display) mirrored No. 7 in the regular line from 1934, its box was painted royal blue instead of red.

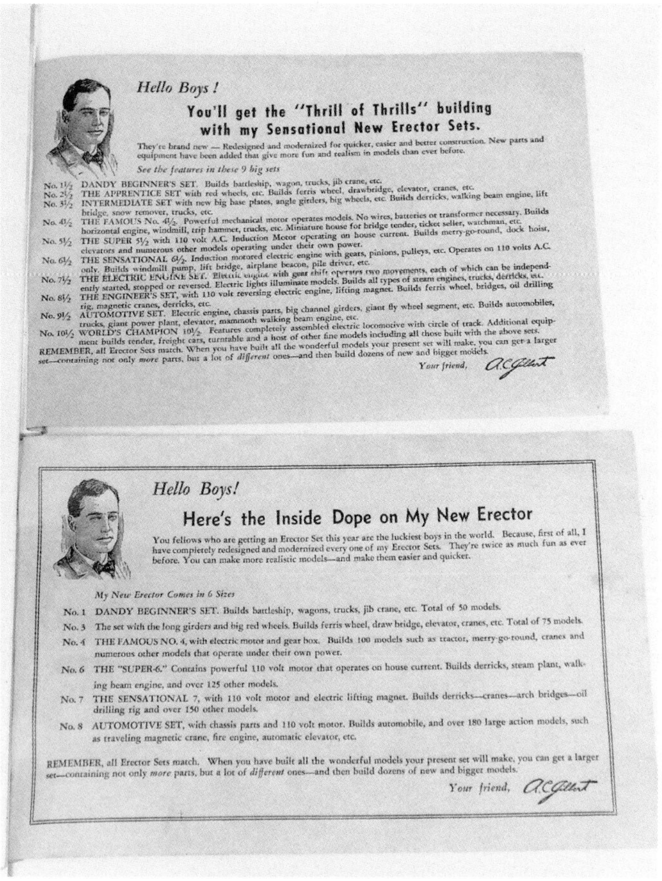

Hello Boys !

You'll get the "Thrill of Thrills" building with my Sensational New Erector Sets.

They're brand new — Redesigned and modernized for quicker, easier and better construction. New parts and equipment have been added that give more fun and realism in models than ever before.

See the features in these 9 big sets

No. 1½ DANDY BEGINNER'S SET. Builds battleship, wagon, trucks, jib crane, etc.
No. 2½ THE APPRENTICE SET with red wheels, etc. Builds ferris wheel, drawbridge, elevator, cranes, etc.
No. 3½ INTERMEDIATE SET with new big base plates, angle girders, big wheels, etc. Builds derricks, walking beam engine, lift bridge, snow remover, trucks, etc.
No. 4½ THE FAMOUS No. 4½. Powerful mechanical motor operates models. No wires, batteries or transformer necessary. Builds horizontal engine, windmill, trip hammer, trucks, etc. Miniature house for bridge tender, ticket seller, watchman, etc.
No. 5½ THE SUPER 5½ with 110 volt A.C. Induction Motor operating on house current. Builds merry-go-round, dock hoist, elevators and numerous other models operating under their own power.
No. 6½ THE SENSATIONAL 6½. Induction motored electric engine with gears, pinions, pulleys, etc. Operates on 110 volts A.C. only. Builds windmill pump, lift bridge, airplane beacon, pile driver, etc.
No. 7½ THE ELECTRIC ENGINE SET. Electric engine with gear shift operates two movements, each of which can be independently started, stopped or reversed. Electric lights illuminate models. Builds all types of steam engines, trucks, derricks, etc.
No. 8½ THE ENGINEER'S SET, with 110 volt reversing electric engine, lifting magnet. Builds ferris wheel, bridges, oil drilling rig, magnetic cranes, derricks, etc.
No. 9½ AUTOMOTIVE SET. Electric engine, chassis parts, big channel girders, giant fly wheel segment, etc. Builds automobiles, trucks, giant power plant, elevator, mammoth walking beam engine, etc.
No. 10½ WORLD'S CHAMPION 10½. Features completely assembled electric locomotive with circle of track. Additional equipment builds tender, freight cars, turntable and a host of other fine models including all those built with the above sets.

REMEMBER, all Erector Sets match. When you have built all the wonderful models your present set will make, you can get a larger set—containing not only *more* parts, but a lot of *different* ones—and then build dozens of new and bigger models.

Your friend, A.C. Gilbert

Hello Boys!

Here's the Inside Dope on My New Erector

You fellows who are getting an Erector Set this year are the luckiest boys in the world. Because, first of all, I have completely redesigned and modernized every one of my Erector Sets. They're twice as much fun as ever before. You can make more realistic models—and make them easier and quicker.

My New Erector Comes in 6 Sizes

No. 1 DANDY BEGINNER'S SET. Builds battleship, wagons, trucks, jib crane, etc. Total of 50 models.
No. 3 The set with the long girders and big red wheels. Builds ferris wheel, draw bridge, elevator, cranes, etc. Total of 75 models.
No. 4 THE FAMOUS NO. 4, with electric motor and gear box. Builds 100 models such as tractor, merry-go-round, cranes and numerous other models that operate under their own power.
No. 6 THE "SUPER-6." Contains powerful 110 volt motor that operates on house current. Builds derricks, steam plant, walking beam engine, and over 125 other models.
No. 7 THE SENSATIONAL 7, with 110 volt motor and electric lifting magnet. Builds derricks—cranes—arch bridges—oil drilling rig and over 150 other models.
No. 8 AUTOMOTIVE SET, with chassis parts and 110 volt motor. Builds automobile, and over 180 large action models, such as traveling magnetic crane, fire engine, automatic elevator, etc.

REMEMBER, all Erector Sets match. When you have built all the wonderful models your present set will make, you can get a larger set—containing not only *more* parts, but a lot of *different* ones—and then build dozens of new and bigger models.

Your friend, A.C. Gilbert

***Top:* The inside back instruction manual cover for the regular line. *Bottom:* The inside back cover for the Sears sets. Note the different numbering systems (1936–42).**

Starting in 1936, three Sears sets came in metal boxes. Set No. 6 was identical in contents to the 1935 offering, but Gilbert designed a new box to house it. This box, which measured 17" x 9" x 3", was unique to the Sears line and never used in the regular Erector line. Gilbert must have sold a great many sets through Sears to justify the creation of a special box for this one customer.

This box for No. 6 was painted green and came with the same 14" x 6" yellow background inside lid parts display that was used in 1935. The set number was rubber-stamped in black ink on the upper right corner of the inside of the lid. Surprisingly, only four metal tabs were used to hold the inner lid parts display in place. The old box had used six.

Set No. 7 fell in the middle among the metal box sets sold through Sears beginning in 1936. As with No. 6, it maintained the same contents as in 1935, but came in a smaller box. This new box, which measured 18" x 10" x 3" and was painted royal blue, had been used for No. 6 the previous year. The 17" x 9" inside lid parts display was used on this set as it had been in 1935. However, because the box was smaller, the parts display so filled the inside of the lid that there was no room to rubber-stamp the set number in the corner. Instead, it was stamped on the display insert, on the lower right side, the only place with enough space.

The line of Sears sets expanded in 1936, with the addition of a new top-of-the-line set, No. 8. Actually, there is some question as to whether "The Automotive Set," as it was known, was introduced in 1936 or 1937. By examining the instruction manual for the Sears sets from 1936, I concluded that Gilbert had this set ready to go, but No. 8 was not included in the Sears catalog. Perhaps it was just not ready in time to make the deadline for publishing that catalog.

The No. 8 was the first Sears set to contain the chassis parts, and its contents and the metal box it was packed in were identical to No. 7 from 1933. The same inner lid cardboard parts display was used on Nos. 7 and 8, but more parts were displayed and the display arrangement differed. The set number was rubber-stamped on the upper right corner of the inside of the lid.

Starting in 1936, an interesting practice occurred with instruction manuals. The manuals for Sears sets from this year are easy to identify because on the inside of the back cover the Sears line was fully described. This was consistent on all Sears sets through 1942 and different from the inside back cover for any set from the regular line, where the standard sets were promoted.

In reviewing the models illustrated in the Sears instruction manuals, the section for No. 1 models is combined with the regular line No. 1½ section. The same is true for the Sears section for No. 3 and the regular line section for No. 2½, and the Sears section for No. 4 and the regular line section for Nos. 4½ and 5½ (through 1940). In each case the Sears section (whole-numbered-set section) did not illustrate as many models as did the regular line section. As confusing as this practice was, it made sense because it reduced printing costs.

Beginning with the No. 6 section (and the No. 4 section in 1941), each section for the manual illustrated only models

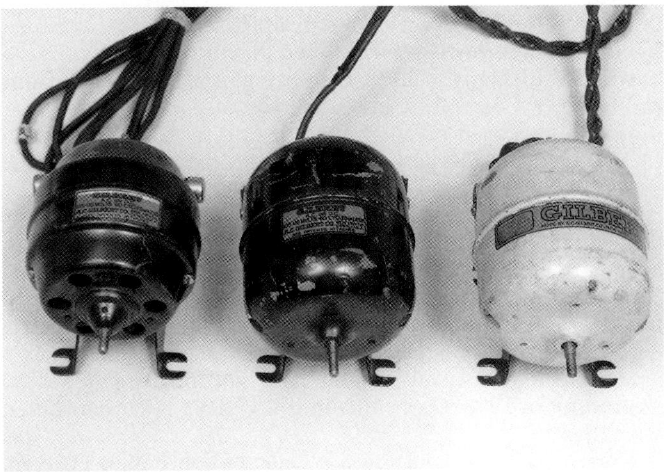

Over the years, three versions of the (P56G) 110-volt electric motor were used in Sears sets, including a scarce light brown version (right).

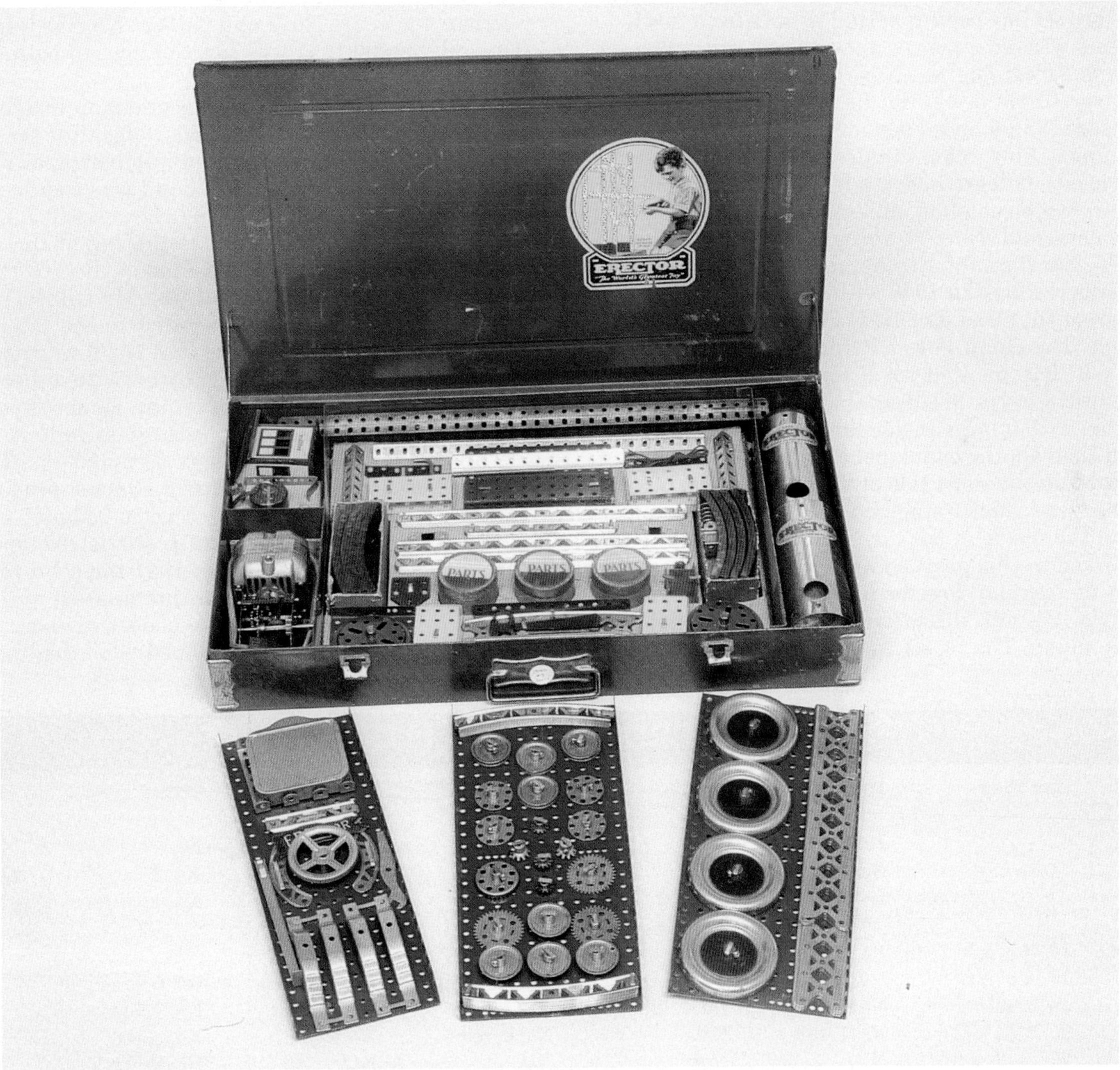

In 1940 a seventh set (No. 9) was added to the Sears roster. This top-of-the-line set did not include the parts to build the Parachute Jump (as did its counterpart in the regular line). Most unusual was the inner-lid adornment, which consisted of only the oval outer-lid label.

built with the Sears sets. This practice was logical because models created for the larger sets in the regular line were markedly different in 1936 when compared with those from the larger sets in 1933. Likewise, the manuals for the regular line sets split off at this point and make no reference to the even-numbered sets. The sole exception was No. 9 from 1940.

After seeing no changes in the 1937 line of Sears sets, I discovered some modifications in 1938. To start, Gilbert dropped the metal parts cans and began using parts containers with cardboard bodies. This change carried over into the Sears line for all the metal box sets and even affected cardboard box No. 4. In the past, the nuts, bolts, and other small parts had been packed in a cardboard parts box. Beginning in 1938, they came in the 1"-deep parts container with a metal lid.

More interesting was a new version of the (P56G) 110-volt electric motor that came with some metal box sets from 1937 through 1942. The new (P56G) was a bit larger than its predecessor and its ends were more rounded. Both the old and new versions show up randomly in sets dating from 1937 to 1942, though the egg-shaped one is more common. Also, both were painted black, though a rare variation painted light brown has been reported in sets from 1941.

In 1939, Sears wanted a more elaborate and expensive set to offer through its catalog, so Gilbert added a seventh one to the line. Surprisingly, it was the No. 9½, straight from the regular line, packed in a metal box measuring 22" x 13" x 3" and painted royal blue. This created a conflict, however, because previously Gilbert had made sure the discounted sets from Sears were somehow different from the full-price sets other dealers sold. Now, however, a top set was available for $11.95, less than the Erector catalog price of $14.95.

This issue was resolved in 1940 with the creation of a new top-of-the-line set that was specific to Sears. Designated No. 9, it was called "The Giant Power Plant Set," and packed in a 22" x 13" x 3" box painted royal blue. It was, with one exception, identical to No. 9½ from the regular line of 1939. The latter came with a large inside lid label, and No. 9 from Sears did not. Instead, the oval label found on the outside of the box was used on the right side of the inside of the lid and the set number was rubber-stamped in black on the upper right corner of the inside of the lid.

This set worked in this position in the Sears line because of changes to the regular Erector line. At this time Gilbert upgraded its No. 9½ with the special parts required to build the Parachute Jump. The Sears No. 9 never received these parts. So, starting in 1940, it had fewer parts than the No. 9½ and could not build the Parachute Jump. Sears promoted its set as the Giant Power Plant Set, and its marked-down price did not conflict with what was in the regular line.

Although No. 9 continued in the Sears line through 1942, it did not match the rest of the Sears sets. Set No. 9 came with an (A49) Electric Engine or sometimes a (P51) instead of a (P56G) motor. Besides having base plates painted blue or yellow (not red like the rest of the Sears line), this set had (MN) Base Plates not the old (S) Base Plates as did other metal box Sears sets.

Likewise, only nickel-plated boilers appeared in No. 9. All other metal box Sears sets came with boilers painted black. Finally, this was the only metal box set in the Sears lineup lacking a cardboard inside lid parts display.

The instruction manual from 1940 did not follow the pattern established for the larger sets back in 1936. In the past the sections for small sets were combined, but for large sets the Sears manuals and the regular line manuals went their separate ways with either whole-numbered sections (No. 6, No. 7, and so forth) for the Sears sets or fractional sections (No. 6½, No. 7½, and so forth) for the regular sets. But like the instruction manual sections for small sets, the sections for Sears No. 9 and Gilbert No. 9½ were combined. The only model that was not common to both sets was the Parachute Jump.

(This practice of combining sections in instruction manuals continued well into the 1950s, long after these Sears sets were gone and the complicated numbering at the top of the pages had any significance. When I was a child playing with my 1955 Amusement Park Set, I remember seeing all the different set numbers listed at the top of the pages in my instruction manual and marveling at the assortment of sets Erector produced. Maybe that was Mr. Gilbert's aim.)

Another item of interest related to the later instruction manuals for the Sears sets is that No. 9 was never listed on the inside page of the back cover with other Sears sets. Although this top-of-the-line set ran for three years, the promotional page was never updated to include it.

Three other modest changes occurred in the Sears sets before World War II interrupted Erector production. First, the large nickel-plated (MJ) Electro Magnet used in 1939 gave way to the smaller, more realistic red version Gilbert introduced in 1940. Second, in 1941 the solid red (MH) Disc Wheels came with a new color combination in the small sets (Nos. 1 through 7). Now these wheels had black tires and red hubcaps. Third, No. 1 was dropped from the line in 1942.

SEARS ERECTOR SETS 1935–42

	Box Size	1935	1936	1937	1938	1939	1940–42
Cardboard Box Set		No. 1 No. 3	No. 1 No. 3 No. 4	No. 1 No. 3 No. 4	No. 1 No. 3 No. 4	No. 1 No. 3 No. 4	No. 1[1] No. 3 No. 4
Metal Box Sets	16" x 8" x 3"	No. 4, red	N/A	N/A	N/A	N/A	N/A
	17" x 9" x 3"	N/A	No. 6, green	No. 6, green	No. 6, green,	No. 6, green	No. 6, green
	18" x 10" x 3"	No. 6, green	No. 7, blue	No. 7, blue	No. 7, blue	No. 7, blue	No. 7, blue
	20" x 12" x 3"	No. 7, red	N/A	No. 8, red	No. 8, red	No. 8, red,	No. 8, red
	22" x 13" x 3"	N/A	N/A	N/A	N/A	No. 9½, blue	No. 9, blue

1. Dropped in 1942.

Contents Equivalency Chart

The contents of Sears sets were, with just a few exceptions, identical to those of the regular line of Erector Sets from 1934.

Sears Set	Erector Set
No. 1 (1935–41)	No. 1 from 1934
No. 3 (1935–42)	No. 3 from 1934
No. 4 (1936–42)	No. 4 from 1934
No. 6 (1936–42)	No. 6 from 1934
No. 7 (1935)	No. 7 from 1934
No. 8 (1937–42)	No. 7½ from 1934
No. 9½ (1939)	No. 9½ from 1939
No. 9 (1940–42)	No. 9½ from 1939

Listings of 1936–42 Sears Erector Sets

	Gd	VG	Exc	Inv	Org

NO. 1 (1936–41) The Beginner's Set

Built 50 models. Came in a cardboard box 12½" x 8¾" x ⅝"; sold for 79 cents.

30	50	80	+15	+20

NO. 3 (1936–42) The Big Girder Set

Built 75 models and featured the large wheels. Came in a cardboard box 18¼" x 10¼" x 1"; sold for $1.79 in 1936, $1.98 from 1937 to 1940, $2.19 in 1941, and $2.45 in 1942.

40	60	100	+20	+25

NO. 4 (1936–42) The Famous Battery Motor Erector

Built 100 models and featured battery-operated (P58) Motor. Came in a cardboard box 18¼" x 10¼" x 2½"; two-layer set with removable cardboard parts display tray; sold for $3.98 from 1936 to 1941 and $4.49 in 1942.

60	90	150	+30	+45

NO. 6 (1936–42) The 110 Volt Electric Motor Set

Built 125 models and featured 110-volt (P56G) Motor and (T) Boiler. Came in a green metal box 17" x 9" x 3" with parts display on inside of lid; sold for $5.98 in 1936, $6.79 from 1938 to 1941, and $7.19 in 1942.

80	120	200	+40	+50

NO. 7 (1936–42) The Electric Lifting Magnet Set

Built 160 models and featured crane models built with (MJ) Electro Magnet. Came in a royal blue metal box 18" x 10" x 3" with brass corner trim and parts display on inside of lid; sold for $7.98 in 1936, $8.79 from 1937 to 1941, and $9.89 in 1942.

120	180	300	+60	+75

NO. 8 (1937–42) The Super Automotive Set

Built 180 models and featured automotive and truck models built with chassis parts. Came in a red metal box 20" x 12" x 3" with brass corner trim and parts display on inside of lid; sold for $11.98 from 1937 to 1941 and $12.75 in 1942.

160	240	400	+80	+100

NO. 9 (1940–42) The Giant Power Plant Set

Featured (A49) Electric Engine and giant flywheel and built Giant Power Plant. Came in a royal blue metal box 22" x 13" x 3" with brass corner trim and same oval label on inside of lid as on outside. Two-layer set with three removable parts trays constructed from (MN) Base Plates; sold for $14.95 from 1940 to 1941 and $15.98 in 1942.

140	210	350	+70	+90

NO. 9½ (1939) The Automotive Set

Featured truck parts and giant flywheel and built Giant Power Plant. Came in a royal blue metal box 22" x 13" x 3" with brass corner trim; two-layer set with three removable parts trays constructed from (MN) Base Plates; sold for $14.95.

125	195	300	+65	+80

THE 1946 SEARS ERECTOR LINE

Considering the disruption caused by World War II, it was somewhat surprising that Gilbert continued to offer special Erector Sets to Sears after 1945. In fact, several component parts were unique to the Sears sets. For example, the (S) Base Plates came only in these offerings, though they were not complicated to produce. Also unique to the Sears sets were the (P58) battery-operated motor and (P56G) 110-volt motor, both of which required much assembly. Evidently, Gilbert still regarded Sears as a very important customer to provide it with so much effort.

Like the regular Erector line, the Sears line was scaled down in 1946. Four years earlier, six sizes of sets had been available from Sears: Nos. 3 and 4 were packed in cardboard boxes, and Nos. 6, 7, 8, and 9 came in metal ones. In 1946 Sears cataloged only five sets, with just the largest coming in a metal box.

Other interesting anomalies occurred in the Sears sets from 1946. Although most of the regular Erector Sets featured mustard yellow inserts in 1946, the color of these inserts began a transition to blue. However, the inserts used in the Sears sets continued to be green. Also, the (MC), (MD), and (MF) Base Plates continued to be painted red, as before the war. Color discrepancies characterized some of the components of these sets, with (BN) Turret Plates being red and (MH) Large 3" Disc Wheels showing up with black-painted tires and red hubcaps.

Cardboard Box Sets

Four sets came packed in cardboard boxes for Sears. Set Nos. 3 and 4 were back, identical to the 1942 versions. But as was true with the regular line, the Sears line felt the impact of postwar steel shortages. Set Nos. 6 and 7, both packed in steel boxes before the war, came in cardboard boxes in 1946.

Set No. 6 (packed in a green metal box before the war) came in a box about the same size as the one used by Gilbert for its No. 6½. It had a lift-off lid (with the same cover picture as all the small cardboard box sets) that was unadorned on the inside. The contents of this set was unchanged from 1942.

Meanwhile, No. 7 (packed in a blue metal box before the war) came in the same, highly unusual box as did No. 7½ in the regular line. The body of the box was covered with flat blue paper, and the lid was covered with shiny blue foil. The oval Erector label was used on both the inside and outside of the lid, which was hinged. Cords on each side of the lid supported it when the box was open. Like No. 7½, the box for No. 7 was much too big for the number of parts that came in it. After the cardboard display inserts were discarded, it looked only half full.

Metal Box Sets

Sears offered only one metal box set in 1946: No. 8, called "The Giant Automotive Set." A continuation of a prewar set, it was indistinguishable from the 1942 version except for the parts can lids, which now were painted creamy white. Before the war, they were nickel-plated (with a paper "PARTS" label).

THE 1947 SEARS ERECTOR LINE

Sears cataloged the same five sets in 1947, although they had changed. The same parts changes that occurred in the regular line were carried over to the Sears sets. These changes included the modification in the pattern in the (C) 10" Girders, the improvement in the (MJ) Electro Magnet, and the metal bottom on the parts can, among others.

The most striking difference occurred with No. 7. In 1946 the box was blue, with shiny foil paper on the lid. This year, the color of the cardboard box was changed to maroon. This modification mirrored a similar change that occurred with No. 7½ in the regular line.

No special sets were available in the years after 1947. Looking at the Sears catalog for 1948, the largest set offered was No. 7½ from the regular line. Collectors remain fascinated by the variety of Sears sets cataloged between 1935 and 1947, particularly because they resembled the memorable sets that first appeared in 1933 and 1934.

Listings of 1946 and 1947 Sears Erector Sets

	Gd	VG	Exc	Inv	Org

NO. 3 **The Girder Set**

Built 75 models and featured the large wheels. Came in a cardboard box 18" x 10" x 1"; sold for $2.69.

	Gd	VG	Exc	Inv	Org
	40	60	100	+20	+25

NO. 4 **The Battery Motor Set**

Built 100 models and featured battery-operated (P58) Motor. Came in a cardboard box 18¼" x 10¼" x 2½"; two-layer set with removable cardboard parts display tray; sold for $5.89.

	Gd	VG	Exc	Inv	Org
	40	90	150	+30	+45

NO. 6 **The 110 Volt Electric Motor Set**

Built 125 models and featured 110-volt (P56G) Motor and (T) Boiler. Came in a cardboard box 16¼" x 8¼" x 2¾"; two-layer set with removable cardboard parts display tray; sold for $8.79.

	Gd	VG	Exc	Inv	Org
	75	110	180	+35	+50

NO. 7 **The Electric Lifting Magnet Set**

Built 150 models and featured crane models built with (MJ) Electro Magnet. Came in a box 20¼" x 13½" x 3½" with hinged lid (blue cardboard with foil-covered lid in 1946; maroon cardboard in 1947). Two-layer set with removable cardboard parts display tray; sold for $11.98.

	Gd	VG	Exc	Inv	Org
	120	180	300	+60	+75

NO. 8 **The Giant Automotive Set**

Built 180 models and featured automotive and truck models built with chassis parts. Came in a red metal box 20" x 12" x 3" with brass corner trim and cardboard parts display on inside of lid; sold for $15.98.

	Gd	VG	Exc	Inv	Org
	160	240	400	+80	+100

THE 1960–62 SEARS AND WARD ERECTOR LINES

An interesting event occurred in 1960, when Gilbert rekindled its old relationship with Sears, Roebuck & Company and Montgomery Ward. Although it had been wholesaling sets to both retailers throughout its early history, no special sets had been made for Sears since 1947 and Ward since 1932. Now Gilbert launched a new marketing arrangement known as the Science Series.

Both Sears and Ward sold almost the entire range of Erector. What was most unusual about the new marketing arrangement was that it affected only three of the midrange sets. Also, the packaging for each retailer was different.

For Sears, the special sets were part of the "Science-Career Series," which was composed of sets similar to the three smallest metal box sets in the regular line. But their appearance was different, as the lithography on the outside of the lid was unique. Done in blue, orange, and white, the lid read "Science-Career Series" and had the silhouette of a boy building the set's featured model.

Sears No. 10044, known as "The Automatic Radar Scope Set," was analogous to No. 10042 in the regular line, "The Automatic Radar Scanner Set." The only difference in contents was that the Sears set contained the (P15B528) Remote Control in place of two (NJ) Battery Holders.

Set No. 10057, the version of The Electric Engine Set offered by Sears, was packed in a box the same size as the one used for The Rocket Launcher Set in the regular line. But the box for No. 10057 was analogous to the one used for No. 10051 from 1957, a precursor to this set. Both came packed with cardboard inserts and not Styrofoam.

The largest set in the Science-Career Series was No. 10064, called "The Automatic Conveyor Set." It was identical to No. 10063 in the regular line in every way except for the set number and the box lid lithography.

The instruction manuals for the three sets in the Science-Career Series were attached to the inside of the lid with paper fasteners, as were their counterparts in the regular line. These sets remained part of the Sears offering through 1962, the end of traditional Erector production.

The same three sets were modified for Montgomery Ward. The main difference between the Sears and the Ward sets was the lithography on the outside on the lid. The Ward Sets were identified as "American Science Series," and the box lid looked almost like an American flag. It was done in red, white, and blue, and the right side was nothing but red and white stripes.

The American Science Series differed slightly from the Science-Career Series. For example, No. 10043 (called "The Power Model Set") was the smallest and came in a box that was the same size as the one used for Sears No. 10044. All the same, it clearly was analogous to No. 10041 from 1957. On the inside of the lid, the same lithography was used, but with a paper label pasted over the old set number on which appeared the current set number (10043 in 1960–61 and 10301 in 1962). Like the Sears set, it contained a (P15B528) Remote Control instead of (NJ) Battery Holders.

Set No. 10055, Ward's version of The Electric Engine Set, was identical to the Sears No. 10057, except for differences in set numbers and box lithography. The same held true for No. 10065, Ward's version of The Automatic Conveyor Set.

Beginning in 1960, Gilbert produced the Science-Career Series for sale only through Sears. The special lithography on the box lids makes these unique sets favorites of collectors.

Similar to the Sears sets, the American Science Series was produced for sale through Montgomery Ward, another major wholesaler. Like the Science-Career Series, these sets differ from offerings in the regular line.

Its instruction manual was packed loose, rather than clipped to the inside of the lid, as with the Sears version.

The wholesaler sets offered by Sears and Ward represent an interesting area to collect. When exhibited next to their counterparts from the regular Erector line, they create a handsome display that enthusiasts enjoy.

Listings of Science-Career Series Erector Sets

	Gd	VG	Exc	Inv	Org

NO. 10044 The Automatic Radar Scope Set

Featured the (DC3) 3 Volt Motor and (P15B528) Remote Control. Came in an orange and blue lithographed metal box 16" x 8" x 3" that pictured silhouette of boy playing with Radar Scope; two-layer set with removable cardboard parts display tray; sold for $7.44 in 1960 and $8.19 in 1961.

50 70 120 +25 +35

NO. 10057 The Electric Engine Set

Featured the (A49) Electric Engine. Came in an orange and blue lithographed metal box 16" x 10" x 3" that pictured silhouette of boy playing with crane model; two-layer set with two removable parts display trays, one cardboard and one constructed from (MN) Base Plates; sold for $12.49 in 1960 and $12.98 in 1961.

50 70 120 +25 +35

NO. 10064 The Automatic Conveyor Set

Featured the (T) Boiler and Conveyor Belt. Came in an orange and blue lithographed metal box 18" x 10" x 3" that pictured silhouette of boy playing with conveyor model; two-layer set with removable parts display tray; sold for $16.98 in 1960 and $17.66 in 1961.

60 85 140 +30 +35

Listings of American Science Series Erector Sets

	Gd	VG	Exc	Inv	Org

NO. 10043 The Power Model Set

Featured the (DC3) 3 Volt Motor and (P15B528) Remote Control. Came in a lithographed metal box 16" x 8" x 3", with outer lid resembling American flag; two-layer set with removable cardboard parts display tray.

50 70 120 +25 +35

NO. 10055 The Electric Engine Set

Featured the (A49) Electric Engine. Came in a lithographed metal box 16" x 10" x 3", with outer lid resembling American flag; two-layer set with two removable parts display trays, one cardboard and one constructed from (MN) Base Plates.

50 70 120 +25 +35

NO. 10065 The Automatic Conveyor Set

Featured the (T) Boiler and Conveyor Belt. Came in a lithographed metal box 18" x 10" x 3", with outer lid resembling American flag; two-layer set with removable parts display tray.

60 85 140 +25 +35